D0365300

AFRICAN AMERICANS AND U.S. POLICY TOWARD AFRICA 1850–1924

AFRICAN AMERICANS AND U.S. POLICY TOWARD AFRICA 1850–1924

In Defense of Black Nationality

Elliott P. Skinner

Howard University Press
Washington, D.C.

Printed in the United States of America
This book is printed on acid free paper.

Library of Congress Cataloging-in-Publication Data

Skinner, Elliott Percival, 1924–
    African Americans and U.S. policy toward Africa : in defense of
    Black nationality, 1850–1924 / Elliott P. Skinner.
            p.   cm.
    Includes bibliographical references and index.
    ISBN 0-88258-142-2 : $39.95. — ISBN 0-88258-159-7 (PBK.) $24.95
    1. Afro-Americans—Relations with Africans.   2. United States—
-Foreign relations—Africa.   3. Africa—Foreign relations—United
States.   I. Title.   II. Title: African Americans and US policy
toward Africa.
E185.625.S56   1992
327.7306—dc20   92-17588
                                                                        CIP

For Gwen
who understood and encouraged

Contents

vii

Preface

The object in researching and writing this book was to disprove the charge that, unlike many other ethnic groups in the United States that attempt to influence American policy to help their embattled homelands, African Americans have done little or nothing to aid the continent of their ancestors. Very often, those who made the charges could honestly claim to know so little about the general history of African Americans that their ignorance of this arcane information could be forgiven. More disturbing was to encounter otherwise well-informed Africans and Americans, among others, who knew little about the often acrimonious debates that took place among earlier generations of African Americans about helping to protect the black nationality in Africa. Moreover, many doubted that the debates ever took place. My decision was that if I was not to consider such persons simply malicious and ignore them, then the story needed to be told.

I had always believed that being of African descent, I ought to know more about that continent and its peoples. The late Professor E. Franklin Frazier of Howard University, who interviewed me for a Ford Foundation Foreign Area fellowship in the mid-nineteen-fifties, simply smiled at this assertion. He indicated that this reaction was not as common as I believed, but he was apparently impressed enough with the interview that I was sent off to Upper Volta to do ethnographic fieldwork on labor migration and political change among the Mossi people. This experience

led not only to my career as an anthropologist but to my interest in the
process by which a colonial territory was moving toward independence.

My interest in the decolonization of Africa led people at the Foreign
Service Institute of the Department of State to ask me to give lectures for
them, and this fed my general concern with United States foreign relations. Imagine my surprise when Secretary of State Dean Rusk called and
asked whether I would consider being nominated by President Lyndon B.
Johnson to be his ambassador to the Republic of Upper Volta. A number
of factors influenced my decision to accept the offer. One of my mentors,
Dr. Hugh H. Smythe of Brooklyn College, City University of New York,
was serving as ambassador to Syria, and this led me to believe that I, as a
specialist on the Upper Volta, might make a special contribution. Except
for Professor Edwin O. Reischauer of Harvard University, who was then
serving as United States ambassador to Japan and had learned Japanese as
a child of missionaries, I would be the only other chief of mission on
speaking terms with an "exotic" language, and an African one.

While I received the normal briefings from the State Department before
going off to Ouagadougou, I had an extraordinary four-hour session with
Ambassadors Smythe and Franklin H. Williams, and Dr. James Moss,
who was then working in the State Department. Not only did they share
their professional knowledge with me, but they attempted to alert me to
the pitfalls awaiting an unwary political appointee. Thanks to this brief-
ing, I was better prepared than some of the diplomats whose stories I have
told in this book to deal with the intricacies of diplomatic life. I remain
eternally grateful to two of these excellent teachers who have now gone to
their reward, and I continue to salute Jim Moss and the diplomats with
whom I served. The latter (two of whom later became ambassadors)
taught me a great deal, though I heard through the grapevine that they
often felt that I conducted the "country team" meeting of all my staff like
a tough and demanding postgraduate seminar. It will be fascinating to find
out later what other comments have surfaced in the archives of the foreign
service.

As an anthropologist accustomed to participant observation, which can
be alternately exciting and tiresome, I was not prepared for the years of
looking at microfilm of diplomatic correspondence and the often brittle
pages that provide data for historians. I gained more respect for their
scrupulous attention to detail when I was forced to return and to hunt
incessantly for a telegram whose content I may have missed in my eagerness to get to the end of a story. It was this experience, more than any
other, that curbed my dissatisfaction with the dearth of studies such as I

was undertaking. Professional historians are such nitpickers that they refrain from coming to conclusions until they are assured that there are no more bits of evidence that might give their story another slant. This being the case, I shall not be unduly disturbed if they resent the audacity of an anthropologist to enter their arena. In fact, I am pleased that Professors Joseph E. Harris and Arnold Taylor, both of Howard University, and my longtime friend, Professor John Henrik Clarke, consider me to be a historian manqué and predict that in my next reincarnation I will fulfill my destiny.

I feel privileged to have been able to profit from the work of such illustrious historians as John Hope Franklin, Rayford W. Logan, Charles Wesley, Benjamin Quarles, and others. Without the prodigious work of the editors of the *Booker T. Washington Papers,* the *Marcus Garvey and UNIA Papers,* and the correspondence, books and articles of W. E. B. Du Bois, and other important historical papers, my task would have been more difficult. I also profited from the many unpublished dissertations that unfortunately remain unseen by many students and scholars.

Without the assistance of the many librarians at the Library of Congress and the United States National Archives who directed me to often obscure files and collections, my work would have been impossible. Virginia Butler, chief of the reference and publications operations at the State Department, was so excited by this project that she placed surplus copies of the *Foreign Relations of the United States* at my disposal. Jeanne Blackwell Hudson of the Schomburg Collection (now Center for Research in Black Culture) of the New York Public Library had probably given up trying to keep tabs of the requests of a person who, from college days up to now, always needed help with references. Dorothy Porter of the Moorland-Spingarn Collection at Howard University was always eager to help, and with her retirement, Doris Hull and Elinor Sinnette continued the tradition. When I could not or did not personally seek help from those listed above, my work-study students or research assistants, now too numerous to mention, were gladly received by them.

This book has taken me so long to research and to write that many of the institutions that provided financial support to the project probably despaired of ever seeing it come to light. In my defense, let me say that in a number of cases, time to do this research or writing was sandwiched between anthropological and other projects. I am grateful for a Guggenheim Foundation fellowship, which together with a fellowship from the Social Science Research Council, enabled me to profit from the generosity of the Center for Advanced Study in the Behavioral Sciences at Palo

Alto, California, to start the basic research for this book. I still remember with gratitude the wise counsel of Gardner Lindzey, the former director of the CASBS, and the intellectual stimulation from the fellows of the center. Incidentally, it was at Palo Alto that Dr. St. Clair Drake, then professor at Stanford University, approved of my decision to write this book. A grant from the Woodrow Wilson International Center for Scholars at the Smithsonian Institution in Washington, D.C., was invaluable for getting me to the nation's capital with its vast resources. Finally, Columbia University, especially the Department of Anthropology, provided me with the sabbatical leaves and release from committee assignments I needed to finish the project.

It is difficult to remember all the people who helped me intellectually or programmatically with this project so that they may be thanked. Charles Harris, former director at Howard University Press, appreciated the need for such a study and he assigned Renee Mayfield to goad me on. Ruby Essien, who inherited the task of procuring "an acceptable manuscript," succeeded in doing so, even though it meant using her purple pencil quite liberally. My colleagues at Columbia, especially the late Robert Francis Murphy, were intrigued with this project but could relate to it only when I recounted my delight at finding the "ethnographic" reports that some of the early African American diplomats sent to the State Department in an effort to explain the local scenes. Murphy never failed to remind me that Franz Boas, whose chair I now occupy in the department at Columbia, appreciated history as a tool in understanding peoples whose cultures were disappearing.

Gwen, to whom I dedicate this book, gamely tolerated my tendency to share with her my excitement at finding unknown connections between the principals of history, the contradictions and foibles of members of our species, and the struggle of an oppressed people to influence the course of events. Our daughter Luce is not overly impressed that this book is finished because she is convinced that I love to write books and books and books.

AFRICAN AMERICANS AND U.S. POLICY TOWARD AFRICA 1850–1924

Introduction

Until quite recently, any interest that African Americans showed in the conduct of United States foreign policy was viewed as quixotic by most white Americans.[1] This, of course, was due to the historic difficulty of whites in accepting people of African descent as organic members of a society created by both. True, there is now a grudging acceptance that African Americans are interested in United States policy toward Africa and possibly toward the Caribbean, but this admission is still accompanied by a concern that such interest might not be in the national interest. That African Americans might desire a voice in America's global policy is only acknowledged by the most enlightened white Americans.[2]

This reluctance to accept the participation of African Americans in the conduct of United States foreign policy is rooted, of course, in the nature of the foreign policy-making process as well as in the position of African Americans in American society.[3] Nevertheless, African Americans have almost always known that in order to gain equal status in America, they must have a say in how their country relates to the rest of the world. In order to accomplish this, African Americans have used both *formal* and *symbolic* means to deal with America's foreign policy. It might be useful to see this issue in theoretical perspective before embarking on a study of the early initiatives of African Americans to influence United States policy toward Africa.

1

It is almost axiomatic that the foreign policy of any society, be it a village community, a small city-state, a feudal kingdom, a large imperial system, or a modern nation-state, is designed to protect that entity from all outsiders, whether friends or enemies, actual or potential. In their effort to do so, societies have normally assigned their foreign policy-making and executing processes to an elite—persons endowed with either achieved or ascribed superior status and judged to embody their particular society's salient values. Historically, sovereign figures were the persons who made and conducted foreign policy. And although many monarchs were too modest to make the claim, the more arrogant ones boldly proclaimed (though not perhaps in so many words): "L'état, c'est moi."[4] When, as sometimes happened, sovereigns could not fulfill their obligations as representatives of their people to the outside world, they designated members of the royal family or other high status persons to do so. These persons were often granted plenipotentiary powers to act in the place of their leaders.

In a few well-known cases in the ethnographic and historical records where powerless societies were forced to negotiate with more powerful ones, they frequently substituted false leaders (often called chiefs of straw) to parley for them. These substitutes were intended to protect the integrity of their true sovereigns and, by extension, of their collectivities by being able to make decisions that monarchs could not make without jeopardizing themselves or their societies. Societies were then in a position to claim ritual ignorance of what had been done in their name and to deny that these acts ever took place. The true sovereigns and their collectivities were thereby protected.[5]

In contrast to monarchies whose ascribed leaders personally conducted their foreign affairs, democracies often had difficulty choosing persons to perform these tasks. Viewing themselves as sovereign, the citizens of democratic polities often hesitated to yield this awesome power to any person for fear that it could be used against them at home. The founders of the American Republic attempted to deal with this problem by granting only their presidents the right and duty to represent the nation-state in foreign relations and to choose persons to help them do so.[6] Yet the Founding Fathers reserved to the people, as represented by the Senate, the duty and right to judge actions taken either by the president or his representatives. Some American presidents have found this practice irksome, but most have accepted the strictures placed upon them by their constituents.[7] A few presidents and their immediate subordinates have been known to resent these limitations on their power and have at times even attempted to bypass the Senate, with the result that they have been accused by acting "imperially" and, in a few cases, have been threatened with impeachment.[8]

While in the past the presidents of the United States, like their royal counterparts, usually had the prerogative to choose those who could help them conduct their foreign policies, they invariably chose persons from their own political party, social class, background, or region, or persons who possessed specific attributes deemed useful to the foreign policy enterprise. Not only did they have to have confidence in the skills of their envoys but they also needed the assurance that their representatives embodied the values of American society and would protect it against all enemies, foreign or domestic. Finally, American presidents often sought to demonstrate to foreigners that the persons sent as envoys possessed the qualities most valued by the American people and their leaders. Until quite recently, and some scholars would argue even until today, such considerations often governed which persons were chosen by American presidents as envoys and where they were sent. Reciprocally, the same considerations were often uppermost in the minds of American administrations when they recognized countries or accepted envoys sent from them.[9]

While even in democratic societies such as the United States the president and his administration have tended to monopolize the foreign policy-making process, this monopoly does not go unchallenged. The attempts of the clergy and merchants to influence their monarchs' foreign policy were the bane of earlier European states. In the United States, the monopoly was not only constitutionally modified by Congress but has constantly been challenged by prestigious business, labor, military, ethnic, academic, and ideological groups.[10] The latter have increasingly demanded that their concerns be taken into consideration by whatever administration exercises power. Significantly, except in moments of international crisis requiring a national consensus, the mass of Americans have generally been held by many officials or elites to be ignorant of, and largely indifferent to, foreign affairs. And though this attitude should be alien to the equalitarian and democratic ideals of the United States, a number of American leaders have found it a necessary or valuable help in making their foreign policy.

Largely because of the cosmopolitan nature of the emerging United States of America, a number of the Founding Fathers, such as Madison and Washington, were deeply worried that factionalism might hurt the young Republic. In the *Federalist Paper* Number 10, Madison warned against combinations of citizens who "united and actuated by some common impulse of passion or of interest" may be averse to the rights of other citizens or to "the permanent and aggregated interests of the community."[11] Intimately involved in the divisive Genêt affair (1793) and with the Alien and Sedition Acts (1798), George Washington also cautioned in his farewell address that the primary allegiance of all Americans should be to the nation:

> Citizens by birth or choice of a common country, that country has a right to concentrate your affections. The name of American, which belongs to you in your national capacity, must always exalt the just pride of patriotism more than any appellation derived from local discriminations.[12]

Washington primarily feared those "local discriminations" due to ethnic concentrations within the United States of America. He felt that it was only in "union" that Americans would experience that "security from external danger, a less frequent interruption of their peace by foreign nations, and what is of inestimable value, they must derive from union an exemption from those broils and wars between themselves which so frequently afflict neighboring countries."[13]

Obviously what Washington had in mind was an America whose population was so united that any pluralistic tendencies would be subordinated to the common good or national interest. The question is, What is in the national interest? Historically, the answer for American democracy has been that the "national interest" is whatever the public or the electorate wants it to be. As Charles Evan Hughes once remarked, "Public opinion in a democracy wields the scepter."[14] In his famous debate with Senator Stephen Douglas, Abraham Lincoln declared, "With public sentiment on its side, everything succeeds; with public sentiment against it, nothing succeeds."[15] The problem, of course, is that public opinion is often awkward to describe, elusive to define, difficult to measure, and impossible to see, even though it may be felt. This is true in our domestic affairs, and it is even truer in foreign affairs. A far greater conundrum for the citizens of the United States is that while equality is a basic political tenet, this ideal has always been affected by the reality of cultural pluralism, economic ranking, ethnic stratification, and racialism within the society. There have always been groups of Americans who believe their view of the national interest superior to that of their fellow citizens.

While many Americans were content to accept the views of this elite, many of the so-called ethnics were not quite so quick to do so. They often resented the "nativistic" or typical American attitudes about their ancestral lands, especially when these views were defined in terms of the national interest. Even newly arrived migrants who considered themselves "sojourners" or "strangers" (in that they had not yet decided whether they would remain in the United States) often resented disparaging remarks made about their homelands.[16] This resentment increased when they decided to settle in the United States in order to have better lives for themselves and their children. One important reason for their attitude was the fear that negative views about their lands of origin might be designed to frustrate their ability to prosper in their adopted country. As a result they tended to monitor and even change the views of their neighbors and leaders about their homelands.

Viewing the behavior of immigrants on behalf of their ancestral lands, some scholars and publicists have asserted that the attitude of immigrants or ethnics has been "the single most important determinant of American foreign policy."[17] Of course, these scholars recognize that United States foreign policy "responds to other things as well," but they have insisted that "probably *first of all*" attention should be paid "to the primal facts of ethnicity."[18]

Over the years, many statespersons and elite groups have not only noted the ethnic factor in our foreign policy but have bitterly resented it. President Theodore Roosevelt was particularly hostile to the attempts of ethnic groups (often referred to as "the hyphenates") to influence American foreign policy. In a speech in 1895 he lashed out at the particularism of "the hyphenated Americans—the German-American, the Irish-American, or the native-American."[19] He warned that unless all of these groups considered themselves "American, pure and simple," the future of the nation would be impaired.[20] Roosevelt would later agree with the statement of Woodrow Wilson that the propensity of many American ethnic groups to defend their ancestral lands was because "only part of them has come over" from the old countries. Roosevelt said of ethnic Americans: "When two flags are hoisted on the same pole, one is always hoisted undermost. The hyphenated American always hoists the American flag undermost."[21]

Despite the attitudes of the American elite about the ethnic consciousness or loyalties of pre–World War I immigrants, there is little evidence that many of them were disloyal to their new country. What they resented was the often "know-nothing" attitude of the commonalty of their neighbors about foreign countries and the often subtle use of these prejudices to delay the social and economic mobility of immigrants. Between World Wars I and II, ethnicity among European migrants was widely judged as posing a danger to the United States. When the United States was preparing to enter World War II, the editors of influential *Fortune* magazine warned that "there is dynamite on our shores."[22] They felt that while some immigrant European groups unqualifiedly supported the war, others somewhat reluctantly supported it, while still others submitted to the war effort with traces of subversive defiance. The editors wondered whether the United States could transform this mélange into a "working model of political warfare."[23]

What should be noted about this fear that the allegiance of some Americans to their lands of origin might jeopardize America is that the identities of the groups so considered changed as a function of their assimilation or assimilability into United States society. Whereas in World War I the Germans were so vilified that even sauerkraut became known as "Liberty Cabbage," by World War II, and despite the presence of the Hitlerite German-American Bund, there was no sustained public reaction against the Germans. This group was well on its way to full assimilation in the United States.[24]

The contrast between the plight of the Chinese and Japanese in the United States during World War II is instructive. Until this period, most Americans continued to hold American-born Chinese and their ancestral land in disdain as posing no threat to them. This was not the case with the Japanese, whose nation was viewed as a formidable enemy of the United States, and who as a people viewed themselves as a master race, albeit in Asia. Thus when the war broke out, many Americans questioned the loyalty of even second-generation Japanese Americans; these were systematically rounded up and incarcerated in concentration camps. Nevertheless, Japanese Americans succeeded in gaining permission to fight in Europe in the American army and acquitted themselves with distinction.[25]

Despite America's mixed historical experience with ethnicity as a factor in its foreign policy, this issue was always present and accounted in part for the attitude toward the attempt of African Americans to participate in its foreign affairs. Unfortunately, it is still not recognized that this concern is linked to the attitude about granting ethnic groups the right to participate as equals in society. Jimmy Carter, whose presidency witnessed enormous pressure from America's ethnic groups to influence his foreign policy, complained accordingly in his farewell address. He declared bluntly that Americans were increasingly being drawn to single-issue groups and special interest organizations that attempted "to ensure that whatever else happens, our own personal views and our own private interests are protected. This is a disturbing factor in American life."[26]

Supporting President Carter's concern was Senator Charles McC. Mathias, Jr., of Maryland. He bitterly attacked the efforts of minorities in the United States to influence American foreign policy, declaring that "ethnic politics, carried as they often have been to excess, have proven harmful to the national interest."[27] Mathias echoed George Washington's concern that factionalism—in this case ethnicity—could generate "unnecessary animosities" among Americans and create among them "illusions of common interest" with outsiders, whether in fact any existed. He expressed alarm at the attempts of American ethnic groups to put pressure on both the domestic and foreign policy-making institutions of the United States to adopt measures in favor of their lands of origin. This included African Americans lobbying on behalf of Africa; Caribbean peoples lobbying on behalf of the people of the Caribbean basin; Greeks lobbying both the presidents and Congress against granting arms to Turkey, our NATO ally; Jewish groups promoting the cause of Israel; Mexican Americans and Italian Americans supporting immigration policies to benefit the areas from which their ancestors came; and Polish Americans and some central and northeastern Europeans attempting to enlist the aid of the United States against Soviet activities and presence in their ancestral homes. Mathias did not suggest that the ethnic advocacy of Americans was unpatriotic. He did stress, however, that the administration's "resistance to the pressures of a particular group in itself signals neither a sellout nor even a lack of sympathy with a foreign country or cause, but rather a sincere conviction about the national interest of the United States."[28]

While Mathias's linkage of African Americans with other groups in the United States in his general condemnation of their role in the formulation of the country's foreign policy shows a recognition of this group's changing status, their case has historically been significantly different from those of other Americans, even the Asians. Unlike the English, other Europeans, or Asians who arrived on the shores of the future United States of America from recognized nation-states or empires, the Africans were plucked from societies that had no political status in the emerging concert of nations and sold as servants. True, the European privateers or traders along the coasts of Africa had to deal with local African monarchs, either to trade for captives or to fight for them, and therefore recognized both the strengths and weaknesses of the traditional African political organizations. But the English colonists in America who bought the transported persons and transformed them into "slaves for life," knew little about, and cared less about Africa and Africans. Then for reasons that have been thoroughly explored by historians, the builders of the American nation determined quite early that the human characteristics of persons of African descent were questionable and that in any case they could not be members of their society.[29] The early American leaders could and did ignore the political systems of the societies from which the slaves came because the African potentates were powerless to make representations on behalf of their people. So in contrast to many of the white ethnics in America, African Americans were powerless, the countries from which they came were powerless, and as they contemplated struggling for freedom and equality within the United States, they felt that they had to do something about the status of Africa in the global system.[30] The two processes were inseparably linked and had to be dealt with as such.

The particular dilemma of the African American appears to have puzzled certain analysts, but it is more likely that they were unprepared to deal with its full implications. Thus when in his book *Man in the Street* Thomas Bailey criticized American ethnic groups as unduly interfering in American foreign policy, he openly acknowledged his bewilderment over the status of African Americans:

> No mention has thus far been made of the most numerous hyphenate group of all, the Afro-Americans, who constitute about one-tenth of our population. They are racial hyphenates rather than national hyphenates, for they have long since lost any foreign nationality.[31]

For Bailey, as for many other American analysts, "racial-hyphenates," in contrast to "national hyphenates," had no "foreign nationality" and were therefore theoretically as well as programmatically unqualified to participate in the foreign affairs of the United States. But like the owner grown uncomfortably aware of the human characteristics of his chattel slaves, Bailey could not ignore the one attempt he knew of where African Americans exhibited their political awareness in showing an interest in their country's foreign policy. Bailey noted that when Mussolini attacked Ethiopia in 1935, many African Americans were incensed, and one Hubert Fauntleroy Julian (Harlem's "Black Eagle") went to fight in Ethiopia. In Bailey's view, Julian "was an outstanding exception."[32] He asserted that, as far as the Ethiopian war was concerned, "the sympathies of the American Negro, in so far as they had any, were with their colored brethren."[33] Bailey was clearly convinced that African Americans could have had no possible interest in attempting to influence United States policy on behalf of Ethiopia. He felt that the interest of African Americans in the Ethiopian war was based not on the philosophically sophisticated notion of *nationality* but on the more primordial sentiment of *race,* and that race was a questionable basis for loyalty or commitment in the modern world.

Bailey's attitude to the contrary, African Americans had long known and acted on their belief that race was always very much a factor in their lives and in the affairs of contemporary nation-states. They had always believed both race and ethnicity were important in conditioning the behavior of their fellow citizens. Generations of African Americans had understood all too well that it was race that was largely responsible for their inability to share equally in the affairs of their nation-state. Returning to the example of the Ethiopian war (even though this occurred quite recently and is not discussed in this book), as Roi Ottley observed:

> From the beginning, the Ethiopian crisis became a fundamental question in Negro life. It was all but impossible for Negro leaders to remain neutral, and the position they took toward the conflict became a fundamental test. The survival of the black nation became the topic of angry debate in poolrooms, barber shops and taverns.[34]

Contemporary African American leaders were terribly frustrated by their inability to mobilize United States and world opinion against Italy. Writing in *Foreign Affairs* about the "Inter-Racial Implications of the Ethiopian Crisis," W. E. B. Du Bois voiced the "lost faith" of African Americans "in an appeal for justice from the United States in this war or in any affair that concerned black people."[35]

The Ethiopian war was also a litmus test for African American leaders because it forced them to deal with a widespread concern among their followers that they were unable to influence the foreign policy of their nation on an important issue. Here was an issue defined in terms of race, the very issue that had conditioned their lives in American society but which their leaders could do little about. True, United States policy-makers may have seen this problem solely in terms of power and national interest and without relevance to race.[36] But the black Harlemites who nightly battled their Italian neighbors made no distinction between race and nationality. They saw Italian Americans as white of Italian origin and fought against them on that basis. For their purposes, African Americans saw the Ethiopians as "blacks" and sought to engage their nation-state on behalf of a black nation judged to have been unjustly invaded by a white nation. They simply wanted to enlist the aid of their nation, the United States, on behalf of the Ethiopians, judged to be members of their race.[37]

The Ethiopian war provides yet another good example of the ambivalence that confronted early African Americans when they sought to deal with the foreign affairs of the United States. It should never be forgotten that African Americans shared with many other Americans a certain ambivalence toward foreign countries—and even more so toward Africa. The ancestors of almost all white Americans who came to North America and who subsequently lobbied for their ancestral lands were also ambivalent about those countries. They might extol the virtues of the "fatherland" or "the ole sod" or "Zion," but they recognized that America held out the possibility of a better future for them and for their children.

The ambivalence of African Americans toward Africa was of a different order. As we have seen, in marked contrast to the Europeans, most of the Africans came involuntarily to America and, even after being freed from chattel slavery, bore the obloquy of their origin. For African Americans, then, America was not originally a land of hope and glory, nor was it the mother of the free. It was a land of slavery, prejudice, and discrimination from which their forebears would have fled had they been able to do so. Nevertheless, Africa was never universally viewed by the descendants of the bondpersons as a land of bliss. Many took a dim view of an ancestral land whose military and political weaknesses permitted its inhabitants to be carried off and enslaved. They were scorned when Africa was conquered and colonized by outsiders who, convinced of the sub-humanity of its inhabitants, felt called upon to Christianize and civilize them. Moreover, some African Americans, though certainly not the majority, remained ashamed of Africa's legacy, their black skin, which remained a badge of low status despite individual accomplishments.[38]

Because of an often virulent racism, over the centuries African Americans remained structurally linked to Africa whether they had any emotional bonds to that "mysterious" continent or not. This ambivalence increased when they had to acknowledge that the global position of Africa was so very low that its peoples were treated with contempt wherever they went. Thus, whenever African Americans sought equality with Americans of European descent, they were reminded that their Africanness precluded such aspirations.

Faced with the dilemma of being forced willy-nilly to relate to Africa, early African Americans adopted a number of strategies: some attempted to ignore their African past and, through the processes of acculturation and miscegenation, sought to eliminate all sociocultural and biological links with that continent; others vaunted Africa's ancient glories in the attempt to combat white arrogance by proving that their ancestors once civilized the world; still others wished to go back to Africa and, by helping to Christianize and civilize it, improve its status and theirs in the global system; and finally, some sought to take advantage of America's growing power in international affairs to help build a strong Africa, which through a "reflex" action could demand that African peoples everywhere be treated with dignity and respect. Interestingly, early as well as contemporary African Americans, individually and collectively, tried all of these approaches to deal with the African problem. Some individuals vacillated between these different strategies throughout their lives.[39]

While early African Americans ordinarily attempted to deal with their Africanness in sociocultural and biological terms, a significant group of their leaders sought to use international politics to deal with this dilemma and to change the status of Africa in the world. This approach led inexorably to a concern with America and its foreign policy. The more perceptive of these early actors recognized that their ambition had some quixotic aspects since foreign policy was a preoccupation which status they lacked. They were prepared to face the reality that attempts to deal with United States foreign policy toward Africa involved gaining high status within the African American group, as well as being accepted by the white elite structure that controlled the policy. They were aware that, having been systematically excluded from the higher ranks and conditions of American life, they had to employ superhuman efforts to get to the footstool to reach the bottom rung of the ethnic hierarchical ladder of their society. They also fully understood that, given the difficulty of protecting their own position within the United States, they would find it infinitely harder to influence their country's foreign policy. Yet many persevered.

The problem for African Americans who did achieve elite status among their own people was that, with a few notable exceptions, they had to be seen as overtly challenging the country's white power structure. They had to demonstrate by words and deeds that they were dissatisfied with the status of African Americans within American society and were actively trying to change it.[40] Even those who had gained leadership status by not openly confronting the white power structure only escaped the opprobrium of being considered "Uncle Toms" by attempting to show that their conduct, while questionable, did in fact, ameliorate the position of African Americans vis-à-vis whites and was designed to change the society's caste-like structure.[41] Yet to do so was to be perceived by powerful whites as rebels who did not accept the majority's view of the nature of American society.

The structurally ambivalent position of African American leaders in American society was most clearly demonstrated when the subject of their serving as presidential envoys arose. American presidents could choose only important persons to represent them abroad. They also had to be assured that African American candidates for such positions possessed the necessary leadership qualities and shared most of the values and aspirations of the American elite. But all Americans were also aware that racial factors conspired to prevent most African Americans from participating fully in American life, thus frustrating any opportunity to acquire the requisite values. Many American presidents used important whites or highly regarded African American allies to vouch for candidates for diplomatic posts. It is quite clear that even during this early period, pragmatism obliged American presidents to accept African American envoys on the faith that they would be politically astute enough to perform their duties.

There is enough evidence in this book that some of the envoys had to use all the skills they had to perform their tasks honorably. Their efforts were affected by the structural equivalence of what Du Bois once described in psychological terms as a "double-consciousness."[42] They were both insiders and outsiders. As insiders, they knew the strengths and especially the weaknesses of American society in a way white Americans could not know and still they accepted the obligation, indeed the duty, to protect and to defend that society. Yet as outsiders, they often had a different perspective from American whites about American society and about its conduct in the global arena.[43] Better than most of their white counterparts, African American envoys could readily understand, even if they could not accept, the views of foreigners about American society. Yet this greater insight was not always an unmixed blessing. African American envoys have been known to exhibit a sense of moral superiority over white Americans who, in their arrogance, did not often realize how their attitudes affected the status of America. For many an African American member of the foreign service, participation in America's foreign policy-making process was viewed not only as serving the country but also as making it better than it really was.[44]

That early group of African American envoys who gained their posts as a function of membership in, and service to, the Republican party were quite conscious of the duality of their roles both to Africa and to the United States. The ease with which many of these men moved from local and national politics to serving as United States ministers to Liberia was indeed remarkable. That they shared many of the attitudes of white Americans toward Africa is also clear, and in their zeal some were not completely averse to the idea that America should establish protectorates in Africa.[45] But also important was that these men believed in the redemption of Africa and were prepared to engage both themselves and their country in the task of attempting to forestall European conquest and colonization of the entire continent. They held to these views even when their own lowly status in the United States was the subject of frustration in working with Africans.

A number of the envoys both understood and rejected the problems faced by American presidents in assigning them to specific posts. They knew all too well that the presidents had to weigh both the attitudes of Americans and those of the foreign countries in which the envoys wished to be placed.[46] Nevertheless, African American leaders hoped that fundamental domestic and international change would persuade American presidents to assign them as envoys to black as well as nonblack countries and to receive envoys from all foreign lands. Their endeavor was always to increase the political power of African Americans in the United States so that they would be more acceptable as presidential representatives. Moreover, they sought to strengthen the position of Africa within the global system so that persons of African descent would be welcome as diplomats the world over.

We shall see that a number of early African American envoys desired to break out of the limited number of posts to which they were traditionally assigned. In fact, no early American president sent any African American envoy to an important country, white or Asian, for fear that his appointee would be disdained and for fear that the country to which he was sent would take umbrage at the United States. The hope of African American leaders was that the rise of a powerful Africa and the changing position of blacks in the United States would resolve the problem. Their role was to bring this change about. Unfortunately (or perhaps fortunately) for the early envoys, the global political situation did not change fast enough for them to lose their structural ambiguity and to appear indistinguishable from their white counterparts.

Not all of the early African American leaders wanted to deal with their domestic and African concerns through the official American foreign policy apparatus. Either they lacked access to governmental officials or had too great an aversion to the United States government to desire to use its foreign policy to achieve their end. Consequently, they were left with what can be called, neologistically, "symbolic structures" to articulate their African interests. These structures were educational, emigrationist, and religious organizations or messianic or millenarian "pan" movements. The object was to avoid or to bypass the political systems of the United States, its foreign policy agents, and the European colonial powers in dealing with Africa.[47] Yet, as citizens of the United States, this was almost impossible to do, given the importance of citizenship in the nation-state system.

The United States, for its part, could and often did attempt to ignore most of the activities of its early African American citizens in Africa or on behalf of Africa. Many white Americans believed that when these activities were not futile, they could only lead to conflict between the United States and powerful European imperial powers. Nonetheless, both the United States and European governments were periodically forced to recognize the foreign policy initiatives of African Americans or even of immigrant blacks in America whose activities concerned them. In a number of cases, both the United States and the Europeans found it necessary to use the unofficial activities of African Americans in Africa as the basis for interstate activities and relations. Thus, although largely symbolic in nature, these structures did have an important impact on the evolution of Africa and on America's relationship to that continent and its peoples. Some of these symbolic activities did have the desired reflex action on American society that enabled African Americans to move beyond their limitations at home and deal with the realities of the global system that embraced both themselves and Africa.

What was especially characteristic of the early attempts of African Americans to influence United States policy toward Africa was their hope to build and to protect a "black nationality" there.[48] The nature of this black nationality and even its site were never clearly delimited, because for most African Americans the entire continent, and not one specific area, was the focus of their attention. They all hoped that once created, this black nationality would have a powerful impact within the global system. It would demonstrate the capabilities of the black race on its ancestral continent, thereby securing the worldwide emancipation of people of African descent from slavery, subjugation, and scorn. The conflict that rose was whether this black nationality should be created and maintained by the emigration of African Americans to Africa and whether it was the duty of African Americans in the United States to do everything in their power to accomplish this end.

We shall see that the issue of emigration to Africa, or a "return to Africa," became and remained an important source of tension among African Americans in their attitude toward Africa during the early years. This issue was often linked to, but was never strictly indicative of, class and color differences among native-born African Americans, or between them and migrants from the Caribbean and Africa who had joined the African American community. On one occasion an influential African American joined forces with a Jamaican immigrant to launch a civilization program in Africa. Later on an African American leader and an immigrant from Jamaica quarrelled incessantly over whether the struggle for Africa's redemption should be fought in the United States or in Africa. We shall see that the issue may well have turned on the elite status of the African American and his belief that he could enlist the support of the United States for Africa, and the feeling of the Jamaican that he was only a sojourner or "stranger" in the United States and only wished to have the support of a group of African Americans to go and redeem Africa. The manner in which this conflict was resolved was surprising as well as paradoxical, but it did indicate that most African American leaders, emigrationist or not, supported the idea that the United States should help to create, protect, and defend a black nationality in Africa and, by extension, protect all of Africa from conquest and colonization, so that a rejuvenated continent could help its people the world over.[49]

The early African Americans were often sophisticated about changes in the United States and beyond that demanded the use of different types of structures for articulating their foreign policy concerns, especially about Africa. Thus when it became clear that the end of Reconstruction had diminished the opportunity of the post–Civil War African American leaders to affect United States policy toward Africa, a shift was made to the use of close patron-client relations with the White House to pursue their aims. A few of these leaders were not above attempting to work through the colonial structures of European imperialists to accomplish their ends. This gave the impression that some of them had shouldered the "white man's burden," but a careful reading of the data would suggest that they wanted to get the white man off the back of African peoples the world over.

Finally, when it appeared that few activities of African Americans and persons of African descent could actually liberate Africa, a number of leaders resorted to congresses and conventions in attempts to stimulate the United States to take action on behalf of Africa and peoples of African descent. This part of the study comes to an end at a period when it seemed that the efforts of African Americans and others of African descent in the United States to rescue the black nationality had reached their nadir. Yet, viewed in perspective, these congresses and conventions created the ideological networks and laid the groundwork for the activities that would later fulfill the dreams of liberating the black nationality.

This book, then, places the attempts of early African Americans to influence United States policy toward Africa against the canvas of the foreign policy-making process of an important nation-state in which they had very limited power and prestige. These early African Americans used their limited political power in the interest of Africa in the hope that their activities would protect Africa and aid African peoples the world over. These two processes have always complemented one another, now perhaps more than ever. Future studies will show how later generations of African Americans built on the experiences and activities of their ancestors and participated in the foreign policy processes of the United States of their day. They used their growing political power progressively to emancipate themselves fully in the United States of America and attempted to influence how the United States dealt with foreign policy issues relating to Africa and, by extension, to the rest of the world.

Notes

1. Thomas A. Bailey, *Man in the Street: The Impact of American Public Opinion on Foreign Policy* (New York: Macmillan, 1948), 16; Herschelle Sullivan Challenor, "The Influence of Black Americans on U.S. Foreign Policy," in *Ethnicity and U.S. Foreign Policy,* ed. Abdul Aziz Said (New York: Praeger, 1981), 143; Sylvia M. Jacobs, *The African Nexus: Black American Perspectives on the European Partition of Africa, 1880–1920* (Westport, Conn.: Greenwood Press, 1981), xi–xiv. Writing in 1974, Francis O. Wilcox, Dean Emeritus of the Johns Hopkins School of Advanced International Studies, lamented that the number of black ambassadors serving in U.S. missions abroad "remains discouraging low" and admitted that "the record is not as good as it ought to be." But, like other white foreign service specialists before and since, he declined to recognize the serious obstacles faced by blacks interested in the foreign policy enterprise. Wilcox claimed that until "very recently, many able black students simply have not realized the fine career potential available to them in the field of diplomacy." Unfortunately, he was

more sanguine about the chance for blacks to enter the foreign service than the record suggests. Despite Wilcox's feeling that the "door is open" and that what was needed was a planned program to attract qualified blacks, as of this writing (1990) there are about six black ambassadors serving overseas—about the same number he recorded in 1974. Foreword to Elmer Plischke's *United States Diplomats and Their Missions* (Washington, D.C.: American Enterprise Institute for Public Policy, 1975), 5–6.

2. Rupert Emerson, "American Interests in Africa," *Centennial Review* 4 (1960): 416. See also Melville J. Herskovits, *Study of United States Foreign Policy in Africa,* prepared for the Committee on Foreign Relations of the United States Senate, 86th Cong. 1st sess. 23 October 1959, 14; Elliott P. Skinner, "Ethnicity and Race as Factors in the Formation of United States Foreign Policy," in *American Character and Foreign Policy,* ed. Michael P. Hamilton (Grand Rapids Mich.: William B. Eerdmans, 1986), 89ff.

3. Henry A. Kissinger, *American Foreign Policy* (New York: W. W. Norton, 1969), 11ff.

4. Kissinger, *American Foreign Policy,* 27–43; Elliott P. Skinner, "Black Foreign Policymakers," *Urban League Review* 9 (Summer 1985): 114.

5. W. E. F. Ward, "The Colonial Phase in British West Africa," in *A Thousand Years of West African History,* ed. J. F. Ade Ajayi and Ian Espie (Ibadan: Ibadan University Press, 1965), 385–402; J. A. Ballard, "The Colonial Phase in French West Africa," ibid., 431–41; Karen E. Fields, *Revival and Rebellion in Colonial Central Africa* (Princeton: Princeton University Press, 1985), 30–90; Michael Crowder and Obaro Ikime, eds., *West African Chiefs: Their Changing Status Under Colonial Rule and Independence* (Ile-Ife: University of Ife Press, 1970), vii–xxix.

6. P. A. Varg, *Foreign Policies of the Founding Fathers* (East Lansing Michigan: Michigan State University Press, 1963), 11–69.

7. Bailey, *Man in the Street,* 7–13; Jimmy Carter, "Farewell Address," *Vital Speeches* 47 (February 1981): 226–28; Skinner, "Ethnicity and Race," 89–92; Charles McC. Mathias, Jr., "Ethnic Groups and Foreign Policy," *Foreign Affairs* 59 (1981): 975ff.

8. Ibid. See also Roger Morris, *Uncertain Greatness: Henry Kissinger and American Foreign Policy* (New York: Harper and Row, 1977), 1–25.

9. Elmer Plischke, *The Conduct of American Diplomacy* (New York: Van Nostrand, 1950).

10. Ralph Hilton, *Worldwide Mission: The Story of the United States Foreign Service* (New York: World Publishing, 1971).

11. James Madison, *The Federalist Papers,* ed. Henry B. Dawson (New York: Charles Scribner, 1863), 1:56.

12. George Washington, *Washington Farewell Address: The View from the Twentieth Century,* ed. Burton I. Kaufman (Chicago: Quadrangle Books, 1969), 18.

13. Ibid., 19.

14. Quoted in Thomas A. Bailey, *Man in the Street,* 1.

15. Ibid.

16. Elliott P. Skinner, "Strangers in African Societies," *Africa* 33 (October 1963): 307–20.

17. Nathan Glazer and Daniel P. Moynihan, eds., *Ethnicity: Theory and Experience* (Cambridge, Mass.: Harvard University Press, 1975), 23–24.

18. Ibid.

19. Louis L. Gerson, "The Influence of Hyphenated Americans on U.S. Diplomacy," in Said, *Ethnicity and Foreign Policy,* 21; Bailey, *Man in the Street,* 15.
20. Bailey, *Man in the Street,* 15.
21. Ibid., 15.
22. Gerson, "Hyphenated American," 25.
23. Ibid.
24. Frank P. Zeidler, "Hysteria in Wartime: Domestic Pressures on Ethnics and Aliens," in *Ethnicity and War,* ed. Winston A. Van Horne and Thomas V. Tennesen (Milwaukee: University of Wisconsin Press, 1984), 72ff.
25. During World War II, Polish Americans exerted a great deal of pressure on President Roosevelt during his negotiations with the Soviet Union on the projected postwar boundaries between the USSR and Poland. These persons felt that the settlement at Yalta made a mockery of the Atlantic Charter and urged congressmen and senators not to ratify the agreement. Significantly, however, the loyalty of Polish Americans was not questioned. When Eisenhower came to office, many citizens of central European origin wished the United States to "liberate" their ancestral lands. Again the loyalty of these groups was not questioned, and while it is generally admitted that these groups failed in their effort "to force the government to do something it did not want to do, on occasion they have been able to sabotage steps that Washington would have liked to undertake." George F. Kennan, America's brilliant ambassador to the Soviet Union, remarked bitterly in his *Memoirs* that Croatian Americans "never failed to oppose any move to better American-Yugoslav relations or to take advantage of any opportunity to make trouble between the two countries." George Kennan, *Memoirs, 1950–1963* (Boston: Little Brown, 1972), 2:286–87.
26. Carter, *Vital Speeches,* 226–28.
27. Mathias, "Ethnic Groups and Foreign Policy," 997.
28. Ibid.
29. Winthrop D. Jordan, *The White Man's Burden: Historical Origins of Racism in the United States* (New York: Oxford University Press, 1974), 3–51.
30. Carl Degler, *Out of Our Past: The Forces That Shaped Modern America* (New York: Harper and Bros., 1959), 31.
31. Thomas Bailey, *Man in the Street,* 30.
32. Ibid.
33. Ibid., 31.
34. Roi Ottley, *New World A-Coming* (Boston: Houghton Mifflin, 1943), 109.
35. W. E. B. Du Bois, "The Inter-racial Implications of the Ethiopian Crisis," *Foreign Affairs* 14 (1935): 88, 92.
36. There are many contemporary examples of the role that race plays in United States foreign affairs. Roger Morris, who worked daily in the presence of President Nixon, Chief of Staff Alexander Haig, and Secretary of State Henry Kissinger, declared:

There is no documentary evidence—save perhaps the inaccessible White House tapes on national security subjects—that . . . racism was the decisive influence in Kissinger-Nixon policies in Africa, Vietnam, or elsewhere, policies for which there were other arguments and reasons, however questionable. But it is impossible to pretend that the cast of mind that harbors such casual bigotry did not have some effect on American foreign policy toward the overwhelming majority of the world which is nonwhite. (Roger Morris, *Uncertain Greatness: Henry Kissinger and American Foreign Policy* [New York: Harper and Row, 1977], 131–32).

37. Oliver C. Cox, *Caste, Class and Race. A Study in Social Dynamics* (1948; reprint ed. New York: Modern Reader Paperbacks, 1970), 317.
38. Elliott P. Skinner, *Afro-Americans and Africa: The Continuing Dialectic* (New York: The Urban Center, Columbia University, 1973), 4.
39. Hugh H. Smythe and Elliott P. Skinner, "Black Participation in U.S. Foreign Relations," in *The Black American Reference Book,* ed. Mabel M. Smythe (Englewood, N.J.: Prentice-Hall, 1976), 638–47.
40. E. U. Essien-Udom, *Black Nationalism: A Search for an Identity in America* (Chicago: University of Chicago Press, 1962); John H. Bracey, Jr., August Meier, and Elliott Rudwick, eds., *Black Nationalism in America* (Indianapolis: Bobbs-Merrill, 1970); Sterling Stuckey, *The Ideological Origins of Black Nationalism* (Boston: Beacon Press, 1972).
41. The classic case, of course, was Booker T. Washington, whose activities are chronicled in this volume. See Louis R. Harlan, *Booker T. Washington: The Wizard of Tuskegee, 1901–1915* (New York: Oxford University Press, 1983).
42. W. E. B. Du Bois, *The Souls of Black Folk* (Greenwood, Conn.: Fawcett, 1961), 17.
43. Smythe and Skinner, "Black Participation in Foreign Relations"; Skinner, "Black Foreign Policymakers," 112–22.
44. Ibid.
45. Walter L. Williams, *Black Americans and the Evangelization of Africa, 1877–1900* (Madison: University of Wisconsin Press, 1982).
46. The archives of the Department of State are filled with information of this type, but oral interviews with older black members of the foreign service would provide the best source of data.
47. Skinner, *Afro-Americans and Africa;* Sylvia M. Jacobs, "The Historical Role of Afro-Americans in American Missionary Efforts in Africa," in *Black Americans and the Missionary Movement in Africa,* ed. Sylvia M. Jacobs (Westport, Conn.: Greenwood Press, 1982), 1–29.
48. Adelaide Cromwell Hill and Martin Kilson, eds. and comps., *Apropos of Africa* (London: Frank Cass, 1969).
49. Elliott P. Skinner, "Personal Networks and Institutional Linkages in the Global System," in *Dynamics of the African/Afro-American Connection: From Dependency to Self-Reliance,* ed. Adelaide M. Cromwell (Washington, D.C.: Howard University Press, 1987), 15–31.

1
The Roots of Destiny

> The fact that Negroes arrived in English America as the cargo of the international slave trade unquestionably fostered a sense of superiority among Englishmen. If the noble and commanding Othello could be stigmatized as a "thing", how much more likely it was that degrading terms be applied to those wretches newly spilled out of slave ships! It was to be anticipated that from the beginning a special inferior position would be assigned black men.[1]

Africa always loomed large in the consciousness of early African Americans because it was that continent's economic, political, and military weaknesses that made the slave trade possible and consequently made its inhabitants the object of prejudice and discrimination. Africa's legacy remained on the skin of African Americans in the United States and long influenced their lives. Thomas Jefferson, like most of the Founding Fathers, did not believe that persons of African descent could ever be incorporated into the social and political system of the Union:

> Deep rooted prejudices entertained by the whites [he wrote]; ten thousand recollections, by the blacks, of the injuries they have sustained; new provocations; the real distinction which nature has made; and many other circumstances, will . . . produce convulsions which will probably never end but in the extermination of the one or the other race.[2]

Perhaps because they sensed these attitudes, almost all the early Africans who were brought to America wanted to return to Africa. But much to their surprise, those who lived in the coastal regions discovered that they could not cross the big river that separated them from their ancestral continent. They could, and did, dream that death would release them from slavery and that their spirits could fly back to Africa. In real life, only the Europeans could help them to return. When Ayuba Suleiman Diallo of Bondu finally convinced his owners in Maryland that he was indeed a noble personage from West Africa and should be repatriated, only they had the power to permit it. In fact, Diallo's royal relatives did attempt to secure his release from slavery in far-off America and had even attempted to penalize his abductors. But they had neither the international power nor the mechanism to force the repatriation of their kinsman.[3] Similarly, it was only through the good offices of English philanthropists that Olaudah Equiano of Benin was liberated from American slavery and sent to England, where he later participated in the antislavery crusade.[4]

Taking advantage of the political agitation in prerevolutionary America, African Americans began to petition several state legislatures for their freedom and for permission to return to Africa. In 1773 four slaves pledged to the Massachusetts legislature "to submit to such regulations and laws as may be made relative to us, until we leave the province, which we determine to do as soon as we can from our joynt labours procure money to transport ourselves to some part of the coast of Africa, where we propose a settlement."[5] In January 1777 a number of Africans petitioned the General Court of Massachusetts to legislate the gradual abolition of slavery in the state, because "Every Principle from which Am[e]rica has Acted in the Cours of their unhappy Dificultes with Great Briton Pleads Stronger than A thousand arguments in favours of your pe[ti]tioners."[6] Many of these men again petitioned the general court on 4 January 1787 for assistance in removing themselves to Africa. Not believing that they or their children could achieve happiness in the New World even if freed, they wished to "return to Africa, our native country, which warm climate is much more natural [and] agreeable to us . . . And where we shall live among our equals and be more comfortable and happy, than we can be in our present situation."[7] Importantly, they hoped to help their African brethren "by the means of inlightening and civilizing those nations, who are not sunk in ignorance and barbarity."[8]

Clearly recognizing the growing importance of their Africanity in the world of nation-states, many free Africans in the United States of America began self-help organizations under the banner of Africa. Already in Boston in 1775, Prince Hall, a man of Barbadian origin, had become a Master Mason in an English military lodge and had requested and received permission from the Grand Lodge of England to establish an African lodge. He urged the members of his organization to be "good subjects to the laws of the land" and to "have no hand in any plots or conspiracies or rebellion, or side or assist in them."[9] No doubt this was to calm the fears of many whites who feared Freemasonry and who were alarmed that Africans who had links with England might also be in touch with rebellious Africans in other lands. Prince Hall sought every means to improve the economic, social, and spiritual condition of free African Americans.

He also told his followers they had a special duty to their "distressed brethren," and that while many of the slaves could not read, "by our searches and researches into men and things, we have supplied that defect."[10]

On 10 November 1780, in Rhode Island, Newport Gardner and a few of his friends founded the African Union Society. The express purpose of this association was to promote "the welfare of the colored community by providing a record of births, deaths and marriages; by helping to apprentice Negroes; and by assisting members in time of distress."[11] Smarting under the accusation that some free blacks were guilty of immorality, the society took upon itself the responsibility to watch over the moral conduct of its members. Seven years later, on 12 April 1787, in Philadelphia, the Reverends Richard Allen and Absalom Jones organized the Free African Society. The preamble to the articles of this association stated that "two men of the African race, who, for their religious life and conversation have obtained a good report among men . . . [have] from a love to the people of their complexion whom they beheld with sorrow, because of their irreligious and uncivilized state,"[12] decided to form an organization for the purpose of enabling African Americans to help themselves and to provide for their widows and fatherless children. The members of this society established fraternal relations with similar philanthropic organizations that arose in African American communities throughout the nation. These included the Brown Fellowship Society, established at Charleston, South Carolina, in 1790 and the African Society of Boston, established in 1796.[13]

While many of these early organizations were secular in nature, they had been established by highly religious individuals. One reason for creating secular organizations was to enhance solidarity and to prevent conflicts between the members of different religious denominations. This was especially true of the Free African Society established by Allen and Jones. Needing some religious rituals at their meetings, the leaders compromised by using the articles of faith of the Society of Friends. However, it was difficult for small weak groups involved in a struggle of major proportions not to seek strength in their own religious values. In July 1791 Allen and Jones decided to transform the organization into a religious body, the African Church, but could not agree on what form of church they wanted. In 1794 Jones, along with most of the members of the society, transformed the African Church into the African Protestant Episcopal Church of St. Thomas, of which he was chosen leader. Allen, with a few other persons, organized the Bethel African Methodist Episcopal (AME)

Church, which was dedicated that same year. In 1796 Peter Williams and Francis Jacobs of New York City, despite ostensibly good relations with the white Methodist Episcopalians, wanted their own church, for they had a "desire for the privilege of holding meetings of their own, where they might have an opportunity to exercise their spiritual gifts among themselves, and thereby be more useful to one another."[14]

In 1797 they founded the African Methodist Episcopal Zion Church, so called to distinguish it from the churches of Allen and Jones. These three denominations soon spread among the African Americans, often collaborating but sometimes competing for the allegiance of both free blacks and slaves. These African churches took as their maxim the biblical prophecy, "Princes shall come out of Egypt; Ethiopia shall soon stretch forth her hands unto God." In time these churches became not only the cradle for generations of African American leaders but also the training ground of ministers who would carry out symbolic religious work and political activities throughout the United States and Africa. Many of these clerics descended from their pulpits to become practitioners in the realm of secular politics.

Conscious that education was an important weapon in their struggle to redeem "the African race" after the Revolution, African Americans sought additional schools for their children. For example, in 1797 Paul Cuffe of New England—a man who would later take African American immigrants to Africa—was frustrated at not being able to procure education for many more African American children and proceeded to build a school with his own funds. In 1798 Prince Hall established the African School and hired two young scholars from Harvard College to teach there. Perhaps the most famous of these schools was the African Free School, established by the New York Manumission Society in 1787. This school became the nucleus for a number of African Free Schools, which in time produced such black leaders concerned with Africa as Alexander Crummell and Henry Highland Garnet.[15]

The belief of most American whites that African Americans were so biologically inferior to them that they could not and should not be permitted to form an integral part of the emerging United States of America led many African American leaders to take a more active part in defending their race and the continent from which it sprang. They could not leave unchallenged the views of persons such as Thomas Jefferson, who wrote in his *Notes on the State of Virginia* that "whether originally a distinct race, or made distinct by time and circumstances, (blacks) are inferior to the whites in the endowments both of body and mind."[16] Nor were African Americans happy with Jefferson's corollary that the two races, equally free, could not live in the same government, that nature, habit, and opinion, had drawn indelible lines of distinction between them.[17]

Stung by the views of Jefferson and others, African Americans who had the power of pen and other talents reacted. In 1792 Benjamin Banneker, a free man who, in his own words, "freely and cheerfully acknowledge, that I am of the African race, and in that color which is natural to them of the deepest dye,"[18] sent a copy of his *Almanac* to Jefferson in an attempt to demonstrate that a black man was capable of astronomical and mathematical accomplishments. Banneker knew that Jefferson did not think highly of the skill of the African American poet Phillis Wheatley, but he hoped that a man who considered himself an equal to the French philosophers would examine another bit of evidence attesting to the intellectual capacity of African Americans.

In a letter accompanying his work, Banneker challenged Jefferson's view of blacks as presented in his *Notes on the State of Virginia* and regretted that so distinguished a man as Jefferson had contributed to "the almost general prejudice and prepossession, which is so prevalent in the world against those of my complexion."[19] Banneker conceded, "We are a race of beings, who have long labored under the abuse and censure of the world; . . . we have long been looked upon with an eye of contempt; and . . . we have long been considered rather as brutish than human, and scarcely capable of mental endowments."[20] But he urged Jefferson to take fully into consideration the "state of degradation, to which the unjustifiable cruelty and barbarism of men" had reduced African Americans.[21]

Banneker recalled that Jefferson himself had railed against such tyranny when it came from the British Crown. He also cited the contradiction between the high principles of the Revolution and the subsequent behavior of white Americans "in detaining by fraud and violence so numerous a part of my brethren under groaning captivity and cruel oppression, that you should at the same time be found guilty of that most criminal act, which you professedly detested in others, with respect to yourselves."[22] Finally, Banneker suggested that were Jefferson to try to place himself in the shoes of African Americans, he would be convinced that he needed "neither the direction of myself or others, in what manner to proceed herein."[23]

In response to Banneker's letter, Jefferson wrote: "No body wishes more than I do, to see such proofs as you exhibit, that nature has given to our black brethren, talents equal to those of the other colors of men and that the appearance of a want of them is owing merely to the degraded condition of their existence, both in Africa & America."[24] He added that he, too, wished to see those circumstances arise in which African Americans could be raised from the "imbecility of their present existence." Jefferson sent a copy of Banneker's *Almanac* to Monsieur de Condorcet, secretary of the Academy of Sciences at Paris and member of the Philanthropic Society, because, as he told Banneker, "I consider it as a document to which your whole colour had a right for their justification against the doubts which have been entertained of them."[25] But Jefferson later confessed that he was not at all impressed with Banneker's mind. He suggested that although Banneker knew spherical trigonometry, he might have been helped in the preparation of his *Almanac* by "Ellicot, who was his neighbor and friend, and [who] never missed an opportunity of puffing him."[26] Jefferson kept his doubts about the intellectual capacity of African Americans and of their ability to live on a plane of equality with white Americans.

The Reverends Richard Allen and Absalom Jones of Philadelphia also challenged the calumnious statements of whites about African Americans. In a letter of 1794 denouncing slaveholding, they argued that slaves were stigmatized as persons "whose baseness was incurable" and who therefore should be held in bondage. But though whites prevented slaves from rising from the state of barbarism they were said to be in, they also looked to them for superior moral conduct. Allen and Jones asked whether, having reduced them to degradation, it was fair of whites to assert that this showed an incapacity of African Americans for freedom and therefore that they should be content with oppression. They suggested that if whites "would try the experiment of taking a few black children, and cultivate their minds with the same care, and let them have the same prospect in view, as to living in the world, as you would wish for your own children, you would find them upon the trial, they were not inferior in mental endowments."[27] It was wrong, they concluded, for Jefferson and other slaveholders to expect African Americans to be moral supermen while held in bondage and subjected to hostility and discrimination. "Why will you look for grapes from thorns, or figs from thistles? It is in our posterity enjoying the same privileges with your own, that you ought to look for better things."[28] The two pastors consoled themselves that God worked in mysterious ways to achieve his purposes, and that African Americans might be instruments of his scheme "until the princes shall come forth from Egypt and Ethiopia stretch out her hand unto God."[29]

It was in part this same belief—that the Almighty had a special role for Egypt and Ethiopia and, by extension, for the black race in the redemption of all peoples—that led Paul Cuffe to contemplate colonizing African Americans in Africa. Though a successful merchant and sailor, devout Quaker, prosperous taxpayer, and pillar of the Boston African American community, Cuffe had failed in his attempt to secure the vote in Massachusetts, his home state. His eulogist, Peter Williams, said of him:

> It was in his active commiseration in behalf of his African brethren, that he shone forth most conspicuously as a man of worth. Long had his bowels yearned over their degraded, destitute, miserable condition. He saw, it is true, many benevolent men engaging in releasing them from bondage, and pouring into their minds the light of literature and religion, but he saw also the force of prejudice operating so powerfully against them, as to give but little encouragement to hope that they could ever rise to respectability and usefulness, unless it were in a state of society where they would have greater incentives to improvement, and more favorable opportunities than would probably be ever afforded them where the bulk of the population are whites.[30]

Paul Cuffe had come to believe that the "state of society" where African Americans could improve themselves was Africa. He had made several commercial voyages to Africa, including one to South Africa, and had observed the attempts of the British to resettle African Americans from England and Nova Scotia in Sierra Leone. He had even corresponded with members of the African Institution, a London-based organization interested in helping Africans. This was the background that led Cuffe to sail for Sierra Leone on New Year's Day, 1811, on board his own ship, the *Traveller,* with an all–African American crew to survey conditions for missionary work, commerce, and the introduction of his people as settlers.

The British governor and the local people were sympathetic to Cuffe's venture, and in an effort to demonstrate his organizing ability and interest in the country, he founded the Friendly Society of Sierra Leone to promote the interests of the incoming African Americans as well as those of the colonists. When Cuffe received word in Freetown that the British government had sanctioned his project, he decided to go to London. He was well aware that Africa was gradually being brought directly under European control and that free blacks who wanted to return to Africa had to have the concurrence of Europeans. Once in London he held a meeting with the directors of the African Institution who, we are told, stood to profit by the opportunity of inducing Cuffe to settle in Sierra Leone, and carry over with him "a few colored persons of good character, to instruct the colonists in agriculture and the mechanical arts."[31]

Paradoxically, Paul Cuffe's plans to help African Americans go to Africa were frustrated by the War of 1812—a conflict caused in part by America's resistance to Britain's impressing seamen who, while claiming American citizenship, were deserters from the Royal Navy. On his return to America, Cuffe visited a number of cities and talked to prospective emigrants. He also formed a number of societies—one in Baltimore, one in New York, and another in Philadelphia—to further the work he had undertaken. When the outbreak of war threatened the departure of the colonists, Cuffe traveled to Washington, D.C., to speak with government officials. President James Madison graciously received him and carefully evaluated Cuffe's plans, because "many objections had occurred to him against it."[32] And while a number of other important men in the capital applauded Cuffe's aims, the government refused him permission to leave because its wartime policy "would not admit of such an intercourse with an enemy's colony."[33] Since the British government also refused to sanction the voyage, Cuffe's plans had to be scrapped.

During the course of the war, Cuffe consulted with the Quakers and other whites interested in colonizing free blacks in Africa. He sought more funds from the United States for his project and managed to maintain correspondence with sympathizers in both America and Great Britain. The captain received little material help from these groups, but on 10 December 1815, at the war's end, using some $3,000 or $4,000 of his own (Congress by a 72 to 65 vote refused to aid him financially), Cuffe sailed for Africa with thirty-eight African Americans. After fifty-five days of travel he arrived in Freetown, completing the first successful project in what would become a major effort to return African Americans to Africa. Cuffe did not mind the expense because he had not undertaken the trip with financial profit in view. Yet after later calculating the cost, he concluded that in view of the expense of ameliorating the condition of "that part of the great family of Africa" in the United States, "Nothing: Nothing of much amount can be affected by an individual or private bodies until the government removes the obstruction in the way."[34] This experience helped Cuffe to understand that despite his ambition to aid African peoples, he had to accept the reality of the nation-state in world affairs.

While many African American leaders in the United States, such as Absalom Jones and Richard Allen, initially welcomed Cuffe's initiatives and reports on life in Africa, they grew increasingly hostile to the notion of large-scale return of free blacks to that continent. What disturbed them was that, independent of Cuffe's colonizing expeditions, a number of whites had begun to push for colonization of free African Americans or manumitted slaves outside the United States. Moreover, whites did so without consulting black leaders or taking their advice or attitudes into consideration. Already, by 1814, unknown to Cuffe and other African Americans, Robert Finley, a white Princeton graduate who became a Presbyterian minister, had developed an interest in African American colonization. In 1815 Finley said of free African Americans:

> Everything connected with their condition, including their color, is against them; nor is there much prospect that their state can ever be greatly ameliorated, while they shall continue among us. Could not the rich and benevolent devise means to form a colony on some part of the coast of Africa, similar to the one at Sierra Leone, which might gradually induce many free blacks to go there and settle, devising for them the means of getting there, and of protection and support till they were established? Ought not Congress to be petitioned to grant them a district in a good climate, say on the shores of the Pacific Ocean? Our fathers brought them here, and we are bound if possible to repair the injuries inflicted by our fathers. Could they be sent to Africa, a three-fold benefit would arise. We should be cleared of them; we should send to Africa a population partially civilized and christianized for its benefits; our blacks themselves would be put in a better condition.[35]

Perhaps unknown to prospective white colonizationists was the fact that Cuffe was already on his way to Sierra Leone in 1815 with colonists. Benjamin Lundy of the newly founded antislavery Union Humane Society in Ohio called for concerted action by all persons interested in easing the condition of the black race and in removing all blacks from "beyond the pale of the white man." Later the same year the members of the Kentucky Colonization Society petitioned Congress for a suitable territory to

> be laid off as an asylum for all those negroes and mulattoes who have been, and those who may hereafter be, emancipated within the United States; and that such donations, allowances, encouragements, and assistance be afforded them as may be necessary for carrying them thither and settling them therein; and that they be under such regulations and government in all respects as your wisdom shall direct.[36]

In the spring of 1816 Charles Fenton Mercer (a slaveholder who had just discovered secret resolutions urging emancipation and colonization passed in the Virginia assembly in the wake of the Gabriel insurrection) proposed that the assembly petition the federal government to select a territory in the North Pacific to settle free African Americans and those subsequently emancipated in Virginia. Thus by the time Cuffe returned to America in the summer of 1816, whites were busily organizing a colonization scheme.

The white participants in the colonization movement held varying and often contradictory ideas about African Americans, free and enslaved, and motives for why they ought to emigrate. Robert Finley, the prime drive behind the movement, believed sincerely that the prejudice of whites against African Americans was too deep to be eradicated and that everyone, including African Americans, would be better off if they left the United States. This was Finley's motive for calling a meeting at Princeton on 6 November 1816 to plan further meetings in Washington City and for writing to Paul Cuffe on 5 December 1816 seeking information about Sierra Leone. Finley frankly told Cuffe that "the great desire of those whose minds are impressed with this subject is to give an opportunity to the free people of color to rise to their proper level and at the same time to provide a powerful means of putting an end to the slave trade and sending civilization and Christianity to Africa."[37]

On the evening of 20 December, Finley and the Reverend Samuel J. Mills, a pastor from New York, met at the home of Elias B. Caldwell, Finley's brother-in-law, to pray for "divine direction . . . when the expediency of forming a Colonization Society was to be publicly discussed."[38] Finley's enthusiasm was reportedly so boundless, and he believed so strongly that he was working with God, that he promised to contribute $500 from his meager parson's salary.

The first formal meeting of the colonizationists was held on the evening of 21 December at the Davis Hotel in Washington and was attended by such illustrious men as Henry Clay, Francis Scott Key, Bishop William Meade, John Randolph, and Judge Bushrod Washington. During his principal address, Elias B. Caldwell argued the "expediency and practicability" of settling African Americans in Sierra Leone, where the climate agreed with them, where "they could live cheaply," and where "they could carry civilization and Christianity to the Africans." African Americans could never be happy in the United States because they would never achieve equality with whites; to settle them in the western part of the country might be dangerous because they could unite with the Indians against whites. Caldwell admitted that the cost of settling them in Africa would be great, but he felt that America should atone for the wrongs done to Africa and African Americans. Moreover, he believed that "with a promise of equality, a homestead, and a free passage," African Americans would not refuse to depart. He concluded that the proposed colonization "is a plan in which all interests, all classes, and descriptions of people may unite, in which all discordant feelings may be lost in those of humanity, in promoting 'peace on earth and good will to man.' "[39]

Some of the conferees took a more cautious view of the colonization scheme. Senator Henry Clay, serving as chair, felt that the speaker had not emphasized strongly enough that no attempt would be made "to touch or agitate in the slightest degree, a delicate question, connected with another portion of the colored population of this country."[40] Colonizationists would have to reassure many gentlemen from the South and West that there would be no discussion of the question of emancipation, or of the abolition of slavery, if their cooperation was sought. It was upon this condition alone, he said, that "he himself [a slaveholder] had attended."[41] John Randolph of Roanoke, Virginia, who supported Clay's opinion, was concerned that the conveners had not emphasized enough that the meeting had nothing to do with African American slavery. Randolph advised the gathering that if they wished to gain the cooperation of all citizens of the United States, they should attempt "to secure the property of every master in the United States over his slaves." He told the gathering that free African Americans were considered to be a great evil, "a nuisance," and "a bug-bear to every man who feels an inclination to emancipate his slaves." Randolph concluded that he was sure that if a place could be found to send freed African Americans, "hundreds, nay thousands of citizens" would send their slaves.[42]

There is no record of Finley or of any other person there taking issue with the opinions of either Clay or Randolph. To the contrary, the delegates appear to have generally approved of Randolph's characterization of free blacks. In Samuel J. Mills's view, the movement would "transfer to the coast of Africa the blessings of religion and civilization; and Ethiopia will soon stretch out her hands to God."[43] It was therefore not difficult for the delegates to pass resolutions approving the formation of an association for the purpose of colonizing African Americans in Africa or elsewhere. They delegated one subcommittee to draw up a petition to Congress requesting that a suitable territory be secured and another subcommittee to prepare a constitution and rules to govern the association once formed. The session adjourned until 28 December 1816, when the delegates met in the Hall of the House of Representatives of the United States.

At this meeting the delegates adopted a constitution under the title, "The American Society for Colonizing the Free People of Color of the United States." Its sole purpose was "to promote and execute a plan for colonizing (with their consent) the Free People of Color residing in our Country, in Africa, or such other place as Congress shall deem most expedient."[44] Fifty prominent white Americans, including Henry Clay, Daniel Webster, John Randolph, and Bushrod Washington signed the constitution of the society. When the delegates met again on 1 January 1817 for their first annual meeting, Henry Clay presided and Bushrod Washington was elected president. Other important officers were Clay, Key, and General Andrew Jackson of Tennessee.

The founders of the colonization society must have known that Paul Cuffe was in the United States, but the race question would have prevented them from inviting him to attend their meeting. However, on 26 December 1816 Samuel J. Mills wrote to Cuffe about the conference and also sought information about conditions in Sierra Leone. In reply Cuffe stated that he had observed "from the paper, the ardent engagement of the body of that meeting" and gave Mills information on Sierra Leone and the Gambian region. He also suggested that the Sherbro region of Sierra Leone might do for a "small settlement or [at least] a small beginning."[45] In an offhand manner Cuffe added that "were there a willingness for a pretty general removal of this people, . . . the south part of Africa (viz.), the Cape of Good Hope, if it could be obtained, I think . . . looks most favorable. However, I only mention the subject and leave all to the judgement of my superiors."[46]

Cuffe was more forthcoming in a letter he wrote his friend James Brian on 16 January 1817, in which he stated that while some had suggested colonizing the free African Americans either in Africa or in the United States, "I have taken the liberty to propose two colonies: one in Africa and another in the United States, as it is not at all likely all may be prevailed on to emigrate to Africa. But before we wreck our understanding too much, [they should] liberate those already in bondage."[47] As far as Cuffe was concerned, the American Colonization Society should endeavor to get the United States government to stop the slave trade and to authorize the British government to detain American citizens found engaged in it, sending them home as common criminals to be tried by American laws. Then in the characteristic tone he used when speaking of his "superiors," Cuffe added, "However, I wish not to say more than becomes me; neither do I wish for my zeal to lead me before wisdom['s] best guide."[48]

Cuffe became the center of controversy between African American leaders and whites when the colonization society attempted to get him to go to Africa on its behalf. A number of African American leaders, while not openly criticizing Cuffe, made it clear they were not in favor of colonization. James Forten, a personal friend, warned Cuffe on 25 January 1817 that Finley had mentioned to Absalom Jones about sending a letter to Cuffe and that "the whole continent seems to be agitated concerning the people of color."[49] Forten observed:

> Indeed, the people of color here was [sic] very much frightened. At first they were afraid that all the free people would be compelled to go, particularly [those] in the southern states. We had a large meeting of males at the Rev. R[ichard] Allen's church the other evening. Three thousand at least attended, and there was not one soul that was in favor of going to Africa. They think that the slaveholders wants [sic] to get rid of them so as to make their property more secure.[50]

Knowing that Cuffe favored colonization, Forten confessed he was a secret sympathizer of the scheme because, in his opinion, the African Americans "will never become a people until they come out from amongst the white people. But as the majority is decidedly against me, I am determined to remain silent, except as to my opinion which I freely give when asked."[51]

Caught in a cross fire, Cuffe admitted to Mills that African Americans were generally hostile to colonization. In response, Mills betrayed his innocence about the psychology of African Americans by insisting that when Finley visited Richard Allen and other African American leaders, the latter "gave a unanimous expression of their perfect conviction that benevolence to them and the land of their fathers guided the movements that were made at Washington, and that the hand of God was securely moving this business. They acknowledged the desirableness of being separated from the whites."[52] There was apparently little that Cuffe could or wanted to say about this response.

As Forten told Cuffe, what really troubled the African Americans was the suspicion that whites were less than honest about their alleged reasons for fostering the colonization of African Americans outside the United States. African Americans found it difficult to understand how white colonizationists could suggest that they wished to "remove a dangerous element" from the United States and at the same time expect this element to "civilize and Christianize Africa." Even Cuffe, sympathetic as he was to colonization, felt that whites could have shown their good intentions by asking for the amelioration of the plight of the slaves and by petitioning the United States government to help England stop the slave trade, then primarily in the hands of American ship captains. And though Cuffe never actually criticized the plans of the whites, he "cautioned his brethren to watch its operation for a year or two before taking sides for or against it."[53] Cuffe never wavered in his support of colonization. Until his dying day "he remained convinced that by establishing a colony in the United States as well as one in Africa, blacks would be helping, not fleeing from, their brethren in chains."[54]

African American leaders such as Richard Allen, Robert Douglass, James Forten, and Absalom Jones mobilized three thousand men in Philadelphia to deplore the "unmerited stigma" that the colonizationists had "attempted to be cast upon the reputation of the free people of color."[55] They resented the notion that they were "a dangerous and useless part of the community" and vowed "never to separate themselves from the slave population of this country as they were brethren by 'the ties of consanguinity, of suffering, and of wrong.' "[56] They organized a committee to communicate their feelings about colonization to Joseph Hopkins, a congressman from Philadelphia. On 10 August 1817 this group addressed a message to the "Human and Benevolent Inhabitants of Philadelphia," in which they declared, "We have no wish to separate from our present homes, for any purpose whatsoever."[57] They renounced and disclaimed any connection with the plans of the colonization society and firmly declared their determination not to participate in any part of it. The African American leaders maintained that slaves left behind as a result of the colonization project would face greater suffering because their smaller number would make the slave masters more ruthless: "The southern masters will colonize only those who it may be dangerous to keep among them. The bondage of a large portion of our members will thus be rendered perpetual."[58] These free African Americans, while desirous of seeking greater opportunities for themselves and for their children, did not wish to go to Africa. They would prefer being settled "in the remotest corner of the land of their nativity" rather than leave the United States of America.[59]

The directors of the colonization society, pursuing their own agenda, ignored the protestations of the African Americans. They petitioned Congress for funds and asked President Monroe to instruct his ambassador to inquire whether the British would permit a large number of African Americans to enter Sierra Leone. The ambassador did so and on 6 April 1818 reported to the secretary of state that, taking advantage of a dinner with the British Lord Bathurst, he had seized the opportunity to allude to the existence of a society formed at Washington for the colonization of free African Americans in Africa. "I did not fail to say, how large a portion of character and respectability it comprised, or to recapitulate the enlarged objects of philanthropy to the accomplishment of which its exertions looked," the ambassador wrote.[60] He concluded, "Both the dukes expressed themselves favorably towards the plan, and Lord Bathurst avowed in like manner his approbation."[61]

Elated by such reports from the State Department, the officials of the society trumpeted its designs throughout the country and sent Samuel J. Mills and Ebenezer Burgess to England and West Africa on a fact-finding tour. Mills died before he could return to America, but Burgess brought back glowing reports on the possibility of settlement. He also attempted to allay the fears of African Americans by suggesting that the colonization project would indeed eliminate the slave trade as well as lead to the manumission of more slaves. Meanwhile, Congressman Mercer from Virginia pushed his antislave trade bill, which the society hoped would really provide funds for purchasing land in Africa for the colonists. On 3 March 1819 the bill, entitled "An Act in addition to the acts prohibiting the Slave Trade," became law and authorized President Monroe to spend $100,000 for resettling recaptured slaves in Africa. Despite the prodding of the colonizationists, President Monroe hesitated to use the money to purchase land in Africa. He was troubled by the argument of John Quincy Adams, his secretary of state, that while the money could be used to settle recaptured Africans, it might be unconstitutional to use it to purchase land. Besides, Adams distrusted the motives of the supporters of colonization. Some of them he viewed as "exceedingly humane, weak-minded" but relatively harmless individuals; others he felt were speculators who hoped to profit from the colonization scheme; and still others he considered to be "cunning slaveholders" who hoped to raise the price of slaves.[62] Eventually President Monroe came out on the side of the colonization society and interpreted the bill to mean that he did have the right to send to Africa agents who were free to acquire land.[63]

African Americans who opposed colonization faced formidable foes. While never able to get as much money as they needed, the directors, agents, and supporters of the colonization society did manage to win the sympathy of those who feared and despised free blacks and wanted to get rid of them. They succeeded in securing letters from Paul Cuffe's emigrants to Sierra Leone denouncing African American opponents of colonization: "You cannot enjoy yourselves in America as free men . . . because you are captives in a strange land."[64] At home the anti-emigrationists were also criticized by some African Americans who really wanted to leave the United States.

By 31 January 1820 the society had found eighty-six African Americans ready to go to Africa. They arrived safely in Sierra Leone, but after a series of mishaps they, and subsequent arrivals, left and traveled southward to the area of Cape Mesurado. There, after a great deal of confusion, a white naval officer forced at gunpoint King Peter, the local potentate, to sell land to the colonists for $300. The colonists called their new home Liberia, thus emphasizing that it was the "love of liberty" that led them there and away from their homes. They asserted that they were prepared to "suffer hunger and nakedness for years" in Africa rather than tolerate serfdom and inequality in America.[65]

Given their suspicion that the settling of Liberia under the auspices of the American Colonization Society was a ruse of whites to get rid of free blacks, African American leaders initially took a hands-off policy toward the African colony. Moreover, like many of the colonists in Liberia, African American leaders at home did not appreciate the colonization society's practice of sending whites as its agents in Liberia. In 1825, before leaving America, the Reverend Lott Cary declared: "I am African, and in this country, however meritorious my conduct, and respectable my character, I cannot receive the credit due to either. I wish to go to a country where I shall be estimated by my merits and not by my complexion, and I feel bound to labor for my suffering race."[66] He resented the role that Jehudi Ashmun, a white agent of the society, was playing. The opposition group that Cary led allegedly proclaimed, "We have come here to be free, and nothing but real freedom will suffice."[67] Writing to a friend in America Cary declared: "If you intend doing anything for Africa, you must not wait for the Colonization Society, nor for government, for neither of these are in search of missionary ground, but of colonizing grounds; if it should not sow missionary seeds, you cannot expect a missionary crop."[68] Cary was convinced that "if the colored people of Virginia do not think [it] proper to come out [to Liberia], the Lord will bring help . . . from some other quarter. . . . I mention these circumstances that you may look through them to the time foretold in prophecy; i.e. Ethiopia shall stretch out her hands unto God."[69]

The dilemma that the African American leaders at this time faced with respect to Africa was that America was pushing them out more forcibly than Africa was pulling them in. The thousands of free African Americans who lived in the Midwest and in the old Northwest during the early 1820s, and the additional hundreds of manumitted slaves who went there annually to avoid being reenslaved, felt increasing discrimination and hostility from resident whites and newly arriving white immigrants. The whites sought to limit the influx of African Americans by suggesting that their "wives and daughters may and no doubt will be insulted and abused by those Africans" coming into the territory unless measures were taken.[70] An Illinois senator expressed the prevailing sentiment when in 1828 he declared that the presence of African Americans in that state "is productive of moral and political evil. . . . The natural difference between them and ourselves forbids the idea that they should ever be permitted to participate with us in the political affairs of our government."[71] One writer in Illinois suggested, "We want neither slaves or free negroes. They are both unprofitable members of society, and ought to be avoided rather than invited."[72] Ostracized by his neighbors for having rented land to African Americans, George Flower maintained that he could not break his contractual relations with his clients. He was told that "black men had no rights that white men need respect."[73] In Indiana, one David Dobson, hearing a delegate to the state constitutional convention support the right of African Americans to vote, retorted, "Whenever you begin to talk about making negroes equal with white men, I begin to think about leaving the country."[74] In Ohio, William Sawyer had a similar reaction to the suggestion that African Americans should vote: "The United States were designed by the God in Heaven to be governed and inhabited by the Anglo-Saxon race and by them alone."[75]

African Americans faced similar problems as they moved farther West. Initially, blacks in California were valued as miners, some people believing that they had special luck finding gold. But as many more arrived, the issues of slavery and exclusion arose. Although Californians prohibited slavery and voted against excluding them, African Americans faced discrimination on many sides and would have fared worse had the Chinese not also become the object of prejudice. In Oregon African Americans found that white migrants from the Midwest had brought their discriminatory attitudes with them, with many settlers rejecting both slavery and free African Americans, their aversion to the latter greater than their distaste for the former.[76]

Free African Americans resisted exclusion from Middle America and the Far West, but they especially resented the attempts of the branches of the American Colonization Society to get rid of them. In 1824 the Ohio legislature branded slavery a national evil and begged Congress to adopt colonization as a means of eradicating it. The legislators were in favor of the emancipation and colonization of the adult children of slaves in an

attempt to win support for the colonization movement. Judge Isaac New-
ton Blackford of the Indiana Supreme Court warned in 1829 that failure
to support the colonization society would result in the influx of "a low,
ignorant, degraded multitude of free blacks" into his state.[77] The leaders
of the Indiana Colonization Society asserted: "Our black population
adds nothing to the strength, and little to the wealth of the nation. . . .
Let them be removed and their places be supplied with intelligent
[white] freemen, and we venture to say that a saving equal to the cost of
their removal would be gained in the expense of courts of justice and
poor houses."[78] Some twenty years later the Indianans still advocated
"colonizing the Negroes in their native Africa," considering it unsuita-
ble for a "refined and superior class to keep in their midst an uncultivated, degraded and inferior race."[79] During the debates at the Illinois
constitutional convention of 1847, one D. J. Pickney declared: "I am in
favor of removing [African Americans] not only from this State, but
from all the States."[80]

In 1830 a riot of African Americans in the Cincinnati ghetto known as
Little Africa and the decision of the whites there to enforce their laws
against blacks forced African American leaders to meet in "convention"
to protect the rights of free blacks to live in America rather than to have
to flee to Canada or elsewhere. They feared that "if the act is enforced,
we, the poor sons of Aethiopia, must take shelter where we can find it.
. . . If we cannot find it in America, where we were born and spent all
our days, we must beg it elsewhere."[81] This development placed African
American leaders in New York and Philadelphia on the horns of a
dilemma. They had long opposed any kind of emigration. Even those
who had not initially attacked the American Colonization Society regarded the organization as a tool designed by planters and bigoted whites
to remove unwanted blacks.

Thus when on 16 February 1830 "the respectable people of colour, of
the city and county of Philadelphia" met under the chairmanship of
Peter Gardner in the "first coloured Wesley Methodist Church," they
passed eleven resolutions commiserating with and supporting their
"brethren recently from Ohio, but now in Canada."[82] They requested
that the colony in Canada be supported by all philanthropists and by
"every man whose sable skin divests him of his freedom, and impairs his
usefulness in this country."[83] With tongue in cheek, the delegates hoped
that their resolutions would not prove "offensive to the American people" since they were engendered out of concern for their oppressed

brethren "in a country whose republican constitution declares, *that all men are born free and equal.*"[84]

Even before the meeting in Philadelphia, free African Americans in the northern urban centers had started to reexamine their condition. First of all, through manumissions, natural increase, and escapes, their numbers had substantially increased from only 59,000 in 1790 to over 319,000 by 1830. Second, being more numerous, they had become the object of increasing prejudice and discrimination from native-born whites and white immigrants who resented economic competition with them. Third, many free blacks, especially those with poor education and ignorance of their very few civil rights, faced the daily prospect of being deemed runaways, seized, and reduced to slavery. Fourth, they felt threatened by the colonization society, which they believed was conspiring to expel them from the United States. Fifth, they felt that while African Americans in the West Indies were moving toward freedom, their own plight, as well as that of the slaves, was getting worse.

Faced with what seemed insurmountable problems, the African American educated class felt it was time to take their destiny into their own hands and develop vehicles for self-expression. In 1827 Samuel Cornish and John B. Russwurm started a newspaper called *Freedom's Journal.* Their goal was to plead their "own cause" since "too long have others spoken for us." They lamented the tendency of whites to belittle "things which concern us dearly, though in the estimation of some mere trifles," while at the same time exaggerating "the least trifle, which tends to the discredit of any person of colour." Cornish and Russwurm vowed to struggle for the civil rights of all African Americans, free and slave; to educate African American people about the civilizations of Africa; and to report on the progress of Haiti and the South American countries where "despotism has given place to free governments, and where many of our brethren now fill important civil and military stations."[85]

It was with a sense of urgency that Bishop Richard Allen, Cyrus Black, Junius C. Morel, Benjamin Paschall, Jr., and James Cornish issued a call to their "brethren through the United States, inviting them to assemble by delegation, in Convention to be held in the city of Philadelphia, on the 20th of September, 1830."[86] With Allen in the chair, the delegates and honorary guests meeting at the Bethel AME Church formed the American Society of Free Persons of Colour (ASFPC). In a speech addressed "to the Free People of Colour of these United States," Allen invoked the Declaration of Independence and suggested that the time had come for African Americans to "devise and pursue all legal means for the speedy elevation of ourselves and brethren to the scale and standing of men."[87] He insisted that the aim of the society was to help the persecuted and that while he did not question the sincerity of those who worked with the American Colonization Society, he insisted that his group would not accept assistance from that organization.

The delegates encouraged the formation in other states of auxiliary groups of the parent institution in Philadelphia; recommended rules for the organization of these auxiliaries and their representation at general conventions; and resolved that the proceedings of the convention be publicized by the daily papers of Philadelphia. What split the members of the ASFPC in the United States was the issue of support for free blacks forced to flee to Canada. True, all African Americans wished to help those persons in distress; but they were troubled by the implications of supporting any colonization movement, since the majority wished to remain at home and because there were slaves still in bondage. Moreover, the members of the ASFPC grew alarmed when the American Colonization Society, citing African American support of the emigrants to Canada, was able to persuade many trained youths to migrate to Liberia.

In 1832 the sentiments of the leadership of the ASFPC turned against the tide of emigration. Questioning whether any African Americans should emigrate unless literally forced to do so, the next year the ASFPC's committee on colonization strongly criticized emigration to Liberia, concluding, "There is not now and probably never will be actual necessity for a large emigration of the present race of free coloured people."[88]

Even while African American leaders were voicing these concerns, a resolution was presented in the House of Representatives authorizing "that a committee be appointed to inquire into the expediency of making an appropriation for the purpose of removing from the United States and her Territories the free people of color, and colonizing them on the coast of Africa or elsewhere."[89] Much to the satisfaction of African American leaders, consideration of this proposal was postponed until 16 January 1832, and it appeared doomed. But on 31 January 1832 one Mr. Archer sent to the committee a memorial of the Rahway Colonization Society, which recommended an amendment to the Constitution of the United States appropriating revenue to aid in "the removal of such portions of the colored population of the States as they may, respectively, ask aid in removing."[90] Significantly, while it was proposed that Congress govern the territories to which blacks were taken until these areas could be declared a state (or states) independent of the United States, there was the additional proposal that "neither of which States shall, in any event, or at any time, be admitted into the Union of the United States."[91]

The problem for some African American leaders during this period was how to deal with those who despaired of ever gaining equality and liberty in America and were stirred by the spirit of self-improvement through emigration. Some of these leaders longed for "islands" of liberty where African Americans could dwell in relative peace and freedom.[92] In contrast to the directors of the American Colonization Society, many African American leaders saw emigration as a salvation for their followers' individual needs and not as a solution to America's racial dilemma. Moreover, actual and potential African American emigrants resented any role that whites wanted to play in their decision to emigrate. They were especially hostile to African Americans who supported the white policy of emigrationism.

One target of this hostility was John B. Russwurm, the popular co-founder of *Freedom's Journal,* who had emigrated to Liberia. Russwurm's decision had pleased the American Colonization Society, but African American leaders were infuriated when he wrote back to his friends in America, "Before God, we know no other home for the man of color, of republican principles, than Africa."[93] Not only did they resent Russwurm's desertion, but they hinted openly that he had left the United States because he was unsuccessful. One man declared with bitter sarcasm that "it was real necessity that drove him [Russwurm] to seek in Africa an abiding home, as he terms it."[94] Yet in contrast with the 1820s, when most African Americans did not question their leaders' decision to stay at home and struggle to succeed in America, the 1840s saw the publication in African American newspapers such as the *Ram's Horn* of invitations to prospective emigrants to Liberia, which by 1847 had declared itself a republic and had made provisions for all African Americans to become citizens.

With the fever of emigration rising, a number of prominent former anti-emigrationist and neutral African Americans began to suggest the necessity or desirability of leaving the United States. One such person was the Reverend Henry Highland Garnet. A former firebrand, Garnet acknowledged that emigration was a legitimate goal for those seeking power and wealth, even though he recommended no specific area. Later, while on an antislavery lecture tour of Britain, Garnet accepted the invitation of the United Presbyterian Church of Scotland to pastor one of its churches in Jamaica. Another important recruit to the cause of emigrationism was Dr. Martin R. Delany. This Harvard-trained medical doctor had abandoned the position that African Americans should not leave the United States even for Canada. With the active support of James M. Whitfield and J. Theodore Holly, Delany defended emigration at many state and national conventions.

The 1854 national emigration convention voted to accept Delany's philosophy of emigrationism as outlined in his lengthy speech, "Political Destiny of the Colored Race."[95] In it Delany insisted that emigration was the salvation of the African American and of all African peoples. Believing in the equality, if not superiority of African Americans to whites in certain areas of endeavor, Delany felt that "no enterprise, institution, or anything else, should be commenced *for us,* or our general benefit, without first consulting us."[96] He asserted that there was "a great principle of political economy" that African Americans should understand: "No people can be free who themselves do not constitute an essential part of the *ruling element* of the country in which they live. Whether this element be founded upon a true or false, a just or an unjust basis, this position in community is necessary to personal safety. The liberty of no man is secure, who controls not his own personal destiny."[97] Delany suggested that African Americans were sick; they suffered from a terrible disease. "We propose for this disease a remedy," he declared. "That remedy is emigration."[98]

In a letter to Frederick Douglass dated 23 July 1852, Delany had argued that in order for blacks to make any progress, "We must have a position, independent of anything pertaining to white men and nations."[99] He was tired, he wrote, "of whining and sniveling at the feet of white men."[100] To the abolitionist William Lloyd Garrison he had explained that he was "not in favor of caste, nor separation of the brotherhood of mankind, and would as willingly live among white men as black, if I had an *equal possession and enjoyment of* privileges."[101] But he did not look forward to struggling and fighting for these in a country where he had no hope of ever achieving equality. He concluded that he preferred "Heathenism and Liberty, before Christianity and Slavery."[102] Delany did not advocate immediate exodus for all African Americans, but he felt that emigration, like any remedy, must be applied skillfully and carefully "within the proper time, directed to operate on that part of the system whose greatest tendency shall be to benefit the whole."[103] In these remarks Delany echoed the views of his contemporaries that a rejuvenated Africa, like an independent Haiti, through a reflex influence would "irradiate, not only to uproot American slavery, but also to over-throw African slavery and the slave trade throughout the world."[104]

While African American leaders were debating the pros and cons of emigrating to Africa and the possible effect of that emigration on the future of African peoples, whites in the American Colonization Society were the only Americans with the prestige and power to influence American policy toward that continent, especially Liberia.[105] The African American colony of Liberia had limped along with only the help of the American Colonization Society and of the United States which, much to the opposition of some congressmen, had appropriated to Liberia $5,000 in 1823, $56,710 in 1827, and $30,000 in 1828.[106] It was, however, Liberia's willingness to condone the slave trade in its territory and to expand its boundaries that created difficulties for itself and for the United States.

The British government was particulary anxious that the United States clarify its relationship with Liberia. The British minister wrote Secretary of State Abel P. Upshur on 9 August 1843 asking that "Her Majesty's Government should be accurately informed, what degree of official patronage and protection, if any, the United States Government extend to the Colony of Liberia; . . . how far, if at all, the United States Government hold Themselves responsible, toward Foreign Countries, for the acts of the Authorities of Liberia . . . [or] whether the authorities of Liberia are themselves alone responsible on the spot for their public acts; or whether, if they are under the protection and control of the United States Government, it is to that Government that application must be made when the occasions . . . may require it."[107]

The American secretary of state was very careful in his response to the British:

> The Colony or Settlement of Liberia was established by a voluntary association of American citizens under the title of the American Colonization Society. Its objects were to introduce Christianity and promote civilization in Africa; to relieve the slave-holding States from the inconvenience of an increase of free blacks among them; to improve the condition, and elevate the character, of those blacks themselves; and to present to the slave-holder an inducement to emancipate his slaves, by offering to them an asylum in the country of their ancestors, in which they would enjoy political and social equality. It was not, however, established under the authority of our Government, nor has it ever been recognised as subject to our laws and jurisdiction."[108]

The secretary insisted that the United States government did not undertake to settle differences between outsiders and the Liberians and that the local authorities were responsible for their own acts. Nevertheless, because "they are themselves nearly powerless, they must rely for the protection of their own rights on the justice and sympathy of other Powers."[109] He suggested to the British that the United States government regarded itself as "occupying a peculiar position, and as possessing peculiar claims to the friendly consideration of all Christian Powers" with respect to Liberia and "that this Government will be at all times prepared to interpose its good offices to prevent any encroachment by the Colony upon any just right of any Nation; and that it would be very unwilling to see it despoiled of its territory rightfully acquired, or improperly restrained in the exercise of its necessary rights and powers as an independent settlement."[110]

Uppermost in the mind of the American secretary of state was the role of race and slavery in the establishment of Liberia and in the life of the United States. He was concerned that the British might have been using the issue of slavery and of suppression of the slave trade to interfere not only in Liberia but also in Texas. In a cable he sent to his ambassador in London, Secretary of State Upshur suggested that whatever the reaction of United States if "Texas by her own free act should liberate her slaves, we have every reason to object to the agency of England in that measure."[111] He felt that whatever the British did "to embarrass our movements, or impede our progress, is a positive advantage to her."[112] As far as the abolition of slavery in the United States was concerned, the secretary echoed Jefferson: that given the relations of African Americans to whites in the United States as masters to slaves, the two races could never live together as equals, in the same country and under the same government. Therefore, if slavery were abolished, the one or the other race must leave the country or be exterminated. He concluded that the slaves would be the ones to leave because they were the "weaker party." The secretary of state insisted:

> The chances then are that the African would be a persecuted pauper, even as a free citizen of a free State. But even if he should be permitted to share fairly in the labor of the country, that labor would soon come to be considered as his appropriate sphere, and as unworthy of the white man. It is not the policy of our States, nor of England, thus to degrade labor. To all this may be added the certainty that the African race, existing in large numbers as freemen, in countries whose Governments and laws recognise no difference of color, would not long be satisfied to be excluded from any political right, or civil privilege, or social advantage, allowed to the white man. The discords and angry contest which would grow out of this state of things, and the effect which they would have upon the tranquillity and prosperity of the country,

may be easily imagined. A wise Government would avoid them, by once shutting the door against the emancipated slave. The only alternative would be the extermination of his race.[113]

The American minister to the Court of St. James's was especially concerned about the anomaly of Liberia within the world system and about the racial and constitutional reasons that prevented the United States from assuming responsibility for the fledgling state. He wrote the secretary:

It must be admitted that the Constitution of the Liberian community is rather anomalous. It is not a Colonial dependency of any of the great States which compose the family of Christendom;—and its connection with the Colonization Society, itself an American Corporation, seems to take from it the Character of an Independent Commonwealth. Had the Government of the United States thought fit to found a Colony on the Coast of Africa, the Powers of Europe,—who have lined that Coast with their Colonial Settlements—could have made no reasonable objection. On the other hand, had the settlers avowedly constituted themselves an Independent Commonwealth, although difficulties might have been apprehended incidental to the peculiar nature of the Establishment, I do not see how the great Powers could have refused to regard it, as an humble member of the family of States. But constituted as it is, and governed by authority vested in a foreign Corporation, and that not of a nature usually exercising political jurisdiction, I am not confident that its character as an Independent Commonwealth will be recognized, particularly if it is found to conflict with private Mercantile interests.—

The meritorious design of the settlement and its relations with the United States will certainly justify us in all the demonstrations hitherto made of interest in its welfare.[114]

Faced with an untenable diplomatic position in the family of nations, the Liberians had no choice but to move toward the status of an independent state. After some reflection, the colonization society, working through its agents, agreed to permit the territory to develop politically and so notified the United States government. With the American government's position clarified, Liberia moved to declare its independence and asked that "documents of this proceeding, duly certified by the Colonization Society, be presented to the British as well as to other governments, and by that means obtain from Great Britain and the other powers a just and formal recognition of the Government of Liberia."[115] In their declaration, the Liberians wrote:

We, the people of the Republic of Liberia, were originally the inhabitants of the United States of North America. In some parts of that country, we were debarred by law from all the rights and privileges of men; in other parts, public sentiment, more powerful than law, frowned us down. We were everywhere shut out from all civil office. We were excluded from all participation in the Government. We were taxed without our consent. We were compelled to contribute to the resources of a country which gave us no protection. We were made a separate and distinct class, and against us every avenue to improvement was effectually closed. Strangers from all lands of a color different from ours were preferred before us. We uttered our complaints, but they were unattended to, or met only by alleging the peculiar institution of the country. All hope of a favorable change in our country was thus wholly extinguished in our bosom, and we looked with anxiety abroad for some asylum from the deep degradation. . . .

In coming to the shores of Africa, we indulged the pleasing hope that we should be permitted to exercise and improve those faculties, which impart to man his dignity; to nourish in our hearts the flame of honourable ambition; to cherish and indulge those aspirations, which a beneficent Creator hath implanted in every human heart, and to evince to all who despise, ridicule and oppress our race, that we possess with them a common nature, are with them susceptible of equal refinement, and capable of equal advancement in all that adorns and dignifies man. . . .

THEREFORE in the name of humanity, and virtue and religion; in the name of the Great God, our common Creator and our common Judge, we appeal to the nations of Christendom, and earnestly and respectfully ask them, that they will regard us with the sympathy and friendly consideration, to which the peculiarities of our condition entitle us, and to extend to us that comity, which marks the friendly intercourse of civilized and independent communities.[116]

The racial and political climate in the United States forced the State Department to be circumspect in dealing with an independent Liberia. Recommending the independence of the new state was out of the question given the previous experience with Haiti. When in June 1838 "certain citizens of the District of Columbia" (whether African Americans or whites is not clear) sent a petition to the Senate "praying that a diplomatic representative be sent to Hayte and commercial regulations be entered into with that Republic," the matter was tabled despite the support of John Quincy Adams.[117] When another petition to recognize Haiti was submitted to the Senate on 19 December 1838, Senator Legare of South Carolina declared:

As sure as you live, Sir, if this course is permitted to go on, the sun of this Union will go down—it will go down in blood and go down to rise no more. I will vote unhesitatingly against nefarious designs like these . . . They are treason.[118]

So many petitions of this nature were presented to Congress on behalf of the recognition of Haiti that the Senate Committee on Foreign Affairs asked to be discharged from considering the matter further. Henry Wise of Virginia voiced the feelings of many that agitation on behalf of Haiti's recognition was "but part and parcel of the English scheme set on foot by [William Lloyd] Garrison, and to bring abolition as near as possible."[119]

Secretary of State John M. Clayton thought it best to secure a presidential appointment for the Reverend Ralph R. Gurley of the American Colonization Society as a special agent of the United States to visit Liberia and to report on the situation there. In his letter to Gurley of 31 July 1849 the secretary indicated that many Americans continued to take a "lively interest in the success of the settlement of persons of African descent, but principally natives of this country, now known as the Republic of Liberia."[120] Moreover, given the fact that the governments of Great Britain and France had recently acknowledged Liberia's independence, the United States government wanted to know whether the Liberians could "assume the responsibilities and discharge the duties of an independent state." Gurley was to find out about the limits of Liberia's territory and its population, form of government, economic prospects, and state of education. The State Department especially desired to know "whether in the event that we should recognize the Independence of Liberia that government would deem it indispensable to appoint persons of African extraction as diplomatic agents or Consuls whom it might have occasion to employ in the United States."[121] Gurley was advised to suggest to the Liberians that the best way to get the United States to acknowledge Liberian independence was through a treaty of commerce and that they should find a suitable representative. But Gurley was also advised to warn the Liberians that unless the facts he presented to the secretary were satisfactory, no treaty would be approved by a constitutional majority of the senate.[122]

The declaration of independence by Liberia certainly heightened African American consciousness of Africa even though this was accompanied by continued uneasiness about the role of the American Colonization Society in Liberia's development. The subject of emigration, which had been the source of so much acrimony during the African American conventions of the 1840s, was on everyone's agenda in the early 1850s.

Martin R. Delany and those who convened the National Emigration Convention of Colored Men in Cleveland in August 1854 expressly barred persons "who would introduce the subject of Emigration to the Eastern Hemisphere—either to Asia, Africa, or Europe—as our object and determination are to consider our claims to the West Indies, Central and South America, and the Canadas." Yet in their "Secret Sessions" the delegates made their goal "Africa, with its rich inexhaustible productions, and great facilities for checking the abominable Slave Trade."[123] The alleged reason for this subterfuge was that the delegates did not wish to give comfort to the predominately white members of the American Colonization Society, who were still anxious to send African Americans to Africa. However, by 1856 when Delany, as the president of the convention, called a second emigration convention at Cleveland, he and his supporters openly discussed the prospects of emigrating to Africa.

In 1858 the Reverend Henry Highland Garnet, who had long shown an interest in Africa, organized the African Civilization Society and became its president. Ten years before, the younger and very radical Garnet had shocked even African American abolitionists such as Frederick Douglass by his call for the slaves to rebel, and during the same period he had made a spirited defense of African civilization. He stated, among other things, that almost by common consent, the modern world appeared determined to pilfer Africa of its glory. It was not enough "that her children have been scattered over the globe, clothed in the garments of shame—humiliated and oppressed—but her merciless foes weary themselves in plundering the tombs of our renowned sires, and in obliterating their worthy deeds, which were inscribed by fame upon the pages of ancient history."[124] Garnet implied that white skin was the result of divine punishment, that when Miriam murmured against her brother Moses marrying an Ethiopian woman, she was smitten by the Almighty and "became white."[125] Finally, he claimed that at the time when the "representatives of our race were filling the world with amazement, the ancestors of the now proud and boasting Anglo-Saxons were among the most degraded of the human family."[126]

The principal aims of Garnet's new society were to secure the "immediate and unconditional abolition of slavery" and the slave trade in the United States and in Africa; to destroy "prejudice against colored people in the United States," especially in the North, by urging the abolitionists to give jobs to the freedmen and their children; to spread the gospel and enhance the civilization of Africa by cultivating cotton which, by underselling that grown in the United States, would "strike the death-blow to American slavery"; and to establish a great "centre of negro nationality, from which shall flow the streams of commercial, intellectual, and political power which shall make colored people respected everywhere."[127] This was to be accomplished by "the voluntary cooperation of the friends of universal freedom, irrespective of color, either by working with the Society here or assisting its objects in Africa."[128]

Like many of the contemporary emigrationists, Garnet asserted that it made no sense for African Americans to refuse to go to Africa while whites were doing so well economically there. He believed that African Americans would do much better in Africa than whites and that their economic progress would gain them the respect of all peoples. But his suggestion that his society was willing to cooperate with all "the friends of universal freedom, irrespective of color" did not sit well with the opponents of the American Colonization Society. Delany, Douglass, and other African American leaders immediately accused Garnet of accepting funds from Benjamin Coates, a prominent member of the colonization society—Douglass charging that Coates was "the real, but not ostensible head of the African Civilization movement."[129] The preacher vigorously denied this allegation when questioned about it by the African Americans of Boston on 29 August 1858, and he convinced most, but not all, of his interlocutors that the coincidence of the African Civilization Society and the American Colonization Society choosing the same means to help African Americans did not prove that they were collaborating. Nevertheless, Delany insisted that Garnet could not have launched his society and a project to explore the Niger River area as a site for emigration had he not received help from whites—especially from the hated colonizationists.

Whether galvanized by Garnet's activities or motivated on his own, Delany, then living in Chatham, Canada West, summoned the National Emigration Convention to hold its third meeting in August 1858. He resigned the presidency of the organization to accept the title of foreign secretary and the authority to "make a Topographical, Geological and Geographical Examination of the Valley of the River Niger in Africa" and to choose a staff to do so.[130] What Delany never satisfactorily explained was why, like Garnet, he had chosen the Niger River Valley or why he advocated almost the same program as did the African Civilization Society. In any case, he claimed to have been vilified by the whites of Philadelphia (presumably those in the American Colonization Society), who judged him mentally and physically unfit to lead the project. To confuse the matter even more, Delany learned that Robert Campbell, a young Jamaican whom he had recruited for the trip to Africa, had established contact with the colonizationists and had gone off alone to Africa by way of London.

Delany was dismayed to hear that, without his knowledge or consent, the African Civilization Society had started to collect funds in England on behalf of the exploring party. He accused the colonization society of refusing to accept the regeneration of his African "Fatherland" except through themselves. Delany fumed that "it was too great an undertaking for negroes to have the credit of, and therefore they *must go under* the auspices of some white American Christians. To be black, it would seem, was necessarily to be 'ungodly'; and to be white was necessarily to be 'godly,' or Christian, in the estimation of some."[131] Fired by what he considered to be Campbell's treachery, Delany scraped up funds, and on 24 May 1859 he too left for Liberia, on his way to the Niger River valley.

Delany was overcome with joy on reaching Africa and was well received in Liberia by the Americo-Liberian elite, especially by such recent immigrants as Alexander Crummell. These persons voiced their disapproval of Delany's criticism of the American Colonization Society, but he was able to explain the nature of, and reason for, his hostility to that organization. Delany was given the opportunity to lecture before various societies in the major towns and to investigate the nature of the country and its people. He loved Liberia but pressed on to Nigeria, where he was also well received by the indigenous Yoruba and repatriated New World slave (the so-called Brazilians) populations living in Lagos. Curiously, Delany recorded without rancor his meeting with Robert Campbell in Nigeria and the two of them collaborated while there. They collected materials for two interesting and complementary reports and were cosigners of a treaty with Egba people whose principal clause read:

> That the King and Chiefs on their part agree to grant and assign unto the said Commissioners (Martin Robinson Delany and Robert Campbell, of the Niger Valley Exploring Party), on behalf of the African race in America, the right and privilege of settling in common with the Egba people, on any part of the territory belonging to Abbeokuta not otherwise occupied.[132]

In return for these privileges, the Africans of North America were to provide the Egba people with education and knowledge of the arts and sciences, agriculture, and other mechanical and industrial occupations. (Interestingly, nothing was said about Christianity, the Africans having made a spirited defense of their own religion and civilization.) The Americans also solemnly promised to abide by all the laws of the Egba people. So pleased was Delany with his trip that on reporting the end of the African part of his journey he intoned the biblical prophecy,

"Princes shall come out of Egypt; Ethiopia shall soon stretch her hands unto God."[133]

Delany and Campbell returned to the United States via Britain and while there met several English groups "interested in the progress of African Regeneration."[134] One such group included Lord Alfred Churchill, M.P. (Brother of the Duke of Marlborough); his father-in-law, Lord Calthrope; Sir C. E. Eardley; and pastors of several evangelical sects. These men proposed to the African Americans that they jointly form an African Aid Society. Of course Delany welcomed this overture, although he soon sensed such a feeling of paternalism on the part of the British that he was led to complain to them that "we desired to be dealt with as men, and not children."[135] But the African Americans also realized that they could do little in Africa without the support of the British and would have to reach a compromise with their hosts. The final communiqué stated that "in furtherance of the objects of this (African Aid) Society, the Executive Committee, with the generous aid of friends to this movement, have already assisted Dr. Delany and Professor Campbell (two colored gentlemen from America) with funds to enable them to continue their labors and to lay before the colored people of America the reports of the Pioneer Exploration Expedition into Abbeokuta in West Africa, from which they have lately returned."[136] The society accepted Delany's formula to "aid the *voluntary* emigration of colored people from America in general, and our movement as originated by colored people in particular," declaring that "the assistance of all friends to Christianity, Freedom, and lawful Commerce, as opposed to the Slave Trade and Slavery, is earnestly solicited."[137]

Delany's visit to Britain was personally satisfying and was highlighted by a diplomatic incident involving the American minister to the Court of St. James's. The British hosts of the International Statistical Congress meeting in London on 16 July 1860 took the opportunity of Delany's presence to invite him to their sessions. They did so despite Delany's lack of accreditation in the United States, which had sent its delegation headed by Augustus Baldwin Longstreet, jurist, author, and at that time, president of the University of South Carolina. Seated on the dais at the opening session of the congress were Prince Albert and the diplomatic corps, including the American minister, George Mifflin Dallas of Pennsylvania. What happened then is controversial, but by all accounts the chairman, Lord Brougham and Vaux, called Dallas's attention to the presence of a "*negro*" hoping that the minister would feel "no scruples on that account."[138] Thereupon Delany arose and declared: "I rise, your

Royal Highness, to thank his lordship, the unflinching friend of the negro, for the kind remarks he had made in reference to myself, and to assure your royal highness and his lordship *that I am a man.*[139] This remark was greeted with such applause that the American delegation took umbrage and walked out, led by Mr. Longstreet, but Minister Dallas kept his seat. Longstreet afterward called the whole incident "an ill-timed assault upon our country, a wanton indignity offered to our minister, and a pointed insult offered to me."[140]

The resulting controversy pitted British newspapers against each other and started a spate of correspondence between the minister and Washington. In his report to Secretary of State Lewis Cass, the minister wrote: "You will, of course, perceive the extremely unpleasant position in which this matter places me socially here, and I shall therefore anxiously wait the sentiments of the President."[141] President Buchanan and the cabinet did discuss this "insult" to the United States and concluded that the British government should have apologized officially. Moreover, they felt the minister should have walked out with the delegation.[142] For his part, Secretary of State Cass told Dallas that the incident "was designed as a reproach upon a large portion of the American people, among whom slavery is an established institution and upon a still larger portion of them, of whom I am one, who consider the negro race as an inferior one and who repudiate all political equality and social connection with its descendants."[143]

News of Delany's experience preceded his return to the United States and elicited support of him and the British even from those who did not approve of his trip to Africa and emigrationism. Frederick Douglass wrote in his newspaper: "Never was there a more telling rebuke administered to the pride, prejudice and hypocrisy of a nation. It was saying, Mr. Dallas, we make members of the International Statistical Society out of the sort of men you make merchandise out of in America. Delany, in Washington, is a *thing!* Delany in London is a *man.*"[144]

On their return to America, Delany and Campbell had to face the reality that it was not easy for African Americans to go to Africa. Free blacks had little or no money to support emigration schemes. Even one of their most affluent supporters, William H. Day, a newspaper publisher, had to go to England to secure funds to educate free blacks in Canada, in the hope that some of them would go to Africa. Campbell maintained an active interest in Africa, and left with his family for Lagos, Nigeria, where he published a paper. Delany also kept an interest in Africa but threw in his lot with the African Civilization Society, taking the vice presidency under Henry Highland Garnet. He accepted the compromise that the policy of selective emigration be underscored and that African Americans should play a dominant role in the society's program. Meanwhile, in Great Britain the African Aid Society pressured the British government to establish a consulate at Abeokuta so as to open up the Yoruba region to commercial exploitation. In Africa the Yoruba king and his lords, with the advice of the British, reneged on their treaty with Delany and Campbell. They were allegedly convinced that the African Americans could be as dangerous to their rule as were those who settled in Liberia.[145] Nevertheless, both Delany and Garnet still entertained the hope of establishing a colony on the Niger River. They did not abandon these plans until the outbreak of the Civil War induced them to help the Union forces. After a great deal of difficulty, Delany secured a commission as a medical officer in the United States Army; Garnet went to Britain as a self-proclaimed propagandist for the Union cause.

The outbreak of the Civil War significantly changed the relations of the United States with Africa and laid the basis for African American participation in policy formulations toward that continent. Specifically, the absence of many rebel southerners from the Thirty-seventh Congress enabled the United States to consider recognizing both Liberia and Haiti. Not all southerners, however, were against recognizing Liberia. Senator Henry Clay of Virginia, one of the early officers of the American Colonization Society, wrote in 1851 that he had thought for years that the United States should recognize the independence of Liberia and that he had consistently urged administrations to do so. But it was not until President Lincoln sent his message to Congress in 1861 that the subject of recognizing the two African American states was officially broached. He wrote:

> (I)f any good reason exists why we should persevere longer in withholding our recognition of the independence and sovereignty of Haiti and Liberia, I am unable to discern it. Unwilling, however, to inaugurate a novel policy in regard to them without the approbation of Congress, I submit to your consideration the expediency of an appropriation for maintaining a Chargé d'Affaires near each of these states. It does not admit of doubt that important commercial advantages might be secured by favorable treaties with them.[146]

As to be expected, African Americans were overjoyed by this announcement. Meeting in national convention in Syracuse they passed a resolution praising Congress for honoring the president's request. Their sentiments were echoed by many white papers in the North.

The submission of a bill "authorizing the President to appoint Diplomatic Representatives to the Republics of Haiti and Liberia respectively" by Senator Charles Sumner of the Foreign Relations Committee to the full Senate on 4 February 1862 created a veritable storm.[147] Leading the opposition was Senator Garrett Davis of Kentucky. He stated that he had supported the work of the American Colonization Society in the creation of Liberia and that he felt that America should trade with the "infant republic," protect it, and even recognize it; "but," he insisted, "I oppose the sending of ambassadors of any class from our Government to theirs, upon this consideration: it would establish, diplomatically, terms of mutual and equal reciprocity between the two countries."[148] He warned that "if a full-blooded negro were sent in that capacity from either of those countries, by the laws of nations he could demand that he be received precisely on the same terms of equality with the white representative from the powers of the earth composed of white people."[149] Davis felt that passage of the bill would exacerbate relations between the embattled northerners and southerners.[150]

Mr. Charles John Biddle lamented the ill-timed submission of the bill in the midst of a grave civil war. He specifically objected to the establishment of diplomatic relations between the United States and both Haiti and Liberia "because it will be taken, and by those who at this time are its prime movers, it is intended, as an acknowledgement of the equality of the races."[151] The senator felt that "the African policy of the majority of this Congress is spreading far and wide a just alarm for the future of our country and of our race."[152] Lastly, Senator Willard Saulsbury of Delaware complained:

> How fine it will look, after emancipating the slaves in this district, to welcome here at the White House an African, full-blooded, all gilded and belaced, dressed in court style, with wig and sword and tights and shoe-buckles and ribbons and spangles and many other adornments which African vanity will suggest . . . If this bill should pass both Houses of Congress and become a law, I predict that in twelve months, some Negro will walk upon the floor of the Senate of the United States and carry his family into that gallery which is set apart for foreign ministers. If that is agreeable to the taste and feeling of the people of this country it is not to mine.[153]

Defenders of the Haitians and Liberians, such as Sumner, attempted to calm the fears of their fellow senators about the propriety of African Americans who might be sent as representatives of the United States. Moreover, the supporters of the president had the votes. The bill passed the Senate by 32 yeas to 7 nays, and the House by 86 yeas to 37 nays. With the president's signature the bill became law, and treaties of "friendship, commerce, and navigation" were signed between the United States and the countries of Haiti and Liberia. The African Americans in the United States, speaking through the AME Church meeting in convention in August 1862, adopted a resolution stating that "in the noble act of the United States Senate, in passing a law recognizing the independence of Haiti and Liberia, we see the hand of God in a movement which we regard as ominous of good to our race."[154]

The Civil War occupied the government and people of the United States of America completely for many long years, but the government fulfilled its promise to Liberia by appointing John J. Henry of Delaware as United States commissioner and consul general on 11 March 1863. Henry resigned his commission soon after, stating, "Circumstances of a purely domestic nature have arisen which render it entirely impracticable for me to go [to a] distant country."[155] It was not until 22 February 1864 that Abraham Hanson, a white man long associated with the colonization society, arrived in Liberia as commissioner and consul general of the United States. The Liberians were extremely pleased with the gesture of United States approval. Its president told Hanson that he brought with him "a commission and credentials of a higher grade than any it has hitherto had the pleasure of receiving from the hands of any other foreign public functionary commissioned to this country."[156] It was therefore with great shock and sadness that the Liberians heard that President Lincoln had been assassinated and Secretary of State Seward wounded. The president of the Republic of Liberia and his cabinet in council sent a joint message to the people of the United States declaring "sincere regret and pain," as well as "feelings of horror and indignation," at the news of the "foul assassination of the honorable Abraham Lincoln," a man described by them as one who "utterly abhorred slavery—a friend of the negro race and a promoter of the interests of Liberia."[157] In a letter congratulating Andrew Jackson on his elevation to the presidency of the United States, Liberian President D. W. Warner stated that the Liberians in view of

> millions of their race in America, and being so sensibly and gratefully impressed with a knowledge of the numerous favors directly and indirectly received from the United States government, first in their struggle to gain these shores from oppression, and then in their efforts to establish here a home and build up a negro nationality this side of the waters for themselves and their children after them, it were impossible for them to be indifferent to the grave events now taking place in that country.[158]

With no access to diplomatic correspondence, African Americans could not have been aware of the sentiments expressed by the Liberians at that important juncture. Nor was it likely that any of them knew of the equally solicitous sentiments expressed to Secretary of State William H. Seward by a group of Africans and African Americans in the Gold Coast of Africa on 10 July 1865 concerning President Lincoln's death. The letter read:

> We, the undersigned, representing the natives of this part of Africa, as well as persons of African race resident here, desire to show, by the expression of our sorrow for the death of President Lincoln and our hearty abhorrence of the manner in which that death was brought about, that we are able to appreciate the benefits that our race has derived from the results of events that occurred during the administration of that great and good man. [159]

They cited among other things "the emancipation of millions of unfortunate persons of our race and color held in bondage," and assured the American public that "all true sons of Africa will mourn for the cruel and untimely fate of President Lincoln," a man they described as presiding over the fate of the United States "when events took place having such immense importance for the children of our country." Among the signatories were John Aggery, king of Cape Coast; Quow Attah, chief of Donasie; Samuel Wood, Sr., interpreter to the governor; Koffee Affadie, king of Anamaboe; Henry Arquah, king of Winnebah; Chas. H. Gardner, colonial schoolmaster of Massachusetts, U.S.A.; and Josiah M. Abadoo, "on behalf of the People." [160]

What these messages from Liberia and the Gold Coast indicated was that Africans on the continent and their brethren in the New World had become conscious of each other and were recognizing the importance of significant world events to their common fate. At the time, both groups had little power to influence their positions in the world system, and whether in the United States of America or in Africa, they were beholden to the patronage of others. Even those dissatisfied with conditions at home, like the immigrants to Liberia from the United States and the West Indies, could only get to Africa through the generosity of whites. The displeasure of free blacks in the United States over being encouraged to quit a land their ancestors had slaved to develop and in which millions of their fellows still languished in slavery, as well as the fear of an unknown and reputedly backward Africa, prevented many others from wishing to go at all. The interplay between African Americans willing to remain in an increasingly strong and prosperous America and to fight for full rights there, and those wishing to migrate to Africa in an effort to protect and defend a continent being brought increasingly under the control of whites, would preoccupy African Americans in the United States for the period following the Civil War.

Notes

1. Carl Degler, *Out of Our Past: The Forces That Shaped Modern America* (New York: Harper and Row, 1970), 31.
2. Thomas Jefferson, *Notes on the State of Virginia,* ed. William Peden (Chapel Hill, N.C.: University of North Carolina Press, 1955), 137–43, cited in Winthrop D. Jordan, *White Over Black: American Attitudes Toward the Negro, 1550–1812* (Baltimore, Md.: Pelican Books, 1969), 457–58. Robert G. Harper, a proponent of the repatriation of free blacks to Africa, wrote in 1822 that "the distinctive and indelible marks of the Negroes' color and the prejudice of the people" is an "insurmountable obstacle . . . to placing them on a footing with their brethren of the same family" (cited in Philip J. Staudenraus, *The African Colonization Movement, 1816–1865* [New York: Columbia University Press, 1961], 10).
3. Philip Curtin, *Africa Remembered: Narratives by West Africans From the Era of the Slave Trade* (Madison, Wis.: University of Wisconsin Press, 1968), 17–59.
4. Ibid., 60.
5. "Petition of Peter Bestes, Sambo Freeman, Felix Holbrook, and Chester Joie, Boston, April 20th, 1773," in Dorothy Porter, comp., *Early Negro Writing, 1760–1837* (Boston: Beacon Press, 1971), 254–55.
6. Herbert Aptheker, ed., *A Documentary History of the Negro People in the United States: From Colonial Times Through the Civil War* (New York: Citadel Press, 1951), 1:7–12.
7. Floyd J. Miller, *The Search for a Black Nationality: Black Emigration and Colonization, 1787–1863* (Urbana, Ill.: University of Illinois Press, 1975), 5.
8. Ibid.
9. Porter, *Early Negro Writing,* 64.
10. Ibid., 5–8.
11. Irving H. Bartlett, *From Slave to Citizen: The Story of the Negro in Rhode Island* (Providence, R.I.: Urban League of Greater Providence, 1954), 35.
12. Aptheker, *Documentary History* 1:17.
13. Porter, *Early Negro Writing,* 6.
14. Carter G. Woodson and Charles L. Wesley, *The Negro in Our History,* 11th ed. (Washington, D.C.: Associated Publishers, 1966), 150–52.
15. Ibid., 104.
16. Peden, *Notes on the State of Virginia,* 143.
17. Ibid.
18. "Letter From Benjamin Banneker to the Secretary of State, Philadelphia, 1792," quoted in Aptheker, *Documentary History* 1:24.
19. Ibid., 23.
20. Ibid.
21. Ibid.
22. Ibid., 24–25.
23. Ibid., 25.
24. Paul L. Ford, *The Works of Thomas Jefferson* (New York: G. P. Putnam's Sons, 1904–1905), 6:309–11.

25. Ibid., 310.
26. Ibid., 11:121.
27. "Two Negro Leaders Reply to Slanders—and Denounce Slaveholding, 1794," quoted in Aptheker, *Documentary History* 1:32–38.
28. Ibid.
29. Ibid.
30. Benjamin Brawley, ed., *Early Negro American Writers* (Chapel Hill, N.C.: University of North Carolina Press, 1935), 103–8.
31. Ibid.
32. Sheldon H. Harris, *Paul Cuffee: Black America and the African Return* (New York: Simon and Schuster, 1972), 59.
33. Brawley, *Early Negro American Writers,* 108.
34. Henry Noble Sherwood, "Paul Cuffe," *Journal of Negro History* 8 (April 1923): 202.
35. Isaac V. Brown, *Biography of the Reverend Finley of Basking Ridge, New Jersey* (Philadelphia: n.p. 1857), 60–61.
36. Henry Noble Sherwood, "The Formation of the American Colonization Society," *Journal of Negro History* 2 (July 1917): 211.
37. Ibid., 218.
38. Ibid., 220–21.
39. Ibid., 221–23.
40. Ibid.
41. Ibid.
42. Ibid., 223.
43. Ibid., 223–24.
44. Ibid., 224.
45. Harris, *Paul Cuffe,* 235.
46. Ibid.
47. Ibid., 241.
48. Ibid.
49. Ibid., 244.
50. Ibid.
51. Ibid.
52. Ibid., 255.
53. Sherwood, "Formation of the American Colonization Society," 224; Sherwood, "Paul Cuffe," 227, cited in Miller, *Search for a Black Nationality,* 52.
54. Miller, *Search for a Black Nationality,* 51.
55. Louis R. Mehlinger, "The Attitude of the Free Negro Toward African Colonization," *Journal of Negro History* 1 (July 1916): 277.
56. Ibid., 277–78.
57. Ibid., 278.
58. Ibid.
59. Ibid., 276.
60. Robert L. Keiser, *Liberia: A Report on the Relations Between the United States and Liberia* (Washington, D.C.: Government Printing Office, 1928), 3.
61. Ibid.
62. Staudenraus, *African Colonization Movement,* 51–55.
63. Ibid.
64. Ibid.
65. Ibid., 57–65; Mehlinger, "Attitude of the Free Negro," 276.
66. Clinton Caldwell Boone, *Liberia As I Know It* (Westport, Conn.: Negro Universities Press, 1929), 27.

67. Ibid., 23.
68. Adelaide Cromwell Hill and Martin Kilson, eds. and comps., *Apropos of Africa: Sentiments of Negro American Leaders on Africa From the 1800s to the 1950s* (London: Frank Cass, 1969), 81.
69. Ibid., 83.
70. Eugene H. Berwanger, *The Frontier Against Slavery: Western and Anti-Negro Prejudice and the Slavery Extension Controversy* (Urbana: University of Illinois Press, 1967), 20.
71. Ibid., 31.
72. Ibid., 27.
73. Ibid., 30.
74. Ibid., 39.
75. Ibid.
76. Walter C. Woodward, "The Rise and Early History of Political Parties in Oregon," *Oregon Historical Quarterly* 12 (1911): 125–63.
77. Berwanger, "Frontier Against Slavery," 52.
78. Ibid.
79. Ibid., 53.
80. Ibid.
81. Richard C. Wade, "The Negro in Cincinnati, 1800–1830," *Journal of Negro History* 39 (January 1954): 53.
82. Aptheker, *Documentary History* 1:102–3.
83. Ibid., 103.
84. Ibid.
85. Ibid., 82–85.
86. Ibid., 105.
87. Ibid., 106.
88. Howard H. Bell, *A Survey of the Negro Convention Movement* (New York: Arno Press and the New York Times, 1969), 32.
89. Keiser, *Liberia*, 7.
90. Ibid.
91. Ibid.
92. Leslie H. Fishel and Benjamin Quarles, eds., *The Black American: A Documentary History* (New York: Morrow, 1967), 127.
93. Carter G. Woodson, *The Mind of the Negro As Reflected in Letters Written During the Crisis, 1800–1860* (Washington, D.C.: Association for the Study of Negro Life and History, 1926), 161–63.
94. Ibid.
95. Bell, *Negro Convention Movement*, 157.
96. Sterling Stuckey, *The Ideological Origins of Black Nationalism* (Boston: Beacon Press, 1972), 197.
97. Ibid.
98. Ibid., 199.
99. Victor Ullman, *Martin R. Delany: The Beginnings of Black Nationalism* (Boston: Beacon Press, 1971), 150.
100. Ibid.
101. Ibid., 147.
102. Ibid.
103. Stuckey, *Ideological Origins*, 200.
104. Philip S. Foner, *History of Black Americans* (Westport, Conn.: Greenwood Press, 1983), 3:161.
105. Staudenraus, *African Colonization Movement*, 34.

106. Ibid., 59–65.
107. Keiser, *Liberia*, 13.
108. Ibid., 13–14.
109. Ibid., 15.
110. Ibid.
111. Ibid., 18.
112. Ibid., 17.
113. Ibid., 17–18.
114. Ibid., 19.
115. Robert Earle Anderson, *Liberia: America's African Friend* (Chapel Hill: University of North Carolina Press, 1952), 79.
116. Nathaniel R. Richardson, *Liberia's Past and Present* (London: Diplomatic Press, 1959), 64–65.
117. *Congressional Globe*, 25th Cong., 2d sess., 1838–1839, 457.
118. *National Intelligencer*, 19 and 21 December 1838, quoted in Charles H. Wesley, "The Struggle for the Recognition of Haiti and Liberia as Independent Republics," *Journal of Negro History* 2 (October 1917): 374–75.
119. Wendell Phillips Garrison, *William Lloyd Garrison, 1805–1879: The Story of His Life Told by His Children* (New York: Century, 1885), 2:248.
120. Keiser, *Liberia*, 23.
121. Ibid., 24.
122. Ibid.
123. Martin R. Delany and Robert Campbell, *Search for a Place: Black Separation and Africa (1860)*, reprint ed. Howard Bell (Ann Arbor: University of Michigan Press, 1969), 28–33.
124. Henry Highland Garnet, *The Past and Present Condition and the Destiny of the Colored Race: A Discourse at the 50th Anniversary of the Female Benevolent Society of Troy, New York, February 14, 1848* (Troy, N.Y.: J. C. Kneeland, 1848), 6–12.
125. Ibid.
126. Ibid.
127. Stuckey, *Ideological Origins*, 182–83.
128. Ibid., 184.
129. Philip S. Foner, ed., *The Life and Writings of Frederick Douglass* (New York: International Publishers, 1950), 2:443.
130. Delany and Campbell, *Search for a Place*, 39–45.
131. Ibid.
132. Ibid., 248.
133. Ps. 68:31, quoted in ibid., 122.
134. Ibid.
135. Ibid., 122–24.
136. Ibid., 128.
137. Ibid., 129.
138. Ullman, *Martin R. Delany*, 238–40.
139. Ibid., 240–41.
140. Ibid., 243.
141. Ibid., 242.
142. Ibid., 242–43.
143. Ibid., 243.
144. Ibid., 244.
145. A. H. M. Kirk-Greene, "America in the Niger Valley: A Colonization Centenary," *Phylon* 23 (Fall 1962): 225–39.

146. *Messages and Papers of the Presidents* 4:47, quoted in Wesley, "Recognition of Liberia and Haiti," 379.
147. Ibid., 380.
148. *Congressional Globe,* 37th Cong., 2d sess., 24 April 1862, 1806.
149. Ibid.
150. Ibid.
151. Ibid., 2501–6.
152. Ibid.
153. Wesley, "Recognition of Liberia and Haiti," 381.
154. *African Repository* 38 (August 1862): 255.
155. Ibid. 40 (June 1864): 179.
156. Ibid.
157. Ibid. 43 (January 1867): 102.
158. *Appendix to the Diplomatic Correspondence of 1865* (Washington: Government Printing Office, 1866), 472–74.
159. Ibid., 197–98.
160. Ibid.

2

In Defense of Black Nationality

> Our policy toward Africa . . . should be to encourage our people to
> watch and study the developments of that wonderful country . . .
> Africa is the land of our ancestral kindred and the duty is ours, in a
> peculiar sense, to give to that land civilization physical, material,
> mental, moral and spiritual. We show ourselves wanting in the com-
> monest as well as the most sacred instincts of humanity if we are not
> permeated with a profound and growing interest in the land of our
> forefathers. (The Reverend C. H. Thompson, D.D., Rector of St.
> Philip's Church, New Orleans, Louisiana, October 1885)[1]

Sir:

I am instructed by the President to tender you the post of Minister Resident and Consul General of the United States at Liberia.

It is the object of the President to place the interests of the Africo-Americans in that Republic in charge of an American citizen of
African descent who is believed to have at heart the advancement of
his people, and to possess qualifications to render them service and
do credit to this country.

Your name has been presented by the American Colonization Society with such favorable recommendations that the President, in
the interests of Liberia, as well as the United States, now tenders
you the position.

I await your early reply, and am,

Very respectfully yours,

T. F. Bayard
[Secretary of State][2]

When the Civil War failed to gain equality for African Americans, many
of them considered emigrating to Africa, and their leaders sought to
engage the United States in protecting the "black nationality" that was
developing in Africa, especially in Liberia. Perhaps naively, they had
hoped that the same forces that led Abraham Lincoln to emancipate the
slaves would also induce his successors to preserve and increase the
rights of those now free. What they could not foresee were the pressures

that would lead the North and the South to compose their differences so that a reunited nation could take its rightful place in the emerging society of nations.[3]

Although a few African American leaders kept up an interest in Africa during the Civil War, by and large most of them were so committed to the war effort that they all but ignored the wartime appeals of the Americo-Liberians for support. Facing severe financial problems, the prescient of Liberia sent a commission to the United States in 1863 composed of Edward Wilmot Blyden (who was born in St. Croix, Virgin Islands, had studied in the United States, and had later migrated to Liberia), Alexander Crummell (an American-born cleric who had gone to Liberia as a missionary), and J. D. Johnson (born in Liberia). The president invited African Americans to "aid in building up a negro nationality of freedom and Christianity on the continent of their ancestors." Much to the chagrin of the visitors, their presence had little effect on the "Colored People of the United States."[4]

Alarmed that African Americans were not placing the Civil War, their own condition, and the needs of Africa in full perspective, the prescient Blyden attempted to warn their leaders of what the end of the Civil War could mean for them and for Africa:

> For, supposing that it were possible for black men to rise to the greatest eminence, in this country, in wealth and political distinction, so long as the resources and capabililities of Africa remained undeveloped—so long as there was no Negro power of respectability in Africa, and that continent remained in her present degradation—she would reflect unfavourably upon them. . . . If no Negro state of respectability be erected in Africa—no Negro government permanently established in that land—then the prejudice in question will make its obstinate stand against all the wealth, and genius, and skill that may be exhibited by Negroes in North and South America. . . . The work is to be done in Africa.[5]

The Liberian commissioners attempted to combat what they considered adverse propaganda against Liberia in the American press. Crummell sincerely felt that free African Americans at home had duties toward Africa. He wrote to a friend in the United States that it seemed to him that there was a "natural call upon the children of Africa in foreign lands, to come and participate in the opening treasures of the land of their fathers. Though these treasures are the manifest gift of God to the Negro race, yet that race reaps but the most partial measure of their good and advantage." Crummell admitted that he could not understand why when the "resources of Africa are being more and more developed, the extent of *our* interest therein is becoming more and more diminutive."[6]

Crummell said that he understood why there was a class of people of African descent "who repudiate any close and peculiar connection with Africa. They and their fathers have been absent from this soil for centuries. In the course of time their blood has been mingled somewhat with that of other peoples and races." These people, he said, were "brought up and habituated to customs entirely diverse from those of their ancestors in this land." But, insisted Crummell, "other great facts" bound African Americans to the "darkened wretched Negro race" in Africa. "There is the fact of kinship, which a lofty manhood and a proud generosity keeps them now, and ever will keep them from disclaiming. There are the strong currents of kindred blood which neither time nor circumstances can ever entirely wash out."[7] He conceded that African Americans had "bitter memories of ancestral wrongs, of hereditary servitude, which cannot be forgotten till 'the last syllable of recorded time.' " Then there were still "the low imputation of Negro inferiority, necessitating a protracted and an earnest battle, creative of a generous pride to vindicate the race, and inciting to noble endeavor to illustrate its virtues and its genius." Yet despite these realities, Crummell felt that it was "the duty of black men to feel and labor for the salvation of the mighty millions of their kin all through this continent." He asked, "How then can these men ever forget Africa?"[8]

Concerned that African Americans were getting a distorted picture of life in Africa, he pleaded with them to make a "flying" visit to Liberia so that they would learn the truth. But the African American population of the Union concentrated on winning the war in the hope of securing new freedoms. They even ignored Lincoln's colonization schemes. Yet here and there were African Americans who had maintained the interest in Africa sparked by Paul Cuffe and kept alive by the American Colonization Society and the National Emigration Conventions. The Savannah *Republican* (27 July 1865) reported that the colored people of Georgia celebrated the seventeenth anniversary of the Republic of Liberia.[9]

Significantly, as the first signs of the coming resurgence of white oppression appeared in the South, a number of African Americans began to make plans to go to Africa, especially to Liberia. The U.S. government apparently supported this migration, for on 26 January 1867, Johns Seys (a white West Indian, formerly a missionary and an agent for recaptured slaves), who had been named the United States minister to Liberia, wrote to Secretary of State William H. Seward expressing the gratitude with which the corresponding secretary of the American Colonization Society received "the timely supply from the United States government of nearly one hundred barrels of meats and breadstuffs, and the free transportation, with efficient officers to protect them, of various companies of emigrants from Knoxville, Tennessee, Macon, Georgia, Columbia and Newberry, South Carolina."[10]

Delighted with what he sensed was the start of a new emigration current to Liberia, Minister Seys wrote the secretary of state about "a Mr. Purman, of Marianna, Jackson county, Florida, an intelligent colored man representing a population of 5,000 freedmen, [who] wishes information about Liberia, its resources, climate, and the means of getting here."[11] Seys informed Seward that thousands of African Americans from South Carolina had added to the momentum of settling in Liberia. He felt that they were aiding the "noble scheme of African colonization, resulting as it has already done, in the rearing up of this interesting republic, this negro nationality developing the immense internal resources of this rich country, and blessing thousands of heathen people with the light of civilization and Christianity."[12] Then in a statement that betrayed his continued insensitivity to the reasons why many African Americans opposed white-sponsored migration to Africa, the minister told the secretary of state, "That United States government favors . . . the immigration to Liberia of such colored persons as think they can better their condition by coming here, is no more to be doubted than that they favor the emigration of Europeans to the United States."[13]

It was Seys's view that if, despite the end of slavery, "the United States government still favors even now, since all are free to choose their homes, the removal to their father land of such of the freedmen in our country as prefer to leave America for Africa," then the need existed for a "regular systematic method of favoring such immigration that would . . . be wise as well as philanthropic and humane."[14] What Seys had in mind was for the United States government to pass a law appropriating "one dollar *per capita* for every freedman who voluntarily chooses to leave the United States and settle in Liberia, and that such appropriation, upon proper representation on the part of the American Colonization Society, be paid into the treasury of such society, to be strictly accounted for by them."[15]

The secretary of state was properly diplomatic in his response to Seys's suggestion that the government support African American emigration. He advised the minister that only Congress could pass a bill authorizing such an appropriation but that Congress had adjourned for the session.[16] What Seward did not tell Seys was that the former abolitionists and most African American leaders were still set against supporting emigration. Speaking in Washington, D.C., on 22 January 1868, at the fifty-first anniversary celebration of the founding of the American Colonization Society, Senator F. T. Frelinghuysen of New Jersey, a stalwart abolitionist and future secretary of state, declared that "no black man with my consent should ever leave this country without his intelligent desire to do so."[17] Much to the delight of African Americans, the senator felt that they had as much right to live in the United States as his Celtic forebears, but he was willing to admit that African Americans could do great things for Liberia.

More to the point, however, was that the colonization society increasingly began to lose its chief source of revenue—the slaveholders. Congress was now no more interested in appropriating money to get rid of African Americans than it was in ameliorating their economic, political, and social position. Lincoln was dead and the South needed cheap African American labor. These new realities troubled African American leaders, many of whom toyed with the idea of emigrationism. Even Martin R. Delany, now a major in the U.S. Army, equivocated over whether African Americans should opt to go to Africa or stay and fight for greater freedom in America. Criticized for confusing these two objectives, Delany answered: "There are now, in different parts of the South, several thousand freed people, who are determined not to remain, desirous of going to Africa, and really impatiently anxious to get off. It is not to be a question why this is so; in fact, it gives its own question and answer: simply because they are the people, therefore, just like all other peoples under similar circumstances—Germans and Irish for example, leaving their nativity in Europe—when dissatisfied."[18] Delany explained that he was staying in America for the benefit of his race and what he conceived to be in its interests. Nevertheless, he wished Godspeed to those thousands who would go to Africa and only hoped that they would be assured an opportunity to do so. Delany expressed conviction that the coming exodus would not "prejudicially affect that part of our brethren who never will leave America, but rather favorably; because experience and observation teach us, that wherever there are the *fewest* colored people in the United States, there is the *least* objection to them."[19]

Noting the crucial role that the African American vote played in the election of General Ulysses S. Grant to the presidency of the United States, Delany felt that among the "plums" they ought to receive was the diplomatic post in Liberia. Moreover, emulating Ebenezer E. Basset, the Connecticut-born African American educator appointed by Grant as

minister resident and consul general to Haiti, Delaney wished to be the
first African American minister resident and consul general to Liberia.
In February 1869 Delany wrote to Major General Robert K. Scott,
governor of South Carolina, about this ambition, stating: "I have fully
matured all the contingencies and issues which may arise nationally and
internationally and consequently will be prepared to meet any question
at the Department of State."[20] Delany also sent petitions to President
Grant and Secretary of State Hamilton Fish, and mobilized members of
the electoral college who had voted for Grant, as well as businessmen,
judges, and publishers (both African American and white). Delany won
the support of the bishops' council of the AME Church, which on 5 July
1868 signed the following petition to President Grant:

> We the undersigned Bishops of the African Methodist Episcopal Church in
> the United States, representing the largest number of colored Christians in
> the United States and also the largest numbers of Colored voters.
>
> Would recommend to your Excellency's favorable consideration, Major
> Martin R. Delany late of the United Army and now residing in Xenia, Ohio,
> for the position as minister to the Republic of Liberia, Africa.
>
> In our opinion, Major Delany possesses the educational ability to fill the
> place that we now ask for him.
>
> He was commissioned by President Lincoln as a Major in the regular Army
> which position he filled with great acceptibility as his record will show.[21]

Neither these petitions, nor a personal visit to the president, nor subsequent correspondence elicited any response from the chief of state or
from Secretary of State Fish.

Delany was so disappointed by the administration's failure to appoint
him minister to Liberia that he initiated a debate among African Americans whether or not they should demand patronage from the political
parties they supported. He demanded that "the Republican party—or
any political party appealing to blacks—share the patronage of public
office on a 'pro-rata' basis."[22] Arguing that while it was understandable
that the Republican party appointed no African Americans to federal
positions in the North because only one out of every thirty in that region
was African American, Delany insisted that this should certainly not be
the case in the South, where one-third to one-half of the population was
African American.

Whether he believed that this concept was self-serving on Delany's
part or plain wrong, Frederick Douglass took a position that would be
echoed by whites in the 1960s when the issue of affirmative action was
raised by African Americans. Speaking for many northern blacks,
Douglass equivocated over whether the Republican party had in fact let

African Americans down. He conceded that while the lion's share of offices did go to whites, this was due to their superior qualifications. Douglass did hold out the hope that in time this factor would disappear as African Americans, too, became educated. He also conceded that Delany's position was "admirable in theory" but wondered aloud whether the major did not think it absurd as a matter of practice. Teasing Delany, Douglass declared:

> The fact is, friend Delany, these things are not fixed by figures, and while men are what they are cannot be so fixed. According to the census, the colored people of the country constitute one-eighth of the whole American people. Upon your statistical principle, the colored people of the United States ought, therefore, not only to hold one-eighth of all the offices in the country, . . . but they should, of course, be equal in everything else. They should constitute one-eighth of the poets, statesmen, scholars, authors, and philosophers of the country. . . . Now, my old friend, there is no man in the United States who knows better than you do that equality of numbers has nothing to do with equality of attainments. You know, too, that natural equality is a very different thing from practical equality; and that though men may be potentially equal, circumstances may for a time cause the most striking inequalities. Look at our newly emancipated people, read their history of ignorance and destitution, and see their present progress and elevation, and rejoice in the prospect before them. You are too broad not to comprehend, and too brave to shut your eyes to facts; and in the light of these your octagonal principle certainly will not work.[23]

Whether the debate among African American leaders about political patronage reached the ears of the president and his secretary of state or not, the White House appointed an African American as minister resident and consul general to Liberia on 1 March 1871. J. Milton Turner of Missouri met the criteria suggested by Delany in the debate over patronage. This man had apparently impressed the president by being able to control the votes of African American delegates at the 1870 state republican convention held in Jefferson City. He was instrumental in helping to defeat a proposal to reenfranchise former Confederates and in getting the twenty thousand African American voters to support Grant for the presidency. Thanks to this political action, African Americans for the first time in history became official participants in the foreign policy-making process of the United States of America relating to an African state.[24]

When Turner presented his credentials to President Edward James Roye of Liberia, who was born in Ohio and had migrated to Liberia at the age of thirty-one, he did not forget to invoke black nationality. He thanked the Liberian president for receiving him in the capacity of minister resident and consul general from the United States to Liberia, and added:

> I cannot consent to allow the present opportunity to pass without offering to your Government the congratulations of the country I have the distinguished honor to thus represent. In the true spirit of laudable progress, you have *planted upon these shores the germ of a Republic, that is destined not only to develop a civilization worthy of the respect and admiration of unborn generations; but by means of the Christian religion to debarbarize and benefit for almost immediate usefulness thousands of human beings, whose intellects are today debased by the destructive potency of heathenish superstition* [emphasis added].[25]

President Roye, obviously touched by this ceremony, replied that he hoped that Liberia would be a source of brotherly love at home and abroad, "Because," he declared, "a great negro nationality is to be reared on the West Coast of Africa." He was profuse in his welcome to Turner, receiving him most cordially "in the name of the infant Republic, Liberia. I welcome you as the accredited representative of the parent Republic of Republics." He concluded by declaring that "on behalf and in the name of the Liberian Republic," Turner was doubly welcomed. "Six times seven, thou art made welcome to our shore. . . . I have the exquisite pleasure to represent you with your exequatur, which, may God grant, could not be placed in more worthy hands."[26]

Being very much an interested participant-observer in all of this, Mrs. Turner wrote to a friend in St. Louis how delighted she was with the reception given her husband by the president and his cabinet. "Persons from many different parts were present," she said. "A few evenings afterwards he arranged for us a select gathering at his residence, which was simply *elegant*. The mayor of the city also gave us a reception at his residence." What especially pleased Mrs. Turner was that the company was "very intellectual. Just to think of generals and colonels in uniform, Cabinet officers, city councilmen, lawyers, doctors, other professional characters, authors, editors, poets, and other distinguished literary people, together with a live President . . . and they, every one, colored!" Pleased to be in the company of the ministers for England, Germany, Norway, Sweden, Haiti, and other countries, she concluded, "I declare it was the nicest affair that I have ever seen."[27] Mrs. Turner may not have known it, but it was the fear of such affairs being staged and attended by black diplomats and their wives at the White House that caused many United States senators initially to oppose the recognition of both Haiti and Liberia.[28]

The Liberians had welcomed Turner with open arms, but soon a number of interrelated events would test his mettle as a diplomat. The issue that was to plague the new minister resulted from Liberia's difficult financial state. Caught between the necessity to support a modern state structure with all those ministries and their appurtenances, and the lack of means to collect the little revenue generated by the aboriginal population, Liberia was perennially broke. On 31 March 1871 President Roye wrote his "Great and Good Friend," President Ulysses S. Grant, appealing for a loan of $500,000. In his response Grant notified Roye that both the Constitution and policy of the United States permitted such loans only with the "express authority" of Congress and that that body "has hitherto abstained from any such measure and . . . could scarcely, under existing circumstances be expected to adopt any other course." Grant suggested that the Liberians might enter the "money market of the United States as an applicant for loans" and promised to ask Congress about a loan for Liberia. However, he did not do so, leaving the Liberians with the task of seeking funds elsewhere.[29]

Much to the concern of many Liberians, the Roye administration was so short of funds that it was forced to negotiate a loan in Great Britain on fairly usurious terms. Then in London President Roye approved the loan without the normal consultation of the Liberian legislators. This action so infuriated Secretary of State Johnson that he returned to Monrovia, sparking rumors that Roye had received a kickback for accepting the loan.[30]

The situation worsened when the president became engaged in a bruising political battle with the Liberian Congress about extending the presidential term from two years to four years. To forestall any action on the part of President Roye, the Congress authorized an election that was held to replace him at the end of his two-year term. A former president of Liberia, J. J. Roberts, was elected to take office in 1 January 1872, but on 20 October some of Roye's supporters attempted to seize buildings in Monrovia, precipitating a battle during which a cannonball was shot into the president's house.[31]

Faced with a potential revolution, Roye summoned Turner in an attempt to enlist the support of the United States. The president claimed that the loan arrangements had been in order, but when on 23 October he was unable to restore order in this country Roye reported to Turner that revolution was imminent. Roye then promised to resign the presidency, swore allegiance to the government of the United States, and claimed its protection from mob violence in the city of Monrovia. Throughout all of these events Turner resolutely emphasized the neutrality of the United States when asked by African American immigrants to Liberia in the St. Paul River area to give them the protection of the United States "for the sake of humanity, and to prevent a civil war which is now imminent."[32]

The Liberian Senate and House of Representatives, increasingly hostile to Roye, met in executive session on 26 October and deposed the president, but they did not count on Roye's tenacity. He attempted to flee the country rather than resign but was apprehended and arrested by an armed guard that had anticipated his action. On 10 February 1872 the now ex-president was tried for corruption, convicted, and placed in jail. That night he allegedly removed all of his clothing save a filled money belt and fled the prison. Reports indicated that he procured a boat and attempted to reach a British ship then in the harbor but drowned when the boat capsized.[33]

These bizarre events created many problems for Minister Turner. Not only was Roye a head of state and a native of the United States, but prior to his trial and conviction, he had reclaimed his United States citizenship and had asked for the protection of the United States legation. Under the circumstances, Turner found it necessary to find out all he could about Roye's death, because he did not quite believe the account he had been given. He reported to the State Department that an autopsy had found a wound in the occipital region of the ex-president's head. However, passions were so aroused against Roye in Monrovia that no one was implicated in his death, and his estate, said to amount to more than $100,000, was seized by the Liberian government.[34]

Unfortunately, Turner was caught in the fallout of the Roye affair and had to use all the diplomacy at his command in order to avoid disaster for himself, the United States government, and African Americans. One Spencer Anderson, who had been in London with Roye when the loan with the British was negotiated, allegedly arrived in Monrovia carrying some $25,000 of that loan with him. But upon learning about Roye's imprisonment, he refused to land. He did return to Monrovia when the ship called there during its home voyage and disembarked when promised immunity from arrest by the Liberian government. However, the government promptly broke its word, arrested him, and then released him on bail until the March term of the High Court. Not trusting the local postal officials, Anderson sent a package of three letters to Turner at the American legation for transmittal by diplomatic pouch to persons in the United States and Great Britain. This Turner refused to do, and because he was going on tour, he charged a servant to return the mail personally to Mr. Anderson. Unfortunately for all concerned, the messenger to whom Anderson had given the letters to take to Turner reported the event to the Liberian authorities, who promptly rearrested Anderson. When Turner's servant did not find Anderson at home, he brought the three letters back to the legation, where they remained until the minister returned from up-country.[35]

When they learned about these episodes, the members of the Liberian Senate decided to summon Turner to appear before them. A committee of the Senate called upon the minister and inquired whether he had the letters and whether they could obtain them. Turner explained his involuntary role in the matter but expressed concern for his personal honor and that surrendering the letters might jeopardize the strict neutrality of the United States in the entire Roye affair. Asked whether he would accept a summons from the Senate, the minister respectfully declined but suggested that a personal request from that body for him to appear would be given the greatest consideration. Turner subsequently went to the Senate and, after reserving the right against self-incrimination, satisfied the senators of his innocence in the entire affair. Nevertheless, the matter of Anderson's letters still remained. This was resolved, and United States rights were respected when Turner agreed to accept a "writ" of arrest of the letters issued by the Liberian Senate. Upon examination, the letters were found to be harmless, and Anderson was released.[36]

During this entire episode, Turner's main concern was whether the Department of State would have approved of his conduct. When the department finally responded, it suggested that its minister could have resisted dealing with the Liberians but concluded that no harm had been done to the prestige of the United States. More serious for Turner's morale was his anxiety over the effect of the Roye affair on Liberian attitudes toward him and his status and role as a United States minister. Conscious of the suspicion that he might have favored the American-born Roye, Turner was especially solicitous in his relationship with Roye's successor, President J. J. Roberts. Representing the diplomatic corps at a reception given by this now perennial president in honor of his fifth inauguration, Turner declared:

> I am by no means callous to the fact that my station places me officially between two of the most remarkable characters of the nineteenth century, one of whom is no less distinguished for marked justice and great practical comprehension in his administration of the affairs of the Government of the United States, than for the peculiar talent, which makes him "First Military

Captain of the Century,["] the other—called by the independent suffrages of his countrymen from the retirement of age, to preside on the affairs of the Government of his country, the fifth time within two and a half decades. For this latter circumstance, I think, there can be found no parallel in the history of Democratic Institutions.[37]

Turner knew how to flatter Roberts, but he was also discreet. He attempted to get to the bottom of the Roye affair but warned the Department of State that the Liberians were anxious not to have their problems bruited about—a situation that "renders my position both official and social exceedingly delicate. It also renders my personal habits somewhat reticent and recluse."[38]

Given these circumstances, one can imagine the chagrin with which Minister Turner confessed to Secretary of State Hamilton Fish that some Liberians at least were not enthusiastic at having African American diplomats accredited to their country. This development was yet more fallout from the Roye affair and highlighted one of the dilemmas that faced African American envoys of the United States. As recounted by Turner in a rather long and detailed telegram to the State Department, this problem arose because of his dealings with Mrs. Roye. Needing some English currency to pay for his wife's passage from Sierra Leone to Great Britain, the minister advertised for it. The widow of ex-President Roye heard of Turner's need and offered him £200 "for my personal Draft." But aware of the suspicion in which the Roye family was held, Turner notified President Roberts of the transaction and was granted permission to pursue it.[39]

Unknown to Turner, his Liberian landlord had viewed with alarm the visits of Mrs. Roye to the Turners' rooms and suspected foul play. He therefore took advantage of Turner's trip to the country to search the minister's lodgings and discovered the money. Turner was surprised and mortified when he returned and overheard his landlord telling neighbors: "Now if these niggers (referring to the Turners) have that much of Mr. Roye's money, they must have the money the Government is looking for, the black thieves. We have enough thieves here without getting more from America. I don't see what they want to send a nigger here as Minister for anyhow. We can't respect no nigger as Minister." According to a cable Turner sent to the department, the landlord was more abusive than could be reported.[40]

Again, Turner's main concern was not to "disgust the Department" with the unpleasant details but "to discreetly take such measures as would prevent the reasonable attachment of accusation or even suspicion to the Legation of the U.S." He reported that activated solely by this motive, he proceeded to the executive mansion, where he gave President Roberts a full account of what had transpired and of his ability to prove the truth. Turner assured the president that while appreciating the "great confidence the Government of Liberia had hitherto reposed" in him, it was his intention to notify the Department of State of the entire affair, and he was quite willing to submit his wife's baggage to customs inspection to allay any suspicion that it might contain moneys resulting from the Roye affair.[41]

Turner was philosophical about this incident but apparently had had enough from Liberians who, proud of their independence, always suspected that the United States was not above trifling with them. Turner assured the State Department that the current officials were courteous and desired to have good relations with the United States, but he also confessed:

> Having been more than once (and "I" may say repeatedly) subjected by officials and others to gross personal indignities, I am forced to the apprehension that the policy of our President in appointing a Negro citizen of the U.S. to this country is not fully appreciated, nor thoroughly agreed with by some. I fear I cannot err upon this point inasmuch as some intelligent and eminent Liberian citizens have of their accord sorrowfully expressed convictions similar to my apprehension. I am fully aware and highly appreciative of the importance of the position taken by the Administration in the presence of our entire country in elevating one like myself to a position of such great responsibility, trust, and confidence. I have therefore made it my highest acme to be in every sense true to the interests of the Government of our own country. Meantime I am frank to confess that I have desire to be of service to this immature State which is composed of men with whom I am identified by blood and race.[42]

Turner confessed to the department that it was with the most "poignant reluctance" that he felt obliged to report the "humiliating statements" contained in his despatches. But he insisted that he had no intention of inciting the department against the Liberians or of suggesting action against profoundly ignorant persons. What he did desire to do was "to report to the Department, every occurrence of interest to the Legation here" and to let it know about his personal feelings and conduct. Then in an effort to put the best face on conditions in Liberia, Turner reported in a later despatch that in "larger and more mature governments, the recent difficulties experienced in Liberia would have little or no palpable effect upon channels of industry or the usual quietude of citizens." This was in stark contrast to "all small and immature governments, especially those whose organisms are democratic, [where] the conscious individual, and collective sovereignty of the citizens, brings them into such close intimacy that they not only assume a domestic appearance, but might frequently be classed as national families."[43]

Turner was troubled that Liberia had proved itself no exception to this general rule with respect to the conduct of small nations, but he sought to put the little progress that the country had made in perspective:

> I deem it unnecessary to say to the Department that there can be no radiating force so potent in the civilizing and Christianizing [of] Africa as a Christian commonwealth, a religious Negro nationality, under the auspicious control of democratic institutions of government.[44]

It was fair, he insisted, to compare the development of Liberia with that of the United States. The former was first settled by men extracted from "centuries of barbarism, and from other centuries of thralldom." These persons, "aside from a deep-seated love for liberty, brought to the work nothing but a degraded manhood and a wealth of illiterate experience." He compared this with the United States, whose founders were heirs to seven centuries of civilization. In a statement reflecting his views of the historical development of human societies, he declared: "Past experience shows Liberia's need to be men, education, and wealth; these alone can give her sound policy and successful government."[45]

Turner's views about the needs of Liberia and about what the policy of the United States implicitly ought to be toward this black nation were shared and supported by Captain (later Commodore) Robert W. Shufeldt, U.S. Navy, commanding the USS *Plymouth,* who had visited Liberia during 1873. Reporting upon this visit to George M. Robeson, Secretary of the Navy, Shufeldt recommended the establishment of a steamship connection between the two countries. The captain was "fully convinced that immigration, with a moderate amount of capital, is all that is now required to place Liberia upon a permanent footing and to insure an increasing prosperity." Liberia was "essentially an American outpost upon the frontiers of barbarism, and it deserves on this account the fostering care of the American people. It is struggling against a thousand adverse circumstances—ignorance and poverty within, heathenism without—and yet it appears to receive from us but little private sympathy and no public aid." The Liberians, he maintained, were "essentially American in feeling, yet they find themselves at present being gradually shut in and circumscribed by the ever-increasing extension of British power upon this Coast."[46]

Turner's problem was that the United States not only failed to aid Liberia financially but kept on dunning the poor country for the repayment of a loan it had secured in 1869 to buy arms during a series of military skirmishes with the aboriginal population. The settlers had promised to repay the bill with interest in the future but had told Minister Seys they could not do so. In 1873 Turner received a series of messages instructing him to ask the Liberians to pay their bills or at least the interest on their credit. He dutifully spoke to them and, like Seys before him, reported back to the department that the Liberians insisted that they could not pay at that time. Now, however, the Liberians added a new wrinkle. They told Turner that given the similarity of institutions between the United States and Liberia and the American origin of the principal inhabitants of the country, the debt should be forgiven or some alternatives should be worked out. In fact, once when Turner requested the repayment of the loan, the Liberian secretary of state replied that the Liberians were having difficulty making their payment to Great Britain and hinted that the minister should encourage the United States not to press for the repayment of the loan given the traditional friendship between Liberia and the United States.[47]

In an effort to help the State Department to understand the attitude of the Liberians, Turner asked the secretary's permission to send a copy of the response, with all its sentiments of special friendship and other innuendos, on to Washington. To this Turner appended his own sentiments about the Liberian loan. He told the department that while he had no instructions to suggest that a request for the cancellation of the loan be entertained, "I know of no fact more strikingly apparent to the most casual observation than the general absence of money throughout the Republic of Liberia." He conceded that this state of affairs was due to the Liberians' habit of living above their means, and he suggested that unless they stopped consumption without production and "resolve 'to harvest home' to and for themselves," they would never succeed in being independent.[48]

Turner did succeed in impressing upon the Liberians the nature of the constitutional separation of powers within the United States government—a practice they probably viewed as quixotic since it differed so greatly from their own. When Liberian President Roberts gave his 1874 annual report to Congress stressing the continuing friendly attitude of the United States toward Liberia, he remarked: "I indulged the hope that our Government would be relieved by that of the United States from the pecuniary obligation incurred by [the] purchase [of arms]." He said that he was aware that President Grant had the interest of Liberia at heart but that the United States Congress was the responsible body. Nevertheless, he added, "I am fully persuaded that an appeal to Congress would not fail of its object."[49] Roberts was wrong, and Turner never was able to persuade the United States to forgive the loan. Badgered by the Liberians to do exactly that, he had done his best. In response to his requests, the department repeatedly stated that Congress, not the president of the United States, was solely empowered to cancel the loan. Some historians have found this attitude of the United States toward Liberia curious in view of its tolerance toward other international debtors even at this early period.

Turner did play an important role in the decision of the United States to help Liberia in a conflict with the Grebo people, even though he had serious reservations about the Americo-Liberians' attitude toward the indigenous populations. Apropos of this, he periodically reported to the Department of State when such local leaders visited the legation. He was not only impressed with some visiting Vai leaders but also took the opportunity to tell them of the power of the United States and of its wish to see the local people benefit from the civilization that was being brought to them.[50] On 7 September 1875 Turner notified the Department of State that the " 'Grebos'—a tribe of Africans numbering about 30,000 souls have declared war against Liberia." He explained that this altercation was the last in a series of battles going back to at least 1857 between the Grebo and the then Maryland Colony and that this conflict continued when Liberia absorbed that colony. This struggle, he intimated, was not too different from the one between the Liberian colonists and the Vai, and was due to differences between the Liberians and the native populations over whether the latter had really sold or had only ceded their land to the colonists. Turner reported that the situation was further complicated by a claim from the president of Liberia that the American Episcopal Church missionaries, in addition to educating the Grebo, had given them the military training that now enabled them to revolt.[51]

In an attempt to explain "the root of the present misunderstanding [so] that the Department may better appreciate the necessity of the Republic of Liberia to defend with arms against a tribe with whom she is in treaty relations," Turner engaged in a bit of ethnography:

> Albeit, I have discovered that there exists among several of the African tribes with whose habits and traditions of government I have become somewhat acquainted, a rule making it impossible for any King or Chief of a tribe to enter into any compact agreement or treaty of whatever nature, by means of which the lands owned by the tribe may be permanently alienated. When we reflect how that the farms are all planted, worked, and the crops garnered and shared in common,—that the houses are built and repaired on a day or at a time set apart for the purpose, by the allied or consociate labor of the entire

community of each tribal town, we are, perhaps better able to understand how the land itself is also the property of a common ownership; which ownership the tribal tradition renders perpetual, and undertakes to enforce the perpetuation thereof, by making the title non-transferable; hence no individual or collective power within the tribe,—even though it be kingly authority itself, is regarded by the people of the tribe as being sufficient to make permanent cession of the tribal lands. The tribal lands being considered the rightful inalienable inheritance of their posterity held as a thing in trust for generations yet unborn, it would indeed be difficult to conceive of any cause for which an African tribe would contend with greater pertinacity than for that of conducting the unborn descendancy of their lands to their posterity. . . . It would seem quite probable that although the "Grebo" tribe may be vanquished in the field, it may prove quite difficult by any coercive policy to eradicate or even to diminish the force of a tribal tradition that it has been the fixed custom and practice of the tribe to observe, perhaps, for many centuries,—and for which they at present show unwillingness and determination to die if necessary. It is an unhappy circumstance, that the policy of the Republic during the years of her existence in the midst of the very tractable tribes of Africans within Liberian boundaries and who vastly outnumber her civilized citizens has not been sufficiently assimilative to have so intermixed the interests of these two classes of her citizens as to be able now to avoid violent contact with the traditions of a tribe so powerful and influential as is the "Grebo" tribe. For twenty years or thereabout, those American Episcopalian schools have been taught upon a very commendable system among the "Grebo" men, and about as many of their young women have acquired a fair common school training, while quite a number are classical scholars, some are able to read the Holy Scriptures in the original tongues and in some instances to translate them into the "Grebo" language which has been reduced to grammar. Now it seems plain that as this kind of intelligence increases and spreads within the tribe, the people thereof will become better able to know and appreciate their just rights, and to form combinations for the resistance of wrongs perpetuated from without the tribe. It would therefore seem "a far more excellent way" should the probity of Liberian statesmen adopt toward the aborigines of the country, a policy the friendliness and wisdom of which would be capable of inducing at least the intelligence of the tribes, to enter and become an integral [part] of the sovereign state of Liberia, and assist in bearing the responsibilities of the nation. It seems that some such policy would at once obviate many perplexing difficulties that may hereafter spring up to harass and trouble the Republic, and accomplish a grand effectual act in the laudable work for which these colonies, evidently, were planted upon the border of this unknown land—vis: The evangelization and civilization of this portion of this vast continent.[52]

Despite his reservations about the behavior and policies of the Amer-ico-Liberians, Turner did not hesitate to remind the Department of State that Liberia's African policy had many features in common with the

United States' Indian policy. He held that, like the Americans, Liberians desiring new territories and faced with the reluctance of the local people to alienate their lands often promised to pay a form of rent either in stipends or ammunition. The problem for the Liberians, according to Turner, was that in contrast to the Americans, they were often too financially strapped to pay. The result was that the local people resented the Liberians, and those on the coast insisted on trading with foreigners, thereby increasing the conflict between themselves and the settlers. But the minister was not sanguine about the ability of Liberian statesmen to learn a lesson from their country's difficulties. This, he suggested, was regrettable given the need of these leaders "to adopt sufficient means for the elevation of aboriginal Africans, and for assisting to bring Africans into closer and more desirable commercial relations with the civilized world."[53]

The Americo-Liberians had a more intractable problem with the native Africans than the United States had had with the Indians. Whereas the American policy toward the Indians was somewhat successful because of

> the continued decrease and restiveness of the Indian tribes . . . [t]he Indian's utter absence of longevity, together with his absolute devotion to savage life, has incapacitated him to withstand the encroachment of saxon civilization . . . [That] cannot be truthfully applied to the aboriginal African.[54]

Turner believed that

> the African is not restive of the restraints of civilization, nor does he lack longevity; here in his tropical home, beneath the generous ample foliage of his own picturesque scenery, the aboriginal African stands undisturbed by that fell disease so thick in this atmosphere; and which is so deadly of influence to the health and lives of all, of whatever clime or people, who come to make Africa their adopted home.[55]

Turner was convinced that foreign people who entered any country in Africa with the idea of "ignoring, or of creating of the aboriginal African an inferior class," or of regarding him in any way other than a principal and indispensable factor in development of the resources and of the country itself would certainly fail.[56]

Turner could not help feeling a wry sympathy for the Americo-Liberians. He reported with obvious satisfaction: "The alacrity with which this country responds to the call for troops presents a degree of patriotism highly commendable."[57] His major fear was that the five to seven thousand but poorly armed troops that the Grebo could field might just manage to defeat the one thousand well-armed Liberians, with grave results for the lives and property of American citizens in the territory. Yet Turner was not unmindful of the pressure the Liberians could put upon the United States by using the excuse of their inability to protect American lives and property, by requesting that these persons remove themselves and their property to "Native Towns," and by appealing for an American vessel to aid in this process. He was aware that Article VIII of the Liberian-United States Treaty of 1862 stipulated that the United States should never "interfere unless solicited by the Government of Liberia, in the affairs of the aboriginal inhabitants and the Government of Liberia."[58] Turner also realized that this provision was inserted in the treaty as much to protect the Liberians from unwanted interference in their internal affairs by the United States as to obviate the United States being drawn into an African war by the Liberians. The question now was whether the time had come for the Liberians to invoke this provision.[59]

Reviewing the situation in Liberia for the Department of State, Turner reported that Liberia's "little army" of one thousand men was already in the field and that the government could not recruit more than an additional fifteen hundred soldiers, whereas the Grebo had a huge population to draw upon. Moreover, while the Liberians were short of supplies, the Grebo were in their natural habitat and had all the resources of their land. What troubled Turner most of all was the "baneful influence a defeat of the Liberians would have on the remaining sixty or seventy thousand native Africans in Liberia's territory." Already there were reports in Monrovia of "the contemplated uprisings of the tribes in Montserrado County in the vicinity of St. Paul's river. Should they possess the hardihood to combine and rise, Monrovia is defenseless and must fall before them. Americans here are unanimous in their appeal to me for the presence of an American Man-of-War."[60]

The Liberian president, acting through his secretary of state, told Turner that the situation in Liberia was so grave as to force him to consider invoking Article VIII of the treaty. In Turner's opinion, while the Grebo were well armed for land fighting, "they could offer no resistance to a ship-of-war. One ship-of-war could disable their campaign in a few hours, by destroying their towns, and demolishing their works. Indeed, very many agree with me that the mere presence of the ship-of-war would be sufficient to restore peace; and to create for Liberia a moral influence with the tribes now so generally restive." At Turner's request, the United States ordered the USS *Alaska,* Captain A. A. Semmes, U. S. Navy, commanding, to Monrovia. And as Turner predicted, peace was soon restored between the Republic of Liberia and the Grebo reunited kingdom. A treaty was signed between them at Harper, Cape Palmas, on 1 March 1876, witnessed by Captain Semmes.[61]

While the Liberians appreciated Turner's aid in securing help from the United States during the Grebo war, they subsequently turned against him because he questioned the wisdom of unlimited African American emigration to Liberia. Turner was becoming increasingly concerned over the American Colonization Society's propagandizing African Americans to come to Liberia. He appears to have been more optimistic about the effects of the policies of Reconstruction on the lives of African Americans than the facts warranted. In a report he sent to Secretary of State Hamilton Fish in 1872, Turner wrote:

> Now that such signal changes have occurred in the United States with reference to the condition of this class of persons, the wisdom of continuing such a policy [to emigrate exiled Africans to Liberia] is thought by many at least to be questionable. While none would discourage such as desire to leave the United States for Liberia, all must concede that the number who desire to leave is comparatively small, and of a class whose degraded manhood and absolute dependence but ill adapts them to the wants of the primary economy of a young and aspiring democratic government. Many of those who come here are lured by impossible hopes, and possess dispositions rather to acquire affluence and ease than to realize successful empire. Of an emigration that arrived in December, 1871, numbering 243 persons, 45 or 50 persons have died of fever, many are acclimating, thirty-five or forty are intending to return, the remainder are quite despondent, and those who remain here will be little else than a burden on the country.[62]

Personally, Turner did his best to help destitute immigrants. He wrote long despatches to the department concerning the plight of people who came to Liberia under the auspices of an organization known as the Colonization Society for Liberia and personally brought to his home in Liberia one of three children from Sierra Leone whose parents had died and were now homeless. Both he and the department must have been quite satisfied when a congressman from Alabama, not knowing about Turner's action, subsequently asked that these children be found.[63]

What Turner did not bargain for was that the growing disenchantment of both white northerners and southerners with the federal Reconstruction policies led to a compromise at the expense of African Americans and a renewed interest of freedpersons in emigration. New World émigrés to Liberia such as Edward Wilmot Blyden and Alexander Crummell continued to encourage their erstwhile countrymen to join them. Alexander Crummell wrote a series of letters to the "Colored Students, undergraduates at Xenia, Lincoln, Howard, and other colleges in the

United States of America, on matters pertaining to the Conversion of Africa." In a blistering article he declared, "Gentlemen: I have seen the statement, namely, that American black men have no more special obligation with respect to Africa than any other Americans." He suggested to these college students that "it is the duty of black men in America to live and labor for the evangelization of the land of their fathers." First, on the "grounds of humanity"; second, because these men are "the descendants of Africa," and this "bond of family and race is one of the holiest of our native sentiments"; and third, "because they are Christians."[64]

Meanwhile, in the southern states of America things went from bad to worse. In January 1874 Major John M. Orr of Leesburg, Virginia, wrote in the *Southern Review* that African Americans should migrate to Africa or face extinction if they remained among whites in the United States of America. Faced with this threat (which they may have viewed as an opportunity), the officers of the American Colonization Society meeting at the end of 1875 took what for them was a "new departure" by electing two African American vice presidents to their board: the Reverend Jabez P. Campbell, D.D., J. Delaware and Bishop Henry McNeal Turner of Savannah, Georgia. In accepting this honor, Bishop Turner asked, rhetorically, whether now that slavery was dead, the American Colonization Society should continue to exist? His response was that "just so long as we are a people within a people vastly our superiors in numbers, wealth, . . . having no government of our own, we shall be nothing, and be so treated by the civilized world." He felt that African Americans should go to Africa and create the "United States of Africa."[65]

In the person of Bishop Turner, the American Colonization Society had a man who was destined to play a major role in articulating the symbolic policy of African Americans toward Africa. Discovering the African Methodist Episcopal church in 1858, after his seminary training at Baltimore, he was given a church on Capitol Hill in Washington, D.C. Somewhat like David Walker (an early antislavery activist and sometime contributor to *Freedom's Journal*) and Henry Highland Garnet, Bishop Turner had openly urged the slaves to take advantage of the Civil War and to defend themselves vigorously when attacked and insulted, and he had urged a reluctant President Lincoln to use African American troops in the Union army.[66] Accepting the post of chaplain in an African American regiment, he performed heroically during the war and afterward worked as a party organizer in Georgia, being elected to that state's Republican constitutional convention in 1867 and to its legislature in 1868. Then, reacting bitterly to the attempts of white legislators to disqualify African Americans from holding public office, Bishop Turner openly declared that whites should not be trusted; that African Americans should not fight for a country that did not grant them civil rights; and that a revolution was in the offing in the South. These protests did not protect either him or the African Americans, and when dismissed from the Georgia legislature he sought but did not receive the office of United States minister to Haiti. Bishop Turner received instead an appointment as postmaster of Macon, Georgia, but after two weeks in office he was charged with fraud, counterfeiting, and theft and was again dismissed. He was later granted an appointment as customs inspector in Savannah, Georgia, but retreated to the AME Church, convinced that there was no place for African Americans in America.

Significantly, Bishop Turner was converted to emigrationism by the Reverend Alexander Crummell, one of the commissioners on emigration whom the Liberians had earlier sent to the United States.[67] As the young pastor achieved a position in the AME Church that permitted him to travel widely, he too began to spread the "dream of Africa." This message came as a balm to African Americans throughout the South, but especially in South Carolina where they formed a feared majority. Deprived of political and civil rights, denied economic opportunities, their insecurity heightened by the violent political presidential campaign of 1876, these people looked longingly to Liberia for salvation.[68] H. N. Bouey, a twenty-eight-year-old African American teacher from Edgefield County, South Carolina, who had heard Bishop Turner speak, wrote to him:

> Dear Sir: I write to inform you, that as soon as I can arrange my business in America, I am going to Liberia to teach school. Not to come back either. I am a colored man or yellow man as you may have it. I have become satisfied that the colored man has no home in America. I have manhood in me that I would sooner die than compromise. . . . In five years from now the public schools will be closed on the negro. . . . You know educations make unprofitable labor in the south,—hence my people must, and will, be kept ignorant. Some of their leaders such as have property own farms, and some ministers, who have fine congregations supporting them, are standing against immigration to Liberia. But you know, our people must be kept poor and ignorant, so that they may be profitable laborers. . . . Every pulsation of my heart prays god to speed next fall, when I shall leave for Liberia.[69]

With such sentiments leading to what had been called the exodus movement, Martin R. Delany reentered the picture. Together with Bouey, a man from New Guinea named George Curtis, and the Reverend B. F. Porter, an AME pastor and educationist from Charleston, South

Carolina, he founded the Liberian Exodus Joint Stock Steam Ship Company in the fall of 1877. The reaction to this project was instantaneous and terrific. According to one account, "Even before the stock was issued the rumor ran all through South Carolina, Georgia, and as far as New Orleans that a ship was to sail out of Charleston harbor for free Liberia on November 15. Hundreds of families left their homes for Charleston. . . . It was estimated that by the summer of 1877 approximately 30,000 families were in the process of joining the movement."[70]

The reaction of the American minister to Liberia, J. Milton Turner, to the news of this emigration movement almost led to his undoing. Keeping abreast of developments in the United States, he wrote Secretary of State William M. Evarts on 3 September 1877 about several articles he had seen. One in the New York *Evening Post* of 17 July 1877 stated, "The promoters of a Liberian emigration scheme in Charleston assert that they have enrolled the names of two thousand five hundred colored persons in that city, and thirty thousand in the State, who consent to emigrate." Another was a report in a New York paper, *Le Messager Franco-Américain,* of the same date that said, "Il parait que les Sud-Caroliniens ne voient pas avec plaisir cette entreprise d'émigration nègre," the translation of which was, "It seems that the South Carolinians do not view with pleasure this enterprise of negro emigration." Finally, Turner cited an article in the Washington *National Republican* of 20 July 1877, which said that despite a shortage of money to go to Liberia "some families did go, but from the report which they sent back they found Liberia anything but an El Dorado. A few of them wrote urgent appeals to their friends at home to assist them to return, and by means of subscriptions so obtained managed to make their way back."[71]

Apparently taking for granted that the people in the Department of State were closely following the continuing dialectic between African Americans and Africa, Turner wrote the secretary:

The reasons which have influenced me to omit in my correspondence . . . the scheme for the emigration to Liberia of negro citizens of the United States, as propagated by the organizations in the United States known as the American Colonization Society, [et]c., are manifold; the principal one of which is, no doubt, obvious to the Department. But as the determined agitation of the agents of those associations appears of late to attract the attention of a class of Americans whose ignorance of all the real facts in the case leaves them exposed to ex parte statements, which, in many instances, may induce them to leave homes and situations in life where they enjoy, at least, comparative comfort, and are able at the same time to supply an important demand for labor, only to experience disappointment in a foreign land, without hope, in nine cases in ten, of even being able to acquire the means to return to their homes, it now suggests itself as my duty to give only a very few of the more cogent reasons why I cannot advise or encourage the migration by subscription of negro citizens of the United States to Liberia.[72]

Turner wanted to assure the secretary that he meant no condemnation or misunderstanding of the high motives of American philanthropists who wished to help an "unfortunate class, and at the same time aid . . . the evangelization and civilization of Africa." His concern was that the emigrants were not being told that "the abundant wealth which nature has lavished upon Africa" was "locked securely within the environs of these deadly climatic influences." Turner then proceeded to describe the ravages of the Liberian climate, the primitive state of agriculture found there, the high cost of living, and the difficulties that previous groups of migrants had encountered. He also praised "the Spartan-like patriotism and stoic indifference to suffering, put forth so persistently by the first settlers of Liberia. They gained a foothold upon the shores of this country by persuasion when possible and by conquest when necessary." Yet Turner believed that "when taken comparatively, the policy employed by the English and other Europeans seems productive of as great, if not greater results than the plan adopted by Americans."[73]

Turner was especially doubtful whether the settlers' policy of assimilating the local people to Western ways, rather than helping them to modernize themselves while taking the African reality into consideration, was a good one. He said that he did not believe the theory that African Americans, "after three centuries of absence from Africa, the long, weary years of which were not altogether devoted to training [them] . . . in the higher walks of knowledge," were "better prepared than other foreigners, physically or otherwise, to carry civilization" to the unfortunate Africans. From his experience, when the African American confronted the realities of Africa, he was "as much a foreigner as any other people, and can only extend to the barbarous African the same philanthropic sympathy." Overwhelmed by the difficulty of "evangelizing, civilizing, and colonizing Africa," the migrant often gave up and desired to return home. The result was that "after sixty years we find that those who have remained with praiseworthy determination, if possible, to conquer these obstructions, have not assimilated a single tribe of native Africans, but have caused the extinction as such of perhaps as many of the aborigines."[74]

Trying as best he could to forestall criticism of his candor, Turner concluded that while his object was "not to encourage the persuasion of citizens of the United States to exchange their homes and country for Liberia, neither is it desired to dissuade any from coming to Liberia who may wish to do so." He felt it was necessary "to present the facts and difficulties attendant upon such a course, with a view that none, if possible, may emigrate without full knowledge of the probable result." He ventured that "a fact generally recognized by many thoughtful and prominent Liberians" was that persons "of any consequence to the wants of Liberia" were able "to pay their own expense of travel, and if desirous to come, would be willing and would prefer to do so." Finally, Turner said that "whether Liberia succeeds or fails, she cannot be accepted as a fair test of the negro's capacity or incapacity for self-government."[75]

What the diplomat did not realize was that his candor would be used against him. Whether Turner's despatch was leaked to the American Colonization Society and that organization notified the Liberians about it or, as Turner sought to convince himself, the news of the report reached Monrovia because the American government "thought proper to honor that despatch with a place in the *Foreign Relations of the United States*" is still a mystery. But a number of American newspapers got hold of it and culled from it extracts which were intended to show that Turner was somewhat unfavorable to "the wishes of those who desire to emigrate the American negro." The proponents of emigration within the United States made a few attempts to deny views attributed to Turner in the despatch but could not completely refute them.[76]

When news of the report reached Monrovia, some Liberians reacted so abusively that on 15 April 1878 Turner complained to the Liberian secretary of state about "a series of unfriendly behavior and indeed downright mistreatment directed against me with a degree of persistence during the last two or three months by Liberians high in official station in their country."[77] Included among these acts was a memo which the Liberian secretary of state sent to the minister stating, "It is with extreme regret that the Government has cause for grave apprehension that on your part is wanting a kindred feeling so important and so greatly desired."[78] Turner had made the mistake of believing that the "many thoughtful and prominent Liberians" who privately questioned the pro-emigration activities of the American Colonization Society would be willing to see their views in print.

Turner correctly attributed his difficulties to agents of the colonization society in Washington, Philadelphia, and other places, who he claimed had a great influence upon the destiny of the government and people of

Liberia—"an influence infinitely more potent in giving texture, color, and direction to Liberian affairs than perhaps the combined influence of all other sources." He felt that it was unfair for the agents of the emigrationists and the Liberian government itself to criticize the disclosure of some unpleasant facts, especially when the two groups tended to withhold these problems "from the emigrant until the last possible moment after his entrance into Liberia."[79] In its pique, the American Colonization Society in America attempted to use its influence with those who favored emigration to remove Turner from office.[80]

Meanwhile, in Liberia, the secretary of state and others began to spread unkind rumors about Turner, and the attorney general secured a copy of an American article containing derogatory statements about Liberia attributed to Turner and read it to the president and his cabinet. To complicate matters, a group of migrants who had recently arrived in Monrovia and were disgruntled by conditions delegated one of their members to meet with Turner. They wanted to make sure that in coming to Liberia they had not lost their American citizenship, and Turner informed them that they had not. News of the incident further annoyed Liberian officials, who retaliated by refusing to permit a few emigration agents dissatisfied with conditions to see the president. Then a gang of toughs cut the lanyard of the legation's flagstaff and threatened to mob Turner's house until dissuaded by officials who feared the displeasure of the United States.[81]

The State Department inadvertently compounded Turner's difficulties by choosing this inopportune time to instruct its chief of mission to seek either a repayment of the 1869 arms loan or at least payment of the interest. The Liberians blamed the minister for this turn of events and charged that he was responsible for the United States government not cancelling the debt in the first place. The Liberian harbormaster, attempting to get back at the United States for seeking repayment of the loan, tried to impose a port tax on an American ship. The port commander took offense when Turner protested but had to back down. Assuring the Department of State that he had carefully rebutted all allegations of any wrongdoing or disrespect to the Liberians, Turner wrote:

> Appreciating as I have always done in Liberia, that we are a great and powerful Christian nation recognizing and morally defending the confraternity of the nations, and pledged by our own very origin and the richness of the legacy of our principles to the promotion of international friendships and unity, and to the universal brotherhood and amity of man, I

have in consideration of that great fact, as well as the origin of the people composing this far off and struggling Republic, striven to have the United States always occupy the highest ground in her effort to extend the moral influence of her friendship to Liberia.[82]

Turner was later vindicated. He reported to the Department of State that in a conversation with the Liberian president about the disrespect shown to him by Secretary of State Johnson, the president told Turner that Mr. Johnson "had misrepresented the Government of Liberia in the caustic nature of that note and that Mr. Johnson had attempted similar misrepresentation in connection with certain official documents instructing the Liberian Minister to Her Majesty's Government at London." The president said that on the very morning of Turner's visit, and in view of the secretary of state's activities, he had accepted "that gentleman's resignation of the portfolio of State." The president also intimated to Turner the possibility of receiving the resignation of the secretary of the treasury who was then not in Monrovia.[83]

While Turner viewed with a certain equanimity the actions of the Americo-Liberian people, he felt otherwise about the American Colonization Society and its agents. He resented reports that the organization and its people had tried to effect his recall. He also resented their profiting from their paternalistic relationship with the settlers to influence United States policy toward Liberia, which frustrated his own mission. Turner found out that very often the society's agents in Washington knew about United States intentions in Liberia and notified the locals before he could do so. For example, on 20 April 1876—and long before his altercation with Secretary of State Johnson—tired, ill, and suffering from abscesses, Turner asked for leave. On 14 July 1877 he again expressed the desire to be recalled from Liberia, promising to remain until his successor should arrive, but heard nothing about his two requests. On 30 August 1877, in a manner uncharacteristic of him, Turner wrote the secretary of state complaining that while it was "perhaps of little consequence to the Department," he resented being told that William Coppinger, secretary of the American Colonization Society, had written to former Liberian President Warner that the USS *Essex* was scheduled to visit Monrovia and that "one J. B. Penny, a prominent and enthusiastic advocate of the emigration of negro citizens of the United States to Liberia, has been named by the President as Minister to Liberia with a view of facilitating that emigration scheme."[84]

Turner was understandably furious to hear secondhand about the appointment of a new minister, primarily to facilitate emigration, and the arrival of a warship. It appeared to him, first, that he was being sanctioned for supposedly being an anti-emigrationist, and second, that the department did not take into consideration that the visit of a warship to Liberia was normally an event of great ceremonial and political importance. Queried by the Liberians about what he thought of the rumor, Turner replied sarcastically, "If the President has thought proper to make the appointment mentioned, I believe that he has not been actuated by the views to which allusion is made, as the Government has never announced any policy with the view to facilitate the emigration of any class of her citizens."[85]

The president of the United States may not have been explicitly enunciating a pro-emigration policy to get African Americans to migrate to Liberia, but this was an important factor in America's African policy during the late 1870s and the early 1880s. Turner's departure from Liberia on 7 May 1878 coincided with heightened African American interest in the possibility of emigrating to Liberia, and a fierce debate took place in the pages of the New York *Herald*, the New York *Times*, the Savannah *Republican*, and the American Colonization Society's own *African Repository* about the pros and cons of emigration. William Coppinger not only blasted the Department of State for facilitating the diffusion of Turner's despatches but attempted to enlist the aid of African American leaders, the AME Church, and the Congress of the United States to further the society's enterprise. Coppinger insisted that "colored people are not listless spectators of these movements in behalf of that country [Liberia]." He pointed out that "some prominent ministers of the A.M.E. Church have taken decided ground in favor of a general movement to colonize Africa, and to gain a denominational foothold there." He added that their aim was not to remove people to the region, but to strengthen the West Coast Settlements.[86]

In May 1878 President Rutherford B. Hayes nominated John H. Smyth to succeed Turner as minister resident and consul general to the Republic of Liberia. Smyth had studied law at Howard University, was a member of the third constitutional convention of North Carolina, and had supported the nomination of Grant for a second term and Hayes for the presidency. What was intriguing about this appointment was that Smyth, a fervent emigrationist and an Afrophile, was recommended to Hayes by Frederick Douglass, a man known for his anti-emigrationist stance and lack of sustained interest in Africa. No sooner had the new minister arrived in Monrovia than he had the task of welcoming the first batch of emigrants sent on the SS *Azor* by the Liberian Exodus Association. The Liberians were happy to see the new arrivals, but President Anthony William Gardner complained that the 242 migrants were "poorly prepared for self-support, as had been announced by the 'Liberian Exodus Association.' " Nevertheless, he praised the immigrants, reporting that they "labored hard, and [did] much to help themselves." President Gardner added that since "a spirit of immigration" pervaded every state in the American Union and more arrivals were to be expected, the Liberian legislature should pass a law to spread the newcomers all over the country, without prejudice to any single locality.[87]

Smyth would find that while the American Colonization Society and the Liberians wanted African Americans to emigrate to Africa, the two groups had different agendas. Turner and Smyth wanted to protect the black nationalities that still existed in Africa and felt that African Americans in the United States, having understood the larger currents in the global system, could help, but they were both aware of the difficulties involved. The Liberians wanted immigrants who would not only help Liberia but who would also enlist the support of the United States. The aims of the American Colonization Society remained ambiguous, but many African Americans felt that it had difficulties viewing them as organic members of American society. Reacting to the president's description of the plight of the immigrants and perhaps aware of Turner's earlier concerns, Smyth wrote the American Colonization Society that while Liberia's future might be "glorious," it was also "full of responsibility." Like Turner before him, Smyth warned that one responsibility "the Africo-Liberian and his friends abroad [had was] to present faithfully and honestly to the Negro in exile the condition of Liberia, and to discourage the coming of emigrants, however anxious they may be to come, who cannot willingly, from a conviction of duty to the race of Africa, sacrifice comfortable homes, and the long-delayed but possessed boon of liberty, equality and preferment now enjoyed in the United States."[88]

Notes

1. *African Repository* 64 (July 1888): 95.
2. *African Repository* 64 (July 1888): 95.
3. Rayford W. Logan, *The Negro in African Life and Thought: The Nadir, 1877–1901* (New York: Dial Press, 1954), 3–36.
4. *African Repository* 39 (January 1863): 23; ibid. 44 (October 1868): 313.
5. Hollis Lynch, ed., *Black Spokesman, Selected Writings of E. W. Blyden* (London: Frank Cass, 1971), 18.
6. Alexander Crummell, "A Letter to Charles B. Dunbar," quoted in Adelaide Cromwell Hill and Martin Kilson, eds. and comps., *Apropos of Africa: Senti-*

ments of Negro American Leaders on Africa From the 1800s to the 1950s (London: Frank Cass, 1969), 87–93. See also *African Repository* 48 (February 1872): 55ff.

7. Hill and Kilson, *Apropos of Africa*, 93.
8. Ibid.
9. *African Repository* 41 (September 1865): 273.
10. Mr. John Seys, Legation of the United States, Monrovia, to Mr. William H. Seward, 26 January 1867, no. 10, *Foreign Relations of the United States, 1867* 2:327–28.
11. Ibid.
12. Ibid.
13. Ibid.
14. Ibid.
15. Ibid.
16. Seward to Seys, 4 April 1867, no. 7, ibid., 328.
17. *African Repository* 44 (April 1868): 105.
18. Victor Ullman, *Martin R. Delany: The Beginnings of Black Nationalism* (Boston: Beacon Press, 1971), 500–501.
19. Ibid.
20. Ibid., 411.
21. Ibid., 412.
22. Ibid., 414.
23. Frederick Douglass, "Letter to Major Delany," in *New National Era*, 31 August 1871, cited in Philip S. Foner, *The Life and Writings of Frederick Douglass* (New York: International Publishers), 4:280–81.
24. After Seys departed Monrovia, Francis E. Dumas of Louisiana was commissioned on 21 April 1869 to go to Liberia, but he declined. On 29 March 1870 James W. Mason of Arkansas was named minister to Liberia, but he never did go to Monrovia (see James A. Padgett, "Ministers to Liberia and Their Diplomacy," *Journal of Negro History* 22 [January 1937]: 57–58. For biographical data on J. Milton Turner, see *Register of the Department of State, 1870,* 10, 22, 47; *Register of the Department of State, 1931,* 73; Padgett, "Ministers to Liberia," 58).
25. *African Repository* 47 (October 1871): 309–10. President Roye's response was as eloquent as Turner's:

    I have listened to your words, as to those of devoted patriotism for your country, expressive, appreciative, and worthy of your accredited ministerial mission to Liberia, and which words have been so eloquently set forth, leaving the persuasive sentiments, founded upon facts, of the onward march and that high exemplary destiny of the great model Republic. . . .

    Here, it becomes me to record briefly and sadly the evils slavery has done against brotherly love.

    Slavery, in days gone, I trust, never to return, being the reverse of that brotherly affection, which slavery in the interests of cruel masters has fastened, is a most baneful incubus upon the unfortunate individuals composing societies made up from both the slave States and the free States. . . .

    O, Almighty Father, bless all nations. Bless especially the great parent Republic, and its negro child, the little Republic, Liberia.
26. Ibid., 311–13.
27. Ibid., 344.
28. When on 3 December 1861 President Lincoln in his annual message to Congress suggested that both Haiti and Liberia be granted recognition by the

United States on the grounds that this action would bring important commercial advantages to the country, a number of congressmen from the border states were scandalized. They feared both countries would send black diplomats to Washington, and these men and their families would expect an invitation to the White House when their colleagues were similarly invited (Charles H. Wesley, "The Struggle for the Recognition of Haiti and Liberia as Independent Republics," *Journal of Negro History* 2 [October 1917]: 379. See also *Congressional Globe,* 37th Cong., 2d sess., 27 February-2 May 1862; 6 May-23 June 1862).

29. Robert L. Keiser, *Liberia: A Report on the Relations Between the United States and Liberia* (Washington, D.C.: Government Printing Office, 1928), 27.

30. J. Milton Turner to Department of State, 30 November 1871, no. 4, Despatches from U.S. Ministers to Liberia, 1863–1906, Record Group 59, National Archives, roll 2.

31. Turner to Department of State, "State of Public Affairs in the Republic of Liberia," 14 February 1872, no. 39, roll 3.

32. Ibid.

33. Ibid.

34. Ibid.

35. Ibid.

36. Ibid.

37. Turner to Department of State, 15 January 1872, no. 170, roll 2.

38. Turner to Department of State, no. 39, roll 3.

39. Turner to Department of State, 30 March 1872, no. 40, roll 3.

40. Ibid.

41. Ibid.

42. Ibid.

43. Turner to Secretary of State, 25 May 1872, no. 45.

44. Ibid.

45. Turner to Secretary of State, 3 September 1877, no. 273, roll 6.

46. Report of Captain Shufeldt, USN, USS *Plymouth,* to George M. Robeson, Secretary of the Navy, 26 March 1873, cited in *African Repository* 49 (June 1873): 185–86.

47. Turner to Secretary Hamilton Fish, 14 May 1873, no. 74, U.S. Ministers to Liberia, roll 3.

48. Ibid.

49. *African Repository* 50 (June 1874): 173–74.

50. Turner to Department of State, 7 September 1875, no. 178, U.S. Ministers to Liberia, roll 5.

51. Ibid.

52. Ibid.

53. Turner to Fish, 3 November 1875, no. 189.

54. Ibid.

55. Ibid.

56. Ibid.

57. Turner to Secretary of State, 13 September 1875, no. 180.

58. Turner to Secretary of State, 11 October 1875, no. 184.

59. Ibid.

60. Ibid.

61. Turner to Department of State, 8 March 1876, no. 220.

62. Turner to Secretary of State, 25 May 1872, no. 45, roll 3.

63. Turner to Department of State, 2 October 1875, no. 182, roll 5.

64. Turner to Secretary of State, 27 October 1875, no. 189.
65. *African Repository* 52 (July 1876): 84–86.
66. John Hope Franklin and Alfred A. Mossi, Jr., *From Slavery to Freedom* (New York: Alfred A. Knopf, 1988), 159; and for Henry Highland Garnet's call for rebellion, see Herbert Aptheker, ed., *A Documentary History of the Negro People in the United States: From Colonial Times Through the Civil War* (New York: Citadel Press, 1951), 1:226.
67. *African Repository* 48 (January 1872): 55.
68. *African Repository* 52 (July 1876): 85.
69. Ullman, *Martin R. Delany,* 502.
70. Ibid., 503.
71. Turner to Mr. Evarts, 3 September 1877, no. 273, *Foreign Relations of the United States, 1877,* 370ff.
72. Ibid.
73. Ibid.
74. Ibid.
75. Ibid., 375.
76. Turner to Department of State, 15 April 1878, no. 302, U.S. Ministers to Liberia, roll 7.
77. Ibid.
78. Ibid.
79. Ibid.
80. Ibid.
81. Ibid.
82. Ibid.
83. Ibid.
84. Turner to Secretary of State, 30 August 1877, no. 272, roll 6.
85. Ibid., 85.
86. *African Repository* 53 (July 1877): 78–79. See also ibid. 55 (January 1879): 1ff.; (April 1879): 37; (October 1879): 118ff.
87. Annual Message of the President, enclosed in Smyth to Secretary of State, 9 January 1879, no. 9, U.S. Ministers to Liberia, roll 7. See also Smyth to Secretary of State, 15 January 1880, no. 5, roll 8.
88. *African Repository* 56 (December 1880): 130–31.

3

Resisting the Partition of Africa

> Through our ministers at London and at Monrovia, this Govern-
> ment has endeavored to aid Liberia in its differences with Great
> Britain touching the northwestern boundary of that republic. There
> is a prospect of adjustment of the dispute by the adoption of the
> Mannah River as the line. This arrangement is a compromise of the
> conflicting territorial claims, and takes from Liberia no country
> over which it has maintained effective jurisdiction. (President
> Chester A. Arthur, Annual Message to Congress, 1883)[1]

Both the African Americans in the foreign service and those at home
viewed with alarm the news coming from Brussels and Berlin concerning European imperialistic designs upon Africa.[2] In contrast, the
United States government and most of its citizens sought to dissociate
themselves from the plight of the Africans. Fortunately, a number of
African Americans were in the diplomatic service and knew what moves
the Europeans were taking with respect to Africa. They tried to encourage often reluctant administrations to adopt policies toward Africa in
keeping with their views of the nature of American national interests as
well as what they thought would be helpful to Africa and its peoples.
African Americans with symbolic power sought to make their views
known both at home and abroad with respect to United States foreign
policy.

Very much aware that the events unrolling at Berlin spelled disaster
for the still-independent African states and their people, John H. Smyth
in Liberia agonized over what he could do. He soon discovered that his
major task was to see whether he could induce the United States to help
Liberia negotiate with Britain and France over their continued aggression against its territory. Foreshadowing the processes that would eventually lead to the conquest and partition of Africa, the British took
advantage of Liberia's poor relations with its aboriginal population to
stimulate rebellions and wars.

95

Even before he was recalled, James Milton Turner had heard Liberian President James Spriggs Payne implicate the British in the Grebo war. Payne had told his Congress in December 1877:

> The influence of a vast nationality upon our coast, acting frequently through unscrupulous agents, makes the manifestation of this concern of the government of the United States welcome and opportune; and the people of Liberia would do well to invite a more active interposition of the mother Republic. Any form of alliance to it would be of immense service to the infant State—whose intermediate position cannot fail to make it an inconvenience to the great commercial visitants of this part of the coast with unwillingness to comply with civilized law entirely strange to a civilized people.[3]

The president felt that if the settlers had "the native population alone to deal with we might hold our own and live in peace and prosperity." The continuing problem, as he saw it, was that the settlers had "also to contend against an extraneous influence decidedly pernicious and un-principled, [which] gives the future of this country a sombre aspect—un-less under the protection of the United States Government or in some form allied to it." He said that the circumstances of Liberia were "so unique" that he was forced "to entertain the belief that we shall have to either seek this connection, or prepare to become part of the British possessions or be worried incessantly by the depredations of the English shipping and English merchants."[4]

At that time, obviously agreeing with President Payne's analysis of Liberia's position, Turner "invited" the

> attention [of the State Department] to the allusion which His Excellency the President thought proper to make to the relations subsisting between the United States and Liberia; and to remark that while the admission that Liberia will prove unable without material aid, to sustain her Independence is both suggestive and significant, it is regretted that the purport of the President's conviction is in no sense too sombre.[5]

It was not too long afterward that the Liberians had to ask the United States to permit Commodore Robert W. Shufeldt to participate as an arbitrator in an ongoing controversy with the British over the northwest boundary with Sierra Leone. Unfortunately, the boundary commission adjourned without determining to which government the disputed terri-tory belonged. Then, much to the frustration of the Liberians, the Grebo and Kru peoples formed an alliance and issued a manifesto declaring that their ancestors had never alienated lands to the settlers. The leaders of these two groups also reported that on two separate occasions, once on board the USS *Essex* and again on board the USS *Ticonderoga,* they had refused money and flags from the Liberians and had vowed never to accept those symbols of Liberian sovereignty. Moreover, they declared, "We consider our people under the protection of England, whose flag was sent to us many years ago by that government, and which we will fly and also call upon in our present difficulty."[6]

Like Turner before him, Smyth was critical of the way in which the Americo-Liberians treated the indigenous people and felt that the settlers were their own worst enemies. Yet he was more concerned about European imperial aims in Africa and therefore looked askance at any United States policy that, while protecting the local people from the Americo-Liberians, might jeopardize the weak black nationality that was Liberia. Smyth made sure that the Department of State knew about the Americo-Liberians' desire to resolve their problems with the Grebo and Kru by "all pacific and gentle means," but was careful to add that if this proved unsuccessful, the Liberian government would resort to "ulterior measures." He felt this approach was the right one, since "experience has demonstrated that to a failure to so act in the past many present complications may be traced." Nevertheless, the minister could not refrain from adding, "It is to be regretted that the government is not in condition to put such force in the field, should it become necessary to coerce these recalcitrant chiefs and their followers."[7]

Smyth found it difficult to turn the attention of the United States to Africa, and he constantly sought to demonstrate why to do so would be in America's national interest and, barring that, in the interest of African Americans. He did his best to convince the Department of State that Commodore Shufeldt should arbitrate in the British-Liberian controversy over the northwestern boundary with Sierra Leone. Smyth argued that Liberia's possession of the interior would open "a mart for many of the manufactured commodities of the United States, which would be a source of material advantage to our industrial classes, to the government, and would greatly aid in the stability of this republic, which has existed thus long amid most untoward circumstances . . . Then [he concluded], when it is remembered how potent an agent of civilization commerce is and how much the United States, in common with the remainder of the civilized and Christian world, owe to Africa and the negro race, it does seem that our Government might take, with propriety, some part in aiding this struggling government in the accomplishment of some results for Africa."[8]

Smyth bombarded the Department of State with information about European imperial activities in Africa. He even sent the secretary of state articles clipped from British, French, and West African newspapers and periodicals on France's plans to build a railroad between Algeria, the Sudan, and Senegal. The tenor of these articles undoubtedly alarmed Smyth, for one article stated: "There exists in Soudan a large population, a fertile soil, and natural riches which are uncultivated. It is very important to open outlets for commerce through the French possessions, which are the most favorably situated for this purpose. France ought to follow the example of England, and do her best to induce the caravans to cross French territory instead of only coming to its borders." An editorial in the same paper referred to a speech by Victor Hugo in which the novelist held forth that

> Africa [was] the common property of the European nations, to be appropriated for European purposes with or without the consent of its inhabitants, who, according to another authority, are only lazy, palavering savages. In making their allotments of this big farm [the editorial continued], of course not the slightest regard will be paid to such insignificant obstacles as Ashantees and Zulus, notwithstanding the reminder which a recent magnificent funeral should furnish to the French nation.[9]

Betraying his growing frustration with official United States indifference to developments in Africa, Smyth wrote Secretary of State Seward, "I have the honor to again remind the Department of the importance to the government of securing some direct influence in Africa, for the commercial advantages to be thereby obtained." The minister warned that "it would be idle to indulge the thought that the English and French governments are influenced by humanitarian, civilizing motives, solely in the acquisition of territory on this continent. Beyond all such thought is the opening up and development of Africa for the prospective commercial wealth that will accrue to these governments and peoples from such effort." Then in an obvious attempt to goad the department into action, Smyth conceded that while the United States believed that it did not need additional territory, with "our great West rolling in mineral richness from the Mississippi to the Pacific, . . . yet we need more markets for our manufactured articles, and the need increases with every new invention made, every article for which we have not an immediate customer which we produce."[10]

Smyth went so far as to compare French projected activities in Africa with the plans for the American polar expedition reported in the Washington *Star* of 28 June 1879. He felt that this enterprise was all to the good since everyone would get much information about the North Pole, but he believed that the results would only be of importance to science and of no material benefit to humanity at large. He argued that had the same attention been directed to the "known and unknown womb of wealth" embedded in central Africa, "the benefit to our revenues and 40 millions of our nation cannot readily from a commercial view be estimated. When France, England, and Belgium shall have occupied this great field bristling in commercial importance, should we have any relation to it, that relation must of necessity be secondary." Although he must have known that the American secretary of state did not necessarily see his despatches, Smyth ended this one "with earnest hope that Africa may not be wholly neglected by us commercially" and begged the indulgence of the secretary for the "length to which your attention has been taxed by the perusal of this."[11]

Smyth repeatedly warned the Department of State that the Europeans were preparing for the great "scramble" for Africa and had started to put pressure on Liberia. As President Payne had intimated to his Congress in 1877, the sentiment of "protectorates" was in the air, and it afflicted Africans as well as the predatory Europeans. It was with this concern in mind that Minister Smyth dashed off a despatch to the secretary of state on 30 May 1879, reporting that the Liberian secretary of state had told him of a report from France that "the French government desired that Liberia should become a dependency of France."[12]

The Liberians revealed to Smyth that there was also some sentiment in Monrovia for an "alliance of the Government with the United States," even though the "distinct and unequivocal policy" of the Liberian Government was "averse to anything savoring of a protectorate." Smyth somewhat disingenuously called the secretary's attention to the need "to correct some statements that have been recently made which are calculated to mislead that portion of our citizenship which may have some interest in [the] present and future of the young Republic . . . [that] if Liberia is the nation's foster child, the people of the U.S. have never so recognized her, however potent a sense of justice has dictated the recognition of the relationship." Possibly with tongue in cheek, the minister heaped scorn upon "a mere supposition based upon no reliable data" that "England and France will absorb it [Liberia], if it is not protected by the United States." What Liberia most needed was "moral support, which may keep England, France, and ourselves from giving the Republic such protection as would make it English, French or American, and thereby destroy it as a future negro Republic and make it useless, in its influence for good to the millions of negro Africans."[13]

There is little doubt that Smyth was subtly warning the Department of State that both the American Colonization Society and African American leaders desired that Liberia be protected from the Europeans. He was not to be disappointed. Acting Secretary of State W. Hunter wrote to Edward F. Noyes, minister to France, informing him of Smyth's despatch, supported by a despatch to the secretary of the navy from Commodore Shufeldt, who had recently visited West Africa on board the USS *Ticonderoga*. Hunter reminded Noyes that the United States government

> founded and fostered the nucleus of native representative government on the African shores and . . . must feel a peculiar interest in any apparent movement to divert the independent political life of Liberia for the aggrandizement of a great continental power which already has a foothold of actual trading possession on the neighboring coast. . . . If so, it is desirable at least that the United States should be cognizant of the true tendency of the movement. You are, therefore, instructed to make such judicious and confidential inquiries as shall, without communicating undue importance to the matter, put you in possession of the facts. Your report thereon is awaited with interest.[14]

Noyes responded to the department that there had indeed been a great deal of talk about "the advantages which would accrue to France by extending her protectorate over Liberia" between two Frenchmen who were Liberian consuls general to Bordeaux and Paris, respectively. The American minister stated that the Liberian consul general in Paris admitted to attempting to secure the " '*commercial* protection' of France for Liberia, but denies having had anything to do with the *political* scheme." Noyes assured the department that "the French Government has never proposed or expressed a desire that Liberia should be placed under its protectorate; it has, on the contrary, declined to entertain any scheme looking to such result." He concluded that the United States had no cause for apprehension that the French government would listen to propositions dealing with protection for Liberia.[15]

Smyth at the scene in Liberia was more realistic—or cynical—about France's intentions. When he learned that the British and French were squabbling over an island claimed by Liberia he immediately notified the department, and again Washington queried the minister to Paris. This time Noyes was less trustful of France's intentions.

> As the Department is aware, great jealously exists between the English and French Governments, regarding affairs on the coast of Africa in the vicinity of Liberia, both Governments making incompatible claims regarding the islands on the African coast under one color of right or another. Sierra Leone

and Senegal forming centres from which English and French pretensions radiate.[16]

Smyth was convinced that the French were out to conquer all of West Africa, and he did not hesitate to use the black nationality argument in an effort to get the United States to react. He cabled the Department of State:

> I regard the recent movement of the French, and it is regarded by experienced men in Western Africa, as one of the most important in the history of this particular portion of Negroland. They seem determined to work their way down along the interior of the western coast and to establish an invincible prestige among the tribes. . . . The Liberians are trying to push their settlements to the interior, and to make treaties with the powerful tribes within three or four hundred miles of the coast, but in their feebleness it is very little that they can do. They deserve all the assistance and encouragement which it may be in the power of the government to render, in view of the intimate relations which a portion of the Negro race bears to the United States, and which has been borne by their immediate ancestors for upward of two hundred years.[17]

Smyth was so anxious to safeguard the interest of the black nationality that he inadvertently overstepped the bounds of diplomacy. In an effort to convince the Department of State that Liberia's policy toward its indigenous populations was improving, Smyth reported that when the president of Liberia had asked his advice about a treaty with a local monarch, he had responded: "Sir, should you make a treaty with King Blanca Sissi, and this trade be diverted from Sierra Leone and come here, your administration would be regarded as the most illustrious of Liberian administrations."[18]

There is no record of the department's reaction to the episode, but on another occasion, Smyth's unsolicited advice to the Liberian president almost got him into trouble. Smyth had reported to the secretary of state that while he was on a visit to Sierra Leone to gain a surcease from the Liberian climate (but still anxious about the country's tough new policy toward the aboriginal population), he had written the Liberian president asking forgiveness for what "under other circumstances than these which influence my action" might be regarded as presumption. Smyth wrote, "Aside from any official relations with your Government, I have both privately and publicly, shown myself not indifferent to the best interest of your young state, nay more, [I am] a friend to its rightful progress." Nevertheless, Smyth felt constrained to tell the president that his "interior policy"—one which his minister of state and other prominent officials approved—might cause him problems in the future, even though he, Smyth, hoped he was wrong.[19]

The American minister added that history, experience, and the correct interpretation of the reason for the establishment of the colonies and of attitudes of the founders of the Liberian republic clearly indicated that the policy toward the indigenous population was designed to benefit the government and to bring "good results both Christian and secular, to the portion or portions of the interior that you may pierce with your enlightenment." What Smyth was presuming to tell the president was that "conciliation, Sir, is the true policy to be pursued. Neither hostility nor the show of it should constitute any part of your interior plan. It would be better, for a time, to retire after all judicious effort to succeed fails rather than impair your ultimate success by show of force." Smyth added that he would not have dared to give this advice to the president had it not been based on the experience of "so learned a statesman and ecclesiastic as Cardinal Richelieu whose course in great matters was characterized by the use of all means to conciliate, [and] failing in these, then [use] all means to crush."[20]

Smyth then called the attention of the president to a conversation Smyth had had with "a distinguished African" who held an important post in the service of "the English government," a person whose views should "not be unworthy of your consideration," to the effect that people who had conflict with the British should understand that "they are a formidable enemy; and ought always to be conciliated and tolerated." Smyth finally told the president that "the desire of my Government, and my desire, is for the entire success of your effort interiorward." The minister was properly respectful in sending the president this letter, begging to be excused "for what may savor of presumption in the foregoing." He assured the president of his "personal esteem and earnest hope . . . for the Republic of Liberia."[21]

Secretary of State William M. Evarts, apparently feeling that his minister to Liberia had exceeded his instructions and had attempted to formulate policy, cabled indicating great displeasure at the text of the letter that Smyth had sent to the "President of the Republic of Liberia, giving him unsolicited criticism and counsel with respect to the conduct of the domestic policy of his government and also its relations to the neighboring territories and interior tribes." The secretary observed with regret that however strongly Smyth may have been convinced personally of the solidity and value of his views and the benefit that might have resulted from their becoming known to the Liberian government, in communicating them as he did he had departed from two very fundamental rules of diplomatic intercourse:

> In the first place a minister resident has not the personally representative character, and it is a serious violation of etiquette for him to address the ruler of the state directly, especially in writing, instead of his foreign minister. And secondly, for you to tender unsolicited advice of the character shown in your letter, even to the foreign minister, would be an entirely unwarranted proceeding, inasmuch as you follow no instructions in so doing, and the matter presented in no way concerns the diplomatic relations of the two countries.[22]

Evarts said that he would have willingly spared himself "the pain of rebuking you for your course, were it not that the uniformly complimentary and personally friendly tone of your letter to the president" was "marred by a very plain suggestion that a failure of conciliatory policy on his part should be followed by temporary retirement [from the interior]." The American secretary was especially displeased that Smyth had intimated that it was the "desire" of the American government that the success of the president's "interiorward" effort be pleaded as an excuse for his letter.[23]

Because Secretary Evarts could find no indication in Smyth's letter to show that it "was *not* written in pursuance of orders from this Department[, i]t is impossible to allow any inference to subsist that it *was* so written." Evarts "therefore, instructed [Smyth] to cause the Liberian Secretary of State to understand, and request him to inform the President on your behalf, that your letter to the latter was a purely personal and unofficial matter, and in no respect based on any instruction received by you." Smyth was further instructed "to communicate to the Department of correspondence you may have with the Secretary in compliance with this instruction."[24] Smyth did as he was instructed. He wrote the Liberian secretary of state reemphasizing the personal nature of his correspondence to the president. The official responded:

> I have the honor to inform you that the President directs me to assure you, he received the communication as an unofficial document embodying friendly suggestions—prompted by the deep interest you have uniformly manifested in the welfare of this Republic. His Excellency highly appreciated the views therein expressed, as well as the generous spirit from which they emanated, and but for a press of engagement in connection with the session of the Legislature, would have conveyed this assurance to you before this moment.[25]

The zeal with which the Europeans were pushing their efforts to take over Africa placed the United States government in a quandary. It was unwilling to become too involved on the African continent, but its growing strength and the desires of many of its influential citizens were pushing it to do so. Apparently wishing to mollify his minister in Monrovia after rebuking him for attempting to make policy, Secretary of State Evarts sent the following despatch to Smyth on 2 February 1880:

> Liberia is regarded by us with peculiar interest. Already the home of many of who now enjoy citizenship in this republic. This going out to a greater or less extent of our citizens of African descent is but a question of time, and if Liberia be in proper condition to receive and care for such emigrants from the United States, her territory will be chosen by them in preference to that of any other country. A large and valuable commerce between Liberia and the United States may be developed if the countries can be brought to see their true relations toward each other.[26]

Yet at the same time that he was writing these words to Smyth, Evarts was explaining to his minister to France that the reason the volume of *Foreign Relations* for 1879 devoted so much more space to the affairs of Liberia than "would seem to be warranted" was "the peculiar relations which this country holds towards Liberia, and which are likely to become of increased importance." Evarts warned that it was "quite suitable that the great powers should know that the United States publicly recognizes these relations, and is prepared to take every proper step to maintain them."[27]

Apparently not satisfied with the increasing interest of the secretary of state in the unfolding events in Africa, in April 1880 the American Colonization Society broached the notion that the Monroe Doctrine, which stipulated that European nations should not interfere in New World affairs, should be extended to Liberia.[28] It was supported by Commodore Shufeldt who, emphasizing his growing concern for American foreign policy, suggested that all the United States government had to do was to publish a statement declaring that it would protect Liberia.[29] The Department of State was not prepared to go this far, since it was not quite ready to change its basic noninterventionist policy toward Africa. In fact, a dispute between Germany and Liberia gave the United States an opportunity to demonstrate its impartiality.

In February 1881 the German minister in Washington had complained to the secretary of state that some of the "Kroubah" people of Liberia, taking advantage of the wreck of the German steamer *Carlos,* plundered the wreck and robbed the survivors. When notified of this action by Germany, the government of Liberia "showed the sincerest wish to punish such proceedings but declared itself unable to exert authority to that end over the lawless Kroubahs." This response so infuriated the Germans that they ordered their warship *Victoria* to proceed to Liberia to "assist the government of the Republic in the pursuit and punishment of the offenders." But concerned about the possible reaction of the United States, Berlin asked that the American minister in Liberia be informed of the matter. The American secretary of state complied and told Smyth that should the Liberian secretary of state consult with him, he was "at liberty" to express the view that had the case involved an American vessel and its crew, the United States government "would not have failed to consider in a proper spirit any request made to it by . . . Liberia for aid such as Germany is now prepared to render." The secretary advised Smyth, however, that it was not necessary for him to make this statement if the subject was not brought to his attention.[30]

Careful to keep Washington abreast of all important events in Liberia, Smyth had already sent off a despatch dated 3 March 1881 that confirmed the Germans' account of the attitude of the Liberian government. Smyth explained that Liberia "made no effort to detect and punish the guilty parties, it is believed, not from any reluctance on its part to punish crime, but on account of its inability to do so." He also reported that on 28 February, Commander Von Valois of the *Victoria* had visited him, indicating that while his orders were to help the Liberian government take the initiative in punishing those who committed the piratical acts, Germany wished to continue its "historically friendly relations" with Liberia and to that end desired "the aid of the U.S. government through its representative in effecting his purpose."[31]

Smyth reported that he found the German government lenient in demanding only that the warship destroy the settlement of the malefactors and that the government of Liberia pay an indemnity of $3,500. The president of Liberia and Edward Wilmot Blyden, his secretary of the interior, witnessed the destruction of the Kroubah town and had the "culprits" brought to Monrovia. Then in quixotic diplomatic style, the chief executive gave a luncheon in honor of Germany and the United States. According to Smyth:

> The health of our [United States] President was proposed and drunk, to which sentiment I responded in a brief speech, in which I characterized the action of the Liberian government, in the matter of their recent difficulty as "stalwart," and premised my utterance with the relation the term bore to the President of the U.S.[32]

In response to the secretary's telegram of 28 February, Smyth indicated that he had anticipated the instructions from Washington, and on the absence of the German Consul from Monrovia, he tendered his good offices to Commander Von Valois, conferring with him at some length upon the matter. Smyth reported that subsequently, in an informal meeting, the secretary of state of Liberia explained the problems. Smyth "gave his views upon the legal and commercial bearings of the matter, with which the Secretary concurred."[33]

The American minister also reported that he was invited to a conference with the president, his cabinet, and other distinguished citizens at which the *Carlos* affair was discussed, and he explained the American secretary of state's position had the case affected the crew of an American vessel. Smyth added that this timely and correct opinion "tended to soften the asperities created among Liberians—on the bringing of the culprits to Monrovia and their incarceration." Then in a passage that must have raised some eyebrows in Washington, since it so well accorded with Smyth's own views, he explained:

> The recollection of past oppression borne in the United States and the West Indies by negroes, inflicted by Caucasians, had the effect of awakening sentiments and feelings of revenge toward the Germans when they returned to Monrovia with the offenders and hostages, this was principally among the ignorant, although some—other—intelligent persons shared in the contagion; where the preservation of the reputation of the country for doing right and justice, and respecting treaty stipulations should have characterized the sentiments of the people.[34]

By now the Department of State must have been accustomed to Smyth's attitudes on the subject of race and his attempts to defend Africa against the invading Europeans. Thus his sudden recall to Washington was surprising. The department's archives yield no explanation, and a cryptic statement in the American Colonization Society's organ, the *African Repository,* reports only that Minister Smyth was "recalled to make way for Dr. Garnet."[35]

It appears that Henry Highland Garnet had long expressed an interest in becoming minister to Liberia, and his good friends at the American Colonization Society were finally able to get him the post. As Minister Turner had learned, these people had close personal and political relations with American presidents and secretaries of state. In addition to these strong supporters, "the leading merchants of New York joined in the application for Garnet's appointment as 'Minister Resident' to Liberia."[36]

That Henry Highland Garnet would have desired to represent the United States of America in Liberia was not only ironic but serves as an example of the theoretical issues raised by blacks serving as American diplomats. By no stretch of the imagination could one have predicted some forty years before that Garnet could ever have come to terms with the United States of America. The alleged grandson of a Mandingo prince captured in war and sold into slavery, Garnet was a fiery abolitionist who, at the age of twenty-seven, had shocked William Lloyd Garrison and even Frederick Douglass with his radical "Address to the Slaves of the United States of America." In it he had advised the slaves that it was sinful in the extreme for them to submit voluntarily to slavery, since "Neither God, Nor Angels, Or Just Men, Command You To Suffer For A Single Moment." He told them: "You had far better all die—*die immediately,* than live slaves, and entail your wretchedness upon your posterity. . . . If you must bleed, let it all come at once —rather *die freemen, than live to be slaves.*"[37] Later as president of the African Civilization Society in association with Martin R. Delany, Garnet had an ambiguous relationship with the American Colonization Society. He subsequently served as a missionary in Jamaica from 1853 until 1855. Garnet only barely escaped lynching in 1863 during the draft riots in New York City, where he had been recruiting troops for the Civil War.

Honor came to Garnet when, on 12 February 1865, he was invited to preach a sermon in the House of Representatives entitled "A Memorial Discourse," commemorating the passage of the Thirteenth Amendment. He was the first black ever allowed in the Hall of the House of Representatives except in a menial capacity. From this point on Garnet became a recognized black leader, serving as president of Avery College and pastor of the Shiloh Presbyterian Church in New York City. During this period he apparently maintained excellent relations with William Coppinger of the American Colonization Society and was involved in the emigration of blacks to Liberia. This service was noted by Edward Wilmot Blyden, who wrote to William Coppinger about the help Garnet gave to some "refugees" from Arkansas on their way to Liberia. Blyden noted that "true to the race and Fatherland," Garnet, "though on a sick bed, [had] worked hard and successfully" on behalf of the refugees. Blyden felt there was a great deal of "difference between such men as Garnet inspired and guided by a self-sustaining consciousness of ultimate success in the Fatherland," and the many "doubters and traducers." He concluded, "If we had had men like Garnet in the lead in Liberia during the last thirty years we should now be able to show very different results . . . Dr. Garnet has impressed upon me the importance of presenting the cause of Africa."[38]

As fate would have it, Garnet was not to serve as United States minister to Liberia for more than three months. Although he was suffering from asthma while in New York City, his health did improve during the voyage to Monrovia, where he arrived on 16 December 1881 with his daughter, Mrs. Barboza, a missionary teacher. A personal friend of many Americo-Liberians, the new minister was entertained by Blyden, then serving both as secretary of the interior and president of Liberia College, at a reception attended by President Gardiner and about seventy other persons including cabinet ministers, foreign representatives, members of the legislature, and others. Garnet was reportedly in an excellent humor; he "expressed his agreeable surprise at everything he had seen in Africa, and [w]as more than pleased with the country. He said that he believed great things were in store for Liberia, and that these were the beginning of good days for the Republic."[39] Unfortunately, the minister's health deteriorated from this point on, and although he thrived under the care of his daughter and granddaughter and visited many parts of the country, he grew worse and died on 13 February 1882.

The Liberians buried the American diplomat with full military honors and laid him to rest in Palm Grove cemetery, overlooking the Atlantic. Clergymen from the Baptist, Episcopal, Methodist, and Presbyterian churches conducted an ecumenical funeral service, during which Edward Wilmot Blyden preached a sermon based upon the biblical verse, "Know ye not that there is a prince and great man fallen this day in Israel?" (2 Sam. 3:38).

Eulogizing Garnet on 4 May 1882 during a visit to the Union Literary and Historical Association in Washington, D.C., Alexander Crummell stated, among other things, that Garnet's nomination as minister resident to the Republic of Liberia

> came as a recognition of his high character, his honorable career, his splendid services to the cause of freedom, and his grand qualities, both intellectual and moral. It was an offer honorable to the Government which made it, and to the grand man to whom it was tendered.[40]

Recognizing that John H. Smyth had served brilliantly as the United States minister to Liberia, the American Colonization Society recommended that he be returned to Monrovia. The editor of the *African Repository* wrote:

> We violate no secret in making known the fact that Secretary Frelinghuysen invited the American Colonization Society and its zealous President, Mr. Latrobe, to nominate a successor to Dr. Garnet, and that they promptly suggested the name of Mr. Smyth—with the result just stated. He expects to

return to his post of duty, via Liverpool, early in July, accompanied by his wife and daughter.[41]

The *African Repository* added that the nominee had "already resided some four years at Monrovia to the satisfaction of his Government and the acceptance of the authorities and citizens of Liberia."[42]

No sooner had Smyth unpacked than he found himself deeply involved with the United States' growing concern over Great Britain's continuing boundary quarrel with Liberia. Acting Secretary of State John Davis asked his minister to tell Her Majesty's government that the American President

> is entirely unwilling to suppose that, in a case like this, where the issue, as between her Majesty's world-wide Empire and a weak African State is so disproportionate, Her Majesty's government will not give willing need to the views of the Government of the United States—itself in a measure a party to the determination of the controversy . . . by such means as may be still adopted in accordance with those principles of justice and equity which honors nations alike with individuals, in their common intercourse.[43]

Now considering himself a veteran diplomat, Smyth was more aggressive in his relationship with Washington. Reporting upon the seriousness of the situation from Liberia's perspective, Smyth sent a long despatch to Secretary of State F. T. Frelinghuysen about the "threatening demonstration" that her Majesty's consul for Liberia, the governor of the West Africa Settlements, Hon. Arthur E. Havelock, made when he visited Monrovia with four warships.

Smyth reported that the British denied that they were threatening Liberia, but he was convinced that they intended to seize Liberian territory "upon the pretext that the native races were adamant in not yielding any of their rights in the Northwest territory." Enclosing copies of the reports that emanated from a conference between the British and Liberians, Smyth suggested that the secretary

> will be competent to make comment and approach a proper decision as to the matter; and if not incompatible with the relation of a foreign mutual friend of England and Liberia, you will make such suggestions favorable to the Negro nation's rights as may tend to a final and speedy settlement of the matter in justice and equity to both nations, should you feel called upon to interpose, and your suggested views should be heeded. This, I am advised, is the desire of the [Liberian] President.[44]

Smyth also suggested that if Britain gained the territory she was after, the local people would become her vassals and "the oil and forest possession will be guarded and protected for the enrichment of England with little reference to whether the Negro benefitted or not."[45]

Smyth was fairly realistic about the relative advantage to the aboriginal populations if they were taken over by the British rather than by the Liberians. He wrote Frelinghuysen that precedent left little doubt that if England should take over Liberian territory, she would "afford more immediate and ample facilities for cultivation among the native races of Western civilization than Liberia can now afford." Nevertheless, Smyth believed that England would "make the Negroes here subservient to her too frequently incompetent and unsympathetic . . . representatives and traders, and thereby destroy that self dependence that heathen and barbarous races must in a measure retain in taking upon themselves alien civilizations." Africans needed independence "if they are to amount to anything more than a servile and imitative class." With imperial control, he felt, "the benefits of such control will be on the side of the civilizer, England, and the civilized will possess doubtful good, questionable advantage. With nations as with the individuals, elevation should be from within—by growth, not from without—by mounting upon others."[46]

In a revealing postscript, the minister raised the issue of black nationality:

> There is a prospective result that may be looked for to follow the taking from Liberia of this long possessed disputed territory; the lowering of her prestige among the native races within Liberia and contiguous to Liberia. Power always commands respect. Denude Liberia of any portion of her territory, and she so far is injured, and falls in the estimation of native races. Should England take the disputed territory, and the native races be forced into a recognition of a foreign, alien power, they will never feel any respect for it. The change must affect injuriously Liberia, and injuriously the aboriginal Negro's self respect.
>
> The civilized Negro in Africa under foreign domination, as the civilized Negro out of Africa under like control, suffers in his liberty, because it has not the element of imperium. "Imperium et Libertas" must be the motto and the practice of the Negro, if he is to have self respect; if he is to merit the respect of others.
>
> I hope it may be found in consonance with the foreign policy of our Government to aid Liberia in a retention of her self respect unimpaired, her control of her territory, her prestige which is the consequence of her control.[47]

Still refusing to become overly involved in this West African struggle, Frelinghuysen advised Smyth that "if in your discretion it seems to you advisable, impress upon them [the Liberians] the friendly interest which the United States takes in the welfare of Liberia and their desire that the controversy may be settled in a just, equitable and friendly spirit; and you may, also, say that representations of this nature have been made to the Government of Her Majesty."[48] He added that Smyth might also advise the Liberians that it would be in their interest "to arrive at an amicable understanding with the British Government, as it is the utmost importance to the growth and prosperity of Liberia that the two governments should work in harmony for the promotion of civilization of the West African Coast," and suggested if the president of the United States were to have been asked for a boundary decision, he would have recommended the Solyman River, "which, without encroaching upon the actual settlements of Liberia, or sacrificing any material advantages, would satisfy Her Majesty's Government."[48]

The British Foreign Office told the Department of State that the Liberian president had offered the "Maffa River" as a boundary with the "Mannah River" as a substitute should Her Majesty's Government so desire. Emphasizing its forbearance on this matter, and expressing sympathy for "Negro civilization" and the desire to promote the well-being and prosperity of Liberia,

> Her Majesty's Government therefore desire to invite the Government of the United States to exercise their influence with the Liberian Government with a view of inducing it to take a more becoming and reasonable course than it has hitherto done, and to terminate at once by a frank and loyal acceptance of the favorable terms now offered to it, a controversy, the prolongation of which is very prejudicial to the good relations which ought to exist between Liberia and the neighboring British Settlements.[50]

Faced with what appeared to be "an apparent ultimatum for the settlement on the dispute of the basis of the Mannah River as a compromise boundary," Frelinghuysen told Smyth that attempts would be made to have the British accept the Solyman River as a compromise made to them by the president of the United States, but if that failed, the Liberians should be urged to accept the Mannah River compromise. He warned Smyth that "in the event of Liberia's rejection of both these boundaries, it is felt that this Government cannot usefully exert itself further."[51] In a later despatch the department told Smyth that the United States did not regard itself as an arbiter in the boundary dispute, and it constrained Liberia to accept the compromise,

> which offers a pledge of future concord between Liberia and Great Britain, and a moral guarantee to the United States as well as a conventional guarantee to Liberia that that Republic shall be permitted to extend its domestic development and increase its prosperity within limits under effective administrative control, and with assurance of no further disturbance to its affairs by unadjusted disputes.[52]

Frelinghuysen was either too trusting or too naive in his appraisal of European imperial designs in Africa. The French soon joined the British in coveting parts of the area in dispute between Britain and Liberia. Notified by Smyth of this new development, the secretary wrote the French foreign minister referring to the "quasi-parentage" relationship between the United States and Liberia, and Britain's recognition of this fact: "It is not thought possible that France can seriously intend to assert any claim to territory so notoriously in dispute between two parties only, and where no French right of possession has heretofore been recognized by either."[53]

Smyth grasped at every opportunity to emphasize to the Department of State the need for the United States to keep a close watch on events in West and Central Africa. He responded in exhaustive detail to a query from Washington about commercial prospects in the area and possible sites for United States consulates. He recommended that consulates be established in such places as Abeokuta, Abomey, Bathurst, Bonny, Cape Coast, Coomassie, Dakar, Gaboon, Goree, Grand Taboa, Saint-Louis, Lagos, Niger, Sierra Leone, and Whydah. The reasons he gave are instructive:

> Coomassie, the capital of the dominions of the King of Ashantee, is a place at which the United States government should be represented, on account of the influence for good our government would exercise over that wealthy country, and over a people deservedly renowned on account of the practical wisdom displayed by its rulers during three-quarters of a century, and the progress of the people. The difficulty which presents itself to our presence in this country would be that the seacoast of Ashantee is under the domination of England. . . . What has been asserted of Coomassie, as to the possible effect of the presence of a representative of the United States near the kingdom—may be said also of Abomey the capital of Dahomey.[54]

Smyth sought to whet the appetite of American traders by reporting that he had been told by "an educated, wealthy Dahomean" that Whydah was the "principal seaport of the King of Dahomey, a powerful heathen monarch" and that the principal commerce of that country was palm oil, palm nuts, and ivory.[55] To the charge that West Africa was unhealthy and that suitable persons could not be found to serve as consuls there, Smyth countered that if there were no Americans available, he recommended "the appointment of educated native gentlemen to such posts." He reflected that "this would not only accrue to our commercial importance in Africa" but "would be a display of tact in African affairs that has not been heretofore shown."[56]

Smyth's suggestion that the United States might use educated Africans as consuls in its diplomatic posts on the continent demonstrates how anxious he was to safeguard the black nationalities in Africa. By this time Smyth had few illusions about either the Africans or the Americo-Liberians. He knew their foibles and their prejudices against African Americans but felt it was in their interests, and in those of the United States and its black citizens, that his country display a "tact in African affairs" that had not been shown by outsiders. Very much a man of his time, he used an economic argument, even though for him and for most African Americans the issue was primarily political in nature. A strong and independent black Africa was, in their opinion, a necessity for the salvation of blacks both on the continent and throughout the world. Smyth along with other black diplomats and ordinary citizens faced one of the biggest challenges that would face that continent and its people: the determination of European peoples to conquer and to colonize the African continent.

Whether prompted by the Liberians or acting on his own initiative, Smyth cabled the secretary of state on 29 January 1885 about the British loan to Liberia due in 1886. He reported, "Liberia is on the eve of a financial crisis through which the nation will pass successfully by being able to borrow sufficient money to pay English creditors, the 100,000 [pounds] sterling with fifteen years accrued interest."[57]

Smyth doubted whether any European government would lend the Liberians money on as fair terms as would the United States, and he feared the "ulterior motive of any European state aiding Liberia, would be the final acquisition of Liberia as a dependency" for reasons he believed the secretary would readily understand, namely, Europe's need for Africa. Once again using the issue of black nationality as a tool in dealing with the secretary of state over African affairs, Smyth expressed the hope that with new opportunities opening "to the Negro population of our country, it is not reasonable to anticipate any considerable exodus of that portion of the nation toward this or any other part of the orient." But he added, "It is fair to expect that in those hopeful changes going on in the interest of this class throughout our common country that their enlightened self respect will, under more favorable circumstances, cause them to turn their attention to Africa, the habitat of their race. They will take an interest in the work of civilization there, which will manifest itself by some seeking the country as missionaries, educational and evangelical, others for commercial reasons, and the many aiding the work of civilizing Africa through mission efforts at home."[58] Smyth then asked:

> May not these connections existent between Africans in Africa, and
> America-Africa represented in our country by millions, give the United
> States a hold upon the African continent, as a race link; should Liberia
> continue as a Negro state, more potent and permanent than Europe can ever
> have though its African interests be guarded by fleets and standing armies?[59]

He concluded:

> The foregoing is suggested with direct reference to our interests as a great
> and growing nation, and with due regard to Liberia's interests. . . . I have to
> express the hope that our Government may find it within the scope of its
> foreign policy, and its friendly relations with the Republic to assist Liberia's
> successful passage through this crisis, which is probably the only one of
> serious moment that [it] is likely to confront, and which threatens Liberia in
> the near or remote future.[60]

An official in the State Department made an intriguing marginal note on the despatch, suggesting that the United States had no responsibility for bailing out Liberia. Indeed there is no evidence that this was done.

No sooner had the Berlin Conference ended than the French began their aggression against Liberian territory. Smyth reported to the Department of State on 7 December 1885 being informed by the Liberian secretary of state that the "French had been tampering with the chiefs in the Liberian territory south east of Cape Palmas . . . to the end of making a treaty with the Grebo native race in that locality."[61] Apparently a French naval commander had paid a courtesy call on the president of Liberia and had reported a visit to the Grebo region. The officer was allegedly surprised when told that this was Liberian territory. Secretary of State Barclay indicated that in view of European, and especially French, interest in the area, the United States should be notified immediately. Smyth did so in his last formal despatch to the Department of State, since he had submitted his resignation to the newly elected President Grover Cleveland and was awaiting the arrival of his successor before returning home.

Smyth had served long and hard in Liberia and had done everything possible to encourage the United States government to protect the black nationality in Africa from European imperialism. The Liberians recognized his worth, and the republic conferred upon him its honor of Knight Commander of the Humane Order of African Redemption.[62] During his tenure at Monrovia, Smyth had sensitized the Department of State to the new realities in Africa, but the tide that affects the affairs of men was running against him and against the Africans. Much to the dismay of many, especially blacks, the State Department did initial the General Act of the so-called Congo Conference at Berlin.[63] This indicated clearly that it took more than the valiant efforts of a few black diplomats to effectuate a United States policy beneficial to African peoples.

Minister Smyth's hope that incoming President Cleveland would be sympathetic to Liberia's plight was partially met when the new secretary of state, Thomas F. Bayard, warned France not to encroach upon that country's territory.[64] But despite his attitude, the prospects for an African policy really helpful to the Liberians were less than sanguine. President Cleveland's choice of the Reverend Moses A. Hopkins as his new minister to Liberia reflected United States domestic politics much less than its foreign policies. Men such as John H. Smyth and J. Milton Turner had gained their positions through their support of the Republican party and its standard bearers—blacks had played only limited roles in Democratic party affairs. Thus while Hopkins's appointment may well have reflected "credit upon the judgment of President Cleveland," as the American Colonization Society believed, the new minister resident and consul general did not have the fire of a Turner or a Smyth.[65] Born in slavery of "unmixed African blood," the unschooled Hopkins served as a cook in the Union army and began to educate himself. Hopkins was described as "an independent in his political thinking" but impressed people with his interest in Africa. This trait had endeared him to the American Colonization Society, which recommended him to Cleveland.[66]

Hopkins arrived at Monrovia on 10 December 1885 and hardly had time to acclimate himself to the country and acquaint himself with its political problems before becoming involved in Europe's attempts to carve it up. Smyth's last despatch from Monrovia about France's activities on Liberia's southeastern border had so alarmed the Department of State that Bayard instructed his minister in Paris to warn the French that while the United States "exercise(s) no protectorate over Liberia," because that republic

> originated through the colonization of American citizens, and was established under the fostering sanction of this Government, [this] gives us the right, as the next friend of Liberia, to aid her in preventing any encroachment of foreign powers on her territorial sovereignty, and in settling any dispute that may arise. The southeasterly boundary at the river San Pedro has never been questioned, and has the powerful sanction of general admission for many years.[67]

When on 25 February 1886 the French man-of-war *Voltigeur* arrived at Monrovia commanded by Captain E. Dumont, the Liberians hastily sought the help of the United States. According to Hopkins's report, the French officer told the Liberian president of France's desire to enforce a treaty of protection it had signed with the inhabitants of the southeastern Liberian territory in 1833. He insisted that while the people had initially resisted the landing of the French crew, it did take place, and the French were determined to protect the people there. The French captain also suggested that the Liberians should avail themselves of French protection against the imperial designs of Great Britain and Germany. In response, the Liberians insisted that this area was their territory and showed the officer a French map indicating that it was so. Concerned about the French demands, the Liberians asked Hopkins to use his good offices to see whether the United States could immediately place a warship of between five and six hundred tons at their disposal to increase communications and to defeat insidious efforts to seize their southeast territory.[68] Upon receiving Hopkins's despatch, the secretary of state wrote his minister in France indicating that the United States was committed to preserving the territorial integrity of Liberia. Bayard stated that the United States "learned with much concern that French officers have recently been carrying on intrigues with tribes within the long established and universally recognized boundaries of the Liberian Republic, and treating with said tribes as independent."[69]

Not completely trusting the U.S. State Department to take action, the Liberians also notified the American Colonization Society of events in their country. The society appealed to the United States Senate and House of Representatives for funds to explore Liberia and West Africa. It wanted to be able to assure all and sundry that Liberia was a

> country extending northwardly to the Niger at Timbuctoo, and including the headwaters of that great river, that Liberia affords an access, the advantages of which are peculiar to the United States; not by virtue of any treaty stipulation, but through the natural sympathy of the Liberian people, to whom the United States is the mother country to which they are to look for the increase of population, which is alone wanting to the development of their power, and which emigration from this country can alone supply.[70]

More important, the American Colonization Society felt that such an endeavor would help the commercial interest of the United States.

In fact, neither the State Department nor the Congress of the United States was willing to pay more than lip service to help Liberia. Bayard told Hopkins to notify the Liberians that the navy had no vessels available; moreover, he indicated that law had required the navy to dispose of its vessels immediately after they were decommissioned. Congress did not even respond to the appeal of the American Colonization Society for funds to explore the interior part of Liberia. Frustrated, increasingly ill, and unable to keep up with his work, Hopkins died at his post on 3 August 1886, having served fewer than nine months.[71]

Whether he was resorting to political rhetoric to please the friends of Liberia or actually trying to encourage Congress to aid the African nation, in his annual message to Congress on 6 December 1886 President Cleveland declared that "the weakness of Liberia and the difficulty of maintaining effective sovereignty over its outlying districts, have exposed that republic to encroachment." He reminded Congress:

> This distant community is an offshoot of our own system, owing its origin to the associated benevolence of American citizens, whose praiseworthy efforts to create a nucleus of civilization in the dark continent have commanded respect and sympathy.[72]

The president said that while creating a formal protectorate was "contrary to our traditional policy," the United States had a "moral right and duty" to protect Liberia. He formally recommended that a small naval vessel be presented to the Liberians to help them protect their coastal revenues. Pursuing the president's lead, Bayard expressed to his minister in Paris his disbelief that the French were still attempting to seize Liberia's territory. He requested the minister

> to lay the facts proving the validity of the Liberian title to the territory in question before the French Government, accompanied by such observations as may seem, in your discretion, best calculated to promote the end in view, namely, the recognition of Liberia's right. If it be impossible to obtain this, a definite declaration in regard to the line dividing French and Liberian territory may be made, which will fix a boundary such as France and all the powers can recognize and respect.[73]

The Secretary of State was thus willing to aid Liberia but was not prepared to incur the enmity of the French on its behalf.

Because of the growing intransigence of the French, the United States felt it necessary to find a new minister to Liberia as soon as possible. On 11 March 1887 President Cleveland appointed Charles Henry James Taylor as his minister resident and consul general to Liberia. Like his immediate predecessor, Taylor was born a slave in Alabama in 1857. But unlike Hopkins, Taylor was an active Democrat. He was the first black person to hold the office of city attorney in Kansas City, Missouri, and after campaigning for Cleveland was awarded the post as minister to Liberia.[74]

From all appearances, Taylor fully intended to be an active diplomat. En route to Monrovia, he visited Britain and conferred with officials and businessmen there. He next visited Sierra Leone, where he was entertained for a day by Captain J. A. Lewis, the United States consul, and met briefly with the inimitable Edward Wilmot Blyden, who was then living there. The perceptive and race-conscious Blyden was not impressed with Taylor and reported to William Coppinger of the American Colonization Society that he saw the visitor for only a few minutes at the consulate, but "in that short time he talked about everything especially giving us his autobiography and personal exploits and achievements in detail." Blyden said that Captain Lewis was also not impressed with Taylor and had remarked, "I prefer for the Legation in Liberia John H. Smyth with all his faults."[75]

As ill luck, destiny, or God would have it, Taylor's tenure in Monrovia was a disaster. The new Minister arrived at Monrovia on 31 May 1887 and did not like the place. A self-made man and a "race man" who had struggled to rise up from slavery, he, like many African Americans before and after, was shocked by the state of Liberia. In a hasty, though required, report on the "state of affairs" in Liberia, Taylor could not refrain from expressing his dismay at the conditions he encountered. Determined to honor his oath of office but appalled by what he saw in Liberia, Taylor decided to tell all.[76] As he wrote Secretary of State Bayard, "It is a great 'trust' to represent a great people like ours in a foreign country, but in my opinion, a sacred duty to state the 'facts.' " True, he was aware of the State Department's counsel that he be careful in criticizing foreign governments, but he felt "that wherever a government can be found holding and sustaining the relation which has always been found to exist between the United States and Liberia that the plain unvarnished facts should be known." Thus Taylor confessed that it caused him great pain and "regret more than language can express, takes possession of me, at not being able to say more, to the credit of this 'Republic' that I can, and be truthful. I do not believe it to be proper to unnecessarily obstruct the business of the State Department, or tax your valuable time in the perusal of lengthy despatches; but believing as I do, that I would be false to myself, to these people and to the Country, which I have the honor to serve, did I not disclose to you the observations and discoveries I have made in this place."[77]

Despite having read the post reports of J. Milton Turner and John H. Smyth, Taylor could not contain his disappointment over the physical state of Monrovia. The lack of new buildings troubled him, and he was scandalized by the state of the existing ones, built at least ten years before "by a class of American emigrants who are all either dead or too old to repair the decaying and crumbling walls which may be observed on every side." Taylor was concerned that despite fertile soils, "the 'American Negroes' and 'Americo Liberians' would starve to death, here in this land of Fruit, Sunshine and Flowers if Yates and Potterfield and other companies did not bring them food to eat from foreign lands. The emigrants (to this country) eat nothing indigenous to this country, nor will the children, of such parents."[78]

Taylor did not like the climate, especially the rains, but found it "not half so disagreeable as some other characteristics of this place." He also did not think highly of the commercial possibilities of Liberia because "the Liberians do not work, they are as a class indolent, lazy, indisposed to activity except when actuated by the odor, or delightful smell proceeding from something well cooked to allay hunger." However, he insisted that if this "Republic" was to be judged at all, it should be judged by the "works of the citizens." By this he meant by those who "have a voice in controlling the affairs of this Republic, no native being allowed to vote." Taylor complained that "since no citizen engages at manual labor no credit can be given to them, for the exports sent out of the country."

Taylor was equally critical of the morals of the Liberians, and attributed the country's lack of progress to the behavior of its inhabitants. He wrote, "There are at least four females here to every male, Mr. Secretary, you will please let me draw the curtain over this subject, for it will not bear going into the records of your department."[79] Nor did the minister resident feel that religion was helpful. He reported:

Churches, you will find many, including the catholics, the presbyterians, . . . the methodist episcopals, the free Methodists and the Mohamedans, some seven different sects, now what are they doing? The catholics are doing absolutely nothing, the people of the Republic being naturally suspicious, the fact that the Jesuit Father is a frenchman and accompanies Capt. Dumont as interpreter to the President's Mansion was sufficient to make them believe that he was an intriguer or emissary of the French Government, here to help in their overthrow, which I must say, that no government in the world can prevent, for their foes within the country can destroy their institutions at any time they see fit, or may desire to do so.[80]

Taylor reported that the political institutions of Liberia were a farce. It was incomprehensive to him that only twenty-five-hundred males in the country were eligible to vote and that in the elections the "vote exceeds the number of voters." Moreover, he found the differences in the doctrines and tenets of the two parties, the Whigs and the Republicans, vague and ill-defined. But what alarmed him most was the relative absence of civic virtues. According to law, each able-bodied citizen-voter had to join the militia and appear for duty at specific times. Instead of doing so, many men escaped their duty by fraudulently obtaining lifelong disability certificates. Yet most voters sought titles and honor, and almost every man imagined himself a "politician," being "busy day in and day out, scheming and plotting to gain recognition abroad as the only Negro in Liberia."[81]

Like Turner and Smyth before him, Taylor was distressed by the relations between the Americo-Liberians and the indigenous population and concluded that this posed a danger to the republic:

> Every Liberian, matters not how poor, enjoys the labor of from six to eight natives. They do not call it enslaving the natives in this land but I hope soon to personally give you such an account of their treatment of the natives as will enable you and all enlightened citizens to easily find the name by which it shall be known. Suffice it to say, that the Liberian children do not even condescend to carry their books to school on Sunday but compel the little naked natives to carry the books for them. There are no horses, mules, nor donkeys, here the natives are forced to carry negroes in this country, who at home in the United States hold the position of ordinary laborers, the only thing for which they are qualified.[82]

Taylor was convinced that if the indigenous people decided "to oust the Liberians," he was sure that they could "run the most of them into the ocean." He cited a recent Cape Palmas war in which the "Grebo's" had defeated the settlers and indicated that just the previous night General Sherman of the Liberian army had informed him:

> The Natives at Cape Palmas are now in open revolt, and [in] rebellion against the laws of the Republic and in a conference yesterday with the Liberian Department of State's representative here Hon. E. J. Barclay it was hinted, that he would send me a communication in which . . . aid would be asked of the United States, to help them in putting down the "Rebellion" at Cape Palmas by landing there a Man of War, a commander, seamen, war equipment, etc.[83]

So frustrated was Taylor with conditions in Liberia that he did not take seriously the country's fear of foreign aggression. He wrote the department that the Liberians had "no means of protection whatever," and he was certain that they had no more than "fifty guns, rifles or muskets in good working order." The gunboat or sailing vessel called the "quail," which England gave the republic, was then "aground at 'Grand Bassa' entirely ruined." Taylor said that a brief tour of the country which he had taken had given him an insight into "why it is that Liberia is the weakest from all standpoints and most non progressive republic in the world." He discounted all references to climate and health as the reasons and attributed the lack of progress and the " 'whole condition' to these people and their habits." This being the case, Taylor was not sure whether the United States had served its own interests in helping the Liberians: "When I consider the interest [that] the government of my country and especially the present administration has taken in this Negro Republic you cannot imagine the pain it gives me to have to narrate to you what the truth compels."[84]

Taylor not only discounted the fears of the Liberians but also sprinkled throughout his report on the conditions within Liberia statements condemning the reports of his predecessors at the legation in Monrovia. He complained that the records were in very bad shape when he arrived, and he suggested that the Liberians had the opportunity to take copies of whatever despatches they desired. More shocking to him, however, was the "custom here to always have a jug of alcoholic stimulants, say brandy, whisky, rum, gin etc., handy for every comer to partake of in order to maintain the dignity of the United States Government." This he "refused to countenance," even though he felt that he would suffer in comparison with his predecessors, with the exception of Mr. Hopkins who "discontinued and put a stop to the disgraceful leveés given as it was claimed to uphold the dignity of our Government." As soon as he reached Monrovia, the Liberians petitioned him to resume the receptions, but this he also refused to do since he had his standards and, unlike earlier chiefs of mission, had no wish to get too close to the Liberians.[85]

The conclusions that Taylor drew from his all-too-brief look at Liberia and the recommendations that he gave to the secretary of state reflected his disappointment and perhaps his naïveté. "There are many 'things' connected with this country which I am sure you ought to know," he told Bayard. "I am satisfied it would change your opinion of this country and people materially as I am [sure?] it has mine. I have great hopes for a people who are sober, industrious, economical and more; but for people . . . [without these qualities] I have no hopes, no respect, nor sympathy."[86]

Taylor ended his report with the opinion, "Notwithstanding my love for my race and all mankind, I am sure that I could never consent to remain near the government of Liberia. I detest hypocrisy in all its forms, and especially am I disgusted with the 'state of things' at this place." He suggested that the government of the United States should have only a field consular office in Monrovia. Taylor did admit that he had been well received by the Liberians, "from the chief officer of the Government, to the most humble citizen of this Republic. I have been even urged to report the condition of the 'Republic' so as to gain for it favorable comment." Nevertheless, he felt that his report was correct and that it could "be verified by any conscientious man whom the Government may be pleased to send here, as a special envoy or otherwise." He said that he had "great regrets" that he had "to end so soon what I hoped would be a 'long service.' "[87]

Just three days after Taylor had sent off his report to Bayard, he was visited by a delegation composed of "the principal officers and most prominent citizens of the Republic's capital Monrovia." These men had undoubtedly heard about Taylor's reaction to their country (or perhaps had even gotten wind of the nature of his despatch) and, in his words, "came seeking my opinion of their country and to assure me, of their friendly feeling towards the Government of the United States and 'its' present representative near their dominion. Being a firm believer, in the doctrine, of our friends being those who will tell us of our faults, I did not hesitate to vent my feelings." Taylor confessed that his despatch was prepared "while sick with disgust" and done to "deliver my soul," but felt that his interview with the delegation had convinced him that "all is not yet lost in the 'Republic.' "[88]

The Liberians assured Taylor that they would "commence the work of retrenchment and to take hold where their fathers had left off and to see that the Republic is made a success." This gratified the minister resident, who explained to Washington how shocked he was by the high salaries and other perquisites of the government officials. He did try to persuade the secretary of state that the Liberians' "love for the 'Parental care' of the United States is so great" that instead of resenting his despatch, they were quite prepared to mend their ways. Recognizing that he had perhaps done irreparable harm both to himself and to the Liberians, Taylor told the delegation that, subject to the instructions he received from the secretary of state, he would be pleased to "remain and watch their work, of reducing the 'expense' of carrying on their government." He voiced the hope that his "officiousness" would not be "condemned" by the secretary of state, for "after thinking about the matter fully," Taylor had concluded that it was his "duty to the Government of the United States to keep this Republic from being a failure if I find it within my power to prevent it. I hold that in working here to (indeed) encourage the Liberians to quit the position of mendicants that I am serving my race. I am confident it would be cowardly, to run away from the fray, at the appearance of the first danger or difficulty." Taylor was anxious that Bayard know how earnestly he wished to "free" the Liberians "from their extravagances" and that he awaited a reply to his cable, "praying that my 'course' may be approved."[89]

Unaware of the effects his precipitous request to resign had had, Taylor busied himself with the affairs of Liberia. Early in 1887 the United States had learned of the arrival of indigenous Liberian workers in Panama and queried its minister whether the Liberian government was aware of this event and of the dangers to its people in the rather unhealthy isthmus. Still distrustful of Liberian officials, Taylor responded to Washington that they were aware of the emigration, and were themselves party to the contract and receiving benefits from it. He reported somewhat cynically that encouraging "the emigration of the natives to the isthmus of Panama is in some way thought by the Government to be to the 'natives' benefit, but in what way I am unable to discern or see."[90] Subsequent black diplomats in Liberia would be troubled by this issue, and African Americans would later defend Liberia when a "scandal" about exporting laborers broke out in the 1930s.

Liberia's persisting conflict with its indigenous population continued to be a source of a great deal of the cable traffic between the U.S. minister and Washington. The problem was now compounded by the attempts of black merchants to open their own ports of trade without the government's permission though with the sympathy of American Christian missionaries. The latter also supported their converts, who they felt were unjustly expelled by the local people for not participating in a war against the government. Supporting the rebels were the British, who expected to profit from the troubles in Liberia. In seeking help from the United States through its legation, the Liberians complained that they were being penalized for not adhering to the Berlin pact. They indicated to Taylor that they had not been invited to Berlin, and since Liberia was not a European country, it was not bound by the decisions made at Berlin. Moreover, it refused to "commit suicide" by yielding its territories to whites.

This argument must have impressed Taylor, because he "beseeched" Bayard to grant the "Prayer of the Liberian Government, praying for aid to put down a 'rebellion' near Cape Palmas." He assured the secretary that the Liberian government was doing everything in its power to have its people "respect, adhere to, and obey the law." He added that "it would be not only an act of kindness to aid Liberia, in the matter of compelling her subjects to submit to the laws of this Republic, but I seriously maintain that it would be showing those good offices toward her which ought so much be desired on the part of the United States." Taylor tried to impress upon Bayard the importance of considering that the Liberian people were "nearly all from America. I therefore would most earnestly beseech you to grant if possible, the presence of a 'man-of-war' on this coast to remain until this crisis is satisfactorily settled for the good of this Republic."[91]

Aware that some missionaries were suggesting to the State Department that the indigenous people's point of view should be considered along with that of the Liberian government, Taylor stated categorically that there were not two sides to the issue and reiterated that the United States should support Liberia. He concluded, "I have the honor to state most respectfully that the time is far distant when the United States shall feel reluctant towards helping the former citizens or inhabitants of America."[92]

Taylor was now so committed to his task that he retreated from his abstemiousness and welcomed the opportunity to give the traditional Fourth of July celebration. He did so "in order to keep and retain during my stay here that friendly consideration, which was so richly enjoyed by all my predecessors."[93] He was therefore deeply distressed to find out that almost immediately upon receiving his despatch no. 10 requesting recall, Bayard had "acquainted the President with the urgent request . . . to be permitted to return to the United States." Under the direction of the president, the secretary granted Taylor "a leave of absence for the purpose of returning home in order to resign your office."[94]

What is not clear is whether Bayard had received Taylor's despatch retracting the offer to resign before talking to President Cleveland or whether he simply decided to ignore the retraction. Someone in Washington did put brackets around the section of the despatch in which the request for resignation appears and wrote "please leave out" in the margin. Whether this was put there before or after the fact is not known. However, Taylor reacted bitterly to his recall. He complained that he really wished to serve in Liberia and that he had accepted a one-third decrease in his income in order to accept the post. Then in a 115-page letter to the President, he poured out his feelings of bitterness and deception at what he had encountered in Liberia. He wrote, among other things, "I pictured in my mind a country peopled by my own race, destined in the near future to show the world **A Great Negro Nationality** [emphasis his]."[95]

Taylor admitted that he felt betrayed by Liberia and had a deep sense of shame that his people had not lived up to his expectations. He suggested that only legal prohibitions prevented him from going public with his views about Liberia. Finally, Taylor told the president that he was convinced that nothing could save Liberia "except two or three thousand negro emigrants from the United States."[96]

In retrospect, Taylor's initial reaction to Liberia was no different from that of either J. Milton Turner or John H. Smyth. Like them he despaired that Liberia would ever become the black nationality of which blacks in the diaspora dreamed and hoped. Taylor did not hold President Cleveland responsible for recalling him. He vigorously campaigned for the president's reelection to office in 1892, and as a reward, he was offered the position as minister resident and consul general to Bolivia. He declined the offer, perhaps because he had had enough of diplomatic service. Taylor accepted the post of recorder of deeds for the District of Columbia, a position he held until his death in 1898.[97]

Despite Taylor's promise upon leaving office to respect the law forbidding him to criticize the people to whom he had been accredited, it was impossible for him to remain silent about his experiences in Liberia. For one thing, he had had a difficult experience in that troubled land; for a second, with the progressive failure of Reconstruction and emigration fever growing throughout the United States, he felt obliged to warn fellow blacks against going there. Taylor took a radically anti-Liberia position. He functioned as a one-man truth squad against Edward Wilmot Blyden and the "emigrants." He wrote letters to the editors of several papers advising against emigration and even wrote a pamphlet on Liberia entitled *Whites and Blacks and the Questioned Settled* (Atlanta, 1889). To complicate matters, the issue of the conflict between mulattoes and blacks, both in the United States and in Liberia, where it took the form of relations between Americo-Liberians (mulattoes) and the "Native tribes" (blacks), became the subject of much debate.

So strong were the sentiments for and against Liberia among African Americans that President Cleveland and his secretary of state had a difficult time deciding upon a nominee for minister to Liberia. Early on it was reported that Thomas F. Bayard had invited John H. Latrobe, president of American Colonization Society, and his executive committee to suggest the "name of a competent and proper man" for the position as minister to Liberia. After "careful deliberation," these persons proposed the name of the Reverend Joseph C. Price, president of Livingstone College, Salisbury, North Carolina, for "appointment to that honorable position."[98] Probably unknown to the Department of State was the correspondence between the American Colonization Society and Edward Wilmot Blyden about the vacancy in Monrovia. In a postscript marked "private" to a letter dated 23 January 1888 at Sierra Leone, Blyden suggested to William Coppinger, secretary of the society:

> I hope you may succeed in having Price appointed Minister to Liberia. I know him. He cannot go far wrong on the question of Africa. I hope he will call here on his way to Monrovia. Urge him to come out as soon as possible. . . . Try and warn him against seeking advice from [John H.] Smyth or [J. Milton] Turner. They are apt to give him erroneous impressions to start with and thus bias all his views. Tell him to come and see for himself. I should be glad if Mr. Bayard could advise him to appoint me to act for him in his absence; this would have great weight with him. President Johnson and Mr. C. T. O. King are now friends and working together. The presence of a man like Price on the spot under proper guidance would be a most useful thing for the country. Being with him I could shape his despatches here.[99]

On 8 February 1888 Bayard wrote Price that "it is the object of the President to place the interests of the Africo-Americans in that Republic in charge of an American citizen of African descent who is believed to have at heart the advancement of his people, and to possess qualifications to render them service and to do credit to this country."[100] On 5 March 1888 Price replied to the secretary of state that while he was profoundly grateful and appreciative of "the distinguished recognition given me by the offer of this 'post' of trust, duty and honor attended, as it is, with an emolument of some consideration," his work at Livingstone College compelled him to decline the appointment. He added that while his work had "for its primary object the education of the Negroes, and the bringing about of a better state of things in the South generally, still it also has in view, as an ultimate objective, the enlightenment of Africa and the final redemption of the Dark Continent, which will be greatly advanced by the Christian education and the industrial development of the Negroes in this country."[101]

Having failed to have Price sent to Liberia, the American Colonization Society next proposed as a candidate the Reverend Ezekiel Smith of Fayetteville, North Carolina. Smith was described by the society as "a licensed minister of the Baptist Church and an educator of the first rank, zealous and practical in his efforts for the elevation of his race. He is of good personal appearance, dignified in manner, and much esteemed by those who know him. He is recommended as having at heart the eleva-

tion of his people." Smith, a self-made man like many of his prede-
cessors at Monrovia, was also a race man. Born during slavery in 1852
in North Carolina of African-born parents, he enrolled at Shaw Univer-
sity and graduated with an A.B. in 1878. He served as a major of the
Third North Carolina Infantry during the Spanish-American War. When
Smith returned to North Carolina he became the principal of the State
Colored Normal School at Fayetteville, founded the North Carolina
Industrial Association, and founded and edited the Carolina
Enterprise.[102]

Given his background and the support of the American Colonization
Society, which knew about his long interest in Africa, Smith had no
difficulty being confirmed by the Senate. He left for Monrovia on 2 June
1888, accompanied by his wife and son, and arrived at his post on 10
July. From all indications, Smith was under no illusions about the difficulty of his task in Monrovia but felt that he was amply compensated
politically as well as financially—especially the latter since his yearly
salary was $4,000 a year (whereas the Liberian president received a
salary of $2,500, and the secretaries of state and treasury only $1,000
each). The problem for Smith was that the Liberians were still miffed
over the resignation of Taylor and the 115-page letter to President Cleveland. They retaliated by making the envoy cool his heels for several
weeks before permitting him to present his letters. On 10 August 1888
Smith wrote Secretary of State Bayard that when he arrived in Monrovia
with his family, he found a "considerable feeling of hostility toward my
predecessor. The inimical feeling, in measure, has been transferred to
me."[103] He gave as an example that he had duly notified the Liberian
secretary of state on the day of his arrival, but that it was not until a
month later that he was given an audience and granted the opportunity to
deliver to the president the sealed letter of credence. Smith wrote that he
waited patiently without the slightest murmur.[104]

Not content to delay the American diplomat's reception, the Liberians
reportedly embarrassed him on 26 July, the forty-first anniversary of the
independence of the republic. He had received an invitation from the
mayor and city council to attend the anniversary exercises. Smith said
that he was annoyed "when the orator of the day availed himself of the
opportunity to pay his respects to the Negroes of the United States, by
dealing them a full dose of vituperation. "This, too," reported the minister, "I passed by unnoticed." Smith said that so far he had "not given the
slightest attention to any act of discourtesy shown. I shall studiously and
earnestly labor to merit only the good will of all; to perpetuate the

amicable relations between the two countries and above all, it shall be my constant endeavor to worthily represent the great government of which I am a member and which has honored me as its representative."[105]

Smith also complained that Monrovia "must be the least desirable of any post occupied by any Minister representing our government abroad."[106] First of all, he felt "separated from the world" and without the opportunities of self-improvement; second, the climate was deadly; and third, the cost of living was very high. Yet he promised to do his best.

No sooner had the Liberians ended their boycott of Smith than they asked him to seek the help of his government in their problems with the indigenous people still acerbated by the hostility of the missionaries and by the designs of both Britain and France. The situation had not changed since Taylor was minister, and Mr. Barclay, the Liberian secretary of state, had sent a letter to the American secretary by way of Taylor giving a full account of the attack by some local people on the missionaries and seeking the assistance of the United States in punishing the malefactors. Relations between the Liberians and the United States were becoming strained as a result of these conflicts. Even before Smith had arrived at Monrovia, a cleric, the Reverend Rives, had sent him a letter dated 23 June 1888 informing him that an American missionary, Miss Mary B. Meria, had complained to a justice of the Supreme Court, Oliver Wendell Holmes, of an attack upon her by the people in her jurisdiction. Rives felt that the Liberian government was to blame and wished Smith to do something about it. Smith dutifully notified the State Department of the troubles and was instructed to assure both the Liberians and the missionaries that the United States government would do whatever was in its power to help them.[107]

In an effort to understand the basis of Liberia's problems with its indigenous populations, Smith started to travel widely and, as he wrote John H. Latrobe, he availed himself of every opportunity to get acquainted with "the customs of the people, learn something of their different institutions, and thereby draw conclusions as to the future prosperity of the Republic." In general, he was impressed with the "earnestness and zeal which are being exerted by the leaders—the teachers, religious and others—to instruct the masses properly in their several duties as citizens." The preacher in Smith was pleased with the "Aborigines" to whom he spoke (through an interpreter) "of Jesus the mighty to save," and he believed them not only "susceptible to light—the true light—but many of them anxious to receive the truth."[108]

Smith was also coming to terms with the Americo-Liberians and was reportedly pleased that their leaders were "learning by degrees that Liberia is not the United States. I mean by this remark alone that the people here are beginning to un-Americanize themselves and are slowly but surely adapting themselves to Liberia and the peculiar but natural surroundings and circumstances of the country." He felt that the "progressive and aggressive citizens, teachers and leaders of the masses, with the permanently established institutions, warrant the indulgent hope for a great and glorious future for the lone star Republic of Liberia."[109]

Nevertheless, the continuing strife between settlers and indigenous populations created conditions that jeopardized Liberia's independence and engaged the attention of, and perhaps were the source of wry amusement for, Smith and officials of the American Department of State. In his despatch of 22 April 1898, Smith reported that the local politicians were squabbling over the nomination for the presidency. President Johnson, the incumbent, had formerly been the unanimous choice of both the Republican and Whig parties but had then declared himself a Whig and had defeated the Republican candidate in the subsequent election. In the January 1889 national convention of the Whig party, however, he was opposed by none other than his wife's sister's husband, one A. D. Williams. The convention was leaning toward Williams when Johnson supporters asked for a two-week adjournment. Then, much to the disconsertion of Williams's supporters, a group of delegates met two days before the end of the adjournment and renominated Johnson. Taking advantage of the scandal, the Republicans met in their national convention and, eschewing their own candidate, supported A. D. Williams, who they felt had been cheated out of the Whig nomination. Intrigued by all the goings-on, Smith reported that the election campaign was warm, and the outcome impossible to predict. What did bother Smith, however, was the lack of party platforms and the absence of issues, especially those "looking to the development of the country." In a later despatch he indicated that Johnson had been reelected by a vote of 1,750 out of a total vote of 2,783.[110]

More serious for Liberia and the United States was the outcome of the mayoral election in Monrovia the following year. The defeated candidate not only protested the results but also organized a secret society known as the Side Clap, which terrorized the capital. The founder of Side Clap was eventually arrested, but while awaiting trial he escaped and sought asylum in the German consulate. The consul hoisted his national flag and, with five fully armed Europeans at his side, refused to surrender the accused. Alarmed that this "diplomatic incident" might be used by the Germans to declare war on Liberia and to provide an excuse for taking over the country, a number of friends of the accused finally persuaded him to leave the German consulate.[111]

The German consul was mortified by this turn of events, and though criticized by both the Europeans in Monrovia and the Liberians for interfering in the internal affairs of his hosts, he continued to bluster. To Smith's relief, the Liberian government ended the impasse by revoking the exequatur of the German consul on 10 February 1890, thereby declaring him persona non grata, and asking him to leave. Smith's last despatch to the Department of State was similar to his first one: a report that the two Gola chiefs, dissatisfied over the division of spoils taken in war against the Mandingo, had started to fight and were devastating the country. Smith reported that failing to make peace among the combatants, the Liberian government had issued an ultimatum to the belligerents to cease fighting or be attacked.[112] The minister left Monrovia and arrived back in North Carolina on 22 June 1890, satisfied that he had done his best to help preserve a black nationality. On 26 June "the colored . . . citizens" of Goldsboro, North Carolina, gave Smith a big reception and both the mayor of the town and the editor of the *Argus* newspaper spoke in his honor.[113]

While Smith was still en route home, the United States found itself having to defend Liberia's honor and sovereignty at an African slave-trade conference that took place in Brussels in June 1890. Now sensitized by its black envoys in Africa to the European practice of using lofty humanitarian projects as excuses for seizing parts of Africa, the American secretary of state James G. Blaine, expressed deep concern at Liberia's not being invited to a conference at which the issue of the slave trade (with important implications for Liberia) was discussed. Blaine insisted that "full respect should be paid to the independent and sovereign place of that Republic in the family of nations." Then, so no one would misunderstand what he meant, "the representative of the United States made an explicit declaration of the relation of the Republic of Liberia to the United States and the desire of this Government that the general act [of the Berlin Conference] should contain an express stipulation to the effect that the Liberian Republic would be invited, as a sovereign power, to adhere to the treaty."[114]

So forceful was the United States' intervention that the president of the conference, Baron Lambermont, supported the United States' position, adding that although "all the world knows" Liberia was founded "with the object of affording a home to certain freed American slaves desiring to return to the mother country, it was destined at the same time to fulfill a civilizing mission upon the Guinea coast." Whether he meant it or not, Lambermont said that "the creation has produced happy results. It began, it is true, under great difficulties, but this often happens in the early life of new states. This young Republic none the less deserves the sympathies of all those who are interested in the cause of humanity in Africa. It is an independent and free state. . . . Moreover," he added, "the conference has every interest in associating it with its work, not only because of the mission Liberia is called upon to fulfill, but also because it is also in a position to lend indispensable assistance toward the execution of several of the clauses of the general act." Not to be outdone, the British delegate, Lord Vivian, welcomed the position taken by the United States and the conference, but this did not prevent Her Majesty's Government from pursuing their aggression against the territorial integrity of Liberia.[115]

President Benjamin Harrison nominated Alexander Clark of Iowa to be his minister resident and consul general to Liberia on 16 August 1890, thereby honoring black support of the Republican party. Born in Washington County, Pennsylvania, in 1826, Clark was educated in its public schools and, after learning the trade of barbering, moved to Muscatine, Iowa, in 1843. He became active in the abolitionist movement and in 1853 was a delegate to the Convention of Colored Men, which met in Rochester. Quickly identifying himself with the newly formed Republican party, Clark became one of its stalwart supporters and orators and was a perennial delegate to its conventions. In 1869 he was chosen as a black delegate to the national convention of the Republican party meeting in Washington, D.C., but he soon despaired at the lack of progress being made by blacks. In 1882 he bought a newspaper, the Chicago *Conservator* (which he successfully published until 1889) and enrolled at the University of Iowa Law School. Clark graduated in 1883 and shortly afterward was admitted to the Chicago bar. He had no difficulty being confirmed by the Senate and arrived at Monrovia on 18 November 1890.[116]

For Clark, as for Henry Highland Garnet before him, the ministerial appointment to Liberia represented the culmination of his career and of a life devoted to improving the lot of black people. In presenting his letters of credence, the sixty-four-year-old Clark stated, "The government and the people of the United States regard with no ordinary interest the conditions and destiny of a republic charged with high responsibilities of Liberia." He added that the United States not only believed that Liberia stood for "popular government on a vast continent, ancient in history but new to modern civilization," but that many distinguished black citizens of the United States looked to that country to help solve "one of the greatest problems of the century—the enlightened, general substantial and permanent amelioration of a vast and powerful race hitherto largely unknown and unknowing to the blessings of Christian civilization." Clark concluded, "As a representative of that race as well as of the great republic whose credentials I bear, I profoundly share in the friendship of my government and its citizens of Liberia and in their lofty anticipation for her future."[117]

In his response, the president of Liberia said, "I see in your countenance the scars of many hard fought political battles, as well as in other spheres—of usefulness so well written in the history of your country, that you are no stranger to the people of Liberia."[118]

The Liberian president was correct in his view that the scars of many hard fought battles had severely affected the new American representative. Clark was thrilled by the great displays and the pomp and ceremonies in the Liberian capital, but there is no indication from the despatches that he did very much. On 1 April 1891 he asked for leave, pleading such a "severe attack of African fever and [so] greatly reduced in health" that his physician had advised him to return home. This was not to be, for Clark died in Monrovia on 3 June 1891 at a most inopportune time for Liberia.[119] While Clark was on his deathbed, Liberia was coming under increasing pressure from European attempts to carry out the intentions of the Berlin Conference. Moreover, it was becoming clear to many African Americans that although the United States did not readily acquiesce in the partitioning of Africa, it was not prepared to take forceful action on behalf of the peoples of that continent. Like his predecessor, who had warned the Europeans not to ignore Liberia's sovereignty, in May 1891 Secretary of State James G. Blaine vigorously protested to France through his minister in Paris, Mr. Coolidge, when he heard rumors of France's intention to annex the Liberian littoral between the Cavally and San Pedro rivers, and to seek to establish a protectorate over the coast.[120]

Blaine placed Liberia's position in historical perspective by indicating to the French that while Liberia was "peculiar and almost isolated," being "one of the few independent sovereignties of the vast continent, and the only one on the whole of the Atlantic seaboard," it was also one of the few countries that at no time had "trespassed on the domain of its neighbors or invaded their comparatively recent sphere of influence." Indeed, Liberia was bound to the United States "by special ties which, strong in their origin, have been further strengthened by half a century of intimate relationship" and that it was "apparent that this Government and people could not behold unmoved, much less acquiesce in, any proceeding on the part of the neighbors of Liberia which might assume to dispose of any territory justly claimed and long admitted to belong to the Republic, without the concurrence and consent of Liberia as an independent and sovereign contractant."[121]

Blaine was loath to criticize France without giving it "an opportunity of frankly disclaiming any intention to encroach upon the recognized territory of Liberia." But he told his envoy in Paris that, by President Harrison's direction, he was to call upon the French minister of foreign affairs and inform him "that the Government of the United States does not accept as valid or acquiesce in the protectorates announced by Mr. Desprez's note of November 3 1891, or by Mr. Patenotre's later note of January 26, 1892," so far as those announcements related to territory pertaining to the Republic of Liberia westward of the San Pedro River, unless Liberia itself was "a consenting party to such transactions." Blaine added, "The President is so firmly convinced that the just rights of independent Liberia will be duly respected by all that he is indisposed to consider the possible contingency of such expansion of the territorial claims of other powers in Africa as might call for a more positive assertion of the duty of the United States."[122]

While such diplomatic maneuvering about Liberia's territorial integrity was taking place, Clark had died in Monrovia, and Bishop Henry McNeal Turner had arrived on his first visit to Liberia and to Africa. This cleric was in the vanguard of an impressive group of African Americans, who, while being rapidly disenfranchised at home, would attempt to elaborate a symbolic black foreign policy toward Africa. The bishop was no stranger to the officials in the Department of State. They knew from despatches sent by former diplomats in Liberia such as Smyth that Turner had been involved with the Liberian Exodus Joint Stock Steam Ship Company, whose vessel, the SS *Azor,* had taken emigrants from South Carolina to Liberia in 1878. Since that period, Turner had been very much in the forefront of the emigration movement but had never visited Africa. Finally, the presiding bishops of the AME Church authorized him to visit Africa to confer with several pastors of the church who had migrated with their congregations to Sierra Leone and Liberia.[123]

For Turner this visit to his "fatherland" was a dream come true because, as everyone knew, he had longed to "look over the ground" to facilitate the "emigration of blacks." Turner scorned the negative reports on Liberia by Charles Taylor and others and was convinced that he would see or hear nothing to change his conviction that Africa was the only hope for African Americans. He felt that conditions for blacks in the United

States had so deteriorated that emigration was the only solution to their position within America and in the world. Turner believed and hoped that the increasing acts of violence against blacks in the South—lynchings, the oppressive convict labor regime, and segregation—would lead to "war, efforts of extermination, anarchy, horror and a wail to heaven." He declared, "Yes, I would make Africa a place of refuge, because I see no other shelter from the stormy blast, from the red tide of persecution, from the horrors of American prejudice."[124]

Turner firmly believed that building and defending a strong black nationality in Africa would help blacks all over the world. He did "not believe any race will ever be respected, or ought to be respected, who do not show themselves capable of founding and manning a government of their own creation."[125] Nor did he feel it possible for any race to amount to much if its people were excluded from "all honorable positions, from being kings and queens, lords, dukes, presidents, governors, mayors, generals." He proposed establishing a state in Africa of some half-million civilized Christians, where blacks could have not only their own high officials and dignitaries, but also ordinary artisans and mechanics, and such institutions as railroads, corporations, telegraph offices, commercial enterprises, and colleges. Under these conditions, the racial stigma would disappear and blacks would not have to fawn upon whites or plead for mercy from them. Glory could only come to the race from seats of power and influence. "Till we have black men in the seat of power, respected, feared, hated and reverenced, our young men will never rise for the reason they will never look up."[126]

Turner could scarcely conceal his anger toward black leaders who, in the face of the Europeans' scramble for Africa, looked askance at his "symbolic African nation." He suggested that these persons were prepared to do nothing but "wait till the whites go over and civilize Africa, and homestead all the land and take us along to black their boots and groom their horses. Wait till the French or English find some great mines of gold, diamonds or some other precious metal or treasures, so we can raise a howl over it and charge the whites with endeavoring to take away our fathers' inheritance, and lift a wail for the sympathy of the world."[127] Having lost all confidence in whites, especially in the United States government, Turner felt that blacks had to redeem Africa on their own and in any way possible for them.

Just as he had hoped, Turner was enamored with his visit to Africa. His first contacts with Africans on board ship were rewarding, and these were followed by joyous welcomes when he arrived. He reported that when the people of Freetown heard of his arrival, they streamed to the waterfront to greet him. Overcome with joy, the bishop wept when he set foot on the soil of Africa. He reported with pleasure that he did not see the miasmic swamps that many had warned him to expect in Sierra Leone. Instead he saw the clean city of Freetown built on hills and the pleasant homes owned by proud and prosperous black men, and he heard glowing reports of progress from the British governor. Turner was even more impressed that Liberia had its own black president and government. He wrote, "One thing the black man has here, and that is manhood, freedom and the fullest liberty; he feels like a lord and walks the same way."[128] Liberia's undeveloped aspects did not bother Turner in the least. Indeed, they only increased his interest in encouraging blacks to come to the country and to take advantage of the opportunities in agriculture, mining and trade. "I get mad and sick," he wrote, "when I look at the possibilities God has placed within our reach, and to think that we are such block-heads we cannot see and use them."[129]

The bishop confessed that he shared the dismay of native Africans who could not understand why "the black man is at home across the sea." During a visit to the inland plantations where he found salubrious conditions, he remarked that if white missionaries could live and prosper in that area, he did not understand why African Americans refused to believe that it was possible to do so. By the time Turner left for the United States, he was firmly convinced that his views of emigration were correct: "I see the wisdom of my position now as I never dreamed before. If the black man rises to wealth . . . he will never do it by trying to be white or snubbing his native country [Africa]."[130]

Encouraged by Turner's visit, but now more concerned with European ambitions and also more sensitive to African American criticism of conditions in Liberia, the Liberian government tried a new approach in its immigration policy. On 27 January 1892, in a joint resolution, the Liberian Congress declared:

> Whereas in the opinion of the Legislature of Liberia, some measure should be adopted to encourage Negro Immigration to this country, in order to colonize our unoccupied territory thereby avoiding international questions and disputes, as regards our Sovereignty over certain portions of our Coast as well as interior possessions, and also in view of the long, and indefatigable efforts of the American Colonization Society in the cause of Liberia, it is meet and proper that this government should in some way recognize the noble, and philanthropic service rendered this country for the past seventy years by the Society . . . [it is] granted an annuity of Six Thousand dollars in gold to aid them in sending Negro immigrants to Liberia.[131]

The irony here was that the Liberians did not turn this money over directly to the African Americans. They either did not know or did not appreciate that the American Colonization Society had never fully recovered from the initial mistrust in which it was held by many African Americans.

Meanwhile, in Washington, Secretary Blaine remained concerned about France's interest in Liberian territory, and on 11 January 1892 President Harrison named William D. McCoy to replace Clark.[132] He left New York on 17 February 1892 and arrived in Monrovia on 25 March.[133] Whether because of his own unflappable character or because of changing sentiments in the country, he made no reference in his letters of credence to the black nationality invoked by so many of his predecessors. What he immediately had to do, however, was deal with Liberia's boundary disputes. Like his predecessors, McCoy was faced with explaining to the department how Liberia's persisting problems with its aboriginal populations contributed to the problem. His despatch of 14 June 1892 reiterated how limited the Liberians' control over the local people was. In this case one Julla, a Mandingo chief, alleging that his grandfather was once insulted by a Vai chief, sought revenge by making war on the Vai and their Gola allies, forcing the latter to flee. This action brought the Liberians, including the president himself, to the rescue of the Vai and the Gola. Before this situation could be brought under control, however, the Tana, a subgroup of the Vai, counterattacked and defeated the Mandingo. Moreover, the Tana swore vengeance on the other Vai for permitting marauding Mandingo to attack both Vai and Gola without resistance. This renewed fighting brought the Liberians to the field, and they arrested and fined chiefs of the Tana but left the Mandingo alone for fear of exacerbating relations with France. The situation was complicated by the presence of American missionaries in Half-Cavalla. Fearing that the American missionaries near Cape Palmas would become involved, McCoy reported to the State Department that he advised them "to remain strictly neutral." He reported that while he had no fears for their safety, should an emergency arise, he was prepared "to adopt whatever measures are necessary for their protection."[134]

What concerned McCoy most of all was the effect of Liberia's internal affairs on its future and on United States policy. He was convinced that the Liberian government knew of the plans and activities of indigenous groups. McCoy reported that the Liberian president said to him that the Mandingo were good traders whereas the Gola did little commerce. On the other hand, the Mandingo were cruel and dealt in slaves. What the

Liberian president wanted was for "the natives to fight it out," but this action, according to McCoy, was "an abrogation of the alliance which has heretofore existed between American-Liberians and the Mandingos, and it effectively closes trade with the interior."[135] The minister frankly believed that the Liberians could do a better job and was concerned that Washington was not pushing them to do so. He wrote to the Department of State:

> Permit me to say that the policy of this Government with respect to the native wars has driven nearly all of the interior trade from Monrovia. There is much disquietude because of uncertainties attending the future, towns and villages have been broken up, farms deserted, and many of the natives, especially in the vicinity of Cape Mount, are on the verge of starvation.
> The Government is fully able to assert and maintain a different policy but I fear the necessity for it will not be realized until the industries of the community are completely destroyed.[136]

What really did alarm McCoy was the increasing evidence that certain Western Europeans seemed determined to exert unwelcome influence on the Liberian government. Intermixed with his despatches about Liberia's African policy were reports on the visits of European warships. On 19 September 1892 he reported that during the trouble at Half-Cavalla, the British warship *Trush* had evacuated from the area British subjects who had refused to pay taxes to the local people. On 15 November McCoy reported that the Dutch man-of-war *Alkmaar* had visited Monrovia and had taken the president on a visit to Cape Palmas. Again, on 30 November, the envoy reported that the German cruiser *Falk* had paid a one-day visit to Monrovia. Whether out of patriotism or out of fear of foreign intervention, some Americo-Liberian settlers asked for the visit of American vessels of war. McCoy notified the secretary of the navy that the president of Liberia, his cabinet, and many leading citizens had requested a visit by an American warship to ports along the coast. He added that "most of the inhabitants are from the United States, and as there are but few American vessels that are engaged in this trade—and being small at that, the people naturally long to see the majestic and powerful vessels that they read about and to greet once more the Stars and Stripes . . . I would suggest that December be the month most suitable. Then the Legislature will be in session and the weather pleasant and comparatively healthful."[137]

To McCoy's surprise and to the concern of the Department of State, Liberia decided to dicker with France over the San Pedro region. Earlier Liberian regimes, supported by such ministers as J. Milton Turner and

John H. Smyth and backed by the United States, had refused even to consider yielding territories to Britain or France. This long tradition led the American Secretary of State to order his minister in Paris to reject French claims and to tell his minister to the Court of St. James's to notify the British that "the position of this Government as the next friend of a republic founded in Africa by American enterprise" was unchanged toward either France or Great Britain, that the United States had acted in the past "to avert any diminution of such just rights to African territory as Liberia possessed, and that due representation would be made against the apprehended encroachments of France westward of the long recognized boundary of the San Pedro River."[138]

So serious did the United States consider France's designs on Liberian territory that in his annual message to Congress on 6 December 1892 President Harrison declared:

> In consequence of the action of the French Government in proclaiming a protectorate over certain tribal districts of the west coast of Africa, eastward of the San Pedro River, which has long been regarded as the southeastern boundary of Liberia, I have felt constrained to make protest against this encroachment upon the territory of a Republic which was founded by citizens of the United States and toward which this country has for many years held the intimate relation of a friendly counselor.[139]

Whether the Liberians considered negotiating with France because they had lost confidence that the United States would go beyond mere rhetoric in defending their cause or because they simply needed the money the French were offering them is not clear from the records. The American diplomats in Paris kept abreast of the negotiations between the Liberians and the French, and kept McCoy informed. On 16 January 1893 the department told McCoy that Liberia "cedes to France that portion of the country lying between the Calvally and San Pedro Rivers, receiving in return a recognition of its independence and the sum of twenty-five thousand (25,000) francs [$4,825]." The despatch added that although the land the territory ceded was said not to be at all valuable and scarcely settled, the officials in Washington felt that the "compensation received by Liberia seems inadequate."[140]

The Liberians apparently felt that since the United States was not prepared to provide much help, they had little choice but to negotiate loans with Europeans. The State Department, in turn, felt that the Europeans were taking advantage of the Liberians. Washington expressed surprise to McCoy that the Liberians did not ask him to see whether the American minister in Paris could help them in their negotiation with

France. Washington was unhappy with the results but could then do little about what had transpired. Nevertheless, the State Department instructed McCoy to visit the Liberians to verify whether they had been forced to sign the agreement with the French. [141]

Washington's cable to McCoy notifying him of the agreement between France and Liberia arrived just after he had sent a cable to the department indicating that as soon as President Joseph James Cheeseman had taken office on 28 March 1892, the Liberians had decided to solve their boundary dispute with France. McCoy indicated that he personally did not like the terms of the projected accord, and in a note marked "personal" appended to the text of the treaty, he wrote that

> the map illustrating the proposed changes of the boundary by the Franco-Liberian treaty is inclined to impress one favorably except when it is remembered that France has not established any proof of her claims; that Liberia has developed and still occupies all the territory desired by France and that her claim thereto has been recognized by all nations (France included), and that France is yielding no territory but gaining a very rich section from a country that can ill afford the loss. [142]

Most of the senators and representatives from Cape Palmas and Maryland County (the areas affected by the treaty) were opposed to it, and they were supported by a few of the leading men in Monrovia. On the whole, however, the sentiment seemed to McCoy "overwhelmingly in favor of ratification." He concluded the only thing that friends of Liberia could do was to hope that the republic could surmount its difficulties so that it could "continue to be a portal through which civilization may reach the interior in spite of the impending crisis." [143]

Instructed by the department, McCoy queried the Liberians whether in fact they had been pressured by the French to sign the treaty. G. W. Gibson, the Liberian secretary of state, said that he had been instructed by President Cheeseman to state that the treaty with France was not satisfactory to his government. In a secret memorandum that he gave to McCoy to transmit to Washington, Gibson said that in the first place, Liberia did not wish to "alienate any portion of her territory *whatsoever;* and second, if pressed by circumstances to do so, it would have preferred that the consideration offered by the French Government to the Republic . . . be equivalent in view of the valuable tract of territory in question." [144]

President Cheeseman had also directed Gibson to say to McCoy that Cheeseman "appreciates very highly the interest manifested by the same and regrets that he did not feel at liberty to solicit more active interference in the negotiation of the boundary question." Then in what may have been an attempt at determining whether the United States was willing to do more than give verbal support to them, the Liberian officials said that the treaty had still not been ratified by the senate, but added, "It is possible that under the circumstances it will be ratified as the best thing to be done in view of the fact that we are not able to cope with so great a power as the French Government."[145] Then in an attempt to put the United States on the spot, the Liberians stated bluntly that "if the Government of the United States of America would protect and defend Liberia, throughout against French encroachment in case the treaty is not ratified, . . . [then] it will not be."[146]

The Liberians lost this gambit because Washington was in no mood to jeopardize its relations with France over Liberia, nor as we shall soon see in a later chapter over Madagascar or any other place in Africa. McCoy recognized this United States policy and did not push. He simply passed on to the State Department a manifesto from many persons, including African Americans, who had lived or settled in the affected region, which read in part: "We beg to state that we are not savages living in degradation like many African tribes whose territory . . . [the French] Government has acquired possession of. We are civilized Africans who have been brought back to these shores—our fatherland—through the benevolence of American philanthropists; and there are some, too, among us who have been directly brought out of the darkness of the heathenism into the light of civilization and Christianity, since our arrival here." The petitioners appealed to "all civilized Negroes wherever they may dwell. Whatever may be your present political connections, you have an interest in Africa as your fatherland." McCoy's only comment to Washington was that since this appeal was from some persons living in Liberia, and not from the government of Liberia, "no action could be taken."[147]

McCoy's low-key reaction to the Franco-Liberian treaty was probably due to a combination of factors: his health was deteriorating rapidly, and the Liberians were reacting testily to what they considered to be a lack of congruency between America's rhetoric about friendship and its half-hearted support.

Although Bishop Turner was on a visit to Liberia during this period there is no evidence that McCoy briefed him on the Franco-Liberian treaty. Apparently the Bishop spent a great deal of time outside of Monrovia on missionary activities. According to McCoy, Turner returned to the capital on 6 April 1893, accompanied by one of his elders, the Reverend G. G. Vreeland, wanting to travel to Grand Bassa to hold an AME Church convention. The only ship available was the Liberian warship, the *Gorronammah,* then on the point of departure. Unfortunately for the bishop and his suite, the Liberian president refused to delay the departure of the warship even though the bishop offered a sum of $50 for transportation and promised that the vessel would be delayed only one hour. The bishop had no recourse but to open the conference in Monrovia and then adjourn it to be continued at Grand Bassa at a later date. [148]

What is curious about this episode (and what apparently disturbed both McCoy and Turner) was that until then the bishop appeared to have been well received by the Liberians. It is also unclear from the archives whether the president's decision was based on a national emergency that demanded the departure of the ship or whether he was miffed at not getting the support of the United States and its citizens, including the bishop. We shall see later that no less a person than Booker T. Washington would suggest that the Liberians were their own worst enemies because they did not know how, or refused, to curry favor with the United States.

Seemingly unfazed by having to change his plans, Bishop Turner continued his activities. On 14 April 1893 the president of the College of Liberia invited both Turner and Minister McCoy to attend a lecture at the college given by Mr. Gibson, the Liberian secretary of state. [149] Shortly after this event, McCoy reported to the Department of State that Bishop Turner had been appointed consul for Liberia in the United States by the Liberian president, and unless the bishop declined the offer, he would eventually present his credentials to the United States. [150]

McCoy's health was deteriorating rapidly, and he was anxious to return home. With the election of President Cleveland, he sensed that he was to be replaced, and he sent a long despatch to the Department of State giving advice to his successor on domestic and foreign affairs. By this time, McCoy had taken the pulse of the diplomatic service and the role of Africa and of African Americans within it. He had previously written a private letter to the secretary of state complaining that the salary paid to the chief of mission in Monrovia suggested discrimination against that legation. He said that Monrovia was the only diplomatic post with a salary less than $5,000, when it ought to have ranked with Bolivia ($5,000), Costa Rica ($10,000) and Korea ($7,000). Moreover, he felt that the time allotted to travel between the United States and Monrovia was too short and that at least fifty days should be allowed for transit.[151] Nevertheless, he was quite prepared to remain at post until time and the climate permitted him to leave and a successor to be named. This was not to be. On 16 May 1893 his aide, Vice-Consul Beverly Y. Payne, notified the State Department that McCoy had died on 15 May of a bilious attack excited by the climate and had been interred in Palm Grove cemetery.[152]

Worried about affairs in Monrovia, on his return to the United States Bishop Turner called on Secretary of State W. Q. Gresham in Washington. Turner was reportedly alarmed by the void left by McCoy's death and the danger this posed both for Liberia's sovereignty and for the United States, since the French were about to implement the Franco-Liberian Treaty of 1893. He had written from Sierra Leone that, more than ever, the increasing number of whites in Africa meant "the capture of the only spot upon the face of the globe [where] the black man can ever hope to be in power and demonstrate the ability of self-government."[153] Turner also reported Cheeseman's offer to him to become Liberia's consul in the United States and requested some gesture of support for that black nationality against European pressures. Secretary Gresham reiterated to Turner America's support for Liberia's independence but was unwilling to go any further.[154]

The Liberian president's offer to Turner to be his consul in the United States created a problem for the Department of State even though Turner would have been stationed at Baltimore, rather than in the capital, namely, that Liberia had never had a black representative to the United States, and the United States had never before accepted a black diplomat from any country. The group that took offense at this nomination and opposed it was none other than the American Colonization Society, which argued that Bishop Turner was neither a Liberian citizen nor a resident of Washington, D.C. Not wishing to lose its dominant position with respect to United States policy toward Liberia to an African American, the society conveniently forgot that when it needed supporters for its emigrationist policies it had named Turner one of its vice presidents. Bowing to pressure from the society, the Liberians revoked the first appointment and instead named Turner consul to the southern states. Neither the American Colonization Society nor the Department of State could deal with the possibility of African Americans playing a more dominant role in foreign policy. Bishop Turner abandoned all hope of becoming a diplomat and became an ardent emigrationist, believing that blacks could not achieve full equality in America.[155]

McCoy was the last of an important group of African Americans who served as ministers to Liberia during the scramble for Africa. Like almost all of his predecessors, he was anxious to have his country protect the black nationality on the West Coast of Africa, and he served at the expense both of his health and his pocketbook. Whether it was because so many of these persons were "black nationalists" or because they were clergymen, they do not appear to have attempted to use their offices to garner riches for themselves. These men were struggling against incredible odds to help the Liberians, even when it often appeared that their efforts were appreciated neither at home nor at their posts. The problem for African Americans at this juncture was that the changing political climate in the United States was whittling away their political clout. They were therefore forced to shift the locus of their attempts to influence United States policy toward Africa from the politico-diplomatic realm to that of symbolic structures.

Notes

1. Message of the President to the Congress of the United States, *Foreign Relations of the United States, 1883,* ix. See also *African Repository* 60 (January 1884): 29.
2. See Sylvia M. Jacobs, *The African Nexus: Black American Perspectives on the European Partitioning of Africa, 1880–1920* (Westport, Conn.: Greenwood Press, 1981).
3. *African Repository* 61 (March 1885): 127–28.
4. J. Milton Turner to Secretary of State, 18 December 1877, no. 285, Despatches from U.S. Ministers to Liberia, 1863–1906, roll 7, Record Group 59, National Archives.
5. Ibid.
6. J. H. Smyth to Secretary of State, 17 June 1879, no. 31, *Foreign Relations of the United States, 1879,* 719.
7. Smyth to Department of State, 17 July 1879, no. 38, ibid., 719–20.
8. Smyth to Department of State, 24 March 1879, no. 21, ibid., 712.
9. Smyth to Department of State, enclosures no. 1 and 2 in Consular Series no. 32, 28 August 1879, ibid., 723–24.
10. Smyth to Department of State, 7 August 1879, Consular Series no. 27, ibid., 722–23.
11. Ibid.
12. Smyth to Department of State, 30 May 1879, no. 30, ibid., 718.
13. Smyth to Secretary of State, 3 July 1879, no. 34, U.S. Ministers to Liberia, roll 7.
14. Smyth to Secretary of State, 17 July 1879, no. 38; *Foreign Relations, 1879,* 341.
15. Noyes (Paris) to Secretary of State, 20 August 1879, no. 256, *Foreign Relations, 1879,* 341–42.
16. Noyes (Paris) to Secretary of State, 13 May 1880, no. 350, U.S. Ministers to Liberia, roll 8.

17. Smyth to Secretary of State, 12 February 1880, no. 69, *Foreign Relations, 1880*, 1:701–2.
18. Smyth to Secretary of State, 13 August 1879, no. 42, ibid. 1:691–92.
19. Smyth to Department of State, 20 November 1879, no. 54, U.S. Ministers to Liberia, roll 7.
20. Ibid.
21. Ibid.
22. Secretary of State (Evarts) to Smyth, 7 January 1880, no. 63, roll 8; *Foreign Relations of the United States, 1880*, 34; Secretary of State from Smyth, 19 March 1880, no. 2, U.S. Ministers to Liberia, roll 8.
23. Ibid.
24. Smyth to Department of State, 19 March 1880, no. 2, roll 8.
25. Department of State to Smyth, enclosure no. 2 in Smyth to Evarts, 20 March 1880, no. 74.
26. Evarts to Smyth, 2 February 1880, no. 68.
27. Evarts to E. F. Noyes, American Minister to France, 7 April 1880, no. 76.
28. *African Repository* 56 (July 1880): 66.
29. *African Repository* 57 (July 1881): 127–29.
30. Evarts to Smyth, 28 February 1881, cited in Robert L. Keiser, *Liberia: A Report on the Relations Between the United States and Liberia* (Washington, D.C.: Government Printing Office, 1928), 38–39.
31. Smyth to Secretary of State, 3 March 1881, no. 107, U.S. Ministers to Liberia, roll 8.
32. Ibid.
33. Smyth to Secretary of State Evarts, 19 April 1881, no. 116.
34. Ibid.
35. *African Repository* 58 (July 1882): 95.
36. Alexander Crummell, *Africa and America: Addresses and Discourses* (New York: Negro University Press, 1969), 297.
37. Henry Highland Garnet, "An Address to the Slaves of the United States of America" [1843], reprinted in Garnet, *A Memorial Discourse by Reverend Henry Highland Garnet, Delivered in the Hall of the House of Representatives* (Philadelphia: Joseph M. Wilson, 1865), 44–51.
38. Hollis Lynch, ed., *Selected Letters of Edward Wilmot Blyden* (Millwood, N.Y.: KTO Press, 1978), 290–91.
39. *African Repository* 58 (April 1882): 56.
40. Crummell, *Africa and America*, 302–3. Crummell's summary of Garnet's views about service to Africa gives a sense of the attitude of some of the Afrophiles of the period. The eulogy continued:

The offer was gladly accepted by my friend. It was the very thing he desired. He had long been wishing to see the Coast of Africa, to tread the soil of his ancestors. If this public position had not been offered him, he would, I have no doubt, sought some other mode, either as a missionary or a teacher, of reaching the Western Coast.

Gratifying as the offer was to him, it brought dismay and sorrow to a large circle of his best friends. For my own part, I felt it my duty to oppose its acceptance with candor, warmth, and decision. I had not doubt of its unwisdom, and I pressed my conviction very earnestly upon him.

Alas, all dissuasion was useless. "What," said he, "would you have me linger here in an old age of neglect and want? Would you have me tarry among men who have forgotten what I have done, and what I have suffered for them?

To stay here and die among these ungrateful people?" "No," was his ejaculation; "I go gladly to Africa! Please the Lord I can only safely cross the ocean, land on the coast of Africa, look around upon its green fields, tread the soil of my ancestors, live if but a few weeks; then I shall be glad to lie down and be buried beneath its sod."

Thus grandly, nobly did this high soul turn from baseness and ingratitude to a final far-distant haven of repose and death.

The Lord listened to the desires of his servant.

41. *African Repository* 58 (July 1882): 95.
42. Ibid.
43. Acting Secretary of State to the Minister in Great Britain (Lowell), 15 September 1882, no. 460, U.S. Ministers to Liberia, roll 9.
44. Smyth to Secretary of State, 2 October 1882, no. 12.
45. Ibid.
46. Ibid.
47. Ibid.
48. Secretary of State to Smyth, 21 December 1882, no. 9.
49. Ibid.
50. The British Secretary of State for Foreign Affairs, Mr. Granville, to the American Minister, Mr. Lowell, Foreign Office, 30 December 1882, cited in Keiser, *Liberia*, 47–52.
51. Secretary of State to Smyth, 8 April 1883, no. 14, U.S. Ministers to Liberia, roll 9.
52. Secretary of State to Smyth, 19 June 1883, cited in Keiser, *Liberia*, 53.
53. Secretary of State to the French Minister, Roustan, 22 August 1884, cited in ibid., 54–55.
54. Smyth to John Davis, Assistant Secretary of State, 13 June 1883, no. 32, U.S. Ministers to Liberia, roll 9.
55. Ibid.
56. Ibid.
57. Smyth to Secretary of State, 29 January 1885, no. 108.
58. Ibid.
59. Ibid.
60. Ibid.
61. Smyth to Secretary of State, 7 December 1885, no. 149, roll 10.
62. Smyth to Secretary of State Thomas F. Bayard, 17 December 1885, no. 150. During a touching farewell visit made to the Liberian president, Minister Smyth declared:

In view of the uniformly cordial, friendly and pleasant relations that have almost uninterruptedly, existed between your two immediate predecessors in the high office of President of this Republic and their ministry and myself; and between your Excellency and cabinet and myself; I give expression to a simple fact, when I beg to assure Your Excellency that, contending and alternate emotions of pleasure and pain pass [through] me at this time. The prospect of returning to the country which cradled my infancy, fostered my youth, and sustained and honored my manhood, and to the association of my nearest and best friends, cannot but be full with anticipations of pleasure; the conscious severance of the pleasant relations which have subsisted with Your Excellency and co-adjutors whose labor and efforts have been so praiseworthy in your day and opportunity in the aid given your guidance of this ship of state, demonstrating, as far as you have been able to do, the capacity of the Negro race to govern itself, and to civilize the heathen in this, the home of our race, gives a poignancy to separation which is akin to pain. . . .

It may not be improper for me to say Excellency that, I feel grateful to my country that circumstances so conspired as to have brought me in the relation I so recently bore, for a period of seven years, to Your Excellency's Government and people, which gave me an opportunity to know this and other portions of our common fatherland which knowledge dearly cherished, has increased, intensified, and elevated my self respect, and confirmed my race loyalty,—as no other position however superior in grade or emolument, at home or abroad, which my generous country could have conferred—could have done. . . .

May your country be always blessed with prosperity, and may blessed influences of civilization radiating from here fill with Christian light a continent. May your State never be subject to a foreign race, and may your sons and daughters never be diseased with indifference or disloyalty to the prejudice of your country's best interests; and may Africa's children and their descendants in other lands practically sympathize and aid the work of civilization so happily begun and being so well carried on here, at times, mid adverse environment and internal embarrassments.

In response to this oration, the President of Liberia declared:

It is with mingled feelings of pleasure and regret that I have today to bid good-bye to you in your official capacity. It is pleasing to me, to reflect that our relations, both officially during my incumbency in office, and unofficially previous to my coming into power, have been such as will leave behind a record of friendship and confidence. I experience regret because, regarding the situation more in the aspect of race, than of international interests, and considering the wealth of men possessed by your greater Republic and the poverty in that respect of our infant nation, the moment is not opportune for you to cast in your lot with a people whose greatest need is men.

I am aware that in this remark I am digressing from the purely diplomatic line, but it must be admitted, that the actual situation of the two governments and countries in respect to each other has been peculiar from the beginning; and I trust that this will furnish sufficient justification for this digression.

Regarding the first principle of diplomatic intercourse which requires the representative of a foreign power to be on the best terms of friendship with the Government and people of the country to which he is sent, I am pleased to bear record of the fact, that your relations with the government and people of the Republic have been of the most cordial and friendly sort.

I cannot forget how earnestly you have labored to elicit for us the sympathies of your Government in the difficult and vexed questions that we have been striving to solve for the past seven years, in some instances taking the initiative in bringing to the notice of your Government questions of vital importance to the Republic.

The study you have made of the race in their own fatherland, and the inferences you have no doubt drawn of the potentialities of the people and the country, will render you but the more efficient advocate of the cause of Liberia and Africa. . . .

You bear with you our best wishes for your welfare and prosperity. I say "non pas adieu, mais, au revoir," or, in other words, while today I bid you "good bye" in your official, diplomatic capacity, it is with the hope, that in the near future, we may meet again on the soil of our beloved fatherland, in some other, but still important, relations.

63. Edward Younger, *John A. Kasson, Politics and Diplomacy From Lincoln to McKinley* (Iowa City: State Society of Iowa, 1955), 336–39.
64. Thomas F. Bayard, Secretary of State, to Mr. McLane, American Minister to France, 13 January 1886, no. 67, *Foreign Relations of the United States, 1886,* 298; Bayard to McLane, 12 July 1886, no. 142, ibid., 304.
65. *African Repository* 62 (October 1885): 127–28.
66. At the end of the Civil War he worked as a porter in Pittsburgh and later attended Avery College in Allegheny City, Pennsylvania. He matriculated at Lincoln University where he graduated as valedictorian of his class. In 1877 Hopkins became the first black graduate of Auburn Theological Seminary, after which he went to Baltimore as an evangelist. He then became pastor of the Presbyterian Church at Franklinton, North Carolina, and served as principal of its Colored Normal School (James A. Padgett, "Ministers to Liberia and Their Diplomacy," *Journal of Negro History* 22 [January 1937]: 74; Jake C. Miller, *The Black Presence in American Foreign Affairs* [Washington, D.C.: University Press of America, 1978], 292).
67. Bayard to McLane, 13 January 1886, no. 67, *Foreign Relations, 1886,* 298.
68. Hopkins to Department of State, 18 March 1886, no. 12, U.S. Ministers to Liberia, roll 10.
69. Bayard to McLane, 16 July 1886, no. 142, *Foreign Relations, 1886,* 304.
70. *African Repository,* Memorial of the American Colonization Society to the Senate and House of Representatives of the United States, 62 (April 1886): 65–67.
71. Ibid. 62 (October 1886): 131–32.
72. Annual Message, President Cleveland, 6 December 1886, *Foreign Relations, 1886,* vii.
73. Bayard to McLane, 22 March 1887, no. 386, *Foreign Relations of the United State, 1887,* 291.
74. *National Cyclopaedia of American Biography* (New York: James T. White, 1904), 12:113, 5:551. Determined to advance in the world, he ran away to Georgia at the age of twelve, changed his name, did odd jobs, and graduated from the University of Michigan with a law degree in 1874.
75. Edward Wilmot Blyden to William Coppinger, 6 June 1887, in Lynch, *Letters of Edward Wilmot Blyden,* 373. Blyden's letter to Coppinger needs to be quoted at length to elucidate the racial issues involved. There are indications that Smyth was a philanderer, and for Captain Lewis to prefer him to Taylor was not complimentary to the new minister. Blyden wrote:

    Captain Lewis says, that besides telling him of his great intimacy with President [Grover] Cleveland and [U.S. Secretary of State, Thomas A.] Bayard, he referred to his Caucasian antecedents—to the blood of some great white man in his veins. He did not refer to this in my presence but I could see that he was full of the idea that Liberia would be honored by his residence in it.

    You know me well enough and the history of the work in this country to know when I say I deeply regret that to such a man should have been entrusted such great interests, that it is no mere sentimental grievance.

    The only colored men now who represent the United States abroad are mulattoes. This is very sad, considering the large population of Negroes in that country. Of course this result must have been brought about by the conditions of politics which alone influence politicians who have the appointments largely in their hands.

    Let us pray, however, and hope that God who has the hearts of all men in his hands may use Mr. Taylor for the good of Africa. I am sure He will do this ultimately, but I mean that He may spare us the inconvenience and care, which sometimes comes from His permitting the folly of men to prevail for a time.

76. Charles Taylor to Department of State, 7 June 1887, no. 8, U.S. Ministers to Liberia, roll 10.
77. Taylor to Department of State, 8 June 1887, no. 10.
78. Ibid.
79. Ibid.
80. Ibid.
81. Ibid.
82. Ibid.
83. Ibid.
84. Ibid.
85. Ibid. In Taylor's opinion, one of his predecessors had "conducted himself in such a manner, that I am sure that the most exemplary life passed here by a minister of the United States for the next sixteen (16) years would not remove the stain left. I need only say that there are two children here, who claim that one of my predecessors caused their coming into this world."
86. Ibid.
87. Ibid.
88. Taylor to Bayard, 13 June 1887, no. 13.
89. Ibid.
90. Taylor to Bayard, 14 June 1887, no. 14.
91. Taylor to Bayard, 15 June 1887, no. 15.
92. Ibid.
93. Taylor to Department of State, 5 July 1887, no. 17.
94. Secretary of State to Taylor, 29 July 1887, no. 8, in reference to no. 10.
95. Taylor to Grover Cleveland, President, [received 11 November 1887].
96. Ibid.
97. *National Cyclopaedia of American Biography* 5:551.
98. For appointment of Price, see *African Repository* 64 (July 1888): 95.
99. Lynch, *Letters of Edward Wilmot Blyden*, 384. One of the reasons the American Colonization Society recommended Price for the position in Liberia was his strong support of that organization's program. Price spoke at an Emancipation Day celebration at Columbia, South Carolina, on 3 January 1888 on the subject, "The American Negro, His Future and His Peculiar Work." The *African Repository* reported that Price's

advice to his race was to pay less attention to the past and look to the glorious future. He said the Negroes had the mind and ability; all they needed was confidence. The Negro could do what any other man could. He was opposed to amalgamation, and he did not believe in it. The peculiar work of the American Negro was the redemption of their race in Africa, which was their own country. If the white man could find gold, diamonds, and other riches in Africa, why not the Negro? *It was the duty of the American Negro to go to Africa and reclaim their country, civilize* the Negroes there, give them manual and intellectual education, and show them the way to build up the country. The speaker was a well-educated man. (*African Repository* 64 [July 1888]: 99)

100. See appointment letter of Price in *African Repository* 64 (July 1888): 95.
101. *African Repository* 65 (April 1889): 60–61.
102. *Register of the Department of State, 1888,* 183; James A. Padgett, "Ministers to Liberia," 75.

103. Ezekiel Smith to Department of State (Private), 10 August 1888, U.S. Ministers to Liberia, roll 10.
104. Ibid.
105. Ibid.
106. Ibid.
107. Smith to Department of State, 28 September 1888, no. 14.
108. *African Repository* 65 (April 1889): 60–61.
109. Ibid.
110. Smith to Department of State, 22 April 1889, no. 30, and 7 May 1889, no. 32, U.S. Ministers to Liberia, roll 10.
111. Smith to Department of State, 3 May 1890, no. 51.
112. Ibid.
113. *African Repository* 66 (October 1890): 127.
114. James Robert Spurgeon, Chargé at Monrovia, to Department of State, 18 April 1888, no. 81, Subject, "Adhesion of Liberia to Act of June 8, 1899," *Foreign Relations of the United States, 1892,* 166–67; and Mr. Blaine, Secretary of State to Mr. Coolidge, American Minister to France, 4 June 1892, ibid.
115. Ibid.
116. Padgett, "Ministers to Liberia," 77–78.
117. Clark to Assistant Secretary of State, William P. Wharton, 18 November 1890, no. 1, U.S. Ministers to Liberia, roll 10.
118. Ibid.
119. Chargé d'Affaires in Monrovia to Wharton, 1 April 1891, no. 16.
120. Liberian letters uncataloged, King to Coppinger, Monrovia, 31 July 1891, and Blaine to Coolidge, 4 June 1892, *Foreign Relations, 1892,* 166–67.
121. Blaine to Coolidge, *Foreign Relations, 1892,* 166–67.
122. Ibid.
123. Edwin S. Redkey, *Black Exodus: Black Nationalist and Back-to-Africa Movements, 1890–1910* (New Haven: Yale University Press, 1969), 43.
124. Turner to *Christian Recorder,* 22 February 1883 and editorial in ibid., quoted in Redkey, *Black Exodus,* 31–34.
125. Ibid., 34.
126. Ibid.
127. Ibid., 36.
128. Ibid., 43–46, based on Turner's letters in *A.M.E. Church Review* 8 (April 1892): 446–98.
129. Ibid., 45.
130. Ibid., 45–46.
131. Ibid.
132. Padgett, "Ministers to Liberia," 78. Born of free parents in Cambridge City, Indiana, on 14 November 1853, McCoy was taken to Boston, Massachusetts, while a child and was educated in its public schools. He returned to Indianapolis, Indiana, after his training and served as principal of a colored school for twelve years until appointed to the Monrovia post.
133. *National Cyclopaedia of American Biography* 14:58 states incorrectly that McCoy was unmarried.
134. McCoy to Blaine, 28 February 1893, no. 56, U.S. Ministers to Liberia, roll 11.
135. Ibid.
136. Ibid.
137. McCoy to Secretary of State, John W. Foster, 20 September 1892, no. 36.
138. Foster to Mr. Lincoln, American Minister to Great Britain, 12 July 1892, no. 806, *Foreign Relations, 1892,* 229.

139. Annual Message of 6 December 1892, of President Harrison, ibid., xiv.
140. Foster to McCoy, 16 January 1893, no. 19, U.S. Ministers to Liberia, roll 11.
141. Ibid.
142. McCoy to Foster, 1 February 1893, no. 52. McCoy wrote:

> That section is known as the "Grain Coast" and the commercial importance of
> Cape Palmas depends largely upon the trade between the two places.
>   Under the "Hinterland Doctrine" Liberia has been claiming interior terri-
> tory as far as the Niger River but the treaty retreats the claim . . .
>   It is rather unfortunate that Baron de Stein [a Belgian citizen serving as
> Liberia's Consul in Brussels] was appointed to cope single handed with Com-
> missioners thoroughly posted in details and in their own citadel, yet it will be
> still more unfortunate for Liberia when the Treaty is ratified. I think, how-
> ever, that it will be done for most of the officials think that is the best they can
> do.

143. Ibid.
144. Gibson to McCoy, 10 March 1893, no. 123.
145. Ibid.
146. Gibson to McCoy, 24 October 1893, no. 99.
147. McCoy to Gibson, 27 April 1893, no. 70.
148. McCoy to Department of State, 20 July 1893, no. 90.
149. McCoy to Gibson, 15 April 1893, no. 66.
150. McCoy to Gibson, 22 April 1893, no. 67.
151. McCoy to Foster, 24 October 1892, no. 39.
152. Ibid. McCoy was interred at Palm Grove cemetery near the grave of Henry
    Highland Garnet. Members of the Liberian government, the diplomatic corps,
    and the Masonic Order attended the ceremony. Later on his widow requested
    that his remains be disinterred and shipped back to Indianapolis, Indiana
    (Chargé d'Affaires at Monrovia to Department of State).
153. Redkey, *Black Exodus,* 180.
154. Ibid., 180ff.
155. Ibid.

Pan-African Initiatives

The colored man who will stand up and in one breath say that the Negroid race does not want social equality and in the next predict a great future in the face of all the proscription of which the colored man is the victim, is either an ignoramus, or is an advocate of the perpetual servility and degradation of his race variety. . . . I believe that two or three millions of us should return to the land of our ancestors, and establish our own nation, civilization, laws, customs, style of manufacture, and not only give the world, like other race varieties, the benefit of our individuality, but build up social conditions peculiarly our own, and cease to be grumblers, chronic complainers and a menace to the white man's country or the country he claims and is bound to dominate.[1]

This Congress will have a large, practical tendency. It has definite aims in view. . . . One of the vital and urgent problems before us is the relation of the American Negro to the civilization and redemption of his Fatherland. God's hand must be recognized in his presence in America. This is now the home and heritage of these American[s] born of the colored race. Here he will stay. . . . But Africa now needs the best brain, and the best heart, the finest moral fiber, and the most skilled genius and power that the American Negro can furnish for her civilization and redemption.[2]

The triumph of European peoples in the global system at the end of the nineteenth century forced African Americans to rely primarily on symbolic acts and structures to articulate their interests in Africa, in the hope that these would come to the attention of white Americans. The Berlin West African Conference of 1884–85 had legitimized the conquest and colonization of the African continent. The United States of America had launched its own imperial thrust into Asia, Latin America, and the islands of the seas. European peoples bestrode the world like giants, viewing the conquered people with a mixture of scorn and pity.

The American voice that epitomized his country's attitude was that of Theodore Roosevelt, a firm believer in the "white man's burden." Roo-

151

sevelt held that the black race was inferior to the white, whether for physiological or environmental reasons, or a combination of the two. He was in favor of European imperialism or colonialism. In his book *Winning of the West*,[3] he rationalized the defeat of Native Americans on the grounds that they, like the inhabitants of the Philippines, China, India and Africa were "backward" peoples. As far as he was concerned, it made no difference that the land was often taken as a result of "primeval warfare . . . where no pity is shown to non-combatants, where the weak are harried without ruth, and the vanquished maltreated with merciless ferocity."[4] Roosevelt felt that "the most ultimately righteous of all wars is a war with savages, though it is apt to be also the most terrible and inhuman. The rude, fierce settler who drives the savage from the land lays all civilized mankind under debt to him. American and Indian, Boer and Zulu, Cossack and Tartar, New Zealander and Maori—in each case the victor, horrible though many of his deeds are, has laid deep the foundations for the future greatness of a mighty people."[5] Persons with such attitudes could only view with amusement or disguised contempt their minions' call for exodus, their presentations of petition and prayers, and their engagement in other such symbolic activities in the effort to secure relief for themselves and others.

In keeping with this global trend, the domestic mood of the United States was "white solidarity" and "farewell to the bloody shirt" of the Civil War. In his inaugural address in March 1896, President William McKinley had promised "to do nothing, and permit nothing to be done, that will arrest or disturb this growing sentiment of unity and cooperation, this revival of esteem and affiliation which now animates so many thousands in both the old antagonistic sections, but I shall cheerfully do everything possible to promote and increase it."[6] McKinley would tolerate in 1898 the bloody pogrom of Wilmington, North Carolina, and the institution of the grandfather clause in Oklahoma, and in 1900 the disenfranchisement of blacks in North Carolina. Congress would treat with contempt the attempt of the last surviving black congressional representative of the Reconstruction, North Carolina's George H. White, to introduce a bill making the lynching of an American citizen a federal crime. Nor did it take seriously White's farewell address to the Congress of the United States on 29 January 1901 in which he declared, "This, Mr. Chairman, is perhaps the Negroes' temporary farewell to the American Congress; but let me say, Phoenix-like he will rise up some day and come again. These parting words are in behalf of an outraged, heart-broken, bruised and bleeding, but God-fearing people, faithful, industrious, loyal, rising people—full of potential force."[7] Apologizing for his "earnestness," White beseeched Congress to understand that he was "pleading for the life, the liberty, the future happiness, and manhood suffrage for one-eighth of the entire population of the United States."[8]

Largely bereft of all but symbolic power, African Americans took two opposing but dialectically related positions: to agitate and pray for their own salvation and that of Africa, and to compromise with the power of whites for the same ends. Three African American leaders would dominate this period and would chart guidelines for the foreign policy initiatives for generations of their successors. The fully established Bishop Henry McNeal Turner, a fiery nationalist-missionary and emigrationist, would be suspicious of and would hold in disdain the principal of Tuskegee Institute, Booker T. Washington, a purported accommodationist. Washington would concentrate his energy in dealing with the issues of blacks within the United States. He would help but would be held in contempt by the still younger W. E. B. Du Bois, who saw the plight of African peoples in a global perspective. But whether competing or cooperating to help black peoples, these three shared the burden of powerlessness.

Significantly, it was at the Columbian Exposition at Chicago in October 1893, a panegyric to America's growing power, that Bishop Turner of the AME Church launched his crusade on behalf of African peoples. In a weeklong "Congress on Africa," over a hundred persons (explorers, travelers, missionaries, scientists, and sociologists), including the aging Frederick Douglass, read papers and gave speeches on Africa. Turner trumpeted the need for blacks to take a greater interest in Africa. Announcing that the first man, Adam, was black and that African Americans had a special obligation to their kinsmen across the seas, Turner shocked whites and hoped that blacks would rally to his cause.[9] He won the support of a few black leaders such as Bishop William H. Heard (a future minister to Liberia).

There were, however, dissenting voices. Secretary to the Congress Frederick P. Noble remarked that had Turner's "audience been southern negroes, he could have carried his point; but these negroes [at the Congress] belong to the best classes . . . and show no signs of race duty."[10] Nevertheless, Noble was convinced that with more information about Africa and increasing racial violence, more influential black leaders would favor emigration to Africa and there build the black nationality that he believed would ameliorate the condition of black people everywhere. Turner issued a call for a national convention of African Americans in

Cincinnati for November 1893. He appealed to the "friends of African repatriation or Negro nationalization elsewhere, to assemble and adopt such measures for our future actions as may commend themselves to our better judgement."[11] The call of the convention would have "no application to party politics or to the stay-here portion of our race."[12] What such persons chose to do or not to do was immaterial to Turner, whose overriding concern was that "at the present rate [the African American's] extermination is only a question of time."[13]

Much to Turner's delight, over three hundred "responsible Negroes" from all over the nation indicated that they would attend the convention, and a widely read black newspaper, the Indianapolis *Freeman*, reported that the Turner convention would be a timely and important gathering. But the editor of the *Freeman* confessed that he was anti-emigrationist himself and that he hoped the convention would give emigrationism its "death blow." The editor also polled important black leaders on the prospects of the convention. Of the thirty-nine respondents only two allegedly supported emigration. Fifteen persons (among whom were such highly respected leaders as Ida B. Wells, P. B. S. Pinchback, John M. Langston, Bishop Alexander Walters, and Frederick Douglass), while opposing a mass exodus of African Americans, felt that educated and skilled individuals should go to Africa. Frederick Douglass's reply to the *Freeman* epitomized the attitude of this group. He wrote, "Every friend of the race will rejoice that Bishop Turner has bravely called his convention. . . . Nevertheless I do not believe in any wholesale plan of colonization to Africa. Emigration? Yes. Exodus? No."[14] Twenty-two persons, representing the overwhelming majority of those responding, rejected emigration to Africa or to anywhere else. Yet they indicated a deep concern for the plight of black people, and they felt that everything should be done to halt the lynching of blacks and to protect their declining civil rights.

One of the most interesting of the negative replies came from a then relatively unknown Dr. Booker T. Washington of Tuskegee, who was not in favor of the convention and who disparaged emigrationism. Washington felt that "if those who compose the Turner Convention shall show themselves able to hide themselves behind a great cause, it will succeed; otherwise, [it would] fail. Men cannot exhibit themselves and do the best thing for a great cause at the same time."[15] As far as emigration was concerned Washington declared, "This talk of any appreciable number of our people going to Africa is the merest nonsense, and it is surprising that it has engaged the attention of serious minded people for a minute."[16] He was convinced that it "does no good, but on the other hand does a great deal of harm among the more ignorant of our people, especially in the far South, where some are led to feel that there is a power in the government or somewhere that can move them to Africa or to the West as it sees fit . . ."[17] Writing afterward, some of the naysayers would accuse Turner of speaking "of the United States as Hades and of Africa as Eden; yet even he still holds his residence in Hades, only paying Eden a brief visit once a year."[18] For his part, Turner considered some of his detractors as reactionary at worst, accommodationist at best. He asserted that they would rather serve in hell than reign in heaven. He ignored the views expressed in the newspapers and proceeded with his convention.

Delighted that some eight hundred delegates had shown up to join the throng of local blacks, Turner was eloquent about the need for blacks to leave the United States and build their own nationality. Yet he was realistic enough to gauge the temper of the delegates and to take it into consideration. Confessing that he had seen too much of American prejudice to have any hope of a solution to the race issue except through emigration, the bishop felt that no amount of education could help unless a person could say, "I am somebody, that I am a man much as anybody else, that I have rights, that I am the creature of law and order, that I am entitled to respect, that every avenue to distinction is mine. For where this consciousness does not form the substream of any people, ultimate degradation will be the result." If America was to be the home of the Negro, then "the Negro must be a self-controlling, automatic factor of the body politic or collective life of the nation. In other words, we must be full-fledged men."[19]

The participants at the convention were reportedly enthusiastic, and to the surprise of none, the committee on emigration, chaired by Professor William H. Council, an Afrophile and president of Alabama Normal Institute, and including the bishop's son, John T. Turner, recommended emigration:

> We fail to find in any part of the United States, outside the colored man himself, any considerable influence which encourages African genius and progress. . . . The oppressed of all ages have had recourse to revolution or emigration. . . . To adopt the former is to court utter extermination. The latter may bring relief. . . . We recommend the colored people of the United States to turn their attention to the civilization of Africa as the only hope of the Negro race as a race.[20]

This recommendation was viciously attacked by none other than Charles H. J. Taylor, who had been so disappointed with his tenure as United States minister to Liberia in 1887. Sensing a defeat for the recommendation Turner returned the report to the committee, postponed its discussion on several occasions, and finally disposed of it by accepting a compromise. This urged the executive committee of the convention to study conditions among blacks all over the nation in order to recommend emigration from sections where racism was most virulent. This motion passed unanimously, but a disappointed Turner was determined to use all the power at his command to pursue emigrationism.[21]

At the root of Turner's determination was his refusal to accept the basic commitment of most African Americans to the United States. Returning to Atlanta from Cincinnati, he mused, "What under heaven would [I] want with a national convention of over seven hundred delegates to endorse African emigration, when at least two million of colored people here in the South are ready to start to Africa at any moment, if we had a line of steamers running to and fro."[22] The growing reality, however, was that despite the increase in prejudice, discrimination, and especially lynching, most African Americans, aware of their powerlessness, were apparently prepared to listen to black voices urging moderation. The voice they heard would urge accommodation with white domination, if only as a tactic, to deal with white power.

Booker T. Washington had not only rejected Turner's invitation to the Chicago convention but had also long been on record as opposing emigration from the United States as a solution to the problem of blacks in the United States. In one of his early public speeches (given before the National Education Association on 16 July 1884 at Madison, Wisconsin), Washington said that "in spite of all talks of exodus, the Negro's home is permanently in the South."[23] He would use variations on this theme when he was chosen to speak for the "Negro race" at the Cotton State and International Exposition at Atlanta, Georgia, in September 1895. This speech, later derisively called the Atlanta Compromise, would determine for a generation how blacks would attempt to deal with the power of European peoples, not only in the United States of America but also in Africa.

Caught between the emigrationists and those who wished to ameliorate the plight of blacks at home, Washington chose to side with the latter. His Atlanta address would later be viewed even by his detractors as "one of the most effective pieces of political oratory in the history of the United States."[24] He realized that the weight of history would be upon his shoulders when he spoke to an audience in which there would be the elite of southern society (former slave holders), in which northern liberals would be seated, and where there would be black folk. And while he was determined to say nothing that was not "true and right," he was also determined to say nothing that would give undue offense to the South and prevent it from thus honoring another Negro in the future. He was equally determined to be "true to the North" and to the interests of his own race.[25] This was a tall order and would turn out to be the black man's version of the white compromise that ended Reconstruction.[26]

In his well-known phrases Washington stated that in America's domestic affairs, the "wisest among my race understand that the agitation of questions of social equality is the extremest folly" and that in "all things that are purely social we can be as separate as the fingers, yet one hand in all things essential to mutual progress." He lamented that "in the great leap from slavery to freedom we may overlook the fact that the masses of us are to live by the productions of our hands, and fail to keep in mind that we shall prosper in proportion as we learn to dignify and glorify common labor, and put brains and skill into the common occupations of life; shall prosper in proportion as we learn to draw the line between the superficial and the substantial."[27]

Washington suggested that given the ignorance and inexperience of blacks coming out of slavery, "it is not strange that in the first years of our new life we began at the top instead of at the bottom; that a seat in Congress or the state legislature was more sought than real estate or industrial skill; that the political convention or stump speaking had more attractions than starting a dairy farm or truck garden."[28] With white help he believed he could change these things. Washington felt that the South could not do without the help of one-third of its population. Then in an effort to appease the southerners, he suggested that blacks held toward whites "a devotion that no foreigner can approach, ready to lay down our lives, if need be, in defense of yours, interlacing our industrial, commercial, civil, and religious life with yours in a way that shall make the interests of both races one."[29]

In return for this, Washington insisted that it was "important and right that all privileges of the law be ours, but it is vastly more important that we be prepared for the exercises of these privileges." He hoped that the time would come when there would be a "blotting out of sectional differences and racial animosities and suspicions, in a determination to administer absolute justice, in a willing obedience among all classes to the mandates of law." To emigrationists such as Henry McNeal Turner, Washington had this to say: "To those of my race who depend on bettering their condition in a foreign land or who underestimate the importance of cultivating friendly relations with the Southern white man, who is their next-door neighbor, I would say: 'Cast down your bucket where you are'—cast it down in making friends in every manly way of the people of all races by whom we are surrounded."[30]

Washington's address took the country by storm. It drew the praise of whites from the president on down, catapulted him into the role of a black leader, and even impressed his detractors. President Grover Cleveland regarded the speech as one whose "words cannot fail to delight and encourage all who wish well for your race; and if our colored fellow-citizens do not from your utterances gather new hope, and form new determinations to gain every valuable advantage offered them by their citizenship, it will be strange indeed."[31] The editor of the Atlanta *Constitution* wrote to a New York paper stating, "I do not exaggerate when I say that Professor Booker T. Washington's address yesterday was one of the most notable speeches, both as to character and as to the warmth of its reception, ever delivered to a Southern audience." The address, he said, was a revelation, "a platform upon which blacks and whites can stand with full justice to each other."[32] Probably taking their cue from the white elite, the black elite all over the world initially warmly welcomed Washington's speech. Francis James Grimké wrote, "It is a great satisfaction to us all to know that you had the opportunity of speaking on so important an occasion, and that you acquitted yourself so nobly. I am greatly delighted with the extracts from your address that I have seen."[33] William J. Cansler, a black educator in Knoxville, Tennessee, wrote saying, "You are our Moses destined to lead our race out of the difficulties and dangers which beset our pathway and surround us on all sides. . . . Upon you has fallen the mantle of the illustrious Douglas[s], to you we accord the title as leader, all intelligent and thinking colored men will follow."[34] From Wilberforce College one young professor, Dr. William Edward Burghardt Du Bois, wrote, "Let me heartily congratulate you upon your phenomenal success at Atlanta—it was a word fitly spoken."[35]

Edward Wilmot Blyden of Liberia and Sierra Leone wrote to Washington stating that he was sure that Providence had made of him "the instrument of such a message to the whites and blacks of this country at the present times." He assured Washington, "Your address was an inspiration. It will go down to posterity with such documents as [President] Washington's Farewell Address." The irascible Blyden could not refrain from adding, "I am particularly pleased that you did not introduce the word 'Afro-American,' as a descriptive of the race in so important and dignified a public document. That word excludes in discussing race questions, the whole of the people of the Fatherland. It excludes me." Blyden felt that the concept "Afro-American" limited all views and discussions of the race question. It was "narrow and provincial and not a statesmanlike word. I am glad to see that Southern leaders of the race, as a rule, ignore that word."[36]

Henry McNeal Turner could not ignore Washington's speech. He sarcastically noted that the "great professor" had judged it "prudent and discreet to pass by those phases of [America's] barbarous civilization, as well as the efforts being made to disfranchise the Negro in some of the states." The bishop felt that Washington and his audience should have recognized that many blacks knew "national sociology enough to know that social equality carries with it civil equality, political equality, financial equality, judicial equality, business equality, and whatever social equality is denied by legislative enactments and judicial decrees, the sequel must be discrimination, proscription, injustice, and degradation." Turner was concerned that if Washington meant that any enactment of laws favoring equal rights for blacks was "artificial forcing," then he feared that the Tuskegean was implying that blacks were not prepared to exercise "all the privileges enjoyed by whites," and further implying that they were "not prepared for freedom . . . [or] for citizenship." Claiming to have respect for the principal of Tuskegee, Turner concluded that Washington "will have to live a long time to undo the harm he has done our race."[37]

The negative stereotypical depiction of Africa and of Africans during the Atlanta exposition at which Washington spoke convinced Turner that this emerging black leader was playing into the hands of the detractors of the race. The bishop had been asked to contribute artifacts to a pavilion honoring the "New Negro," but to his chagrin the samples of iron-work, leather and cloth goods, vegetable products, and a copy of a silk quilt made for Queen Victoria by a Liberian woman, were placed in a small corner labeled "uncivilized Africa." Not too far away was an exhibit titled "Dahomey Village," in front of which stood "a big-nosed white man urging the visitors to not miss seeing the wild cannibals from the west coast of Africa." The sight of this insult to Africa was too much for Bishop Turner. He turned on the white barker and exclaimed, "Why do you white men pursue the negro to Africa with your lying? You have for years lied about the negro in this country, and now, when you are being found out, you are lying about the negro at home on his native heath."[38]

The reporter for the Chicago *Inter Ocean* who later described the heated exchange between the bishop and the showman said that the "crowd shouted, the showman looked stupefied, and the bishop walked on down the Midway, telling me that there was no new negro. He was simply the same old negro, showing his capacity as he was given opportunity by the new white man; and I am not sure that he is wrong." The reporter commented that Washington and Turner were not very far apart, "except on the question as to where the Negro is to work out his own salvation. Washington insists that by applying the industry and capacity that made the Negro valuable in slavery to the new condition of freedom the Negro can do the work and become independent here in America. Bishop Turner wants the Negro to go to Africa and apply these new conditions in a new country."[39]

The relationship between Africa and African Americans was the theme of a Congress on Africa held 13–15 December 1895 under the auspices of the Stewart Missionary Foundation for Africa of the Gammon Theological Seminary in connection with the Cotton States and International Exposition. For many years previously, the Stewart Foundation had offered prizes "to encourage thought and investigation, spread intelligence and stimulate personal and property consecration among the American Negroes for missionary work in Africa."[40] The conveners of the congress invited to Atlanta such Africa specialists as Edward Wilmot Blyden, Alexander Crummell, T. Thomas Fortune, John H. Smyth (ex-minister to Liberia) and Bishop Henry McNeal Turner. Both President Thirkield of the Stewart Foundation and Professor Bowen of Gammon Seminary knew Booker T. Washington and had corresponded with him concerning the Atlanta address and other matters. There is, however, no evidence that they invited him to the congress.

Bishop Turner must certainly have felt some vindication when Thirkield declared in his welcoming address, "This . . . Congress indicates that God is stretching forth his hands to Ethiopia—to that 'Dark Continent' which, through long and dolorous ages, has been vainly stretching forth its hand unto God." Thirkield asserted that after the curse of the *"stealing of Africans from Africa,"* the European nations were now engaged in the effort to *"steal Africa from the Africans."* In the face of this situation, he believed that "one of the vital and urgent problems before us is the relation of the American Negro to the civilization and redemption of his Fatherland." There was now no question that America was the home and heritage of blacks born there. They were there to stay, and it made no sense for the weak and poor among them to go to Africa because they would only relapse into barbarism. "But," he concluded, "Africa now needs the best brain, and the best heart, the finest moral fiber, and the most skilled genius and power that the American Negro can furnish for her civilization and redemption."[41]

Papers presented at the conference included sketches of traditional life in Africa, the slave trade, health conditions in central Africa, the languages of Africa, missionary successes and failures in Africa, and the position of the African American in America. There were remarkable papers by Smyth and Turner on the African American and Africa. Crummell (who had long served as a missionary in Liberia) spoke on "Civilization as a Collateral and Indispensable Instrumentality in Planting the Christian Church in Africa." He stressed that Christianity alone was not enough for the heathen "man-child" of Africa. Civilization was also necessary if the African was to make any progress. For the African, this would mean that "all the childishness of inheritance is gradually to be taken out of his brain, and all the barbarism of ages to be eliminated from his constitution."[42] Interestingly, the Crummell who in years gone by had castigated African American students for ignoring their responsibilities to Africa now said not one word about the African American and Africa. One observer concluded that now that Crummell had become a "staid Episcopal priest in Washington," he had retreated from emigrationism and considered emigrationists such as Turner to be "turbulent, screeching and screaming creature[s]."[43]

Bishop Turner used his essay, "The American Negro and the Fatherland," to reemphasize his emigrationist sentiments and to attack Booker T. Washington. He declared, "The heathen African, to my certain knowledge, I care not what others may say, eagerly yearn for that civilization which they believe will elevate them and make them potential for good." Using a theme developed by the black historian, Colonel George Washington Williams, Turner challenged the view that whites stole ordinary blacks from Africa. He insisted that the bulk of blacks brought to America were the children of hereditary slaves and that these were destined to remain in slavery until they could learn about God. Now that blacks were free long enough to begin to think for themselves, he added, they ought to realize that *"there is no manhood future in the United States for the Negro* [his emphasis]." Turner insisted that the chasm between blacks and whites was such that there could not be social contact between them. He believed that Senator John Tyler Morgan of Alabama told the truth when he declared that the "Negroid race" could expect nothing without social equality, but that whites would never grant it.[44]

John H. Smyth, profiting from having served as United States minister to the Republic of Liberia, addressed the subject, "The African in Africa and the African in America." He lamented that having been made citizens of America because of the Civil War, blacks in America

> as a class . . . are averse to the discussion of Africa, when their relationship with that ancient and mysterious land and its races is made the subject of discourse or reflection. The remoteness of Africa from America may be the reason for such feeling; the current opinions in the minds of the Caucasians, whence the American Negroes' opinions are derived, that the African is by nature an inferior man, may be a reason. The illiteracy, poverty, and degradation of the Negro, pure and simple, as known in Christian lands, may be a reason in connection with the partially true and partially false impression that the Negroes, or Africans, are pagan and heathen as a whole, and as a sequence hopelessly degraded beings. These may be some of the reasons that make the subject of Africa discordant and unmusical to our ears. It is amid such embarrassments that the lecturer, the orator, the missionary must present Africa to the Negro in Christian America.[45]

Somewhat like Turner, Smyth was very concerned about the spate of articles critical of Liberia and emigrationism by "men of African descent of prominence, and by men of like prominence of uncertain descent [Booker T. Washington?], and by men of other races than the Negro." He felt it was his duty as an American citizen, and a Negro, to vindicate those who were maligned. Smyth felt that it was important to understand that most of the emigrants to Liberia were from the South, with the result that the civilization they developed in that country bore a certain likeness to the southern United States. Therefore, the Liberians needed to assimilate "the sentiment of liberty and rule, the general heritage and possession of the native African." Nevertheless, he insisted that the Liberians had built an educational system and the only democratic republican form of government on the continent of Africa. They did this, he noted, despite the heritage of slavery, which robbed them of their best racial peculiarities and characteristics. Smyth conceded that Caucasians might not like his views, but he felt that "the Negro who has grown up to manhood under their alien Christian civilization, alien to the Negro and [in many respects] to Christ, is in his virtues as vices more Caucasian than African." He felt that the civilized Negro in America, while still a Negro African, was without the peculiarities of that race because he was thoroughly Americanized. The result, according to Smyth, was that the African American was unable to understand himself and was now convinced that because of the interracial nature of the United States, "his end must be reached by pursuit of the same line followed by the controlling races."[46]

Reviewing at length the history of contact between foreigners and Africans on the continent, Smyth felt that contemporary Christians were not alone in having made mistakes in attempting to Christianize the African. He despaired of any attempt to Christianize the African if that meant subverting African humanity. In Smyth's view, the African "may be forced to accept a dogma or a religion, but will not receive either under such circumstances. Alien races can aid the progress of Christianity and civilization among Africans, but cannot control it with hope of ultimate success in Africa." In view of these differences between the reaction of Africans in America, and of Africans in Africa to Western civilization and to Christianity, Smyth wondered whether the African in America should feel that defending his Africanness "would be injurious to the best interest of the American nation"? Smyth thought not:

> I would gladly impress upon persons entertaining such thoughts, that race allegiance is compatible with patriotism, with love of the land that gave us birth . . . Though we are a part of this great national whole, we are a distinct and separate part, an alien part racially, and destined to be so by the immutable law of race pride, which is possessed by our white fellow-citizens, if not by us. The sentiment, the something stronger than sentiment which makes an English American proud of his connection with Britain, a French American proud of his connection with La Belle France, and a German American fondly attached to the memories of the fatherland, and all European races of their Aryan descent, has something that partakes of the moral sublime. Truly "language and religion do not make a race."[47]

One question still remained for Smyth: What should be the attitude of the African in America toward those in Africa, especially to those in Liberia? He wished to impress upon the Africans in America that they were descendants of African races and, as a consequence, were different from people of the Caucasian races. Moreover, he felt that the best work they could do must be in accord with the "bent of [their] genius." This, he believed, would permit them to work "in harmony with God's design in his creation," of his "race line." Africans in America could help those in Africa provided that they had skills and fixity of purpose:

> Unless the Negro out of Africa goes to Africa seeking a home because he has none; goes of his own volition, with as correct a knowledge of Africa as may be obtained from the writings of trustworthy African travelers and explorers and missionaries, reinforced by race loyalty, and with greater confidence in himself and his race than in any alien self and alien race; goes from a sense of duty imposed by his Christian enlightenment, and not unprovided with ability and previous experience to organize and control labor, with as ample means as he would go with from the Atlantic coast of the United States to the Pacific slope for the purpose of engaging in business, he is wholly and

entirely unsuited for Africa, and would impede by his presence not only
the progress of Liberia (if he went thither), but any part of Africa by his
unprofitable presence, and ought to be denied the right to expatriate
himself.[48]

Smyth was not against upsetting his audience if the results would be
beneficial to Africa. He felt that it was his duty as a Negro to be "clear
in his conviction of the high destiny in reserve for Africa and its races,
and of [their] duty to be loyal to the race." In Smyth's opinion, true
allegiance would "make us sharers in that glory which the sacred writing
declares shall come, when Ethiop[i]a shall stretch forth her hand unto
God."[49]

At the end of this congress Bishop Turner went off to South Africa to
establish links with the "Ethiopian" churches there, while his nemesis,
Booker T. Washington, had not only increased in stature but was being
sought after by leaders of African descent whose goals were, ironically,
more similar to Smyth's own than to those of the principal of Tuskegee.
Among those seeking help from Washington were a group of Africans,
African Americans, and persons from the Caribbean then resident in
London but eager to help black people everywhere. These men had
attempted to aid the delegates whom King Lobengula of the Ndebele
nation had sent to London to seek help from Queen Victoria against
Cecil Rhodes's South Africa Company, which had seized their lands in
1891. The best they could get was an audience with Colonial Secretary
Neville Chamberlain, who said that while his sovereign sympathized
with them, there was little or nothing he could do.[50]

Alarmed by this experience, and by the existing condition of peoples
of African descent throughout the world, Henry Sylvester Williams (a
Trinidadian who had studied in Canada and had a law degree from
Gray's Inn in London), the Reverend Henry Mason Joseph (of Antigua,
British West Indies), and others decided on 24 September 1897 to found
the African Association, "to encourage a feeling of unity and to facilitate friendly intercourse among Africans in general; to protect the interests of all subjects claiming African descent, wholly or in part, in British
colonies and other places, especially in Africa, by circulating accurate
information on all subjects affecting their rights and privileges as subjects of the British Empire, by direct appeals to Imperial and local
Governments."[51]

As secretary general of the organization, Williams wrote Booker T.
Washington on 27 September 1898 informing him about the group
whose object, he indicated, was to effect "a fuller [and] perfect sympa-

thy of all our people claiming African descent." Williams informed the Tuskegean that he took for granted that Washington was "alive to the necessity of a general union amongst the children and descendants of Ham, as it would tend to create a respect for us which today is non est." The end sought by the organization, according to Williams, was to "endeavor to promote, [and] to make representations in cases of oppression effecting [sic] our people wherever found."[52]

Williams's assumption that Washington would feel the necessity of cooperating with "people claiming African descent" was based on the hope that the Tuskegean would have positive views about Africa. In fact, Washington's initial views on Africa were fairly ambiguous, if not unfavorable. They had been formed from childhood memories and had been influenced by his opposition to the emigrationism of Turner and others. "As I recall my first definite impressions of my race in Africa, [he wrote] . . . the books I read when I was a boy always put the pictures of Africa and African life in unnecessarily cruel contrast with pictures of the civilized and highly cultured Europeans and Americans." He recalled in his geography book a "picture of George Washington placed side by side with a naked African, having a ring in his nose and a dagger in his hand." Moreover, the young Booker not only understood that "God was white and the Devil was black," but that even in Africa, "the lowest and most degraded type of man was black, and the blacker he was the further down in the scale of civilization I expected him to be."[53]

Washington later revealed that he looked to find the best traits in Africans and looked with disfavor on blacks who sought "to get away as far as possible from association with our own race, and to keep as far away from Africa, from its history and from its traditions as it was possible for us to do."[54] He would later use his own personal diplomacy to mobilize United States support for Liberia. Nevertheless, Washington believed that the sojourn of blacks over centuries in the United States had made them quintessentially American. He once observed, "It has often occurred to me that people who talk of removing the Negro from the Southern states and colonizing him in some distant part of the world do not reflect how deeply he is rooted in the soil."[55] Washington believed not only that blacks had contributed greatly in life and labor to building America, but also that they had added something of their inner life and temperament to the areas in which they lived. He was convinced that during the antebellum period, the lives of blacks and whites were so interwoven that they had no "separate history" and that it was only with emancipation that the "masses of the Negro people began to think of themselves as having a past or a future in any way separate and distinct from the white race."[56] Moreover, he felt that blacks were better off in the United States than in any other part of the world that was totally under white control.

Washington's first real opportunity to view Africa in a slightly different perspective came during a visit he paid to Great Britain in 1899, at the height of the Anglo-Boer War. He had received a notice about the African Association from Henry Sylvester Williams and had written an article in the *Atlantic Monthly* concerning southern Africa. So he looked forward to getting some firsthand information about Africa during his trip to London. Writing to the editor of the *Colored American* magazine of Washington, D.C., from London on 20 July 1899, Washington said that outside of Africa itself, London was perhaps the best place to study events in Africa because the British controlled so much of that continent. He explained that he needed to look into African affairs because people advocated that blacks emigrate there. He added, perhaps maliciously, that "because of my respect for those who have thus advised, especially Bishop Turner, I have tried to make a careful, unbiased study of the question, during my sojourn in England, to see what opportunities present themselves in Africa for self-development and self-government."[57]

From his conversations with Henry Morton Stanley, the explorer, Washington said he was convinced that there was "no place in Africa where we of the United States might go to advantage." This was because the Europeans had "gobble[d] up the greater part of Africa, and there is practically nothing left. Old King Cetawayo [former king of Zululand] put it pretty well when he said, 'First come Missionary, then Rum, then come Traders, then come Army'; and Cecil Rhodes had expressed the prevailing sentiment more recently in these words, 'I would rather have land than niggers,' and Cecil Rhodes is directly responsible for the killing of thousands of black natives in South Africa, that he might secure their land." The Tuskegean concluded that it was impossible for Africans to escape the spheres of influence of the Europeans and that as far as African Americans were concerned, "If we are to go to Africa, and be under the control of another government, I would think we would prefer to take our chances in the 'sphere of influence' of the United States."[58]

Nevertheless, when in London Washington encountered a "large number of Negroes, some from Africa, some from British Guiana and others from the West Indian Islands, and not a few from America," he modified his views about educated Africans—really about highly educated blacks. Much to the amusement of white Americans, Washington used to talk about the incongruity of semi-naked Africans who could read Cicero in Latin but could not sew a pair of trousers. What impressed him about the blacks he met in London was that they took themselves quite seriously. He remarked, "It is surprising to see the strong intellectual mould which many of these Africans and West Indians possess."[59] Moreover, when he met with Henry Mason Joseph and Henry Sylvester Williams, president and honorable secretary, respectively, of the African Association, they invited him to discuss with them "a very important movement [that] has just been put upon foot. It is known as the Pan-African Conference."[60]

Washington was pleased to receive an invitation to participate in the meeting setting up the "preliminary program." He agreed with the decision of the planners to take advantage of "the Paris Exhibition of 1900 (which many representatives of the race may be visiting), to hold a conference in London in the month of May." He reported that the goal of the conference was to take steps "to influence public opinion on existing proceedings and conditions affecting" the welfare of blacks in various parts of the world such as South Africa, West Africa, the West Indies, and the United States. It was hoped that during three days some of the following subjects would be discussed: the conditions favoring the development of a high standard of African humanity; the cruelty of civilized Paganism of which blacks were the victim; the industrial development of black people in the light of current history (no doubt stimulated by Washington himself); Europe's atonement for her blood guiltiness to Africa; the problem of organized plunder versus human progress which had made blacks its battlefield; and Africa as the Sphinx of history in the light of its unsolved problems.[61]

The name of Booker T. Washington figured prominently on the conference's list of sponsors. The other persons named were Bishop J. Theodore Holly of the Episcopal church in Haiti, where he had settled after promoting emigrationism with Martin R. Delany in the 1850s; Bishop James Johnson of Sierra Leone, who had been a missionary in Lagos, Yorubaland, and the lower Niger delta; Bishop Henry McNeal Turner, militant leader of the AME Church; the Reverend Majola Agbebi, a Baptist minister and headmaster of a school in Lagos; the Reverend C. W. Farquhar, a West Indian missionary in West Africa; Judge David Augustus Straker of Michigan, U.S.A.; Professor W. S. Scarborough, of Wilberforce University, Ohio; Henry Richard Cargill, a Jamaican planter and politician; J. Tengo Jabavu, a South African and product of Lovedale Mission, who edited the African weekly *Imvo Za-bantsundu* (African Opinion) in Cape Town, South Africa; and J. Oton-ba Payne, chairman of the board of Hope School in Lagos and a good friend of Edward Wilmot Blyden.[62]

Writing to the editor of the Indianapolis *Freeman*, Washington held out high hopes for the conference:

> I beg to advise as many of our people as can possibly do so, to attend this conference. In my opinion it is going to be one of the most effective and far reaching gatherings that has ever been held in connection with the development of the race.[63]

Williams not only welcomed this interest of the principal in the conference but personally wrote him several letters about attending it. In one letter, Williams wrote that the conference was likely to be a major "precentor [*sic*] to the 20th Century" and that his only anxiety was for "our folks" to attend. He indicated that he would like the various professions to be represented and papers to be read and discussed on the various phases. Williams intimated that a kindly suggestion from Washington on the usual procedure of such a conference would be gratefully appreciated. He added, "If any of our Coloured American Papers have taken up the matter may I thank you for the opportunity to read their references. Our Womanhood must be represented also. They deserve a prominent position in the Conference, [and] it must be given them."[64] Williams followed up this letter with another, giving more detail and ending with hope for the "fullest co-operation from our People across the 'blue pond.' "[65] On 1 June 1900 Williams wrote Washington again, indicating that some delegates had already arrived, inquiring about when he should be expected, and "anxiously expecting" him to take part in the proceedings.[66]

While Washington was prepared to patronize the Pan-African Conference and was largely responsible for acquainting African Americans with it, he preferred to attend to American domestic politics and its effect on blacks at home. He was deeply involved in the presidential race of McKinley and Roosevelt against Bryan and Stevenson and wrote to Williams that this obligation prevented him from attending the conference. A disappointed Williams replied, "The Pan African Conference Committee regrets the cause hindering your presence at the greatest gathering our race as a people has ever witnessed. We certainly would like to press you, but as you know best the circumstances referred to . . ." Nevertheless, Williams was determined to extract some contribution from Washington for the conference and asked him to prepare a paper "on the industrial development of the people in the light of current history to meet the exigencies of an adapted civilization." Williams promised the professor that this paper would be read and given due publicity. The secretary expressed the hope that Washington would influence "many who are coming over to support the project" in view of the opposition of such white groups as the Aborigines Protection Society, which resented blacks themselves having organized the conference. He concluded in the words of many supporters, "We must do for ourselves in order to demand and ultimately gain the respect of other races."[67]

It is perhaps one of the ironies of history that while domestic concerns kept Booker T. Washington from attending the Pan-African Conference in London, his domestic prestige may have facilitated W. E. B. Du Bois's presence there. About a year earlier, on 4 October 1899, Thomas Junius Calloway, managing editor of the *Colored American* and the leader of what was then known as the "Bookerite" faction in Washington, D.C., had written Washington asking for support for "a Negro Exhibit in connection with the United States Exhibit" at the Paris exhibition scheduled for 1900. Calloway noted that while deploring, as any black person would, the drawing of the color line at the exhibit in Paris, he wished to counter the slander against blacks sent abroad by American whites whenever a black person was lynched. The editor wanted to show European audiences that African Americans were not a "mass of rapists, ready to attack every white woman exposed, and a drug in civilized society." This he planned to do by developing an exhibit of blacks in their homes, professions, and elsewhere in the hope of "convincing thinking people of the possibilities of the Negro."[68] Calloway also assured Washington that the directors of the United States exhibit had agreed that the Negro exhibit "can not fail to correct many misapprehensions which now exist and to give a very complete and valuable view of the status of the Negro in this country."[69]

Washington immediately spoke to President McKinley on Calloway's behalf and again on 24 October 1899 reminded the president of their conversation "in regard to a separate educational exhibit representing the progress of the Negro race at the Paris Exposition." Washington told the president that the officials in charge had agreed to it and that they had also discussed "the means for the salary and other expenses of a competent person to prepare and install this exhibit." Washington added that he was "convinced that the best person to have charge of this exhibit is Mr. Thomas J. Calloway, who was formerly one of our teachers at Tuskegee and who has had large experience in this kind of work, and I hope you can see your way clear to bring about his appointment."[70] Washington's efforts were successful. On 25 January 1900 Calloway wrote him, "Our bill for $15000.00 has now passed both houses of Congress and I suppose will be signed by the President within 24 hours. Public sentiment was so unanimous in its favor that the only questions asked me have been 'Is it enough?' "[71] It is not known whether it was Calloway who thought of recruiting Du Bois to develop the Negro exhibit for Paris or whether it was Washington who suggested it. Washington was then in close touch with Du Bois. In fact, just two days after his letter to McKinley seeking support for the Negro exhibit, Washington had written Du Bois from Tuskegee offering him a position at the school.[72]

Du Bois did not respond to Washington until 17 February 1900. He said then that while he still had not made up his mind about Tuskegee, he had turned down an offer from Howard University "without hesitation" because the institution was poorly run. What Du Bois wanted from Washington was a recommendation to serve as superintendent of the schools for blacks in Washington, D.C. He asked, "Could I not serve both your cause [and] the general cause of the Negro at the National capital better than elsewhere? I wish you'd think this matter over seriously [and] give me your best advice."[73] In a subsequent letter Du Bois stated, "I do not of course want you to do anything which would compromise you or make you appear to be 'in politics' but if without prejudice to your position [and] the school's you could endorse me I shall appreciate it."[74]

To the dissatisfaction of Washington's friends in the nation's capital, who did not consider Du Bois sympathetic to him or them, the principal did endorse Du Bois, but Du Bois did not get the appointment. Then on 10 April 1900 Du Bois wrote Washington turning down the offer to teach at Tuskegee, giving as his reason that he was not convinced that the opportunities at Tuskegee were sufficient to warrant leaving his position at Atlanta. He added, "The only opening that would attract me now would be one that brought me nearer the centres of culture and learning and thus gave me larger literary activity. I thank you very much for the offer and for other kindnesses and I need not assure [you] that you will always have in your work my sympathy [and] cooperation."[75]

During all this correspondence neither Washington nor Du Bois mentioned the Pan-African Conference, but it was undoubtedly at this time that Calloway commissioned Du Bois to prepare the Negro exhibit for the U.S. pavilion in Paris. The editor was a good friend of both of them.

While seeking a position at Tuskegee, Du Bois had even asked Calloway to send a recommendation to Washington.[76] The problem for Du Bois and Calloway was that the budget allowed by Congress for the exhibit was too small. Du Bois later reported that the task of finishing the job was terribly difficult with little money, limited time, and not too much encouragement:

> I was threatened with nervous prostration before I was done and had little money left to buy passage to Paris, nor was there a cabin left for sale. But the exhibit would fail unless I was there. So at the last moment I bought passage in the steerage and went over and installed the work. It was an immediate success . . . The American press, white and colored, was full of commendation and in the end, the exhibit received a Grand Prize, and I, as its author, a Gold Medal.[77]

There is no evidence that Du Bois had planned to go to the Pan-African Conference before leaving for Europe. He knew both Washington and Bishop Alexander Walters, two Americans closely associated with planning the conference, and had attended the Afro-American Council meeting in Chicago in 1899, where the idea of a Pan-African Conference to follow the Paris exposition was discussed. Du Bois was later to claim that both he and Bishop Alexander Walters had received invitations to attend the conference, yet no correspondence between him and Henry Sylvester Williams prior to the conference has come to light.[78] Of course, once in Paris it was the easiest thing for Du Bois to go to London—a possibility foreseen by the planning group that had linked the conference with the Paris exposition to facilitate the attendance of blacks who could only have attended if others had paid their way as far as Paris. In any event, Du Bois got to Paris, and given his interest in the problems of black people, he could not have resisted going to the London conference.

Like Booker T. Washington, Du Bois was also exposed to the negative images of Africa held by almost all contemporary whites and most blacks in America. Yet he never flinched from acknowledging his links with that continent and its peoples. In an early biography, Du Bois noted that his birth coincided with "the Abyssinian expedition and opening of the Suez Canal, so fateful for all my people."[79] In his second biography, he waxed more eloquent about the memory of his earliest knowledge about Africa. He tells us that on his mother's side he was "descended from Tom" (later known as a Burghardt) who was born in West Africa about 1730 and who had been "stolen by Dutch slave traders and brought to [America]." He recalled that in his family's tradition there was a song, "Do bana coba—gene me, gene me, / Ben d' nuli, ben d' le—," sung by "a little black Bantu woman" who was either "Tom's mother or wife" and who "never became reconciled" to life in America.[80] It was also in attempting to get to the root of the black problem in America that Du Bois prepared and presented as his doctoral thesis at Harvard University in 1896 "The Suppression of the African Slave-Trade to the United States."[81] Yet Du Bois was not then as interested in what the slave trade did to Africa as in attempting to make "a small contribution to the scientific study of slavery and the American Negro."[82]

It was Du Bois's growing concern with the pathological social problems of African Americans—crime, poverty, and family organization— that led him to focus on black life in Africa prior to the slave trade. He developed an intellectual interest in a black nationality and saw the obligation of African Americans to Africa in secular and political terms. In an early and much cited essay prepared for the American Negro Academy in 1897, Du Bois challenged the social Darwinists of his day and maintained that, specifically in the case of the Egyptian civilization, the "Negro did make some contributions to world history."[83] Moreover, Du Bois insisted:

> If the Negro is ever to be a factor in the world's history—if among the gaily colored banners that deck the broad ramparts of civilization is to hang one uncompromisingly black, then it must be placed there by black hands, fashioned by black heads and hallowed by the travail of 200,000,000 black hearts beating in one glad song of jubilee.

He further asserted:

> The 8,000,000 people of Negro blood in the United States of America—must soon come to realize that if they are to take their just place in the van of Pan-Negroism, then their destiny is not absorption by the white Americans. That if in America it is to be proven for the first time in the modern world that not only Negroes are capable of evolving individual men like Toussaint, the Saviour, but are a nation stored with wonderful possibilities of culture, then their destiny is not a servile imitation of Anglo-Saxon culture, but a stalwart originality which shall unswervingly follow Negro ideals.[84]

While the London conference was a fitting forum for Du Bois, he was far from being the most illustrious figure among the fourteen or so African Americans there. That honor went to Bishop Alexander Walters, D.D., of the AME Zion Church (cofounder with T. Thomas Fortune of the Afro-American League and its successor, the National Afro-American Council) from New Jersey. Walters, who had attended religious conferences in Britain in 1889, 1890, and 1891 and had

preached in its Methodist churches, was asked to preside at the conference.[85] Setting the tone with his address, "The Trials and Tribulations of
the Colored Race in America," Walters viewed the conference as a
remarkable feat. He said that for the first time in their history, "blacks
had gathered from all parts of the globe to discuss how to improve the
condition of the race," to assert their rights, and to organize themselves
to strive for an equal place in the company of nations.[86] Walters added
that despite living in a society whose traditions, prejudices, and laws
were arrayed against them, and gaining personal emancipation after
some two hundred years at the end of the Civil War, blacks in America
were "engaged in a long and severe struggle for full social and political
rights."[87]

Echoing Bishop Walters, Mrs. Anna J. Cooper of Washington, D.C.,
spoke about the situation of blacks within the United States of America,
and Miss Anna H. Jones from Kansas spoke about "The Preservation of
Race Individuality." Mr. D. E. Tobias addressed the topic, "Africa, the
Sphinx of History in the Light of Unsolved Problems"; Mr. C. W.
French of St. Kitts "claimed equality for blacks" in his paper, "Conditions Favoring a High Standard of African Humanity"; and Mr. Benito
Sylvain of Haiti presented a paper entitled "The Necessary Concord to
be Established Between Native Races and European Colonists." Other
speakers addressed the subject of black people from their own perspectives. Henry F. Downing, the only African American present who had
served in the foreign service of the United States (as a United States
consul in Loanda, Angola), "declared that blacks had no intention of
complying with the wishes of those who desired them to remain slaves
forever."[88]

W. E. B. Du Bois, who chaired the committee and whose task it was
to prepare "An Address to the Nations of the World," impressed everyone with the ease with which he took the conference in stride.[89] His
approach was probably collaborative since he did not claim sole credit
for drafting the statement. Yet the style of the address was Du Boisian,
and in it he used many ideas that he had used before and would later
elaborate on. Always viewing the plight of blacks in historical perspective, Du Bois had declared as early as 1897 that blacks should not forget
that they lived "upon the threshold of the twentieth century." Their
relationship to other peoples was seen by the fact that "on our breakfast
table lies each morning the toil of Europe, Asia, and Africa, and the isles
of the seas; . . . [W]e have made the earth smaller and life broader by
annihilating distance, magnifying the human voice and the stars, binding

nation to nation, until today, for the first time in history, there is one standard of human culture as well in New York as in London, in Cape Town as in Paris, in Bombay as in Berlin." For Du Bois, this meant that blacks had an obligation to each other the world over and, by extension, to the downtrodden of the earth.[90]

Du Bois felt that a general appeal to the nations of the world was necessary because of the "inviable position of our people everywhere today" and because of the spirit of the conference. Placing the group's work in perspective, he wrote, "In the metropolis of the modern world, in this the closing year of the Nineteenth Century, there has been assembled a Congress of men and women of African blood, to deliberate solemnly the present situation and outlook of the darker races of mankind." He went on to predict that "the problem of the Twentieth Century is the problem of the color line, the question as to how far differences of race, which show themselves chiefly in the color of the skin and the texture of the hair, are going to be made, hereafter, the basis of denying to over half the world the right of sharing to their utmost ability the opportunities and privileges of modern civilization."[91] Du Bois admitted that at this period in time the darker human races did not approach the Europeans' standard of cultural development. Nevertheless, he insisted that "the world's history, both ancient and modern, has given many instances of no despicable ability and capacity among the blackest races of men."[92]

Fully aware of the might and power of European peoples, Du Bois appealed to them to ameliorate the plight of African peoples under their dominion. Suggesting that race should not be seen as a barrier between peoples and that Africa should not be exploited under the pretense of bringing civilization and Christianity to its peoples, he urged the British, in the name of their more enlightened fellow citizens such as Wilberforce, Clarkson, and others, to "give, as soon as practicable," the rights of responsible government to the Black Colonies of Africa and the West Indies—at least to grant them autonomy within the framework of the British Empire. He urged the French and Germans to consider that justice was necessary for the prosperity of their colonies. To Leopold II, he urged that the Congo Free State should become a great black nation. And he urged his white fellow citizens of the United States, in the name of such great abolitionists as Douglass and Garrison, to grant full equality to African Americans. He then called upon all the imperialist powers to respect the integrity and independence of the black states of Abyssinia, Haiti, and Liberia. Lastly, he urged the "independent tribes of

Africa, the Negroes of the West Indies and America, and the black subjects of all Nations" to take heart, and to try unceasingly and struggle bravely to "prove to the World" that they were indisputably entitled to belong to the "great brotherhood of mankind."[93]

The delegates to the Pan-African Conference passed a number of resolutions thanking such groups as the British, the Foreign Anti-Slavery Society, and the Quakers for helping to ameliorate the plight of blacks throughout the world. They were particularly concerned about Africans in southern Africa, and sent a memorial to Queen Victoria, inviting her "august and sympathetic attention to the fact that the situation of the native races in Southern Africa is causing us and our friends alarms." Among these concerns were the compound system of African labor then used in South Africa and Rhodesia; the internship of Africans to white colonists; the system of forced labor and pass laws; the segregation of Africans in public places; and the difficulty for Africans to acquire real property and the franchise.[94]

Since the conference was held in their capital, the British could not ignore the sentiments of its members. True, Queen Victoria did not have the time to meet them, but a few months later her Colonial Secretary, Joseph Chamberlain, Sr., at Her Majesty's command, informed the conferees that "in settling the lines on which the administration of the conquered territories is to be conducted, Her Majesty's Government will not overlook the interests and welfare of the native races."[95] There is no evidence, however, that the United States embassy in London reported any news of the conference to the State Department. And while few white Americans paid any attention to what took place in London, one Elizabeth Bartlett Grannis, a white feminist who often marched to the polls demanding the vote, wrote to Booker T. Washington on 21 March 1901 stating:

> I was never present at a Convention when I realized that any person or persons were so thoroughly justified in blowing their own Race Trumpets, as at the International Negro Convention held in London, England, last July! The Eloquence of Delivery, with the Quality of Matter which was listened to on this occasion, would certainly have astonished the best types of Ante-Bellum-Masters of their Slaves. And you were not there! The year before I learned that your Wife was present at one of the Sessions of the International Council, but *I* neither met or saw her![96]

The news of the conference was reported to black America through its press. The *Colored American* of September 1900 reported that "July 23–25, 1900, marked a new era for the colored race throughout the world.

Under the eaves of the Parliament in Westminster Town Hall was held a three-days' conference for the discussion of the native races question." The report mentioned the highlights of the conference, and indicated that its main goal was "to protect Africans from the depredations of the Empire builders."[97]

When Du Bois returned to the United States from London, the experience of the conference was very much on his mind as he addressed the officers of the American Negro Academy at its third annual meeting in October 1900. Reviewing the prospects of blacks the world over and the ability of African Americans to deal with their problems, he suggested that as one considered "The Present Outlook for the Dark Races of Mankind"

> it is but natural for us to consider that our race question is a purely national and local affair, confined to nine millions [sic] Americans and settled when their rights and opportunities are assured, and yet a glance over the world at the dawn of the new century will convince us that this is but the beginning of the problem—that the color line belts the world and that the social problem of the twentieth century is to be the relation of the civilized World to the dark races of mankind. If we start eastward to-night and land on the continent of Africa we land in the centre of the greater Negro problem—of the world problem of the black man.[98]

Coming as it did, some sixteen years after the Berlin Conference that gave Europe the green light to conquer and colonize Africa, the Pan-African Conference of 1900 was the first determined effort of blacks to liberate their ancestral continent. The blacks who launched the movement and who were responsible for creating the very concept of Pan-Africanism were primarily those whose ancestors had been plucked away from Africa and who had thereby gained a larger view of the world. Du Bois emerged as the spokesman at the London conference because he belonged to a nation-state that was clearly seen as the heir to European global power. He was obviously prepared to do battle with this global power but felt that this was best pursued by direct agitation for the rights of blacks within the United States. Only after that battle had been won did he believe that blacks in America could successfully help Africa. This meant, however, that he had to abandon any attempt at assisting Africa to Booker T. Washington who, having compromised with powerful whites in the United States, was able to influence United States policy toward an Africa increasingly dominated by Europeans.

Notes

1. Bishop Henry McNeal Turner, in *Respect Black: The Writings and Speeches of Henry McNeal Turner,* ed. Edwin S. Redkey (New York: Arno Press and the New York Times, 1971), 168–69.
2. J. W. H. Bowen, *Africa and the American Negro* (Miami, Fla.: Mnemosyne, 1969), 13–14.
3. Theodore Roosevelt, *The Winning of the West* (New York: G. P. Putnam's Sons, 1889–96).
4. Howard K. Beale, *Theodore Roosevelt and the Rise of America to World Power* (New York: Collier, 1956), 149–50.
5. Ibid.
6. Rayford W. Logan, *The Negro in American Life and Thought: The Nadir, 1877–1901* (New York: Dial Press, 1954), 88.
7. Ibid., 92.
8. Ibid.
9. Redkey, *Black Exodus,* 181ff.
10. Frederick P. Noble, "The Chicago Congress," *Our Day* 12 (October 1893): 279–300; *Voice of Missions* (October 1893); *A.M.E. Zion Quarterly Review* 4 (October 1893): 120.
11. Redkey, *Black Exodus,* 184ff.
12. Ibid.
13. Ibid.
14. Ibid., 185–86.
15. Booker T. Washington, "To the Editor of the *Indianapolis Freeman,*" 25 November 1893, in Louis R. Harlan and Raymond W. Smock, eds., *The Booker T. Washington Papers* (Urbana: University of Illinois Press, 1972–89), 3:377–78 (hereafter cited as *BTW Papers*).
16. Ibid.
17. Ibid.
18. Statement of Bishop Benjamin F. Lee, quoted in August Meier, ed., *Negro Thought in America, 1880–1915, Racial Ideologies in the Age of Booker T. Washington* (Ann Arbor: University of Michigan Press, 1963), 67.
19. Redkey, *Black Exodus,* 186ff.
20. Ibid.
21. Ibid.
22. Ibid.
23. BTW's speech before the National Education Association, 16 July 1884, *BTW Papers* 2:255–62.
24. Logan, *Negro in American Life,* 275.
25. Booker T. Washington, *Up From Slavery: An Autobiography* (New York: Doubleday, 1949), 211–12.
26. Meier, *Negro Thought,* 25.
27. *BTW Papers* 2:583–87.
28. Ibid.
29. Washington, *Up From Slavery,* 218–25.
30. Ibid.
31. Grover Cleveland to BTW, 6 October 1895, *BTW Papers* 4:50.
32. Washington, *Up From Slavery,* 225–26.
33. Francis J. Grimké to BTW, 20 September 1895, *BTW Papers* 4:25.
34. William J. Cansler to BTW, ibid., 30.
35. William Edward Burghardt Du Bois to BTW, 24 September 1895, ibid., 26.

36. Edward Wilmot Blyden to BTW, 24 September 1895, ibid., 27–28.
37. Henry McNeal Turner, "Critique of the Atlanta Compromise," in Redkey, *Respect Black,* 165–78.
38. Chicago *Inter Ocean,* 2 October 1895, 7, cited in *BTW Papers* 4:42.
39. Ibid.
40. Bowen, *Africa and the Negro,* 10.
41. Ibid., 13–14.
42. Ibid., 119–20.
43. Redkey, *Black Exodus,* 230.
44. Bowen, *Africa and the Negro,* 195–98.
45. Ibid., 69.
46. Ibid., 69–76.
47. Ibid., 77, 75.
48. Ibid., 82–83.
49. Ibid., 83.
50. Owen Charles Mathurin, *Henry Sylvester Williams and the Origins of the Pan-African Movement, 1869–1911* (Westport, Conn.: Greenwood Press, 1976), 341.
51. Ibid.
52. Henry Sylvester Williams to BTW, *BTW Papers* 4:475.
53. Booker T. Washington, *The Story of the Negro: The Rise of the Race From Slavery* (New York: Associated Press, 1909), 1:8, 23.
54. Ibid., 12.
55. Ibid., 7.
56. Ibid., 7–8.
57. BTW to Editor of *Colored American* Magazine, *BTW Papers* 5:164–66.
58. Ibid.
59. Ibid., 155–56.
60. Ibid.
61. Ibid.
62. Mathurin, *Henry Sylvester Williams,* 50–51.
63. BTW to the Editor of the Indianapolis *Freeman,* 15 July 1899, *BTW Papers* 5:156.
64. Williams to BTW, 17 July 1899, ibid., 158–59.
65. Williams to BTW, ca. July 1899, ibid., 167.
66. Williams to BTW, 1 June 1900, ibid., 556.
67. Williams to BTW, 29 June 1900, ibid., 569–70.
68. Thomas Junius Calloway to BTW, 4 October 1899, ibid., 226–67.
69. Howard J. Rogers to Calloway, 23 October 1899, ibid., 244.
70. BTW to William McKinley, 24 October 1899, ibid.
71. Calloway to BTW, 25 January 1900, ibid., 227.
72. BTW to Du Bois, 26 October 1899, ibid., 245.
73. Du Bois to BTW, 17 February 1900, ibid., 443–44.
74. Du Bois to BTW, 26 February 1900, ibid., 450.
75. Du Bois to BTW, 10 April 1900, ibid., 480.
76. Du Bois to BTW, 27 July 1894, in Herbert Aptheker, ed., *The Correspondence of W. E. B. Du Bois, Selections, 1877–1934* (New York: Citadel Press, 1951), 1:37.
77. W. E. B. Du Bois, *The Autobiography of W. E. B. Du Bois: A Soliloquy on Viewing My Life From the Last Decade of Its First Century* (New York: International, 1968), 220–21.

78. Du Bois wrote to Immanuel Wallerstein (ca. 1961) that a letter of invitation reached him in Paris ("Pan-Africanism As Protest," in *The Revolution in World Politics,* ed. Morton A. Kaplan [New York: 1962], 139). Contee states that Du Bois may have discussed the conference with such persons as Bishop Henry McNeal Turner and Professor William S. Scarborough of Wilberforce University, whom he had met at various conferences. Nevertheless, Contee believed that Du Bois probably read a letter that Booker T. Washington had written to the editor of the Indianapolis *Freeman* in August 1899 approving Sylvester Williams's initiative (Clarence Contee, "The Emergence of Du Bois as an African Nationalist," *Journal of Negro History* 59 [1969]: 51).

79. W. E. B. Du Bois, *Dusk of Dawn* (New York: Harcourt, Brace, 1940), 9.

80. Du Bois, *Autobiography,* 62.

81. Ibid., 148.

82. W. E. B. Du Bois, *The Suppression of the African Slave-Trade to the United States of America, 1638–1870* (New York: Schocken Books, 1969), xxxv.

83. W. E. B. Du Bois, *The Conservation of Races,* Occasional Papers, no. 2 (Washington, D.C.: American Negro Academy, 1897).

84. Ibid.

85. Mathurin, *Henry Sylvester Williams,* 62–63.

86. Ibid., 63.

87. Ibid., 63–64.

88. Ibid., 64–67.

89. Alexander Walters, *My Life and Work* (New York: Fleming H. Revel, 1917), 253ff.

90. Ibid., 253. Cf. Du Bois, *Conservation*; W. E. B. Du Bois, *An ABC of Color: Selections Chosen by the Author From Over a Half Century of His Writings* (Berlin: Seven Seas, 1963).

91. Walters, *My Life and Work,* 257ff.

92. Ibid.

93. Ibid.

94. Mathurin, *Henry Sylvester Williams,* 72–73.

95. Walters, *My Life and Work,* 257.

96. Elizabeth Bartlett Grannis to BTW, 21 March 1901, *BTW Papers* 6:59.

97. S. E. F. C. C. Hamedoe, "The First Pan-African Conference of the World," *Colored American* 1 (September 1900): 223. See also Rayford W. Logan, "The Historical Aspects of Pan-Africanism: A Personal Chronicle," *African Forum* 1 (1965): 90.

98. W. E. B. Du Bois, "The Present Outlook for the Dark Races of Mankind," *Church Review* (Philadelphia), 17 (October 1900): 95ff.

5

Rescuing Black South Africans

Dear Brothers in Christ—

I am trying to draw your attention to the following facts: Our people at home in the Transkei are in a bad state; needing two principal modes of life; first, Christianity and civilization, but in the first place we are sinking down every year through the bad treatment of white men with our Kings or Chiefs. . . .

Brethren, hark to this cry from Macedonia and harden not your hearts. When I saw your paper, your freedom, I could not help shedding tears for my poor native country. You are born of God (as Moses in Egypt). Brothers, consider that clearly. Don't put those talents in safes . . . use them . . . to purchase the freedom of your brothers in South Africa, or in the whole of Africa. I shall await your favorable reply. (Reverend John Tule to Bishop Henry McNeal Turner)[1]

Probably very few of the blacks who heeded the call to attend a congress at the Gammon Theological Seminary in Atlanta to deal with the issue of the relationship of African Americans to Africa were aware that blacks in South Africa were seeking their own way to God, and in the process would link up with them. As early as 1872, the first stirring of what came to be called the Ethiopia Church Movement occurred in Lesotho when black Christians, like their counterparts in the United States, seceded from the Paris Evangelical Mission at Hermon and established their own church. More significant was the secession that occurred in Tembuland in South Africa in 1884, when an African, Nehemiah Tile, left the Wesleyan church and, under the patronage of King Ngangelizwe, established the Tembu Catholic Church. This was soon followed by a secession from the London Missionary Society of Chief Kgantlapane of Taung in Botswana to found the Native Independent Congregational Church. Further secessions took place among the Bapedi in the northern Transvaal and in the Witwatersrand mining area, where some of the rebels had the support of African secular leaders. By now the movement

181

had developed some revolutionary ideas, among which was the notion that the Xhosa god, Dalidipu, was more powerful than the Christian god, Tixo.[2]

The event that ultimately led to the involvement of African Americans was the secession in 1892 of another minister, the Reverend Mangena M. Mokone, from the Wesleyan church, charging racial discrimination. He objected to the creation of separate conferences for black and white ministers and the imposition of a white chairman and secretary on the black group. Probably influenced by the same ideas as Bishop Turner and others about "Ethiopia's hands," he founded the Ethiopian Church in Pretoria in the same year. The problem for Mokone, as for most secessionists before and after, was to gain legitimacy for "apostolic succession" by affiliation with a recognized denomination. Building links between black South Africans and African Americans was to make this possible.

Whites in South Africa, especially the Afrikaners, did not know how to deal with the African Americans who appeared in their midst. In 1890 a gospel choir composed of four men and six women, known as the McAdoo Minstrels and also as the Jubilee Singers (not to be confused with the Fisk University group of the same name), went to South Africa. The question was whether they would be welcome in the Boer republics. On 30 June 1890 the American consul at Cape Town wrote the state presidents of the Orange Free State and the South African republic to enquire about the visits. The state secretary wrote from Pretoria that in answer to the query whether there were "laws of the South African Republic against the performance of a troupe of Colored Musicians, I have the honor to state that there exists no such provision." In July 1890 the state president of the South African republic wrote the burghers of the Orange Free State:

> Having been informed by the U.S. Consul that the "Jubilee Singers" a
> company of colored people from the United States of America, contemplate
> visiting also the Orange Free State, I trust that they will be treated, wherever
> they happen to be, with that consideration and respect which is due to the free
> citizens of a Sister Republic.[3]

The performance of the Jubilee Singers aroused pride in the local blacks because it furnished proof to them that given an opportunity, people of African origin could excel. One editor wrote: "Their visit will do their countrymen [Africans] here no end of good. Already it has suggested reflections to many who, without such a demonstration, would have remained skeptical as to the possibility . . . of the natives of this country being raised to anything above remaining perpetual hewers of wood and drawers of water."[4] The editor was wrong, for while white

South Africans were enthusiastic about the Jubilee Singers, they did not change their attitudes toward native Africans. In contrast, the African community was ecstatic over finding a link with blacks in America and hoped to use this link to reach the black leadership in the United States.

In 1891, due largely to the influence of the McAdoo Minstrels, a black South African named Paul Xiniwe founded a choir with the support of a white man, one Balmer. Variously called the African Choir or the Zulu and African Choir, this group made a tour of South Africa and later went to Great Britain to raise enough money to build technical schools for Africans in South Africa. The group encountered serious difficulties and returned home, but was then invited to participate in the Columbian Exposition in Chicago. Here they met Bishop Henry McNeal Turner who, as we saw above, was one of the principal speakers in a weeklong congress on Africa.[5] After the exposition the choir was invited to make a brief tour of a few American cities, but this venture failed, and the choir was stranded in Cleveland, Ohio. The Reverend R. C. Ransom of the local AME Church came to their rescue and, with the help of Bishop Benjamin W. Arnett and Dr. S. E. Mitchell, arranged for a number of choristers to return to South Africa in 1894. He also arranged for a number of them to attend the AME Church-sponsored Wilberforce University in Xenia, Ohio. These persons became the first group of South African students to attend an American university. One of them, Charlotte Manye, wrote her sister, a Mrs. Kate Makanya in Johannesburg in January 1895, telling her about life in America. Mrs. Makanya showed the letter to their uncle, the Reverend Mangena M. Mokone who, noting Turner's name on the college's stationery, wrote the bishop on 31 May 1895 seeking information about the AME Church.[6]

Mokone, like the Reverends Richard Allen and Absalom Jones, the founders of the AME Church, and other African "separatists," had become disgusted with segregation, high-handedness, salary differentials, and discrimination in the South African Methodist Church. On 24 October 1892 he issued a "Declaration of Independence" from the Methodists, vowed to serve God "in his own way," and on 5 November 1893 launched "the Ethiopian Church." The suspicion is that Mokone had plans to evangelize the entire African continent; therefore, the news that his niece had established links with African Americans may have seemed to him a sign from above that his prayers had been answered. In his first letter to Turner, Mokone explained why he had founded the Ethiopian Church and how he had ordained two ministers or priests and seven deacons. Mokone insisted that the church was "entirely managed by us blacks of South Africa." What he sought from Bishop Turner was help to send black South Africans to be educated at colleges in the United States.[7]

Mokone's letter was welcome news to Turner, who needed some evidence to show African Americans that they had a role to play in the redemption of Africa. Turner had reported that in 1893, while on board the steamship *Majestic* during his second trip to West Africa, he had met a gentleman from South Africa who "wishes me to accompany him [to] Cape Colony, in South Africa; he assures me that I can organize another conference there in a month. Had I the money, I would go at once, may anyway, if I can make ends meet."[8] Turner could not go to South Africa then, but Mokone's letter now renewed his interest in the region. He responded to Mokone encouraging him to build up the Ethiopian Church and enclosed a copy of the AME newspaper, *Voice of Missions*. The South African was delighted with the bishop's reply, and in September 1895 both he and the secretary of the Ethiopian Church, the Reverend Jacobus Gilead Xaba, wrote Turner about subscription rates for the *Voice of Missions*. More important, they asked him to send them a copy of the AME Church's policy or table of organization so that they could learn the rules governing membership in the church. Then without waiting for a response, Xaba wrote Turner saying: "The *Voice of Missions*, your Lordship sent us over, is a very, very important and instructive paper to a Christian community . . . its circulation among us has created an extraordinary revivification . . . We desire much knowledge from it." What Xaba wanted most urgently from the AME Church was missionaries to come to this "southern extremity" of Africa, where he felt Christianity was merely "half-baked, and left uncooked."[9]

Echoing the sentiment of Xaba's letter was one Turner received in November 1895 from John Tule from the Transkei then working in Cape Town. Tule wrote: "Our people at home in the Transkei are in a bad state, needing two principal modes of life; first, Christianity and civilization. . . . Now, my honest brothers, this a cry from Rama; send us ministers. I have found your address in your paper."[10] Afterwards, meeting in their third annual conference in March 1896, the members of the Ethiopian Church of South Africa declared: "This Conference is strongly of the opinion that a union with the African Methodist-Episcopal Church will not only be hailed by our people, but would be the means of evangelizing numerous tribes of this vast continent."[11] Recalling that the same circumstances that led the African Americans to secede from white American Christianity led them to do likewise, the South Africans sent a delegation in the person of the Reverend James Mata Dwane to the United States to negotiate an affiliation.

By the time Dwane arrived in America in June 1896, Bishop Turner had prepared the ground, stating that like Richard Allen's group, which seceded from the Methodist Episcopal Church in Philadelphia in 1787, the South Africans were justified in leaving the white churches in their homeland. Turner recommended that the AME Church's council of bishops approve the union. This took place on 19 June 1896, and the Ethiopian Church of South Africa was absorbed into the AME Church as its Fourteenth District with Dwane as vicar bishop and general superintendent. When Dwane returned to South Africa he convened the first conference of the new district at Queenstown in the Cape in April 1897, reported upon his mission to America, and stressed that the council of bishops of the AME Church expected the loyalty of the South Africans. In return the South Africans expected two favors from their African American brethren: funds to build a school and a visit from Turner. Writing to Turner from South Africa, Dwane stated:

> Our great need in this country is a first-class institution of learning. . . . People in this country are very anxious about higher education. I hope the AME Church will soon take up this question in earnest. You have not the least idea, my Lord [referring to Bishop Turner], how much depends on this question. The failure of the white churches to do so is a source of much discontent and our church must take the matter up.[12]

While Dwane was establishing communication with Turner about help for his separatist Christians, there was a great deal of ferment among African Christians and other Africans in South Africa. Ethiopia's defeat of Italy at the battle of Adowa led many blacks in South Africa, and peoples of African descent in other parts of Africa as well as in the New World, to believe that important political changes were at hand. The biblical prophecy that princes would come out of Egypt and that Ethiopia would stretch forth her hands seemed real to many downtrodden blacks. At least one white missionary, the Reverend Joseph Booth, preached a convoluted doctrine advocating self-determination for Africans on the continent and abroad, as well as the return of African Americans to Africa, with Booker T. Washington playing a key role in the process. Booth, who wished to establish "industrial missions" in South Africa, founded a religious movement, the African Christian Union, in Natal. He succeeded in converting a number of Zulus to his way of thinking and in September 1896 issued a twenty-one-point manifesto, which was reprinted in Jabavu's newspaper, *Imvo*.[13] Among the aims stated were

> To provide capital to equip industrial mission stations.
> To demand . . . by Christian and lawful methods the equal recognition of the African and allied peoples to the rights and privileges accorded to Europeans.
> To solicit funds [from Europeans] to restore Africans [in America] to their fatherland.
> To place on record . . . the great wrongs inflicted upon the African by people of Europe and America and to urge upon Christians, who wish to be clear of African blood in the day of God's Judgment, to make restitution.[14]

Boldly declaring a policy of AFRICA FOR THE AFRICAN, Booth declared:

> Let the African, sympathetically led by his more experienced Afro-American brother, develop his own country, establish his own manufactures, work his own plantations, run his own ships, work his own mines, educate his own people, possess his own mission stations, conserve the wealth accruing from all sources, if possible, for the commonwealth and enlightenment of the people and the glory of God.[15]

It was this religious fervor in South Africa that led Mokone, as presiding elder of the emerging African church, to invite Turner to come to South Africa and Turner, an avowed emigrationist, to accept the invitation. Mokone wrote: "Here in Africa all the nations are gathered except Negroes, my own people, English, Dutch, Germans, Hollanders, French, Russian Jews, Swedish, Arabian, German Jews." He asserted that all the whites were busily colonizing but that blacks were "sleeping and will not come to visit the fatherland." He feared that "then when all is taken . . . we shall begin to cry like Esau." Mokone pleaded for Africans to teach one another, concluding, "I am sure we are not inferior to any [race]."[16] Turner could not turn down this appeal, and he decided to visit South Africa.

Turner's visit to South Africa, while religious in nature and, as such, characteristic of the African American's symbolic foreign policy toward Africa, would have real implications for later diplomatic relations between the United States of America and the peoples of that region. In 1893, and long before Turner thought of visiting the subcontinent, there was a sharp exchange of letters between diplomats in Washington and Johannesburg over the treatment of an African American, John Ross. On 15 January of that year, Ross, a blacksmith working on the Delagoa Bay railroad was verbally abused by a white fellow employee. When he responded in kind, he was accused of being "impudent," tied up, and given fifteen lashes by a white policeman who carried out summary justice.

William W. Van Ness, Jr., the United States consular agent in Johannesburg, resented Ross's being treated like one of the "native Kaffirs" and sent off a report to the Department of State via the American consul in Cape Town. He also informed the secretary of state of the South African republic that the "laws of the United States . . . made no distinction in citizenship between white and colored [*sic*]." When the American consul in Cape Town later saw the chief justice of the South African republic he took the same position. By this time Ross had lodged a claim of damages totaling $10,000 against the South African republic and was supported in his suit by the Department of State. The Afrikaners adopted a conciliatory attitude and apparently settled the case satisfactorily.[17]

Striving to avoid similar incidents in the future since he was cultivating the United States, Paul Kruger, then president of the Transvaal, decided to issue special passports to African Americans. Thus when the bishop requested a travel permit to visit the Transvaal, he was granted the status of "honorary white." As such he was exempted from the provisions of Article 9 of that republic's constitution, which explicitly prohibited "any equalization of the colored inhabitants with the whites."[18] Whether the bishop resented this status is not clear since he did not refer to it in any of his reports on his trip to South Africa.

Turner had no illusions about the political ramifications of his visit to South Africa. He stated openly that his trip, "though made in the interest, and for the extension, of the African Methodist Church, was productive of results that are broader than church lines."[19] Nevertheless, he was determined to avoid as much as possible conflict both with whites and (especially) between church members in America and South Africa. The bishop was conscious of the Africans' criticisms of the missionaries for not ordaining black clergy, and he decided not to have this said about the AME Church. During his six-week trip, he sought to demonstrate his faith in local leadership by ordaining thirty-one elders, twenty deacons, and reobligating at their own request the eight ministers who had been consecrated by the Ethiopian Church. He also confirmed the Reverend James Mata Dwane in the position of vicar bishop, thus giving him the power to ordain ministers for the church. Turner wrote home that everywhere he was well received and that on his visits the "Africans and colored people went wild by the thousands."[20]

Encouraged by what he saw, Turner was often critical of the white missionary bodies in South Africa. In Cape Town on 22 April 1898, he gave a speech in which he complained about the wrongs that Africans had suffered at the hands of whites. The editors of the *Christian Express* attacked him for his insistence that these wrongs were sufficient grounds for creating independent AME churches in Africa. On the other hand, the bishop shrewdly disguised the extent of his political agenda by "judiciously choosing his topics whenever he addressed gatherings at which whites were present."[21] At a meeting in Cape Town on 24 April 1898 he spoke on the wisdom of ecumenism, imploring his audience to welcome "the necessity of all creeds working with one common object, and not shouting each other down and cutting each other's throats." He also urged blacks and coloreds to improve themselves morally, and intellectually through education. A local paper, the Cape *Argus,* known for its liberality as far as the African population was concerned, approved of Turner's remarks, calling him "a powerful man with an equally powerful voice."[22]

Because of what he considered to be its "class" aspects, Turner was not as critical about the racial situation in South Africa as he was about racism in the United States of America. He observed:

> Much has been said about the prejudice to be found in South Africa against the Africanite. I grant that prejudice does exist, but it is not the kind found in America. It is not race prejudice at all, but prejudice of condition. The Europeans came with their civilized ideas among a heathen people, inferior in knowledge and religion; they came with civilized forms of government, and as a natural consequence the natives were rated as any people in a similar condition would be. The Romans had the same estimate of the tribes of Britain when they conquered it though both were white races. It has always been so.[23]

No doubt flattered by the treatment he received personally, Turner said that "in South Africa, a Negro from a civilized country and having the bearing of a gentleman and of a scholar, coming among the English of Cape Colony or the Boers of the Transvaal, is received with all honor, and his color is no barrier to the proffer of courtesies and hospitalities."[24] In a report from Bloemfontein dated 16 April 1898, Turner did admit that progress for Africans was needed, but took care to add: "But most of the Boers, in our opinion, are kind men. We were never treated better. They treated us to everything but whiskey, and that has been offered four times."[25]

When Turner was received by President Paul Kruger of the Transvaal, he reported that while "many, both white and black, give him [Kruger] a

bad name, I was treated throughout the Republic with marked consideration and respect."[26] In fact Kruger told Turner, "You are the first black
man whose hand I have ever shaken."[27] The bishop noted that the president "received our church with great cordiality, though I must confess,
if reports be true, it was not so much from love of it as from distrust of
white missionaries whom he dislikes." Turner concluded that while the
Boer president was patriotic and undoubtedly a statesman of large caliber and shrewdness, the Boers as a rule were not educated and showed
more prejudice than did the English. Turner was equally impressed with
the Afrikaner president of the Orange Free State, who was "a perfect
gentleman in every respect" and from whom he received permission for
the AME Church to solemnize marriages as had been done by the other
churches in that republic.[28]

Turner left South Africa with the conviction that "the presence of a
thousand educated Negroes from America, men of character, courage,
enterprise and property, would be hailed with joy by the natives and, at
the same time, be an object lesson to them, that the same possibilities are
open to them also when they [are] sufficiently elevated to merit and
demand them."[29] Musing about the plight of Africans on the continent
and of those in America he wrote: "I confidently believe that as God
prepared the heart of Simon Peter to receive and instruct Cornelius, and
at the same time taught Cornelius where to find Peter, so He has moved
upon our hearts here in America and theirs in South Africa, to the
building up of His kingdom among men."[30]

What the bishop apparently did not realize at that time was that many
white South Africans, especially the missionaries, felt that the African
Americans were having a nefarious influence on the blacks. The *Christian Express* reported in 1897 that Ethiopianism was inspired by the
Africans' emulation of African American jubilee singers who toured the
country in 1890 and from whom they got the feeling that blacks "might
become more than 'hewers of wood and drawers of water.' "[31] This
charge against African Americans would be expressed in more vigorous
terms in the following years. While Turner had actual experience in
South Africa, his rival, Booker T. Washington, used his growing status
as the most important African American leader to find out more about
conditions in southern Africa. He was in touch with many resident black
missionaries and white officials who wrote to him about conditions
there. Moreover, Africans in many parts of southern Africa knew about
his work at Tuskegee and, more important, about his techniques in
dealing with powerful white Americans. In September 1899 Charles

Satchell Morris, an African American missionary serving in South Africa, wrote to him from the Lovedale Institute: "I am now at the Tuskeege [*sic*] of South Africa, a great school of some 550 students from nearly all tribes of South of Zambesie. I have a little wooden box about two by 4 inches presented to me to give to you. I will take it all around Africa and then bring it home to you. . . . At this writing the war clouds are gathering thick and fast and it looks as if the Briton & the Boer would close in on each other in a life & death struggle for the mastery of all this great region."[32] Washington received this letter shortly after his return from Britain, where, in addition to lecturing about his philosophy of education and race relations, he had informed himself on Africa and its people and had formed views on the subject.

While the British undoubtedly knew about African American opposition to European imperialism in Africa, they correctly sensed that blacks were more concerned with racism, particularly the virulent Boer variety. The British were thus not above bringing the case of Thomas Turnbull's treatment by the Boers to the attention of African Americans. Yet this anti-Boer propaganda was vitiated by Britain's initial decision not to use African troops in what they felt was to be a "white man's war."[33] Further complicating the issue for African Americans was that while the United States government was pursuing a policy of neutrality, many white Americans favored the Boers as "under-dogs," fighting the mighty British Empire in the name of freedom and independence.

So powerful was the Boer lobby, and so desirous were its members of mobilizing all Americans against the British, that a prestigious group of "representatives of American public and private life," including Booker T. Washington, asked President McKinley to mediate between Great Britain and the republics of the Transvaal and the Orange Free State. This group thought it only fitting that the United States should "strive to prevent the wiping out of two of our sister republics, the dissolution of thousands of English and South African homes, the slaughter of thousands of civilized men and drenching of South Africa with blood and tears." Whether Washington saw the irony in attaching his name to a petition endorsed by the Boer presidents is not known, but for possibly the first time in the history of the American Republic a black man was asked to participate as an equal in an "array of representatives of American character, distinction and influence" on a matter of foreign policy. He was in the company of some ninety university presidents, among whom were the presidents of Stanford, Chicago, and Colby; senators; representatives; governors; mayors; clergymen; Alexander Graham Bell

Brown; and such other illustrious persons as Carl Schurz and Adlai E. Stevenson.[34]

African Americans not only witnessed the spectacle of white Americans attempting to influence the country's policy toward South Africa but debated the issue among themselves and, to a limited extent, also sought to influence this policy. As the war waxed hot, the Boers sent envoys to the United States to plead their case. They were aware that "public opinion ruled in the United States, and frequent elections, including the choice of a President, provided the hope that popular sentiment might modify any official indifference which stood in the way of assistance."[35] The Boer propagandists hoped that the "Dutch and German elements in the United States could be relied upon to support their Boer kinsmen, and the Irish could be depended upon to indorse any movement designed to avenge the historic grievances of their compatriots." The Boers also counted on the "many persons who objected to the manner in which British capitalists had exploited the resources of South Africa, and the imperialism in England's decision to uphold the Outlanders [non-Boers] in their demand for a larger share in the control of the Boer republics."[36]

The Boers were well received in the United States, especially by the Dutch and German societies, such as the Holland Society of New York, and the Irish Societies, particularly the Ancient Order of Hibernians. So vociferous were the partisans of the Boers that Theodore Roosevelt, then governor of New York, threatened to clap the "belated Fenians" in jail if they attempted to invade Canada as a way of getting back at the British in South Africa. His ire against the Irish Americans was deeply stirred because of their "violence and indiscretions" but also because Great Britain had so recently supported the United States in its war with Spain.[37]

While a few important African American figures supported the Boers, the overwhelming number supported the British. Fred L. Jeltz, the editor of a Topeka newspaper, felt that the British were up to their old practice of imperialism and suggested that although the situation "[was] in some respects similar to the situation in the Philippines, the sympathy of at least a majority of Americans [could] not but go out to the plucky and patriotic Boers." Similarly, in an address on the "British-Boer Conflict" before the Congressional Lyceum in Washington in February 1900, Henry Y. Arnett, son of Bishop Benjamin W. Arnett of the AME Church, criticized what he termed the "British greed for gold." He "lauded the Boers for 'clinging to their kinsmen' and for 'daring to die

for their personal, civil and religious freedom.' " The young Arnett felt
that the Boer example was worthy of emulation by African Americans.
W. Calvin Chase, editor of the Washington *Bee,* took the position that
African Americans should take a good look at this case of imperialism
which, in his opinion, was comparable to the role of the United States in
the Philippines. For him this was another example of "the mailed hand
of the Anglo-Saxon in his vain attempt to dominate the world under the
hypocritical pretense of civilizing and christianizing it."[38]

Most African American newspaper editors adopted a pro-British position from the onset of the war, and most African Americans became
increasingly critical of the Boers as they heard more about racism in the
Transvaal and the Orange Free State from black missionaries. The *Colored American* of Washington, D.C., was highly critical of the racism of
the Boers and felt that they were bound to lose since the "magic cudgel
of civilization is on the side of the British." Emphasizing that "blood is
thicker than water" and convinced that "the native Africans, from whom
the Boers stole their territory, will fare infinitely better under the statesmanship of Lord Salisbury [the British prime minister] than under the
bossism of Oom Paul [Paul Kruger, president of the Transvaal]," the
editor was at a loss to understand "how a rational colored man in this
land can find in his heart a sympathetic throb for people so begotten with
prejudice" as the Boers.[39] Both the *Freeman* and the *Recorder* felt
compelled to side with the British since the Boers still kept the Africans
in a state comparable to slavery. The editor of the St. Paul-Minneapolis
Appeal wrote that while in the beginning he had some sympathy for the
Boers, having read a letter from an American missionary who had lived
in the Transvaal for fifteen years, he concluded that the Boers "deserved
to be defeated because of their 'brutality to the natives.' "[40]

A number of African Americans advocated a campaign to support the
British cause openly in active competition against the Dutch, German,
and Irish Americans who supported the Boers. Frederic J. Loudin, director of the Fisk University Jubilee Singers, writing to James Edward
Bruce, a distinguished editor and journalist, complained that it was a
pity that the United States was not giving more support to Britain in the
Boer conflict. Concerned that blacks would support "bloody
McKinley," who was doing nothing about lynching, and the "whited
sepulchre Roosevelt who slandered our brave soldiers who saved him
and his Rough Riders from annihilation," Loudin felt that blacks should
combat those whites who "are holding meetings all over the country,
[and] passing resolutions of sympathy with those Boers who would

enslave our people the very moment they free themselves from British rule. In fact it is well known that Britain's refusal to allow that is in a great measure responsible for the present outbreak." Loudin admitted "that British rule in South Africa is not all we wish it were but it is a thousand times better than Boer administration." Loudin felt that if there ever was a time for blacks to "speak out," now was the time. He claimed that white Americans were collaborating with the "oppressors of our race" and that the words of African Americans would carry much "weight for the good of our race in all parts of the world so far as Britain is concerned." Summing up his concern Loudin declared:

> That which I would advise and *strongly* too is that mass meetings be held, resolutions—of which our people are very fond of passing—be passed and sent to the British Ambassador or to Lord Salisbury, but if sent to the British Ambassador requesting him to forward them to his government and don[']t be afraid to make them too strong and let them know *who* we are.
>
> Please do not delay for *now* is the time. We will I am sure in this way make more friends—and God knows we need them—than in any other way. It will influence the treatment of our race in Africa as well; the opportunity is one of a lifetime. It is the one time when the expression of opinion will have *great* weight [emphasis his].[41]

Loudin was perhaps too optimistic about the ability of African Americans to be more effective than the more powerful Dutch, German, and Irish communities in affecting United States policy toward the South African war. Despite an official policy of neutrality, both President McKinley and his successor, Theodore Roosevelt, were said to have strong "pro-British feelings."[42] And although disgusted with the inability of the British to crush the Boers quickly, the pugnacious Roosevelt never wavered in his support for Britain. He was convinced that the Boers were battling "on the wrong side of the fight of civilization and will have to go under." Moreover he felt that it was "in the interest of the English-speaking peoples, and therefore of civilization, that English should be the tongue south of Zambezi." Finally, Roosevelt felt that should England's empire be destroyed, "the United States would be in grave danger from the great European military and naval powers."[43] A few African Americans did attempt to follow the advice of Loudin to support the British. The pro–Booker T. Washington Colored National League of Boston passed a resolution in February 1900 declaring that "colored people the world over should sympathize with England in this great struggle . . . against the thick-headed, hard-hearted and hypocritical Boers."[44] The Negro Progressive Association in Washington and the

Negro Methodist ministers meeting in Delaware passed similar resolutions.

Although not known for favoring any initiatives taken by Booker T. Washington, Bishop Henry McNeal Turner joined in the general support of blacks for the British. Speaking at the 1899 annual meeting of the AME Church in Columbus, Georgia, Turner confessed that, like most African Americans, he sympathized with the British because they were more just to the Africans. Nevertheless, he expressed some doubt about an ultimate British victory.[45] Charles Satchell Morris, a black Baptist minister, was equally pessimistic about the future of Africans in South Africa. Speaking at an Ecumenical Missionary Conference held in New York City, 21 April to 1 May 1900, he warned that "European invaders" of South Africa had a "bitter, unrelenting prejudice" against blacks. He recommended that African Americans "play a greater role in the development of the country."[46]

Despite the concern of the clerics over the course of the war, the church decided to send Bishop Levi Jenkins Coppin to South Africa as the first resident bishop of the AME Church. When he arrived in May 1900, Coppin was denied a permit to visit the embattled provinces in the country. The bishop tended his flock and kept the home church informed about the course of the war. Coppin fully supported the British, while recognizing that the Boers, fighting for their independence, had the sympathy of many Americans. He noted that the policy of the Europeans was to "divide the blacks" one from another and doubted that the Africans would reap any benefits from the war. Moreover, while he noted that the British had a "theory of equal justice for all" the groups, Coppin felt that the "whole South African condition is now a great problem."[47]

A number of African Americans then in South Africa actually fought on the side of Britain during the Boer War. This was ironic in view of the controversy that had arisen earlier when the Boers in the Transvaal attempted to conscript American citizens to fight against Africans. In a memorandum prepared for the guidance of consular officials, the Department of State took the position that Americans in South Africa "may be required to perform service in a local force raised *for the maintenance* of internal order or the defense of territory from an invasion by savages or an uncivilized nation; but aliens could not be forcibly enrolled . . . to defend [a sovereign state] against a civilized power."[48] Since the Boers were fighting against allegedly uncivilized Africans, it was possible for Americans to be impressed for service—but not during a war between Britain and Boers.

Later, when an Anglo-Boer war seemed imminent and Americans feared conscription, the Boers promised not to impress them against their wishes. The American consul in Cape Town was specifically authorized to protest against the conscription of Americans in a conflict "against any 'civilized power' unless such citizens had exercised 'political privileges and assumed political obligations' toward the Transvaal government."[49] When a number of African Americans volunteered to fight for the British (as did some white Americans for both the British and the Boers), the question of their rights as Americans was raised. The Department of State advised Cape Town that Americans "taking up arms in the service of one of the belligerents in the war" did, in fact, "identify themselves with the citizens of the states for which they are fighting." As such they were subject to the "ordinary risks and incidents of civilized warfare" and, while they did not "forfeit their American citizenship," they could "claim no immunities on account of their nationality."[50]

It is impossible to know how many African Americans fought against the Boers (or for the Boers for that matter). H. C. Bruce of Washington, D.C. (brother of Blanche Kelso-Bruce, who served as U.S. senator from Mississippi during Reconstruction), was probably indulging in rhetoric when he suggested that in view of Boer discrimination against Africans, "colored Americans are for England, and if it was possible for troops to be raised in this country for the 'Queens's Army' one hundred thousand colored Americans could be raised inside of a hundred days."[51] True, a black sergeant in the United States Army castigated Henry Y. Arnett for supporting the Boers and was "indignant that an Afro-American would dare praise a people who mistreated 'our kith and kin.' "[52] But there is no evidence that as many blacks ever seriously contemplated raising troops to go to South Africa as did the Irish and Germans.

Among the blacks who saw service against the Boers were H. A. Smith and Horatio L. Scott. Little is known about Smith, but Scott was born in California and went to South Africa in 1896 after working as a sugar grower in Oceania and as a gold miner in Australia. He was working as an explorer and ranger for Cecil Rhodes's South Africa Company when the war broke out, and he joined the Imperial Light Horse, a corps of mounted infantry recruited among foreigners in the Transvaal. Scott took part in the "prolonged siege of Ladysmith and in the relief of Mafeking"—exploits that delighted the black press in the United States. He was reported to have said that while the Africans had "grievances against the British," they could not stomach the Boers, and that his own encounters with racial discrimination in the Transvaal convinced him that as a "man of color" he had no other alternative but to fight for the English, "for the sake of my race."[53]

Ironically, the signing of the treaty of Vereeniging that brought peace between Briton and Boer did not improve the lot of blacks in South Africa, African or African American. Whites became increasingly alarmed about the possible influence of both the African American missionaries and laypersons who lived in South Africa. Despite the end of hostilities and the imposition of British rule in the former Boer republics of the Orange Free State and the Transvaal, the AME Church lost its recognition and privileges in the two areas. Protests were in vain because "the British were beginning to perceive of Afro-American missionaries as threats to colonial rule, because of a fear that they were fomenting revolt among South Africans." Coppin was consequently unable to travel to the areas "where the church had originated and where membership was the strongest."[54]

Although the British feared that the education then being provided by African American missionaries might lead to subversion, they apparently had no such fear of the possible effects of any initiative taken by Booker T. Washington. They had observed "with interest the progress of Negroes in America" under the guidance of Washington and expected advice from him in "promoting the advancement of the Negro tribes that now come under their jurisdiction."[55] Lord Grey of the British South Africa Company, which then controlled Southern Rhodesia, inquired of friends whether Washington might not be encouraged to tour Rhodesia and to advise on the best methods "to raise, educate and civilize the black man." The British South Africa Company was prepared to pay Washington's expenses for a period of about six to nine months. Washington initially welcomed the offer since it reflected his growing worldwide importance to both blacks and whites in the United States. He allegedly consulted President Roosevelt and other prominent Americans about what he should do, and in an interview given to the Boston *Transcript* on 21 June 1903, he declared:

> One very practical reason why I cannot accept the offer is that Tuskegee needs about $100,000 a year which I have to raise. Lord Grey wanted me to examine the condition of the black people, and to make a report as to what methods would increase their industrial and moral value. I considered the offer carefully, but found the task fraught with such responsibility that I decided to reject it at this time. Some day, perhaps, I shall go, but it will be when my labors here are not so great as they are now. The blacks there represent every grade of intelligence and education from savagery to the

college graduate, but the majority of the work of advancement is being done along industrial lines.[56]

What is not known is the nature of the advice given to Washington by President Roosevelt and other whites who may have convinced him that he needed to concern himself more with Tuskegee than with southern Africa. However, there is incontestable evidence that in later years many whites felt that he should not engage in foreign policy even when he was asked to do so. What is clear is that many black African leaders in southern Africa approved of Washington's approach to education, and some, but not all, saw logic in this view of race relations.

John Langalibalele Dubé, who was educated at Oberlin College from 1887 to 1892 and who had visited Tuskegee in 1897, was so impressed with Washington that in 1901 he established the Tuskegee-like Zulu Christian Industrial School in Ohlange "with financial assistance from white philanthropists from America."[57] Known as the "Booker T. Washington of South Africa," Dubé would later become involved in African nationalist politics in South Africa, but at this early period he, like many other Africans, preferred Washington to Bishop Turner. One scholar noted: "Thus, John Tengo Jabavu, the well-known eastern Cape newspaper editor and political leader, could write an editorial praising the work of Booker T. Washington while at the same time condemning Bishop Henry M. Turner of the African Methodist Episcopal Church (AME Church) as a firebrand. . . . Similarly, Pambani J. Mzimba, founder of the independent African Presbyterian Church, could write to Washington about the possibility of South Africans attending Tuskegee: 'The sons of Africa are crying to the Africans in America "Come over & help us.' "[58] A. K. Soga, "editor of the rival newspaper *Izwi LaBantu,* also favored the 'Tuskegee Industrial System for South Africa.' " In the neighboring High Commission territory of Basutoland (present-day Botswana), a student who had studied at Wilberforce University of Ohio also sought aid from Washington.

During the immediate postwar years, South African blacks were as interested in securing the aid of African Americans to procure education as they were to improve their political condition. The Tuskegee brand of industrial education was valued because at this period black South Africans were attempting to acquire the skills of whites. But they also linked this kind of education with the promises of Bishop Turner's AME Church. Testifying on 4 October 1904 before the South African Native Affairs Commission (SANAC), which from 1903 to 1905 conducted inquiries into the condition of local blacks, the Reverend Samuel

Jacobus Brander of the Ethiopian Catholic Church in Zion related how his group "joined the AME Church of America, because we found at that time that it would go better if we joined the American Church, as they had education and other things better than we had. We considered that it would be better for us to join them, so that they could help us, being coloured peoples themselves."[59] However, he added that he and his group left the AME Church and established their own denomination "on account of the promises they gave us when we joined them not being kept. They promised that they would give us a school from America at their own expense, with teachers and all, and this they did not do."[60]

Another complaint of the Africans was that the AME Church people "took all the best positions without telling us a word, sending men from America, and putting them into those positions, and taking us away, without giving us notice."[61] The commissioners did not ask Brander to explain what he meant by the statement that the AME Church was "taking us away," but it is quite possible that the preacher was concerned about the departure of many young Africans to study in the United States. This exodus also troubled the commissioners. They constantly probed for its meaning and its possible effect on South Africa, since it was well known that the AME Church had as its motto, "Africa for Africans." And while some of the witnesses before the SANAC suggested that this only meant "Africa for all nations [ethnic groups]," the commissioners were not convinced. Thus when the Reverend D. D. Stormont, the African principal of a boarding school in the Transkei, appeared to testify and was asked why African students went to America, he responded:

> It is difficult to know the real reason [for African students going to the United States], but you know the reason that is assigned, namely, that they cannot get education in their own country, and that they cannot get advancement in their own country . . . Another reason was that they were sent over there in order to get higher education, so as to be able to enter the Ministry of the African Methodist Episcopal Church, which in the course of its history, has been associated with the Ethiopian movement. Another reason—and I believe this is the chief reason—was that the American negroes were led on by . . . false utterances declared in public speeches and in letters from Natives in this country respecting the treatment of the blacks by the Europeans in South Africa. They were led on to offer, by sentiment, free education, and they offered free education to a number of young Natives, so that they might be sent back here to do mission work in connection with some American or other propaganda. I know that the motive of free education and board figured very prominently in the case of at least a dozen of those who went to America; and the result was that they sent back a message to South

Africa saying they were getting splendid education and board in America for nothing.[62]

A large number of whites in South Africa increasingly protested the growing African connection with African Americans in both church and school and saw in it seeds of disaster. One such person was the Reverend James Scott, a missionary of the Free Church of Scotland in Natal. He told the SANAC:

> I would like to say that there is a danger of a great deal of evil happening through these Blacks from America coming in and mixing with the Natives of South Africa. These men from America for generations suffered oppression, and they have naturally something to object to in the white man. . . . These men from America come in and make our Natives imagine they have grievances when there are no grievances.[63]

Scott suggested that African Americans be declared prohibited immigrants because they were effectively spreading egalitarian views among the Africans. Similar charges were made against the AME Church by one Dr. James Steward of Lovedale, who had visited black colleges in the United States in 1893 and 1903. But more damaging to the AME Church and its religious and educational activities was the testimony of two Africans: the Reverend James Mata Dwane who, now dissatisfied with the AME Church, testified that it was spreading anti-white feelings in South Africa;[64] and Francis Z. Peregrino, a Gold Coaster who had gone to live in South Africa and had initially supported the Ethiopian movement, but who now criticized what he considered to have been the AME Church's nationalist philosophy. Whether, as has been suggested, Peregrino feared that should blacks come to power in South Africa they would expel him along with the whites is unknown.[65]

Significantly, a number of white Americans, both missionary and secular, saw danger in cooperation between African Americans and black South Africans. In May 1904 Roderick Jones, a journalist, published a study of Ethiopianism entitled "The Black Peril in South Africa," which dwelt at length on the influence of African Americans and AME ministers on Africans. The following year Jones again attacked black missionaries and denied that their movement was religious:

> When Ethiopian missionaries, saturated with American democratic ideas, go up and down the land telling the Kaffirs [sic] that South Africa is a black man's country, and that the blacks must 'stand up for their rights,' it is impossible to ignore the political aspect of the propagandism.[66]

Given the amount of hostility against black missionaries among whites in South Africa, it was almost inevitable that the black churchmen would complain to the American diplomats stationed in that country. In 1903 the Reverend A. M. Middlebrooks, a black minister from Pinebluff, Arkansas, wrote Secretary of State John Hay about the refusal of the British authorities to permit him to work in the Transvaal. The department then instructed Consul Bingham at Cape Town to investigate and to protest if Middlebrooks's charge was true. Bingham reported that the protests were justified since, despite the war, both the British and the Afrikaners felt that black missionaries should be prevented from preaching in South Africa unless under white supervision. The consul reported that the whites "claim that if the Kaffir [sic] is given an education he could not be handled as submissively as he could if he were kept in ignorance."[67]

The consuls of the State Department serving in South Africa joined the chorus of South African whites, and even of white American missionaries, claiming that black missionaries were a danger to racial peace in that country. Consul Bingham in Cape Town wrote Ernest Lyon, the African American consul in Monrovia, that

> above all the American colored man should not come here, for there is a great prejudice against him by the whites. They are very fearful that he will teach the native colored man some modern ideas, which will enlighten him. . . .
> The Government is claiming that these men are teaching the doctrine . . .
> that Africa is a black man's country and the white man has no business here. This is all laid to the American Negro some of whom come here with good educations.[68]

The non-missionary African Americans who lived and worked in South Africa also found conditions getting worse and felt they were not getting the help they expected from the white United States diplomats serving there. With the imposition of British rule in the Transvaal and the Orange Free State, African Americans immediately lost the status as "honorary whites" they had received because of the intervention of the State Department in the case of John Ross. What particularly disturbed African Americans in South Africa, who styled themselves "natives and citizens of the United States of America," was that in contrast to the practice of Paul Kruger in the Transvaal, the British attempted to forbid the sale of liquor to them.

Petitioning Consul Joseph E. Proffit to protect their rights in the Transvaal "as civilized people," Thomas Brown et al. wrote:

> We find that our liberty once enjoyed under the late government is abrogated and we are left without protection. We are at a loss regarding our treatment, and therefore appeal to you for the adjustment of the same.

First: We are debarred of a second class railway ticket because of our colour.

Secondly: Prohibition from walking on the sidewalk for which we are thrown about like chattel.

Thirdly: We are not allowed to do any business because we are Americans.

Fourthly: We are told that the Americans are [or?] subjects must expect the same treatment as the Africans. To this and more makes our treatment unbearable, and demands your immediate attention.[69]

In a memorandum accompanying this petition to the State Department, Consul Proffit noted that he had been advised by the British authorities that the prohibitions the African Americans had complained about were in fact abrogated when Britain took over control from the Boers. However, he explained that the maintenance of such prohibitions as that of preventing blacks from using the sidewalks "lies rather in custom than in law."

Proffit asserted that "the sentiment which exists in the breast of the average white man in South Africa against the use of the sidewalks by people of color . . . [was] perhaps a greater deterrent than any law could possibly be." He pointed out that tradesmen's licenses were denied to the petitioners not because they were Americans, as claimed, but because they were "colored men." Then in a revealing statement, Proffit confirmed that prohibitions such as the law relative to railway transportation did "not differ in any essential respects from the laws obtaining in many of our Southern states."[70]

During the trial the South African judge insisted to Proffit that Brown and his fellows were subject to the laws applying to blacks in South Africa. The consul did succeed in having Brown's sentence suspended but was apparently so unsympathetic to the African Americans that they wrote the American Secretary of State from Johannesburg on 28 August 1903, complaining that not only did they not receive any help from American consular officials when the British government insisted that they "wear a pass" like any "native in his barbarous state" but, they charged, one consular official had also treated them as though they "were heathens" and had "advanced the advice that they [black Americans] had no business" being in South Africa.[71] African Americans were urged to recognize that they were guests of the British government as long as they remained in South Africa; that they had known about the pattern of race relations in that country before they arrived; and that they had an obligation therefore "to abide by those rules, however harshly they may press upon . . . [them]."[72] Their letter concluded with the following observation:

> It seems to us that our Government is used to assist the British Government in restricting our rights to live and act as civilized people in this country. I hope that our Republican administration will not make capital for the Democratic Party in Ohio, Indiana and Illinois by permitting their agents in South Africa from driving us from this country.[73]

Like many Americans overseas, Henry Dean and Thomas Brown may have placed too much emphasis on the ability of the United States to protect them. As blacks, they probably did not realize that their "status in the United States was changing for the worse and the American consuls in South Africa were probably influenced by this fact" and did not care to protest the abrogation of their rights.[74]

Captain Henry Dean, who had arrived in Cape Town during the Boer War with a dream of founding an "Ethiopian Empire" in Africa, was especially indignant about the turn of events in South Africa. He resented being classified as a European because of his light skin and had difficulties with the U.S. consul, William R. Bingham, whom he categorized as a useless "anemic old man from Kansas." The consul's sin was that he failed to help another African American from Texas, Kid Gardener, who had been arrested, convicted, and imprisoned for getting into a fight after being refused a drink in a Cape Town bar.[75] Apparently concluding that United States diplomats in South Africa were not prepared to defend their interests, resident African Americans there had recourse to the local courts to defend and secure their rights. They hired one Dacre Tottenham, an attorney in Pretoria. He argued that the "American Negro" was a person of "much higher social standing than the African native." This argument failed to impress the British, who insisted on the application of the same laws to all blacks. The attorney for the Crown insisted that were a distinction to be made between an "American native [sic] and an African native then the spirit of the law would not be carried out" since the law prohibited the sale of liquor to any "colored person."[76] The irony was that African Americans continued to patronize bars legally in British controlled Cape Town and Natal, whereas they were forbidden to do so when the British took over the Boer areas.

Attempting to satisfy the clamor of the Africans for education but preferring that it not be linked to the AME Church, held to be subversive, the colonial officials turned once again to Booker T. Washington.

When Lord Alfred Milner was named high commissioner for South Africa, he appointed E. B. Sargeant commissioner of education, and Sargeant asked Mrs. Grace Lathrop Luling, a friend of Washington's, to get advice. Washington's response to her will be cited in full because it demonstrates clearly his belief in full civil rights for South African blacks even when he was regarded as not advocating the same rights for American blacks. He wrote to Mrs. Luling that after consulting with Mr. J. N. Calloway, a member of the faculty of Tuskegee who had spent three years or more in Africa as the head of a Tuskegee team sent out to introduce cotton raising in the German possession of Togo, he was now in a position to answer her. Washington prefaced his response with the observations made by Mr. Calloway after his experience in Africa that he could

see no very great difference between the native problem and the Negro problem in America, and that the answers to the six questions herewith submitted are based upon the recognition of that fact:

(1) Since the blacks are to live under the English Government, they should be taught to love and revere that government better than any other institution. To teach them this, they should receive their education and training for citizenship from or through the government. It is not always true that the Missions teach respect for the rulers in power.

(2) There is no universal language among the tribes of Africa, and therefore they could have no books that would be of general use to the several tribes in the colonies. They should be given a language that will open up to them a knowledge of the world they live in and of western civilization. No other language will do this so well as the English language. Aside from this, all the laws and business of the colony are to be in English from and by English methods.

(3) The State should not only give a common school education but an industrial training that will fit them to go out into this rich country and be skilled laborers in agriculture, mining and the trades.

(4) As far as native men become educated and refined they should be shown, in a social way, a proper recognition of their worth and in civil standing be the equal of Europeans. To undertake to settle this problem in any other way means, eventually, more or less civil discord.

(5) The tribal system of government should gradually be replaced by an allegiance directly to the government of the land. Some native blacks have already gone to the United States for an education and when they return to their homes in Africa they will not be satisfied to give their allegiance to the old time superstitious chiefs.

(6) Experience shows that the black, as other men, work better and more profitably when induced to this labor by reward and it is voluntarily performed. If proper inducements are offered these people they will labor more and more as their wants are increased by education.

> Thanking you affording me the opportunity to be of service in this matter, I am, Yours very truly,
>
> Booker T. Washington[77]

Washington would have been the last person to encourage Africans to engage in "civil discord" to obtain "civil standing . . . the equal of Europeans," but he was essentially correct in believing that there would be trouble if educated Africans were not granted full equality. For their part, the European officials in South Africa were primarily interested in ruling Africans through traditional chiefs and in getting rural Africans to labor in the mines. But there were a growing number of Christians who eschewed the control of the traditional chiefs. In 1901 they founded the Natal Native Congress with little or no support from the chiefs in order to effect a liaison with the government for "Christians and civilised natives" who had moved away from the influence of the chiefs. Ultimately the congress hoped to represent all Africans.[78]

Most members of the congress belonged to separatist churches, but the spokesmen of the two largest groups, the African Methodist Episcopal Church and the Ethiopian Church, being typical of many of the smaller sects, stopped short of asserting African political autonomy when they stressed that their members wanted political involvement, as well as economic cooperation with whites, in the wider South African society. Spokesmen for the congress told the South African Native Affairs Commission that they desired increased African land-holdings and were concerned about economic relations with whites. They insisted that "education should be structured to fit Africans for a common society based on European standards. Racial distinctions in syllabuses should be discouraged, and industrial and technical schools were needed to provide alternative occupations for a surplus rural population."[79] In addition to this, the congress called for local governments for urban African communities. Thus these Africans were in substantial agreement with the advice that Washington gave Mrs. Luling. African Americans were long held responsible for a rebellion that broke out in South Africa during this period. In 1905 British officials in Durban, Natal, in an attempt to force rural Africans into the mines, passed Poll Tax Act 38, which stipulated that in January 1906 a tax of £1 would be paid by every male, irrespective of color, over the age of eighteen years. The Africans protested, yet on the date specified, some chiefs and their followers promptly paid. But a number of persons, led by two Christian members of the African Congregational Church (an Ethiopian sect), refused to pay. There then ensued several clashes between Africans and whites, during which a number of white magistrates and farmers were killed. The administration invoked martial law, killed a number of Zulus, took others into custody, and tried and executed those found guilty of insurrection.

Reacting to these developments, Bambata, a Zulu chief, allegedly receiving the tacit support of Dinizulu, the Zulu king, organized a revolt against the British. He mobilized his *impis*, or soldiers, and attacked the government army composed of white and African soldiers. In May 1906 Bambata and over five hundred of his warriors then retreated beyond the Tugela River but were pursued by a superior government force, which defeated and killed them. Several bloody clashes subsequently took place between the Africans and the government, and over four thousand Africans were killed. It was not until July 1906 that the government was able to announce officially that the Bambata rebellion was over.[80]

While it is still difficult to assess the role played by the AME Church and the Ethiopian movement in the Bambata rebellion, many European colonists were convinced that "the whole thing was engineered by sedition-mongers from America."[81] They conceded that the precipitating factor was the essential injustice of the poll tax, but correspondents to the Natal *Mercury* blamed African Americans and the Ethiopian movement as the major cause of the trouble. One wrote: "An evil star rose in the American firmament and sent its satellites to preach sedition in Natal."[82] The writer admitted that not all African Christians, the *amakolwa*, were bad, only Ethiopians affected by the AME Church, like the members of the African Congregational Church. The Reverend James Scott, a white clergyman, informed a public meeting "that Natal Natives were being sent to colleges in America." He added that "over 150 young Natives were recently sent from South Africa, including twenty from Natal." This to him was "one of the greatest dangers to the standing of the white men in South Africa." He claimed that he "would be loath to hinder any man getting education, but insisted that the fact to which he had drawn attention was a great danger to their future."[83]

The African American missionaries in southern Africa were so concerned that their work might be jeopardized that a number of them voluntarily appeared before the commission investigating the cause of African unrest. They "persistently denied that the AME Church sowed seeds of discontent or anti-white feelings, maintaining that the Church was politically neutral, but loyal to the British Government and its colonial authorities in Southern Africa."[84] The problem for these missionaries was that the black nationalist views of Bishop Henry McNeal Turner were widely known in South Africa. One Bishop Charles Smith told the commission, "We do not stand for very many of his [Turner's] utterances in regard to Africa."[85] Smith's views were echoed by Bishop Levi Jenkins Coppin, the senior AME Church official in South Africa. Coppin informed the commission that Turner's views on emigration were not always consistent with those of the council of bishops of the church, nor of many individual church members in the United States.[86] This refutation apparently convinced the commission, because in its final report it asserted that the AME Church's pursuit of self-determination was not necessarily a political activity. Moreover, it recommended that the AME Church not be proscribed.[87]

What the commission did not see were the letters espousing black nationalism that Coppin sent home from South Africa. Criticizing missionaries who sang about the Africans, "Pity them, pity them, Christians at home," he was pessimistic about the lot of black South Africans. He thought it not at all likely that the Europeans would do more for the Africans than was being done. Coppin reported wide support among whites to remove Africans "to a location, that is to say, to get a camp outside of the city and place them there, where they will be beyond the reach of civilizing influences." When he inquired how the Africans would make a living, he was told that "a line of cars would extend to their quarters that they might come into town during the day and find work." What disturbed Coppin about this situation was that he felt that the wages they could command were "small at the very best, so by the time they pay car fare, morning and night, to and from their work, there will be little left for them to purchase food and clothing or to make their homes even partially comfortable. The inevitable result," said Coppin, "will be that under this plan they will remain perpetually in their present condition, though living under the very shadow of a civilized and Christian community. Once they owned all the land by inheritance, and now they are not permitted to domicile on it, or, only upon such portions of it as may be allotted to them out of pity."[88]

The bishop could not refrain from comparing the situation of blacks in South Africa with that of those in the United States:

> When we are told that a man in America is denied civil and political rights on account of being a descendant of Africa, we are content to call it unjust, ungodly; but when we are told that an African in Africa is denied civil privileges because he is an African, we feel that besides being unrighteous and unworthy [of] our Christian civilization, it is ridiculous in the extreme.[89]

What gave the bishop some comfort was his conviction that in contrast with the United States, "in Africa, more than any other place upon the face of the globe, it will be difficult to withhold from the black man the measure of justice and privilege to which he is entitled as a man. This is his home. Here he is to the manor born." Coppin firmly believed that interlopers who on account of superior strength would resolve to rob the African "of his country and his privileges must feel that to do so would be to take the vineyard of Naboth." He recounted that 250 years had passed since the Dutch settled permanently in South Africa. Their ability to subjugate the weaker peoples they found occupying the Cape enabled them to move further and further north until they were situated beyond the Vaal. Coppin wrote that "strong in experience and rich in possession, they [the Boers] came to regard the man who is native to the soil as being the man without a soul."[90]

Coppin recounted how grieved he was to see the pathetic Africans "by the thousands scattered about upon islands, in forts, in locations and upon transports, with homes destroyed and property confiscated." But, like the good Christian he was, Coppin did not despair: "Be not deceived. God is not mocked." The bishop also believed that "the colored man, whether in South Africa or elsewhere, has a duty to perform. He must learn to appropriate the light that comes to him. He must show himself worthy of his place among civilized nations. He must profit by the terrible lessons that others have been taught before his face. He must in every sense be a man."[91]

Nevertheless, many African American missionaries resented being associated with Ethiopianism, and protested to the United States government about the increase in the restrictions placed against them and the intensification of general harassment. In a long confidential despatch sent to the State Department early in 1909, Julius Lay, the American consul in Cape Town, reported that the government officials believed that the "influence exerted by the American colored" interfered with "their control of the natives." The consul agreed with South Africa, stating that "American representatives of the AME Church have not always conducted themselves in such a manner as to entitle them to the confidence of the authorities."[92]

The charges that African American missionaries were creating problems for the British in South Africa reached the ears of Theodore Roosevelt. A thoroughgoing Anglophile and imperialist, the former president castigated the missionaries for what he considered to be unwarranted rhetorical interference in South African affairs. In a speech before the annual convention of the AME Church in Washington, D.C., in 1909, he declared that the delegates should not allow the "occasional wrong-doing" to overshadow "the fact that on the whole the white administrator and the Christian missionary have exercised a profound and wholesome influence for good in savage regions."[93]

The South African Natives report for 1909, linking the Ethiopian movement with African Americans, concluded that the "close connection between the Ethiopians and the negroes of the Southern States is viewed with grave misgiving by many South Africans." The fear was that there would be a stimulating "spirit of racial jealousy and exclusiveness" which could have a "sinister influence on the future of South Africa."[94] Nevertheless, the commissioners were convinced that there was a great thirst for education among South African blacks and that unless something were done, the American connection could pose problems.

A number of whites as well as blacks in South Africa denied that either the African Americans or the Ethiopians were responsible for the outbreak. The secretary of the American Zulu Mission denied that the African Congregational Church was Ethiopian and claimed that he was on the best terms with its members. Dismissing the charges that Ethiopianism was a negative force in southern Africa and that the Africans were disloyal to the British government, the newly formed South African Native Congress passed a resolution on 10 April 1906 declaring that "much has been made of the outcry of Ethiopianism, and all sorts of charges have been laid at the door of this new feature." It stressed, however, that there was no proof that "the natives, or any section of them, are disloyal or meditating mischief against the supreme authority." The congress believed that Ethiopianism was a "symptom of progress, brought about by the contact of the natives of Africa with European civilization making itself felt in all departments of the social, religious, and economic structure." The resolution wished to place on record the congress's opinion "that the imposition of taxation without representation is a crime; that to that cause must be traced the origin of the disturbances."[95]

The African leaders in South Africa attempted to keep Booker T. Washington informed about their problems with the British and asked him for both educational and political aid. On 29 January 1907, Pixley ka Isaka Seme, a graduate of Columbia University in New York City who was then studying at Jesus College, Oxford University, wrote the Tuskegean, "We need your spirit in South Africa."[96] Again, on 15 April 1908, Seme wrote Washington informing him about attempts to form a club among African students in England. Seme wanted to take advantage of the presence of the "future leaders of African nations" to have them exchange ideas. However, he thought it wise to warn Washington that "this movement is not fastened to any daring or even lofty star—violence in word or deed has no place in our programme—We meet as brethren, sons of a common fatherland for the interchange of general ideas and for self-education in the problems of the unhappy fatherland receiving her story from the lips of her own sons. . . . In closing I beg to say that publicity and all species of notoriety are not connected with our movement—our programme is very simple but I believe that in God's time this movement will prove very eventful toward bringing about the 'regeneration of Africa.' "[97] On 29 April 1908 Washington responded to Seme, announcing satisfaction with the plan to bring together "the educated young men of our race in England . . . to seriously discuss the problems and conditions of their people in Africa. It is a great task that you have before you; but great tasks have their rewards. . . . More and more I am learning that you face in South Africa, in a somewhat different and more difficult form, the same task we have in this country. . . . I wish you Godspeed in your work and hope that you will keep me informed of your success."[98]

John Langalibalele Dubé, of Phoenix, Natal, sent Washington a copy of the report of the commission that had investigated the Bambata rebellion and a copy of a speech that he had made to the Zulu people, to provide the principal of Tuskegee with "an insight to our life in South Africa." Dubé said to Washington, "[Y]our devoted life in the interest of the Negro race has made me love you dearly." He expressed concern about Washington's possible reaction to his political stance: "You may regard me as a political agitator from reading my speech to the Zulu people," he said, "but I am sure if you knew me, you would know that I am not in the habit of speaking as I did upon that occasion. Things had gone so bad, that I as one of the leaders of the people felt it my duty to speak the whole truth."[99]

Obviously Dubé felt that he needed the support of African Americans for the battle that he and his colleagues had started to wage against the oppression of blacks in South Africa. The sad end of the Bambata rebellion had convinced many of them that the black people in South Africa did not possess the military power to combat the whites. In turning to Booker T. Washington, Dubé stressed that "a great number of civilized natives are anxious to push forward in spite of the prejudice of our white people. The condition is much like that in the Southern States in America. They want our ignorant people to stay in their heathen condition so that they can only use them as beasts of burden. Those who aspire to something higher are not wanted." Dubé hoped that Washington would help with an agricultural program that had been approved by the officials of Cape Colony only because they knew of the Alabaman's reputation for prudence. Recounting the trouble he had had with whites in South Africa, Dubé concluded: "I wanted some one either from your School, or Hampton to teach farming, but the authorities objected to that. They fear that American Negroes would teach our people racial ill-feeling."[100]

Notes

1. From the Reverend John Tule to Bishop Henry McNeal Turner, quoted in J. Mutero Chirenje, Harvard University, "The Afro-American Factor in Southern African Ethiopianism—1890–1906," n.d., 38. This dissertation has now been published. The full title is J. Mutero Chirenje, *Ethiopianism and Afro-Americans in Southern Africa, 1883–1916* (Baton Rouge: Louisiana State University Press, 1987), 43–54.
2. See Josephus Roosevelt Coan, "The Expansion of Missions of the African Methodist Episcopal Church in South Africa, 1896–1908" (Ph.D. diss., Hartford Seminary Foundation, 1961). See also Bengt G. M. Sundkler, *Bantu Prophets in South Africa* (London: Lutterworth Press, 1948), 39ff; Document 8c presented as Testimony in the Minutes of Evidence, South African Native Affairs Commission, 1903–1905 (SANAC), in *From Protest to Challenge: A Documentary History of African Politics in South Africa, 1882–1964,* ed. Thomas Karis and Gwendolen M. Carter (Stanford, Calif.: Hoover Institution Press, 1972–77), 1:39–41; Carol A. Page, "Colonial Reaction to A.M.E. Missionaries in South Africa, 1898–1910," in *Black Americans and the Missionary Movement in Africa,* ed. Sylvia M. Jacobs (Westport, Conn.: Greenwood Press, 1982), 177–96.
3. Despatches from U.S. Consulate in Cape Town, 1800–1906, T191, Record Group 84, National Archives, roll 16.
4. "The Jubilee Singers," Editorial in *Imvo,* 16 October 1890, cited in Chirenje, *Ethiopianism,* 34–36.
5. Ibid., 39–40.
6. South African Native Affairs Commission (SANAC), *Report of the Commission, 1903–5* (Cape Town: Cape Times Limited, 1905), 1:64. See also Anthony Ngube, "Contributions of the Black American Church to Development of African Independent Movements in South Africa," in *For Better or Worse: The American Influence in the World,* ed. Allen F. Davis (Westport, Conn.: Greenwood Press, 1981), 146.
7. Coan, "Expansion of Missions," 442. See also SANAC *Report* 2:634.
8. Turner to Editor, *Voice of Missions,* 23 February 1893 and 15 May 1893.
9. Mokone and Xaba to Turner, 18 September 1895, in "Ethiopian Mission," *Voice of Missions,* December 1895; Xaba to Turner, 26 October 1895, in "South African Letter," ibid., December 1895, cited in Chirenje, *Ethiopianism,* 52ff.
10. Ibid., 54.
11. Ibid.
12. Dwane to Editor, 22 May 1897, in "Grand Letters from South Africa," *Voice of Missions,* July 1897, and Marcus Gabashane to Turner, 25 May 1897, in "Letter from South Africa," ibid., July 1897, cited in Chirenje, *Ethiopianism,* 56.
13. Edward Roux, *Time Longer Than Rope: A History of the Black Man's Struggle for Freedom in South Africa* (Madison, Wis.: University of Wisconsin Press, 1964), 84–85.

14. Ibid.
15. Quoted in George Shepperson and Thomas Price, *Independent African: John Chilembwe and the Origins, Setting, and Significance of the Nyasaland Native Rising of 1915* (Edinburgh: University Press, 1958), 111–12. See also Joseph Booth, "Industrial Missions in Africa," *Missionary Review of the World* 19 (April 1896): 290–94.
16. Mangena Mokone, "Grand Letter From South Africa," Mokone to the Editor, *Voice of Missions*, 22 May 1897.
17. Chirenje, "Ethiopianism," 37–38; Willard B. Gatewood, Jr., "Black Americans and the Boer War, 1899–1902," *South Atlantic Quarterly* 75 (1976): 226–31. Apparently Assistant Secretary of State Edwin F. Uhl was quite concerned about these incidents in South Africa. On 2 October 1894, Consul Charles Benedict wrote to Mr. Uhl:

In reply to your esteemed favor of May 29th 1894, No. 26, I beg to state that the whipping of the colored American citizen, mentioned in my Despatch No. 48 and alluded to in your Despatch No. 220 of May 9th, 1893, was not given for the alleged offense of walking on the side walk but for insolent language used towards a police officer.

I shall endeavor to follow instructions as regards any whipping of our Citizens, and will keep you promptly informed. (Despatches from U.S. Consulate at Cape Town, 1800–1906, Record Group 84, National Archives)

18. Gatewood, "Black Americans and Boer War," 231.
19. *A.M.E. Church Review* 15 (4 April 1899), quoted in *Respect Black: The Writings and Speeches of Henry McNeal Turner*, ed. Edwin S. Redkey (New York: Arno Press and the New York Times, 1971), 178.
20. *Voice of Missions*, November 1898, cited in Edwin S. Redkey, *Black Exodus: Black Nationalist and Back-to-Africa Movements, 1890–1910* (New Haven: Yale University Press, 1969), 249.
21. Chirenje, *Ethiopianism*, 63.
22. Quoted from "An American Bishop at the Opera House," *Cape Argus*, 25 April 1898, in Chirenje, *Ethiopianism*, 63.
23. Quoted in Redkey, *Respect Black*, 179.
24. Ibid.
25. Ibid., 63.
26. Ibid., 180.
27. Chirenje, *Ethiopianism*, 63. See also Coan, "Expansion of Missions," 156.
28. Redkey, *Respect Black*, 180.
29. Ibid., 179.
30. Ibid., 181.
31. "The Colonial Native and the American Negro," *Christian Express*, 6 September 1897, quoted in Chirenje, *Ethiopianism*, 58–59.
32. Charles Satchell to Booker T. Washington, September 1899, Louis R. Harlan and Raymond W. Smock, eds., *The Booker T. Washington Papers* (Urbana: University of Illinois Press, 1981), 5:209–10 (hereafter cited as *BTW Papers*). Cf. R. H. W. Sheppard, *Lovedale, South Africa, 1841–1941* (Cape Province, South Africa: Lovedale Press, 1941).
33. Gatewood, "Black Americans and Boer War," 232.
34. *BTW Papers* 5:230–32.
35. John H. Ferguson, *American Diplomacy and the Boer War* (Philadelphia: University of Pennsylvania Press, 1939), 177.
36. Ibid.

37. Ibid., 210.
38. Gatewood, "Black Americans and Boer War," 233–39.
39. Ibid., 234.
40. Ibid.
41. Letter in the Schomburg Collection, cited in Adelaide Cromwell Hill and Martin Kilson, eds. and comps., *Apropos of Africa: Sentiments of Negro American Leaders on Africa From the 1800s to the 1950s* (London: Frank Cass, 1969), 122.
42. Ferguson, *American Diplomacy*, 206.
43. Ibid., 208.
44. Gatewood, "Black Americans and Boer War," 237.
45. "Bishop Turner on Kruger," Savannah *Tribune*, 4 November 1899, cited in Sylvia M. Jacobs, *The African Nexus: Black American Perspectives on the European Partitioning of Africa, 1880–1920* (Westport, Conn.: Greenwood Press, 1981), 143.
46. Ibid., 145–46.
47. Coppin, *Observations*, 28, 76, 140, cited in ibid., 144.
48. Marcum to Moore, 5 November 1898, Pretoria, Cons. Letters and Memorandum by Mr. Van Dyne, 4 April 1899, cited in Ferguson, *American Diplomacy*, 15.
49. Ibid., 17.
50. Ibid., 68.
51. *Colored American*, 20 January 1990, 1.
52. Gatewood, "Black Americans and Boer War," 238.
53. Ibid., 236.
54. Jacobs, *African Nexus*, 144.
55. Arthur Hawkes, "The Negro Problem in South Africa," *Review of Reviews* 28 (September 1903): 325–30, quoted in Thomas J. Noer, *Briton, Boer, and Yankee: The United States and South Africa, 1879–1914* (Ohio: Kent State University Press, 1978), 112.
56. *BTW Papers* 7:181–82.
57. *BTW Papers* 4:262.
58. R. Hunt Davis, Jr., "The Black American Component in African Responses to Colonialism in South Africa, ca. 1890–1914," *Journal of Southern African Affairs* 3 (January 1978): 66.
59. Document 8c presented as Testimony in the Minutes of Evidence, South African Native Affairs Commission (SANAC), 1903–1905, in Karis and Carter, *From Protest to Challenge* 1:39–41.
60. Ibid., 41.
61. Ibid.
62. SANAC, *Report* 3:1009.
63. Ibid. 2:375. Cf. ibid., 2:634.
64. Ibid. 2:708–15.
65. Chirenje, *Ethiopianism*, 105.
66. Roderick Jones, "The Black Peril in South Africa," *Nineteenth Century and After* 55 (May 1904): 712–23; "The Black Problem in South Africa," ibid. 57 (May 1905): 770–76, cited in Noer, *Briton, Boer, and Yankee*, 120–21.
67. Pierce to Bingham, Washington, 30 December 1903, no. 158, Records of Consulates: Cape Town; Pierce to Proffit, Washington, D.C., 30 December 1903, no. 37, Records of Consulates: Johannesburg; Bingham to Pierce, Cape Town, 7 March 1904, no. 335, Consular Despatches: Cape Town, cited in Noer, *Britain, Boer, and Yankee*, 115–16.

68. Bingham to Ernest Lyon, Cape Town, 7 March 1905, Records of Consulates: Cape Town, cited in Noer, *Briton, Boer, and Yankee,* 121.
69. Petition of Thomas Brown, et. al., to Joseph E. Proffit, Johannesburg, 8 August 1904, in Consular Despatches, Pretoria, T660, Record Group 59, National Archives, roll 2.
70. Proffit to Loomis, Pretoria, 8 August 1904, ibid.
71. Noer, *Briton, Boer, and Yankee,* 165.
72. Proffit to Loomis, Pretoria, 8 August 1904, Consular Despatches, Pretoria, roll 3.
73. Harry Dean and James Brown to Secretary of State, Johannesburg, 28 August 1903, Miscellaneous Letters of the Department of State, M179, Record Group 59, National Archives, roll 1182.
74. Clement Tsehloabe Keto, "American Involvement in South Africa 1879–1915: The Role of Americans in the Creation of Modern South Africa" (Ph.D. diss., Georgetown University, 1972), 164.
75. Harry Dean, *The Pedro Gorino: The Adventure of a Negro Sea-Captain in Africa and on the Seven Seas in His Attempt to Found an Ethiopian Empire* (New York: Houghton and Mifflin, 1929), 78–88. Engaged along the southern African coasts, Dean traveled inland from the Cape as far as Lesotho. He was accused by the Portuguese in Mozambique of being an American agent, lost out in a very costly deal, and finally returned to the United States a broken old man after being forced to sell his shipping business.
76. Clipping from Transvaal *Leader* of 2 August 1904, Consular Despatches, Pretoria, roll 276.
77. From BTW to Grace Lathrop Dunham Luling, 28 January 1905, *BTW Papers* 8:184–85. But compare W. Manning Marable, "Booker T. Washington and African Nationalism," *Phylon* 35 (1974): 398–406.
78. SANAC, *Report* 3:492, 523, 868.
79. A. P. Walshe, "The Origin of African Political Consciousness in South Africa," *Journal of Modern African Studies* 4 (1969): 592–94.
80. H. E. McCallum to Secretary of State for Colonies, Pietermaritzburg, Cd. 3247, 19 July 1906, in *British Parliamentary Papers* 79 (1906): 6–7.
81. Roux, *Time Longer than Rope,* 97–98.
82. Ibid.
83. Ibid.
84. Ibid., 38.
85. SANAC, *Report* 4:964.
86. Chirenje, *Ethiopianism,* 107–8.
87. SANAC, *Report* 1:64.
88. Bishop Levi Jenkins Coppin, *Letters From South Africa* (Philadelphia: A.M.E. Books Concern, n.d.), 210ff., quoted in Hill and Kilson, *Apropos of Africa,* 245ff. See also "American Negro's Religion for the African Negro's Soul," *Independent* 54 (27 March 1902): 748–58; *Observations of Persons and Things in South Africa, 1900–1904* (Philadelphia: A.M.E. Book Concern, n.d.), 205.
89. Coppin, cited in Hill and Kilson, *Apropos of Africa,* 247–49.
90. Ibid., 252.
91. Ibid.
92. Cited in Noer, *Briton, Boer, Yankee,* 123, Lay to Department of State, Cape Town (Confidential), 16 February 1909, no. 111, *Internal Affairs of British Africa, 1037/7544.*
93. Theodore Roosevelt, *The Works of Theodore Roosevelt: National Edition* (New York: Charles Scribner's Sons, 1926), 16:260–61.

94. South African Native Races Committee, ed., *The South African Natives: Their Progress and Present Condition* (London: John Murray, 1909), 199.
95. Karis and Carter, *From Protest to Challenge* 1:46–48.
96. Pixley ka Isaka Seme to BTW, 29 January 1907, *BTW Papers* 9:204.
97. Seme to BTW, *BTW Papers* 9:500–501.
98. BTW to Seme, ibid., 522.
99. John Langalibalele Dube to BTW, 21 September 1907, ibid., 338–39.
100. Ibid.

**Martin R. Delany
(1812–85)** Author of
*The Condition, Elevation,
Emigration and Destiny
of the Colored People of
the United States,* Delany
advocated emigration in
response to the oppression
of black people in America.
With Robert Campbell, he
traveled in Liberia and the
Niger Valley. On his return,
he wrote the *Official Report
of the Niger Valley Exploring
Party* in support of emi-
gration. (Photograph from
Rev. William J. Simmons,
comp., *Men of Mark:
Eminent, Progressive and
Rising,* Cleveland: George
M. Rewall & Co., 1887)

**Henry Highland Garnet
(1815–82)** A militant
abolitionist, Garnet advocated resistance to slavery,
including armed rebellion
to overthrow the institution.
After an eventful life as
clergyman and missionary
in the Presbyterian church,
editor, and emigrationist,
Garnet was appointed
minister to Liberia in
January 1882. He was given
a gala reception by Edward
Wilmot Blyden and the
Liberian political elite. He
died a month later and was
given a state burial in
Liberia. (Photograph from
Rev. William J. Simmons,
comp., *Men of Mark:
Eminent, Progressive and
Rising,* Cleveland: George
M. Rewall & Co., 1887)

Edward Wilmot Blyden (1832–1912) A consistent spokesman for emigration, Blyden served Liberia in various offices — as professor of classics, president of Liberia College, secretary of state, minister of interior, minister to Britain, and later to Paris and Britain as a special envoy. When his bid to become president of Liberia failed, he moved to Sierra Leone, where he lived and worked for over twenty-five years. *(Courtesy of the Library of Congress)*

Henry McNeal Turner (1834–1915) Bishop and historian of the African Methodist Episcopal church, Turner was variously a legislator, editor, agent of the Freedmen's Bureau, president of Morris Brown College, a vice president of the American Colonization Society, and strong advocate of emigration. He traveled to Africa, lectured widely in Europe, and contended that the American government should pay reparations and assist in the repatriation of the slaves to Africa. *(Courtesy of the Moorland-Spingarn Research Center, Howard University)*

James Milton Turner (1840–1915) President of the Freedmen's Association of Oklahoma and St. Louis respectively, an educator, and diplomat, Turner raised money from black soldiers after the Civil War to found Lincoln Institute in Missouri, which later became Lincoln University. He served as minister resident and consul-general to Monrovia, Liberia from 1871–78. (Photograph from Rev. William J. Simmons, comp., *Men of Mark: Eminent, Progressive and Rising,* Cleveland: George M. Rewall & Co., 1887)

George Washington Williams (1849–91) Author of the well received *History of the Negro Race in America* and *History of the Negro Troops in the War of the Rebellion,* Williams was also a soldier, clergyman, lawyer, legislator, and explorer. He exposed the exploitation and brutal oppression of Africans in the Congo Free State under King Leopold of the Belgians after his travels and observation of conditions in Africa. (Photograph from Rev. William J. Simmons, comp., *Men of Mark: Eminent, Progressive and Rising,* Cleveland: George M. Rewall & Co., 1887)

Booker T. Washington (1856–1915) Founder of Tuskegee Institute, Washington became a race spokesman during post-Reconstruction. Although openly opposed to emigration, he quietly assisted in efforts to benefit Liberia. *(Courtesy of the Moorland-Spingarn Research Center, Howard University)*

W. E. B. Du Bois (1866–1963) Scholar, editor, one of the founders of the NAACP, and chief organizer of five Pan-African Conferences, Du Bois was appointed special minister and envoy extraordinary to the inauguration of the president of Liberia in 1923. *(Courtesy of the Library of Congress)*

Marcus A. Garvey (1887–1940) Impressed by Booker T. Washington's message of self-help, Garvey left Jamaica, traveled to Britain, and then came to America, where he organized the United Negro Improvement Association, the largest international black nationalist organization of its time. He supported emigration, but also advocated racial uplift wherever blacks found themselves. *(Courtesy of New York Public Library, Schomburg Collection)*

Charles Young (1864–1922) A graduate of the U.S. Military Academy, a teacher of military science at Wilberforce University, an officer in the Spanish American War, author of *Military Morale of Nations and Races,* and a man of sterling character, Young served with great distinction as military attaché to Port au Prince, Haiti and Monrovia, Liberia. *(Courtesy of the Library of Congress)*

6

Challenging Imperialism in the Congo

> The rich and populous valley of the Congo is being opened to com-
> merce by a society called the International African Association, of
> which the King of the Belgians is the president and a citizen of the
> United States the chief executive officer. Large tracts of territory
> have been ceded to the association by native chiefs, roads have been
> opened, steamboats placed on the river, and the *nuclei* of states es-
> tablished at twenty-two stations under one flag which offers free-
> dom to commerce and prohibits the slave trade. The objects of the
> society are philanthropic. It does not aim at permanent political
> control but seeks the neutrality of the valley. The United States can-
> not be indifferent to this work nor to the interests of their citizens
> involved in it. It may become advisable for us to co-operate with
> other commercial powers in promoting the rights of trade and resi-
> dence in the Congo Valley free from the interference or political
> control of any one nation.[1]

African Americans who closely followed European activities in Africa
largely distrusted Leopold II's venture in the Congo. In contrast, the
White House and the Department of State were apparently less suspicious of his motives, although African Americans did not believe that
their president could be so innocent or naive about the intentions of
Leopold or other Europeans involved in the scramble for Africa. In an
endeavor to obtain the views of leading blacks about the situation in
Africa, the editor of the *A.M.E. Church Review* wrote to them inquiring,
"What should be the policy of the colored American towards Africa?"
The rector of St. Philip's Church lamented that in their opposition to the
attempts of the American Colonization Society to encourage blacks to
migrate to Africa, blacks had not only ignored Africa but also were
openly hostile to a Liberian president who sought their help. The Reverend C. H. Thompson argued that with the emancipation from slavery
and the end of the practice of linking emigration of freedmen with
Africa, blacks could now regard Africa as a continent with which they
had a special relationship. He suggested that many unemployed black

215

youth could find work in Africa, especially in Liberia, which was settled by African Americans.

From Omaha, Nebraska, the Reverend G. W. Woodley sent an appeal to the wealthy colored men of New York, Boston, and elsewhere to unite in opening commercial relations with Africa. Relating how all the explorers insisted that Africa was the "most productive country in the world," he felt that blacks should go to Africa. In the United States blacks crouched at the feet of whites begging for a position, "while [in Africa] they have a country which white men say is better than theirs." He concluded that there was no future for African Americans equal to that which would "follow the opening up of Africa" and, with that, the "civilization and Christianization of [their] own people." Woodley admitted that there could be difficulties in the process but insisted that such problems "are inseparably connected with all great enterprises."[2]

There is every indication that Woodley, a correspondent of the *African Repository* was an emigrationist and quite aware that the supporters of King Leopold hoped to attract the support of the United States and European countries by holding out the hope that the Congo would be a site for the colonization of African Americans. Henry S. Sanford, Leopold's agent in the United States, had written as early as 1879,

> Nearly 5 million of our people are of African race, descendants of slaves. Contact with the white races, and lately, emancipation, education and equality of political rights, have made them far the superiors of the parent race, and will tend to excite a spirit of enterprise, ambition and desires hitherto dormant, and for which central Africa opens a wide and peculiarly appropriate field. The idea of these people to return to Africa and regenerate the parent country—to extirpate slavery and to introduce fertile cultures—is worth while and attractive and should be promoted by the United States.[3]

John H. Latrobe, president of the American Colonization Society (who had also been elected president of the American section of the International African Association, an organization founded by Leopold to lobby for his control of the Congo), agreed with Sanford, but he knew from long and bitter experience that black leaders were generally against emigration to Liberia and would feel the same way about the Congo. He wrote Sanford on 4 March 1884, advising him that

> the better sort of the [black] race in Baltimore are too comfortable, too much respected and too well satisfied to take interest in Africa or things African. Social equality they hope, whatever they may say, will one day come to pass; and they regard the idea of settlement on the Congo or on the coast, attractive enough to increase emigration in that direction as inimical to the hope aforesaid.[4]

Both Sanford and Latrobe, as well as members of Congress, sought to enlist the aid of Secretary of State F. T. Frelinghuysen in their enterprise, and he assigned a special agent, W. P. Tisdel, to the Congo to survey the possibilities for active United States interest in the region. Even before Tisdel reached the Congo, he allegedly sent off a letter to the secretary of state (largely dictated by Sanford), stating that the Congo would be an

> inviting field for the coloured people of our country, as it is within their power to educate and civilize fifty millions of blacks, who in time must become an important element in the new nation of Free States which are so surely being brought into political life through the efforts of the International African Association.[5]

The problem that Sanford, Latrobe, Tisdel, and even the American congressmen faced was the increasing hostility of black leaders to all talk of emigration. This led Latrobe to write on 9 August 1885:

> The questions involved, however, are simple ones, although the interests are might. They grow out of the existence, in the same land, of two races, the white and the black, that cannot amalgamate by intermarriage. . . . The Negro question will remain in spite of the late war. My view, in advocating colonization had been to make Africa for the American African, what America is for the Irish and German who throng our shores. Liberia and the Congo will be co-active.[6]

Only white Americans who supported Leopold's plans for the Congo were invited to Berlin. The so-called West African Conference opened on 15 November 1884 at Chancellor Bismarck's official residence in the Wilhelmstrasse and, after a short break for Christmas and the New Year, closed on 26 February 1885. Although nominally independent and sovereign, neither Ethiopia nor Liberia was invited to join the fifteen powers represented: Germany, Austria-Hungary, Belgium, Denmark, Spain, the United States of America, France, Great Britain, Italy, the Netherlands, Portugal, Russia, Sweden, Norway, and Turkey.[7] A few white Americans, such as Henry Morton Stanley and Henry S. Sanford, agents or partisans of Leopold II, king of the Belgians, hoped that the conference would ratify the king's control of much of central Africa as his personal fief. Sanford, as Leopold's executive, was interested in the prospect of amassing great wealth in Africa. And Collis P. Huntington, a railroad magnate who attended the conference, hoped to do likewise.

Commenting on the conference for the black world, J. Theodore Holly, the first black Protestant Episcopal bishop, said of the events in Berlin, "They have come together to enact into law, national rapine, robbery and murder."[8] In contrast, broader American opinion held that "no prospect of commercial advantage warrants a departure from the traditional policy of this Government," which was to resist engaging in the "broils" of Europe, and that becoming involved with Africa and the Congo could lead to a serious situation and "engraft upon the peaceful precedents of our diplomacy." Both President Chester A. Arthur and Secretary of State Frelinghuysen opposed recognizing Leopold's leadership of the International African Association and his interest in securing personal control of the Congo for fear of departing from the established policy of keeping distant from African affairs. Frelinghuysen was leery of American participation in the proposed conference but was under pressure from his minister in Berlin, John A. Kasson, Henry Morton Stanley, and Senator John Tyler Morgan to take part. In assenting to be represented at Berlin, Frelinghuysen cautioned his minister that the United States was interested only in freedom of trade in the Congo Basin; freedom of trade and navigation on the waters of the Congo and Niger rivers; humanitarian policies such as insisting upon religious freedom for the inhabitants of the area; and the abolition of the slave trade. Aware that one of the main reasons for the conference was to formulate rules for avoiding conflicts between European powers committed to partitioning Africa, Frelinghuysen nevertheless instructed Kasson to insist on "neutral control of Central Africa as promised by the International Association."[9]

Only with difficulty did Kasson "conceal his inner urging for imperialism." He was most anxious for the United States to occupy a position of éclat and prestige and threw himself into the conference with great enthusiasm. Constrained by attitudes at home and by his instructions, he ostensibly had to confine his discussion to nonpolitical matters, but since political and nonpolitical affairs were inextricably interwoven, Kasson relentlessly advocated the broadest application of every liberal principle that came up. This must have appeared naive to the other delegates, but he carried out his instructions faithfully and insisted that the conference deal with those issues that accorded with the neutral interests of the United States. Observers at the conference later said that Kasson was a good influence there.[10]

What Kasson could not do, and there is no indication that it was possible, was to protect the "existing rights" of the Congolese people to dispose freely of themselves and their lands. It was also clear to him that there was a great deal of cynicism at the conference since the European delegates refused to accept the prohibition of liquor in central Africa. Yet the American delegation was pleased with the agreement to suppress the Arab slave trade and, considering that the political arrangements made by the Europeans were outside its instructions, initialed the General Act when the conference ended on 26 February 1885. Back home, Senator Morgan, believing that the Berlin accord presented yet another opportunity to encourage the emigration of African Americans to Africa, increased pressure on the administration to ratify the General Act. Despite a great deal of skepticism in Washington and in other European capitals, Morgan insisted that Leopold's actions were basically humanitarian—that they were designed to stop the slave trade and would bring civilization and commerce to the Congo. Morgan even convinced the secretary of state that the United States should support Leopold's enterprise if only to prevent European commercial monopoly in the region. The senator won his case, and with the initialing of the treaty by the Department of State, the Congo Free State was born. [11]

Many Americans, especially blacks, feared that the Senate might actually ratify the General Act. [12] Their only hope was that it would be opposed by Grover Cleveland, the first Democratic president since Buchanan. Most African Americans were still Republicans, but they knew that Cleveland fervently opposed imperialism, and disliked protectorates and foreign entanglements. They hoped he would somehow prevent the ratification of the "treaty of the Congo Conference." Fortunately, for those who opposed Leopold, the president and many members of Congress were firmly set against the treaty.

In January 1886 the Democrats on the House Foreign Affairs Committee, flushed with their recent electoral victory and prompted by rumors of a pending "alliance" between Belgium and the United States and of commercial deals between Sanford and Leopold II, asked to examine all the correspondence relative to the Berlin Conference. This group produced a negative report to the president and expressed the fear that, aside from a lingering distaste for European politics, United States participation in a European conference to settle African affairs would encourage Europeans to seek a voice in New World affairs such as the Panamanian isthmus canal issue. [13]

In his inaugural address, President Cleveland echoed George Washington and warned the country against "meddling in 'foreign broils and ambitions in other continents.' " Then, as if to emphasize his point, Cleveland immediately withdrew the protocols of the Berlin Conference submitted to the Senate by the previous administration. Later, in his annual message to Congress, the president declared that to share the obligation of enforcing neutrality in the far-off Congo valley smacked of entangling "alliances." Cleveland suggested that the only role the

United States should play in the whole affair was to take a " 'friendly attitude' toward the conference declarations." Of course, the United States was prepared to protect its economic interest in central Africa, but ratifying the treaty was another matter indeed. That document "gathered dust" in the Department of State despite the attempts of certain senators to resurrect and ratify it.[14]

Senator Morgan of Alabama was especially anxious for the United States to help Leopold obtain the Congo and transform it into a homeland for African Americans. In one memorable speech that he made on the floor of the Senate he declared:

> It occurs to me that if there is a country in the world that is open to enterprise of the negro race, it must be the great valley of the Congo. We ought not to shut the doors to such an enterprise as that. We ought to encourage it. If these people can not attain to the highest reach and power and civil capacity of every kind in our midst, do we not owe them the duty, having brought them as slaves from that country, to open the gates of Africa to them, so that they may go back and traffic with their own people and promote commerce in the midst of the African population? Have they not a better natural right to reap the wealth of Africa than any other race of people in the world?[15]

Most African Americans ignored what they rightly viewed as the racist sentiments of Senator Morgan, but a number of emigrationists welcomed the support of the Alabaman. Paradoxically, one of the few African Americans inclined to support Leopold's control of the Congo turned out to be the person who launched the attack that ultimately helped to deprive the king of his prize. George Washington Williams— Civil War veteran, participant in a Mexican war, legislator, pastor, nominee for the post of minister to Haiti, and the first celebrated historian of Negroes in the United States—had carefully followed European activities in Africa. While on a visit to Brussels in 1884, he tried unsuccessfully to meet with Leopold II. When he heard that there would be an international conference in Brussels in November 1889 to deal with the problems of the slave trade and liquor, he sought but failed to be part of the official United States delegation. Undeterred by this failure, Williams, a confirmed race man, was determined to attend the conference in Brussels and later to visit the Congo in an attempt to use African Americans to improve conditions in that country. He sought and received employment from S. S. McClure, a well-known syndicated columnist, who sent him to Brussels as a "representative of the Associated Literary Press of the U.S.A." to write a series of articles on the conference.

When Williams arrived in Brussels, he finally succeeded in interviewing Leopold II. Williams reportedly found the king to be "one of the noblest sovereigns in the world; an emperor whose highest ambition is to serve the cause of Christian civilization, and to promote the best interests of his subjects, ruling in wisdom, mercy, and justice." Leopold told Williams that most people had two motives in developing the Congo: "One is trade and commerce, which is selfish . . . and the other is to bring the means and blessings of Christian civilization to Africa, which is noble." Asked by Williams about his own motive, the king replied, "What I do there is done as a Christian duty to the poor African; and I do not wish to have one franc back of all the money I have expended." His great reward, he said, would be the gratitude of the Congolese people, who would have enjoyed a lawful government and the administration of justice.[16]

While Williams had hoped to influence the work of the congress through the agency of Edwin H. Terrell, the United States minister to Belgium and the official delegate, he was apparently unable to do so. President Harrison, who had defeated Cleveland in 1888, was cool toward this Brussels conference; so it was not surprising that Terrell was given instructions to participate fully in the affairs of the conference, and report upon proposals made there, but not to sign anything.[17]

What Williams did succeed in doing in Brussels was to receive a commission from Leopold and from Captain Albert Thys, chief administrative officer of the Belgian Commercial Companies operating in the Congo, to recruit African Americans to assist in developing that territory. This project was supported by Henry S. Sanford, who had written in 1886 that African Americans would have the type of "civilizing influence" in the Congo that whites could never hope to provide. "What an opening for our people of African descent, awaiting another Moses to show them the way to the new land of promise, their fatherland," he remarked.[18] Captain Thys agreed to pay Williams $150 a month to recruit forty African Americans and escort them to the Congo. Whether Williams knew it or not, Leopold had told Sanford that if American blacks went to the Congo, "they must not remain a separate colony, distinct from the State, but become citizens of the country and obey its laws."[19]

While in Brussels, Williams was also able to attract the attention of Collis P. Huntington. This was indeed a fortuitous meeting for Williams, because Huntington was not only interested in building a railroad in the Congo but, like many wealthy whites of that epoch, also had an interest in the education of blacks and was a trustee and major benefactor of Hampton Institute in Virginia. Huntington helped to fund Williams's trip to the United States.

Williams arrived in New York in December 1889, but though supported by the American Missionary Society, he was largely unsuccessful in recruiting blacks to serve as clerks, blacksmiths, and engineers in the Congo. Then with an introduction from Huntington, Williams set off for Hampton to talk to its founder, General Samuel C. Armstrong, and its faculty and students about the possibility of going to Africa. Here again, he failed to recruit anyone. According to Armstrong, the Hampton students were not "developed enough to stand the test in Africa." Nevertheless, Armstrong felt that Williams's visit was not a failure and had "sown much good seed."[20]

Perhaps hoping to ingratiate himself with Leopold II, Williams visited the White House on 23 December 1889 to tell President Harrison about his projected trip, and to discuss with him the possibility of ratifying the Berlin Act. The president showed an interest in Williams's project but still had serious reservations about a treaty that would enable Leopold to acquire the Congo Free State. Harrison felt that to approve the act presented the "danger of annulling the traditions of a century; of violations [of] the Monroe Doctrine, and of approaching the stormy circle of European politics."[21] Faced with this attitude, Williams promised to prepare for the president a memorandum dealing with the international, legal, and sentimental reasons why the United States should ratify the act. After he left the White House, Williams visited Senator John Sherman, a man he had known in Ohio, then serving as chairman of the Senate Committee on Foreign Relations. Sherman had the same reservations as did the president about the Berlin Act, but according to Williams, the senator promised to suspend action on the matter until Williams had visited the Congo.

It was a personal tragedy for Williams to have to return to Brussels without African American recruits. Captain Thys understood his predicament and paid him for his services. Then, eager to proceed to Africa, Williams sought aid from officials at the royal palace. To his consternation, they tried to dissuade him from going to the Congo, pleading that the climate was deadly during the rainy season, that the expenses for the trip were heavy, and that it was difficult to travel by caravan. When, despite these arguments, Williams insisted that he would make the trip, the king sent for him. Leopold received Williams cordially enough but also attempted to dissuade him from going to Africa. The king turned down Williams's request for employment in the Congo stating that this was reserved for his Belgian subjects. Leopold reiterated that travel to the region was difficult, that it was almost impossible to get wholesome food for "white men," and that it might be well for Williams to wait five years before traveling—the time that Henry Morton Stanley felt was necessary to complete the projected railroad. When these entreaties failed and Williams indicated that he planned to leave for the Congo almost immediately, the king retorted, "Then you cannot go on the State-Steamers, and must rely upon the Mission-Steamers." Undaunted, Williams completed the proper courtesies and left the palace.[22]

It had become increasingly clear to Williams that Leopold's sentiments had turned against him. He discovered that there was a growing fear in Europe of the impact of African Americans on the Africans. Whether the Europeans were aware of the attitudes of the African Americans who served as diplomats in Monrovia is not known, but Williams was even refused an interview with Sanford, who had formerly favored the emigration of blacks to the Congo. He learned that Sanford was disappointed at not being consulted during Williams's recruiting attempt. He also learned that Sanford, who had opposed the abolition of slavery before the Civil War, strongly believed that blacks, whether in the United States or in the Congo, should be subordinated to whites and that he allegedly mistrusted intelligent blacks such as Williams.

Sanford was reportedly also resentful of the relations between Williams and Huntington, fearing that this African American, as a representative of an American company planning to trade in the Congo, might join those who sought to demonstrate that the Congo was not so fertile, nor its volume of trade so abundant, as Sanford had claimed.[23] It appeared that both Sanford and Leopold had been deeply disturbed when the king received a cable from the Belgian minister in Washington stating that Williams was "very shrewd," and that he intended to go to the Congo as the representative of the "vastly rich" Huntington and would attempt to purchase large tracts of rubber lands as a way of getting a foothold in that country.[24]

Ignoring the feelings of the Belgians and Sanford, Williams proceeded with his plans to visit Africa. He had a few assets, such as the agreement with S. S. McClure that a series of articles he planned to write would be distributed by the Associated Literary Press to its subscribers. Williams also hoped to achieve a certain notoriety by making a detailed report to President Harrison on the state of affairs in the Congo. But Williams's greatest asset was his friendship with Huntington. The philanthropist had already invested $50,000 in a railroad that the Belgians planned to build along the Congo River from Matadi to Stanley Pool, and he wished to know something about the feasibility of that scheme. Huntington, who was somewhat of a gambler and who had invested in the railroad from the

East Coast of Africa to Lake Victoria Nyanza, was not too concerned about losing his money. He allegedly felt that he would gain satisfaction from aiding "the opening of the country and thereby promoting civilization."[25]

Huntington provided Williams with a check for £100 as help to travel to the Congo and a letter indicating confidence in him. Huntington wrote that he was looking forward to Williams's report on the Congo as coming from someone "well qualified to enlighten Americans upon this subject—particularly as to the actual condition and extent of civilization of the native population, concerning which I believe much misapprehension exists."[26] With this letter and money in his pocket, Williams sailed to Africa on 30 January 1890, visiting Sierra Leone, the Ivory Coast, the Gold Coast, and Nigeria; visiting churches; and examining the cultures of the people. His biggest regret was that the Europeans still sold arms and liquor to Africans with the result that "with an unrestricted trade in fire-arms and rum it will not be long ere the African will perish by his own hands."[27] Williams also picked up the reports on the Congo from fellow passengers and at stops along the way. These convinced him that there were a "dozen excellent reasons" why his visit was "in the Providence of God, the best thing that could happen for the poor native and the mis-guided Belgian [Leopold II]."[28]

By the time Williams arrived at Boma, the Atlantic port of the Congo, he was convinced that Leopold and his agents were out to sabotage his trip or even to do him bodily harm. While en route, he had already mailed off a letter to Sanford accusing him of instigating opposition to his trip. He reported having complained to President Harrison and to Senator Sherman of the opposition and having requested protection as "an American citizen visiting a country that had been opened to a great international commerce and free trade." Moreover, he told Sanford that he would hold him respon-sible for any mishap. In a letter to Huntington, Williams vowed that he would "take every precaution to preserve my life, and shall do my duty to history and humanity with unflagging zeal and dauntless courage."[29]

Once on shore, Williams wrote Senator George F. Hoar asking that his mail be forwarded to Holland to escape the eyes of Leopold's spies. Furthermore, he asked Hoar to "request the President to ask the King of the Belgians to give me safe conduct through the State of Congo" and to send a "man of war here and enquire for me of the Governor General of the Congo State and of the Dutch House." Williams thought it wise to take measures to prevent harm to himself and to ensure that in the event of his death his personal effects would be sent to the United States and turned over to the senator.[30]

Williams was actually not unreasonable in asking for a warship to be sent to rescue him, since this was almost the order of the day. There is no evidence that he expected to receive responses either from the senator or from President Harrison, but he may have felt that it did no harm to convince persons in the Congo that he had friends in high places. With what he hoped were assurances, Williams bravely proceeded on a perilous projected six-thousand-mile trip to the headwaters of the Congo River. He was appalled by what he witnessed and called the attention of missionaries on the spot to what they were not reporting to the outside world. Calling the Congo "the Siberia, of the African continent, a penal settlement," Williams concluded that not only had Leopold acquired the country by the "most brutal frauds" but that he continued to mistreat its people. He attempted to retrace the travels of Henry Morton Stanley and to investigate the labor system, transit methods, and the food and quarters for workers on the prospective railroad.[31]

Williams also visited and interviewed such missionaries as George Grenfell, who, while courteous to him, suspected that he might have been seeking information concerning the possible emigration or repatriation of African Americans to the Congo. Grenfell, who would later accuse Leopold of barbarism in the Congo, wrote his superiors in London saying that during a visit to him, Williams had questioned "the King's disinterestedness in his Congo enterprises, and [had] hinted that among future possibilities was that of the sale of the royal interest to a big Belgian Company."[32] Significantly, while many of these residents in the Congo shared Williams's concern for the conditions of the Congolese people under Leopold's rule, they were not prepared to jeopardize their activities by putting their views into print.

By the time Williams reached Stanley Falls, at the end of his upstream travels, he was distressed enough about what he had experienced to write "An Open Letter to His Serene Majesty Leopold II, King of the Belgians and Sovereign of the Independent State of Congo, by Colonel the Honorable Geo. W. Williams, of the United States of America." Like the lawyer he was, Williams addressed Leopold as "Good and Great Friend," indicating that he wanted to submit to "[His] Majesty's consideration some reflections respecting the Independent State of Congo, based upon a careful study and inspection of the country and character of the personal Government you have established upon the African Continent." Suggest-

ing that the king would want no less than the truth, Williams said that he
was inspired to write in the firm conviction that Leopold believed that his
government of the Congo was "built upon the enduring foundation of
Truth, Liberty, Humanity and Justice."[33]

Williams confessed to Leopold that he was "disenchanted, disappointed
and disheartened" by what he saw and that he felt obliged to lay specific
charges against His Majesty's Government and to deposit the requisite
documentation of his charges with Her Britannic Majesty's secretary of
state for foreign affairs. His hope was that an international commission
could be created with powers to send persons to "attest to the truth or
falsity of these charges." Specifically, Williams charged that Congolese

> everywhere complain that their land has been taken from them by force; that
> the Government is cruel and arbitrary, and declare that they neither love nor
> respect t[h]e Government and its flag. Your Majesty's Government has
> sequestered their land, burned their towns, stolen their property, enslaved
> their women and children, and committed other crimes too numerous to
> mention in detail. It is natural that they everywhere shrink from the "*the
> fostering care*" your Majesty's Government so eagerly proffers them.[34]

Williams leveled twelve specific charges against the government of
the king, including deficiency in the "moral, military and financial
strength" needed to govern such a vast territory; hiring and not paying
mercenary slave-soldiers; violating contracts made to workmen; cruelly
subjecting prisoners to chain gangs; importing women for immoral purposes; monopoly trading and punishing Africans who traded with others;
slave-trading; not punishing soldiers who engaged in cannibalism; enslaving for military purposes; having illegal contract with Arabs; and
misrepresenting the nature of the country to foreigners such as railroad
builders. In summation, Williams declared:

> Against the deceit, fraud, robberies, arson, murder, slave-raiding, and
> general policy of cruelty of your Majesty's Government to the natives,
> stands their record of unexampled patience, long-suffering and forgiving
> spirit, which put the boasted civilization and professed religion of your Maj-
> esty's Government to the blush. . . . All the crimes perpetuated in the Congo
> have been done in *your* name, and *you* must answer at the bar of Public Senti-
> ment for the misgovernment of a people, whose lives and fortunes were en-
> trusted to you by the august Conference of Berlin, 1884–1885. I now appeal
> to the Powers, which committed this infant State to your Majesty's charge,
> and to the great States which gave it international being; and whose majestic
> law you have scorned and trampled upon, to call and create an International
> Commission to investigate the charges herein preferred in the name of Hu-
> manity, Commerce, Constitutional Government and Christian Civilization.[35]

True to his commitment to President Harrison, Williams sent a report to him from St. Paul de Loanda, Angola, on 14 October 1890. In it he reviewed in some detail his own involvement with the Congo and that of such other Americans as Henry Morton Stanley, Henry S. Sanford, Secretary of State Frelinghuysen, and Senator Sherman. He also informed the president that while it was true that the United States had no commercial interests in the Congo, it was the United States "which introduced this African Government [the Congo Free State] into the sisterhood of States." And that while the United States may have been guided by "noble and unselfish" motives when it did so, the United States was morally responsible for what had happened in the Congo. Williams felt that the people of the United States had to be told the whole truth "respecting the Independent State of Congo, an absolute monarchy, an oppressive and cruel Government, an exclusive Belgian colony, now tottering to its fall. I indulge the hope," wrote Williams, "that when a new Government shall rise upon the ruins of the old, it will be simple, not complicated; local, not European; international, not national; just, not cruel; and, casting its shield alike over black and white, trader and missionary, endure for centuries."[36]

Williams's letters to Leopold II and to President Harrison, along with a report to Huntington on the proposed Congo railroad, created a sensation in the diplomatic, financial, political, and missionary circles in Europe and the United States. Under circumstances never made clear, Williams had sent the letters to Europe to be printed, and copies of these were circulated before they reached their addresses. One of the first persons to get copies was Sir William Mackinnon, head of the British East Africa Company, and a close friend of both Leopold and Huntington. Sir William wrote Huntington regretting that his African American protégé had been so critical of the king and predicting that no good could come of the affair, since the "King is the last man in the world to permit or sanction any inhumanity on the part of his officers or servants."[37] Huntington, however, apparently felt that there might have been some truth in what his beneficiary had said and, though still willing to support Williams, at least financially, was careful not to alienate Sir William. Huntington wrote the head of the British East Africa Company that he, too, did not like the report and that Leopold was "solicitous of the best welfare of the natives of the country and would not, if he knew it, tolerate any departure from the rules of honest and kind administration that I know he laid down for the guidance and government of those he sent to the Congo country."[38]

Henry Morton Stanley, to whom Sir William had sent a copy of the letter, was highly critical of its author, not only because of what he had said about Leopold but because of what he had said about Stanley himself. Moreover, Stanley was embarrassed that the New York *Herald* ran a series of letters on the "Open Letter," identified Williams as a truthful man, and suggested that the report had made "the gravest charges of the cruelties and deceptions by the government of the Free State."[39] In response to questions by a reporter of the New York *Herald* who visited him in his hotel in New York to talk about the affair, Stanley attacked the character of George Washington Williams. He said that he had warned his friends not to have anything to do with Williams since he, Stanley, saw the letter as a "deliberate attempt at blackmail" designed to force the king to turn over the concession to build a railroad in the Congo to Huntington, Williams's benefactor, or face future besmirching in a book that Williams planned to write. Stanley recalled to the reporter that he had met Williams, "who was negro," as far back as 1884, when Williams had applied for a position in the government of the Congo State. Stanley said that he had even recommended Williams to King Leopold, dwelling particularly on the applicant's good education and record. Unfortunately, Stanley said, the king was not "particularly smitten with Williams," and the negotiations had fallen through. Stanley added that this was the last time that he had seen Williams and insisted that Williams's assertion of having been in "charge of the surveys of the Congo railroad are absolutely false."[40]

What Stanley neglected to tell the New York *Herald* was that Williams had claimed to have made a survey not on behalf of the Belgians but on behalf of Huntington. Nor did Stanley reveal how Williams hoped to blackmail Leopold with a letter that was already in the public domain. Yet Stanley's statement to the newspaper about Williams's character was supported by Alfred LeGhait, the Belgian minister to the United States, who sent a letter to the editor of the *Herald* protesting the publication of Williams's letter without any commentary. The diplomat was particularly incensed that no attention was called to his sovereign's civilizing mission. LeGhait associated himself with the "illustrious" Mr. Stanley and repeated the charge that Williams was attempting to blackmail the king of the Belgians. He also complained to his superior, Baron Lambermont, minister of state, that in contrast to the silence in Brussels, he, LeGhait, was attempting to defend the honor of Leopold before the Americans.[41]

LeGhait was only partly correct when he hinted that Leopold was not being fully supported in Europe against charges leveled against him in Williams's "Open Letter." The British minister to Brussels, Lord Vivian, warned his foreign minister, Lord Salisbury, that "a certain Colonel Williams, a mulatto and citizen of the United States," had intended to send off a letter containing scandalous and utterly unfounded charges against Leopold. This act was allegedly taken in revenge and in an attempt to blackmail the Belgian king for not giving Williams a job in the Congo. Lord Vivian submitted that any impartial enquiry would absolve the king, and that the United States minister in London would confirm the reports about Williams. Nevertheless, Lord Vivian warned Salisbury that although Williams may have been all that the king and his supporters said about him, "I suspect there is a good deal of disagreeable truth in his [Williams's] pamphlets."[42]

For reasons of their own, a number of persons in Europe took Williams's letter seriously. In Britain, R. Cobden Phillips of the Manchester Chamber of Commerce assumed that Leopold was guilty as charged. The radical and anti-monarchist elements in Belgium were also prepared to accept Williams's charges against the king. A number of newspapers complained that the public would have been better served if instead of ad hominem attacks on Williams—such as questioning whether he was a regular colonel in the U.S. Army rather than a soldier who had fought for Juárez in Mexico against Austrian aggression or why he had flitted from one profession to another—Leopold and his administrators had replied to the charges leveled against them. One paper even suggested that while Leopold believed that the conquest of a large part of Africa would "increase his patrimony and civil list," it appeared that his search for commercial gain had led him to "neglect the interest of civilization" and adopt the slave practices for which the Arabs were being reproached. Passions in Brussels reached such a height that there was a debate in the Belgian Parliament that only ended when the prime minister promised an official report.

What was significant about Williams's intervention in Congolese affairs was the "furor raised by a relatively brief statement by a relatively obscure black American about the conduct of one of the most important and most powerful men in the world." John Hope Franklin, Williams's biographer, writes that Leopold and the administrators of the Congo "were deeply embarrassed, to say the least." But given the Congo's enormous potential and strategic importance, and their own lack of capital to develop it, the Belgians were prepared to exploit the local people to that end. Williams, for his part, did not have the political clout to get the United States to act. Neither President Harrison nor the senators to whom Williams had written were prepared to take steps to protect the black nationality. Williams did his best to sensitize them to many of the practices he felt were delaying the development of the Congo. But his persistent refrain, "My cry is *Africa for the Africans!*" fell on deaf ears.[43] Persons such as Williams, along with some black missionaries, were constrained to employ symbolic structures in an often vain effort to influence United States policy toward Africa.

George Washington Williams might have been able to recruit the Reverend William Henry Sheppard of Hampton Institute for service in the Congo had he visited that school several years earlier. By the time Williams arrived at the Institute in Virginia in 1889 to recruit students, the young preacher who would do much to end Leopold II's personal rule over the Congo had already graduated.[44] In 1882, while at Hampton, Sheppard had heard Edward Wilmot Blyden give a visiting lecture on the responsibility of the African American to Africa. Sheppard decided to become a missionary and, after Hampton, went to Stillman College for religious training. He later preached in Montgomery, Alabama, and Atlanta, Georgia, and in 1887, apparently despairing at the rise of racism in urban America, petitioned the Presbyterian Board of Foreign Missions to send him to the Congo.

The officials of the American Presbyterian Congo Mission were reluctant to send blacks to head missions in Africa and refused to accept Sheppard's request until they could find a white missionary to accompany him. As fate would have it, the missionary they found was the Reverend Samuel Norvell Lapsley, who, strange as it may seem, had developed an interest in the Congo from listening to Alabama Senator John Tyler Morgan. This racist senator who, as indicated above, had supported Leopold II's appropriation of the Congo in the hope that African Americans could be "repatriated" to Africa was Lapsley's father's law partner.

Despite Lapsley's background as a scion of slaveholders, he welcomed the opportunity to go along with Sheppard to the Congo. With letters of introduction from Sanford, Secretary of State James G. Blaine, and Belgian officials, the two missionaries left Rotterdam and arrived in 1890 at Luebo, in the Kasai region where they established their mission.[45] From all indications these two Americans, some nine hundred miles up-country and far from other Westerners, got along well and braved the climate and diseases until Lapsley died in March 1892. Frustrated with his lack of progress among the Bakete, who preferred their own religion to that preached by the Americans, Sheppard proceeded to Bakuba country. This was quite a feat since the Bakuba, proud of their society and culture—especially their political organization—had managed to keep out all foreigners until Sheppard arrived. He so impressed them with the speed with which he learned their language and with his eagerness to visit their country that they were convinced he was a reincarnated Bakuba. But though they welcomed him in their midst, they, too, preferred their own religion to that of whites.[46]

While Sheppard mourned the loss of Lapsley, he apparently felt increasingly at home among the Bakuba. Upon leaving the United States, he had lamented leaving his family and friends but he had written to the Presbyterian *Missionary,* soon after arriving in Africa, "I am certainly happy in the country of my forefathers."[47] He had also written a letter about his work to the Indianapolis *Freeman,* thereby keeping the African American public informed. When the time came for home leave in 1893, Sheppard passed through Britain where he was named a fellow of the Royal Geographical Society in recognition of his travels among the Bakuba. He proceeded to the United States, lectured widely throughout the South about his Congo mission, and received help from various black congregations. A talk he gave at the Hampton Institute was published in the *Southern Workman*. He acquired a wife in the person of Miss Lucy Gantt, a former member of the Fisk Jubilee Choir who shared his missionary fervor.

Sheppard was tireless in his efforts to recruit black missionaries for the Congo and was able to take three other black missionaries with him when he returned to the Kasai in 1894. These were joined by another black missionary in 1895. In 1896, Sheppard wrote to friends, "We are happy and feel at home; [we] seldom speak of returning to America."[48] He later reported that he had built the "First Presbyterian Church of Luebo." Sheppard never tired of inviting other blacks to join him in his missionary activities. In one of his letters to the *Southern Workman,* he pleaded, "So we beg of you that you lift up your eyes and see the fast ripening harvest field and hear our soul's pleading cry, 'Come over into Macedonia, and help us'."[49]

Sheppard's autonomy ended in 1897 when the Presbyterian Mission Board sent out two white missionaries, the Reverend Samuel Phillips Verner and the Reverend William McCutchan Morrison, to head the Kasai mission. Sheppard apparently took no exception to this development and worked quite well with Morrison. Verner posed a problem, however, because as soon as he arrived in the Congo he insisted that "it was absolutely essential that Caucasians be placed in charge of all of the mission's affairs." Verner wanted to make the Congo "a stronghold of Caucasian power," held that blacks were inferior to whites, and completely agreed with the racist sentiments of the local Belgian administrators. He firmly believed that the Congo should not be a "proving ground or homeland for intelligent blacks, [and] he was not in sympathy with many of the aspirations of the mission."[50]

While Verner was willing to remain as quiet as Grenfell did in the face of the atrocities committed by the Belgians and their auxiliaries on the Congolese, both Morrison and Sheppard decided to complain and took a harder line when Verner left missionary work in 1899 and went home. Noting an increase in the atrocities that he frequently witnessed in the Kasai, Sheppard wrote a long report in 1900 about the treatment of the local people by the so-called Zappo-Zaps, who worked as an African auxiliary force for the Belgian government. We are told that "Sheppard's graphic description of the carnage and cannibalism he had observed shocked his fellow evangelists. Because such barbarity was inconceivable to them," they sent another missionary to confirm the report. This investigator reported that he had counted "fourteen incinerated villages and forty-seven corpses, some of them partially eaten," and over a distance of seventy-five miles had encountered deserted villages of people "compelled to take refuge in the bush."[51]

The Presbyterian Mission was determined to arouse the conscience of the Christian world and sent Sheppard's report to both Britain and the United States. While the Belgians, supported by Catholic missionaries, who saw the report as a plot to take over the Congo for Protestantism refuted its findings, the executive committee of the Board of World Missions in the United States found themselves in a quandary. They wished to render to Caesar what was his, namely the Congo, but at the same time they wanted to protect the missionaries. However, political factors led them to take a stronger stand, perhaps, it was suggested, "because the United States was beginning to play a more aggressive role in the world. In the spirit of manifest destiny, the Presbyterians refused to allow any obstacles to stand in the way of their expansion."[52] They filed a complaint with the State Department in 1900 against the Belgian authorities in the Congo.

Morrison returned to the United States in 1903 and galvanized the American mission boards and their supporters to a sense of their responsibility toward the Congo peoples. He even managed to persuade the general assembly of the Presbyterian Church to send delegations to complain both to Secretary of State John Hay and President Theodore Roosevelt. Morrison and two associates did get an appointment to see President Roosevelt, but he told them frankly that "the government would not be in a position to take any direct action in the case unless there was some specific instance of personal maltreatment of one of our American missionaries."[53] He pledged decisive remedies should events warrant it. Surprisingly, the missionaries even succeeded in gaining the support of Senator John Tyler Morgan of Alabama. A member of the Senate Committee on Foreign Relations, Morgan was a strong character who often led rather than followed public opinion.

Meanwhile, in Great Britain, acting on evidence produced by Sheppard, the Reverend William McCutchan Morrison, Roger Casement, a British consul, and Edmund D. Morel, a former British consul in the Congo, joined the battle against the Belgian king and his private companies. Morel felt it necessary to unite in one group "all men whose hearts were touched, whatever their standing, profession, political opinion and religious belief in a common aim."[54] At the suggestion of Casement, he organized the Congo Reform Association in March 1904, with the option of having international affiliates. Morel visited the United States, and despite State Department concern over a presidential election and the Russo-Japanese War, he did meet with both Secretary of State John Hay and President Roosevelt. Hay considered it impertinent that "Englishmen" would come to Washington to take up the Congo quarrel. He was also concerned about dealing with Britishers when Roosevelt needed the votes of Irish Americans who supported Leopold because he favored Catholic missionaries in the Congo.[55]

The public speeches of Morrison and Morel, and the assistance of New England women, American missionaries, and ministers exerted a great deal of pressure on the State Department. The problem was that having just concluded the Spanish-American War, the United States did not wish to get embroiled in another colonial venture. What concerned the State Department was that

> the very people who are most ardent against entangling alliances insist most fanatically upon our doing one hundred things a year on humanitarian grounds, which would lead to immediate war. . . . The Protestant Church and many good women were wild to have us stop the atrocities in the Congo. The fact that we were parties to some earlier treaties gave some basis for an interest. . . . People kept piling down on the Department demanding action on the Congo. We went the limit which wasn't far.[56]

The State Department ordered Lawrence Townsend, the American minister in Brussels, to query Leopold about conditions in the Congo. This enquiry did not get very far allegedly because "Townsend was most reluctant to jeopardize the good relations that existed between Brussels and Washington by asking too many questions about developments in Africa."[57]

Not to be deterred, the various pressure groups formed an American branch of the Congo Reform Association (ACRA). Thomas Seymour Barbour, foreign secretary of the American Baptist Foreign Missionary Society, was named its chairman. Meeting at the Thirteenth International Peace Congress in Boston, the delegates raised questions concerning Leopold's mandate in the Congo. Specifically, they wanted to know whether "the Congo Free State [was] still to be regarded as the trustee of the Powers which recognized the flag of the International Association" and what the position of the Congo Free State was in international law in view of the grave questions raised about its conduct.[58]

Feeling the need to mobilize the African American community to support their efforts in the Congo, the ACRA turned to the most important black person in the land, Booker T. Washington. Barbour invited him to become a member of the board of the ACRA, and on 21 May 1904 Washington replied, stating that he was prepared to serve in any capacity "in calling the attention of the country to the awful conditions prevailing in the Congo." Probably aware that Senator Morgan was preparing a memorial to Congress appealing to the American government to intervene actively in the Congo affair, Washington told Barbour that he would be "disappointed" if something could not be done to change conditions there. He added:

> When Congress meets in December, if you approve of the plan I shall be very glad to call personally upon as many members of the Foreign Affairs Committee as possible and urge action. I have also thought of another plan by which I might assist. If I could have a short but pointed statement of the case which I might put before the President . . . I could give the same statement out to the press, making the point at the same time that I had placed the matter before Mr. Roosevelt, that would give the matter a publicity that perhaps it could get in no other way as the newspapers are always anxious to give greatest publicity to whatever is even remotely connected with the White House or the President.[59]

With the editorial assistance of Robert E. Park, executive secretary to the Congo Reform Association, Washington published an article in the *Outlook* magazine of 8 October 1904. Recounting the history of European perfidy in central Africa, he charged that instead of honoring the pledge to uplift the black man, "wherever the white man has put his foot in the Congo State the black man has been degraded into a mere tool in the great business of getting rubber." Placing the Congo crisis in global and racial perspective, Washington warned, "The oppression of the colored race in any one part of the world means, sooner or later, the oppression of the same race elsewhere."[60]

Meanwhile, King Leopold mobilized pressure groups in favor of his Congo rule. Within the United States one of his spokesmen charged that the missions had been infiltrated by "quasi-political agents who believe that they find advantage in depreciating the Government . . . in whose territory they are labouring." The Reverend Samuel Phillips Verner, while not completely supporting Leopold, criticized what he called "idealistic missionaries." Possibly referring to Sheppard, he declared that one did not have to "leave Virginia to find Negroes abused" and suggested that "before the church presumed to lecture people about race relations, . . . [it should] put its own house in order."[61]

Leopold intimated to the Brussels correspondent of the New York *American,* to whom he had given an interview, that his detractors were really seeking Protestant control in the Congo. This charge was designed to gain the support of Catholic Cardinal Gibbon of Baltimore, Maryland. Leopold also used in his propaganda machine the Belgian minister in Washington, Professor Nerinx of Louvain, and two lobbyists, Henry Wack and the California lawyer Henry Kowalsky. Then in a bold stroke, Leopold encouraged the formation of the American Congo Company in an attempt to win the support of American capitalists for the Congo State.

In the person of Booker T. Washington, Leopold's friends believed they had a formidable foe. Kowalsky wrote the king that "Dr. Washington is no small enemy to overcome." Nevertheless, he felt that he ought to win over the principal of Tuskegee. By means of letters and a personal interview Kowalsky sought to convince Washington that Leopold was being slandered by the missionaries, including William Henry Sheppard. When these efforts proved inadequate, Kowalsky offered Washington a trip to the Congo. He said that Washington could select his own route. "Be your own master, free from suggestion or dictation—the fullest and widest latitude of your own choice alone shall map your footsteps, and every dollar of expense I will place in the bank for you to defray your wants. All I want is 48 hours' notice of the fact that you will go."[62] When Washington still did not relent, the Belgian ambassador to the United States and one Professor James H. Gore invited him to speak at a

Congress on Economic Expansion in Belgium. Washington was intrigued by the offer, and he was encouraged by Park to accept it in the following words:

> I say by all means "go." I believe that it will give you an opportunity to say something, at once for your school and our own colonial system, more fundamental than has yet been uttered. The difference between our colonial system and others consists in the fact that we are preparing the peoples we govern for citizenship, either in the United States or as independent states; other countries are interested only in the *economic development* (a vague term, which may be interpreted in many ways) of their possessions.[63]

Park did warn Washington that "the King of Belgium hopes to win you over to his theory of dealing with the Blackman. It is part of his cynical view of things in general that everyone can be purchased with money or flattery."[64] Washington decided not to go to Belgium.

Throughout 1905 and into 1906 Washington spoke out vigorously on the plight of Africans in the Congo. He often shared a platform with Mark Twain, but after this his interest appears to have slackened for reasons that are not clear. On 29 June 1906 Park wrote Washington stating that "there seems to be a feeling here that you have not as much interest in the work of the association as [you] formerly did."[65] The Tuskegean denied this and agreed to collaborate with Park on yet another article on the Congo problem. Then in December 1906, the New York *American* published a number of letters purloined from Kowalsky. In one letter Kowalsky related to Leopold that in attempting to silence the uproar about the Congo, "I then reached out and got to Dr. Booker T. Washington." Much to Washington's sorrow, Kowalsky did not explain what he meant by that statement, and it never became clear what exactly had transpired. For his part, Washington denied having ever given Kowalsky or Leopold any help. Moreover, there is no proof that he helped the enemies of the Congolese people. It appears that as early as 1905 Washington felt he had done all that he could do. One of his biographers concluded, "There is no other known evidence to support a view that Washington aided Kowalsky or faltered in his support of Congo reform."[66]

Despite pressure from many Americans, black as well as white, the Department of State continued to temporize on the Congolese issue until it became clear that the president had to do something. Roosevelt expressed "sympathetic interest" in the missionaries' struggle, but he had no intention of committing the United States to any action. Secretary of State Hay even told Baron Moncheur, the Belgian minister, that since the

United States was not a signatory to the Berlin Act, it should not have been pressured to interfere in the Congo affair. Nevertheless, in order to pacify the missionaries and their supporters, the State Department named Clarence Slocum as consul general to the Congo Free State. The pressure did not stop, however. There was still a great push among both black and white Republicans to make the Congo issue an important one in the next election. Roosevelt warned Senator Henry Cabot Lodge that with respect to their party's platform, "the only tomfoolery that any one seems bent on is that about the Congo Free State outrages, and that is imbecile rather than noxious."[67]

But the Presbyterian missionaries refused to give up their protests. They petitioned the administration in May 1906 to "bring about by any means that may be practicable an immediate concert of action on the part of all civilized nations," and particularly those which participated in the Berlin convention out of which emerged the Congo Free State, to "abate the atrocities which have been and are being committed on the natives" and to grant to all nations and missionary bodies, especially the Protestants, "access to all parts of the State." Elihu Root, the new secretary at the State Department, insisted that the United States had not signed the Berlin Act and with the exception of Liberia had no political interests in Africa. Moreover, he submitted that if the United States possessed "in Darkest Africa a territory seven times as large and four times as populous as the Philippines," it might "find good government difficult and come in for our own share of just or unjust criticism."[68]

In December 1906 Senator Lodge introduced a resolution in the Senate assuring President Roosevelt of congressional approval for any measure he might judge necessary to ameliorate conditions in the Congo. There was now pressure on the president to withdraw any recognition that America might have given to the Congo flag and to use his power to rid the world of an evil as bad as the slave trade. Roosevelt still equivocated. In his message to Congress on 3 December 1907 he held that "our aim is disinterestedly to help other nations where such help can be widely given without the appearance of meddling."[69]

What Sheppard and the other missionaries wanted, however, was nothing less than for Leopold to be forced to relinquish ownership of the Congo. This desire was the subject of great angry debates in the Belgian Parliament. The Belgian state had not previously shown an interest in taking over the Congo from its king, but Anglo-American pressure forced it to do so. Leopold himself proved difficult since he wished to protect what he considered to be his rights. But the transfer was finally approved by the Belgian Chamber and Senate in the summer of 1908, and the king signed the agreement in the fall of that year. Sheppard's denomination felt vindicated by the transfer, but many others felt that it might have been better had Britain or the United States annexed the territory. Secretary of State Root was warned by some missionaries that the transfer of power to Belgium would bring little change. It would be like "cutting off a twig, expecting thereby to kill the poisonous tree."[70]

The Department of State was pleased with the transfer of the Congo Free State to Belgium, since it considered the missionaries obstacles to normal diplomatic relations with Belgium. The problem was that the Kasai Company, which controlled the area where Sheppard and the other Presbyterian missionaries worked, continued some of the practices of the Congo Free State. Sheppard and another missionary, Lachlan Vass, complained that Bakuba who declined to fill their rubber quotas were flogged, imprisoned, or even killed. In February 1909 Sheppard and Morrison were summoned to appear at Leopoldville in May 1909 to answer a charge of libeling the Belgian government.[71]

The immediate reason for this charge was an article that Sheppard had published in the *Kasai Herald* (edited by Morrison), in which he alleged that the conditions of the Bakuba people were happy and prosperous until they were incorporated into the Congo Free State. Then the towns were neglected and became full of weeds and dirt, and the people no longer had any time "to listen to the missionaries." "Why this change?" Sheppard wondered. He continued, "You have it in a few words. There are armed sentries of chartered trading companies who force the men and women to spend most of their days and nights in the forests making rubber, and the price they receive is so meager that they cannot live upon it."[72] The officials in the Congo reacted angrily to the article, and charged that Sheppard and Morrison had violated a royal decree of February 1906 prohibiting any calumnious denunciation of a state official. The penalty was a fixed term of five years penal servitude (or a fine). The Kasai Company also claimed damages because, it alleged, the missionaries' charges had ruined the price of its stocks.[73]

The American Congo Reform Association and Edmund D. Morel welcomed the indictment of the missionaries, because they hoped that "the trial of American citizens in the Congo would concern the American government" and would provide the ACRA with an opportunity to plead for consular jurisdiction. The ACRA, the Presbyterian Mission Board, and many congressmen immediately appealed for both a change of date and of venue. The American consul at Boma, William W.

Handley, appealed to the Belgian governor-general for a lawyer for the two missionaries. The Belgians refused, stating, "You know the Rev. Drs. Morrison and Sheppard have not spared the administration on the occasion of their attack on the Kasai Company."[74] It was evident to him but not to Handley that the missionaries could not ask their lawyer, who would have been a colonial officer, to associate himself with the administration's attackers. Moreover, the governor-general felt that conflict of interest would prevent any Belgian lawyer from being free to act. As for granting the missionaries consular status, the Belgians absolutely refused and affirmed the competence of the Congo courts to try American citizens.[75] News of the legal problems of Sheppard and Morrison created an uproar in Washington. To make matters worse, Secretary of State Philander Chase Knox did not acknowledge the letter sent to him by the missionaries, forcing them to use their political clout to make him meet them. And even though Knox instructed the American legation in Brussels to delay the trial and seek a change in venue, the ACRA, the Southern Presbyterian Church, and the Alliance of Reformed Churches met in New York City in June 1909 and "importuned"

> the President of the United States to insist upon the observation of the Berlin and Brussels Acts and the provisions of the treaty between the American Government and the Congo Independent State so far as the interests of these missionaries are concerned, and protests for justice.[76]

The churchmen sought out former Secretary Root, the Governor of Massachusetts, "John Marshall Harlan (on behalf of Sheppard's mother) [,] and Senator Joseph F. Johnston of Alabama, as a service to James Rutherford Lapsley," to meet with Knox and the president. Given such pressure, Taft instructed Knox to cable his minister in Brussels to inform the Belgian government that the United States viewed the trial with "acute interest and no little concern." The note indicated that American recognition of Belgium's role in the Congo might depend upon the outcome of the trial.[77]

After numerous delays the Congolese government finally agreed to change the trial date to September and the site for the trial to Leopoldville. It also named Emile Vandervelde as a lawyer to defend Morrison and Sheppard. People in the United States followed the trial with great interest and, as it coincided with a general Protestant missionary conference in Leopoldville, the court was crowded out with missionaries. The lawyer for the defendants insisted that Sheppard had intended no malice in writing the article. Moreover, he asserted that the stock of the Kasai Company had fallen, not because of the article, but because of reports of other atrocities in the Congo. Vandervelde also challenged the prosecution to prove that Sheppard's statement was untrue. This the prosecution refused to do.

The American consul general, who had faithfully attended the trial, reported to the State Department that he had "never heard anything like it and he believed that it was one of the finest appeals for the natives of the Congo that had ever been made." After due deliberation, the judge, Charles Louis Gianpetri, ruled that Sheppard had no malicious intent to harm the interest of the Kasai Company; that he had no intent to blame the company or challenge its honesty; that he did not attribute to the company the acts committed by its agents; and that the article in the *Kasai Herald* could not refer to the company, which disconnected itself from the abuses that Sheppard denounced. Finally, the judge stated that since the Kasai Company failed to show that Sheppard's article caused it serious moral or material damage, he dismissed the suit and ordered the plaintiff to pay the court costs.[78] Sheppard retired from the Congo in April 1910, some two decades after he had entered the mission field. We are told that "as an evangelist, he lamented his inability to convert the Kuba; but as a man he could be proud of his role in helping to bury the rubber regime in the Kasai."[79]

What the activities of Sheppard, George Washington Williams, and Booker T. Washington demonstrate is that African Americans outside the foreign service establishment did use whatever symbolic power they had to influence American policy toward the Congo. Of the three, only Washington had viable relations with the political leaders of the day, and his influence had to be mediated through the screen of racism. One can say that all three men were used by whites whose paternalistic views of the Congo were largely unacceptable to them. Nevertheless, they all attempted to use American power and prestige against the king of the Belgians, thereby enabling those who wanted to ameliorate the plight of the Congolese to exert pressure for reform.

Notes

1. President's Message to the Congress of the United States, *Foreign Relations of the United States, 1883*, ix.
2. *African Repository* 61 (October 1885): 120–21.
3. Henry S. Sanford, "Report of the Hon. Henry Shelton Sanford, U.S. Delegate from the American Branch to the Annual Meeting of the African International Association in Brussels, in June 1877, to the Hon. John H. B. Latrobe, Brussels, July 30, 1877," *American Geographical Society Journal* 9 (1877): 103–8. See also his ideas in "American Interests in Africa," *Forum* 9 (June

1890): 409–29. See also Joseph A. Fry, *Henry S. Sanford: Diplomacy and Business in Nineteenth-Century America* (Reno: University of Nevada Press, 1982), 133–63.

4. Cited in J. Njuguna Karanja, "United States' Attitude and Policy Toward the International African Association, 1876–1886" (Ph.D. diss., Princeton University, 1962), 111.

5. Special Agent Tisdel to Frelinghuysen, 23 November 1884, cited in ibid., 128.

6. Ibid.

7. George Shepperson, "The Centennial of the West Africa Conference of Berlin, 1884–1885," *Phylon* 46 (1985): 38.

8. Quoted in Sylvia M. Jacobs, *The African Nexus: Black American Perspectives on the European Partitioning of Africa, 1880–1920* (Westport, Conn.: Greenwood Press, 1981), 71.

9. Edward Younger, *John A. Kasson: Politics and Diplomacy From Lincoln to McKinley* (Iowa City: State Society of Iowa, 1955), 327ff.

10. Ibid.

11. Ibid.; *Congressional Record,* 50th Cong., 1st sess., 28 June 1888, pt. 6, 19:5671–72.

12. Younger, *John A. Kasson,* 336–39.

13. Ibid.

14. Ibid.

15. *Congressional Record,* 50th Cong., 1st sess., 28 June 1888, pt. 6, 19:5671. See also an article in the same vein by Senator Taylor entitled "The Race Question in the United States," *Arena* 9 (September 1890): 385–98.

16. John Hope Franklin, *George Washington Williams: A Biography* (Chicago and London: University of Chicago Press, 1985), 178ff.

17. Ibid.

18. Henry S. Sanford to the Editor, New York *Herald,* 17 July 1886, quoted in ibid., 185.

19. Stanley Shaloff, *Reform in Leopold's Congo* (Richmond, Va.: John Knox Press, 1970), 21.

20. Franklin, *George W. Williams,* 186.

21. Ibid., 187.

22. Ibid.

23. George Washington Williams, *A Report Upon the Congo-State and Country to the President of the Republic of the United States of America* (1890: reprinted as Appendix 3, pp. 3–4), as cited in ibid., 188.

24. Ibid., 189.

25. Ibid., 188.

26. Ibid.

27. Ibid.

28. Ibid.

29. Ibid., 190.

30. Ibid.

31. Ibid., 191.

32. Ibid., 201–2. John Hope Franklin remarked that "of all the 1890 observers and critics of Leopold's rule in the Congo—Grenfell the missionary, Casement the diplomat, Conrad the novelist, Williams the reporter, and doubtless others— only Williams saw fit to make his unfavorable views widely known immediately" (ibid., 220).

33. Ibid., 243.

34. Ibid., 243–46.
35. Ibid., 243–53.
36. Ibid., 264–79.
37. Ibid., 208.
38. Ibid.
39. Ibid., 208.
40. Ibid.
41. Ibid., 209.
42. Ibid., 210.
43. Ibid., 210–16; Williams quoted in Jacobs, *African Nexus,* 86.
44. Born in 1865 in rural Virginia, Sheppard was sent in 1877 at the age of twelve to Hampton, where he came under the influence of General Armstrong, a man known for his ability to instill the "ideal of manhood" in young blacks, among them Booker T. Washington. None of the historians of this period, including John Hope Franklin, Sylvia Jacobs, or Walter L. Williams, have indicated that these two persons ever met each other. It is possible that they heard about each other.
45. Walter L. Williams, *Black Americans and the Evangelization of Africa, 1877–1900* (Madison: University of Wisconsin Press, 1982), 23–29.
46. William H. Sheppard, *Pioneer Missionary to the Congo* (Louisville, Ky.: Pentecostal Publishing Co., 1917), 93–106. See Ruth M. Slade, *English-Speaking Missions in the Congo Independent State, 1878–1908* (Brussels: A.R.S.C., 1959), 106.
47. Williams, *Black Americans,* 23–24. See William H. Sheppard, *Southern Workman* 29 (April 1900): 220–21.
48. Williams, *Black Americans,* 24–28.
49. William H. Sheppard, "Into the Heart of Africa," *Southern Workman* 12 (December 1893): 182–87; "Light in Darkest Africa," *Southern Workman* 24 (April 1905): 218–227.
50. Shaloff, *Reform in Congo,* 49. See S. P. Verner, "The White Man's Zone in Africa," *World's Work* 8 (November 1906): 8227–36.
51. Shaloff, *Reform in Congo,* 77.
52. Ibid., 85.
53. Ibid., 91.
54. Ibid., 93. See W. M. Morrison, "Personal Observations of Congo Misgovernment," *American Monthly Review of Reviews* 28 (July 1903): 38–42.
55. Ibid., 94ff. Cf. S. J. S. Cookey, *Britain and the Congo Question, 1885–1913* (London: Longman, 1968).
56. Philip C. Jessup, *Elihu Root, 1905–1937* (New York: Dodd, Mead, 1938), 2:61–62.
57. Shaloff, *Reform in Congo,* 91.
58. Ibid., 95–96.
59. Booker T. Washington to Thomas Seymour Barbour, 21 May 1904, Louis R. Harlan and Raymond W. Smock, eds., *The Booker T. Washington Papers* (Urbana: University of Illinois Press, 1981), 7:510–11.
60. Booker T. Washington, "Cruelty in the Congo Country," *Outlook* 78 (8 October 1904): 375–77.
61. Shaloff, *Reform in Congo,* 85. Cf. S. P. Verner, "The Affairs of the Congo State," *Forum* 36 (July-September 1904): 150–59.
62. Henry Kowalsky to Booker T. Washington, 1 and 10 March 1905, quoted in Louis R. Harlan, "Booker T. Washington and the White Man's Burden," *American Historical Review* 71 (January 1966): 451.

63. Ibid., 451.
64. Ibid.
65. Ibid.
66. Ibid., 452.
67. Paul McStallworth, quoting from letter of Roosevelt to Lodge, Washington, 2 October 1906, cited in "The United States and the Congo Question: 1884–1914" (Ph.D. diss., Ohio State University, 1954), 233.
68. Shaloff, *Reform in Congo*, 96–97.
69. McStallworth, "United States and the Congo," 235. See also *Foreign Relations of the United States, 1907,* 61.
70. Shaloff, *Reform in Congo,* 102.
71. Ibid., 110ff.
72. Ibid. Cf. Slade, *English-Speaking Missionaries,* 317ff.
73. Shaloff, *Reform in Congo,* 110ff.
74. Slade, *English-Speaking Missionaries,* 369ff.
75. Ibid.; Shaloff, *Reform in Congo,* 118.
76. Shaloff, *Reform in Congo,* 118.
77. Ibid., 119.
78. Ibid., 125.
79. Ibid., 170.

7
Supporting Madagascar and Ethiopia

> It might not be expedient to give Mr. Waller any diplomatic discretion at the Hova [Malagasy] capital. The eventual supremacy of the French in Madagascar, is a foregone conclusion, which it is not incumbent upon us to avert or contest. (Advice from a desk officer to the Assistant Secretary of State, Josiah Quincy, on 2 June 1893.[1]

> I am making special notes of this trip, which carries some significance. I believe, partially through my efforts I have succeeded in getting the United States to establish diplomatic connections with the country. Thus Americans may have an opportunity to assist in developing the country. The President of the United States and Secretary Hay are especially interested, looking to the securing of a treaty between the United States and Abyssinia [Ethiopia]. Therefore, on my return to New York, I shall be proud to avail myself of the opportunity of a personal interview, in order that I may give you a few facts regarding this country, etc. (William H. Ellis to Andrew Carnegie, 24 September 1903).[2]

Two African Americans, John L. Waller and William H. Ellis (also known as Guillaume Enriques Ellesio), played largely unknown roles in the early history of United States relations with Madagascar and Ethiopia, two independent states that were still resisting the attempts of European imperial powers to conquer and colonize them. Both Waller, who served as United States consul in Madagascar, and Ellis, a romantic adventurer, had dreams of establishing black colonies and business enterprises in the two countries at the turn of the century and wanted the United States to establish close diplomatic relations with them. Both men exhibited the acquisitive tendencies found among many Americans of their "robber-baron" generation, but they also struggled against the racism so endemic in American life. And in their own way they both attempted to use United States power in the global system to protect black nationalities and to help blacks deal with the overwhelming power of whites. Waller's experiences in Madagascar led to a diplomatic scandal and long negotiations between France and the United States. Ellis's more romantic experiences in Ethiopian-United States relations remain an intriguing footnote in diplomatic history.

John L. Waller, who served as United States consul in Tamatave, Madagascar, from 1891 to 1894, found himself in the ambiguous position of an official who sought to protect the independence of the Malagasy people, while his country had conceded their conquest and colonization by France. Like many of the early African American diplomats, Waller (one of twelve children) was born on 12 January 1850 to slave parents in New Madrid County, Missouri. Liberated in 1862 during the Civil War by the Thirty-second Iowa Infantry, the Waller family was aided by a benevolent white family to rent out and settle on a large farm in Tama County, Iowa. In 1867, at the age of seventeen and only five years out of bondage, young Waller entered high school, earned his diploma, and enrolled in a nearby college. Owing to illness and multiple deaths in his family, he had to interrupt his education until 1874 when he began to read law in Cedar Rapids, Iowa, at the office of a sympathetic white attorney. Waller was admitted to the Iowa Bar in 1877, but perceiving Kansas to be the only nearby state that would give a young black attorney any kind of opportunity, he settled in Leavenworth on 1 May 1878. He promptly sought and received admission to the Kansas Bar, becoming in the process the first black man to practice law in the courts of Leavenworth. Here, despite "prejudice and opposition," he established a brilliant reputation. In 1879 Waller moved to Lawrence, Kansas, where he married one Mrs. Susan Bray, an educated black widow of some means.[3]

Like many of the other early black diplomats, such as Turner, Smyth, and Charles Taylor, Waller had taken an active part in Republican politics. As editor of the Topeka *Weekly Recorder* from 1883 to 1885, he campaigned tirelessly for all Republican candidates and used his paper as a forum to attack the disenfranchisement, lynching, and segregation of African Americans. He won a seat on the Republican state central committee but failed by a margin of only four votes to gain election to the Kansas legislature. This defeat was symptomatic of the growing sentiment among Republicans and other white Americans that the time had come to end the Reconstruction, to seek reconciliation with the South, and to abandon the drive to give full equality to blacks. Nevertheless, with the help of his cousin, Anthony Morton, Waller secured the black vote in Kansas in 1888 for the Republicans in the first Harrison-Cleveland electoral contest. As a reward he was elected to the Kansas electoral college, becoming the first black in the state to be so honored. In 1889 Waller received an appointment as deputy county attorney in Topeka, Kansas, again making racial history.

On 17 April 1889 one A. M. Mason, an attorney in Iowa City, Iowa, wrote President Benjamin Harrison supporting Waller's bid for a post in Haiti. And on 22 June 1889 Waller himself wrote Secretary of State James G. Blaine indicating that if the Haitian post had been promised to another person, he, Waller, was prepared to accept positions in Peru, San Salvador, Manila, and Victoria, British Columbia, among others. Also in June 1890, a senator from Kansas wrote Mr. Blaine calling his attention to Waller's consular ambition, complaining that Kansas had not had its fair share of appointments and that even the District of Columbia had received more appointments. The senator continued the campaign and, in November 1890, was joined by congressmen and businessmen from Kansas who wrote directly to President Harrison on Waller's behalf. Finally in February 1891, Waller was offered, and he accepted, the position as United States consul at Tamatave. He arrived at post on 10 August 1891, accompanied by his wife, four children, and stepson. Waller remained in that port city, but sent his family to the Malagasy capital, Antananarivo.[4]

There has been a great deal of speculation about why Waller sought a diplomatic appointment. One historian has suggested that, in marked contrast with the anti-imperialism of such black leaders as Frederick Douglass, many post–Civil War black leaders favored American overseas expansion. According to him,

> Black supporters of overseas expansion believed that prosperous Negro colonies in Latin America, the Pacific, and Africa would rebound to the benefit of their race in two ways: they would not only enhance the prestige of the United States and thus elicit the approval of white America, but would also augment Blackamerica's economic and political power base and in so doing aid in the fight for justice and equality.[5]

Waller appears to have epitomized the type of person described above. Like Turner, Smyth, and other diplomats, Waller was interested in black nationality, but he also appears to have been interested in his own economic advancement.[6]

Waller's tenure as United States consul at Tamatave was plagued from the very beginning by the aggressiveness of the French and by the refusal of the United States to oppose European imperialism. Yet for many years previously, Americans with their calicos and other merchandise had been the favorite foreign traders of the Malagasy. In November 1862, Radam II, king of Madagascar, had even appointed William Mark, a United States citizen, as his secretary of state for foreign affairs.

This man was characterized by one observer as a "crazy, drunken, unprincipled American,"[7] but Madagascar may have made a calculated move to court the United States, which was then just emerging as a world power. The Malagasy consul at Mauritius had advised his superiors of the importance of cultivating close friendship with the United States. He felt that although the Americans wanted only to gain an economic foothold in Madagascar, such a friendship would stand the Malagasy in good stead should Madagascar face further problems from the aggressive European powers. This official was convinced that the United States of America "was destined . . . one day to weigh heavily in the balance of any European imbroglio."[8]

The Malagasy welcomed the appointment of Major John P. Finkelmeier as the State Department's commercial agent in their country and eagerly concluded the usual treaty of commerce and friendship with the United States on 14 February 1867. They were overjoyed when Finkelmeier returned to their capital in June 1868, bringing with him the protocols of the Americo-Malagasy treaty for ratification. They organized an elaborate ceremony during which the treaty was ratified and took the unprecedented step of introducing the commercial agent to Queen Ranavalona II. He was the first such person so honored after the queen's accession to the throne in April 1868.

Because they had imperialist designs on Madagascar, the French were reportedly very unhappy with the treaty between the Malagasy and the United States. The local French commissioner complained that the United States did not insist that the Malagasy respect "humanist principles," the code words then in use by European powers bent on seizing the countries of "semi-civilized" or "uncivilized" peoples. Nor, he insisted, did the treaty mention the suppression of the slave trade, the pursuit of pirates, or provision for freedom of worship by American nationals. The Frenchman suggested that the tone of the treaty indicated that the Americans only wanted to please the Malagasy, and he doubted that any American citizens would ever settle in Madagascar.[9]

The French may well have been correct, since the United States had only commercial interests in Madagascar and had little regard for that society or its sovereignty. For example, when in the early 1880s the Malagasy, alarmed by their escalating quarrel with the French, sought to enlist the aid of Europe and the United States in preserving their independence, the American consul in Madagascar cautioned moderation. He advised the Malagasy prime minister that the Franco-Malagasy dispute could only be "understood and settled" by the mediation of "friendly powers."[10] He requested and received permission from the Department of State to accompany a Malagasy delegation to Europe and the United States. Washington cautioned its diplomat to avoid "any officious interference in the settlement with France which might imply that this country took sides in the controversy."[11] The Malagasy mission to France and other European states ended in disaster because the emissaries were not empowered to accept what in effect was France's demand to establish a protectorate over their country. The British foreign minister was not helpful to the Malagasy, but when queried about whether a visit to the United States would be useful, he replied, "The sooner they go to the States the better."[12] Fearful of alarming the French, the Malagasy visited Washington on the pretext of ratifying a new Americo-Malagasy treaty concluded with W. W. Robinson on 13 May 1881, replacing the one of 1867.

The American press and general public were sympathetic to the Malagasy in their country's difficulties with France and gave the ambassadors a warm welcome. Secretary of State Frederick T. Frelinghuysen (whom Minister Resident Smyth in Monrovia had sensitized to European designs in Africa) received the ambassadors on 12 March 1883 and introduced them to President Chester A. Arthur. The envoys told the president that, in their country's confrontation with France, "we do not ask you to fight for us, but only to make France, your friend, understand that it is not fair to provoke trouble in Madagascar which is an independent country."[13] They only requested that the United States furnish them with arms.

Unfortunately for the Malagasy, United States officials wished neither to furnish them arms nor to mediate between them and the French in what clearly was a case of aggression. The most the United States was willing to do was to ratify a treaty in which Queen Ranavalona II was recognized as head of the Malagasy state,[14] before she died on 13 July 1883. Disappointed by their American trip, the envoys revisited Europe and concluded treaties with European states that recognized the independence of Madagascar. The problem for the Malagasy was that France refused to abandon its designs. An unequal war broke out between France and Madagascar in June 1883. The valiant Malagasy waged a long and bitter guerrilla struggle in defense of their country, hoping thereby to encourage the United States and Great Britain to mediate.[15]

In May 1884 Lieutenant Mason A. Shufeldt visited Antananarivo, and Queen Ranavalona II gave him a letter for President Arthur in which she complained of difficulties with the French and of the "calamities of a foreign war" that threatened her people. The queen wrote that in this perilous time the one source of help was surely "that great nation in the West who ever has been our kind friend who sets to the world so great an example of success and . . . who, in the remembrance of her own early struggles for independence, can but sympathize with our dominion still young in its new history." The queen added that she understood that the policy of the United States was neither "one of aggression nor of aggrandisement," but only one which sought the "extension of commerce, the increase of learning, the fostering of those manufactures that are of benefit to man and the upholding of all those just laws that protect and make happy her citizens." It was in view of these qualities, said the queen, that she had reason to "solicit from Your Excellency the President of the United States, the friendship and assistance of the United States in these our troubles." She ended her letter with these words:

> I request Your Excellency the President the mediation of the Republic in my present difficulties with the Republic of France. We request of Your Excellency the appointment of a committee of arbitration consisting of equal numbers of American, Malagasy and French members to discuss the causes of my present difficulties and the just settlement of them. We request of Your Excellency a speedy reply to this Our Communication that our troubles may cease, and through your great friendship we may be at peace to pursue our policy of advance and of civilisation."[16]

Seconding the appeal of the queen, the Malagasy prime minister wrote to the American secretary of state and to the secretary of the navy. American traders in Madagascar also added their voices to the call for help, as did Robinson, the American consul. He wrote that the Malagasy were making progress toward civilization; that the guerrilla war with the French was detrimental to this progress; and that the United States policy of non-intervention "is sure to be construed as unfriendly to the [Malagasy], as being the weaker party, and as favoring their opponent."[17] However, all this was in vain. The United States refused to act unless the French agreed for it to do so. The French, for their part, had no intention of permitting outsiders to jeopardize their long-range plans to take over Madagascar.

By the middle of 1885, the French government revealed that its minimal demands included the provision that the Malagasy (or the Hova as the French called them) "agree to receive at Antananarivo a French Resident with an auxiliary escort for his protection to whom all matters and correspondence with all other foreign governments are to be referred."[18] The Malagasy were caught in a bind: accept a rather questionable bargain from a French administration facing elections at home or take the chance of confronting a possibly tougher new French government. They agreed to France's term and signed a treaty on 17 December 1885. Nevertheless, uneasy about the clause specifying the presence of a French Resident in their capital and fearing that this jeopardized their sovereignty, the Malagasy requested a clarification. In response the French insisted that their Resident should have the right to interfere in Madagascar's external relations, to oppose the cession of territory to a foreign nation, and to veto the establishment of military and naval posts. Lastly, the French insisted that "no treaty, agreement or convention with foreign powers can be made without the approval of the French Government."[19]

The terms of the treaty were fuzzy and were not clarified even when the Malagasy accepted a postscript to an explanatory letter from the French on 9 January 1886 that contained a clause stating that the Malagasy government "had the right to negotiate treaties of commerce with foreign powers 'so long as these treaties of commerce would not be contrary to the stipulations of the treaty of 17 December, 1885.' "[20] The appendix temporarily satisfied all the parties, but its vagueness led inexorably to conflict between the Malagasy and the French; and, as we will see, it would prove to be the undoing of John L. Waller when he arrived in Tamatave to take up his position.

As soon as he arrived, Waller applied to the government of Madagascar for an exequatur to conduct the business of consul. Significantly, it did not include dealing with political matters. The State Department subsequently instructed Waller that "any business of a political complexion, if there should be any such between the Government of Madagascar and Foreign Powers, will be in the charge of the French Resident" and that the French Resident General was well aware of these facts.[21] On 4 August 1891 Waller received a letter from the Malagasy prime minister granting him an exequatur "to transact the business of the Consul according to the Treaty of Friendship and Commerce made between Madagascar and the United States of America on the 13th of May 1887."[22]

Whether the French protested these events is not clear from the records, but Waller acknowledged the receipt of a telegram from Assistant Secretary of State William Wharton instructing him to apply to the French Resident General for his exequatur instead of to the Malagasy authorities. In his reply Waller called Washington's attention to his first telegram, in which he had indicated that he had already applied for and had received an exequatur from the Malagasy government. Waller suggested, moreover, that "to make an application to the French Resident General will be taken as an insult by the Malagasy government and will involve the country in war and bloodshed, as the Hovas insist that the French Resident General has no authority to issue an exequatur."[23] Hoping to avoid a controversy, the Department of State then advised Waller to conduct his business as did the consuls of the governments of Britain, Germany, and other great powers.

Waller responded that he could not follow the behavior of the European consuls toward the Malagasy because there was no clear pattern. He wrote that the German consul continued to conduct his official correspondence and business with the Hova authorities, not through the intervention of the French. This the German consul indicated he would continue to do unless the French could secure an exequatur for him (presumably from the Malagasy) or unless he received instructions from his own government to apply directly to the French for one. The Italian consul also indicated that he conducted his intercourse directly with the Hova government and did not seek an exequatur through the intervention of the French. Moreover, as Waller explained to the department, the Malagasy were so jealous of their prerogatives in this matter that during a recent Malagasy New Year's celebration the British vice-consul was virtually not recognized by the Hova government, "because he is now trying to conduct his official intercourse through the medium of the French Resident General."[24]

The Madagascar government was obviously attempting to use the good offices of Waller to resist France's seizure of their country, and the French resented what they considered to be Waller's sympathetic attitude toward his hosts. The Hova governor at Tamatave insisted to Waller that under the terms of the Malagasy-United States treaty of 1881, the United States did not have the authority to send a consul to Madagascar through the aegis of the French. Moreover, the governor declared that the Hova authorities were determined to control their own affairs, including "exequaturs for foreign Consuls." He indicated that he was instructed "not to recognize any foreign representative or official, who had endeavored to hold intercourse with the native authorities through the intervention of the French." The governor concluded that "under no circumstances will any foreign Minister or Consul who did not hold an exequatur from the Hova government direct, be recognized as such by said government."[25]

Waller was obviously impressed and sympathetic to the Malagasy's declaration of independence, and reported that the foreigners in Madagascar, including many of the French, felt that the Hova government and people were still fully determined to persuade the French to respect the postscript to the Franco-Malagasy treaty of 1885. In view of these circumstances, Waller felt that the Department of State should not insist that he apply to the French Resident General for the exequatur.[26]

France's decision to exert greater control over the island by establishing courts with jurisdiction over all foreigners and their property alarmed the American and British communities. The local British vigorously protested the decision as inimical to their interests. Waller reported that he had carefully interviewed Americans doing business in Madagascar and that they, too, believed that the institution of the judicial courts "would be detrimental to American interests, and greatly hamper and disturb American trade and commerce." It appears that both Waller and the Malagasy attempted to use the prospect of increased trade between Madagascar and the United States as a means of staving off French conquest. He reported that the resident American traders believed that there would be a great increase in United States trade in the country when the political situation quieted down. For their part, the Malagasy authorities assured Waller that there would be "no attempt to take their country by foreign invasion." Moreover, they felt that "when the pretensions of the French Protectorate shall be given up as it [sic] inevitably must be, there would be a great demand for cotton goods since a large part of the outlay of money now being made by them for war materials, would then be turned to business channels. Apparently concerned that the Department of State would accuse him of "localitis" (that is, viewing the world through local eyes), Waller begged to "apologize for claiming so much of the valuable time of the Department in one despatch." He explained that he had "sought to place the Department in possession of the whole situation in Madagascar, as I felt it my duty to do so."[27]

In what may have been an attempt to get to the core of the Franco-Malagasy controversy, or to join his family, Waller asked to be assigned to the capital of the island at Antananarivo. On 25 April 1893 he reported to the State Department that a strong French fleet under the command of Admiral Richard had arrived; that the Malagasy had procured "large assignments of arms and munitions of war"; that French residents on the island were quite excited; and that in his own opinion and that of many foreign residents, there was no doubt about the eventuality of a "conflict in a very short time." Waller suggested that in the event of such a conflict, it would be imperative that the department place a "fully qualified and empowered" representative, as well as one familiar in dealing with the Hova authorities, at Antananarivo, to protect American interests in the interior. To meet such an emergency, Waller recommended that the department might do well to "instruct the Consul at Tamatave [himself] to proceed to Antananarivo, leaving a deputy or the Vice Consul to act in his stead at this Port."[28]

Unfortunately for Waller, the department refused to authorize his transfer. Grover Cleveland and the Democrats were now in power and, as customary, the State Department believed that there would be a change in consular representatives as well as policies. On 2 June 1893 a desk officer suggested to Assistant Secretary of State Josiah Quincy that "it might not be expedient to give Mr. Waller any diplomatic discretion at the Hova capital. The eventual supremacy of the French in Madagascar, is a foregone conclusion, which it is not incumbent on us to avert or contest."[29] A week later Quincy was informed that a new consul had been appointed in Mr. Waller's place, and that it might be better to give that person copies of the cables and let him use his discretion in nominating a vice consul.[30]

Given the intimacy of the small diplomatic community in Tamatave, the French probably learned immediately about Waller's impending departure. They then apparently felt free to sanction him for what was clearly his disapproval of their aggressiveness toward the Malagasy. Waller reported to Washington on "the discourteous behavior of the new French Resident at Tamatave toward the U. S. Consul." He was disturbed that although the newly appointed French Resident Governor had called upon the Malagasy governor of Tamatave and on the German, British, and French consuls, as of 22 August 1893, he had neither called upon, nor sent his card to, the United States consul. Moreover, when the French Resident sent the customary letter notifying the United States legation of his country's national day, 14 July, "the U.S. Consul was not invited nor was there any time designated for him to call as is the custom, while the governor and the other Consuls were all invited." Waller in turn did not force himself upon the French Resident. Instead he sought instruction from the Department of State for "future guidance in relations to the discourteous behavior of the newly appointed French resident in Tamatave."[31] There is no indication in the archives that Washington responded to this inquiry.

In contrast, the Malagasy had been so satisfied with Waller's performance that they apparently did not want President Cleveland to replace him. In August 1893 the Hova government wrote Cleveland recounting how it valued "the friendly relations so happily existing for a long time between the two countries" and how out of this had emerged good economic relations and reciprocal confidence. The letter added that the Malagasy were especially pleased by the United States' attitude toward them, as shown by giving its consul "orders to do all communications direct with us. We feel highly satisfied with the friendly way in which your representative, Mr. Waller carries on business transactions with us. We have the feelings of gratitude a pleasant recollection of this friendly attitude."[32] There is no evidence that President Cleveland responded to this letter, but by the time the letter was written, Waller must have known he was to be replaced. He had already made arrangements to get a large grant of land, a prospect that angered the French and would lead to some diplomatic tension between France and the United States.

Waller remained U.S. consul in Tamatave long enough to witness the final act in France's seizure of Madagascar. Included in his despatch of 25 August 1893 to the Department of State was a clipping from the *Madagascar News* reporting that the British foreign secretary, placing the Zanzibar-Madagascar convention before the House of Lords, admitted that Great Britain had recognized French claims to Madagascar in exchange for their acquiescence in Britain's protectorate over Zanzibar. Lord Salisbury had therefore instructed his consuls and ministers to apply for exequaturs through the medium of the French Resident. Waller also reported that the question being asked in Madagascar was whether America would permit Britain to influence its action.[33] The State Department remained silent on this question because it had already made up its mind to straddle the issue. Receiving no reply, bowing before the inevitable, and aware as he must have been that he was being recalled, Waller sent the customary certificate from his doctor, indicating that he was suffering from chronic dysentery, and requested a leave of absence of sixty days to go to the mountainside to receive a cure.[34]

When Edward Telfair Wetter arrived in Tamatave to replace Waller as United States consul, he was instructed "to take no step toward asking a formal exequatur from the Hova Government directly or through the French Resident" so long as he was able to discharge his consular duties with the temporary recognition, and by the mutual consent, of both parties. The State Department wished to take its time "to gain a better understanding of the exequatur question." Moreover, the new consul was cautioned that if he found it impossible to discharge his duties he was to report the facts to the department and await instructions.[35]

Waller's resignation from the consularship and departure for Antananarivo were initially the source of much local amusement until it was
learned that he had been promised a large concession by the Malagasy.
The French newspaper *Le Courier de Madagascar* reported that Waller
had left the previous week for Antananarivo, where he was said to have
opened a grocery store.[36] Another paper, *Madagascar News,* humor-
ously reported:

> In truth the "colored gentlemen" has resigned his high functions to open a
> . . . grocery at Antananarivo. The seat of the boss behind a counter will
> better suit him than the consular armchair. And then since he will necessarily
> become purveyor to the Palais, an advantage so inestimable although only
> honorary, fortune cannot fail long to visit his shop. Mr. Waller proceeded to
> Antananarivo last week after telling his plans to one of our friends.[37]

In a cable to the Department of State Wetter reported that it was more
likely that Waller would remain in Antananarivo if his grocery succeeded but that the chances were against it. Wetter, was, however, more
interested in making contact with Waller because of problems with the
financial records of the consulate than in knowing the ex-consul's plans.
He had sounded an ominous note in his cable to the Department of State
on 27 January 1894, in which he mentioned that there were "rumors
afloat against Mr. Waller's moral and financial character of a most
serious nature." Rumor against Mr. R. W. Geldart, Waller's vice-consul,
"especially in financial matters, seems to be even more unsatisfactory."
Wetter said that the view in Tamatave was that Mr. Waller was a tool in
Geldart's hands, and that if the former consul ever returned to the port,
he would have to account for his stewardship of Crockett's property.[38]

W. F. Crockett, a citizen of the United States and a trader, had died in
Madagascar in June 1892 leaving a local wife and two minor children.
He had stipulated in a will that his property be used for his family and
should be administered by the U.S. consul to escape the fees and expenses that would accrue were the property to be placed in Malagasy
hands. Waller had reported these facts to the Department of State in
November 1892 and had added that because of claims against the estate
he had taken personal charge of it. Since this was normally the practice
of United States consuls, Washington approved Waller's action and directed him to administer the estate in conformity with consular regulations. Waller subsequently reported to the State Department that he had
converted the property into cash but apparently failed to tell the department what he had done with the money.

When Wetter took charge of the consulate in January 1894 and checked its records, he could find no accounting of the Crockett estate after November 1892. The acting vice-consul, a man named Geldart, said that he could throw no light on the matter. The only item in the Crockett file was a letter declaring that his common-law widow had appointed John Waller "as administrator and guardian for the estate of the late W. F. Crockett." This document authorized Waller to rear the couple's daughter in his family and "to lend the money which belongs to me and my children at such interest as will pay for the clothes, board, and care of the children without consuming the principal for that purpose." The widow also stipulated that she wanted "the interest paid at the end of each six months, provided that it shall always be applied to the board, lodging, and care of the children. I want a statement showing the amount of interest the principal has earned at the end of each six months."[39]

Waller was still in Antananarivo when the news reached there that the Malagasy had actually granted him a concession. The resulting uproar both in the port and in the capital would play a crucial role in a drama that would lead to the undoing of the ex-consul of the United States of America. On 27 March 1894 Edward Wetter sent to the Department of State an item in the *Madagascar News* of 17 March 1894, which read in part:

Large Concession Granted to An American Citizen in the Great Rubber District of Fort Dauphin . . . His Excellency the Prime Minister and Commander in Chief of Madagascar had just granted the Hon. John L. Waller, U.S. Consul in Madagascar, a concession measuring in area 15 miles square . . . It is this district which is now attracting such wide attention in commercial circles on account of the abundance and value of the rubber forests there. The District also contains very valuable timbers such as Ebony, Mahogany, Rosewood, Teak, etc., and is admirably adapted to the cultivation of Tea, Coffee, Vanilla, etc. Mr. Waller informs us that he will stop the destruction of the rubber trees and vines by the natives so far as he is concerned and will preserve the product by having the milk extracted in a scientific manner. He will also enter largely into the cultivation of Rubber upon his concession. This intention of Mr. Waller's is a step in the right direction and will add immensely to the value of the concession; which is by far the largest and most important surface concession ever granted in Madagascar and we congratulate Mr. Waller upon his success.[40]

The local papers stressed that the Waller concession of some one hundred and fifty thousand acres was extremely valuable, and that the local people in the area had earned large sums of money from the products there and as a result had been able to import large quantities of goods.

The speculation that Waller had planned to establish an "American Colored Colony" on his land did not initially alarm the editor of the *Madagascar News*. The newspaper was concerned with the size of the grant. It noted in its edition of 3 May 1894 that the concession was equal to one-third the size of the nearby island of Mauritius, where Waller had many close friends. Moreover, it reported that Waller had told his Mauritian friends that he was giving priority to the selection of agricultural holdings, no matter how small or how large, and that it was also his intention to found townships and to facilitate the establishment of industrial enterprises such as sawmills, fiber-works, and so on. This feature of the enterprise, said the *Madagascar News,* was designed to open up profitable areas to the artisan classes of Mauritius, as it necessitated the employment of some skilled Mauritians. In the opinion of the paper, the development of the commercial projects would initially be slow.

In contrast, *Le Madagascar* reflected the outrage of the French community over Waller's concession. This act was deemed an attack upon "Commercial Freedom in Madagascar," and the paper questioned the legality of Mr. Waller's title. It asked, "What profit does Mr. Waller reap from his concession?" The paper did not hesitate to say that no good would come of the affair. It had no doubt that "Mr. Waller may stand personally very high in the good graces of the Prime Minister. Independent of race affinities which always draw individuals close together, Mr. Waller in the exequatur question has exhibited so much consideration for the Malagasy Government, that the latter cannot fail in its turn, to have a great deal for him." Nevertheless, the paper doubted that "the personal sympathies which ex-Consul of the U.S. ought to enjoy at the Silver Place have been the main motive." Nor did the writer of the article believe that "his Excellency Rimilaiarivary whose sleep has never yet been broken by philanthropy, could possibly have permitted himself to be seduced by the beautiful imagery of a colony of American Negroes and Negresses established in any portion whatsoever of Madagascar and owe their happiness to him." The paper was convinced that what prompted the action of the Malagasy was "simply the pleasure of putting a spoke in the wheels of the white man (Vagahas) and above all of the French, who carry on the rubber traffic in the South."[41]

By now Waller's concession had become a cause célèbre between the Malagasy and the French government. The following questions were raised: Was the Resident General of France in Madagascar consulted and did he give consent to the concessions made to Mr. Waller? Did the concession given to Mr. Waller represent such an alienation of territory as to provoke protests from the French government? Did this concession merely prove that the Malagasy government wished to impede the "penetration of the civilized element, and particularly the French element, into the South-East of Madagascar?"[42]

Le Madagascar of 5 April 1894 was certain that the Hova government had made a mistake in granting the concession to Waller. It declared that under normal circumstances, whenever the Malagasy had given a concession to a person of any nationality other than French, care had to be taken that the person was not the "agent of his government and that said government proposed establishing a coaling station or military establishments upon his concession." The paper said that given its "great confidence in the fair dealings of the great American Republic" it could not "suppose for a single instant that such might be the case with the Waller concession." Mr. Waller, it added, was "actuated simply by commercial and philanthropic intentions." It believed that at first he was going to cultivate rubber and afterward he was planning to found "a colony of colored Americans, who will undoubtedly plant vanilla for their leader." The paper stated explicitly:

> We will add that the future American colony will be most detrimental to us. Let us not even suppose that this little Republic should desire to have this Honorable Mr. Waller for President. We doubt indeed that it would constitute for the future of Madagascar an element of peace and very bonafide progress. The example of the American Republic of Haiti is not very reassuring in this respect.[43]

While the French community in Madagascar was angry that the Malagasy had granted Waller a concession, Wetter could not wait until his newsworthy predecessor returned to Tamatave so he could discuss the Crockett account with him. On 8 May 1894 Wetter notified the department that he was anxious to verify Waller's movements, since it was rumored that he and his entire family would leave for the United States on the steamer *Pembroke Castle*. Suspecting that at best Waller had not followed proper procedures under the consular codes, and at worst had mismanaged Crockett's estate, Wetter had tried to get an accounting from both Waller and Geldart on 29 March 1894. By this time Waller was up-country, and Geldart asserted that Waller had not turned over to him any money from the Crockett estate, but had taken it, declaring that he would give an account only to the Department of State. Disturbed by Geldart's report, Wetter prepared a suit against Waller in the name of the

United States, charging him with "negligence and mismanagement of fiduciary trusts."[44]

On 1 October 1894, with Waller back in Tamatave from Antananarivo, Consul Wetter, "acting judicially," opened the case against Waller with several resident Americans to serving as associate judges. The court included Wetter, R. W. Geldart, J. O. Ryder, and Daniel J. Howe, a newly arrived American. Wetter reported that since Geldart was "Waller's most intimate friend and champion," and Ryder and Howe were perfectly neutral, "the utmost impartiality has been secured to Mr. Waller."[45]

The court deliberated and judged Waller guilty of "abuse and negligence of his fiduciary trusts, both as a citizen and as an official." Wetter instructed Waller to pay to the United States consulate within forty-five days "the amount of the balance due said Crockett's heirs now in his hands, to wit, $1,961.67, Madagascar currency," and an additional $294.25 as the interest that would have accrued on the sum had it been loaned out at 8 percent as stipulated in Crockett's will. Wetter also ordered Waller to pay all the court costs and not to leave Madagascar until these payments had been made. In addition to reporting these actions to the Department of State on 26 October 1894, the consul asked for permission to bring criminal charges against Waller.[46]

Because he could not raise the funds to cover the judgment in the Crockett case, Waller was still in Tamatave in December 1894 when new hostilities broke out between the French and the Malagasy. The French bombarded and captured the town, installed a military garrison and established martial law, and placed all mail under surveillance. This last provision was especially distressing to Waller because he needed to be in constant communication with his family in the capital concerning his concession and the raising of funds to settle his accounts with Wetter. For example, on 27 November 1894 he had written to his wife indicating that he had heard that "the State Department recognizes the right of the Hova Government to lease land to American citizens." But he told her that the Department of State had said that the French might invoke clauses in their treaty with Madagascar stipulating that land should be leased for a period of twenty-five years instead of thirty years, as in his lease.[47] As it turned out, Waller's attempts to correspond with his wife got him into difficulty with the French. On 22 December 1894 Waller wrote a letter to his wife in which he warned her:

> Now that Tamatave is under military law and no one is allowed to leave here for the capital, and all communication by post having been cut off, I can not

therefore tell when we shall meet again or when you will hear from me; but I certainly hope that our separation will be brief, and that no harm will befall my loved ones. I am still at Mr. Dublin's, and am waiting anxiously to hear from you regarding the money which was to be sent in time to meet judgment against me here . . . Let me caution you to have nothing to do with or say anything about the troubles between the French and Hova Governments, as such would only tend to embarrass you. Of course, this does not prevent you from keeping up your friendly relations with our friends at the capital, being careful always to avoid any discussion on the present difficulty.[48]

Waller's difficulties with the French arose from his attempts to contravene their military censorship and from unforeseen events that flowed from that. Because of the lack of transportation, he could not mail out the letters he had already written to his wife until two days after the date for the implementation of the French censorship decree, Article III of which prohibited the transmission of mail except through the French military. In an effort to escape French censorship, Waller personally delivered to the steamship *Umlazi* of the Donald Currie Line, a package of letters he had written to his wife and enclosed others for different persons, to be sent to "Antananarivo, via Natal and Vatomandry." Waller would later insist that he knew nothing of the censorship imposed by the French. What he never did explain satisfactorily is why he dated both letters 23 January 1895, when he mailed them on 20 January 1895.[49]

Waller's bad luck was that the package of letters sent to Antananarivo via Natal was mishandled and was returned to Tamatave, where it was seized by the French. The French read in Waller's letter to his wife about their proposed military censorship and also such intimate details as his informing her that the reason for not receiving any money was that Wetter had advised the State Department to withhold his salary and his concern that his wife and his friends could not readily raise the money that he needed. He wondered whether the French had turned over to her the passports that had been forwarded through them.

The French military censors also read Waller's letter to his wife relating how he had charged his lawyers in Washington to consider suing Mr. Wetter for some $20,000 in damages for compelling him to "remain here in the midst of such annoyances, both mental and physical." Waller told his wife that she could not possibly imagine how Wetter had wronged him. He pledged that if his wife could only get help from friends, "I will teach Wetter a bitter lesson if I can only get out of his hands, and get home."[50] What infuriated the French, and led them to arrest Waller on 5 March 1895 and charge him not only with violating their censorship but also with "attempting to correspond with the subjects of a hostile nation, [in an effort] to furnish the enemy with instructions prejudicial to the military and political situation of France,"[51] was his report about the conduct of their soldiers and his suggestion that they had spies in the Malagasy capital. In the letter to his wife, Waller said:

> Geldart, Duder, and Poupard are as thick now as three in a bed, and Wetter is their god. I will inform you that D. and P. are on their way to Antananarivo, and they will likely reach there long before this letter leaves Tamatave.
>
> Please inform M. [George E.] Tessier and our friends that both of these men have been sent up there by the French to find out secretly all the movements of the Hova Government, which they will send to the French authorities from time to time. Therefore the Government had better keep a strict watch of these men and order them from the capital as soon as possible. Both of them are for the French. I shall slip this letter out by English steamer via Natal; then it will not be read by the French, as all letters are here at this time. I shall be anxious to learn that you have received this letter; therefore, when you get it do not mention anything you find in it, but simply say: Your No. 44 received. And please destroy it as soon as you and Mr. Tessier have read it, and not mention to anyone but Mr. Tessier and secretaries about the information which I send you.[52]

A summary of the letter that Waller wrote to Tessier, referred to in the correspondence as "an agent," read in part:

> I send an important letter, under cover to you, to my wife, which I will be pleased to have you hand her in person, on account of its importance.
>
> I need not inform you that she will call your attention to a certain matter therein contained, the importance of which will at once challenge your most careful attention, and place our friends on their guard. This matter is strictly confidential, and I can assure you that our friends can not afford to lose any time in attending to it, etc.
>
> Smallpox, rape, destruction of *embles* [rapid destruction of everything], wretchedness. Supplies of beeves.
>
> Letter sent by British steamer, so that it might not be seen by the colonel.[53]

The French would later claim that they considered Waller's mailing of these letters to be only a minor infraction, but insisted that Waller knew about their imposition of censorship on the mails on 18 January 1895, since he had told his wife in a letter mailed on 20 January 1895, "I shall ship this letter out by English steamer via Natal; then it will not be read by the French, as all letters are here at this time."[54] The French also noted that in a letter mailed to one Ratsimanana on 20 January 1895 Waller stated, "I dare not write you on matters about the French and Hovas here, and when you write do not mention any matter as to the war, but only friendly and business matters, as all letters are opened and read by an officer in the French army here. Therefore, be very careful what you write."[55]

When Wetter found out that Waller had been arrested and was in prison awaiting trial, he wrote several despatches to the French commander, Captain Kiesel, requesting immediate information about Waller's arrest, the nature of the charges, and where the prisoner had been incarcerated. Wetter insisted to the Frenchman that as far as he knew, Waller had been "leading a most peaceful and quiet existence" since his return to Tamatave. The consul therefore expressed his surprise at the action against Waller. Waller's imprisonment, he said, "can only be warranted by a most grave breach of the laws, and [I] sincerely hope for the sake of the good relations and friendship between France and the United States that the evidence in hand will warrant such extreme measures."[56]

The very same day, junior French officials (acting on behalf of their superiors) responded to Wetter's complaint. They gave specific information of the charges levied against Waller and confirmed that he was "arrested to be impeached at the military tribunals."[57] Wetter thus became involved in the Waller case but did not notify the Department of State about the affair until March 11. Wetter reported having "engaged an attorney to represent Mr. Waller, but all his examinations and of the witnesses have been held privately, and so far he has not been granted legal advice, nor has the attorney or anyone else been permitted to see him." Later Wetter would tell the Department of State that, not knowing precisely what to do next, he sent for Paul H. Bray, Waller's stepson, and advised him to secure counsel for the accused. Young Bray allegedly assumed that the consul would pay the cost of counsel and secured a lawyer for his stepfather. The lawyer initially told Wetter that his fee would be minimal since the fine for violating Article III was a paltry 5 to 15 francs. But when the lawyer learned that the case had taken on other dimension, he told Wetter that his fee would be some $150 for Waller's defense. Since, according to Wetter, neither Waller's friends nor the other Americans in town would contribute money for the lawyer's fee, and since Wetter was himself prohibited by law from paying the cost of counsel, "[he] refused to pay . . . with the result that Girandeau [the lawyer] withdrew from the case."[58]

Witter confessed to the State Department that he was at a loss to understand the legal issues involved in the former consul's arrest. If the French had the power to arrest Waller under their statutes, then Wetter, as United States consul, was not justified in interfering unless Waller were ill-treated or denied justice. But if, on the other hand, the French had occupied Tamatave without having formally declared war, then they would have had no right to imprison Waller. Wetter had concluded that "to raise that issue here now would mean so much to the French and would cause such bitter animosity toward every American, that I felt it would be unwise to assume the position unless warranted therein by the law of the nations."[59]

The records in the Department of State indicate that Wetter did far less than he could have done for Waller. He was obviously angry when he had heard about the letter in which Waller had been harshly critical of him and had promised to sue him for some $20,000. But what apparently incensed Wetter was the reference in Waller's letters to "Duder and Poupard," and to "D. and P. . . . on their way to Antananarivo," with the implication that Waller had attempted to betray fellow Americans to the Malagasy. As Wetter explained to the department, "Personally, I have no doubt, nor has anyone else here, white or black, that had Waller's letters of January 23 [1895] reached Antananarivo, Duder and Poupard would have been murdered." Wetter said that while Waller had insisted that "D. and P." referred to one Draper and one Purdy, without questioning the prisoner's veracity, it appeared strange to him that no one had ever heard of Draper or Purdy and that both Duder and Poupard were supposed to be in Antananarivo when Waller wrote the letters. Nevertheless, in Wetter's opinion "none of this business concerned the French. If Waller were scoundrel enough to attempt to have these men's lives taken by the Hovas, as they were Americans it would concern this consular court and not the French."[60]

Wetter's first report to the State Department about the Waller affair was factually correct but somewhat self-serving. His claim that he immediately engaged "an attorney to represent Mr. Waller" belied his reluctance to do so. Wetter did not report that he was so angry that he rejected out of hand Waller's attempt at apology and an appeal for help. Waller had written Wetter from the military prison at Tamatave on 18 March 1895 stating that he was told by a Mr. Ethelbert G. Woodford that the consul was doing all he could to effect his release and that this had come as a surprise since he had previously been informed that "you would not aid me in any manner." Waller said that if he had had the benefit of Wetter's "official influence," the outcome might have been different, but he asked "your assistance and aid as an American citizen, as I have taken an appeal from judgment of to-day." Waller asked Wetter's "pardon for the manner in which I mention your name in a letter to my wife, dated, I think, January 23, 1895. It was done in the heat of passion and under great mental pressure; therefore I here and now recall and expunge every reference to you from said letter." Declaring that he had offered to do this, but that Wetter had refused to acknowledge the gesture, Waller concluded, "Please aid me as an American, as you are the only official representative we have here."[61]

Acknowledging the receipt of Waller's letter, Wetter responded that he would have answered immediately had he not wished to clarify certain issues raised in the letter. He said that Waller should know of the regulations specifying that a consul could not intervene if an American had been "willfully guilty of an infraction of the local laws." He could understand Waller's surprise at his using his "consular position for the purpose of in any way protecting or attempting to secure you any amelioration of the penalty you have thus willfully laid yourself open to." Nevertheless, he asked Waller to understand that he could not take any action on his behalf which did not "come within the rights of every American, nor can I raise on your behalf any issue that may result in jeopardizing American interests or rights here unless such action be fully warranted in my opinion by the law of nations or be directly ordered by the Department of State."[62]

However, Wetter categorically refused to discuss with Waller the question of an apology since, as he said, there was "no apology or excuse that you can possibly offer for same that will at all excuse it." He bore Waller no ill will and did not indulge "in the cowardly habits of 'back-biting' and of kicking a man when he is down; therefore whatever I can lawfully do for you in my official capacity, I repeat, I have done and will continue to do." The consul declared that he would lay before the Department of State the full details of Waller's case and request its consideration. But he could not hold out any great hope of immediate action, "as I greatly fear your dastardly attempt on the lives of D. and P. will be apt to prejudice the mass of your fellow-countrymen against you. Absolute justice and protection against oppression will undoubtedly be accorded you, but you ought scarcely to expect clemency." Wetter promised to call at the jail to find out whether Waller had any specific request to make to the department and whether there was anything that he could officially do to help the prisoner.[63]

Surprisingly, after this rather tough response to Waller, Wetter complained to the French commander, perhaps to protect himself, that although notified of Waller's arrest, he had really received no formal reply to the notes asking why Waller had been detained. In his angry response to Wetter, the French commander almost accused him of dereliction of duty or worse for waiting until the trial was over and the verdict pending to show this concern. Captain Kiesel acknowledged the receipt of Wetter's several letters and suggested that Waller's lawyer had overstepped judicial bounds in his handling of the case. He pointed out that though the consul himself had daily followed the affair, he had not officially involved himself in the proceedings. Kiesel said that he was "led to conclude that it was intentionally [that] you kept aloof of the suit begun by the military authority." It was of course no business of his to seek reasons for Wetter's behavior, but "I should have held it a point of honor to confirm our friendly intercourse by enabling you to follow the Waller case."[64]

What especially troubled Kiesel about Waller's case was "finding an American citizen full of hatred for France" and willing to accuse "two American citizens, Messrs. Duder and Poupard, whose lives should have been greatly imperiled had the accusations, as cowardly as false, of J. Waller reached the Hova officers they were to have been imparted to." Kiesel concluded that justice had "run its course" and was now beyond his intervention. Nevertheless, he indicated that the appeal would be open to the public, and that he would order that Wetter be "officially notified of the date and hour of the judging."[65]

On 24 March 1895 Waller was sentenced to twenty years' imprisonment; his appeal was rejected by the French military tribunal.[66] Both he and Paul H. Bray, his stepson, were shipped out of Tamatave on 25 March 1895 on the French steamer *Djeunah*. Waller would later allege that he had been subjected to cruel treatment on board. He said he was chained to the floor by his arms and legs, kept on his back in that condition for seven days, and exposed to other such indignities.[67] Despite his protestations that there were no American officials on the island, Bray was put off ship at Zanzibar while Waller was kept on board. Bray finally had to pay his way to France, where the U.S. consul at Marseilles sent him to Paris. From there he was shipped at government expense back to the United States.

Bray would later testify before Department of State officials that while on board ship he had no opportunity to contact his father, who was consigned to fourth-class accommodations, but he was told by a fellow passenger that the guards brought Waller "nothing but rice, a little curry and water, and not even a spoon or a fork or anything to eat with." Waller complained that he was treated like a dog. "He had offered to buy a little wine or a little lemonade, because he could not stand the change of water," but was denied that privilege.[68]

The departure of Waller and Bray left Mrs. Waller and her children destitute in Antananarivo until Ethelbert G. Woodford, a businessman and friend of Waller's, agreed to pay their passage to Mauritius out of his own pocket. There the United States consul took care of them and sent them on to Marseilles, from where they were sent first to Paris and then back home. For reasons unknown Mrs. Waller evinced no desire to visit her husband while she was in Marseilles and not far from Aix-en-Provence, where he was imprisoned. Nor did she wish to go there from Paris when the American ambassador and French authorities offered her the opportunity to do so.[69]

The Waller case drew much attention in the U.S. Congress. Both the Senate and the House of Representatives passed resolutions requesting the president to furnish them with the correspondence at the Department of State concerning Waller if in his judgment this was not incompatible with the public interest.[70] Therefore, as soon as the Department of State heard the verdict, it took action. On 10 April 1895 Secretary of State Walter Q. Gresham instructed the American ambassador in Paris, Mr. J. B. Eustis, to ask the French government for a record of all the proceedings in the Waller case, including a copy of the evidence. Gresham also ordered Assistant Secretary of State Edwin F. Uhl to conduct an in-house investigation of the matter.

On 30 April 1895, the American ambassador in Paris reported to the secretary that he had seen Foreign Minister Albert Hanotaux and had been informed that the papers related to the Waller case were en route to Paris and that he would be notified when they arrived. Meanwhile, the diplomats at the State Department reviewed their records and questioned all the witnesses who came to Washington or agreed to answer questions by mail. Their attempt to get to the bottom of the Waller affair in order to effect his release revealed a tangled web of personal ambition, possible fraud, hatred, spite, personal vendetta, and virulent racism. All of this was played out against the background of French imperialism, the Malagasy's attempt at self-protection, and the refusal of the United States to do little more than seek a narrow commercial interest in Africa.

As soon as John H. Bray arrived in Washington, he was summoned to the State Department and interviewed by Assistant Secretary of State Uhl. Commenting upon his stepfather's position and role in Madagascar, Bray asserted that the whole affair had been very peculiar. He insisted that the French Resident's claim that the Malagasy did not have the right to grant any concession without his approval was a personal one and did not have the sanction of Paris. Bray also asserted that the Malagasy had the right to reject France's claim to review the granting of concessions, since their prime minister had assured the French Resident that the grant "was only a commercial enterprise, and that he had no intention to throw any obstacle in the way of France."[71]

Waller's undoing, according to Bray, was that the merchants in Madagascar and in neighboring Mauritius were so unsure of the legality of Waller's concession that they feared to invest in it. With the fall of Tamatave, the French officials systematically harassed and attempted to expel both him and his stepfather, threatening them with imprisonment. Bray lamented that Waller was arrested and examined without benefit of counsel because Wetter had refused to advance the lawyer's fee or to pay for it. Yet Bray admitted that Consul Wetter had been kind to him, and that he had housed and aided him when he was being harassed by the French.[72]

The State Department was especially interested in finding out what Bray knew about the identities of "D. and P." Bray told Uhl that the French had "asked me if I knew anybody by the name of Draper and Purdy. I told them that I did not know anyone by that name."[73] He admitted that he knew one Poupard, but he maintained, that Waller had testified that "D. and P." referred to Draper and Purdy, and not to Duder and Poupard.[74] When Mrs. Waller arrived in Washington, she was summoned to the Department of State and was accompanied by a lawyer, a man from Howard University, when interviewed by Mr. Uhl. Like her son, Mrs. Waller could not throw any light on the identities of Draper and Purdy. She did admit to knowing two Americans named Mr. Duder and Mr. Poupard. Mrs. Waller's major complaint concerned Wetter's treatment of her husband. She said she knew little about the Crockett legacy except that her husband had sent Wetter a report as requested and had turned over the whole estate to him under protest. Mrs. Waller reported that her husband felt that he had no obligation to do so, but he complied rather than court difficulty. She thought it odd that Wetter had the reports for three months without making any complaint and unfair that when Waller returned to Tamatave on his way home, Wetter first demanded money and the estate from him and then detained him. Mrs. Waller had attempted to raise funds to activate her husband's concession and to settle the Crockett affair but failed to do so because "the men there were not used to dealing with a woman, and they did not think the papers signed by a woman were good, and they said Mr. Waller must come up and sign them."[75]

Ethelbert G. Woodford was also summoned to the Department of State to give testimony on the affair. He was emphatic in his testimony that Waller and his family were objects of racism and shabby treatment by almost all the Americans in the Madagascar region. Woodford said that he arrived at Tamatave on 9 March 1895, four days after Waller's arrest, and was permitted to land only after the vigorous intervention of Consul Wetter. Being a friend of Waller, Woodford said that he tried to help the prisoner before trial and had to bribe a jailer to see him after the trial was over.[76]

Woodford painted a dismal picture of life in Tamatave, among the members of the American trading community and between Wetter and Waller. Because the traders were all involved in the same enterprise, there was a great deal of "scandal, gossip, lying, and everything like that . . . so much of it that it would simply disgust anyone." He noted, moreover, that men who one day would be deadly enemies would then become fast friends, a trait Woodford attributed to the traders being "a low class of men, not very refined ideas nor very high moral principles."[77] Woodford was highly critical of the role that Wetter played in the Waller case but was also somewhat understanding of the personal characteristics of the consul. He said that he found Wetter to be "a very peculiar man, with a singular, overbearing, bullying style of speaking to anyone. He is a man of very commanding appearance, of sharp manner, and curt address."[78] Woodford noted that while Wetter disliked Waller, he was highly agitated about the ex-consul's imprisonment and trial. At the same time, Woodford could not understand why Wetter did not make more of an effort to raise the $60 fee needed to defend Waller. He admitted that Wetter did not personally have the money to pay for a lawyer but also felt that the reason for his lack of action was that Wetter felt that "it was a foregone conclusion that the French court would condemn Waller, and it would do no good to pay this money to this mulatto lawyer; that if I wanted to spend my money for Waller [it would be better if] I would give it to his wife and family, where it would do more good."[79]

Despite his attempt at objectivity, Woodford stressed to Uhl that he did not believe that Wetter had done enough to help his predecessor. In fact he said that he told Wetter that the case against Waller "was outrageous." He added:

> To take this man off and to give him twenty years in prison is to practically give him his death warrant. I argued it out very strongly with Wetter at the time. In the first place, the French have no legal standing there, and are simply filibusters occupying this place. There has been no declaration of war. They simply wanted to get rid of Mr. Waller because he had obtained his large concession. His was a business matter, just as mine.[80]

Woodford's conclusion was that Wetter was "a man of small ideas, a man easily inflamed to anger and very vindictive. I believe that the man at the bottom of his heart tried to do the best that he could. The thing was too deep for him. He would get into a terrible fit of passion about what Waller would say." Woodford reported saying to Wetter, "Why do you take any notice of what the man says about you?"[81] Woodford said that Wetter would not forgive Waller and extended this animosity to Mrs. Waller and her children. When Woodford had to pay to transport them from the capital to Tamatave and sought help from Wetter to send them onward, the consul refused, saying, "It has nothing to do with this consulate."[82] Like Bray and Mrs. Waller, Woodford could not help the Department of State identify the persons referred to by Mr. Waller as "D. and P." He did observe that since there were a lot of "rascals running over that island," it was impossible to "know who is who."[83] Woodford was nevertheless highly critical of Waller for mentioning the names of the two men in his letters and told the Department of State that he had said to Waller, "If the two men whom you said were spies, what right had you, as an American citizen, to denounce them?" Waller reportedly replied, "You do not understand, neither can I explain it to you." Woodford told the Department of State that Waller's reference to D. and P. was the only criticism he had of him, adding:

> Of course I have my own views about the whole affair. I had the opinion from the moment the French seized Waller that they intended to get rid of him. They thought he was a nigger, had no money, and that we white Americans, like Wetter, myself, and a few others, would not bother our heads about him. My opinion is that the war was caused through Waller's concession; and that was the origin of the last French expedition. There was tremendous opposition to the granting of his concession by the Queen, and the French looked with suspicion on this grant and upon all American enterprise. I myself moved on a larger scale than Waller, and was negotiating for several concessions, and had addressed a memorandum in 1891 to the prime minister, a copy of which had been sold by an employee of mine, in which I outlined the whole policy of granting concessions on a very large scale to Americans, with, of course, a view to my own advantage."[84]

While the diplomats of the Department of State in Washington questioned everyone they could find who knew about the Waller affair, even seeking information from Madagascar, the American diplomats in Paris also badgered the French for the papers dealing with the case and demanded access to the prisoner. When on 31 May 1895 Ambassador J. B. Eustis of the United States had not received word from the French foreign minister about Waller, he wrote Albert Hanotaux, the French minister, stating: "The case of Mr. Waller has been much commented upon in the United States, and as it was specially recommended to me by my Government, I shall feel obliged if a reply to this last question could reach me at an early date."[85]

The problem for Hanotaux was that the French government could not decide whether to give the United States a copy of the evidence in the Waller case. The French officials stalled by claiming that the papers had been retained in Madagascar. This response did not please Washington, and on 2 August 1895 the department complained to the French that their refusal to provide the documentary evidence was disturbing, and insisted that the French government's denial of access to Waller by the American embassy was "not only unjust and oppressive to him, but discourteous to the Government of the United States."[86]

The French finally permitted American diplomats in Paris to communicate with Waller, but they refused to provide the record of the trial. On 16 October 1895, Hanotaux wrote Ambassador Eustis that while the Waller papers had arrived in France, "the general principles of our criminal law do not allow that a legal procedure which ended in a definitive decision can be the object of any communication whatsoever." He asserted that those principles were "more strictly applied in the case of a prosecution conducted in conformity with military laws, according to which the procedure is secret until the accused appears before the council of war." Under these conditions, Hanotaux wrote, "I can only express to your excellency my regrets that I am not in [a] position to comply with the desire you made known to me."[87] The French foreign minister took pains, however, to defend his country's actions and to call into serious question the behavior of Waller.[88]

Faced with what they considered to be nonnegotiable positions, the diplomats of both France and the United States embarked upon conversations and an exchange of letters in the hope that a solution would present itself. The French foreign minister suggested that the American ambassador should personally look over the evidence and satisfy himself about the guilt or innocence of Mr. Waller. But Hanotaux refused to turn over the evidence to the United States government. The American ambassador, for his part, refused to study the evidence while in the presence of the French, since in his opinion Washington would not agree to that procedure.

In what the American ambassador described as the French foreign minister's "individual musing" as to how the issue should be resolved, Mr. Hanotaux proposed "release of Waller on his part, and acceptance of this on our part, as a final settlement of the case." Hanotaux added that while he was not yet in a position to make such a suggestion, he would promise to spare no effort to persuade the president of France and the other members of the French cabinet to accept the compromise.[89]

Hanotaux received the American ambassador the following week and reported that the French president was susceptible to a proposal to free Waller. Meanwhile, Eustis had asked for and received permission for the ailing prisoner to be transferred to Nîmes, in the south of France. The American ambassador then advised the secretary of state that in his opinion the French were adamant about not releasing the testimony and requested permission to negotiate a release of Waller, whose health was rapidly deteriorating. Unfortunately for all concerned, this process was halted when a French election resulted in Hanotaux's replacement as France's foreign minister. This development revived the Americans' interest in securing the record of the Waller trial. Secretary of State Gresham instructed Eustis to "renew application for record and evidence with new French minister for foreign affairs. Urge prompt action in view of Waller's health. Ascertain if compromise release suggested by his predecessor can be effected." Eustis cabled back that he believed the compromise suggested by the foreign minister would end the matter, since he had ascertained unofficially that this was agreeable provided that Waller not seek any sort of indemnity for his arrest, trial, and ill-treatment.[90] The American secretary of state replied bluntly to Eustis that Waller's death while in French confinement would greatly embarrass relations between the two countries. Secretary Gresham also informed Eustis that the French ambassador in Washington, concerned about the complexity of the case and fearing that the affair had gone on long enough, had suggested to his government that Waller be released because of ill health and on humanitarian grounds.[91]

It took some time for the new French foreign minister, Marcellin Berthelot, to master all the intricacies of the Waller case. When he had done so, he supported his predecessor's refusal to surrender the trial records. Meanwhile, Waller, who had been kept informed of the developments in Paris, decided to maintain his right to claim an indemnity from the French government. Citing unlawful imprisonment, mistreatment, great expense, and financial loss, he demanded $10,000 as a reasonable and satisfactory indemnity for his nine months' imprisonment, and additional cost for his counsel.

Once more at an impasse, the State Department decided on a two-pronged approach: to ascertain whether the French offer to the American ambassador to review the Waller case record was a personal favor to him "as ambassador" or whether French opposition to releasing the documents was really categorical; and to get the opinion of a good French lawyer on whether Waller's arrest, trial, and conviction were justified according to French law. The department really wished to review the record so that it could protest to the Quai d'Orsay if the evidence against Waller were insufficient to prove his guilt. Nevertheless, both Gresham in Washington and Ambassador Eustis in Paris were uneasy about where this approach could lead. Eustis feared "the danger of attempting to establish a precedent which might be used against us," but he followed his instructions to read the Waller record even under the guise of "personal privilege" and to convey his conclusions to Washington.

On 6 December 1895 Eustis cabled the Department of State, "Have permission to inspect Waller record. Will report conclusions."

On 7 December, convinced of Waller's guilt, he sent the following telegram from Paris:

> It is proper to state that before examining the evidence I had been inclined to believe, from the information I could gather, that Waller was, perhaps, convicted on insufficient evidence, and that on account of the prejudice against him he might not have had a fair trial. After examining the original letters of Waller, I have no doubt whatever of his guilt.
>
> It was not a case of inadvertent or imprudent writing, but was a deliberate attempt to give information to the enemy to the prejudice of the military situation of France. The evidence fully sustains the charge. The whole tenor of the correspondence discloses his guilty intention, and no court could have hesitated to condemn him. Will communicate more fully by mail.
>
> Now, that by access to the record my Government has obtained the information desired as to the evidence, it seems to me that we ought to reach a speedy solution of the matter. Being satisfied of Waller's guilt, the proposition of the French Government as to his pardon, in my judgment, ought to be accepted. In the face of the evidence establishing his guilt, Waller's pretension to a claim for indemnity, on the ground of his innocence, could not for a moment be seriously considered. The proposition of the French Government could not be viewed as a compromise or as conditional, for we have nothing to compromise. We waive no rights, because we have no such rights. The French Government desires only an assurance from us that his pardon will terminate the matter. I can see no other possible solution.
>
> Our Government has done everything in its power. It has obtained the needed information, and secures the pardon of a guilty man.[92]

This cable to Washington indicated that Eustis accepted at face value the French contention that "D. and P." were American citizens and that Waller's exposure of them was a terrible act, tantamount to condemning fellow citizens to death as French spies. The ambassador simply ignored Waller's assertion that "D. and P." were English miners whom he simply wanted the Hovas to expel from their capital. The State Department specifically queried Eustis on this point, but the ambassador pleaded ignorance of Waller's position. Meanwhile, the State Department's French legal consultant found that although Waller's trial record did show some gross procedural irregularities, he was not sure that much could now be done about it. The Department of State did not raise the issue of the French not having declared war, but neither was it prepared to ignore Waller's demand for indemnity. He, meanwhile, continued to press the issue. On 4 January 1896 Waller wrote to the embassy denying the legality of his trial and conviction and maintaining the right to claim indemnity against the French government for unlawful detention and deportation. He insisted that the amount of damages he claimed was based on precedent. Waller cited the case of a British missionary the French had detained for two months at Tamatave in 1883. "For the two months' detention of the latter," said Waller, "France paid $5,000. I have been detained ten months."[93]

The Department of State wished to resolve the Waller case without a confrontation between the United States and France and at the same time protect the ex-consul's right to sue the French government. Washington specifically queried its ambassador in Paris whether only the French government or private individuals also could be charged with wrongfully imprisoning Waller. The French legal consultant in Paris held the view that "a Frenchman can sue the State, but not before ordinary judicial tribunals. Such suits can only be brought before what are known here as 'administrative' tribunals. No difference in this respect between an alien and a Frenchman." The lawyer said that he did not know whether the French government could be blamed for Waller's mistreatment while en route from Tamatave to Marseilles. Eustis reported that the consul at Marseilles was "unable to find out positively under whose charge Waller was during the voyage" but believed that the prisoner was under the control of the captain of the vessel. In response to a query from the Department of State whether Waller's release could "close the incident . . . leaving Waller the same rights and remedies before the French tribunals as would, under like circumstances, be available to a Frenchman," Eustis replied that all that was needed was "an exchange of letters" between his embassy and the French stating that the "incident is closed between the two Governments."[94]

On 4 February 1896, nearly two years after Waller was arrested, tried, and jailed by the French, the American secretary of state cabled Ambassador Eustis permission to "effect [the] release of Waller on terms proposed by the French government, making necessary exchange of notes.

Cable when Waller is actually released. If necessary, you can furnish him with transportation to the United States." The ambassador was also instructed that should Waller upon release desire to bring suit in French courts about ill-treatment suffered during the voyage, the embassy should furnish the ex-consul with such security costs as would enable him to do so.[95]

The American ambassador called at the Quai d'Orsay with the necessary protocols concerning the Waller case and was told that the minister would see the French president and the cabinet "at once," and that there was every reason to believe that Waller would be released within a week. The ambassador was overjoyed at this news, but he did not count on French legalisms and the nature of French bureaucracy. Days passed, and in apparent despair, Eustis cabled Washington, "Have been disappointed at the delay of Waller release. The ministers could not agree at first which one should prepare a decree for the President's signature." Finally, it was decided that the Ministry of Marine should sign the release, and Berthelot informed Eustis on Wednesday that it would be done at once. When the ambassador did not receive the protocol on the specified date, believing that it was now a mere question of formality, he personally visited several departments to accelerate the process. A frustrated Eustis cabled Washington that he was using every means to secure Waller's prompt release. Finally on 20 February 1896 Eustis cabled, "The President signed this morning Waller's pardon. Orders are issued for his release."[96] Waller insisted to the end that he would sue the French, but nothing came of these threats.

While the United States' commercial interest in Madagascar led to the long and complicated Waller affair, its relative lack of interest in Ethiopia's commercial possibilities initially prevented African Americans from taking little more than a biblical interest in that ancient Christian land. This was all the more ironic since for generations blacks had hoped for the fulfillment of the biblical prophecy that "Ethiopia shall stretch forth her hands unto God." Even if white Americans had noted the references, they no doubt would have joined the scriptural skeptics who had asked of another place, "Can anything good come out of Nazareth?"

While the United States ignored Ethiopia and even Liberia, its own creation, both Great Britain and France had opened consulates in the coastal regions of Ethiopia in the 1840s, thereby formalizing earlier unofficial contacts between their explorers and missionaries with the fabled land of "Prester John."[97] The news that in the 1860s the Ethiopian king Tewodros II felt powerful enough to have imprisoned European diplomats (including a special emissary from the Court of St. James's), insisting that the Europeans should receive his diplomats with equality, would have seemed incredible to Americans, black and white.[98]

Black American diplomats such as J. Milton Turner and John H. Smyth, who served in Liberia during the 1870s and 1880s, at the beginning of the scramble for Africa, were certainly aware that Ethiopia was endangered. Through its diplomats in European capitals, the American Department of State kept abreast of the conflicts between the Ethiopian Emperor Yohannes IV (1871–89) and Great Britain, France, and Italy over trade and missionaries. Some American military officers in the army of the khedive in Egypt did indeed fight against the Ethiopians, and were aware that in June 1884 Rear Admiral Sir William Hewett visited "His Majesty the Negoosa Negust" to ensure free transit of British goods through the port of Massawa on the Red Sea.[99]

Ethiopia's real troubles with the Europeans began in 1885 when Italy, profiting from the carte blanche it had received at Berlin, established a garrison at Massawa. The Italians replaced the Egyptian khedives who, under the British, had replaced the Turks in the area. Yohannes, whose troops had fled before the might of the Italians, felt betrayed by the British. The Italian prime minister, Francesco Crispi, was convinced not only that African colonies were indispensable to his country's greatness but also that Rome had a duty to Christianize and civilize the Ethiopian barbarians. In pursuing their scheme, the Italians sought "a perfect understanding with the cabinet of London" about the future of Ethiopia. What they had planned to do was to take advantage of Article XXXIV of the General Act of the Berlin Conference of 1884–85 to edge into Ethiopia and to establish relations with dissident vassals of Yohannes and with such peoples as the Galla and Sidamo.[100]

Aware of the ambitions of the Italians and fearing their designs on the whole of Ethiopia, Yohannes wrote his ambitious and rebellious vassal, Menelik of Shoa, in 1886: "The Italians will not tire us, and with the help of God, we shall be victorious."[101] The negus had the opportunity to prove to Crispi that the Ethiopians could fight when, in January 1887, his troops intercepted a column of Italian legionnaires on the move, trapped some 550 of them, and ended up killing 430 men and wounding 82 others. Writing to Queen Victoria, the Ethiopian emperor declared that he had not sought war with the Italians but that they were interfering in the affairs of his country, something they had no right to do. Victoria, as was her wont, responded to Yohannes that she was sorry that he had "disputes" with the Italians, who were "a powerful nation, with friendly and good intentions."[102]

In October 1887, still pursuing their imperialist ambitions in Ethiopia, the Italians signed a convention of friendship and mutual support with Menelik, king of Shoa. The Italians assured Menelik that they did not wish to annex any territories and attempted to mediate between him and the emperor. Then, when Yohannes was killed in battle with the Mahdist forces on the Ethiopian border, Menelik became emperor. He signed a treaty with the Italians on 2 May 1889, hoping thereby to get military aid to consolidate his rule. The Italian text of Article XVII of the Treaty of Wichale stipulated, "His Majesty the King of Ethiopia consents to avail himself [or use, 'servirsi'] of the Italian Government for any negotiations [or for all business] which he may enter into with all the other Powers or Governments." In contrast, the literal Amharic version of this article specifically stated that "the Emperor of Ethiopia, for all matters that he wants with the Kings of Europe, it is possible for him to communicate with the assistance of the Italian Government."[103] This difference in the texts suggests that both signatories had their own aims in mind: Menelik sought to use the Italian representation in Europe to conduct his own diplomatic affairs, and the Italians saw their version of the treaty as giving them protectorate right over Ethiopia.

The Italians sought to convince the other important European states that they had a protectorate over Ethiopia. Only the French and the Russians disputed this ploy. The French suggested that since Italy had not occupied Ethiopia, its treaty with that country was only a political transaction and had nothing to do with the questions that the Berlin Conference had sought to address. Russia, for its part, did not recognize Italy's claim of protectorate status since the czars felt that they had to protect the interest of a state whose religion had many features resembling their own.[104] Menelik initially knew nothing about Italy's claim over his country but discovered, to his chagrin, that some European states, especially Great Britain, preferred to deal with him through Italy. Early in July 1890 Queen Victoria, answering a letter from Menelik, responded that taking note of a clause in the Italo-Ethiopian treaty, "We shall communicate to the Government of our Friend . . . the King of Italy copies of Your Majesty's letter and Our reply."[105] When Menelik received Victoria's letter, he wrote to King Umberto of Italy complaining that the responses to his letter from Queen Victoria and from the German kaiser were "something humiliating for my kingdom." Referring to Article XVII of his treaty with Italy, the emperor reiterated that he was under no obligation to use Italy as an intermediary with other powers. He added that he hoped the king would "rectify the error committed in Article XVII, and announce this mistake to the friendly powers to whom you have communicated the said article."[106] Menelik warned King Umberto that he had "no intention of being an indifferent spectator if far-distant Powers make their appearance with the idea of dividing Africa." Menelik declared that for fourteen centuries "Ethiopia [had been] an island of Christians among a sea of Pagans" and warned, "As the Almighty has protected Ethiopia to this day, I am confident He will increase and protect it in the future."[107]

Relations between Ethiopia and Italy went from bad to worse, and the Italians, convinced that they could defeat Menelik, sought to portray the emperor as a barbarian king of a primitive African people.[108] Then like the French in Madagascar, the Italians attempted to gain the cooperation of the world and other powers by accusing the Ethiopians of savagery and especially of slavery. Italian Prime Minister Crispi insisted that the disputed Treaty of Wichale was "one of those accomplishments that do honor to Italian policy" and "one of the most civilized acts concluded in recent times." He charged that Menelik did not honor the treaty because he was unwilling to give up the slave trade. Crispi asserted, "We even got him to go so far as to have Ethiopia represented at the Conference of Brussels for the abolition of the slave trade. This laid a restraint on Menelik, a restraint which he did not like, and this was also one of the reasons why he failed to abide by his obligations."[109]

Despite his earlier military experiences with Ethiopia, Crispi asserted that Italy could not accept defeat in Ethiopia and vowed that his aim was to "assert Italy's name in the regions of Africa and to show to the barbarians also that we are strong and powerful . . . The barbarians understand only the thunder of cannons: very well, at the opportune moment, the cannons will thunder, and let us hope that they will thunder with the victory of our arms."[110] Meanwhile, Crispi successfully prevented Ethiopia from receiving arms from Germany, Austria-Hungary, and Great Britain. In April 1895 the British India Office directed the governor of Aden to refuse the transshipment of some four thousand arms to Ethiopia because "Her Majesty's Government have reason to believe that they are intended for use against a friendly Power."[111] Only because of its own imperial ambitions in the valley of the Nile did the French not join the arms embargo against Ethiopia.

Fully aware of the military power of Italy and of the support it was receiving from the major world powers, Menelik sought to compromise.

But the Italians refused and continued both their diplomatic and military offensives against Ethiopia. Attempting in vain to break the diplomatic blockade fostered by Italy, the emperor sought close relations with Russia, but this effort, too, failed. Italy was bent on war. On 17 September 1895 Menelik reportedly issued this mobilization proclamation to his troops:

> Hitherto, God has graciously preserved our native land. He has permitted us to conquer our enemies, and to reconstitute our Ethiopia. . . .
> An enemy is come across the sea. He has broken through our frontiers, in order to destroy our fatherland and our faith. I allowed him to seize my possessions, and I entered upon lengthy negotiations with him, in the hope of obtaining justice without bloodshed, but the enemy refuses to listen. . . .
> Enough! With the help of God I will defend the inheritance of my forefathers, and drive back the invader by force of arms. Let every man who has sufficient strength accompany me. And he who has not, let him pray for us.[112]

The nature of the battle of Adowa (Adwa), which took place between Ethiopia and Italy on 1 March 1896, is too well known to bear repetition here. Suffice it to say that the battle was disastrous for Italy. About 4,000 European troops and 2,000 African troops (mainly Eritrean allies of Italy) lost their lives; 1,428 lay wounded. Italian casualties numbered 7,500, "nearly 43 percent of the force engaged. Ethiopian losses have been estimated at 7,000 killed and 10,000 wounded, or 14 percent of the emperor's army." The Ethiopians captured large numbers of rifles and artillery from the battlefield and some eighteen hundred Italian soldiers. Menelik's victory was so complete that, "five days later, Italy sued for peace."[113]

Ethiopia's victory over the Italians shocked white America and thrilled African Americans. Black newspapers and preachers waxed lyrical about Menelik's victory, seeing in it God's hand and the realization of their dreams and hopes for Ethiopia. An editorial in the Savannah *Tribune* of 21 March 1896 declared, "The Abyssinians [Ethiopians] are defending their homes and native land; they are perfectly right in expelling foreign aggressions. This overbearing spirit exercised by European nations over African natives should be stopped."[114] Echoing this sentiment, the Cleveland *Gazette* editorialized on the same day, "King Menelik is proving himself more than a match for civilization's trained and skilled warriors, with all their improved machinery of war. More power to him!"[115] Black newspapers all stressed the determination with which the Ethiopians, with their well-trained army, defended their territory from the yoke of protectorship. African Americans viewed this struggle as symbolic of the determination of Africans to maintain their independence against the widening imperialistic designs of European peoples. The implication for blacks all over the world was not only that a united and determined people could be victorious, but that in so doing they could demonstrate their humanity for all to see.

Ethiopia's success stimulated blacks in Haiti and the United States to seek close relations with that state. In late 1896 or early in 1897, Benito Sylvain, who since 1889 had served as a Haitian diplomat in both London and Paris, was sent "on a diplomatic mission for his president to the court of the Emperor Menelik of Abyssinians."[116] Sylvain was later to attend the Pan-African Conference in London in 1900 and to be identified there as "aide-de-camp to Emperor Menelik." Very much a race man, Sylvain had founded the Black Youth Association of Paris in 1898 and was on his way back to Ethiopia when he encountered Robert Skinner, a United States consul returning from Addis Ababa. According to Skinner, "Commandant Benito Sylvain, envoy of His Excellency the President of the Republic of Haiti to His Imperial Majesty the Emperor of Ethiopia," was wearing the decoration of the Order of the Cross of Solomon upon his breast. Skinner reported having been told that Sylvain had "conceived the happy idea some years ago of seeking the Emperor Menelik, in order to secure His Majesty's adhesion to a programme for the general amelioration of the negro race. To Mr. Benito Sylvain it seemed especially appropriate that the greatest black man in the world should become the honorary president of his projected society."[117] Skinner, sharing with many whites a common perception of the possible danger of an alliance between continental Africans and blacks in the diaspora, maliciously reported a rumor in Addis Ababa that Menelik, while willing to help uplift the "negro," insisted to Sylvain that he, Menelik, was of Caucasoid origin. What Skinner failed to report was the obvious incongruity of this statement, since Menelik was more "negroid" in appearance than most Ethiopians.

As United States consul in Marseilles, Skinner had long recognized the absurdity of the United States having no diplomatic representation in Ethiopia while maintaining a relatively large amount of trade with that country. On 8 January 1900 he wrote to Assistant Secretary of State David J. Hill that "although we maintain relations with many of the better African trade centers, our people know next to nothing of the situation and possibilities in Abyssinia." He indicated that his "chief object in raising a question foreign to my duties in Marseilles is to suggest that in Abyssinia we maintain not even the semblance of official representation, although there exist a vast population politically independent and capable of absorbing our products."[118] A month later, a junior officer in Washington replied to Skinner that while the secretary of state recognized "the force" of his observation, the Department of State did not consider it advisable to make any recommendation to Congress upon the subject at that time.[119]

Skinner was disappointed by this reply because, like John H. Smyth in Liberia before him, he feared that if the United States postponed action, "this rich and unexplored territory will become definitely tributary to one of the Great Powers, and unless we act promptly, we shall see ourselves barred out of Abyssinia as we are now in a measure in various other portions of Africa." Skinner then wrote directly to Secretary of State John Hay urging an economic treaty with Ethiopia. The secretary acknowledged receipt of the letter and instructed a junior officer in the department to indicate to Skinner "how impossible" it was to react positively to his request.[120]

While Consul Skinner was being rebuffed by the Department of State over sending a mission to Ethiopia, a remarkable African American appeared on the scene and sought to influence United States policy toward Ethiopia. He was William H. Ellis, about whom one of the foremost historians of Ethiopia wrote, "Little is today known of [the] bearer to Emperor Menelik of the signed copy of the first Ethiopian-United States treaty of 1903–4, [and] probably the first black American to discover Ethiopia, and an early advocate of the return of Negroes to Africa."[121] From the available evidence, it appears that Ellis, who was "apparently" born in Victoria, Texas, claimed to have been the son of a Cuban father and a Mexican mother, although he looked "like a negro— dark-skinned, full-lipped and kinky hair."[122] Involved in an unsuccessful scheme to colonize blacks in Mexico during the late 1880s, Ellis participated with Norris Wright Cuney (1846–98) in Texas Republican politics. He later "drifted" to New York where he became a "confidential employee" of Henry H. Hotchkiss, the noted millionaire gun inventor. Becoming financial adviser to Mrs. Hotchkiss when her husband died, Ellis speculated unsuccessfully on Wall Street but lived in style at the Plaza Hotel, where he was noted for his sartorial splendor and his generosity.

According to Ellis's own account, he first met Ethiopian "Crown Prince" Ras Makonnen in London in 1902, while both of them were attending the coronation of Edward VII. Again, according to Ellis, the crown prince invited him to visit Ethiopia and to assist Emperor Menelik and his people in developing the country. When Ellis returned to the

United States later in 1902, he bought and read all the books on Ethiopia that he could find and sought to encourage the Department of State to send him to establish commercial relations with Ethiopia. By this time, however, Assistant Secretary of State Francis B. Loomis had finally authorized Consul Skinner to proceed to Ethiopia with a draft "treaty of Amity, Reciprocal Establishments and commerce" to serve as the basis for negotiations with the Ethiopians.

Ellis, who by this time had become an important news item in the United States, was reportedly greatly disappointed by his missed opportunity to have initiated commercial relations between Ethiopia and the United States. He complained bitterly to the New York *Herald Tribune,* the New York *Times,* the Baltimore *Sun,* and the Washington *Post,* not to mention lesser known white newspapers and important black ones, about what he considered to be an official rebuff. It is not clear, however, whether he knew about the early efforts of Skinner to establish commercial relations between the two countries. Undaunted by his failure, Ellis wrote letters to the British foreign secretary seeking the help of the British agent at the Ethiopian court in order to get to Addis Ababa. Then, as had Waller in Madagascar, Ellis let it be known that he would attempt to "obtain a concession of land and colonize American negroes in the Negus' domains in Africa." He also said that he planned to take his bride, Miss Ida Maud Lefferts Sherwood (an English woman "said to be the grand-niece of the late Lord George Armstrong of Craigside, Durban and London") on a honeymoon trip to Africa. All these reports made good copy for American and British newspapers. On reaching Marseilles sometime around 24 September 1903, Ellis wrote to the American millionaire and philanthropist Andrew Carnegie explaining the reason for his trip and giving detailed information about the Ethiopians. He had hoped to interest Carnegie in the prospect of Americans helping to develop Ethiopia.[123] Ellis then proceeded to Addis Ababa and returned to London in late December 1903, giving ecstatic reports about his reception by Menelik. He told the London Bureau of the Pittsburgh *Post* that Menelik was prepared to welcome Americans to the country "in peace and without fear" and that Consul Skinner, who was then at Addis Ababa, would have no difficulty negotiating a treaty with the emperor. The monarch was said to believe that, in contrast with the European powers that had sought to colonize Africa, "America was alone without land in Africa and wanted none. She only wanted liberty to trade."

Menelik reportedly had also shed tears when told that Lincoln had freed the slaves and had expressed a great deal of interest in American affairs, "especially the development of the coloured race from slaves to the status of whites." Ellis said that Menelik had promised gradually to free his own slaves. He also told members of the London press that he had in his possession a letter from Menelik that ended with the peroration, "I and all my chiefs and subjects thank you, so when you and all Americans come to visit me and my country we will accept you in love. Our aim is one—Christianity and independence. And now may God bless you and your country and bring you safe in health and peace to your home; also soon to return to me and my country." This letter was signed at the court in Addis Ababa in "this the 7th (17th) day of November, 1896 (1903), in the year of Our Salvation." The emperor had reportedly also given Ellis a letter to Andrew Carnegie and would also have sent the millionaire a lion until dissuaded by Ellis from doing so.[124]

When Ellis returned to the United States he continued to embellish the report of his trip to Ethiopia. He reported that he had met Consul Skinner in Marseilles and was assured by him that the American-Ethiopian commercial treaty under consideration would mean an increase of trade between the two countries to about $25 million from the current $7 million. Ellis then started a lengthy correspondence with Carnegie about possible investments in Ethiopia and sent him Menelik's letter. Hearing that the treaty, which Consul Skinner had previously taken to Addis Ababa, had been signed by the two nations in December 1903, ratified by the United States Senate on 12 March 1904, and signed by Theodore Roosevelt on 17 March 1904, Ellis suggested to the State Department that he, being "a coloured man already familiar with the country and its ruler, should be chosen as the official emissary to carry the ratified document back to Addis Ababa."[125]

Assistant Secretary of State Francis B. Loomis was reluctant to confer this honor upon Ellis. The Department of State finally entrusted the task to Kent J. Loomis, a brother of the assistant secretary, who offered to take the treaty to Addis Ababa at his own expense while on a lion-hunting expedition. Ellis was understandably disappointed but accepted as a compromise the opportunity to go to Ethiopia in the company of Kent J. Loomis. Then, under circumstances that read like a mystery thriller, sometime between 14 June and 20 June 1904, between New York and Plymouth, England, Loomis disappeared from the stateroom he shared with Ellis on board the S. S. *Kaiser Wilhelm*. And although the embassies in London and Paris were concerned over Loomis's disappearance, Ellis was able to convince them that it was imperative that he be permitted to take the treaty to Addis Ababa by the time specified by Menelik.

The news of Loomis's disappearance struck the press in the United States like a bombshell. Ellis was well known by reporters, and there was a great deal of speculation in the newspapers. The Washington *Post* speculated that Ellis might have been responsible for Loomis's disappearance and, in all probability, may have murdered him. How else could one interpret the question posed by the newspaper, "Who is the sole visible beneficiary of our diplomatic efforts in Abyssinia up to date? Solve the conundrum, and all the rest is simple."[126] The American embassies in London and Paris launched their own investigations of the tragedy.

Public interest in Loomis's disappearance was heightened when his body washed ashore near Cherbourg, France, on 27 June 1904. By now many newspapers had reported that, among other things, Loomis was an alcoholic. American newspapers also regaled their readers with stories such as one claiming that Ellis had hoped to be "Abyssini's King"; that his past life had revealed questionable episodes, such as his friendship with Hotchkiss's widow; that he had plans to interest Carnegie in business ventures in Ethiopia; and that he had designs for settling blacks on large estates obtained from Emperor Menelik.

Undoubtedly ignorant of developments surrounding the recovery of Loomis's body and the aspersions cast on his own character, Ellis reached Addis Ababa in early August 1904 and dutifully deposited the commercial treaty, thereby rendering what he considered to be a great service to the United States, to Ethiopia, and to African Americans. Ellis also wrote Carnegie a long letter dealing with economic matters and enclosed a copy of a letter from Menelik to the millionaire. He wanted to allay any suspicion that the letter the monarch had previously sent Carnegie was not authentic.

When he arrived in Paris during his passage through Europe on his way home, Ellis reported to the press that he had received from the emperor concessions for all the diamond mines in Ethiopia and for some quarter million acres of land on the Blue Nile, where he hoped to experiment with cotton cultivation. But when he arrived in the United States in November 1904, Ellis heard all about the whispers concerning his possible role in the death of Loomis. He immediately insisted that the Department of State issue a public statement absolving him of any complicity in the affair and traveled to Washington, D.C., on 21 November 1904 to clear his name. Ellis was accompanied by General James S. Clarkson, surveyor of the Port of New York. His first stop was the White House, where he gave the president gifts sent to him by Menelik.

The following morning, again accompanied by Clarkson, Ellis called at the State Department, where he was received by Assistant Secretary of State Loomis. Later queried about this visit, Ellis told newsmen that while they had treated him "roughly," he fully expected that the State Department would clear up the matter. Ellis intimated that the department would also explain why he had not commented publicly about Kent J. Loomis's behavior while on board ship. On 22 November 1904 the State Department issued the following statement:

> Mr. Ellis reported at the Department of State today and deposited the receipt which he received from King Menelik upon delivery to him of the signed copy of the commercial treaty with Abyssinia. Mr. Ellis has fully and cheerfully answered the searching questions put to him by officials, who made careful inquiry into all the circumstances connected with his trip to Africa. It was stated at the Department that Mr. Ellis's explanations were of a satisfactory nature and that no blame is now attached to him in connection with the tragic episode which occurred on his trip from New York to France in June last." [127]

Ellis was furious that the diplomatic language used by the State Department did not more forcefully proclaim his innocence. He intimated to the press that the State Department knew the facts of Loomis's death as well as he did. Ellis also suggested that he might reveal things that could create "indigestion in certain circles," since the truth always hurt. The Washington *Post* complained that "the behavior of Ellis since his return from Abyssinia had been characterized by a distinctly insolent menace and swagger which leave a very painful impression on the thoughtful mind." The paper added that Ellis's attitude toward the assistant secretary of state had been particularly amazing and was "the attitude of a man who knows his power and is prepared to use it ruthlessly." The paper concluded that while "from first to last," it had "sought enlightenment" on the Abyssinian affair, it resented Ellis's "arrogant speech and conduct in Washington, his repeated threats of vengeance in case that absolution was withheld. Manifestly there is some ugly reservation touching this affair." [128]

For its part, the Department of State remained silent in the face of Ellis's remonstrances, and the story of Loomis's death disappeared from the news. Nevertheless, the scandal accompanying Loomis's disappearance and the uproar it created in the press apparently soured Carnegie's attitude toward

Ellis. The adventurer tried to interest the millionaire in Ethiopia but without success. Ellis also tried unsuccessfully to interest the German government in his enterprise. His subsequent and frequent enquiries to the State Department about commercial possibilities in Ethiopia received the polite responses due a man who had sought to influence United States policy toward Africa, but his services were clearly not welcome.

While it is possible that Ellis was involved in the death of Loomis, his conduct was more likely that of any nineteenth-century adventurer not averse to lining his own pockets while helping the United States establish relations with Ethiopia. Waller's experience, on the other hand, raises some disturbing questions about the role of the United States in the conquest and colonization of Africa during the scramble. This case also demonstrates how racist notions of the day conditioned the ability of blacks to serve in the foreign service of their country. At least one historian has suggested that had Waller been a white consul, his fate would have been different. This historian's reasonable view was that "France did not have an established government in Madagascar by any definition and neither Waller nor the United States was obligated to side with France in her war."[129] More instructive for this study was the attitude of many Americans of Waller's day toward the role of blacks in foreign policy. The New York *Times,* writing about the Waller affair, said that this case proved that "of American Negroes, the better class are not seeking or accepting offices." Then without providing any evidence, the paper added that the Waller case was simply the "worst example of the general failure of Negroes as diplomats."[130] What the editor did not mention was that the United States usually chose from among its best citizens to conduct its foreign policy. What we will never know is what effect the experiences of Waller and Ellis had on the collective memory of State Department officials during this period in the evolution of the American foreign policy. Did they contribute to the biased view that only a white elite could direct this country's foreign policy?

Notes

1. Note from anonymous official in the State Department to Assistant Secretary, Mr. Quincy, 2 June 1893, Notes from Madagascar Legation to Department of State, 1883–94, T806, Record Group 59, National Archives, roll 8.
2. William Ellis to Andrew Carnegie, 24 September 1903, quoted in *Ethiopia Observer* 15 (1972): 92.
3. John L. Waller Application and Recommendation File, General Records of the Department of State, Record Group 59, box 158, National Archives. See also Randall B. Woods, "Black America's Challenge to European Colonialism:

The Waller Affair, 1891–1895," *Journal of Black Studies* 7 (September 1976): 57–77. See also Allison Blakely, "The John L. Waller Affair, 1895–1896, *Negro History Bulletin* 37 (February-March 1974): 216–18.

4. Ibid.
5. Woods, "Black America's Challenge," 58.
6. Blakely, "Waller Affair," 218.
7. Phares M. Mutibwa, *The Malagasy and the Europeans: Madagascar's Foreign Relations, 1861–1895* (London: Longman, 1974), 78–79.
8. Ibid., 152.
9. Ibid., 158.
10. Ibid., 212.
11. Ibid., 216–17.
12. Ibid., 236. It should be pointed out that the Hova people did not believe they needed the protection of outsiders. One early British missionary remarked that the Hova "had a civilisation of their own, differing very much, it is true, from our nineteenth century civilisation, ages before they ever came in contact with Europeans. They had established forms of government, gradations of rank, and laws affording considerable protection of life and property" (A. Davidson, "Customs and Curiosities of Madagascar," pt. 2, London Missionary Society (LMS) Miscellanies, iii, 651, as quoted in Mutibwa, *Malagasy and Europeans*, 1).
13. Ibid., 236ff.
14. Ibid.
15. Ibid., 267–68.
16. Ibid.
17. Ibid., 268–69.
18. Ibid., 283–84.
19. Ibid., 288.
20. Ibid., 292.
21. Department of State to Waller, Notes from Madagascar Legation, roll 7.
22. Ibid.
23. Waller to Josiah Quincy at Department of State, 26 December 1892, no. 40, roll 8. In contrast to his antipathy to the French, Waller was quite sympathetic to the Malagasy. He was also scornful of the perfidy of Great Britain. Unfortunately for him, this was to be his undoing. Almost as an afterthought, Waller informed the Department of State of "the death of Hon. R. Mc Whitney, the late U.S. Vice Consul for Madagascar and the strained political situation existing between the French and the Hova Government in Madagascar which has been augmented by the recent establishment of the French Court in Tamatave. And the eminent danger to American interests in the event of war between these dual governments—necessitated the prompt appointment of a successor to the deceased U.S. Vice Consul."
24. Waller to Department of State, 7 December 1891.
25. Ibid.
26. Ibid.
27. Waller to Department of State, 16 January 1891.
28. Waller to Department of State, 25 April 1893, no. 53.
29. Note in the Despatches of the Madagascar Legation, 2 June 1893, roll 8.
30. Note to Quincy, Department of State, 10 June 1893.
31. Waller to Department of State, 22 August 1893, no. 64.
32. Enclosed in no. 65, August 1893, Waller to Quincy, Assistant Secretary of State.

33. Waller to Quincy at the Department of State, 25 August 1893, no. 66.
34. Waller to Quincy at the Department of State, 30 December 1893, no. 77.
35. Secretary of State to Assistant Secretary of State, 5 June 1893.
36. Wetter to Department of State, 16 January 1894, no. 126.
37. Ibid.
38. Wetter to Department of State, 27 January 1894, no. 130.
39. Ibid.
40. Wetter to Department of State, 27 March 1894, no. 21 (Enclosure: *Madagascar News*, 17 March 1894).
41. Wetter to Department of State, 8 May 1894.
42. Ibid.
43. Wetter to Department of State, 3 May 1894, no. 3, enclosing clippings from *Le Madagascar* and the *Madagascar News*.
44. *Papers Relating to the Foreign Affairs of the United States with the Annual Message of the President, 1895* (Washington: Government Printing Office, 1896), 54th Cong., 1st sess., H. Doc., pt. 1, 252.
45. Ibid., 253.
46. Ibid.
47. Ibid., 254, 382.
48. Ibid., 382–83.
49. Ibid., 320.
50. Ibid., 322.
51. Ibid., 326.
52. Ibid., 332.
53. Ibid.
54. Ibid., 254.
55. Ibid., 332.
56. Ibid., 322.
57. Ibid., 321.
58. Ibid., 315–16.
59. Ibid.
60. Ibid., 320.
61. Ibid., 315, 322.
62. Ibid.
63. Ibid., 322–23.
64. Ibid., 321–26.
65. Ibid.
66. Ibid. 326–28.
67. Ibid., 282.
68. Ibid., 282, 351.
69. Ibid., 273, 281–85.
70. Ibid., 251.
71. Ibid., 356.
72. Ibid., 335ff.
73. Ibid., 344.
74. Ibid., 340.
75. Ibid., 366.
76. Ibid., 370ff.
77. Ibid., 370.
78. Ibid., 372.
79. Ibid.
80. Ibid., 373.

81. Ibid., 379.
82. Ibid.
83. Ibid., 371–72.
84. Ibid., 347–77.
85. Ibid., 264.
86. Ibid., 274.
87. Ibid., 286.
88. Ibid. Hanotaux wrote to Eustis that after examining the papers when they arrived in Paris, he could have come to no other conclusion than that the gravity of the charges brought against Waller warranted condemnation. He insisted:

   The letters seized allow one to come to the conclusion that Waller had already previously sent to the Hovas information on our military situation, and that his stepson, Paul Bray, also carried on with Mrs. Waller correspondence which might have had for him the gravest consequences had it fallen into the hands of the French authorities.

   At that period Tamatave was occupied by our troops, and had been placed under martial law; military operations against the Hovas had been commenced. The acts of Waller therefore constituted doings admitted to be punishable by the military laws of all nations. Finally, in that same correspondence, Waller, under transparent initials, denounced to the prime minister, as French spies, two American merchants who were about to proceed to Tananarivo, thus designating two of his fellow-citizens to the vengeance of the Hovas.
89. Ibid., 285–86.
90. Ibid., 285–88.
91. Ibid., 288.
92. Ibid., 299–300, 302.
93. Ibid., 312.
94. Ibid., 312–13.
95. Ibid., 313–14.
96. Ibid., 314.
97. Sven Rubenson, "Aspects of the Survival of Ethiopian Independence 1840–1896," in *Nineteenth Century Africa,* ed. P. J. M. McEwan (London: Oxford University Press, 1968), 349ff.
98. Ibid., 351.
99. David Levering Lewis, *The Race to Fashoda* (New York: Weidenfeld and Nicolson, 1987), 100.
100. Rubenson, "Survival of Ethiopian Independence," 354.
101. Lewis, *Race to Fashoda,* 100.
102. Ibid., 103–4.
103. Harold G. Marcus, *The Life and Times of Menelik II, Ethiopia 1844–1913* (Oxford: Clarendon Press, 1975), 114–15.
104. Ibid., 115–16.
105. Ibid., 124.
106. Ibid., 127.
107. Robert P. Skinner, *Abyssinia of Today* (London: Edward Arnold, 1906), 145.
108. Marcus, *Menelik II,* 162.
109. Donald A. Limoli, "Francesco Crispi's Quest for Empire—and Victories—in Ethiopia," in *Partition of Africa: Illusion or Necessity,* ed. Robert O. Collins (New York: John Wiley and Sons, 1969), 134.
110. Ibid.
111. Marcus, *Menelik II,* 158.

112. Skinner, *Abyssinia Today,* 145–46.
113. Harold G. Marcus, "Imperialism and Expansion in Ethiopia from 1865 to 1900," in *Colonialism in Africa, 1890–1960,* ed. L. H. Gann and Peter Duignan (Cambridge: University Press, 1969), 1:420–61; Marcus, *Menelik II,* 173
114. Sylvia M. Jacobs, *The African Nexus: Black American Perspectives on the European Partitioning of Africa, 1880–1920* (Westport, Conn.: Greenwood Press, 1981), 195.
115. Ibid., 194.
116. Owen Charles Mathurin, *Henry Sylvester Williams and the Origins of the Pan-African Movement, 1869–1911* (Westport, Conn.: Greenwood Press, 1976), 48–49; Tony Martin, *The Pan-African Connection: From Slavery to Garvey and Beyond* (Dover, Mass.: Majority Press, 1983), 201.
117. Skinner, *Abyssinia Today,* 130–31.
118. Department of State, Consular Letters from Marseilles, unnumbered letter, dated 22 March 1900, Record Group 59, National Archives, vol. 18, roll 1182.
119. Frank J. Manheim, "The United States and Ethiopia: A Study in American Imperialism," *Journal of Negro History* 27 (April 1932): 144.
120. Skinner, *Abyssinia Today,* ix.
121. Richard Pankhurst, "William H. Ellis—Guillaume Enriques Ellesio: The First Black American Ethiopianist?" *Ethiopia Observer* 15 (1972): 89–121.
122. Ibid., 89.
123. Ibid., 89–91.
124. Ibid., 90–93.
125. Ibid., 95–97.
126. Ibid., 97–102.
127. Ibid., 101–5.
128. Ibid., 106.
129. Blakely, "Waller Affair," 216–18.
130. *New York Times,* 22 February 1896, 4, quoted in ibid.

8

Booker T. Washington: Diplomatic Initiatives

The whole trend of imperial aggression is antagonistic to the feebler races. It is a revival of racial arrogance. It has even been the boast of the proud and haughty race or nation that God has given them the heathen for their inheritance and the uttermost parts of the earth for their possession. . . . Will the Negro stultify himself and become part of the movement which must end in his own humiliation? (Kelly Miller, October 1900)[1]

We must come to the rescue of our people over here. The grasping policy of these nations [England, France, and Germany] must be checked if it can [be done]. They now have everything on the west coast, yet Ahab like, they covet Naboth's little vineyard.

What can you do? Our Government I am confident will act if the proper influence is brought to bear on it. *I simply ask that the source of information be withheld for diplomatic reasons.* God give you wisdom to act in this crisis. (Ernest Lyon, U. S. Minister to Liberia, to Booker T. Washington, 10 August 1907)[2]

Mr. Emmett J. Scott, my secretary, went to Washington for the purpose of having an interview with the President [Theodore Roosevelt] concerning the interests of Liberia. I have just received a telegram from him, a portion of which I quote—"Liberian matter amicably settled. President says he will go limit of all power and moral force to protect Liberia." (Booker T. Washington to Ernest Lyon, 28 September 1907)[3]

African Americans debated long and hard the position they should take when the United States joined the Europeans in an effort to dominate the world. While it was true that except for seizing Liberia for its former slaves, America had been loath to intervene in African affairs, the United States was actively involved in the Caribbean and Latin America and had imperial designs in the Pacific and Asia. What should be the position of blacks? As Americans, many blacks felt it their duty to fight for their country, and in the final analysis, this was the position that most of them adopted.[4] Nevertheless, they could not agree with whites who spoke patronizingly about "our little brown brothers" or about the "white man's burden," for they fully realized that, for most whites, African Americans were also judged to be "half-devil and half-child."[5]

Blacks rejoiced when Ethiopia defeated Italy to protect its sovereignty, grieved when Madagascar and most of Africa were conquered and colonized by Europeans, and attempted to protect the black nationality that was Liberia. They were deeply embarrassed by Haiti which, because of its backwardness and instability, was cited by white supremacists as evidence of the incapacity of blacks to run a country when they had full civic rights. Yet while deploring the sad conditions there, they did not despair of the ability of blacks to be responsible citizens either of Haiti or of the United States. They believed that Haiti should be left alone "to work out her mission for the children of Africa in the New World and to fulfill her destiny among the Nations of the Earth."[6]

Frederick Douglass, who discovered that American racism could create grave problems for a black diplomat when he served as United States minister to Haiti (1889–91), condemned what he termed America's "unwarrantable intermeddling" in Hawaiian affairs and confessed that "the stories afloat to blacken the character of the Queen [Liliuokalani] do not deceive me."[7] When President William McKinley submitted a proposal to the Senate to annex Hawaii, some black leaders opposed its ratification, fearing it was a plot to overthrow the government of the "dark-faced natives."[8]

Significantly, Booker T. Washington did not join the chorus of African Americans condemning the administration for its imperialist policies. In a speech in Boston in August 1898 he stated that the "domination of Americans in Hawaiian commercial and social life was the inevitable result of superior physical and mental stamina, not of trickster or brutal disregard of native rights."[9] No doubt Washington's support of the president was due to his close association with him—an association that had even led to speculation and to an implausible rumor that Washington was being considered for a place in McKinley's cabinet. Nevertheless, like most African American leaders, even Washington felt that America's record in race relations made it unlikely that his country's imperialist ventures were in the best interests of native peoples. A more widespread feeling, and one voiced by a writer in the *A.M.E. Church Review* of that period, was that the colonial thrust against the "dark races in Africa and Asia" had initiated a "startling world movement . . . which is no less than the stirring of the spirit of civilization and prowess among the dark-skinned races."[10]

A growing problem for African Americans was that with their increasing loss of the vote and their exclusion from Congress, they had lost any political power they possessed. Washington was the only person among them who had the ability to articulate their interest in world affairs in general and in Africa in particular, and his prestige and some symbolic power depended upon the good will of his powerful white patrons. As we saw above, he preferred to work unobtrusively, and while he was quite willing to lend his name to actions in support of Africa, he was not yet willing to take the lead in such matters.

The Europeans who were in the process of developing Africa so as to exploit it more effectively were aware of Washington's work at Tuskegee. They knew his opinions on race relations and considered his school a model for their African activities. Yet many Europeans were also skeptical of his real attitude toward European rule in Africa and of that of most African Americans. The Germans were anxious to have Tuskegee help them introduce cotton cultivation into Togo, but debated long and hard before approaching its principal. In September 1990 Baron Beno von Herman auf Wain, representing the Kolonial Wirtschaftliches Komitee, asked Washington "to select for us two negro-cottonplanters and one negro-mechanic who would be willing to come over to said company's land in the colony of Togo in West-Africa to teach the negroes there how to plant and harvest cotton in a rational and scientific way."[11] Nevertheless, the baron warned:

Some members of the company have certain misgivings whether your negro-planters might find some difficulties in starting and developing their work in Togo, in finding the necessary authority towards the native population and in having at the same time the necessary respect towards the German government official who of course would try to help them as best they could in their work.[12]

Whatever his views, aside from possible feelings that he was being flattered, Washington replied:

I am very glad that your Company has agreed to the suggestions which you made to it. We have already selected three of our best men to go to Togo. . . . I do not think in any case that there will be much if any difficulty in the men who go from here treating the German officials with proper respect. They are kindly disposed, respectful gentlemen. I believe at the same time they will secure the respect and confidence of the natives.[13]

As it turned out, Washington had every reason to be pleased with the initial reports from his staff and students who arrived at Lomé, Togo, on 30 December 1900. They kept him informed about the differences they noted in the Africans under various colonial regimes. For example, they found in the English colonies that young boys were adept in the pursuit of education "but not inclined to manual labor. They seek to imitate their masters and become English Gentlemen." In Togo, on the other hand, "German exactness is in evidence. The natives are made to do their work in order and promptly."[14]

Like other visitors to Africa, the Tuskegeans were amazed and intrigued by the local customs. Shepherd Lincoln Harris reported that the people "like to work and will work if they get plenty of 'chop' [food] as they call it, but they are not able to do much hard work. They soon give out." In many ways, these African Americans felt clearly superior to the whites attempting to develop Africa. Harris wrote Washington, "I know to some it will sound like too much praise, but since we have been here, we have done more and better work than any other company here at work." There were some white groups doing the same kind of work as the Tuskegeans, but "all those who know anything about either put our work in the lead. . . . I feel safe in saying that we all are doing all that there is in our power to reflect credit upon our race in America, and above all[,] credit upon Tuskegee our dear old Al."[15]

The Tuskegeans did not escape tragedy. Two young men who had been sent out to Togo drowned in the surf in May when their landing boat overturned. It was difficult for Washington to replace them because others wanted to strike out on their own among the Africans. The German company, for its part, insisted that all land developed remain in company hands and that all the cotton should be sold to them. Moreover, most young Americans found the five-year contract too long and the pay grossly inadequate.[16] When the Germans did increase the pay, one of Tuskegee's students remained in Togo. He reported success in training people to grow cotton and was largely instrumental in laying the basis for the cultivation of cotton in Togo. This man, John W. Robinson, was determined to "make good" in Africa. He said, "I am doing nothing that most people would consider great or noble, or either very honorable—'Growing Cotton' because it is commonly thought that any fool with a mule could do that . . . Yet it has become the main object of my life to do most successfully that so-called simple thing, 'Grow Cotton' . . . How well I am succeeding my work must tell, not my words."[17]

Washington became involved with many others attempting to cultivate cotton commercially in various parts of Africa. Among them was Henry Francis Downing, a blackman who had attended the Pan-African Conference in 1900. Born in New York City, Downing had served in the U.S. Navy. He was appointed a U.S. consul in West Africa in 1887 but resigned the next year to become president and manager of the United States African News Company in New York. He wrote Washington from

London in 1902 stating that he had been advised that Tuskegee could provide a cotton expert for his company, New Cotton Fields Ltd. Downing said, "It may be interesting to you to know that the Company in carrying out its operations has in view the locating on its properties in Africa of American families (coloured) experienced in Cotton growing."[18]

Leigh S. J. Hunt, a hard-headed white American capitalist who, with British associates, had acquired land on the banks of the Nile in the Anglo-Egyptian Sudan, wanted the services of African Americans, including a carpenter trained at Tuskegee, to organize a cotton plantation on which he hoped to settle African American colonists. He wrote to Washington in December 1903, in care of the American Embassy in London, extolling the possibilities of his colonization scheme. Hunt insisted that his project was not philanthropic, but practical and commercial. Hoping to flatter Washington, he asked, "What race of men is best adapted to assist in this pioneer work,—to serve as model farmers, to train the natives and teach them how to make the best use of these lands?" and answered, "I should like to try the American Negro as I believe him best fitted to work with advantage to himself and to the Sudanese."[19] Noting that Hunt had copied the letter to Lord Cromer, then the British agent and consul general in Egypt, with broad diplomatic power to oversee its economic and political modernization, Washington replied, "As I think I have said to you, I am not in favor of wholesale colonization of the Negro people in Africa, or anywhere else, but the opportunities which you suggest that Sudan offers are opportunities which, it seems to me, large numbers of our Negro people should take advantage of."[20]

True to his word, Washington did encourage young men to go to the Sudan. Hunt later reported that "if their beginning is a true index of their character and worth then I congratulate you upon the kind of men Tuskegee sends out into the world. To tell you the truth I am delighted with these boys and therefore very hopeful that my experiment in blazing the way to this land of promise is going to prove beneficial to at least some of your race."[21] Hunt was pleased that his men had recommended others and wanted Tuskegee to encourage them to go off to the Sudan. In his reply, Washington ignored Hunt's reference to "boys" and referred to his students as "men." He wrote, "I have also talked to the men and find them in entire sympathy with your proposition. I believe then that they will meet your desires most satisfactorily."[22]

Anxious that these young men represent the race with distinction, Washington wrote to them, "I shall watch your work there, with a deep interest and anxiety. . . . You will have in your keeping, the reputation of the school in your hands and in your work and deportment." He sought to impress upon them that "a great many persons going to a warm climate, go to ruin from a moral standpoint. I hope you will all keep this in mind and remember that if you yield to the temptation and lower yourself in your moral character, you will do yourself, the school and the race the greatest injustice, but I feel sure you are going to stand up and be men."[23]

Washington's increasing skill in dealing with whites, both at home and abroad, steadily bolstered his reputation as the black leader par excellence. More by pluck than by luck, Washington did not join such black leaders as Bishop Henry McNeal Turner, Archibald H. Grimké, Kelly Miller, and Bishop Alexander Walters in criticizing President McKinley's expansionist policies. This had paid off in his ability to obtain the funds with which W. E. B. Du Bois went off to Paris and then on to the Pan-African Conference in London. Washington was disappointed with Colonel Theodore Roosevelt's denigration of the valor of the black troops who had actually saved the Rough Riders' hides at San Juan Hill in Cuba.

In his own book, Washington used reports of the heroism of black soldiers to correct Roosevelt's scandalous views of the incident. He quipped that what Roosevelt said might make "very nice reading, but it is not history, in which it is always hazardous to sacrifice truth 'to make a period' [sic]."[24] Nevertheless, Washington did not join the outcry when McKinley chose then Governor Roosevelt as running mate and later established good relations with the vice president-elect. Responding to a telegram that Washington had sent him just after the election, Governor Roosevelt invited him to visit Albany, New York, when next up North.[25] In turn, Washington invited Roosevelt to visit Tuskegee.

Roosevelt's accession to the presidency following the assassination of McKinley prevented him from visiting Tuskegee, but Washington now had excellent relations with the highest official in the land. He was in a better position than any other black person in the United States to influence America's domestic policies as well as its foreign ones. On the very day that he was sworn in as president of the United States, Theodore Roosevelt wrote Washington, "I must see you as soon as possible. I want to talk over the question of possible future appointments in the [S]outh exactly on the lines of our last conversation together. . . . I hope that my visit to Tuskegee is merely deferred for a short season."[26] The president kept his word and sought Washington's advice and recommendations for appointing to office both blacks and whites, in both the North and the South.

Although Roosevelt was in the process of developing a fairly amicable relationship with Washington, the country was still retreating from the Reconstruction era with its promise of a better deal for blacks. He was therefore not willing to disturb the emerging pattern of race relations.[27] The country's mood was still "farewell to the bloody shirt."[28] Moreover, in Theodore Roosevelt, the United States had a president who firmly believed in the superiority of the white races, especially of the English-speaking peoples and in the notion of the "white man's burden." A number of scholars have suggested that he was not a racist in the modern sense, as some contend. But there is no doubt that Roosevelt firmly believed that the black race was inferior to the white one, whether for physiological or environmental reasons, or a combination of the two.[29] He was in favor of European imperialism and colonialism. It was in such an era, and with a man holding such views on race and imperialism, that Washington had to contend in order to ameliorate the condition of blacks both at home and abroad.[30]

President Roosevelt's invitation to Washington to dine at the White House on 16 October 1901 stirred up controversy among whites in the South as well as the North, but it was viewed by blacks all over the world as an advance for African peoples. There were few African Americans who did not praise this event. Even Bishop Henry McNeal Turner, still involved in emigrationism (and now chancellor and treasurer of the Colored National Emigration Association, organized "for emigrational purposes to any country where all men have rights regardless of their color"), took time out to congratulate Washington "for all the conditions and circumstances connected with dining with President Roosevelt." He concluded, "You are about to be the great representative and hero of the Negro race, notwithstanding you have been very conservative. I thank you, thank you, thank you. God bless you."[31] From Paris, Benito Sylvain, aide-de-camp of Emperor Menelik of Ethiopia, cabled Washington, "Hearty compliments for President Roosevelt[']s reception."[32]

Not only were blacks in Europe following the fortune of Washington, but people who knew of his earlier support of the Pan-African movement continued to write to him. In a letter seeking Washington's advice on a project to ascertain *"the real facts"* pertaining to "lynchings, the progress, the prosperity and the poverty of the [black] people, and so forth, and so forth," John Elmer Milholland, an editorial writer for the New York *Tribune,* told him about dining "with the Committee representing the Pan-African Association." He added, "I found the organization was in rather a bad shape for lack of funds and proper management. Having in mind what you said, I suggested that they identify themselves with this great International Union which we have started over here, and which I think is ultimately to be a great factor in human affairs . . . I will talk more about this when I see you, because it has a direct bearing upon our Southern problem."[33] People naturally assumed that Washington should have been as interested in southern lynchings as in Pan-Africanism.

Washington's role as a broker between whites and blacks was not always an enviable task given the needs of blacks and the prejudice of whites. This was especially true with respect to the official positions or "plums" that blacks expected from incoming administrations. Among these positions were the prestigious diplomatic posts to Haiti and Liberia, and a few others. With the prompting of Washington, President Roosevelt offered the post of collector of the port of Charleston, South Carolina, to Dr. William Demosthenes Crum. What the President had to overcome was the active opposition to Crum from Benjamin R. Tillman, the vitriolic, racist senator from that state. Then without the Tuskegean's knowledge, both Dr. John R. A. Crossland of Missouri and William A. Pledger (a newspaper publisher in Georgia) sought the diplomatic position at Monrovia. Crossland had the support of the secretary of the interior and simply wanted a federal position, whether to Liberia or as replacement for Henry R. P. Cheatham as recorder of deeds in Washington, D.C. When Roosevelt queried Washington about the qualifications of Crossland, who had declared that he was supported by the entire Missouri Republican party organization, he responded, "Dr. Crossland, so far as I can get information, is a clean, high toned man of ability, but is not known outside of the state of Missouri to any extent."[34]

When Crossland got the nod to go to Monrovia, Pledger was furious. Meeting Emmett Jay Scott, Washington's secretary, Pledger complained bitterly that the only reason Crossland had received the appointment was that the Tuskegean had recommended him for it. Pledger insisted that Crossland had "never been [of] any assistance" to Washington while he, Pledger, had been a "staunch and loyal friend." Scott attempted to mollify Pledger by explaining that when the administration said that Washington had recommended Crossland for a position, it was for the job of recorder of deeds and not for the Liberian legation. However, this explanation did not satisfy either Pledger or other blacks who felt that Roosevelt had in fact reduced the number of federal appointments given to blacks instead of increasing it, and that Washington was not being impartial. Scott reported to Washington that a number of "older politicians," including T. Thomas

Fortune and Pledger, were threatening "to directly approach the President" decrying Washington's power to endorse blacks for public office.[35]

In an effort to protect himself against job seekers and to retain the goodwill of Roosevelt, Washington wrote the president congratulating him for his "strong and clear letter on the subject of appointing Negroes to office." He added that it appeared to him that the letter had resolved "the whole matter for all time" as far as the administration was concerned. Assuring the president that he would only recommend persons of the highest caliber, Washington noted, "The only one I have recommended about whose character I was not sure is Dr. Crossland, Minister to Liberia."[36]

Owen Smith, who was then minister resident in Monrovia, did not know about the competition among the black elite back home for his job. He had visited Washington, D.C., in July 1900 and had suggested to Secretary of State John Hay that if the Republican party were returned to power in the forthcoming elections, he wished to remain in the diplomatic service but would like to go to Cuba or Haiti, rather than stay in Liberia. On his return to Monrovia, Smith had followed the electoral politics closely, even while actively fending off European attempts to take over Liberia. When by May 1901 he had heard nothing about a new appointment, he wrote Hay offering to remain at Monrovia, claiming that his health was better there than it had been in the United States. His only wish was to be able to choose his own secretary. Smith became alarmed when the department claimed that it was the breakdown of the telegraphic services that prevented it from notifying him of McKinley's assassination. He was mortified later to read in the *Times of London* of 27 December 1901 that his successor had been named. On hearing the news, the Liberian government asked Smith to enquire of the State Department whether it could confer upon him the decoration of "Knight Commander of the Order of African Redemption." When the department did not respond, Smith asked that the decoration be placed in the Liberian archives until a reply was received.[37]

Dr. John R. A. Crossland arrived at Monrovia on 10 May 1902 and walked into a hornet's nest created by hard feelings between Smith and the legation's secretary. Moreover, Smith was miffed about not getting a new appointment. Crossland was obliged to share a rented house with an immigrant African American family, the Faulkners, because of Smith's unreadiness to move from the legation. Smith lambasted Crossland for refusing to pay for the domestic help at the legation, and Crossland complicated the situation by removing the legation's business to the Faulkners' house, even though they were behind in their rent. Matters came to a head when Crossland took over control of the house and, after a domestic quarrel, shot Mr. Faulkner. Reporting this incident to the department, the secretary of the legation claimed that Crossland had become so closely involved in the Faulkners' domestic affairs that he refused to expel the couple even when advised to do so by the president of Liberia. The result, said the secretary, was that many Monrovians felt that the Liberian government ought to have considered revoking Crossland's exequatur, thereby making him persona non grata.[38]

It is doubtful whether the State Department had either the patience or inclination to follow all the strands of a conflict bred of ambition, African fever, disappointment, lust, revenge, and retribution when the basic task of the legation was the conduct of United States foreign policy. On 17 October 1902 Minister Crossland wrote the American secretary of state complaining, "Incurable indolence, constant inefficiency, every fact and circumstance connected with this office, urges me to ask for this change. Anxiously await your pleasure. American interest is too great to suffer here." The State Department was thus forced to deal with a messy situation. It was having considerable trouble dealing with European aggression against Liberia, and here it was faced with squabbles among resident diplomats. According to the *American Colonization Society Bulletin,* Crossland was given permission to leave, ostensibly because of "a personal encounter between him and one of the officials of the Monrovia legation. There appeared to be a state of affairs in existence at Monrovia which was not acceptable to the State Department and therefore a change in the mission will be made."[39]

News of the sad state of affairs in Liberia reached Tuskegee even before Crossland returned to the United States and embarrassed Washington no end. True, he had not recommended Crossland to Roosevelt, but he could not bear to confess to the president that he did not personally know every important black leader. On 24 January 1903 Washington sent President Roosevelt a "Personal and Confidential" letter saying, among other things, "I am most anxious to see a really first class man go as Minister to Liberia, and if I can help you find such a man, please let me know."[40]

The man Washington recommended to Roosevelt as a candidate for the post in Monrovia was Ernest Lyon, who turned out to be an excellent choice. Born in Belize, Honduras, on 22 October 1860, Lyon had migrated to the United States and had received both the bachelor's and the master's degrees at New Orleans University. He subsequently took special courses at the Union Theological Seminary in New York and became a

Methodist Episcopal minister. In 1894 Lyon was naturalized an American citizen, and in 1896 he was named pastor of St. Mark's Church in New York City. About this time Lyon also became active in black Republican politics. As a member of the Afro-American Council, he supported both the domestic and foreign policies of McKinley and Roosevelt during the debates in the black community over America's adventures in the Caribbean and the Far East. When the Republicans won the presidency in 1900, Lyon moved to Baltimore, Maryland, where in 1901 he became pastor of John Wesley Church and founded the Maryland Industrial and Agricultural Institution for the education of colored youth.[41] Lyon took leave from these positions to go off to Monrovia.

Ernest Lyon and his family arrived in Monrovia on 23 July 1903, where he found that his predecessors had created an unpleasant atmosphere. But unlike Crossland, who took umbrage at Smith's refusal to vacate the legation when he arrived, Lyon showed a great deal of understanding when Dr. James Robert Spurgean, the chargé d'affaires, still occupied the residence. When he presented letters of appointment, again like his predecessors, Lyon invoked the notion of brotherhood with the Liberians. Lyon declared that he regretted being constrained by protocol from uttering his own thoughts, "but since my government has ordained, for reasons palpable to all, that my words on this occasion together with the response of His Excellency shall be transmitted to the seat of the home government in Washington, I am compelled to sacrifice my own preference, in order that I might conform to the established regulation of the government, whose Minister and Representative I am." Lyon said that he regretted the "groundless insinuation that the black man is incapable of self government" and suggested that "history neither ancient nor modern has furnished any proof of the incapacity of the black man, conditions being equal, to maintain an independent and sovereign government." This being the case, Lyon said that "the perpetuation, therefore, of your national existence becomes more than a Liberian or an African problem. It is a universal problem. It is a problem, the solution of which affects every man of African descent."[42]

Lyon did not believe that he could hide the problems facing blacks in the United States of America from the Liberians. Asking permission to give the Liberians "tidings of the friends and relations whom you left behind you nearly ninety years ago, he admitted that like the Liberians, blacks in America "have had our difficult and perplexing problems to solve, not one but many. They piled upon us, from the hour of emancipation, with alarming rapidity. So difficult were they at times that our friends despaired, and hope grew faint within us." "But," said Lyon, "at no time in our critical history did we ever lose faith in God or confidence in the benevolence of our fellowmen."[43]

Like the earlier ministers to Liberia, Lyon was plagued by the continuing issue of emigrationism. His task was made more difficult by the activities of many important African Americans. T. Thomas Fortune, a longtime friend of Washington, got into the act. In 1902 he had written Washington about "the possibility of getting 100,000 Africans to go to the Congo." Losing his patience, Washington angrily responded, "I would say briefly that I feel very sure that if you could get Bishop Turner, Col. Pledger and Rev. W. H. Heard to go to the Congo and settle there that you would have little trouble in getting the remainder to follow. What do you think of this scheme?"[44]

The problem for Lyon was that the Liberians encouraged the activities of emigrationist African American leaders. Alfred B. King, president of the Liberian Senate, went on record in the pages of the magazine *West Africa* declaring that he welcomed the African Americans because "the treatment of our race is, every year, getting worse in America, and every year sees our people improving in arts and crafts, and in intelligence generally. Circumstances are working steadily for the realization of the great hope of Liberia."[45] Lyon was caught in a dilemma. He supported Washington's anti-emigrationist policy but wished to please his hosts. Almost as soon as he arrived in Monrovia, he wrote Secretary Hays about the plight of fifty-six African American migrants, twenty of whom had died, the remaining thirty-six quite destitute. Lyon complained: "Owing, Your Excellency, to the agitation now going on in the United States, on the subject of Negro emigration to Liberia, by irresponsible persons, whose literature has wide circulation among innocent and poorer classes of Negroes, the question becomes one of gravity for the consideration of both governments."[46]

The minister took a rather hard line on the emigration of poor, unskilled persons to Liberia. He sent the secretary a copy of a letter detailing the perils of uncontrolled emigration prepared by an experienced diplomatic colleague in Liberia. The author of the letter said, "I am most decidedly a well wisher of this country and should like to see it prosper, but if I were really interested in emigration as you must be, I would warn and urge those desiring to emigrate to this country not to do so without proper preparation and without sufficient and necessary means."[47]

Unfortunately for Lyon, this letter, like the one an earlier minister, J. Milton Turner, had sent to the State Department, was leaked to the emigrationists. William H. Heard, a former minister to Liberia, excoriated Lyon in the black press, accusing him of being "maliciously false" and "unjust to Liberia" in his views about emigration. Understandably upset, Lyon sought to convince the State Department, the Liberians, and African Americans that in principle he was not opposed to emigration. "The Legation does not oppose the right kind of emigration," he declared. "The effort is to prevent the coming of that class, which is a tax upon the Legation and the limited resources of the community."[48] In his cable he cited chapter and verse to substantiate his position.

An astute politician as well as a diplomat, Lyon was not above linking the question of African American emigration, the problems facing blacks within the United States, and European pressure on Liberia as a means of seeking support for his mission. Lyon wrote Hay that he felt it necessary to inform the department that "there is a strong impression here as well as abroad that the Colored Citizen of the United States, has no standing in his own country; that he is disbarred from all rights and privileges accorded to other citizens; that he is still 'A hewer of wood and a drawer of water'." It was these concerns, said Lyon, that led him "respectfully to make the following request with which I sincerely trust Your Excellency [the secretary of state] may find it expedient to comply." Lyon said that he believed that if the United States sent African Americans as special representatives to the inauguration of President Arthur Barclay, this would "afford a splendid present, an object lesson of the government's further care and development of its Colored citizens . . ."[49] There is no evidence in the archives that the officials at the State Department bothered to respond. Later administrations did send important black representatives to such affairs.

Lyon attempted to shame the United States into helping Liberia while at the same time improving race relations at home, and he used the same ploy in trying to improve the status of blacks in the United States military. He wrote the secretary of state asking "respectfully that a Military attaché be accredited to the Legation at Monrovia. A Negro military man trained in one of our Military schools, would not only inspire the citizens of the Republic, but would add much to lift the stigma which has been put upon our nation." In lieu of this, the minister wondered if a warship could not be instructed to visit Monrovia during the inauguration of the president, and added, "It has been quite some time since Liberia has had the presence of one of the United States Navy. The presence of one would inspire the whole town and especially the American colony."[50]

By seeking the appointment of a black military attaché to his legation, and requesting the presence of a warship in Liberian waters, Lyon hoped both to augment his woefully understaffed mission and to stem the tide of British, French, and German aggression against Liberia. He complained bitterly of getting little support from his government, and he felt that the lack of response by the Department of State reflected adversely on America's position in Africa. In one of his cables to the department he suggested that "strengthening the working force of the mission will hasten the day when America will share with Europe, the wealth of Africa."[51]

In a bold move to attract the attention of the U.S. Navy and other maritime interests at home, Lyon decided once again to resurrect the issue, previously rejected by the U.S. government, of an American coaling station in Liberia. Wrapping himself in the American flag, Lyon declared that these facilities would contribute toward guarding and strengthening American influence and interests in Africa, which should continue to increase as the "development of Great African Colonies goes forward under the European nations among whom the continent is divided." Lyon felt that such a station "would enhance the prestige of the great American Navy on the high seas":

> The "Stars and Stripes" unfurled to the breeze, somewhere in Liberian territory would have a wholesome moral effect, not only upon the merchant marine of European nations, which do business in Liberian waters, but also upon the Republic herself. . . . It would greatly encourage the efforts of her people who love, admire, and imitate American Institutions. It would strengthen their national confidence, in that it would serve as a lever of protection against any, who would employ "might instead of right" in their political dealing with this weaker nation. It would extend the blessings of Christian Civilization into the interior of her territory among her barbarous population.[52]

Lyon was not above playing the emigrationist card when it suited him. He suggested that by also helping Liberia materially, the United States could make Liberia's "sunny clime more desirable for thousands of other colored persons now on America, who will inevitably seek an asylum in this land whence their ancestors came in 1619."[53]

The propensity of the Liberians to juggle European avarice for parts of their territory, with the lack of firm commitment by the United States to help, often created difficulties for the State Department. In 1905 they faced such multiple problems as new aggression from the French, conflict with Great Britain over the Kaure-Lahun region on the Sierra Leonean border, demands by Germany for new ports, and their own need for money. The Liberians sought to solve some of these problems by inviting Dr. Edward Wilmot Blyden, then living in Sierra Leone, to undertake a diplomatic mission to Europe. They would later claim that his main task was to induce the French to abide by the Franco-Liberian Treaty of 1892. Through their own intelligence, the Germans got wind of other aspects of Blyden's mission and complained to the United States that there was more to his trip than met the eye. The Germans noted that Blyden had called at the British Foreign Office before proceeding to Paris. There were also rumors that he planned to obtain a British loan for Liberia. It seemed that a protectorate might be at issue.

When Secretary of State Elihu Root queried his staff about this report, a rather frustrated second assistant secretary in the department replied that he "had not seen the German memorandum re Liberian protection by Great Britain and France."[54] Moreover, while Lyon's despatch of 11 October did not mention Blyden's mission, the cable did convey Liberia's repeated wish that the U.S. should give it a vessel. The assistant secretary confessed to Root that the duplicity of Liberia had been "a sore trial to us on several occasions." He declared that "our Minister at Monrovia has sent us propositions by the Liberian government in flat opposition to negotiations with England and France then going on and of which our Minister knew nothing."[55] The assistant secretary was obviously troubled that Lyon had not even hinted at the possibility of the events cited in the German report, namely, that the Liberians were in fact preparing to grant concessionary rights to the Monrovia Rubber Company and to the Liberian Development Company, and were attempting to get the concurrence of the French. The State Department instructed Lyon to inquire discreetly about the unknown elements in the Blyden mission.[56]

There is no record of how Lyon felt about possibly being duped by the Liberians, but he went to the president himself to get the information he sought. He reported that the Liberian President had disclaimed knowledge of any instructions to Blyden except to deal with the treaty dispute with France, and had assured Lyon that if Blyden had discussed other matters in Europe, then he had certainly exceeded his instructions; and that Blyden's mission had failed because the French had refused to see him. Lyon then sought to assure the State Department that the Liberians were angry with Blyden and that when the envoy returned to Monrovia, the Liberian officials were barely civil to him before his departure for "Sierra Leone where he enjoys the unique distinction of being the first [person] to be appointed by the British Government as a director of Mahommedan [sic] education in that adjacent colony."[57] Yet Lyon was clearly suspicious of the Liberians and left open the question whether they and Blyden were really telling him the truth.

Shortly after Blyden's departure for Sierra Leone, Lyon reported to the department that he had received reports that Sir Harry Johnston was scheduled to visit Monrovia at the same time as a British naval squadron. He suggested to the department that the trinity of forces combining Sir Harry Johnston, the local British Consul, and the naval squadron posed a threat to the Liberians, and asked for "a visit of our war ships to the City of Monrovia."[58] Lyon was troubled to discover that the Liberians were, in fact, changing their normally cautious policy in dealing with the Europeans. The Liberians' problem was that their treasury was now as bare as it was in 1871 when they had to contract a usurious loan with the British. That episode had led to the scandalous death of President Edward James Roye and long negotiations with foreign bondholders that were not settled until 1898. The black ministers in Liberia during that chaotic period had all done their best to get help from the United States government but had failed. Now once again faced with financial disaster, receiving no help from the United States, and with imperial designs on their territory, the Liberians obviously felt compelled to deal with the British.

Lyon discovered and reported that the éminence grise of this enterprise was none other than Sir Harry Johnston, who had gained a great reputation as governor-general of British East Africa and had advanced British imperial designs in the Niger Delta by deporting such persons as King Jaja of Opobo.[59] Johnston had visited Liberia in 1904 and had waxed lyrical about that country's prospects. Then, with the permission of the Liberians, he was able to amalgamate a number of rubber, mining, and other corporations that had concessions in the country to form the "Liberian Development Company, Chartered and Limited." Johnston promised to "redeem Liberia from the engulfing debt in which it was wallowing, and at the same time [was] quite prepared to start the republic on the highway of national progress."[60]

The news from Liberia led the Department of State to examine its intelligence and to attempt to make sense of the upcoming events. The department finally concluded that this was the project that took Blyden to visit Johnston in London and that had alarmed the Germans. The American consul in Freetown had reported to the Department of State that in December 1906 the British governor of Sierra Leone had "hastily departed from Britain for a conference with Sir Harry Johnston, before Johnston goes to the West Coast (Liberia)." The consul added that Johnston had "negotiated or promoted, the taking, into the hand of the British government, the collection of customs for the Liberian Republic."[61]

Early in January 1907, Lyon reported to the department that he too had heard about the departure of the governor of Sierra Leone for London.[62]

All of these developments were the result of the failure of a scheme that the Liberians had worked out with the British. Fearing economic disaster, the government of Liberia had authorized the Liberian Development Company to secure a loan of $500,000 through such London brokers as "Messrs. Erlanger and company." The Liberians had stipulated, among other things, that the loan would be used in the following manner: $25,000 "for any pressing Liberian obligation"; $125,000 "for paying domestic debts"; $35,000 "to be loaned to the Liberian Development Company"; and the balance "to be devoted to the development of banking and road schemes by the Liberian Development Company." In addition, the British would furnish a number of officials to serve as chief and assistant inspectors of Liberian customs revenue, and the chief inspector would act as financial advisor to the Liberian republic; Liberia would make semi-annual payments of $30,000 as interest until the full sum be received by the Liberian Development Company; and the Liberian Development Company would be charged with the responsibility of repaying the loan from the brokers by paying them "50 percent of the net profits derived from the exercise of the powers and privileges of the charter of the former company, together with profits from the banking and road schemes to be undertaken in Liberia."[63]

According to Lyon's reports, it did not take the Liberians very long to discover that British control of their customs was having a disastrous effect on their incomes, that the expenditures of the Liberian Development Company were out of control, and that their country was not being developed as they had hoped. The Liberians resented paying what they considered to be unreasonably high salaries for customs officials and were scandalized when, after only purchasing a small steam launch for the Saint Paul River and spending $163,882.70 on fifteen miles of a dirt road for automobiles, the Liberian Development Company stated that its funds were being exhausted. The Liberians discovered that "every expense of the Company was being paid out of the 100,000 pounds borrowed on behalf of the Republic, rents, directors' fees, officers' salaries, traveling expenses, and also that the company was sending out prospectors and paying them out of this money."[64]

Concerned about these developments, Liberian President Arthur Barclay visited Sir Harry Johnston in London and asked for an accounting. Barclay later reported to his Congress that Johnston had told him "the Company had no money. That it might be bankrupt any time." Moreover, "he felt the government of Liberia should manage its own affairs. He saw no hope for the company unless the Government took it over." Johnston laid before Barclay in the offices of the bankers a plan proposing that Liberia buy out the company for £100,000 at 2 percent interest.[65] Liberia thus found itself in a financial bind at a time when Britain and France were encroaching on its territories and the Germans were establishing trading centers along its coast, eager to join the other Europeans in dividing up its territory.

Lyon discovered and reported to the State Department that the British consul in Monrovia, Braithwait Wallis, had sent a threatening letter to the president of Liberia stating, in part, that "the time has now gone by when Liberia could re-enact the part of a hermit kingdom, and that she must not lose a moment in setting herself seriously to work to put her house in order, or be prepared, at no distant date, to disappear from the catalogue of independent countries." Insisting that "His Majesty's Government do not consider that the government of the Republic is either stable or effective," Wallis declared that "it is essential that the finances of the country be placed, at any rate for the time being, in the hands of an European financial expert . . . and a trustworthy police force, under European Officers, should be at once established." Finally, warning that Great Britain was "not likely to entertain the proposal of guaranteeing the independence and integrity of Liberia," the consul declared that if the Liberian government did not carry out the reforms within six months, His Majesty's Government would "assist" in placing them into effect, including measures to prevent threat to the Kissi region of Sierra Leone.[66]

The Department of State was so alarmed by Lyon's cable that it instructed Whitelaw Reid, American ambassador to the Court of St. James's, to make discreet inquiries into the question of the British taking over Liberia and so on. The secretary added that the department had an interest "in the welfare and integrity of the Liberian Republic, not only because it is an off-shoot of our own body politic, founded by Americans and built upon American principles, but because of the *very possible racial contingencies of the future* [emphasis added]."[67]

Lyon dutifully kept the Department of State informed about developments in Liberia but was unable to get more than sympathy and interest from its diplomats. He took a leaf from the book of earlier black ministers to Liberia and used "back channels" to achieve his ends. Turning to Booker T. Washington for help, Lyon wrote from Monrovia stating that as he had taken the Tuskegean into his confidence in an earlier letter, "I am under further and more pressing necessity by recent developments to bind you to a stricter confidence in what I shall herein impart." He reported to Washington that negotiations between Liberia and the Europeans about the delimitation of frontiers had reached such an "acute state as to demand the presence of the President of Liberia at a conference in London." Lyon reported that Britain and France each were determined not to let the other suffer any territorial gain from Liberia. "England on the northwest declares that she has no desire for Liberia's territory, but if French encroachments in the southeast are not checked she will be obliged for national defence to imitate France on the northwest."[68]

Lyon sought to persuade Washington that Liberia was unable to check France and insisted that unless the United States intervened "the impairment of the independence of Liberia is inevitable." He stated further that he had received a confidential letter from the Liberians asking for diplomatic interference by the United States. Pleading with Washington to use his influence to get the United States Government to intervene, Lyon asked only that Washington withhold the source of the intelligence "for diplomatic reasons." But he continued, "In conferring with Bishop Scott, he says that if you find it absolutely necessary to give up the source of information why you can use my name."[69]

Washington replied to Lyon on 18 September 1907 that he was trying to decide "what will be the best manner of taking up the case of Liberia. The more I think of it, the more I am convinced that the wisest thing will be to make a perfectly frank statement of the case directly to the President. I feel reasonably sure that he will do something to relieve the situation if it is possible for any American to do so."[70] True to his word, Washington wrote a letter to President Roosevelt the very next day. In it he commented on the National Negro Baptist Convention, the reaction of blacks to the president's position in the Brownsville affair, and the need to replace a deceased white justice of the peace in Washington, D.C., with a black one, and he indicated that he was going to send Mr. Scott, his secretary, to see him within a few days regarding Liberia. Washington reminded Roosevelt about "the history of Liberia, Africa, how it was established by Americans during President Monroe's administration and how its interests have been safeguarded in many ways by America ever since its foundation." He added, "I have information from reliable sources that both France and England are seeking to take large parts of the Liberian territory. I am sure that you will prevent this, if it can be done."[71]

On 28 September 1907 Washington wrote Lyon that Scott had seen the president and had telegraphed to say, "Liberian matter amicably settled. President says will go to limit of all power and moral force to protect Liberia."[72] The problem for Liberia and its black supporters in the United States, however, was that the president and the State Department were only prepared to use "moral suasion" and not "force" to ward off the Europeans. Toward the end of 1907, Liberian President Arthur Barclay went to London en route to Paris to settle his country's boundary disputes and attempted to see Whitelaw Reid. Claiming previous obligations, the ambassador declined to see President Barclay. This rebuff incensed the Liberians, who subsequently complained to their resident American diplomats. Lyon was distressed by Reid's conduct and in a cable to the secretary of state expressed his regret that the meeting did not take place, since it would have been "diplomatically sound" for the ambassador to have received the Liberian president.[73]

Whether the British interpreted Reid's failure to receive Barclay as indicative of the United States' lack of interest in Liberia's affairs is not known, but they too refused to negotiate their boundary disputes with Barclay until the president had visited French officials in Paris. The French, for their part, either because they believed that the United States would not intervene on behalf of Liberia or because they were undeterred by this possibility, took a hard line. Their foreign office confronted Barclay and his suite with a plan for delimiting the boundary. Lyon reported that the French told the visitors that "Liberia would be compelled to accept what had been done unless she was prepared to back up her objections by *something more than moral suasion*."[74] Barclay had no force at his command and was therefore compelled to accept the treaty, and early in 1908 the Liberian Senate ratified it.[75]

Recognizing that the United States could not, or would not, help them, the Liberians were less able than ever to resist the increasingly hard line taken by the British. They were forced to modify the 1906 loan agreement by what became known as the Tripartite Agreement of 1908. This stipulated that Liberia would assume direct responsibility to the brokers for the loan of 1906 and that aside from securing some "advantages from the new agreement secured from the . . . Company the residue of the loan, amounting to £30, 223.8.9," and "practically" dispensed with its services.[76] Nevertheless, the British were not prepared to let Liberia off the hook so lightly. Lyon reported from Monrovia on 4 January 1908 that one Captain McKay Cadell of the British army had arrived "unexpectedly" in Liberia to take charge of the frontier police force. He noted that the Liberians objected to an English officer, contending that the commanding officer should be "the subject of any other government besides England or France." Lyon added, philosophically, that he was afraid that the objection would avail nothing since "the president dominated the legislature and his will is law. Many are of the opinion that this is the first step to a protectorate."[77]

Whether, as it appears, the Liberian president had agreed to this British action when he was in London is not clear, but on 25 January 1908 Lyon cabled the department that the British wanted the Liberians to exchange the territory of Kaure-Lahun for another area. They claimed that the region's half-British, half-Liberian status made for difficult administration, that the Kissi people preferred an exchange, and that the territory was an important outlet for the Sierra Leone railroad. The British also warned that failure to accept this request might lead to the demand that Liberia pay back the sum of £160,000, "the amount expended by Great Britain in keeping order in the Kaure-Lahun district for the last ten years." Lyon told the Department of State that in his view the loss of this territory, what with the lands taken recently by France, would "greatly embarrass the little Republic."[78]

Less than two weeks later, the British decided to tighten the screws again. They demanded that the Liberians reorganize their financial structure and place British officials in charge of customs. They also demanded that the chief inspector of customs be made financial adviser, with a seat in the Liberian cabinet and with veto power over the expenditures of the Liberian government. Lastly, they wanted judiciary reforms and warned that His Majesty's Government would "refuse to treat with Liberia further if her legislature fail to adapt the reformatory measures."[79] Moreover, the British said that barring these changes they would not guarantee the future independence of Liberia.

Reacting to these threats, the French warned that the presence of a British officer in charge of a Liberian force policing the Anglo-Franco-Liberian frontiers would amount to nothing less than a "British army of occupation." They insisted that they be granted equal representation on any such force. In turn, the British replied that if Liberia acceded to the demands of the French, they "would join with France in the disrupture and division of the republic."[80]

Alarmed by this crisis in their national life and possibly not trusting their own executive, a group of Liberian senators had earlier visited Lyon to complain about the initial British demands. These men wanted nothing less than to send a commission to the United States to seek help.

At that time Lyon was relatively noncommittal and had reported to the Department of State that he told his visitors that if they wished the United States to intervene, then the Liberian secretary of state should make an official request to the United States government.[81] He now busied himself with securing permission for a Liberian commission to visit the United States and present its case to the government.

The news from Monrovia that a Liberian commission was coming to the United States provided the "Wizard" of Tuskegee with the perfect opportunity to help an African nation-state and at the same time advance the cause of blacks in the United States. On 21 March 1908 Washington wrote President Roosevelt about "two matters in which I think you can do a great deal, within the near future, to change the attitude of many Colored people and to put a few of the loud talking enemies into an awkward position and, at the same time, accomplish a great deal of good." One of those matters was about "the Liberian Commission, which is coming to this country on an official visit soon, as I understand. The second is the matter of the separate coach law." Washington told the president that the commission was to see him "in reference to the encroachments of foreign governments upon Liberian soil," but pleading ignorance of "the custom of the State Department as regarding such matters," he wondered whether "in some way some special attention" could not be shown to the commission. Washington noted, "This is the first time that any such Commission, composed of Negroes, has visited this country and I am most anxious that they be treated with just as much courtesy as the customs of the United States will allow; even if an exception has to be made, I think it will be a fine thing."[82]

Washington shared with President Roosevelt his own major plans for receiving the commission, consistent with its dignity. In addition to having its members visit Tuskegee, Washington was "willing to bear a good part of the expense of their entertainment, personally, if necessary." He was only waiting for the "command" from either the president himself or the State Department. "Whatever is done, or is not done," he told Roosevelt, "will attract a good deal of attention and result in wide comment among the Colored people."[83]

Despite his claim that he knew nothing about protocol and diplomacy, a false modesty given the pomp and ceremony that usually prevailed at Tuskegee and other black institutions when important guests arrived, Washington began to make plans for the visit of the commission. He sought to assure the president that he had no illusions about either the strengths or weaknesses of the Liberian republic. He wrote briefs for the president detailing the personal characteristics of the visitors and offered to send Bishop Isaiah Benjamin Scott (who had served as a missionary in Liberia) to give Roosevelt firsthand information about them.[84] The president declined the offer but suggested to Washington that "Bishop Scott bring those three gentlemen to see me when they come." Roosevelt also warned: "Unfortunately, I am afraid the Liberian Republic is in a pretty bad way, and I do not think it advisable that any official prominence that can be avoided should be given their visit."[85]

Despite Roosevelt's reservations, Washington attempted to put the best face on the matter. He wrote Lyon a "Personal and Confidential" letter in which he reported that he had arranged hotel accommodations in New York for the commission and that later friends would arrange for their accommodation in Washington, D.C. He said further that arrangements "have been made by which the President will receive these envoys unofficially." Washington rationalized that this procedure "gives them a certain great advantage, as under ordinary circumstances, the President himself would not, I think, receive persons of such a mission, but would let them have their entire business connection with the State Department." Washington also revealed to Lyon that he was planning to invite the commissioners to Tuskegee and would be arranging special railroad accommodations for them. He was hoping to have the commissioners remain several days "to see something of the best life of our people in other parts of the South and in America. I shall propose to bring them to Tuskegee at my own expense."[86] What Washington did not share with Lyon was that "special railroad accommodations" were necessary because black people in the United States were up in arms about growing interstate segregation and discrimination on public transportation.

In a manner typical of him, Washington curried favor with important officials when he wanted to accomplish something. He wanted the commissioners to be received by Secretary of State William Howard Taft so he wrote him that in the opinion of the Tuskegee people he, Taft, was certainly "going to be nominated" for the presidency when the Republican convention met in Chicago. He also wrote Taft that the Liberian envoys wished to see him while they were in the country, adding, "I strong[ly] urge you grant an informal interview to them and myself. I shall probably be in Washington to see President [Roosevelt] with them some time between June eighth and tenth [1908] and if agreeable could see you at your house preferable [sic] evening after they see President."[87]

Taft did see the envoys as Washington requested because he was counting upon the Tuskegean's help in the coming elections, and Washington knew it.[88] Washington told a friend at the time that no one could deny that there had been considerable ill feeling among the "Colored people" against the president and against Mr. Taft because of what they considered to have been the wrongful dismissal of soldiers accused of rioting at Brownsville, Texas. But Washington maintained that "the sensible Colored people, and they are in the majority, take the view that even though a mistake has been made in this one case, they ought to overlook it in view of the many fine things that have been done for the race on the part of the President and the Republican party."[89]

In a confidential report that he sent to Ernest Lyon at Monrovia on 3 June 1908, Washington carefully explained how he planned to help the envoys. He said it was necessary and preferable for the envoys to meet the president at the White House, stating "that this is really the way to get a full, free and frank conference with the President. Whenever I want to accomplish anything of value I get him to permit me to come to the White House at night when he is free from other cares and duties." Explaining why a visit to Taft was necessary, he wrote, "I think in view of the fact that it is practically certain that Secretary Taft will be in the White House during the next four, or perhaps next eight, years it is important that they get acquainted with him, and get his influence and good wishes." Washington confessed that he sought as far as possible to keep the commissioners from attending too many functions given by the black community "until they are through with their diplomatic work at the State Department and at the White House. You of course can easily understand that somebody might make some fool utterance that might damage their mission," he told Lyon, adding, "Of course after they are through with their interviews with the Secretary of State and the President, matters will be different."[90]

Washington could not refrain from telling Lyon that in his opinion the Liberians had made diplomatic mistakes in their dealings with the United States. "If you will permit me to say rather frankly, it is my opinion that Liberia has made a mistake in the last few years in not cultivating the good will of the people in America. The fact is, Americans have in a large degree forgotten Liberia." Washington believed that Americans were interested in Liberia but that their interest had to be kept alive. He feared that the Liberians had drifted too much toward other countries and had not kept alive the original and historic attachment between themselves and America. It was his hope that "the visit of these

Envoys is going a long ways toward re-awakening and reviving the old interest." In a revealing postscript Washington noted: "If it is known in Washington that the three million Negro voters in the United States object to any foreign nation encroaching upon Liberian territory, a way will be found to carry out the wishes, in my opinion, of the American Negroes."[91]

The Liberians were satisfied with the help they received from Washington during their mission to the United States. On 12 June 1908 the secretary of the delegation wrote him, "The Envoys desire me to express to you their cordial thanks and appreciation for the very masterly and helpful service you have so kindly given them in their mission to this Great Government. They will not forget to carry your name, your great work at Tuskegee as well as your worth to the Negro race, to President Barclay when they shall return home."[92] The envoys sent Booker T. Washington copies of documents they had received at the Department of State, containing the declaration that both the governments of Great Britain and the United States appreciated Liberia's desire to remain independent from foreign encroachments, and asked that these matters be kept confidential.[93]

Washington was obviously pleased by his ability to establish contacts between the Liberians and such important persons as the president of the United States, Secretary of War Taft, and Secretary of State Elihu Root. In a letter to Mr. P. O. Gray, editor of the *African Agricultural World* of Monrovia, Liberia, on 15 June 1908, he reported that the commissioners had met the president and secretary of state on two occasions, the secretary of war and Mrs. Taft, Judge R. H. Terrell, the American press, the Negro Business League, and many other luminaries. Washington related that when the president saw the commissioners he "went over in a painstaking and careful manner every detail in connection with their visit. He assured them that the United States would assist and encourage Liberia in every way possible." Washington added that the American secretary of state was said to have even rearranged his schedule to give the envoys a two-hour audience so they could "present their views." Mr. Root assured them that "the United States would do everything within its power to carry out their wishes." Washington's own opinion was that the envoys "impressed us all as being a set of scholarly, dignified, courageous gentlemen, deeply interested in the welfare of their country," and eminently qualified to represent an independent State.[94]

What Washington could not have known was that both the president of the United States and his State Department viewed Liberia's problem in strictly racist terms. Moreover, they were loath to alienate Great Britain on Liberia's behalf. Roosevelt had assured Emmett Jay Scott, Washington's deputy, that he desired to settle the question of Liberia "on the broad ground of the square deal to the Liberia Republic." Yet two days after he had met the Liberian commissioners, Roosevelt wrote to a friend that with reference to the predicament of both Liberia and Haiti, "the question is one of race."[95] Not only did the president believe that these two black republics could not govern themselves, but in the State Department, Second Assistant Secretary Adee, who personally favored "some form of quasi-protectorate" status over Liberia by the United States, lamented that the right justification could not be found for so doing despite a thorough review of Americo-Liberian relations.[96]

Firmly believing that "race and climate" had a profound effect on culture, Adee wrote in a memorandum to Assistant Secretary of State Robert Bacon, "It must always be borne in mind that the climate of Liberia is against any effective Americanisation." He felt that only "full-blooded Africans" could stand the climate, and that "half-bloods have to go through two or three attacks of the fever before they can be acclimated." Adee expressed the notion that "with the experience we have gained in the Philippines, we could administer and self-develop Liberia in practical ways, with the aid of trained African mestizos from Puerto Rico and perhaps some Philippinos, and sending some full-blooded southern Africans. . . . To do that, however, we would have to assume an administrative protectorate, in short a colonial control in all but the name. The practical administration might be under the Secretary of Agriculture."[97] Secretary Root, for his part, had listened respectfully to the Liberian commissioners, but had declined to commit the United States to any action until he, in turn, had sent a commission to their country to investigate conditions and to report back.[98]

In a bald effort to strengthen their hand with the American administration, the Liberians suggested to Washington that their country would be honored if he would accept the post of chargé d'affaires for Liberia in the United States. Flattered by the offer, but prudent to a fault, Washington replied that he would consult the administration. On 16 June 1908 he wrote Secretary Root that he was "really anxious to be of some service to Liberia, but the question arises, whether it would be proper or desirable for me to accept such a position; and the further question arises, whether I could not be of the same value to them, in acting in a private capacity or rather in a seemingly unofficial capacity." Washington claimed that he cared nothing about an official designation; his only object was to be of service. Nevertheless, he said that the Liberians seemed anxious that he should consent to take the position. He continued, "The only element that appeals to me, in favor of accepting the position, is perhaps in the fact that I might speak with some authority in helping the Republic carry out the advice and suggestions which you gave."[99]

Revealing his attitude about race to whites, in a manner unusual for him, Washington told the secretary of state, "Liberia is practically the only portion of Africa, which is now left in control of the black man, and I am particularly anxious that the people of Liberia have a chance to see what they can do." He confessed that he held out little hope for the Liberians "except as they are able to get right down to business and develop the natural resources of that country in a way to give them wealth, and consequently strength and standing before the world." Adopting what he considered to be the "hard-nosed" position of people in the State Department, Washington said that he was too realistic to believe that the mere fact that the Liberians had political control of their country meant anything, "except as they can make themselves of service in the development of the natural resources of the country." It was in this direction that he wanted to be of service to Liberia.[100]

Washington proposed to send to Liberia "some strong men from Tuskegee and [to get] some of their brightest men to come to Tuskegee to get hold of our ideas and methods of work, with a view of returning to Liberia and putting them into practice." He terminated this long letter to the secretary of state, thanking him for being so frank with the Liberians. "I went over your conversation fully with them again, and they realize now, as I think they did not before, that what you have suggested is the wisest course of action for them, and I think they will do their best to follow your advice."[101]

In his response, Secretary of State Root was candid about the nature of the foreign policy enterprise, but he was also not too enthusiastic about Washington taking part in it:

> I do not think it would to any degree increase your usefulness to the Liberians for you to be Chargé d'Affaires. Indeed, it would rather tend to detract from the weight of your independent expression of opinion and interest regarding their affairs. A chargé d'Affaires is a very low grade diplomatic representative, and your own personality would, I think, have greater weight without that small office than with it. It would not be a real relation but a mere false appearance. You can do them good as an American, which you are, not as a Liberian, which you are not.
>
> I think very highly of your idea of sending some strong men from Tuskegee and bringing some of their brightest men to Tuskegee to get hold of your

ideas of methods and work with a view to returning to Liberia and putting them into practice. This would require time, of course, and the first thing, it seems to me, is for you to send some of your men there. I hope you will be able to send them men who have not only the education acquired at Tuskegee, but who have strong characters and capacity for leadership and control.

I am much pleased that you liked the advice that I gave the Commissioners in our recent interview. I have already written to our Ambassador in London to take the subject up with the British Government." [102]

Not really knowing the true attitude of the United States administration toward their country but believing that they had its support, the Liberian envoys went to Europe to inform the Europeans about the result of their American mission. From Hamburg they wrote Washington that they had been well received in Berlin. They told him confidentially that "the Berlin authorities expressed themselves as willing to join in a compact to guarantee the integrity of Liberia and thought that for obvious reasons it should be international [involving] the United States, England, France and Germany." The head of the delegation added that he did not know "what the Washington Government will think of this idea, but perhaps it might allay the jealousy of the other powers better than if England only were invited. We leave this however to the discretion of the United States Government." [103] Whether the United States saw in these remarks a hint that Liberia was willing to deal with the British but not with the French or Germans is not known. What soon became clear was that Minister Lyon distrusted any close relations between the Liberians and the British because of the implications for African Americans dealing with white Americans. He appeared not to trust the Anglo-Saxons.

On 19 September 1908 Lyon wrote Washington from Monrovia reporting that he had "just seen a letter, written confidentially from London to the President of the [Liberian] Republic—informing him that Sir Harry Johnston—of West African fame and author of a history of Liberia—has been invited by President Roosevelt to come to the United States for the purpose of studying the Negro question from the American viewpoint as it relates to his emigration to Liberia." Lyon knew full well that the principal of Tuskegee opposed large-scale emigration of blacks to Liberia or to any other place for that matter. He also knew that Liberia favored emigration and was therefore concerned that President Roosevelt might agree to it. [104]

What especially troubled Lyon was Johnston's alleged antipathy to "the American type of Negroes." He reported to Washington, "Sir

Harry will have nothing good to say of the Liberian Negro—whom he claims is American—but before Sir Harry should be taken seriously—the inside history of the Liberian Development Company and his part in the birth of the organization should be given by some one else." Lyon sought to convince Washington that Johnston was an arch imperialist, instrumental in giving the Uganda protectorate to Britain and therefore not to be trusted. Flattering Washington for accepting to be burdened with affairs of state, Lyon told him, "You have now become diplomatically linked with the future of Liberia. In the capitols of Europe, especially London and Paris—where Liberian matters are discussed in their relations to the United States brought about by the recent commission—your name is mentioned as an important factor." Lyon added that before the commission went to the United States, some "designing persons" (and by this he meant blacks who were followers of W. E. B. Du Bois) misunderstood what Washington stood for. But he assured him that "the condition has changed and what you have always stood for is now appreciated and admired."[105]

Washington found himself courted by some blacks who had despaired that anything could be done in, or for, Liberia. One such person was Henry Francis Downing, who had served as a U.S. consul in West Africa in 1887, and who, as indicated above, had since then lived in London, had attended Henry Sylvester Williams's Pan-African Conference in 1900, and had closely followed West African affairs. Downing wrote to Washington criticizing the Liberians, especially Vice President James Jenkins Dossen and the envoys who had visited London on their way home from the United States. He asked the Tuskegean to place his views before Secretary of State Root and the president.[106]

Whether through disinformation furnished by the British, who may have been in contact with Downing, or by other means, the Liberians were disturbed to hear that Washington had made some suggestions to Secretary Root about how to resolve their boundary dispute with Britain. Vice President Dossen queried Washington about the facts and received the following response from Tuskegee:

> I never talk about such matters, outside of official circles, to anyone, and in this particular case I have not discussed the subject with anyone outside of yourself and Secretary Root; and I am sure that Secretary Root made no such suggestion or gave any such advice when we saw him.[107]

Not only did Washington deny having attempted to see the secretary on any subject since he and the Liberians were at the State Department together, but he added that, for that matter, the president and his entire cabinet had been out of the capital during the whole of the summer and it was impossible to get any information, or do any business, except through subordinates, which was always disagreeable and hardly productive. Washington revealed to Dossen his plan to see the secretary on 13 October and to go over the whole matter fully with him. After this conference, Washington would write Dossen giving more definite information on how matters stood since certainly, by that time, the secretary would have had some report from the agent who had visited Liberia. Meanwhile, Washington asked Dossen to keep him informed: "I wish to know how to present the case to the Secretary. My highest ambition is to see Liberia stand for all time on its own feet without being under obligation to any other nation, and whatever I do will be with that in view."[108]

Through his own intelligence network, Washington had apparently heard disturbing news about Downing's activities in London and was convinced that it was this man who had implicated him as a participant in talks about England's wish to annex Liberia to Sierra Leone. He informed Dossen that for his own personal and private information, he wished him to know that "Downing is a deadly enemy to Liberia, in my opinion, and I think it is through him that many of these reports get scattered. He wrote me a long letter sometime ago in which he made the most damaging statements concerning yourself and fellow Envoys." The principal said that he had paid no attention to Downing's letter and did not even answer it; nor had he brought the letter to President Roosevelt as Downing had begged him to do. Finally, Washington advised Dossen of the necessity of watching Downing, "as he would not hesitate, in my opinion, to do anything that would denationalize Liberia." He added in a postscript, "I have just written for an engagement with the Secretary of State for October 13th, when I shall take up the matter fully relative to Liberia. Of course, I will write you as soon as I have done so."[109] On 12 December 1908 Washington wrote Dossen that during a recent visit to the nation's capital he had had the opportunity to discuss Liberia's affairs with both Secretary of State Root and Lord Bryce, the British ambassador. He reported that he had also previously spoken about Liberia to both Britishers when they had visited Tuskegee. Washington wrote that the three of them "went over Liberian matters pretty thoroughly," adding,

> I am quite convinced that Secretary Root, Mr. Bryce and Sir Harry Johnston are all friends of Liberia, and in the highest degree favorable to maintaining its independence as a nation. Secretary Root has received the report from the special agent who went to Liberia, but it contains nothing that was not known before and nothing that has not been already covered in discussion.

It is possible that there will be some developments in connection with Liberia within the next few days or weeks. This latter matter I am not permitted to mention just now to anyone. I am to have a conference with President-elect Taft regarding the matter within the next few days. So far as I can get hold of the facts, there seems to be no immediate danger of any interference with Liberia.

Whenever I can serve you, please be kind enough to let me know. I might add that Secretary Root is deeply interested in all that concerns Liberia. Of course what is contained in this letter is confidential. We have many pleasant thoughts of you and your fellow envoys in this country. [110]

What Washington hinted at in his letter to Dossen when he said that "there will be some developments in connection with Liberia within the next few days or weeks" was the discussion within the administration about the wisdom of sending an American commission to Liberia. On 14 December 1908 Washington wrote the secretary of state from New York about having taken his advice to speak with Taft concerning Liberia and even to ask about the wisdom of sending a commission to Liberia as the secretary had requested. Washington reported to Root that Taft had indicated that it might be wise to provide for the expenses of the commission in a diplomatic and consular bill that was soon to go before Congress. Washington suggested that if Root wished to pursue the discussion, this could be done on Monday, 21 December as Washington would pass through the capital on his way South, adding:

If the sending of this commission is finally decided upon, and if my name is to be seriously considered in connection with the trip, I ought to say that I should have to give very careful consideration to the matter before deciding whether I could go or not. This will be one of the points I should have to discuss with you further. [111]

On 16 December 1908 Root wrote Washington that the proper steps would be taken to ask Congress for an appropriation for the expenses of the commission to Liberia. The secretary of state recommended that Washington talk with Taft and with some other persons in New York about the other members of the commission. Root thought "it would be desirable to have the other members white men and to have them men who have shown an interest in the improvement and welfare of the black race in our Southern States." Root suggested one Mr. Ogden as a possibility. The secretary also felt it "would be desirable to have one of them at least a man who has some familiarity with practical government, perhaps some one who has had something to do with the building up of government, either Cuba, Porto Rico or the Philippines." [112]

While it appears that Washington would have wished to go as a member of a United States commission to Liberia, he felt it prudent to inquire of his board of trustees whether he ought to consider doing so. For reasons that are not clear, but which perhaps revealed a great deal about the attitude of many important whites about the role of blacks in America's domestic politics as well as in its foreign policy, Dr. Seth Low, president of Columbia University then serving as president of Tuskegee's board of trustees, felt it necessary to write confidentially to Secretary Root about Washington's projected trip.

> As you may know, I am President of the Board of Trustees of the Tuskegee Normal and Industrial Institute, of which Dr. Washington is Principal. Dr. Washington has told me of your wish that he should serve upon an important mission to Liberia, and has asked me for my advice. I shall be very much obliged if you will outline to me, as far as you properly may, the matter as you see it, indicating especially, so far as you are free to do so, why it seems to you desirable that Dr. Washington should serve in this way. I feel sure that the Trustees of the Institute will wish him to co-operate with the government in every proper way, and will give him any necessary leave of absence. On the other hand, it is essential, as you can understand, that I should be able to place the matter before the Board with as much fullness as circumstances permit; and particularly why Dr. Washington appears to be the best man for the purpose.
>
> *I should also be glad to know whether it seems to you that, in accepting this particular mission, he would be likely to expose himself to criticism on the part of the white race for mixing in politics; and perhaps, from the black race, as one who may be looking towards Liberia as an important factor in the solution of our problems at home.* As George Washington once said, "It is impossible for a man to pursue a course that will escape criticism; but it is always possible to pursue a course that is capable of vindication." The object of my questions is to develop as clearly as may be the precise object of the mission, so that the Trustees may form their own opinion as to the wisdom of Dr. Washington's taking part in it . . .[113] [emphasis added].

Buoyed by the prospect of going to Liberia and by discussions with both American and foreign diplomats, Washington was hopeful about Liberia's future. On 7 January 1909 he wrote Liberian Vice President Dossen a long letter recounting the many discussions he had had with Ambassador Bryce and Sir Harry Johnston and reiterating that those gentlemen "have no wish to do anything to disturb the integrity and independence of Liberia." Nevertheless, he warned the vice president that Bryce and Johnston "may not speak of nor know about the designs of those higher in authority than they are." He advised Dossen to keep him informed as "speedily as possible just what further demands England has made upon your country, and what you think I can do in order to help." Washington suggested that the Liberian commission that visited the United States had done as much as possible to allay fears about Germany. The problem, of course, was Great Britain. Washington told the vice president that during his last visit to the State Department he had seen Secretary Root, Secretary Bacon, and Ambassador Bryce at the same time and that they had spent an hour discussing Liberian conditions. "Mr. Root, as he always is, was very frank with the British Ambassador, he told him rather plainly that Liberia feared the further encroachments on the part of England," Washington wrote. He sought to assure Dossen that "in the presence of all Mr. Bryce repeated that his country had no selfish designs on Liberia." Washington impressed upon Dossen that the United States government had almost made up its mind to send a three-person commission to Liberia and that the object of this commission would be threefold:

> 1st. To make a demonstration that will let the rest of the world know that the U.S. has not lost interest in Liberia and that it means in some way to re-awaken and strengthen its former interest and connection.
>
> 2d. To be of any service in the way of suggesting improvements and reforms in the government of Liberia.
>
> 3d. To help strengthen the educational work in your country.[114]

Characteristically, Washington told Dossen that he had "been asked to become a member of this commission" but was not sure that he would be able to accept. Much depended upon the method of transportation and the length of time it would take him and the other members of the commission to look into conditions in Liberia and to make the journey to and fro. "The only danger I can see in carrying out this plan and the further helping of Liberia," he wrote, "is the change of administration which means a new Secretary of State. I am hoping that Mr. Knox, who will succeed Mr. Root, will take as much interest as Mr. Root has." Washington said that at Secretary Root's suggestion, he had already spoken with President-elect Taft about the matter and had received a sympathetic response to the commission's plans. He promised to keep Dossen informed about further developments. He warned Dossen not to leak the news, because "it will be very embarrassing to me if the information that this commission is to be sent should come back to the State Department or should in any way become public before it has been announced by the U.S. Government. Please guard this information most carefully."[115]

Washington was philosophical about the future. He further added:

Whether or not the commission will go if I cannot personally go I am not sure, but my impression is the commission will go at any rate whether I am a member of it or not. I am trying to select high types of men. I think, perhaps, it is just as well to state that the other members of the commission are likely to be white men of high standing.

In regard to your dispatching a second commission to the United States, I hardly think it well for you to move in this direction until the United States has sent a commission to Liberia. If the commission goes from here, that would lay the basis, it seems to me, for another commission being sent to this country from Liberia.

If you will let me know very definitely just what encroachments England and any other country have made recently, I shall be able to help you better.

I shall be glad to hear from you as often as possible.[116]

Due largely to Washington's efforts, Theodore Roosevelt discussed the problems facing Liberia in his last message to Congress. The outgoing president also told Congress on 19 January 1909 that he intended to recommend that President-elect Taft seek Washington's advice about dealing with the concerns of blacks whether about Liberia or other matters. On 18 January 1909 Washington acknowledged this recommendation when he wrote the now ex-president, "I have been intending to write extending my special thanks to you for what you said regarding speaking to Mr. Taft about my relations to your administration and what I have attempted to do. I had not expected any such consideration on your part, but it is in keeping with all the generous and fine things that you have done and are constantly doing. If I can be of any service to Mr. Taft, I shall be more than glad."[117] On 20 January 1909 Roosevelt did write the incoming president reminding him of their conversation about Washington. Roosevelt said, "[There] is not a better or truer friend of his race than Booker Washington; and yet he is so sane and reasonable that following his advice never gives cause for just criticism by the white people."[118]

When news of the formation of a United States commission to Liberia leaked out, a number of blacks besieged Washington with requests to serve. Among them was none other than his nemesis, T. Thomas Fortune. Beseeching Emmett Jay Scott to forward a letter to "the Wizard" before the latter made any commitment to others, Fortune frankly admitted that he wanted to be a member of the Liberian commission because he was "competent," he wanted to see Europe and Africa, and he needed the "emoluments of the position." He requested Scott to tell Washington that he had mended his ways and had even reached an agreement with his wife. He added, "*I have recovered my senses but not my cents* [emphasis his]."[119] Washington was, however, too careful to recommend Fortune for the post, which lack of action led Fortune to request that Washington return the letters that he had previously written to him.[120]

Washington was serious about the composition of the commission for Liberia and wrote to Sir Harry Johnston about it, enclosing a copy of the bill the president had sent to Congress concerning it. Believing that Sir Harry and the British had given up their imperial aims toward Liberia, Washington was forthcoming in his correspondence with him. He told Johnston that Secretary of State Robert Bacon had asked him to participate and to help "in selecting the other members." Washington also told Sir Harry that he had not decided to accept the invitation, even though he had received permission from his board of trustees to do so. He added:

> As to the make-up of the commission. It is the present wish of the State
> Department that the commission be composed of one person who has had
> experience in reorganizing and rebuilding governments such as in the
> Philippines, Porto Rico, San Domingo and Cuba. That another member be
> one who has had experience in reorganizing the finances and customs such as
> was done recently in San Domingo. And the third be one able to help them in
> their educational matters. This is what we have been aiming at. Of course,
> there are few colored people who have had experience in such matters. I hope
> in some way that Mr. Banks, of Mound Bayou, may be made a member of
> the commission. What do you think of that? At any rate, I am quite sure there
> will be one if not two members of the commission white people.
>
> I am very glad that you have given me information concerning the best
> time to visit Liberia. It may be that the trip will have to be postponed until
> November.
>
> I shall be very glad to hear your opinion of Haiti. I am deeply interested in
> the future of that country.
>
> The New York *Sun* a few days ago had a very fine editorial on your letters
> concerning the South in the London Times. Will you not tell me how I can
> get hold of all of these letters?[121]

What Washington did not know was that the British had not abandoned their designs on Liberia and that a crisis generated by their imperial aims was then brewing in Monrovia. Despite the Liberians' conviction their commission had won the understanding of the American State Department, they had taken seriously the preemptory demands contained in the letter from His Majesty's consul and were doing their best to comply with proposed program. This, at least, was the opinion of Lyon, and the Department of State accepted his views.[122] The Liberians had passed a law creating a frontier force under an Englishman, Captain McKay Cadell, and gave him the rank of major. They had also appointed one

Mr. W. J. Lamont as chief inspector of customs and as financial adviser to the republic. Lamont allegedly did a good job, but the Liberians were obliged to pay him several times the salary he had received for doing the same job while in Sierra Leone and, incidentally, a sum which was twice the salary of their president. Tempers flared when Liberia attempted to reduce Lamont's salary.[123]

What complicated matters for Lyon and for the State Department was that local British officials attempted to overthrow the Liberian government. Whether because he wanted a force loyal to himself and to the British government or because he wished to subvert the Liberian government, Major Cadell filled the ranks of the frontier force with Mendi-speaking men from neighboring Sierra Leone. Moreover, Cadell had the uniforms, caps, and other equipment of this frontier force stamped with the crown and emblems of His Britannic Majesty's Service. When the Liberians complained to the major that filling the ranks with non-Liberians was against Liberian law and asked about the reason for the emblems on the uniforms of the soldiers, Cadell equivocated and refused to admit the obvious. He also refused to dismiss the foreign soldiers when the Liberians asked him to do so.[124]

By the time the Liberians realized what was happening, Cadell had entrenched himself in their capital. He had not only persuaded the municipality of Monrovia to give him control of the city police but had otherwise become indispensable in his roles as street commissioner, tax collector, treasurer, and supervisor of many municipal functions—all without charge. With the support of the British consul, Braithwait Wallis, Cadell had started to replace local policemen with persons from Sierra Leone, and he insisted that all communication between himself and the Liberian president should first be submitted to the British consul.[125]

Alarmed by what could only have been considered a form of creeping imperialism, the Liberian municipal authorities consulted Lyon and decided to dispense with the free services of Cadell. The major not only refused to resign these functions but presented the city of Monrovia with a bill for services rendered. He warned that if the bill were not paid, he would not surrender the city's property entrusted to his supervision. Faced with these acts of mutiny, the Liberian president asked Cadell to resign as head of the frontier force. Again Cadell refused, and he then presented the president with an unitemized bill for some $80,000 and a note (copied to the Liberian Senate) threatening the president with violence unless the demands were met within twenty-four hours. The major felt himself to be in a strong military position because he had thrown up rock breastworks six feet deep, with portholes, on all approaches to Monrovia. Moreover, he also sought to repossess some of the guns the British consul had ordered him to send to a shipping company for return to Europe.

Lyon kept the department fully informed about the developing crisis. He reported that on 5 February 1909 His Majesty's consul had cabled London that there was a mutiny in the Monrovia barracks and that a warship should be despatched to protect British lives and property. (There was no such mutiny at the time, but Lyon warned that there was one in the making.) Just as Lyon had predicted, by the time Cadell gave his ultimatum to President Barclay on 13 February 1909, a British war-ship, *Mutiny,* had appeared off Monrovia and had trained its guns on the capital. Working closely with Lyon, the Liberians sought to avoid a confrontation by asking that all British subjects be withdrawn from the Monrovia military barracks so that the Liberians could suppress any rebellion without harming them. Lyon issued a call to all American citizens to seek shelter at the legation to forestall the British claim that they also had to protect American citizens. When Major Cadell and the Britishers left the military barracks and the Liberians assumed control of the establishment, the mutiny was effectively frustrated. This time, due in large part to the efforts of Lyon, this black nationality did not suc-cumb to European imperial trickery. [126]

Meanwhile, in the United States, both Washington and the Taft ad-ministration were still agonizing over whether he should make the trip. On 15 February 1909 Assistant Secretary of State Bacon asked Archi-bald Butt, the White House military aide, if it was a good idea to send Washington to Liberia. Butt replied:

> I agree with you, Mr. Secretary, that the government of Liberia should be preserved for the Negroes, and also that Booker Washington should go on any commission which is sent there. I also believe that a navy vessel should be anchored off the coast, but I do not believe that a navy vessel should be used to convey Booker Washington there. The people will understand why he ought to go, and will not hesitate to endorse it, but they will make a hue and cry against such a marked distinction in sending him on a government vessel. They will not forgive the President for doing it, either. [127]

Recalling the flap over Roosevelt's inviting Washington to dinner at the White House, Butt cautioned the secretary of state, "As you love the President and hope for his renomination some day don't hamper him now with another incident with Booker Washington." [128]

Washington was leaning in the direction of participating in the commission, and on 16 February 1909 he wrote the secretary of state that he thought he could leave for Liberia by the time a vessel could be gotten ready and the other commissioners chosen. He preferred that the trip be as direct and as short as possible so that he could get back to Tuskegee before the end of the school year. Washington apparently had no inkling of the administration's concern that whites might object if he were sent on a navy vessel, because he told Secretary Bacon that he would "prefer going and returning on same naval vessel and without any change of vessels. In that case [I] can keep up much valuable work on vessel which I usually do here." He also said that he would "prefer to arrange to live on vessel while there so commission can keep in good physical shape to do good work." Washington also felt that the appearance of an American man-of-war "will have fine effect not only on Liberians but upon other countries that are interested."[129]

On this same day Washington wrote Seth Low about a long conference he had had with the people of the Department of State, in which it was decided that

> the Liberian matter is practically reduced to the following point. The people in the State Department say they think I can save Liberia by going. If I do not go, they fear that the independence and usefulness of the country will be lost. The Department is so impressed with the importance of my going at once that it is willing to use an emergency fund for expenses, either to defray the expenses of the entire commission of three or for me to go alone. Under the circumstances, using the permission granted me by the Board of Trustees, I have placed myself in the hands of the State Department. It seemed to me that this was the only thing to do as it was a clear case of duty. I have a feeling that if the Department carries out its present plan to have the commission go on a man of war that the time required will not be very great and that I can get back here in time to do a great deal of valuable work before the close of our financial year.[130]

Three days later, Washington wrote to the vice president of Liberia about the British threat and about the United States' decision to send out a commission:

> I am very sorry to hear of developments in your country since your letter was written. I hope that by the present time matters are quieting down. I have been to the State Department several times recently, and am keeping in close touch with developments.
>
> Certainly, I can say to you that the visit of the Liberian Envoys has had the result of deepening and quickening the interest of this country in Liberia, in a way that nothing has done in recent years.

It is the present intention of the State Department to send a Commission to Liberia at an early date, and I have been asked to go as a member of this Commission. I am trying to see my way clear to do so. If the present intention of having a man go directly to Liberia and return, for the accommodation of the Commission, is carried out, I think I shall go.

You can depend upon this, that whoever does go will be high-minded people of large influence and capable of service. I think that Mr. Robert C. Ogden, Mr. John Wanamaker's partner in New York and Philadelphia, is likely to be one of the members of the Commission. [131]

Ironically, and much to Washington's dismay, it was his importance to the incoming Taft administration that made it impossible for him to go with the commission to Liberia. Washington had written to Sir Harry Johnston on 28 February 1909 that when news of the attempted British coup in Liberia reached the United States, Secretary of State Root had telegraphed him to come immediately to the capital. While Washington was there, Root told him he was "ready to send the commission without authority of Congress, that is using an emergency fund, as he felt that the situation justified his doing that." Washington added that he "was urged to consent to go as a member of this commission, or if I thought best, to go alone." Meanwhile, Roosevelt was attempting to get the bill to send the commission through Congress, but the problems of transition to the Taft administration delayed the process. [132]

The replacement of Root by Robert Bacon delayed the departure of the commission. When approached about the commission and about Washington being a member of it, the incoming president objected to Washington "leaving this country especially at this time" since he needed him during the transitional phase of the administration. Washington felt it "unfortunate that the whole matter came up just on the eve of three changes, the change in the office of the Secretary of State, the adjournment of Congress, and the change of Presidents." Nevertheless, he believed that nothing definite would be done until the new administration settled in and gotten to work. Then, he hoped, "President Taft will change his opinion concerning my going. I have had three interviews with him on the subject and in each case he definitely and strongly objected to my leaving this country." Washington concluded with the hope that Secretary Bacon could arrange with the British ambassador for Johnston to be in Liberia when the commission finally arrived there. He also told Sir Harry that while Robert C. Ogden, a partner of John Wanamaker, had almost consented to be on the commission, he was not sure who the other members would be. [133]

After much politicking, leaking of names, and the refusal of some experienced men to go to Liberia, Ronald P. Falkner, an educator in

Puerto Rico, and George Sale, superintendent of Baptist mission schools in Puerto Rico and Cuba, were selected from the list of whites that Washington had submitted to the secretary of state. Because he could not go, Washington chose as his replacement Emmett Jay Scott, his secretary and confidant.[134] Unfortunately, these appointments and the mode of travel to Liberia stirred up racism among whites and backbiting among blacks. A number of reporters from the New York *Times,* learning that Scott was selected to go to Liberia and that he was to travel on the USS *Birmingham,* attempted to stir up the race issue. They not only objected to Scott's being appointed a commissioner but wondered aloud whether the numerous southerners on board the *Birmingham* would accept Scott's presence. A number of officers allegedly indicated that they would seek a transfer or eat below rather than sit at a table with a black man. This report led the administration to transfer the commissioners to the cruiser USS *Chester,* whose captain and other officers were very kind to Scott and his companions. Scott reported to Washington: "We have had our meals in the *Cabin mess* the Captain's sumptuous quarters [*sic*] he only has been a *fellow diner.* So much for the newspaper sensations." Later, while in Liberian waters, Scott "traveled on the *Birmingham* without racial incident."[135]

A number of African Americans charged incorrectly not only that Washington had recommended to the secretary of state a white majority of commissioners but that he had snubbed the Liberians by sending Scott to Monrovia instead of going himself. The Boston *Guardian* headlined: "LIBERIANS INSULTED BY U.S. SENDING COLORED CLERK AND UNKNOWN WHITES."[136] It was of course true that the Liberians were disappointed that Washington did not head the commission. Scott wrote to him, "I must not neglect to tell you that everyone asks for you & your failure to come is a great disappointment. Dossen & the others are here. The Legislature has been called in special session & they have appointed a *Commission* to confer with us—to prescribe us as far as they think they may. They play politics here always."[137]

Vice President Dossen was especially disappointed that Washington did not come with the commission, but he certainly understood why. He wrote Washington about a reception given for the commissioners:

> It was a gala day, the people from all parts turning out to greet the American visitors. The only regret was the absence of "Booker" as our people young and old, are fondly calling you. Ladies had made new costumes to wear on your arrival. When I arrived on the scene and told them that you would not come their hearts sunk. But I assured them that it had become impossible for you to leave President Taft's side during the first months of his

Administration, but that while you were absent in person your great heart was in the movement and that I felt that with you deeply interested in the movement, success was inevitable.[138]

The Liberians were frank with Washington about what they hoped he could do for them. In a long letter, Dossen said that the Liberians' most urgent need was for money to pay off their loan from Britain and to get rid of the English officials. He agreed that reforms were necessary but felt that the Liberians were intelligent enough to gauge which reforms were in the interest of all the people and which ones were not. The institutions of Britain and Liberia were so different that the two countries could not work together. Dossen told Washington that there was a need for immigrants and that while he respected the Tuskegean's opposition to immigration, he felt that the pressure of white emigrants in the United States might so increase prejudice toward blacks that the latter might find a better life in Africa. He concluded:

> It is from this broad, statesman-like view of the question that leaders of the race should view the question of emigration to Liberia, with the view of securing what is already Liberia's and acquiring as much more as it is possible to acquire, so as to keep in tact an outlet and a future field for the American Negro. If we let Liberia slip from our grasp we will have committed one of the greatest blunders a race can commit and one which our children will weep over in future. I shall be very pleased to exchange views with you on the subject. I may mention that in a personal letter to Mr. Taft a few months ago I pointed out this as one of Liberia's greatest needs.[139]

In general the commissioners were surprised and pleased by the way the Liberians received them but felt that they had to disabuse the ordinary folk, if not the official class, of their limited powers to influence United States policy. In a later article, "Is Liberia Worth Saving?" Scott reported that many Liberians "seemed to regard the Commission as being invested with extraordinary powers, as being in a position to settle forthwith for them all of the difficulties which had given, and were giving, them so much concern." The commissioners were compelled to assure them that they were a "Commission of Inquiry only, delegated to ascertain what measures of relief were necessary" to permit Liberia to preserve its independence. Scott added that his group did not hesitate to point out to the Liberians that "at best the Government of the United States could only help them to help themselves" and that the commission "could not and would not recommend that anything be done for them that they could do for themselves."[140]

Carefully shepherded by Lyon, the commissioners visited the disputed boundaries with Britain and France, and met with the British governor of

Sierra Leone, the German consul, and, on innumerable occasions, Liberian officials. Emmett Jay Scott was especially impressed with what he saw. As he reported to Washington: "Liberia has the richest possible possibilities if its resources can be developed. You, I feel sure, will never regret the time, money & strength you have expended to serve the little Republic. The official classes give you full credit for the Commission & your name has been toasted with Mr. Taft[']s & Mr. Barclay[']s at every reception given us." [141]

The other commissioners reportedly shared Lyon's and the Liberians' fear of British, French, and German imperialistic designs on the country. It is perhaps this concern more than any other that led them to present as the first of their recommendations that the United States help Liberia to promptly settle its pending boundary disputes. The commissioners felt that the Liberians alone could not solve this problem because they had neither the power nor the skill to withstand new aggressions against their territory. The commissioners advised that if it were not inconsonant with diplomatic usage, the United States should act as "attorney or next friend of Liberia" and bring to Liberia's negotiations with its enemies "the ability and prestige of the United States." They recommended further that American bankers grant a loan to permit Liberia to pay all of its debts so that it would be free from dependence on any colonial power; that the United States help the Liberians establish an agency to collect and control the revenues of the country for the benefit of any creditors, and for the government itself, and that this agency help to reform the internal finances of the republic; that Liberia be provided with a frontier force as well trained as the one just previously organized by Major Cadell; and that the United States aid Liberia in organizing it. [142] Then, possibly with Tuskegee in mind, the commissioners recommended that the United States "establish and maintain a research station in Liberia" to aid in the development of the agricultural and natural wealth of the country, and to inaugurate the improvements in the line of hygiene and sanitation, necessary in a tropical and insalubrious climate. Lastly, and here one sees the fine diplomatic hand of Minister Lyon, the commissioners recommended that the United States establish a naval coaling station in Liberia. [143]

Not known to neglect any issue that interested him, Washington became active as soon as the gist of the commissioners' report reached him. Using as a lever Taft's interest in retaining the support of blacks who had the franchise, Washington wrote the President on 19 November 1909:

I am very glad that you are planning to take up the matter of the report of the American Commission to Liberia at an early date. I feel quite sure that its publication will accomplish great good in calling attention to the interest of this administration in helping the little Negro Republic. There is very general interest throughout the country among the colored people and many of the white people as well, in the report which this Commission has made. This Liberian report and your interest in the National Negro Exposition project will afford opportunity for letting the colored people appreciate the interest your administration has in those matters which are of interest to them.[144]

Shortly afterward, Secretary of State Philander Chase Knox reported to the U.S. Senate that the Department of State had given careful study to the commission's recommendations and felt that the action suggested was "not only expedient but in the nature of a duty to a community which owes its existence to the United States and is the nation's ward." He said that if the president approved of its recommendations, the department was prepared to lay before the Liberian government a proposal for a treaty designed to accomplish the ends sought. Meanwhile, Knox said that Minister Ernest Lyon was on his way to Monrovia on board the cruiser *Birmingham* to sound out the Liberians on the possibilities of such a treaty.

President Taft did agree with Knox's views and, in a letter to the Senate, urged a favorable response to the recommendations the commission had presented to the Secretary of State. He added, "I cordially concur in the views of Secretary of State and trust that the policy of the United States toward Liberia will be so shaped as to fulfill our national duty to the Liberian people who, by the efforts of this Government and through the material enterprise of American citizens, were established on the African coast and set on the pathway to sovereign statehood."[145]

Unaware of the convoluted processes of the United States government's bureaucracy and under siege from the British and French, the Liberian vice president complained to Washington about the delay at the State Department. On 16 March 1910 Washington replied:

The truth of the matter is, the whole Liberian situation has moved rather slowly. In November, Dr. Lyon, Mr. Scott and I called upon the President and the Secretary of State urging that they take up the Liberian question at once. The Department, however, have just been able to get to it and Dr. Lyon is being held in America so that he may receive definite instructions before departing.

I am happy to say that I believe that matters are going to work out in an entirely satisfactory way.

Upon the same occasion as referred to above, Minister Lyon and I called upon the Secretary of the Navy and urged him to send from time to time a Government war vessel to the Liberian coast. He promised to take the matter under advisement and to do what he could in the matter. I have seen in the newspapers a report of troubles at present brewing between the natives and the Government. I hope that by this time the Government has the situation well in hand. [146]

The following day Washington wrote to Dossen reporting that while he would do all he could to get American war vessels sent to Liberian waters, it was crucially important that the Liberians themselves take the necessary steps to clear up their financial difficulties, which to him were the source of nearly all of their problems. He also tried to impress upon Dossen why it was necessary to carry out all the recommendations of the commission as soon as possible. If this could be done, Washington felt that he could "bring pressure to bear upon the State Department and President Taft in a way to hurry matters up." In conclusion, he implored Dossen:

> You must not become impatient over delays, although I know they are very embarrassing. You must bear in mind that a change in the Washington government always means that everything is thrown back and delayed, and you must also bear in mind that some Secretaries of State do not move as fast as others, although I am convinced that Mr. Knox is just as much interested in your problem as was true of Mr. Root.
> I sent you sometime ago an extract from President Taft's message to Congress bearing upon Liberia. Did you get it?
> Mr. Lyon is being detained in this country waiting for further instructions, that is, waiting until something definite is decided upon in regard to financial and other matters.
> Let me know whether I can serve you. [147]

It is also quite clear that Washington was himself getting a good education about the nature of the foreign policy process. He and Scott "threw the weight of the Tuskegee 'Machine' behind [the commission's] recommendations," because, they said, "subterranean forces are at work to prevent anything being done for Liberia." Both men had to deal with southern racism and northern isolationism which had united in opposition to the United States taking on the role of protecting Liberia. [148] On 10 April 1910, after an interview with both President Taft and Secretary of State Knox, Washington wrote to Scott, "Both are deeply interested and mean to stand by Liberia as far as they can, but of course their hands are tied by the Senate committee." [149] Taking the bit between his teeth, Washington wrote to Henry Cabot Lodge, the arch isolationist in the Senate:

> President Taft, whom I saw a few days ago, asked me to speak to you concerning Liberia. I very much hope that you can see your way clear to favor some of the suggestions which Secretary Knox has put before the Foreign Affairs Committee of the Senate in regard to Liberia. If something is

not done to help Liberia, it will be in a worse condition than it was before the American Commission visited that country. I have gone over the matter pretty fully with both the President and the Secretary of State, and they are deeply interested. The colored people in every part of this country are also deeply interested in saving and helping Liberia.

I called to see you at your residence, but you were not in. I shall be glad to talk with you further regarding the matter sometime when I am passing through Washington if it will be convenient to you.[150]

Senator Lodge was forthcoming in his response to Washington's appeal for Liberia. On 12 April 1910 he wrote Washington that the best way for the United States to help the Liberians "is to use our good offices with France and England, and Germany also, to bring about an arrangement which shall settle the boundaries, arrange for their debt and give them proper persons to train their forces."[151] Washington enclosed a copy of Lodge's response in a letter he wrote to Vice President Dossen from New York City on 19 April. He swore the Liberian to secrecy but promised not to give any encouragement to Lodge's plan without Liberian approval.[152] The Liberians, for their part, sought to explain to Washington that the reason for their boundary problem was that the Europeans were supplying the aboriginal Kroo (Kru) and Grebo populations with modern weapons. Dossen charged:

It is a disgrace to the civilization and honesty of Europe that they should have armed our natives with such arms in the face of the Brussels Act which Europe inaugurated as a means of disarming the native African and thereby destroying his amenities for warfare. But it is but another demonstration of the unjustness of the *role* pursued by the colonies of Europe in West Africa toward Liberia. What is positively a violation of that very solemn international compact and is made the subject of stringent protest when attempted to be practiced in their spheres, is carried out with impunity when it comes to Liberia. Our natives go to the coast to English, French, and German colonies for service; it is at these points they are supplied with rifles and ammunition which they oftener than not, succeed in smuggling into the country.[153]

The Liberians faced another problem when Commander Fletcher of the cruiser *Birmingham,* whom Washington had persuaded the secretary of the navy to send to their coast to help suppress local revolts, displayed a lack of confidence in them. Much to the annoyance of the Liberian government, Fletcher saw his role as arbiter between the native Africans and the settlers. When the Liberian officials rejected his services, he visited the local towns, collected information from the populations, and ignored the government. Alarmed by the implications of what appeared to be a new policy being inaugurated by the commander, Vice President

Dossen appealed to Washington to "lose no time" in trying to prevent Fletcher from poisoning the Navy Department against Liberia. Deeply distressing to Washington, however, was the insistence by the Liberians that the rebellion had to be put down "with a firm hand" so that the rebels and all others would recognize the power of the government. He had already warned the Liberians that Liberia's future hinged upon its ability to manage the native population. He felt that a concerted attempt on their part to redress the grievances of these populations was a sine qua non for both civil concord and the settlement of the chronic border disturbances.[154]

Complicating matters for both the Liberians and Washington was the news that the Taft administration was about to recall Lyon from the legation in Monrovia. Lyon appealed to Washington to try to prolong his tenure or at least to try to get him another diplomatic post. The problem was that many other blacks were seeking the Liberian position. As early as 17 May 1909 the redoubtable T. Thomas Fortune had written a pitiful letter to Washington:

> I am very well, but am prospering not a bit, and have done no work since the close of the campaign. All doors, save those of the poor house, appear to be closed against me . . . I have filed applications with the President and the secretary of state for appointment as Minister Resident and Consul General to Liberia. Mr. Lyon has been Minister for more than ten years. We have had a long string of reverends as Ministers to Liberia, who have paid more attention to the Gospel needs of their denomination than to the commercial relations of the United States and Liberia and to the resources of Liberia and to the character and capabilities of the native people. I would acquaint myself with these matters as well as encourage the Government to introduce and foster your ideal of industrial education.[155]

Washington ignored these self-serving sentiments and Fortune's promise not to ask for another favor and attempted to prolong Lyon's tenure in Monrovia. Unfortunately, he encountered stiff opposition from the Department of State, which had convinced the president that the minister should be replaced. On 11 June 1910 Washington wrote Lyon, "All that could be done in the way of staying your removal was done, but when the Department got to the place where it would simply state that it could not ignore some of the charges that had been brought against you, I was put in a position of not being able to do anything, especially when I could not learn what the charges were."[156] A careful search of the archives of the State Department does not reveal the nature of the charges against Lyon. For what it is worth, the oral tradition among the people of Baltimore is that when Lyon returned from Monrovia, he was, or became, a notorious philanderer and alcoholic.

Given the State Department's strong views about Lyon, the best that Washington could do was to support William Demosthenes Crum as the new envoy to Liberia. This choice did not please the African American community because it appeared to have been made to get the president off the hook. It had been bruited about that Taft, unlike Theodore Roosevelt, heeded the opposition of southerners and did not wish to reappoint Crum to the post of collector of the port of Charleston. Washington had apparently tried and failed to prevent Crum's dismissal and had warned him of the consequences of not submitting a letter of resignation when Roosevelt left the presidency. Now the quid pro quo was obviously the Liberian post.[157]

William Demosthenes Crum was born free in Charleston, South Carolina, in 1859, the son of a black woman and a white man, Darius Crum, whose father (originally Krum) had migrated to the United States from Germany in the nineteenth century. Darius had inherited a plantation near Orangeburg and about forty slaves, and had lived there with his black wife, Charlotte, and their seven children until the end of the Civil War. Although Darius had died almost penniless, leaving his family to fend for themselves, young William was able to attend the Avery Normal Institute with funds supplied by his elder brothers who had migrated to the North. William graduated in 1875 and briefly attended the then-integrated University of South Carolina before entering Howard University Medical School, where he received an M.D. degree in 1880. A racial accomodationist (said by some to have been a "tragic mulatto"), Crum established a medical practice in Charleston and in 1883 married Ellen Craft, the daughter of two prominent escaped slaves. He became active in Republican politics, involved himself in local educational and religious affairs, and in 1894 even ran for the Senate against Benjamin R. Tillman, an avowed racist.[158]

First proposed for the office of postmaster for the port of Charleston by President Benjamin Harrison in 1892, Crum did not receive that position until Roosevelt overcame Senate opposition to have him confirmed in 1905. He remained in that post until Taft forced him out and Washington got him the position in Liberia. Washington took care to alert the mild-mannered minister-elect to the diplomatic hazards of Monrovia. On 13 June 1910 he wrote Crum, "When you go to Monrovia, I very much hope that you will bear in mind that Bishop I. B. Scott, whom you will find there, is one of our warmest and best friends. He has been

of the greatest service to us here, and to your friends and our friends."
The Tuskegean warned, "[There] are certain cliques in Monrovia that
will likely try to alienate you from the Bishop. But I have known him for
twenty years, and during all this time he has proven a staunch, sincere
friend, that you can depend on in season and out of season."[159]

Meanwhile, at home, Washington and Emmett Jay Scott closely monitored the debate about the Liberian bill in the Senate. On 20 June 1910
Washington reported to Scott that Secretary of State Knox had discussed
Liberia at the University of Pennsylvania and had "said in effect that the
State Department had decided to carry out practically all the recommendations made by the Commission."[160] Both men attempted to secure the
implementation of those parts of the commission's recommendations
that did not especially need congressional approval. One of these was the
recommendation that three black officers or noncommissioned officers
from the United States Army be sent to retrain Liberia's constabulary or
frontier force. Washington was sure that given the lack of opportunities
for blacks in the military at that time, service in Liberia "would be
peculiarly attractive to such men and offer them, . . . opportunities for
more rapid advancement in their profession than could be hoped for at
home."[161]

The officer chosen for this job was Benjamin O. Davis of the Negro
Ninth Cavalry, who had just completed the customary four years' college duty at Wilberforce University. He accepted the offer rather than
return to his regiment because, he said, "if I can be of service to the
United States in this capacity, I am willing to undertake the work."
Unfortunately, Davis fell ill with blackwater fever shortly after he arrived in Monrovia. He was recalled in 1911 but was able to give the
general staff recommendations about the military situation in Liberia.
Davis felt that the country needed a force of about fifteen hundred men
and "at least four trained officers, preferably from the [United States]
regular army." Nevertheless, this experience convinced him that the
Liberians would be leery of instituting such major changes, and he
warned that unless the United States insisted that the Liberians put the
agreement in writing, any military advisors would be frustrated.[162]

Reports from Liberia indicated that the government was leery of the
appointment of a customs advisor. Having been badly burned when they
abandoned their traditional caution and permitted Britishers to get too
involved in their government, the Liberians resisted permitting anyone
else, even an American, to do so. Moreover, they were smarting over the
news that both Europeans and Americans were discussing whether the

terms of the commission's recommendations meant that Liberia had not, in fact, become a United States colony or protectorate. The Liberians especially wanted to ascertain that the person being proposed by the United States to oversee their customs was not a racist. When George Augustus Finch, who had served as secretary of the commission to Liberia, heard that Reed Paige Clark, a clerk of various Senate committees, was being considered for the post, he immediately sought to have him meet with Washington. Finch had reported to Scott that "Mr. Clark rightly believes that his prestige in Liberia will be greatly enhanced if he should make the acquaintance of Dr. Washington before he goes down."[163] Washington agreed to have Clark meet with him at his summer home in Fort Salonga, Long Island, toward the end of August, and apparently was quite impressed with him. In a personal and confidential letter to Crum, he wrote:

> Mr. Reed Paige Clark, the new Receiver General and Customs Officer for Liberia, spent a day with me here yesterday at my summer home, and we talked about Liberia. Mr. Clark is a young man from Vermont [actually New Hampshire], but has had much experience in the State and other departments at Washington. In my opinion he is thoroughly equipped for his work, and I feel pretty sure that you will like him. He is thoroughly without race prejudice so far as I can discover. I hope that you and your other friends in Liberia will give him a hearty reception. As I understand it, he plans to reach there sometime in October or November.[164]

Washington also asked Crum to recommend that the Liberian government give Finch "some kind of decoration." He said that Finch, who was then with the Carnegie Peace Foundation in Washington, D.C., allowed "no opportunity slip by to manifest his deep interest in Liberia." Moreover it was largely through Finch's "reminding of the Department and constantly urging and advice that matters [such as the appointment of Clark] have been brought to their present point."[165]

Washington also supported Clark for the position of customs adviser in a letter to Daniel Edward Howard, a Liberian politician and future president, in which he reported having received an offer of some $15,000 from a philanthropist to build an industrial school in Liberia if that country would donate land for it. He extolled Clark's experience "in the departments at Washington," noting also that during the preceding eight or nine months the young man had been making a thorough preparation for his work in Liberia. Washington concluded, "I think you will like Mr. Clark. He is certainly thoroughly in earnest, and is without race prejudice." He also admitted to Howard that "matters regarding Liberia have moved so slowly in this country, but you can easily understand that with all the work that is going on in Washington that everything moves slowly." Nevertheless, he assured him that a number of persons, himself included, "have kept the interests of Liberia constantly before the Department and it looks now as if matters are coming out all right."[166]

Even before Clark left Washington to take up his assignment in Monrovia, he wrote to Tuskegee seeking Washington's advice about "the appointment of a military attaché at Monrovia to aid in the reorganization of the Liberian Constabulary, or Frontier Police." Clark reported his discussion of this appointment with the War Department:

> There seems to be one colored officer on the active list of the Army who is especially well fitted for the work and that is Captain Charles Young, Ninth Cavalry, U.S.A., (now at Fort D. A. Russell, Wyoming), who was recently attached to our legation at Port au Prince, Haiti. He has made an admirable record and is apparently just the man for a position where considerable tact and great executive ability are required. Captain Young is a graduate of West Point. He was highly recommended by Mr. Justice Stewart, of the Liberian Supreme Court, who was in Washington last week.
>
> If you care to write to Captain Young, whom you probably know, and to enlist his active interest in Liberia I shall be very grateful, as I am anxious to have the reorganization of the Constabulary proceed in an orderly manner and with the minimum of delay.[167]

In fact, it was W. E. B. Du Bois who first called Washington's attention to Captain Young. On 6 April 1896 (just one year after he had congratulated Washington for making the "Compromise" speech in Atlanta), Du Bois had written Washington inviting him to be his guest when visiting Wilberforce University the following June. Du Bois lamented that he had no appropriate quarters, but said, "My friend however, Lieutenant Young of the U.S. Army, and [his] mother, cordially unite in inviting you thro' me to be their and my guest at their residence. Answer at your convenience and let us know when you arrive that we may meet you."[168] Washington did receive an honorary master of arts degree from Wilberforce that summer and had kept track of Young's activities.

As it turned out, some eight months before Clark's letter to Washington about Young, the young captain had himself written to Tuskegee from Fort Sam Houston, Texas, on 3 April 1911. He reported to Washington that while each was busy in his own way, they had "the same goal, that of doing something for our own people, for the benefit finally of our country and its welfare, which we all wish for." But the reason for the letter was that Young wanted to allay any anxiety Washington may have had about the behavior of the Ninth Cavalry in San Antonio. Young specified: "The conduct of the soldiers has been exemplary, notwithstanding any reports of newspapers, relative to their disregard of the jim-crow laws or to drunken brawling." Young insisted that both officers and men had admirably succeeded in preventing trouble; that they and the colored people recognized that if the right to be a soldier was taken away from blacks, the result would be their relegation to "a lower caste, far lower than even slavery ever entailed"; and that the lies in the papers about black soldiers were "simply echoes of Brownsville, no more." Obviously aware of Washington's role in attempting to calm a black community that was furious about Roosevelt's and Taft's brutal treatment of the black soldiers involved in the Brownsville affair, Young pleaded with Washington to "speak to the President and to our friends who have faith in us and our ideals, and tell them what I have assured you of in all truth and honesty."[169]

Washington readily assented to Clark's request concerning Young, and queried the cavalry captain about serving in Liberia. Young agreed to serve because, he told Washington, "I am always willing to aid in any work for the good of the country in general and our racc in particular, whether that race be found in Africa or in the United States."[170] Washington responded: "You will have a splendid opportunity I think, to render service in a particular most needed in that important field."[171]

While it was relatively easy for Washington and his friends to gain the appointment of a customs advisor and a military attaché for Liberia, it was more difficult for them to get the Senate to deal with the commission's recommendation for economic assistance. As early as September 1909 Washington doubted that Liberia would ever get substantial aid from the United States government and he sought help from the American private sector. Washington wrote the New York banker Isaac N. Seligman inquiring whether it was possible to "find parties in New York who would like to take up the Liberian debt." Seligman was interested but nothing came of it. Washington received more consideration from Paul M. Warburg, who was a trustee of Tuskegee and a partner in the banking firm of Kuhn, Loeb, and Company. Warburg reportedly "took a philanthropic view" of the matter and in a letter to Secretary of State Philander Chase Knox in November 1909 confessed, "Our associates and we hardly look upon this small transaction as a matter of business, but we rather consider it from the point of view, of attempting to assist that Republic in its struggle to free itself from the oppressive influences, which are well known to you."[172] However, at this time still nothing came of this effort.

Washington was especially concerned about what he considered to be Liberia's apparent failure to "accumulate their own capital by heroic measures of self-denial and enterprise." He sensed only dimly the process by which Liberia was being "underdeveloped" as it was being incorporated into the global economy and firmly believed that self-help and hard work constituted the road to prosperity.[173] In a letter to J. L. Morris, editor of the Monrovia *Liberian Register,* on 5 January 1911 Washington wrote:

> A nation must export more than it imports or financial disaster follows. This means but one thing, that the Liberian people should try to get their living out of the natural resources of their country instead of depending to any extend upon the resources of foreign countries. Every time a Liberian eats a tin of canned goods imported from any other country, it means poverty for the Liberians, it means that the Liberians are paying somebody else to manufacture the tin cans, . . . and paying the freight upon the cans, and all this of course means money taken out of Liberia. . . . All this means another thing, and that is, that a large proportion of the brightest men and women should receive scientific, technical and industrial education in order to enable them to understand and master these natural resources.[174]

Washington recognized that while he was willing to try to help the Liberians by influencing United States policy toward their homeland, they had to rely on themselves if they would preserve the independence of their country. He also realized that for historical reasons, to "a very marked degree the hundred and thirty millions of black people outside of America are looking to the ten millions of Negroes in the United States for guidance and inspiration." Washington believed that these blacks were watching closely to see whether African Americans "surrounded by modern machinery and all the other forces of civilisation" could adapt to their new environment and not only advance but also help Africa. He was convinced that if African Americans could make progress, the other blacks in the global system would believe that it was "also possible for them, in time, to follow, somewhat more slowly, perhaps, but in the same direction."[175]

Notes

1. Kelly Miller, quoted in Willard B. Gatewood, Jr., *Black Americans and the White Man's Burden, 1898–1903* (Urbana: University of Illinois Press, 1975), 222.
2. Ernest Lyon to Booker T. Washington, 10 August 1907, *The Booker T. Washington Papers,* ed. Louis R. Harlan and Raymond W. Smock (Urbana: University of Illinois Press, 1981), 9:332 (hereafter cited as *BTW Papers*).
3. BTW to Lyon, 28 September 1907, ibid., 341.

4. Gatewood, *Black Americans, passim.*
5. Theodore Roosevelt, like many American imperialists, admired Rudyard Kipling. See Gatewood, *Black Americans,* vii, 20. Cf. Howard K. Beale, *Theodore Roosevelt and the Rise of America to World Power* (New York: Collier, 1956), 36–37, 39, 156.
6. E. Don Carlos Bassett, "Should Haiti Be Annexed by the United States?" *Voice of the Negro* 1 (May 1904): 198, quoted in Gatewood, *Black Americans,* 13.
7. Frederick Douglass to Caesar Celso Moreno, March 1894, in Foner, *Life and Writings of Douglass* 4:490, quoted in ibid., 14.
8. *Broad-Axe* (St. Paul), 17 July 1897, quoted in ibid., 15.
9. *BTW Papers* 4:460.
10. *A.M.E. Church Review,* October 1899, quoted in George P. Marks, ed., *The Black Press Views American Imperialism, 1898–1900* (New York: Arno Press, 1971), 154.
11. Beno von Herman auf Wain to BTW, 3 September 1900, *BTW Papers* 5:633ff.
12. Ibid.
13. Ibid., 639.
14. James Nathan Calloway to BTW, 3 February 1901, *BTW Papers* 6:26–27.
15. Shepherd Lincoln Harris to BTW, 15 May 1901, ibid., 110–11.
16. Emmett Jay Scott to BTW, 24 June 1902, ibid., 488–89; Harlan, "Booker T. Washington," 445–47.
17. Harlan, "Booker T. Washington," 445.
18. Henry Francis Downing to BTW, 2 September 1902, *BTW Papers* 6:506–7.
19. Harlan, "Booker T. Washington," 447.
20. BTW to Hunt, 19 January 1904, *BTW Papers* 7:403.
21. Hunt to BTW, 3 February 1904, ibid., 425.
22. BTW to Hunt, 3 June 1904, ibid., 520–21.
23. BTW to Cain Washington Triplett and Others, 12 December 1904, ibid. 8:153–54.
24. Booker T. Washington, N. B. Wood, and Fannie Barrier Williams, *A New Negro for a New Century* (New York: Arno Press and the New York Times, 1969), 50ff.
25. Theodore Roosevelt to BTW, 10 November 1901, *BTW Papers* 5:673.
26. Roosevelt to BTW, 14 November 1901, *BTW Papers* 6:206.
27. Rayford W. Logan, *The Betrayal of the Negro* (New York: Collier Books, 1965), 88.
28. Ibid., 100.
29. Roosevelt to Henry White, 30 March 1896, in Elting E. Morison, ed. *The Letters of Theodore Roosevelt* (Cambridge: Harvard University Press, 1951–55), 1:523; Thomas G. Dyer, *Theodore Roosevelt and the Idea of Race* (Baton Rouge: Louisiana State University Press, 1980), xii-xiii, 168–69; Seth M. Scheiner, "President Theodore Roosevelt and the Negro, 1901–1908," *Journal of Negro History* 47 (1962): 169–82.
30. Beale, *Theodore Roosevelt and America,* 147ff.
31. Henry McNeal Turner to BTW, 5 November 1901, *BTW Papers* 6:287.
32. Benito Sylvain to BTW, 21 October 1901, ibid., 261.
33. John Elmer Milholland to BTW, 30 April 1901, ibid., 99–101.
34. BTW to Roosevelt, 6 November 1901, ibid., 289.
35. Scott to BTW, 17 July 1902, ibid., 495.
36. BTW to Roosevelt, 1 December 1902, ibid., 600–601.

37. Owen Smith to Department of State, 4 February 1902, no. 176, Despatches from U.S. Ministers to Liberia, 1863–1906, Record Group 59, National Archives, roll 13.
38. John R. A. Crossland to Department of State, 6 October 1902, no. 12.
39. *American Colonization Society Bulletin* 22 (February 1903): 76.
40. BTW to Roosevelt, 24 January 1903, *BTW Papers* 7:11.
41. Edwin S. Redkey, *Black Exodus: Black Nationalist and Back-to-Africa Movements, 1890–1910* (New Haven: Yale University Press, 1969), 272–73. According to Redkey, "Lyon, a Methodist pastor and a protégé of Booker T. Washington had worked vigorously in Republican campaigns, and at Washington's suggestion had received the coveted Liberian post from President Theodore Roosevelt" (see also *Who's Who in America, 1914–1915,* 1467).
42. Lyon to J. Hay, U.S. Secretary of State, 1 August 1903, no. 4, U.S. Ministers to Liberia, roll 13, and Lyon to Hay, 20 August 1903, no. 8.
43. Ibid.
44. BTW to Timothy Thomas Fortune, 15 June 1902, *BTW Papers* 6:481.
45. *West Africa,* 3 April 1901, 926.
46. Lyon to Department of State, 23 September 1903, no. 11, U.S. Ministers to Liberia, roll 13.
47. Lyon to Department of State, 14 June 1904.
48. Lyon to Department of State, 15 February 1904. In one of his first cables to the department, Lyon reported that despite the grave problems of boundary settlement "between England on the one side and France especially on the other side," France, Germany, and Great Britain were taking an unusual interest in the inauguration ceremonies of President-elect Arthur Barclay by sending "special Representatives from each country." This he felt was not only in stark contrast to the lack of such representation from the United States but confirmed "the impressions the inhuman practice of lynching and burning Negroes in the United States have upon this and other governments abroad, with regard to the treatment accorded to this particular class of citizens."
49. Lyon to Department of State, 1 September 1903, no. 62.
50. Ibid.
51. Lyon to Department of State, 11 November 1905, no. 56.
52. Ibid.
53. Lyon to Department of State, 2 March 1905, no. 15.
54. Second Assistant Secretary's Room, Department of State, Memorandum of 11 November 1905.
55. Ibid.
56. Department of State to Lyon, 9 November 1905, no. 65.
57. Lyon to Department of State, 18 December 1905, no. 142.
58. Ibid.
59. W. E. F. Ward, "The Colonial Phase in British West Africa," in J. F. Ade Ajayi and Ian Espie, eds., *A Thousand Years of West African History* (London: Ibadan University Press, 1965), 386.
60. Emmett J. Scott, "Is Liberia Worth Saving?" *Journal of Race Development* 1 (January 1911): 288ff.
61. Letter from American Consul in Sierra Leone, W. J. Yerby to Robert Bacon, Asst. Secretary of State, 24 December 1906.
62. Lyon to Department of State, 26 January 1907, no. 223.
63. Scott, "Is Liberia Worth Saving?" 288; George W. Ellis, "Dynamic Factors in the Liberian Situation," *Journal of Race Development* 1 (January 1911): 268–69.

64. Ellis, "Liberian Situation," 268–69.
65. Scott, "Is Liberia Worth Saving?" 291.
66. Lyon to Department of State, 14 January 1907, re Note from British Consulate, Monrovia (Braithwait Wallis to President of Liberia).
67. Department of State, Washington, to Whitelaw Reid, American Ambassador, London 630, 2 February 1907.
68. Lyon to BTW, 10 August 1907, *BTW Papers* 9:332.
69. Ibid.
70. BTW to Lyon, 18 September 1907, ibid., 336–37.
71. BTW to Roosevelt, 19 September 1907, ibid., 337.
72. BTW to Lyon, 28 September 1907, ibid., 341.
73. Lyon to Department of State, 7 December 1907, no. 213, Department of State Numerical File, 1906–10, Record Group 59, National Archives (hereafter abbreviated RG 59, NA).
74. Lyon to Department of State, 8 December 1907, no. 214.
75. Lyon to Department of State, 4 January 1908, no. 216.
76. Ellis, "Liberian Situation," 269–70.
77. Lyon to Department of State, 4 January 1908, no. 217, RG 59, NA.
78. Lyon to Department of State, 25 January 1908, no. 219, 3531/2–3.
79. Lyon to Department of State, 5 February 1908, no. 223.
80. Ellis, "Liberia Situation," 270–71.
81. Lyon to Department of State, 27 January 1907.
82. BTW to Roosevelt, 21 March 1908, *BTW Papers* 9:476.
83. Ibid.
84. BTW to Roosevelt, 12 April 1908, ibid., 498–99.
85. Roosevelt to BTW, 14 April 1908, ibid., 499.
86. BTW to Lyon, 12 May 1908, ibid., 535–36.
87. Cited from *William Howard Taft Papers* in ibid., 542.
88. Ibid.
89. BTW to Charles Knowles Bolton, 12 May 1908, ibid., 534–35.
90. BTW to Lyon, ibid., 548–49.
91. Ibid.
92. C. R. Branch to BTW, 12 June 1908, 9:572. Dossen wrote BTW on 3 July 1908 stating that he hoped that "some action" would be taken in Liberia to "record the nation's appreciation" of what Washington had accomplished (ibid., 589).
93. Branch to BTW, 12 June 1908, ibid., 572.
94. BTW to P. O. Gray, ibid., 575–76. A copy is in 794, 12083/50, RG 59, NA.
95. Quoted in Harlan, "Booker T. Washington," 454, from Scott to Washington, undated [late September 1908] in *BTW Papers*. See also Roosevelt to Ray Stannard Baker, 3 June 1908, and to Johnston, 11 July 1908, in Morison, *The Letters of Theodore Roosevelt* 6:1048, 1125.
96. Memo from Adee to Secretary of State, 24 March 1908, 794, 12083/50, RG 59, NA, cited in Harlan, "Booker T. Washington," 454.
97. Cited in ibid., 455. Memo from Adee to Bacon, 10 November 1908, 794, 12083/50, RG 59, NA.
98. Harlan, "Booker T. Washington," 454.
99. Cited in *BTW Papers* 9:578. The original is in the 794, 12083/30, RG 59, NA.
100. Ibid.
101. Ibid.
102. Elihu Root to BTW, 19 June 1908, *BTW Papers* 9:584. The American ambassador referred to was none other than Whitelaw Reid (1837–1912) who earlier

declined to receive a Liberian president who was visiting London. Reid had been editor of the New York *Tribune* (1872–1905) and U.S. ambassador to Great Britain (1905–12).

103. James Jenkins Dossen to BTW, Hamburg, 1 August 1908, ibid., 610–11.
104. Lyon to BTW, 19 September 1908, ibid., 625–27.
105. Ibid.
106. BTW to Dossen, 1 October 1908, *BTW Papers* 9:629–31.
107. Ibid.
108. Ibid.
109. Ibid.
110. BTW to Dossen, 12 December 1908, ibid., 698–99.
111. BTW to Secretary of State Root, 14 December 1908, ibid., 699–700.
112. Root to BTW, ibid., 703. See also 794, 12083/60, RG 59, NA.
113. Seth Low to Root, *BTW Papers* 9:702–3. See also 794, 12083/60, RG 59, NA.
114. BTW to Dossen, 7 January 1909, *BTW Papers* 10:5–6.
115. Ibid.
116. Ibid.
117. BTW to Roosevelt, 18 January 1909, cited from the *William Howard Taft Papers* in *BTW Papers* 10:14–15.
118. Roosevelt to William Howard Taft, 20 January 1909, *William Howard Taft Papers,* cited in ibid., 15–16.
119. Fortune to Scott, 23 January 1909, cited in ibid., 16–17.
120. Fortune to BTW, ibid., 82–83.
121. BTW to Harry Hamilton Johnston, 10 February 1909, *BTW Papers* 10:28–29.
122. "Affairs in Liberia," Message from the President of the United States, 61st Cong., 2d sess., S. Doc. 457, 25 March 1910, 24.
123. Lyon to Secretary of State, 24 December 1908, no. 257, RG 59, NA.
124. Lyon to Secretary of State, 4 February 1909, no. 268.
125. Ibid.
126. Lyon to Department of State, 11 February 1909, no. 269; 25 February 1909, no. 275.
127. Archibald Butt, *The Letters of Archibald Butt* (New York: Doubleday, Page, 1925), 341–42, quoted in *BTW Papers* 10:29.
128. Ibid.
129. BTW to Bacon, 16 February 1909, ibid., 40–41.
130. BTW to Low, 16 February 1909, ibid., 41.
131. BTW to Dossen, 19 February 1909, ibid., 42.
132. BTW to Johnston, 28 February 1909, ibid., 58–59.
133. Ibid.
134. Harlan, "Booker T. Washington," 455.
135. Scott to BTW, 3 May 1909, *BTW Papers* 10:94–96.
136. Harlan, Booker T. Washington," 456.
137. Scott to BTW, 14 May 1909, *BTW Papers* 10:99–102.
138. Dossen to BTW, 15 May 1909, ibid., 104–6.
139. Ibid. Dossen was also busily involved in sending Liberian students to Tuskegee for training and wrote BTW that he was "sending shortly another young man to be included in the number you promised me to take from Liberia." He also wondered whether Washington thought it wise to confer "the Liberian Order of African Redemption on ex-President Roosevelt and Ex-Secretary of State Root in recognition of their services to Liberia? Write me promptly your views on this point."

140. Scott, "Is Liberia Worth Saving?" 278–79.
141. Scott to BTW, 6 June 1909, *BTW Papers* 10:133.
142. Scott, "Is Liberia Worth Saving?" 298–301.
143. Ibid.
144. BTW to Taft, 19 November 1909, *BTW Papers* 10:237.
145. Message from the President of the United States, transmitting a letter of the Secretary of State submitting a report of the Commission which visited Liberia in pursuance of the provisions of the Deficiency Act of 4 March 1909, "to investigate the interests of the United States and its citizens in the Republic of Liberia, with the consent of the authorities of said Republic," *Foreign Affairs of the United States,* "Affairs in Liberia," 61st Cong., 2d sess., S. Doc. 457, 25 March 1910, 1, 11.
146. BTW to Dossen, 16 March 1910, *BTW Papers* 10:279.
147. Ibid, 280–81.
148. Harlan, "Booker T. Washington," 456.
149. Ibid., 457.
150. BTW to Henry Cabot Lodge, 10 April 1910, BTW Papers 10:317.
151. Lodge to BTW, 12 April 1910, ibid., 321.
152. BTW to Dossen, 19 April 1910, ibid., 321.
153. Dossen to BTW, 3 May 1910, ibid., 324–27.
154. Ibid.
155. Fortune to BTW, 17 May 1909, ibid., 109–10.
156. BTW to Lyon, 11 June 1910, ibid., 336.
157. See *passim* Ellen A. Craft Crum to BTW, 13 February 1909, ibid., 39–40; William Demosthenes Crum to Roosevelt, 27 February 1909, ibid., 57; BTW to Lyon, 11 June 1910, ibid., 336.
158. For biographical data on William Demosthenes Crum see *BTW Papers* 6:147–48, and Rayford W. Logan and Michael R. Winston, *Dictionary of American Negro Biography* (New York: W. W. Norton, 1982), 144.
159. BTW to Crum, 13 June 1910, *BTW Papers* 10:337.
160. BTW to Scott, 20 June 1910, ibid., 340.
161. Marvin Fletcher, *The Black Soldier and Officer in the United States Army, 1891–1917* (Columbia: University of Missouri Press, 1974), 92–93.
162. Ibid., 93–94.
163. George Augustus Finch to Scott, 2 August 1911, *BTW Papers* 11:292–93.
164. BTW to Finch, 8 August 1911, ibid., 292; BTW to Crum, 26 August 1911, ibid., 297.
165. Ibid.
166. BTW to Daniel Edward Howard, 26 August 1911, ibid., 298–99.
167. Reed Paige Clark to BTW, 10 November 1911, ibid., 363–64.
168. William E. B. Du Bois to BTW, 6 April 1896, *BTW Papers* 4:158.
169. Charles Young to BTW, 3 April 1911, ibid. 11:77–78.
170. Young to BTW, 24 November 1911, ibid., 377.
171. BTW to Young, 1 December 1911, ibid., 379.
172. Harlan, "Booker T. Washington," 458.
173. Ibid.
174. BTW to J. L. Morris, editor of *Monrovia Liberian Register,* 5 January 1911, *BTW Papers* 10:531–32.
175. Booker T. Washington, *The Story of the Negro: The Rise of the Race From Slavery* (New York: Negro Universities Press, [1969]), 1:33–35.

9

The Imperative of Unity: "The Tie That Binds"

> There is . . . a tie which few white men can understand, which
> binds the American Negro to the African Negro; which unites the
> black man of Brazil and the black man of Liberia; which is con-
> stantly drawing into closer relations all the scattered African peo-
> ples whether they are in the old world or the new.
>
> There is not only the tie of race, which is strong in any case, but
> there is the bond of colour, which is specially important in the case
> of the black man. It is this common badge of colour, for instance,
> which is responsible for the fact that whatever contributes, in any
> degree to the progress of the American Negro, contributes to the
> progress of the African Negro, and to the Negro in South America
> and the West Indies. When the African Negro succeeds, it helps the
> American Negro. When the African Negro fails, it hurts the reputa-
> tion and the standing of the Negro in every part of the world."
> (Booker T. Washington)[1]

While Booker T. Washington's accommodationist policies did permit
him to use his good offices to persuade the United States to help Liberia,
the whole thrust of President Taft's domestic and foreign policy did not
auger well either for blacks or their foreign policy concerns. The president's "southern policy" removed many of Washington's friends from
power. The administration's foreign policy as articulated by Secretary of
State Philander Chase Knox—that all disputes should be subjected to
international arbitration—placed Liberia in jeopardy. And while these
views were shared by Congress, they created anxieties among African
Americans and Liberians. African Americans were also being drawn
into the spate of local, state, national, and international peace associations that were springing up all over the country and Europe. Some may
even have shared the sentiments of the anti-imperialist movement, the
American Peace Society of William Lloyd Garrison, which preached,
"My country is the world, my countrymen all mankind." But most knew
better. The steady aggression of Europeans against Liberia, the steady
increase of lynching in the South, and the general pattern of discrimina-

349

tion and segregation experienced by African peoples the world over caused many of them to cling to the banner of race.[2]

Given the difficulties in persuading the United States to make an unequivocal commitment to Liberia, Booker T. Washington remained skeptical whether blacks could rely upon the help of sympathetic friends to challenge European and American hegemony in the world. Since 1908 he had expended a great deal of time and energy helping Liberia deal with European imperialism, and while many contemporary blacks knew this, and some of them applauded his efforts, Washington kept his own counsel and followed his own agenda. He would do what he could, recognizing that blacks had limited political power and often had to use symbolic structures to achieve their goals. This policy did not always satisfy his admirers.

For example, a number of South African blacks, beginning with AME Church contacts, had been attempting to globalize their plight and wished to enlist his aid. Pixley ka Isaka Seme from Zululand, who had graduated from Columbia College in New York City in 1903 and had been in contact with Washington since 1906, wrote to him from London about the formation of a club or society of African students in Great Britain for "interchange of ideas." Seme pointed out that in England at that time were to be found "the future leaders of African nations temporarily thrown together and yet coming from widely different sections of that great and unhappy continent and that these men will, in due season, return each to a community that eagerly awaits him and perhaps influence its public opinion." He felt it necessary to point out that "violence in word or deed" had no place in the program of the society and sought to convince Washington that "our programme is very simple but I believe that in God's time this movement will prove very eventful toward bringing about the 'regeneration of Africa'."[3] Washington's response was cautious and reflected his view of global power relations:

> I am sure that English statesmen, the men whose counsels will finally prevail, believe as you and I do, that in the long run Africa can prosper only on condition that, not only the riches of the soil and the mines but the latent powers of the native people are developed in a rational manner. What that implies is a practical problem that can only be solved by study and experiment. You can and should help in the solution of that problem and there are ways that you can be helpful, as no one else can, both to your own people and to the government. More and more I am learning that you face in South Africa, in a somewhat different and more difficult form, the same task we have in this country.[4]

Seme, who even at this time was more eager to challenge English statesmen than to trust their counsel, was apparently disappointed with

Washington's reply. Nevertheless, he still valued contact with the Tuskegean. He wrote a letter to him introducing an American friend and colleague, Alain LeRoy Locke, who was returning home after attending Oxford as the first African American Rhodes Scholar to go there and was "seriously contemplating race work."[5] But when Seme met Washington in London in 1910 and advocated that Americans play a more active role in African affairs, the Tuskegean did not agree. Later Seme sought to make amends by writing to Washington: "I shall always regret that our meeting in London had to be marred by incidents of a personal character . . . Africa is certainly awakening mighty and hopeful. I know that it will be a great cause of inspiration and encouragement to us if you could enlist your interest to our course." Seme had no way of knowing that his hopes for South African blacks would take many decades to be realized, and whether Washington suspected as much will never be known. He simply replied to Seme that he was "sorry that our meeting in London was not more satisfactory than it was."[6]

Washington encountered opposition from many Africans and African Americans who either did not know what he was doing or distrusted his approach to both international and domestic relations, perhaps because of what they felt was his tendency to excuse the behavior of whites in order to maintain his influence in American society. There is no doubt that there was some validity to the views of his critics. He made an extensive tour of Europe during the summer of 1910 "to compare the position of the people there with that of the Southern Negro." His observations were trenchant, and, perhaps as he had expected, he found the position of many of the people there vastly inferior to that of American blacks.

What led to a great deal of controversy both in London and elsewhere was that he was quoted as stating, "There is progress, both moral and material, to report in the condition of the negro, and there is also an improvement in the relations between the two races. People in Europe always hear the worst. You do not hear of progress as quickly as you do of lynchings."[7] The problem for Washington, however, was that the forces and individuals that would ultimately challenge and erode European domination of the globe were already gathering and would challenge his type of leadership.

Increasingly, he felt the competition of such persons as Dr. W. E. B. Du Bois of the National Association of Colored People (NAACP), Professor Kelly Miller of Howard University, and William Monroe Trotter, publisher of the Boston *Guardian*.[8] Primarily because he refused to subject himself unnecessarily to criticism of his leadership, Washington declined an invitation to return to Europe in 1911 to attend an International Races Congress held in London. In attendance were such formidable American liberals as Dr. Franz Boas of Columbia University, Dr. Alfred L. Kroeber from the University of California at Berkeley, and W. E. B. Du Bois. Washington would certainly have found himself among high-powered intellectuals. There is no record whether he sought the advice either of the State Department or President Taft about attending the conference or whether it was Du Bois's name on the list of speakers that discouraged him.[9] Nevertheless, his intelligence system carefully monitored the plans for the conference and kept him informed.

On 13 May 1911 Robert Russa Moton, a longtime protégé who had been contemplating going to the congress wrote to say, "I am convinced that Dr. Du Bois, [Miss] Milholland and Miss Ovington will do everything they can in London this summer to undo the good that you did last year. I have made up my mind that I will go any how now. I wish there were a half dozen or more going. I think we better move together and I hope you will use me in any way you can."[10] Washington urged Moton to go to London along with the other members of the Tuskegee cabal who were attending and offered to give him letters of introduction to several English friends. He observed that since the Anti-Slavery Society, which normally took the lead in matters dealing with race, was having no part in the congress, he would not be surprised if nothing came of it. Moreover, he said that some of his London friends had predicted that the whole affair was going to be disappointing, though he cautioned Moton that these views might well be mistaken.[11]

Writing to Washington from London on 23 July 1911, Moton reported, "There is quite a little interest in the congress in certain quarters. It ought to do some good." He said that he and Du Bois had had a frank discussion about Washington and that while Du Bois felt that Washington's racial strategy had failed and that things had become progressively worse for blacks, this was said in quite an impersonal and very dignified manner. Moreover, when Du Bois referred to Washington at the conference, it was as "the *leading educator* of the *race* and of the *present generation.*"[12]

Reflecting on this congress years later, Du Bois admitted that he was then under a great deal of pressure to attack Washington but that the Tuskegean also had his admirers. These included an American woman who had unsuccessfully tried to prevent Du Bois from speaking at the London Lyceum Club. For his part, Du Bois had welcomed the opportunity to meet so many of the important black leaders in the world, including such South Africans as the Reverend Walter Rubasana and J. Tengo Jabavu. He concluded that the conference was "a great and inspiring occasion bringing together representatives of numerous ethnic and cultural groups and bringing new and frank conceptions of scientific bases of racial and social relations of people."[13] It ranked as the "greatest event of the twentieth century and far . . . more significant than the Russian-Japanese War, the Hague Conference or the rise of Socialism." Du Bois was convinced that the congress "would have marked an epoch in the racial history of the world if it had not been for the World War."[14]

Apparently stimulated by the International Congress of Races and the general peace movement, and eager to retain his position in the field of African affairs, Washington issued a call in March 1911 for an International Conference on the Negro to be held at Tuskegee, Alabama, 17–19 April 1912. Since 1905 Robert E. Park had been suggesting such a conference, but Washington had been too busy with his work at Tuskegee to comply. Now he claimed that for some years he had had in mind to invite to Tuskegee a number of persons from Europe, Africa, and the West Indies who were "actively interested, or directly engaged" in African affairs to assess the work that was going on in Africa and elsewhere for the "education and upbuilding of Negro peoples." At Tuskegee he hoped the delegates might see and study the methods he had employed to help blacks in the United States with a view to deciding whether the methods were applicable to conditions of blacks in other parts of the world.[15] In order to get the people he wanted, Washington wrote Secretary of State Knox about the conference and enquired whether the "Department could give publicity to this Conference, especially to the European governments." He did not fail to remind his white American supporters that as missionaries and European governments had constantly asked about his methods, he felt that this was a fine opportunity for such persons to come to Tuskegee for two or three days to see what actually went on.[16] To make sure that the conference was well publicized, Washington had invitations sent to missionary bodies and to thousands of individuals.

In view of the growing suspicion of the European colonial powers that the colored races of the world were becoming restless under their control, as well as the cost of traveling to the United States, the response to Washington's invitation was good. From South Africa, the Reverend Isaiah Goda Sishuba, president of the Ethiopian Church, wrote Washington, "Thank God to have given the Negro race [a] man of your kind and stamp. A far seeing gentleman and up to date. . . . Myself and Reverend H. R. Ngcayiya[,] Secretary of the Ethiopian Church[,] will attend the above Conference. The executive Board and a Special Conference of our Church has [sic] elected us to become delegates to represent them."[17] The aging Edward Wilmot Blyden wrote from Sierra Leone regretting that he could not attend, but sent a letter commending the conference. J. E. Casely Hayford, one of the Gold Coast's emerging nationalists, also wrote regretting that he was unable to attend. In a letter Washington would later read to the conference, Hayford declared, "There is an African Nationality and when the Aborigines of the Gold Coast and other parts of West Africa have joined forces with our brethren in America arriving at a national aim, purpose, and inspiration, then indeed, will it be possible for our brethren over the sea to bring home metaphorically to their nation and people a great spoil." He praised the work Washington was doing at Tuskegee as a "mighty uplifting force for the race."[18] A number of West Indians representing at least "three colors" came to the conference, as did missionaries representing thirty-six organizations working in colonial lands. In all there were delegates from at least twenty-one foreign countries.

Washington was able to get President Taft to send Ralph Waldo Tyler, a black journalist, to greet the delegates in the United States. In his opening address Washington asked the delegates not to engage in long speeches but rather to engage in "a simple direct, heart-to-heart talk concerning the conditions and concerning the problems that are nearest to the heart of teachers."[19] This request must have been made in jest, because Washington knew his visitors would engage in long-winded oratory. Mark C. Hayford (brother of J. E. Casely Hayford) read a long paper on the subject of industrialism in Africa especially on the historical activities of the ancient Ghanaians who migrated down into West Africa. Not to be outdone, the venerable Bishop Henry McNeal Turner reiterated his view that the African American had a duty to Africa and its peoples.

Representatives of the colonial powers and a number of missionaries at the conference expressed concern about the interests of African Americans in Africa and the role of black missionaries there. Attention was called to the implication of the AME Church in the ill-fated Bambata rebellion. Both the Reverends Sishuba and Ngcayiya, who were at the conference, had been instrumental in preventing a number of Ethiopian churches from seceding from the AME Church and reported that many white South Africans felt that it was dangerous to have black Baptists, the AME Church, the AME Zion Church, and the Colored Methodist Episcopal Church in Africa. They wanted the conference to assert that "their only purpose in going to Africa was to help their brethren there and that in no case did they wish any of the people to be disloyal to the Governments under which they were living." They "urged Washington to go to South Africa and to explain to the whites that their purpose was 'to uplift their brethren and not to incite sedition.' "[20]

Washington had every reason to be pleased with his conference on Africa, but he was frustrated at being unable to expedite a loan to Liberia to help that country protect itself from European imperialism. A few weeks before the conference, President Taft named Reed Paige Clark as general receiver, with Britain, France, and Germany having the right to name three assistant customs receivers. The American president also agreed to designate United States military officers to train the Liberian frontier force.[21] What Washington may or may not have known was that the Europeans feared that if the United States secured a loan for Liberia, it might become Liberia's de facto protector. America would then put a stop to the civil strife there, eliminating one of the presumed justifications for Western European interference in Liberian affairs. Moreover, the Europeans actively engaged the support of American diplomats in their respective countries to dissuade the Department of State from helping Liberia.[22]

When news of European opposition to American help reached the Liberians, they were convinced that the British, French, and Germans were attempting to precipitate violent warfare within and along the Liberian boundaries as a pretext for conquest before the United States could secure the loan. Thus, when conflict again broke out with the Grebo, the settlers requested the United States to send a "fast cruiser" to help put down the rebellion.[23] The Department of State complied, but asked the American ambassador in London to request that Great Britain respect the status quo ante and instructed Minister Crum to arrange a meeting with Liberian and British officials. He was instructed to say that "as a friend of both parties" he was authorized to use his "good offices toward a friendly and equitable settlement of the difficulties" between them. Crum complied with these instructions but sent the department an article in a local paper which reported that in both Europe and America there was growing concern that the United States wished to establish a protectorate over Liberia.[24]

Reports of European concern also reached the Department of State. The Belgians were suspicious that the United States might use the pretext of having to protect American lives and property to seize Liberia. The American embassy in Berlin sent the Department of State a long article written by a member of the Reichstag and Chamber of Deputies, in which a number of fears were expressed: that America would curb Germany's preeminence in Liberian trade; that Germany's cable traffic to South America would be interrupted; that America would strive to protect her own cotton industry by hampering European-supported cotton production in Liberia; and that America might foster African American influence in the continent and "Ethiopianism" (the notion of "Africa for the Africans"). Concerning the latter, the German politician wrote:

> It is also to be considered that the Southern States of the American Union are saddled with a partially decadent negro population, whose removal to Liberia would be unrestricted once Liberia were an American colony. It would also surely eventually happen that the negroes who through their political good conduct and influence in the elections have, according to American custom, earned their right to high official posts, would be provided with such in Liberia, whereby the appointment of hated negro officials at home would be avoided.
>
> This would result in a negro State in Africa which, even though the United States wished it otherwise, could be conducted in pronounced hostility to European colonial policy, which would be especially dangerous since the authority of the United States would continually have to support Liberia. The result would be many unpleasantnesses for Liberia's boundary neighbors, England and France, but might not at the beginning of her development injure German interests. So much is said, however, in the black-inhabited parts of the earth about the solidarity of European civilization, and rightly, that Germans should not take occasion to be happy over the difficulties of her "friends and true neighbors."
>
> But there is more to be considered. Although it has not been much written about in recent years, the "Ethiopian Movement" is known by those who have to do with African affairs not to have reached its end, but to be still smoldering under the surface. It is known that whatever organization the "Ethiopian Movement" now possesses is due to the influence of the North American Christian negroes. The North American negro as the unrestrained master of a fruitful and well-populated territory on the African continent, and powerfully protected by his native State would be . . . a stimulant to the spread of the Ethiopian movement.[25]

Ambassador Whitelaw Reid cabled Secretary of State Knox from London that many businessmen had reported that the Liberians were revoking their concessions so they could give them to Americans when the loan agreement was signed. Reid cautioned that it would be a fatal mistake for United States bankers to lend money to Liberia "unless they obtain permission to put white men in charge of every branch of the administration and to reform it from the bottom."[26] As Crum saw the situation in Liberia, unless the Liberians received the loan they could not support the frontier force that might ensure peace and permit them to proceed with the more difficult task of putting their financial house in order. On 20 October 1911 the French complained to the Department of State that Liberian troops had crossed the border with Guinea, causing casualties among the local people. The department sought to mollify the French by stating that Liberia was endeavoring to get money to appoint a frontier force and that once the arrangements were concluded, "prompt action will be taken towards supporting a proper police force of the Republic."[27] The assistant secretary also instructed Crum to verify the reports of the conflict because "the French Government seems to look to the United States to take steps towards putting an end to what would seem from the [French] Ambassador's note to be a regrettable state of affairs." Crum was also instructed to "discreetly express" to the Liberian minister of foreign affairs that the United States government viewed the situation with grave concern.[28]

From the correspondence between the Department of State and the Europeans it is clear that the United States considered Liberia a bit of a nuisance but was not quite prepared to abandon its responsibilities to that republic. Pressure came from many directions. On the one hand, African American immigrants in Liberia were complaining to President Taft about rigged presidential elections while, on the other hand, the Europeans wanted to seize the country.[29] Taft could do little about the elections, but the secretary of state believed "that it looks as though the new Liberian administration will ratify the loan agreement" and thereby get the funds for the army.[30] Meanwhile, in Monrovia, Crum faced crisis after crisis. On 4 December 1911 he cabled the department that the Liberians had denied that their people had crossed into French territory, but on 6 January 1912 he had to report that there had been a battle near the town of Behlu on the Sierra Leonean border in which four Liberians were killed. The British reacted to this conflict by complaining that had the Liberians accepted their help in policing the frontier in the first place, there would have been no loss of life. Pressured on all sides, the Liberians stopped haggling over the clauses in the agreement for United States army officers to reorganize their frontier force. On 13 February 1912 the department cabled Crum that Captain Charles Young of the Ninth Cavalry was expected to take up his appointment as military attaché as soon as the loan agreement was signed and that he would be accompanied by three ex-army officers. With these developments, both the department and Booker T. Washington hoped for at least some peace on the Liberian frontiers.[31]

Complicating Washington's endeavors to induce the United States to help Liberia resist European aggression were the activities of Henry Francis Downing, formerly United States consul in Loanda, Angola, referred to above. Based in London, but an inveterate Liberia "watcher," Downing sought to stir up conflict between the Liberians and the Americans by writing to President Taft enquiring whether Roosevelt had demonstrated any bigotry to the Liberian commissioners when they had visited the White House. He also wrote Washington about the matter. But whereas Secretary of State Knox replied to Downing that as far as the department was aware the visit of the Liberians went quite well, Washington did not deign to reply to the letter he received.[32]

In Liberia, Crum became ill with black water fever. He was evacuated in September 1912, leaving his black secretary, Richard Carlton Bundy, to assume the position of chargé d'affaires ad interim. Bundy was immediately faced with a series of attacks by disgruntled Liberian youths on the diplomatic community and against Europeans living in Monrovia, and agitation in the provinces. On 12 October 1912 he cabled the department that a number of Dutch, English, and Germans had been stoned but that his investigation revealed no reason for the attacks. Alarmed for their safety, the European consuls wished to ask their governments to intervene. Bundy told the department, "I let it be known that it was my opinion that the situation was by no means beyond the control of the Liberian civil authorities, and that a fair opportunity ought at least be given them to deal with the disorder before any steps were taken by foreign representatives that were likely to involve consequences the end of which could not be foreseen."[33] Unmollified, the German consul threatened to cable for help if another attack occurred, and the British and French consuls requested a conference with the American chargé to deal with the situation. Bundy felt that had the Liberians moved in quickly after the first attack on the Europeans by "a few rowdy incorrigibles," the situation would not have gotten out of hand and assumed "international proportions." As it was, the hesitant official Liberian response led the same "lawless element to make an attack on the American Legation." When stones smashed the legation's windows, Bundy complained to the Liberian secretary of state. The latter apologized profusely and offered to station soldiers to guard the legation.[34]

Although concerned for his safety and for that of the Europeans in town, Bundy refused the offer of protection. He reasoned that accepting it would only confirm "the impression current in the minds of Europeans in Monrovia, that the civil authorities were unable to take care of the situation; and if this information were to get abroad, it would likely be very embarrassing to the Liberian Government." Furthermore, Bundy felt that as the attacks had ceased, the best thing for the Liberians to do was to station troops in the vicinity of the legations. His recommendation was accepted by the Liberian government. Nevertheless, Bundy felt it wise to warn the Department of State that two factors made the situation in Monrovia unstable: first, many townspeople were dissatisfied with the opposition of resident Europeans to the acquittal by the Liberian government of charges against two officials accused of irregularities in the interior; and second, a number of townspeople wanted to embarrass the government by showing it was incompetent to deal with local rioting. Bundy feared that any trivial incident might "cause overwrought foreigners to precipitate a situation that would be quite beyond the control of the Liberian Government. The cause of the unrest is to be found, I believe, in the delay in the effective operation of the new loan agreement and the prevalent local European impression, that it is highly probable that the agreement will never become operative." He concluded:

> There is an ever-increasing opinion among foreigners that the Liberian Government cannot long continue to exist, unless there soon comes an effective supervision of its affairs by forces outside of itself. Meanwhile, the Liberian Government is doing its very best to meet the essential requirements of a most awkward and distressing situation with a fortitude that is, to say the least, commendable.[35]

These views, he told the department, were very much his own, but he felt it prudent to add, "This interpretation does not find very general acceptance among the other foreign representatives here."[36]

Much to Bundy's alarm, a revolt of the Kru people against the settlers in early November led to the sacking of a number of German businesses. Fortunately for Liberia, the American officers seconded to this constabulary succeeded in suppressing the uprising. Bundy again suggested to the department that the reason for the unrest was the government's shortage of funds and the uncertainty about the loan. Nevertheless, he felt that the department should assure the foreign bankers that they should have no fear concerning repayment. His immediate problem was that the owners of the ravaged German businesses had appealed for help, and the gunboat *Panther* arrived in Monrovia on 11 November. Its commander, a rather bellicose officer, formally demanded that the Liberian president take "energetic and decisive measures to guarantee [the] safety of Germans on Bassa coast." If this was not done within twenty-four hours, the commander "reserved liberty to act as he saw fit." This ultimatum disturbed the Liberian president who nevertheless maintained his sangfroid. He told the officer that the situation was under control, and the *Panther* left Monrovia for the Bassa Coast. Bundy reported to the Department of State, "Believe situation in regard to disorder unchanged but cannot forecast German action."[37]

To heighten the tension in Monrovia, the acting Dutch vice-consul refused to attend a reception given by the Liberian president, charging that he had been fired upon near Camp Johnson, where the Liberian frontier force was being trained. Luckily for Bundy and the Liberian government, Major Charles Young, the military attaché, was closely associated with the soldiers at Camp Johnson. Young "instituted such a rigid and vigorous investigation as to immediately explode this theory [that the Dutchman had been fired upon]."[38]

The situation had gotten so far out of hand that the Germans notified Secretary of State Knox of their displeasure with the Liberians. On 30 December 1912 Knox sent Bundy a cable stating that the department had asked the German ambassador to request that his government refrain from giving ultimatums to the Liberians. Meanwhile, he instructed Bundy to urge the Liberians to settle the problem as soon as possible. For their part, the Germans were prepared to compromise but wanted the Liberians to discharge the officials in charge of the Bassa Coast.[39]

The problem for Bundy was that the American officer at Bassa Coast, Major Wilson Ballad, had sent a report to Monrovia exonerating the resident Liberian officials, and the Liberian government had declared that "if compelled to accede to German demands irrespective [of] Ballad's report it will consider usefulness of American officers seriously impaired." Bundy suggested that he could exert "sufficient pressure to secure dismissal [of the Liberian officials] provided incident will be closed and no further demands made by German Government."[40] The department was not prepared to permit Bundy to go that far. It suggested that with regard to the Liberians' note that the usefulness of American officers would be impaired if they had to discharge their officers, the fact remained that no American officers were present at Bassa Coast when the altercation took place. The department told Bundy to suggest to the Liberians that they compromise with the Germans by agreeing to a "provisional dismissal" of the officials until both governments could resolve the issue.[41]

The State Department did feel that the Germans were picking a quarrel with Liberia. On 10 January 1913 Secretary Knox sent a telegram to his ambassador in Berlin stating, "In view of marked consideration of German wishes [which this Government has shown] from the very beginning of the Liberian negotiations, [the United States] feels justified in expecting on the part of Germany a patient and liberal attitude toward Liberia and a cordial cooperation with this Government to save the Liberian government from embarrassments."[42] Apparently this cable was effective, as the next day the American ambassador cabled that the Germans had accepted the compromise of the provisional dismissal of the Liberian officials and that the issue was now closed. Satisfied with the resolution of this conflict, the department congratulated Bundy on a job well done.[43]

The Liberian officials and the resident Americans in Monrovia were so pleased with Bundy's performance as chargé d'affaires following the departure of Minister Crum that they sought to have him appointed minister resident and consul general in Monrovia. However, the situation was complicated by Woodrow Wilson's victory over a divided Republican party, led respectively by Taft and Roosevelt, and by the expectation that the Democratic president might wish to name his own man to the Liberian post. Nevertheless, in the minds of people in Monrovia, Bundy was an eminently qualified candidate for the post. Born in Wilmington, Ohio, in 1870 of African American parents, Richard Carlton Bundy graduated from the Case School of Applied Sciences in Cleveland, Ohio, and then headed the Department of Mechanical Engineering at Wilberforce University until leaving for Monrovia where he had served as secretary to the legation since 1910.

Replying to Liberian President Daniel Edward Howard, who had requested that he support Bundy for the post at Monrovia, Booker T. Washington replied that when, shortly after Crum's death in November 1912, he went to the department to discuss the matter of a new minister for Liberia, he found the secretary of state toying with the idea of recommending Bundy to the post. However, the people at the State Department had second thoughts when they considered that were Bundy to be "made minister the position would become *political* and he might be removed at any time, whereas remaining in his present position he would more likely to be permanent." Major Charles Young had also recommended Bundy to Washington, giving as his reasons that the president of Liberia and the best Liberian citizens supported Bundy; that when Crum was often ill Bundy efficiently ran the legation; and that believing, as the Liberians did, that Washington had the welfare of the republic at heart, securing the appointment of Bundy would place the Liberian president under an obligation to him.[44]

Unfortunately for Bundy, Washington's candidate for the position of minister to Liberia was his longtime friend and collaborator, Frederick Randolph Moore, editor and part owner of the New York *Age*. Born in Prince William County, Virginia, on 16 June 1857, Moore had attended the Washington, D.C., public schools and, after serving two years as a messenger in the U.S. Treasury Department, was assigned in 1877 to its secretary's office. Resigning in 1887, he engaged in banking and real estate in New York City and on Washington's recommendation served for a time with the Internal Revenue Service. When Washington bought the Boston-based *Colored American* magazine in 1904, he named Moore as editor and part owner. Washington sometimes had trouble dealing with Moore's militancy and was not completely happy when his protégé helped to found the Urban League in 1911 and served on its first board. The problem that Moore and his patron faced was that Wilson had already won the election before Taft nominated him for the Liberian position. In a letter to Liberian President Daniel Edward Howard, Washington said, "Mr. Moore's name is now before the Senate, but there is slight hope that he will be confirmed before the new administration comes in." Hinting to the Liberians about possible changes in his influence, Washington confided to President Howard, "There is nothing definite as to what policy Mr. Wilson will pursue regarding the minister after he becomes President, but I shall be glad to do all I can to carry out your wishes."[45]

Washington's problem with the incoming Wilson administration was that while he was still the most important black person in the United States and his link to the Republicans was well known, he had had few dealings with the Democrats. Moreover, he had every reason to consider Wilson unsympathetic to him, to blacks, and to Liberia. Despite these qualms, Washington did attempt to establish contact with the Democratic president-elect. On 24 December 1912 he wrote Julius Rosenwald, inquiring, in view of Wilson's scheduled speech in Chicago on 11 January 1913, "if it might not be worth while for us to try to arrange for a small side meeting for Tuskegee at which the Governor [Wilson] might consent to say a few words. My idea would be to have the audience composed of a small number of selected people."[46] Rosenwald suggested that it might be possible for Wilson to meet a small group from Tuskegee at a luncheon meeting in Chicago, but Washington, fearing that this would "bring up the old question of social equality and might embarrass Governor Wilson," felt that it might be possible to have the luncheon without his presence, in which case, he would be "just as well satisfied."[47]

Very much aware of the possible implications of Wilson's victory for the future of Liberia, President Howard sought direct contact with the incoming administration. He summoned Bundy for a discussion of American politics, leading the chargé to report to the State Department:

It seems that the Liberian Government regards the assistance which is being rendered it by the Government of the United States as policy solely of the Executive branch of our Government. For that reason the President and many prominent officials feel that a change of administration at Washington, particularly when the new administration is of a different political party, is very likely to affect the American policy in Liberia to a considerable extent . . .

I think that for the most part the Liberian Government is very much alive to the difficulties which the government of the United States has had to overcome in order to bring it those measures of assistance which it now enjoys. It is rather generally felt in Government circles, that each of the European nations concerned has considerable interests commercially and otherwise, in the country which it is prepared to safeguard in an uncertain manner, while on the other hand, helpful, unselfish sentiment, is thought to be the chief motive of the interest which the Government of the United States has taken in Liberian affairs. Accordingly it is believed by Liberia, that a consistent, continuous, firm policy, on the part of our Government, is her only hope for national life.

President Howard desires to send a small commission to Washington to get in close touch with President-elect Wilson, for the purpose of soliciting his personal interest, as well as that of his administration in the wellfare [sic] of Liberia. There are many matters which President Howard feels such a commission could lay before President-elect Wilson, and the State Department, from the Liberian standpoint. In this way he thinks, the Liberian Government will obtain a complete understanding of the policy to be pursued by the new administration during the next four years. The Liberian official mind is very much worried lest the Government of the United States may not continue to firmly dominate the international situation in Liberia, and in view of the fact that it is believed that the autonomy of the country is at stake if the American policy is any less firm in the future than it is at present, President Howard is considering this commission as the best means at his command for bringing to the attention of the new administration the needs of his country.[48]

Perhaps because it did not wish to embarrass the incoming administration, the State Department postponed Minister-elect Moore's departure for Liberia. After some hesitation he was sworn in, but as a friend reported to Washington, Moore was informed "that instructions would not be given him by this administration and that for such instruction he would have to look to the administration of Mr. Wilson. He [Moore] seems deeply grateful to you for his appointment." Moore's other problem was that, as usual, many blacks sought the few diplomatic and other positions open to them. As Charles William Anderson, who had secured his appointment as collector of internal revenue in downtown New York with the help of Theodore Roosevelt in 1905, wrote to Washington after Wilson's election, "The black democrats are crowing very loudly, and have already divided the offices now held by colored republicans, among themselves. Du Bois, who prepared their literature during the campaign (for pay) is talked of for Haiti. A half dozen of them are pointed for my place, and each place in Washington is claimed by a dozen candidates. And thus the merry war goes on." In fact, Anderson was one of the last Republican officeholders replaced by Wilson. When, after being told to wait for Wilson's decision, Moore visited the assembled black Democrats in Washington, D.C., he was asked to speak "out of courtesy," but he so infuriated one fraction that its members declared, "He will not go to Liberia." Apparently, these men took themselves too seriously, because Wilson refused to see all African American office seekers. One observer commented that the "hopes of the Negro Democrats" had dropped to zero and that it "really looks as though the brother will get very little if little."[49] Speculating about black prospects under Wilson, Washington wrote to a friend: "I fear the President's high-sounding phrases regarding justice do not include the Negro."[50]

Perhaps suspecting, or hoping, that the Wilson administration might change United States policy toward Liberia, the French ambassador in Washington, D.C., inquired of the secretary of state whether the United States government was still committed to its plans to help that black republic.[51] The French and the British were still disturbed by the conflict on the borders of their colonies with those of Liberia. On 10 May 1913 Bundy cabled the department that trouble had again broken out in the Mambu region, where, in the hope of pacifying the local people, the Liberians had employed one Mr. Cole, a Sierra Leonean "necromancer." The Liberian president then requested more American army officers to train his constabulary and lamented that Major Young, who had to go on leave, was not available.[52]

What appeared more ominous to the Liberians was the refusal of the Wilson administration to receive a commission from them. When this was proposed to Bundy he was prudently noncommittal. It was a good thing that he promised nothing, because the State Department cabled, "It is hoped that you have discreetly made clear the inadvisability of visit."[53] Putting the best face on what was in fact a disappointing response, Bundy did as instructed. He reported back that after he had indicated why such a visit was not possible at the time, "satisfaction was expressed [by the Liberians] with our Government's continued interest, and contemplated visit abandoned with good will."[54] It was this kind of diplomacy that had endeared Bundy to Young and to Clark, had won the respect of the Liberians, and had elicited congratulations from the Department of State. Nevertheless, the Europeans were apparently not pleased with the presence of African American diplomats in Monrovia and sought to use white American diplomats in Europe to change this. On 30 June 1913 Walter Hines Page, the United States ambassador to the Court of St. James's, sent the following cable to Secretary of State William Jennings Bryan:

Sir, on June 25th at the French President's dinner to the King, the Secretary for the Colonies (Mr. Marcourt) sought me out and had quite a long (and of course informal) conversation about Liberia.

There has been, you will recall, a correspondence between the British and the American Governments about trouble that arises at intervals concerning boundary lines. The Secretary for the Colonies intimated that this old trouble would be likely to arise again. But the drift of his conversation was that such specific controversies were really only symptoms of a rather serious condition—that there was convincing evidence that Liberia was going backward; that the high hope with which our Government set up the black republic had surely not been realized; that the negroes, left to themselves, were deteriorating; that no fresh stock went there from the United States and that, therefore, the population got no new ideas nor new impulses and that the men who get control are not and are not likely to be capable leaders; in a word, that the outlook is distinctly discouraging.

His constructive suggestion was that the United States Government send as its Minister to Liberia a strong white man, who by the force of his character might greatly help the Liberian Government and perhaps give it the guidance that it needs. At any rate such a man's study of the situation would be likely to give the Government of the United States a clearer idea of the situation. Mr. Marcourt promised to talk further with me at some early convenient time.

Previously I had a conversation with the Minister of Liberia to the British Government, who strangely enough is not a negro but a Dutchman. But the conversation was only in such general terms as men use while they are becoming acquainted. But the impression that he left on my mind rather confirmed what Mr. Marcourt said.

> Of course I have no independent opinion of my own; but it seems to me worthwhile to communicate this conversation to you. I have a fear, from these conversations and from a conversation that I had two or three years ago with one of our Commissioners to Liberia, that, unless our Government in one way or another comes to the help of Liberia, the land-hungry Powers may move boundary lines inward until at last at some far-off time, the territory of Liberia may consist only of a boundary line.[55]

The intended effect of such actions on the possible choice of black officers in the foreign service of the United States can be gauged by the fact that Page's cable was copied to the State Department's Bureau of Appointments, among others.

Possibly because he was too busy with more important affairs of state, Bryan and his collaborators decided to maintain the status quo with Liberia. When he finally responded to France's inquiry concerning United States policy toward Liberia, the secretary of state simply said that the policy of the previous administration would be sustained. Bryan also acknowledged Ambassador Page's confidential despatch referring to Liberian affairs and, "particularly, suggesting that this Government send as Minister Resident to Liberia a white man and a man forceful enough in characters as to be of real assistance to the Liberian Government. The contents of your despatch under acknowledgement will receive the most careful consideration."[56]

From the appearance of the situation in Washington, D.C., there was no way of knowing whether Ambassador Page's recommendation that the United States should appoint a white man as minister to Liberia instead of a black one was being taken seriously. Booker T. Washington's protégé, Moore, was not sent out as minister. Moreover, President Wilson had systematically cleaned out the black officeholders from the previous administration. They included William H. Lewis, assistant attorney general of the United States, who, until that time, had held the highest position that any black had achieved in the United States government; Ralph W. Tyler, auditor for the Navy Department; and Harry Henry W. Runiss, minister to Haiti. To add insult to injury, Wilson appointed former Missouri Congressman Madison Roswell Smith, a white man, as minister to Haiti, which had traditionally been a black "plum." Booker T. Washington, losing his proverbial sangfroid over this nomination, remarked that the action "would seem to indicate that the present administration is hopeless. I am deeply disappointed in Pres[ident] Wilson."[57]

To everyone's surprise, Wilson maintained the now-hallowed tradition of naming a black man, Dr. George Washington Buckner, to serve as his minister to Monrovia. Born in Green County, Kentucky, in 1855, Buckner was educated at the Indiana State Normal School in Terre Haute, Indiana, and received an M.D. degree from the Indiana Eclectic Medical College. He practiced medicine in Evansville, Indiana, from 1890 until being nominated to the Monrovia legation. As usual, Booker T. Washington had heard of Buckner's success and on 17 September 1913 had written critically of him to Reed Paige Clark, the American customs receiver. Deeply disappointed that Bundy did not get the appointment and dismayed by Washington's report on Minister-elect Buckner, Clark replied:

> Naturally, your letter in regard to the new Minister is disquieting. I had hoped that he would be a man of culture. I knew of course that he would be inexperienced as regards the Diplomatic Service and Liberian affairs, . . . but had hoped that he would be at least cultured and possessed of a certain amount of savoir faire. To learn that there is perhaps but little to expect in this regard is a hard blow to say the least. I shrink from the contrast that will inevitably be drawn by non-Americans between the American Minister and the British, German and French representatives at Monrovia, all of whom are men of intellect, culture and experience and all of whom will be outranked by our Envoy.
>
> The new Minister, however earnest and hard-working he may be, under the circumstances will necessarily lack influence with the Liberian Government and our own Department; the foreign Governments, none of whom are to be counted upon to help Liberia to get on her feet, will be quick to gauge his worth; in the face of the apparent indifference of our State Department to matters Liberian (an indifference from which the foreign Governments are not slow to profit), and the natural apathy of the Bankers, how can those of us who have a real interest in the upbuilding of Liberia expect to accomplish anything of permanent value? It is with great difficulty that the Liberians themselves can be made to realize their own best interests. I am increasingly of the opinion that the officials in power are but little disposed to embark upon the program of reforms that we consider necessary for the Republic's welfare and that they are prone to evolve wild schemes of their own calculated to make matters worse even than they are. With no power at hand to help us force the Liberians to carry out in good faith the tacit pledges of the Loan Agreement I am convinced there is but slight prospect of success here. In what has been accomplished the American Legation has been my chief dependence, and I shall continue, under all circumstances, to do my utmost to co-operate with the American Minister. Please rest assured of this. . . .
>
> I thank you more than I can say for your helpful and kindly letters; your active interest in Liberian affairs is more than ever needed.[58]

Minister-elect Buckner may not have been "cultured," but he was wise enough to visit Washington and Emmett Jay Scott before going off to Monrovia. Moreover, he succeeded in winning their qualified approval. Scott wrote Bishop Isaiah Benjamin Scott in Liberia:

> The new Minister to Liberia has been here for a little conference with the Doctor and me. I took particular pains to emphasize two things: First, that he talk with you as soon as he reaches there, assuring him that you will be glad, unofficially, to advise him in those things where an official would be diffident about it. In the second place, I have urged upon him that he keep Mr. Bundy as his guide, philosopher, and friend because of his familiarity with Liberia and its situation in all of its many phases. He seemed to appreciate these suggestions, and I think will act upon them. He is a singularly abrupt and apparently uncultured man, but nevertheless, seems to have a stratum of good common sense; and I believe he is sincerely anxious to do anything that he can to help our brothers across the Sea.[59]

In turn, Washington confessed to Reed Paige Clark, "In regard to the new minister, I think you will find that while he has a rather crude exterior, deep down at the bottom, he has a lot of common sense and will finally win his way. The more I saw of him and the more I talked with him, the more I was pleased with him, notwithstanding the impressions formed at first sight."[60]

What did trouble Washington was the implication of Wilson's foreign policy for Liberia. Since the president was allegedly not interested in big business, Washington feared that the renewal of the loan agreement with Liberia was in jeopardy because the administration "would not take up such matters with foreign countries in the way that past administrations have been doing." To him this suggested that the "Liberian people will ultimately be led to see the importance of getting right down to business, throwing aside all superficiality and devote themselves to the improvement of their country along fundamental lines of civilization. This, in my opinion, is the last chance for Liberia." Washington told Clark that he wished Bundy would be kept on because the young man had made an impression on all with whom he had any dealing. Moreover, he indicated an interest in keeping in touch with Bundy even after the latter left Liberia. Nevertheless, Washington warned Clark, "As you perhaps know, I am not in such close touch with this administration as I have been with other administrations. I am a Republican and the present administration is Democratic. If you or Mr. Bundy will point out some practical way in which you think I can be of service, I shall be glad to consider the matter."[61]

Meanwhile, the resurgence of African American interest in emigration to Africa attracted Washington's attention, especially since the goal of the emigrants—the Gold Coast of West Africa—made them the subject of United States foreign policy toward Great Britain. Since the days of Bishop Henry McNeal Turner and his later partner William H. Heard, who was formerly minister to Liberia, black interest in emigrating to Africa had waned but had not entirely ceased. Turner himself had effectively lost interest in the movement when he disbanded the *African League* in 1906.[62] But in 1913, much to Washington's distress, one Chief Alfred Charles Sam raised again the banner of emigrationism. Born in the Gold Coast about 1880, the son of an alleged chief, Sam founded the Akim Trading Company in 1911 to trade with the United States. He sailed for New York on 10 February 1912 and, after some misadventures, arrived in Oklahoma, where, in 1913, he began to recruit potential emigrants to go to Africa. As C. G. Samuels, one of Sam's somewhat illiterate collaborators, explained to Governor Cruce of Oklahoma:

> We are working trying to transport the colored people from the State of Oklahoma to Gold Coast West Africa as we thinks it will be better for them since the ballot has been taken from us and we can not act as a man and am peoples are treated so crual as you no yourself our mens and womens are being lynched for most any little frivulus crime with the cord of law and we are jim Croed in the courthouse and in all publick places. So I thought that I would write you a letter to see if there is any method that you may or can or will help us in this great struggle of life in trying to make it to our native land.[63]

Governor Cruce regretted to Samuels that there were no state funds available to help African Americans leave the United States but took the position that as far as emigration was concerned, it was an issue that "each negro will have to settle for himself." Nevertheless, he felt that the black people of his state "ought to be very careful in paying money in installments or in any other way to persons representing themselves to be agents of a society of this nature."[64] The governor was substantially in accord with much of black sentiment in Oklahoma and elsewhere against Sam's venture. The Tulsa *Star* reported in October 1913 that Oklahoma blacks were perplexed by one "Prince Sam, claiming to be an African king, bent on inducing as many as possible of the Colored people of this country to return to their native soil."[65] On 6 October 1913 the Reverend James Fair of Beggs, Oklahoma, wrote Governor Cruce complaining of the extent to which "all of the best community are shot to pieces" over the emigration project and wanting to know "if Chief Sam have any rite to carry citizens from the [U]nited States and carry them to Africa have you given him any authority to do so now . . . if this keeps on there is likely to be a war among the negroes."[66] Alarmed by the news that blacks were paying $25 per share to buy a steamship to transport at least 117 families to Africa, Richard J. Hill, also of Beggs, wrote Robert Owens, a senator from Oklahoma, "Will you kindly inform me as to whether the American Negro as a whole, or those who desire to do so, can acquire title to lands in Gold Coast, West Africa, a British Colony, and if so what is the mode of procedure to do so?"[67]

The British foreign service did not take kindly to reports that Chief Sam was planning to transport blacks to the Gold Coast. The British consul in St. Louis wrote Governor Cruce warning that blacks were probably being swindled by Sam and enlisted the aid of one E. L. Coffey (note the Akan name) of Oklahoma to investigate the nature of the Chief Sam's Clubs that were selling shares in a steamship company. He complained to Cruce, but the governor only replied that if it could be proved that Sam was defrauding blacks, then he would be prosecuted. Meanwhile in Washington, D.C., the British ambassador to the United States, Sir Cecil Spring-Rice, asked the Colonial Office to inquire of the governor of the Gold Coast whether colonization there was a possibility. Spring-Rice wrote Governor Cruce that the Colonial Office had warned that it seemed "very undesirable for any large group of negroes to proceed to the Gold Coast before the land had been obtained." To this he added his personal feeling that African Americans would face health problems in the Gold Coast and that the United States should find some means of delaying the projected emigration until it could be determined whether the emigrants were suitable people who understood the conditions of life on the Gold Coast and whether there was land available for them.[68]

Spring-Rice and his consular staff dutifully kept the United States Department of State fully informed about their actions against Sam's emigration project. Their problem was that John Bassett Moore, deputy to Secretary of State William Jennings Bryan, constantly passed the buck to Governor Cruce of Oklahoma. Moreover, as a British subject, Sam was conducting his business on alien soil and they had no right to prod United States federal and state authorities to take action against the project. When Sam and some twenty persons arrived in New York in February 1914, the British consul there notified both the United States attorney and the New York district attorney of the possibility of fraud on Sam's part. He stressed the necessity of detaining in New York the steamship *Curityba,* rechristened *Liberia,* which was scheduled to leave for Galveston, Texas, to pick up emigrants for the Gold Coast. The consul told the federal and state officials:

> In conclusion it will interest you to learn that I have received telegraphic instructions from His Majesty's Ambassador to inform Sam, Mr. Smith and Mr. Kellogg, and anyone else connected with the enterprise, that the Ambassador has requested the final views of the Governor of the Gold Coast by telegraph, and that until receipt of these final views, His Majesty's Government strongly disapproves of any emigrants sailing from the United States for the Gold Coast.[69]

The British diplomatic community in the United States was perplexed by the determination of the emigrants to go to Africa and the reluctance of the American authorities to do anything about it. In February 1914 Ambassador Spring-Rice met with a delegation of Sam's supporters. He later reported to the State Department that the men "could not be shaken in their faith in Sam's bona fides and stated that he had positive offers from native chiefs on the Gold Coast to receive them in their tribal communities; that some American negroes had already gone over and had written letters testifying to satisfactory conditions, and that as many as 6,000 American negroes intended to emigrate under Sam's auspices."[70] The British also notified Moore at the Department of State that "the Governor of the Gold Coast states that the leases of land which 'Chief Sam' purports to have concluded have not been registered in the Colony." But instead of acting on this information, Moore sent the British reports to Governor Cruce and enclosed a copy of a confidential message which the British Foreign Office had sent to the American ambassador in Britain, Walter Hines Page, urging that the project be stopped. This cable read in part:

> His Majesty's Government . . . are strongly of the opinion that the immigration of these negroes into that colony should not be encouraged for the reason that the land is almost entirely held communally by the native chiefs and communities, so that a negro from the United States could only obtain land by adoption into a native community—which as the immigrant would presumably be Christian and civilized would no doubt be unacceptable to them—or by lease, which would involve lengthy formalities and uncertain results. In addition to these objections, His Majesty's Government consider that the climate and conditions of the colony are entirely unsuited to natives of the North American continent.
>
> Enquiries have, moreover, been made as to the bona fides of the negro Sam, with the result that it has been ascertained that his transactions are not genuine, nor the Company for which he acts reliable. The Gold Coast Government have denied that they have any authorized immigration agent.[71]

Booker T. Washington had heard about Sam's project from his contacts in Oklahoma and activated his network when the would-be migrants and their African leader arrived in New York City. George Wesley Harris, former associate editor of the New York *Age* and editor of the New York *Amsterdam News,* wrote Washington that after a great deal of trouble finding the emigrants' boat "I found about fifty very ignorant, with one or two exceptions, plain, negro farming people on board the old vessel which is in Crane's dry dock for repairs." Harris indicated that while the emigrants still retained an "almost childlike" faith in Sam, that faith had begun to "waver just a little." He was dismayed that the emigrants had paid some $69,000 more (they needed to raise an additional $20,000) for a twenty-seven-year-old ship that many seamen felt could not make an ocean voyage. Harris was more alarmed by the emigrants' white agent, one A. E. Smith, who had the reputation in Harlem of being a "high roller."[72] He enclosed a copy of a New York *Times* article on the emigrants and said that he had offered them any help he could provide. Washington immediately telegraphed to Harris, "How is African party coming on? If you think they are inclined to give up trip and locate in this country we could offer encouragement. Am attending to other matter which I spoke to you about today. Answer my expense."[73] Harris responded in an equally cryptic manner, "African party tells me tonight tied up here indefinitely, but not willing to admit failure. Will report at first break."[74] Two days later, Harris wrote saying, "I am still keeping close watch on the Chief Sam party and something will develop in a very few days. Am going down to the boat again tomorrow."[75]

Washington could do little to help. While he retained the confidence of the majority of African Americans, he was rapidly losing the acclaim of many members of the black elite and had almost no influence with an increasingly racist Wilson administration. A few poor blacks, not knowing about his opposition to emigrationism, actually believed rumors that Washington supported Sam's project. On 27 February 1914 one semiliterate Tom Johnson wrote from Margaret, Alabama: "I was instructed by the Paper that yo an Mr[.] chief-Sam—was caring the colrd Peoples to Aferica, to their own homes an if it is true I wants to go my Self an four other familys. we or wating for an ancer from yo an then we or ready to go as soon as we get a ancer from yo."[76] Washington's response to Johnson is not known, but the New York *Age* and New York *Amsterdam News* increasingly notified the black community of their skepticism over Chief Sam's project.

From across the Atlantic, from Great Britain, Duse Mohamed Ali, the editor of the *African Times and Orient Review,* wrote that Sam's scheme was folly.[77] Dr. Ernest Lyon, former United States minister to Liberia, now serving as Liberian consul general in the United States, joined the chorus against Sam's project. Quoted in the New York *Sun,* this confidant of Booker T. Washington admitted that he did not know Chief Sam, but was nonetheless convinced that the steamer *Liberia* "will never sail" and that if "it does, it will never land on the Gold Coast of Africa because the American Negro is *persona non grata* along that western shore." Putting in a plug for Liberia, Lyon added that with the exception of Liberia, no one else wanted the African Americans. The reason he gave was that "the whole coast is partitioned among European nations, and if the American black man emigrates there he will find himself at sea. He will not be allowed to enter the territory at all. He will find conditions uncongenial, for the prejudice against him on the west coast is greater than it ever was in this country."[78]

Neither Lyon, the British diplomats, nor their white American counterparts, reckoned with either the perseverance of Chief Sam or that of his followers. Constrained to go to Portland, Maine, Sam and his followers remained the object of much diplomatic traffic between the British Foreign Office, the State Department, and the office of the Oklahoma governor. Sir Cecil Spring-Rice kept on insisting that the chief and his entourage would have difficulties in the Gold Coast. He sent a letter to the State Department in which he asserted:

> I have explained that there is no prospect whatever that Chief Sam would be able to fulfill his promises as regards the acquisition of land in the Colony; that the climatic conditions are highly unsuitable for American negroes; and that enquiry here has thrown great doubt on Sam's bona fides; and that therefore His Majesty's Government desires to do all in their power to discourage the movement.

Providing details:

> I have now received a telegram from Sir Edward Grey instructing me to inform the United States Government that it is intended to pass an Ordinance compelling every individual immigrant into the Gold Coast, not being a native of West Africa, to deposit security for his repatriation if required to do so by local authorities. The amount of the security will be 25 pounds per head and the period during which it will become forfeit, if the immigrant becomes destitute, twelve months. The captain or owner of the ship will be obliged to carry back the immigrants who cannot give such security.
>   I have the honor to request that you will be good enough to bring this information to the knowledge of the competent authorities.[79]

The State Department took no action and sent the letter on to Governor Cruce in Oklahoma. Spring-Rice then informed Secretary of State Bryan that "the British vice consul at Portland, Maine, had been instructed not to issue British papers to the steamer *Curityba [Liberia]* which I understand has been purchased by 'Chief Sam' and is the property of the Akim Trading Company of South Dakota."[80] The American diplomats acknowledged the receipt of the information but insisted that "the state department takes the position that it has no right to interfere with the immigration of negroes."[81] Then the assistant district attorney in Portland praised Chief Sam's expedition and concluded that there was no evidence that Sam had violated any laws. Now perhaps embarrassed that they could not help, the British diplomats and the State Department sought to undermine the project. The department published a report on black emigration prepared by Consul Yerby in the Sierra Leone legation. Yerby agreed with Lyon that, with the exception of Liberia, "there is no glad hand of welcome extended towards American Negroes."[82] He sought to dramatize his warning with the following statement:

> Of the few American Negroes who have found their way to West Africa, 99 percent are unprepared to meet the economic conditions and express regret at having left America. These, excepting a few who cannot secure passage money, return to the United States.
>
> My advice [to Chief Sam's followers] is to select some well informed person to make a thorough investigation, visiting the particular section in which they intend settling before they pay any part of their passage money to West Africa. It is quite evident that some of these schemes are in every sense fraudulent. . . .
>
> Those who have come to West Africa suffer untold misery, are for the most part illiterate farmers who have, through a long struggle, managed to save enough passage money for themselves and family, with barely enough to live on through their first certain attack of African malaria. Many have expressed the choice of prison life in America to freedom here. In addition to the above, now and then a misguided independent missionary comes, suffers and dies.[83]

To these warnings from the State Department the blacks who were waiting in Galveston, Texas to board the *Liberia* responded, "We have no rights . . . We were disenfranchised and annoyed. We wanted to go to a place where we could have similar privileges and not have to take our orders from a dominant and unfriendly race. . . . We want to go where we get a square show."[84] Sam's representative summed up their attitude; he told the emigrants that the British "had been forced to admit that the land in the Gold Coast was under the control of the chiefs and that anyone could go to Africa if invited by chiefs."[85]

Faced with a group of expectant but destitute would-be emigrants, Mayor Lewis Fisher of Galveston wired Secretary of State Bryan complaining that Sam was a fraud and lamenting that the blacks "are practically without funds and congregated here a menace to public health and they will become a charge upon this or any other community. Cannot this Government have these people return to their homes and prevent others from coming here?"[86] Bryan replied to the mayor recounting the history of Sam's movement but insisting that "the Department presents these statements and regrets to say that federal government has been unable to take action to frustrate Sam's plans. Should these American Negroes migrate to Africa there is no appropriation at the disposal of this government to pay their return passage to America."[87]

The *Liberia* finally sailed from Galveston with a black crew taking sixty migrants and leaving on the dock several hundred black Oklahomans who had hoped to make the voyage, while hundreds waited in Oklahoma for Sam to return.[88] Shortly before heading to the open sea, the *Liberia* was stopped by HMS *Victoria,* whose captain wanted to make sure that the ship would not employ its wireless to communicate with the Germans with whom Britain was now at war. This hollow excuse permitted the British to seize the *Liberia* and take her to Freetown, Sierra Leone, where they planned to make a more detailed investigation of the ship's papers. Much to the frustration of the British officials, the local court found Sam not guilty of any wrong. People were generous when the *Liberia* arrived at Saltpond, where the Gold Coast *Leader* announced, "REMARKABLE RECEPTION OF CHIEF SAM AND NEGRO DELEGATES IN SALTPOND."[89]

Much as he would have liked to, Booker T. Washington was unable to prevent the departure of Sam's group for the Gold Coast either through his own efforts or by interceding with the British Foreign Office and the Department of State. His once powerful role in America's domestic affairs was rapidly coming to an end, as was his ability to influence his country's foreign policy. Washington's growing bitterness about the inability of blacks to counter white dominance in the world can be gauged from his reaction to an appeal of Rev. Joseph Booth to help "preserve Africa as the natural home of the African-born Negro, & of the Negro of the Dispersion so far as he elects, as the race matures in unity of interests & ideals."[90]

Booth had hoped that Washington would have been willing to select and to send one or two black coworkers to serve as tutors to Africans in central and South Africa. Booth, a former teacher of John Chilembwe of

Nyasaland (who, in 1915, would lead a revolt against the British), had visited the United States and had admired Washington's work. He was now persona non grata in central Africa and wanted Washington to help him secure funds to form the International Fund. Informed by Robert Park that Booth was a "little dinky missionary" who would use any funds received to fight against the British government in South Africa, whose policies he disapproved, Washington wrote Booth that he would be happy to help him realize his plans for racial peace in South Africa, but that he did not believe it possible "to induce any considerable number of American Negroes to emigrate to Africa as long as conditions are as you describe them."[91]

It was now clear that the principal of Tuskegee had done all that he could to help African Americans influence their country's foreign policy toward Africa. His death in 1915 marked the end of an era. African Americans would see their status suffer during a Wilson administration that saw racial segregation fasten itself on the capital of the United States. Only after a war that was fought to make the world safe for democracy would black Americans again attempt to influence United States policy toward Africa. That attempt, when it did appear, was to be largely symbolic in nature.

Notes

1. Booker T. Washington, *The Story of the Negro: The Rise of the Race From Slavery* (New York: Negro Universities Press [1969], 1:33–34.
2. Louis R. Harlan, *Booker T. Washington: The Wizard of Tuskegee, 1901–1915* (New York: Oxford University Press, 1983), 338ff.; Richard B. Morris, ed., *Encyclopedia of American History* (New York: Harper and Brothers, 1953), 298ff.
3. Pixley ka Isaka Seme to Booker T. Washington, 15 April 1908, in Louis R. Harlan and Raymond W. Smock, eds., *The Booker T. Washington Papers* (Urbana: University of Illinois Press, 1981), 9:500–501 (hereafter cited as *BTW Papers*).
4. Cited in Louis R. Harlan, "Booker T. Washington and the White Man's Burden," *American Historical Review* 81 (1966):464.
5. Alain Locke to BTW, 16 March 1910, *BTW Papers* 10:279–80.
6. Seme to BTW, 13 January 1911, and BTW to Seme, 22 February 1911, cited in Harlan, "Booker T. Washington," 464–66. On Seme's career as a nationalist leader, see Edward Roux, *Time Longer Than Rope: A History of the Black Man's Struggle for Freedom in South Africa* (Madison: University of Wisconsin Press, 1964), 108–13.
7. BTW, Interview in the London *Standard,* London, England, 29 August 1910, *BTW Papers* 10:377–78.
8. For a brief summary of the nature of this challenge, see articles on Du Bois, Kelly, and Trotter in *Dictionary of American Negro Biography,* ed. Rayford W. Logan and Michael R. Winston (New York: W. W. Norton, 1982).

9. Harlan, *Booker T. Washington,* 275.
10. Robert Russa Moton to BTW, 13 May 1911, *BTW Papers* 11:155–56.
11. BTW to Moton, 23 May 1911, *BTW Papers* 11:166–67.
12. Moton to BTW, 23 July [1911], *BTW Papers* 11:273.
13. William E. B. Du Bois, *The Autobiography of W. E. B. Du Bois: A Soliloquy on Viewing My Life From the Last Decade of Its First Century* (New York: International Publishers, 1968), 262ff.
14. Ibid.
15. International Conference on the Negro, *BTW Papers* 11:72–73.
16. BTW to Philander Chase Knox, 15 February 1911, *BTW Papers* 10:588.
17. I. G. Sishuba to BTW, 27 August 1911, *BTW Papers* 11:273–74.
18. Harlan, "Booker T. Washington," 465–66.
19. "The Opening Address of the International Conference on the Negro," 17 April 1912, *BTW Papers* 11:521–22.
20. Harlan, "Booker T. Washington," 467.
21. Department of State to Crum, 3 February 1912, no. 21, United States Department of State Decimal File, 1910–29, Records Relating to the Internal Affairs of Liberia, Record Group 59, National Archives (hereafter abbreviated RG 59, NA).
22. Whitelaw Reid (London) to Secretary of State, 4 April 1910; Crum (Monrovia) to Department of State, 23 November 1910.
23. Crum to Department of State, 11 November 1910.
24. Crum to Department of State, 23 November 1910.
25. American Embassy, Berlin to Department of State, 14 October 1910, excerpted from an article by Dr. Arning, Member of the Reichstag, and Member of the Chamber of Deputies, in *Deutsche Kolonialzeitung* of Berlin, for 3 September 1910.
26. Reid to Secretary of State, London, 4 April 1910.
27. Department of State to Crum, 27 October 1911.
28. Department of State to Crum, 10 November 1911.
29. Crum to Department of State, 16 October 1911.
30. Department of State to Crum, 10 November 1911.
31. Department of State to Crum, 13 February 1912, 882.00/443, no. 21, *Foreign Relations of the United States, 1912,* 664.
32. Downing to President Taft, 4 May 1912 and Secretary of State Knox to Downing, 3 June 1912, RG 59, NA.
33. American Chargé to Department of State, 12 October 1912, 882.00/447, no. 53, *Foreign Relations of the United States, 1913,* 655–58.
34. Ibid.
35. Ibid.
36. Ibid.
37. Bundy to Department of State, 15 November 1912, 882.00/450, no. 62, *Foreign Relations, 1913,* 659–62; 882.00/449, ibid., 662.
38. Bundy to Department of State, 15 November 1912, RG 59, NA. See report by Charles Young, 23 November 1912, no. 970/12.
39. Department of State to Bundy, 30 December 1912, 882.00/454, *Foreign Relations, 1913,* 663.
40. Bundy to Department of State, 13 March 1913, 822.00/455, ibid.
41. Department of State to Bundy, 3 January 1913, RG 59, NA.
42. Department of State to Leishman, American Embassy, Berlin, 10 January 1913, 882.00/456, *Foreign Relations, 1913,* 664.
43. Leishman in Berlin to Department of State, 11 January 1913, 882.51/518, RG 59, NA.

44. Young to BTW, 25 January 1913, *BTW Papers* 12:109–10.
45. BTW to Daniel Edward Howard, 21 January 1913, ibid., 107. Reed Paige Clark had also recommended Bundy for the job, and BTW sent him a letter worded in the same manner.
46. BTW to Julius Rosenwald, 24 December 1912, ibid., 92.
47. BTW to Rosenwald, 30 December 1912, ibid., 95–96.
48. Bundy to Secretary of State, 15 February 1913, no. 86, RG 59, NA.
49. Ralph Waldo Tyler to Emmett Jay Scott, 6 March 1913, *BTW Papers* 12:133.
50. BTW to William Henry Lewis, 21 March 1913, *BTW Papers* 12:147.
51. Bundy to Secretary of State William J. Bryan, 10 May 1913, RG 59, NA.
52. Ibid.
53. Department of State to Bundy, 10 May 1913.
54. Bundy to Secretary of State Bryan, 10 May 1913.
55. Walter Hines Page (London) to Department of State, 30 June 1913.
56. Bryan to Page, 16 July 1913.
57. BTW to Oswald Garrison Villard, 8 August 1913, *BTW Papers* 12:246. See also BTW to Charles William Anderson, 6 October 1913, ibid., 305–6.
58. Clark to BTW, 16 October 1913, ibid., 317.
59. Emmett J. Scott to Isaiah Benjamin Scott, 22 October 1913, ibid., 318–19.
60. BTW to Clark, 19 November 1913, ibid., 342–43.
61. Ibid.
62. Edwin S. Redkey, *Black Exodus: Black Nationalist and Back-to-Africa Movements, 1890–1910* (New Haven: Yale University Press, 1969), 275.
63. William E. Bittle and Gilbert Geis, *The Longest Way Home: Chief Alfred C. Sam's Back-to-Africa Movement* (Detroit: Wayne State University Press, 1964), 75–76.
64. Ibid., 73.
65. Ibid., 76
66. Ibid., 77.
67. Ibid.
68. Ibid., 89.
69. Ibid., 116.
70. Ibid., 94.
71. Ibid., 117.
72. George Wesley Harris to BTW, 12 February 1914, *BTW Papers* 12:437–39.
73. BTW to Harris, ibid., 442.
74. Harris to BTW, 18 February 1914, ibid., 445.
75. Harris to BTW, 20 February 1914, ibid., 448.
76. Tom Johnson to BTW, 27 February 1914, ibid., 453.
77. Bittle and Geis, *Longest Way Home,* 102.
78. *New York Sun,* 14 February 1914, quoted in Bittle and Geis, *Longest Way Home,* 108.
79. Ibid., 138.
80. Ibid.
81. Ibid., 139.
82. Ibid., 140–41.
83. Ibid., 141.
84. Ibid., 152.
85. Ibid., 153.
86. Ibid., 153–54.
87. Ibid., 154–55.
88. Redkey, *Black Exodus,* 292.

89. Bittle and Geis, *Longest Way Home*, 183.
90. Joseph Booth to BTW, 14 October 1913, *BTW Papers* 12:312.
91. Harlan, "Booker T. Washington," 462; BTW to Booth, 13 November 1913, *BTW Papers* 12:330.

10

The Versailles Peace Table: Self-Determination for Africa

> Whenever it is proven that African Natives are not receiving just treatment at the hands of any State or that any State deliberately excludes its civilized citizens or subjects of Negro descent from its body politic and cultural, it shall be the duty of the League of Nations to bring the matter to the attention of the civilized world. (Resolution of the 1919 Pan-African Congress)[1]
>
> Today all people are crying out for self-control, self-government. We, in America, realize that there can be no self-government for us here or self-control independent of that which is exercised by the constituted government as elected by all . . . We, therefore, desire a wider expansion. That expansion can only be realized on the continent of Africa, our ancient fatherland. Today, hundreds of us are ready to go back as missionaries in the cause of freedom. Will you stop us, gentlemen, by signing the Constitution of the League of Nations, or will you give us a passport to liberty? (Marcus Garvey's Petition to the United States Congress)[2]

Booker T. Washington's death in 1915, two years before the United States entered World War I, created a vacuum in the ranks of African American leadership, which had the task of dealing with American domestic race relations as well as influencing its policy toward Africa during a struggle that was to make the world safe for democracy. W. E. B. Du Bois and Marcus A. Garvey were to challenge each other about the best mechanism for freeing blacks both in the United States and around the world. Du Bois, who had openly challenged Washington's leadership, especially over domestic race programs, had saluted the dead leader, calling him "the greatest Negro leader since Frederick Douglass, and the most distinguished man, white or black, who has come out of the South since the Civil War."[3]

As indicated above, Du Bois, whose presence at the 1900 Pan-African Conference in London was due to Washington's domestic prestige, conceded that his benefactor's "fame was international and his influence far-reaching."[4] Nevertheless, he faulted the Tuskegean for never truly grasping the nature of political economy and for rejecting the notion that a people could only advance through the efforts of its elite; for accepting the disenfranchisement of blacks; and for fostering the firmer establishment of color caste in the country. Du Bois's position was that African Americans should accept the good that Washington had done and reject the rest. Viewing the plight and future of blacks in global perspective, Du Bois declared:

> Firmly and unfalteringly let the Negro race in America, in bleeding Hayti [then under American occupation] and throughout the world close ranks and march steadily on, determined as never before to work and save and endure, but never to swerve from their great goal: the right to vote, the right to know, and the right to stand as men among men throughout the world.[5]

Marcus Garvey, in far-off Jamaica, also eulogized Washington. His action was prompted by a long correspondence between the two men. On 22 November 1915, at a meeting of the Universal Negro Improvement Association (UNIA), Garvey declared that Washington's rise from slavery to the pinnacle of fame and world power was an accomplishment that should have led to his being "acclaimed head of his race, but since the Negro has no national or set ideal of himself we in our humble way can only acclaim him as the greatest hero sprung from the stock of scattered Ethiopia."[6] The Jamaican leader asserted that Washington had been a godsend to African Americans who, without his leadership, would have shared the fate of the native Americans. Then in an obvious attempt to wrap himself in Washington's mantle, Garvey declared that now that Washington had raised the "dignity and manhood of his race to midway," it was the duty of those who shared his ideals and felt his influence "to lead the race on to the highest height in the adopted civilization of the age."[7] Garvey revealed:

> I read "Up From Slavery," by Booker T. Washington, and then my doom—if I may so call it—of being a race leader dawned upon me in London after I had traveled through almost half of Europe.
> I asked, "Where is the black man's Government?" "Where is his King and his kingdom?" "Where is his President, his country, and his ambassador, his army, his navy, his men of big affairs?" I could not find them, and then I declared, "I will help to make them."[8]

Like many of his West Indian contemporaries, Marcus Garvey, who was born in Jamaica on 17 August 1887, had heard many contradictory reports about race relations in the United States. He was, however, pleased with the work and reputation of Washington and wrote to him on

1 August 1914 about the newly launched Universal Negro Improvement Association and African Communities (Imperialist) League, and the *Negro World*.[9] Garvey intimated that he knew about the split between Washington and W. E. B. Du Bois and informed the principal that, after spending two years in Europe, he was returning there to lecture on the "condition of the West Indian Negro." Wishing Washington well in the "salvation of World Wide Ethiopia," Garvey requested a small donation to conduct his work and a meeting when he passed through the United States in March 1915 while en route to Britain.[10] Washington replied that he hoped Garvey would visit Tuskegee while in the States to see for himself "what we are striving to do for the colored young men and women of the South."[11]

Garvey was pleased to receive an invitation to visit the "great institution" at Tuskegee and requested help during his stay in America since he was "coming there a stranger to those people." Nevertheless, it was also clear that Garvey had decided to do a great deal of public speaking in the South "among the people of our race." He sent "Patron's tickets" for Washington to attend a concert that he planned to organize.[12] Before Washington could respond, Garvey sent him copies of Jamaican papers that commented unfavorably on the work of the UNIA. He warned Washington, however, that the major difficulties preventing the development of the race were with "our own people as some do not like to call themselves 'Negroes.' "[13]

Washington was no stranger to infighting among blacks and no doubt recognized that this implied criticism of Du Bois. But in what turned out to be his last letter to Garvey, he apparently did not wish to fan the flames of dissent. Washington apologized for not having had the time to study carefully the plans of the UNIA, commenting that this was an "age of 'getting together' and everywhere we look, we see evidence of that constructive accomplishment which [is] the result of friendly cooperation and mutual helpfulness."[14]

After Washington's death, Garvey still maintained correspondence with Tuskegee. He wrote Emmett Jay Scott, secretary of that institution, on 4 February 1916 and reported having had a "very nice memorial meeting" for Dr. Washington at the local Collegiate Hall, adding that the Tuskegean was "pretty well heard of in Jamaica of late since the formation of this Association [UNIA]."[15] Garvey also reported that he still planned to come to the United States where he expected support to form a Jamaica Club in the northern states, but requested Scott's help in the southern states.[16] Then as soon as he heard that Washington's successor, Major Robert Russa Moton, was scheduled to come to Jamaica on holiday, Garvey decided to plan his reception and to advise him about the structure of race relations on the island.

The members of the Jamaican elite, for their part, resented Garvey's initiative, and a quarrel broke out between them in the pages of the *Gleaner,* a Jamaican paper. Garvey suggested that a great Negro intellectual such as Moton would quickly "discover the blatant hypocrisy that exists among the people." He planned a meeting in honor of the visitor in which he promised that a "very prominent person" would take the chair, and he promised to send invitations to prominent friends and well-wishers of Tuskegee. Garvey later said that it was reported to him that Major Moton demurred at accepting an invitation that was to be convened without his being consulted, preferring to attend a meeting organized by the elite in which "everybody would have an opportunity of attending and at which representative men from the better classes will be present to meet Major Moton."[17] Furious at this turn of events, Garvey wrote Moton declaring that since Black men were never truly honored in Jamaica, he wished to extend a personal invitation to him and his wife to visit the country. Garvey also advised the new principal not to "believe like coloured Dr. Du Bois that the 'race problem is at an end here' except you want to admit the 'utter insignificance of the black man.' "[18] He also announced his impending departure for the United States and his hope of receiving help to create "an Industrial Farm and Institute here on the lines of Tuskegee Institute where we could teach our people on the objects of race pride, race development, and other useful subjects."[19]

By this time Garvey had already attempted to establish contact with Du Bois. This was in keeping with a well-honed strategy he had developed in Jamaica and in Britain: to seek the support of powerful persons whether he agreed with their views or not. In one of his earlier speeches in Jamaica, Garvey had referred to Du Bois as among those persons he considered to be "making history for the race, though depreciated and in many cases unwritten."[20] Thus when on 30 April 1915 Garvey learned that Du Bois was in Jamaica on vacation, he sent him compliments on behalf of the UNIA, bidding him welcome and hoping that he was enjoying the stay on the island.[21] The two men probably did not meet at this time, but Garvey did not like what he heard about Du Bois's views of Jamaican race relations.

During a farewell dinner held in his honor, Du Bois possibly attempted to flatter his hosts by declaring that Jamaica had "settled the race question" better than most other places. He reportedly said that the problem for blacks in Jamaica was not racial but economic, and could be solved by creating "a large number of small holdings."[22] Yet despite his reservations about Du Bois's views, almost as soon as he arrived in New York City Garvey called at the office of the *Crisis* to invite Du Bois to chair the first public lecture he would give in the United States. In an attachment to this letter, Garvey invoked the numerous services that Jamaicans had rendered to "American capital, American enterprise and American industries, not to mention, our Negro people have helped substantially in pushing through the Panama Canal—to be the world's greatest trade route—and our people are ever willing to work under the progressive leadership of American genius."[23] Du Bois was apparently unmoved by Garvey's flattery and had his secretary decline the invitation, claiming Du Bois had an out-of-town engagement on the date indicated.[24]

Both Garvey and Du Bois were keenly aware that the destiny of all African peoples was inextricably linked to global events. While a student in Britain in 1913, Garvey had been critical of England and its king. He wrote in the *African Times and Orient Review* that he made no apology for prophesying that there would soon be a turning point in the history of blacks "who, before the close of many centuries, will found an Empire on which the sun shall shine as ceaselessly as it shines on the Empire of the North today."[25] Nevertheless, when war came to Britain in 1914, and Jamaica raised a contingent to send to Europe, Garvey and the UNIA held a farewell reception for its members. He rallied to the British flag "and impressed on the men the good wishes of the meeting, and the duty of every true son of the Empire to rally to the cause of the Motherland." It was only later on in the United States, and on the eve of the armistice, that Garvey again addressed the issue of the war. At that time, his concern was over the situation of African peoples during the peace negotiations.[26]

Du Bois, more knowledgeable than Garvey about the intricacies of international relations, noted the preparations for World War I with profound unease. Such activities, he wrote, were due to the disdain of men for each other, and war could only lead to "raped mothers and bleeding fathers," and "Death, Hate, Hunger and Pain!"[27] Du Bois was convinced that the "roots" of the war lay in the struggle of the so-called civilized nations to control the riches of Africa and was appalled when he witnessed these nations "fighting like mad dogs over the right to own and exploit" the darker peoples.[28]

Given his pacifism, Du Bois had no reason to object to President Woodrow Wilson's proclamation of neutrality in World War I on 19 August 1914 and appeal to the people of the United States to be "impartial in thought as well as in action."[29] Indeed, Du Bois had little sympathy for the plight of the Belgians at the hands of the invading Germans because he remembered their unspeakable atrocities in the Congo. He took the same attitude toward the millions of white soldiers of the allies who were being slaughtered on the western front because he recalled that they had also demanded to share in the "spoil of exploiting 'chinks and niggers.' "[30] Nevertheless, he distrusted and condemned the covetous and arrogant racism of the Germans and concluded that the triumph of the Allies "would at least leave the plight of the colored races no worse than now."[31] Du Bois might have preferred to remain aloof from what he viewed as a racially motivated imperialist conflict, but he and other blacks could not help being drawn into the conflict on behalf of the nation-states to which they belonged or on behalf of their friends and masters.

Such was the case of the Liberians, who out of a sense of loyalty to the United States had initially opted for neutrality in the war. This was not, however, in their short-term interest because they relied on British and German trade and now saw their revenues fall by half. The Liberians could not even meet the interest payment on their 1912 loan when it fell due. To complicate matters, the Kru rebelled once again in 1915, and George W. Buckner, minister to Liberia for the United States, who could have pleaded the settlers' case, had returned home to retire, leaving Richard Carlton Bundy as chargé d'affaires. Bundy reported that the Liberians had once again accused the British of fomenting revolt in order to annex Kru territory, that the Liberians requested United States naval support, and that they were prepared to accept United States mediation. The Liberians were especially alarmed when a British ship, *Highflyer,* arrived in Liberian waters on 18 October 1915 with an offer of help.

Suspicious of British motives and notified that the Kru uprising was endangering the lives of American missionaries, the American secretary of state received permission from President Wilson to despatch the USS *Chester* to Monrovia. The secretary also instructed Ambassador Walter Hines Page at the Court of St. James's to ask the British to withdraw their ship since an American warship was en route and the Liberians feared their neutrality would be compromised.[32] For his part, President Daniel Edward Howard did appoint a mixed American-Liberian commission to treat with the Kru, and he accepted the good offices of the USS *Chester* to bring about peace. The commission satisfied itself "that the Krus have no real grievance, that this revolt was initiated for the purpose of subverting, if possible, the Government of Liberia, and that it [*sic*] is not without foreign sympathy and encouragement."[33] The Kru, however, were apparently in no mood to accept Liberian control. Severe fighting broke out during which the Liberian frontier force killed about twenty Kru while losing only two soldiers. The government hanged several Kru chiefs for fomenting the revolt. The Kru accused the crew of the USS *Chester* of using machine guns in support of the Liberians. The American legation denied this charge, claiming that the warship did not fire on the rebels but transported Liberian soldiers and patrolled the coast to forestall foreign intervention.[34]

The Liberians were still attempting to settle their dispute with both the Kru and the British when, in October 1915, James L. Curtis arrived in Monrovia as minister resident and consul general. Born in Raleigh, North Carolina, 8 July 1870, and raised in New York City, Curtis graduated from Lincoln University in Pennsylvania in 1889 and took his law degree from Northwestern University in 1894. He subsequently practiced law in Columbus, Minneapolis, and in New York City. In his letter of application to Wilson to serve in Monrovia, he said that he was encouraged to do so by the suggestions of "many representatives of my race who have an abiding interest in the well-being of the citizens of a Republic with whom they and I are identified by ties of blood." Curtis won the endorsement of the full board of bishops of the AME Church in New York, of Senator James A. O'Gorman of New York, and of Alexander Walters, president of the National Colored Democratic League.[35]

The new minister in Monrovia was able to persuade the Department of State to permit the *Chester* to remain in Liberian waters for three additional months to ensure stability, and he requested money to provide guns and ammunition for the Liberians. Curtis was later able to report to the secretary of state that the defeat of the Kru was so thorough that their country was now under complete Liberian control. His report of the arrival of a British ship, *Prahsu,* in the area with ammunition for the Kru led the American secretary of state to query the British ambassador about his country's intention. The British denied any involvement in Liberia's troubles, and the State Department apparently believed them.

Alarmed at the continued festering of relations between the settlers and the aboriginal peoples and despairing that the Liberian government would reform its operations, abolish the liquor traffic to the interior, consolidate its Departments of War and the Interior, and reduce the salaries of members of its legislature, the United States decided to adopt a hard line. On 4 April 1917 the State Department sent Minister Curtis the following note for the Liberians:

The Department has in the past made known to the Government of Liberia its disappointment in the administration of Liberian affairs, and the time has now arrived when this Government, as next friend of Liberia, must insist on a radical change of policy. The Government of United States can no longer be subjected to criticism from other foreign Powers with regards to the loan agreement.

Unless the Liberian Government proceed without delay to act upon the advice and suggestions herewith expressed, this Government will be forced, regretfully, to withdraw the friendly support that historic and other considerations have hitherto prompted it to extend.[36]

The note contained numerous suggestions: granting the general receiver greater power to control the traffic in arms and ammunition; changing the structure of administering the interior; reforming the financial structure of the country; and restricting the granting of concessions. The note concluded with the warning that "while the Government of the United States will cheerfully accept promises in connection with the above enumerated reforms, it will not be satisfied with promises alone, tangible and permanent results must follow."[37]

Faced with this ultimatum, Curtis met with the general receiver and the major commanding the frontier force to discuss his instructions before meeting with the Liberians. When he did meet the Liberians, he was able to report to Washington that they were disposed "to act without delay upon the said memorandum of reform, as evidenced by the calling of the Legislature in extra session for that purpose for July 16 [1917]." Curtis later reported that the Liberian legislature "for the most part followed the recommendations of the Chief Executive." He was "instructed to keep the Department promptly and fully advised of any action taken by the Liberian Government concerning this matter."[38]

Shortly before he left Monrovia for Sierra Leone to undergo an operation for acute peritonitis and intestinal obstruction, (he died en route on 24 October 1918), Curtis was able to report that the legislators had no difficulty passing laws to control the liquor trade, even though some of them were dissatisfied with the reduction of their salaries.[39] The truth of the matter was that in addition to any self-generated problems, the Liberians were suffering because of their neutrality in the war. President Howard admitted to his legislature that the austerity caused by war had almost driven the country to the point of starvation and that the restrictions "placed on the trade relations of British subjects with Germans residing in Liberia will materially [a]ffect the trade of Liberia and the finance of the Government."[40]

The United States' declaration of war on Germany on 7 April 1917 permitted Liberia to start taking firm measures against the Central powers. When on 5 May 1917 Liberian Secretary of State C. D. B. King revoked the consular exequatur of the German consul at Monrovia, he informed him that Liberia resented Germany's unrestricted submarine campaign that resulted in the "sinking of unarmed ships"; the bombardment, without warning, "of undefended towns and villages"; and a program that threatened the "lives of Liberian citizens travelling on the high seas as passengers or crews of allied and neutral ships."[41]

When President Howard formally declared war against Germany on 4 August 1917, the Liberians restricted and finally expelled German nationals, sequestered their property, and after destroying the cables, converted the German cable station into a hospital. Liberia subsequently recruited and sent hundreds of its nationals to fight with the Allies in France. In retaliation, a German submarine bombarded Monrovia, sank Liberia's only gunboat, and destroyed the French wireless station.[42] Liberia's decision to declare war on Germany out of solidarity with the United States not only resulted in economic chaos but would later place its own sovereignty in danger.

The United States' impending entry into World War I brought Du Bois face to face with what he called "The Perpetual Dilemma": What should his position be? He had grown increasingly bitter about Wilson's domestic and foreign policies toward blacks. The president's first term saw the "greatest flood of bills proposing discriminatory legislation against blacks that had ever been introduced into Congress." Among these were bills advocating the exclusion of blacks from commissions in the armed forces and segregating them in federal accommodations; others proposed barring all immigrants of African descent. Most of these bills failed to pass, but by executive order Wilson segregated black federal employees in eating places and rest rooms and phased out most blacks from the civil service.[43] To make matters worse, the number of lynchings increased so dramatically all over the country that Du Bois and other black leaders of the NAACP felt compelled to stage a silent march of protest down Fifth Avenue in New York City. These leaders were also outraged when the United States seized Haiti in 1915. For Du Bois, "Haiti stood with Liberia as a continuing symbol of Negro revolt against slavery and oppression, and capacity for self-rule; and . . . the killing of at least three thousand Haitians by American soldiers, was a bitter pre-war pill."[44]

Du Bois resented the prospect of black soldiers having to serve "under *white* officers because (save in a very few cases) no Negroes have had the requisite training."[45] Nevertheless his "Philosophy in Time of War" was that blacks should "close our ranks," above all because "This is Our

Country." They should fight for the United States with "every ounce of blood and treasure," and, despite Jim Crow, blacks should face the challenge of the western front as their ancestors had in Egypt, Ethiopia, Babylon, Persia, Rome, and America, so that the world would again know "what the loyalty and bravery of black men means."[46]

The patriotism of African Americans going off to war or on the home front was sorely tested by prejudice and discrimination. Colonel Charles Young, a graduate of West Point who, as we saw above, had served valiantly in Liberia as well as in Cuba, Haiti, Mexico, the Philippines, and the western United States, was retired for physical reasons and thereby denied the command of a black division. The appalling massacre of blacks in East St. Louis in 1917 so enraged Du Bois that he hesitated to consider a possible captaincy on the general staff. His concern was that such a position would have jeopardized his ability to criticize the government in the pages of the *Crisis*, of which he was the editor. The consensus was that he would have accepted the position had it been finally offered to him, despite his conviction that a "strong word" from President Wilson could have stopped the agony of blacks both in the service and outside of it. Despite the opposition of many of his followers and supporters, Du Bois cautioned patience without compromise, silence without surrender. Always a visionary, Du Bois saw this problem in world historical perspective. As he told the "Black Soldier":

> You are not fighting simply for Europe; you are fighting for the world, and you and your people are a part of the world.
>
> This war is an End and, also, a Beginning. Never again will darker people of the world occupy just the place they have before. Out of this war will rise, soon or late, an independent China; a self-governing India, and Egypt with representative institutions; an Africa for the Africans, and not merely for business exploitation. Out of this war will rise, too, an American Negro, with the right to vote and the right to work and the right to live without insult. These things may not and will not come at once; but they are written in the stars, and the first step toward them is victory for the armies of the Allies.[47]

Most African Americans, especially Du Bois, were proud of the gallantry of black troops from the United States, from Africa, and from the Caribbean during the bitter battles on the western front. Moreover, Du Bois had made extensive plans to write a history of black soldiers.[48] He was fortunate in having as a friend in France Major Joel E. Spingarn of the Sixth Army Corps, who, though white, had kept him informed of the odyssey of black troops. On 9 October 1918 Spingarn wrote: "Men from the colored regiments come within my orbit, too, every now and then, and everywhere I hear splendid reports of their labors and fine deeds."

He went on: "You may say for me to all my friends that colored America has more than justified the hopes of those who have always believed in it, and more than earned all that we have demanded for it. I take off my hat to the courage and devoted patriotism of black men in this war." Spingarn also told Du Bois that despite the guns seeming as loud as ever, even louder, there were signs that the enemy was suing for peace.[49]

With the prospect of quiet on the western front, the thoughts of Du Bois turned to the universal problem of black people once the guns fell silent. Already in September 1918 he had proposed to the board of the NAACP that steps be taken immediately to safeguard the future of Africa. At that time, Du Bois had indicated that he had attempted to seize the Wilson administration with the need to do so. The next month, he proposed to the same board that he be sent to France to collect data for a history of the American Negro soldier that he planned to write.[50] Du Bois next presented to the board, and won its approval of, a long "Memorandum on the Future of Africa," which he had devised with the help of George Foster Peabody, a white philanthropist, and P. W. Wilson of the London *Daily News*.[51]

In this remarkable document Du Bois advocated the establishment of "an International Africa with over two and one-half million square miles of land and over twenty million people" that could be created out of the ex-German colonies, the Portuguese colonies, and the Belgian Congo. This entity would be an "Africa for the Africans," but initially it would be under the guidance of "organized civilization" and governed by an "International Commission," which should "represent not simply governments but modern culture—science, commerce, social reform, and religious philanthropy." Central to Du Bois's concern was that the commission "must represent not simply the white world but the civilized Negro world."[52] The latter should be representative of the "chiefs and intelligent Negroes" in ex-German territories, especially those trained in mission and government schools; the "12 million civilized Negroes of the United States," and similar persons in South America and the West Indies; the "independent Negro governments of Abyssinia, Liberia and Hayti"; the educated classes from the French and British African colonies; and the "4.5 millions of colored people in the Union of South Africa."[53]

Du Bois did not underestimate the difficulty of carrying out his program. Somewhat distrustful of missionaries, he insisted that the "real effort to modernize Africa should be through schools rather than churches."[54] The practical policies he envisioned would "involve a thor-

ough and complete system of modern education built upon the present government, religion and customary law of the natives. There
should be no violent tampering with the curiously efficient African institutions of local self-government through the family and the tribe."[55]
Rejecting "sudden 'conversion' " of the Africans by what he called
"religious propaganda," he nevertheless felt that "obviously delete-
rious customs and unsanitary usages must gradually be abolished."[56]
The government for this entity that Du Bois had in mind was one
which followed the example of the "best colonial administrators and
built on recognized foundations rather than from entirely new and theoretical plans."[57] He believed that within ten years of instituting such
a program, twenty million black children would have been to school.
"Within a generation young Africa should know the essential outlines
of modern culture and groups of bright African students could be
going to the world's great universities." These persons would then replace their colored and white teachers in Africa and make it possible
for industrial development to follow. But this development should follow the "newer ideals of industrial democracy, avoiding private land
monopoly and poverty, promoting co-operation in production and the
socialization of income."[58]

Du Bois had no doubt whatsoever that this plan could succeed given
the role that blacks had played in human history and the progress they
had made in the United States and the Caribbean. He felt that the world's
contempt of African peoples had no scientific foundation whatever and
was "nothing more than a vicious habit of mind."[59] Du Bois felt that the
modern world would do well to adopt his scheme, and he was convinced
that "the barter of colonies without regard to the wishes or welfare of the
inhabitants" had been the cause of war and the bane of civilized people.
This, he felt, had led to "unbridled exploitation and an excuse for
unspeakable atrocities" committed against native populations. Du Bois
was convinced that "we can, if we will, inaugurate on the Dark Continent a last great crusade for humanity. With Africa redeemed, Asia
would be safe and Europe indeed triumphant."[60]

The board of the NAACP, while not as internationally minded as Du
Bois, saw the political capital to be gained from his initiative. The
members endorsed his memorandum and voted to appoint a committee
of three to select a group of twenty-five "representative Negroes" to join
Du Bois in selling this plan to the Wilson administration. Miss Mary
White Ovington, acting board chair, who authorized $1,500 for Du
Bois's travel expenses remarked: "[T]he African situation was a live one

in that it would give the Association considerable publicity, that it could be used as a leverage to promote the general cause."[61]

Du Bois, for his part, saw a capital opportunity to internationalize the plight of blacks in America, in Africa, and in the global arena. He was also anxious that the American delegation to Versailles should have black delegates who could defend their cause and that of Africa, and on 27 November 1918 he wrote to President Wilson:

> The International Peace Conference that is to decide whether or not peoples shall have the right to dispose of themselves will find in its midst delegates from a nation which champions the principle of the "consent of the governed" and "government by representation." That nation is our own, and includes in itself more than twelve million souls whose consent to be governed is never asked. They have no members in the legislatures of states where they are in the majority, and not a single representative in the national Congress.[62]

Undoubtedly taking umbrage at this letter, Wilson's secretary responded regretting that "the President finds it absolutely necessary from this time until he leaves for Europe to reserve all his time for what must be done, and done carefully, by way of preparing for his absence."[63]

This rebuff did not daunt Du Bois, however, because he was convinced that the future of Africa was one of the most important questions to be answered after the war. Noting the role that African soldiers under white leadership were playing in defeating the Central powers, he hoped that labor unions or other organizations might demand a new deal for the Africans. Barring that, he feared that an organization such as the proposed League of Nations would address the problems of Africa only as an "afterthought." "This mental attitude toward Africa and its problems," he felt, "builds itself upon unclear thinking based on the tyranny of conventional words."[64] With this in mind, Du Bois wrote to several world leaders and to the American Secretaries of State and of War, outlining proposals for a new deal for Africa. He also notified the board of the NAACP that he had succeeded in placing his memorandum in the hands of the House committee. He told these persons that he planned to convene a small Pan-African Congress during the Paris Peace Conference to which "six representative" colored Americans of the "highest type" would be invited. "It seems to me," Du Bois wrote, "it would be a calamity for the two hundred million of black people to be absolutely without voice or representation at this great transformation of the world."[65] Official Washington kept Emmett Jay Scott, the Negro special assistant to the secretary of war, informed of Du Bois's plans, but had no intention of having blacks on the American delegation for fear they would embarrass President Wilson.[66]

Like many black individuals and organizations other than Du Bois and the NAACP, Marcus Garvey felt that something should be done at the Paris Peace Conference to defend the interest of African peoples. He had spent most of the war years protesting discrimination in the United States and in other parts of the African diaspora, building the UNIA, and spreading its gospel far and wide.[67] Nevertheless, Garvey kept an eye on the war in Europe and occasionally included it in his speeches dealing with race relations. On 5 November 1918 he attempted to get Nicholas Murray Butler, president of Columbia University, to address the Harlem chapter of the UNIA meeting on 10 November (the eve of the armistice), indicating that due to "recent developments arising out of the war conflict in Europe" and about which "all the oppressed peoples of the world" were preparing to present their just claims to the Peace Conference, the UNIA, representing the "new Negro of this Western Hemisphere," was "determined to also formulate and submit to the Conference our plans for the future government of our struggling and oppressed race." Once again, and for the fourth time, the educator at Morningside Heights begged off from meeting with Garvey, claiming prior engagements. Also invited to attend the mass meeting were such other important whites as Theodore Roosevelt, Eugene V. Debs, George McAneny, Robert E. Ford, and Morris Hillquit, most of whom did not respond to Garvey's invitation and none of whom showed up.[68]

Speaking before about two thousand blacks and three or four white men at the Palace Casino in Harlem, Garvey and the UNIA passed a resolution regarding the impending peace treaty that Garvey cabled to all European nations and to the United States government. It contained many of the points detailed in Du Bois's memorandum. Among these were the call for self-determination for all colonies in which African peoples predominated; equal rights with Europeans for Africans in education, work, and travel; the end of discrimination and segregation of African people where they lived side by side with other races; the restoration of lands seized from Africans in South Africa; the eviction from Africa of all those who interfered with or violated African customs; equal representation of blacks in any scheme of world government; and most important, the turning over of "captured German colonies in Africa . . . to the natives with educated Western and Eastern Negroes as their leaders." The conference also voted to send as delegates to Versailles A. Philip Randolph and Mrs. Ida B. Wells-Barnett, with Eliezer Cadet, a Haitian, as interpreter.[69]

The United States government and the European powers were puzzled by and cynical about the desire of a large number of black individuals and newly organized groups to attend the Paris conference. The Hamitic League, a mixed group of African Americans and British West Indians such as John E. Bruce, a journalist who late became a Garveyite, G. McLean Ogle of British Guiana, and Arthur Schomburg, a Puerto Rican bibliophile, was quite interested in the Paris conference. Then there was the International League of Darker Peoples, organized on 2 January 1919 at a conference hosted by Mme C. J. Walker and attended by Marcus Garvey, which had aimed at organizing the various African American delegates elected to go to Paris as a united front among the delegates in France. Under the auspices of the Reverend Adam Clayton Powell, Sr., and of A. Philip Randolph, this group met with a visiting Japanese publisher and editor, S. Kuroiwa, at the Waldorf Hotel in January 1919 in order to seek Japanese assistance to have the race issue brought before the conference in Paris.[70]

The federal, state, and local intelligence agents who reported on Garvey's meeting in Harlem on the Paris conference suggested the possibility that the UNIA was in league with the Bolsheviks and the Irish rebels and, in addition, was looking with favor on the rise of Japan to world eminence in the hope that this "yellow" nation would raise the race issue at Versailles. A few agents believed the rhetoric and perhaps the conviction of the Garveyites "that if the American Negro did not get their rights the next war would be between the Negro and the White man and that with Japan to help the Negro they would win the war."[71]

Faced with the prospect of having African Americans at Versailles who were not only interested in Africa but also critical of the way in which the Wilson administration had treated black soldiers as well as black civilians at home, officials in Washington decided to withhold the passports of African Americans planning to go to France or otherwise make it difficult for them to get there. Neither A. Philip Randolph nor Ida B. Wells-Barnett got to Paris, but Eliezer Cadet did go because he had a Haitian passport. The State Department refused to grant passports to such "delegates" of the National Equal Rights League as Mme Walker, the Reverend Adam Clayton Powell, Sr., and William Monroe Trotter.[72] The latter was personally unacceptable to President Wilson because of his radical stance.[73]

Du Bois was deeply troubled by the refusal of the State Department to grant these persons passports, because he wanted a strong delegation to go to Paris. It is, however, not clear whether he would have received permission from the State Department to leave the country. Du Bois had sent a copy of his memorandum to members of the Wilson administration but did not receive an invitation from Acting Secretary of State Frank L. Polk to come to Washington to discuss it until 1 January 1919, almost a month after he had actually left for Europe. With respect to his departure, he reported somewhat cryptically that "only quick and adroit work on the part of myself and friends got me the chance of joining the newspaper men on George Creel's press boat 'Orizaba.' There was every disposition to refuse me, even as a representative of the *Crisis* magazine."[74]

Ironically, Du Bois shared a "Jim Crow" cabin on board ship with Robert Russa Moton, the successor of Booker T. Washington at Tuskegee, who was being sent to France by President Wilson to visit the black troops. The president was concerned that black troops returning from France would demonstrate their resentment of their treatment by the American army and of the plight of their people at home. Du Bois complained that Moton's duty "was to speak to the returning Negro soldiers, pacify them and forestall any attempt at agitation or open expression of resentment on their return to the United States."[75] Apparently someone leaked to Du Bois that the War Department was hostile to any visit he might make to black troops. On 1 January 1919 General Erwin of the Ninety-second Division, a black unit, advised his intelligence officers that a "man by name of *Dubois,* with a visitor's pass, reported on his way to visit this Division." They were warned not to disclose that they were told about Du Bois's visit but to follow his moves carefully, and immediately report his presence with any unit.[76]

Du Bois saw no conflict between investigating and later reporting upon the plight of black troops in France and holding a Pan-African Congress. The NAACP honored its commitment to him by joining other groups to hold a giant rally on 9 January 1919 in New York City on the future of Africa. Both black and white speakers endorsed Du Bois's memorandum. Among these were Dr. William Sheppard, a black missionary who recounted how he had criticized Belgian rule in the Congo; Dr. Horace M. Kallen, a white professor who stressed the need for a League of Nations; John R. Shillardy, the white secretary of the NAACP; and James Weldon Johnson, field secretary of the NAACP, who underscored the right of Africans to democracy and self-determination and lavished praise on Du Bois, emphasizing the latter's qualification for representing all blacks in Paris. He stressed Du Bois's task of collecting material for a history of the American Negro in the war; his role as special representative of the *Crisis* at the Paris conference; and his duty as representative of the NAACP to bring "to bear all pressure possible on the delegates at the Peace Table in the interest of the colored peoples of the United States and the world" by calling a Pan-African Congress.[77]

Du Bois apparently shared his hopes and plans for holding a congress with white newsmen on board ship. George F. Peabody, with whom he had discussed his memorandum, hoped that Du Bois had taken advantage of sharing his cabin on board the *Orizaba* with four other blacks, including Moton, to plan a common strategy and to be able to map out a program and "further the single-minded-cooperation of the colored people in this great crisis period of the world, when the future of the colored races is of so great moment."[78] Louis Siebold of the New York *World* reported that he had learned in a shipboard interview with Du Bois that "the leading negroes of the United States will ask the Peace Conference to turn back to native control the German colonies in Africa for national organization by those there now and by other Negroes who may wish to live under a government of their own race in the old African land."[79] Intriguingly, Siebold added that "the Peace Conference was going to be asked by Du Bois to commemorate the tercentenary of the landing of blacks in Virginia in 1619."[80]

Du Bois was no stranger to Europe or to Paris, his ultimate destination. He had been there in 1894, in 1900, and in 1906 and knew something about the protocol incumbent upon visitors to that part of the world. Thus, even before he left the United States, Du Bois had notified members of his network and interested others that he had planned to convene a Pan-African Congress.[81] He had the foresight to send a memorandum to Blaise Diagne and others about a Pan-African Congress to be held in Paris in February 1919. In it he noted that he was planning to send personal invitations to "representatives of the Negro race who can attend such a Congress and who represent the Governments of Abyssinia, Liberia and Haiti; the French, English, Spanish, Italian, Belgian, Dutch and former German Colonies; and the descendants of Negroes inhabiting North and South America and the islands of the Sea."[82] He proposed that all "Governments having Negro citizens and subjects should send representatives to address the Congress" and suggested that he was also going to invite representatives from China, Japan, and India who he thought would be interested in the "advancement of the Darker Races."[83]

By 1 January 1919, when he sent off the memorandum to Blaise Diagne, Du Bois had already worked out a tentative agenda for the congress based on the earlier memorandum he had prepared while in the United States. The program included mass meetings to be "addressed by representatives of the Colonial Powers and of the Negro nations"; receptions for the delegates; a closed conference of black delegates during which they would report on conditions in their homelands; reports of committees and resolutions; reports from colonial powers; and a closing session. Du Bois also proposed that the "Conference should form a permanent Secretariat with Headquarters in Paris," charged with "Collating the history of the Negro race," "studying the present condition of the race," "publishing articles, pamphlets and a report of [the] congress," "encouraging Negro art and literature," and "arranging for a second Pan-African Congress in 1920." Finally, he proposed to Diagne and others that a preliminary meeting be called on Wednesday, 8 January 1919, at a time and place specified, signing the memorandum "W. E. Burghardt DuBois, Doctor in Philosophy and Director of Publications and Research in the National Association for the Advancement of Colored People, United States of America."[84]

Thus by the early days of January 1919 the news of this projected event had already spread throughout Africanist circles in Europe and in Africa. Robert Broadhurst, secretary of the African Progress Union founded in 1918 with the full support of Duse Mohamed Ali who had met Du Bois during the Universal Congress of Races in London in 1911, now wrote to him in Paris welcoming him to Europe and wishing him success for the congress.[85] Similarly, the Reverend John Harris, secretary of the Anti-Slavery and Aborigines Protection Society, wrote to Du Bois regretting that the British military authorities had refused to permit the organization to send a representative to the congress. Other well-wishers, such as Mme Colman-Levy, the widow of an influential French publisher, became so enthusiastic about the prospect of a Pan-African Congress that she invited to her salon in Paris groups of interested persons from among the delegations.[86]

The American peace commission, with President Wilson at its head, not only could not have imagined blacks as being among its members but considered African issues ancillary to its treatment of the Central powers. Britain and France were determined to punish Germany, with France seeking reparations, a permanent military alliance against the

Germans, and territorial concessions. The only one of Wilson's fourteen points that bore any resemblance to what Du Bois and other African American leaders were seeking was the fifth, which called for "an absolutely impartial adjustment of all colonial claims, based on the principle that the interests of the population must have equal weight with the equitable claims of the government."[87] The president's insistence on his fourteenth point calling for "a general association of nations to be formed under specific covenants for the purpose of affording mutual guarantees of political independence and territorial integrity to great and small states alike"[88] could only have recalled to Du Bois his own advocacy of an international body to deal with the problems of Africa.

Meanwhile, in the United States, some, but not all, members of the NAACP continued to give him support. Mary White Ovington stated that it was not the intention of the national office to devote an undue amount of time to "the African question, and that a vigorous effort on immediate home front issues would be continued."[89] Du Bois agreed with this proposition and wrote the board stating that to invoke the problems of lynching at the congress might lead to his expulsion but that it was better to deal with the plight of blacks both in the United States and in Africa.[90] When it came down to it, Du Bois did not appear to hesitate having the NAACP make the Pan-African movement a regular part of its program.[91]

What concerned Du Bois in Paris was the debate among the Americans and Europeans about the desirability of permitting the convocation of a Pan-African Congress there. The Americans invariably declared that holding such a congress was "impossible" and moreover that the "French Government would not permit it" because the country was still under martial law. What they understandably did not tell Du Bois was that he was to be trailed around Paris by agents of the American Secret Service.[92] Du Bois later revealed that as soon as he arrived in Paris, he once again sought "to get a conference with President Wilson but got only as far as Colonel [Edward] House, who was sympathetic but noncommittal."[93] In contrast, Ambassador Sharp, Tasker Bliss, and George L. Beer, the chief colonial expert on the United States delegation, felt that a Pan-African Congress was a useless exercise. Using Liberia as an example, they claimed that blacks could not govern themselves. They insisted that "as Liberia does not yet hold out a bright promise for the realization of national desires for the negro, the establishment of other republics would appear undesirable."[94] Moreover, they were convinced that the "content black populations of the British Empire would not go to any new black state."[95]

At times the opposition of Americans and Europeans to the congress appeared so strong that the prospects for holding it appeared as bleak to Du Bois as they did to a correspondent of the Chicago *Tribune*. He reported that Du Bois's memorandum to President Wilson on behalf of an "Ethiopian Utopia" and his attempt to obtain an "international machinery looking toward the civilization of the African natives . . . is quite Utopian, and has less than a Chinaman's chance of getting anywhere in the Peace Conference."[96] Nevertheless, he admitted that it was an interesting action and that since " 'self-determination' is one of the words to conjure with in Paris nowadays, the Negro leaders are seeking to have it applied, if possible, in a measure to their race in Africa."[97]

Faced with these negative reactions from his white countrymen and the lack of interest in a congress by Moton, the most influential African American in Paris, Du Bois activated his black network, especially Blaise Diagne, deputy to the French National Assembly from Senegal, under secretary of Colonies, and commissioner general of black French troops. We are told that Diagne carried great weight within French governmental circles as a result of his role in recruiting Africans for the war[98] (even though, as it would turn out, he was viewed with suspicion by Africans on the continent). Du Bois had the good fortune to be able to witness the ceremony on 28 December 1918 during which Diagne was awarded the French Legion of Honor. He recorded his emotions at that time in the *Crisis:* "Vive la France! 'Mine eyes have seen' and they were filled with tears. . . . Men of Africa! How fine a thing to be a black Frenchman in 1919—imagine such a celebration in America!"[99]

Apparently Diagne was receptive to Du Bois's plans, not only because he empathized with the editor of the *Crisis* over the race issue and welcomed the idea that Paris would be the center for the Pan-African Congress movement, but also because he sought to expand France's interest in Africa. The two men held similar views on the role of the elite in the race movement but differed somewhat over the role that Europeans would play in the economic development of black people.[100] With respect to France's interest in Africa, an agent of the United States Department of State reported:

> As soon as the Liberian Delegates arrived in Paris, the French Government designated Blaise Diagne, a colored delegate to the Chamber of Deputies from Senegal in West Africa, who made quite a campaign on the Liberians, possibly with the object of increasing the French prestige and securing some sort of commitment from them. Owing to the failure of the American Embassy to reserve rooms for the Liberian Delegation, Mr. Diagne secured

these rooms and showered the Liberians with attentions and the expenditure of money.[101]

Regardless of what motive Blaise Diagne had for helping Du Bois, he did intercede with his prime minister for permission for the congress to take place. Du Bois must have been anxious about the chances of getting this permission given the opposition of the United States and his own fear that "radical" delegates might throw a wrench into the works. By the end of January he happily cabled the NAACP: "Clemenceau permits Pan-African Conference, February 12, 13, 14. North, South America, West Indies, Africa represented. Two of our delegates, Haiti, Liberia, sit in Peace Conference. Carefully selected delegates welcome."[102] Several years later he reported that the decision to hold the congress "was held up two wet, discouraging months. Finally we received permission to hold the Congress in Paris. 'Don't advertise it,' said Clemenceau, 'but go ahead.' "[103]

When Du Bois proudly declared that "our delegates, Haiti, Liberia" would sit at the Peace Conference, he was probably unaware that the Liberians had wanted to participate in the concert of nations meeting in Paris and had cleared it with Washington. Richard Carlton Bundy, chargé d'affaires in Monrovia, notified the department that the Liberians wanted to go to Paris and that both Ernest Lyon, now serving as Liberian consul general at Baltimore, and American General Receiver Harry F. Worley at Monrovia had offered to act as delegates for Liberia and in complete harmony with the delegates of the United States. Possible Liberian delegates could be President-elect James Jenkins Dossen, who was then chief justice of Liberia, Secretary of State C. D. B. King, and Attorney General Barclay. The State Department concurred with the choice of a delegation including King, as chairman; M. C. Dunbar, a Liberian senator; Worley, as disbursing agent of the funds needed by the delegation; and M. H. A. Miller, who served as secretary.[104]

The Liberians were anxious to get to Paris because they were still having difficulty protecting their sovereignty from both Britain and France, and these two imperial powers wanted very much to clarify United States policy toward Liberia at the conference, as they wished to deal with the ex-German colonies in Africa. The State Department was aware that Liberia's decision to enter the war on the side of the Allies in no way protected it from the imperial designs of Britain and France. Even when Liberia was neutral and the British and French wanted the German receiver to leave Monrovia, the Americans had insisted he remain in order to curb the appetite of the other Europeans. With the departure of the Germans and the economic crisis of the country, the fear of the Americans was that unless aid came from the United States, the Europeans would gain economic control. The Bank of British West Africa, "the only bank in the country at that time," had been aiding the Liberian treasury by providing a monthly sum to pay local bills. In 1918 it declared that it was prepared to make a substantial loan to Liberia of some $15 million, which would also terminate the 1912 arrangement, "on condition that [British] officials appointed by the bank undertake a far-reaching reconstruction program."[105] Since this would have meant British imperial control, the Liberians asked Ernest Lyon to intercede with the State Department. Lyon told the department that "the trade promised to Liberia before the deportation of the Germans and upon which Liberia depended, has not been realized and the country is in a worse condition today than it was ever before."[106] Informed by Lyon that Congress had passed the Liberty Loan Acts to finance the war and pressed by the United States Department of War for facilities at Monrovia, on 10 January 1918 Liberia requested a loan of $5 million from Washington. In September 1918 the State Department induced the Treasury to open a credit of that sum for the Liberian government under the authority of the First Liberty Loan Act of 24 April 1917. Under the terms of this loan, Liberia was to liquidate its 1912 loan from the various donors, thereby leaving the United States as sole receiver. It would improve its harbor facilities; accept American experts to manage its finances; settle boundary disputes; provide health and police services for the interior; and help reform judicial, municipal, and educational services.

While the American State Department recommended the loan to Liberia, it was concerned about the legality of the request and especially about the importance of the loan for Liberia's sovereignty. Secretary of State Polk had informed President Wilson about the possible impact on Liberia's sovereignty were it forced to accept a loan from the Bank of British West Africa and suggested that the United States Treasury should act, because "it is against the policy of this Government at the present time to permit the State of Liberia to be forced into a position where she will be dominated or controlled by any European Government or its agent."[107] The secretary added that as the "Negro people of the United States were deeply interested, it would be unfortunate if the loan were not made."[108] President Wilson replied to Polk that he was entirely sympathetic to the project. He believed that "this was a case . . . in which common friendship and justice demanded that [the United States] act in as helpful a manner as possible."[109] The department then notified Britain and France of its plans to use the loan to "convert the international receivership into an all-American affair," pointing out that the 1912 plan had proven "expensive and cumbersome" and that "the multiple control of Liberian financial affairs" had not worked.[110]

Joseph Lowery Johnson, appointed by President Wilson on 27 August 1918 as a successor to James L. Curtis, arrived in Monrovia in the midst of the diplomatic activity concerning the loan. Born in Ohio in 1874 and educated in its public schools, he spent several years as a teacher until he went to study medicine at Howard University in Washington, D.C., from where he graduated in 1902. He practiced medicine in Columbus, Ohio, until his appointment as consul general and minister resident to Liberia. With the help of Bundy, now the perennial second secretary, he had to mediate between the Liberians and the bureaucrats in Washington. While the State Department had notified Liberia that the $5 million credit was established, the Treasury did not believe that it was necessary to advance such a large sum of money to the Liberians and ruled that no money could actually be spent until a receivership had been established. The department requested Johnson to judge whether it was politically expedient to establish credit for Liberia. The department for its part wanted to be assured that both the legislative and executive branches were constitutionally empowered to accept such a loan. Then he had to transmit to the department Liberia's revised plans, which attempted to spell out in detail its own commitments and those of the United States.

Complicating Johnson's mission and the plans of the State Department were the aims and activities of the British and French who, with the end of the war in sight, renewed interest in their imperial competition in Africa. On 18 September 1918 the British voiced the concern that while in theory the loan was not in itself a bad thing, they did not believe that the Liberians could accept the dictates of a sole American receiver. In other words, the British believed that the United States wanted to establish a protectorate over Liberia and were therefore reluctant to withdraw their rights under the accords of 1912. The French, for their part, wanted control of the old German cable line from Monrovia to Brazil and urged the United States to consider approving a French railway and harbor concessions in Liberia.

When the French government suggested that a tripartite agreement should be made between the United States, Britain, and France over any plans for Liberia, the British government suggested that the Liberian matter be referred to the Peace Conference at Paris, because the "anarchical conditions in the hinterland" of Liberia were a "source of constant expense and annoyance."[111] While surprised and delighted by the relative speed with which the loan was offered, the Liberians began to have second thoughts. John Lewis Morris, secretary of the treasury of Liberia, arrived in Washington, D.C., and presented a view of the loan that was "at wide variance with the original petitions." He reported that the Liberians were "suspicious of American financial aid, fearing control and ultimate supervision of their Constitution. They wanted Black instead of White officials, except for certain specified officers, and generally speaking believed that the proposed American treaty amounted to a protectorate."[112] In the face of all this diplomatic maneuvering, the United States denied that it had any interest in establishing a protectorate over Liberia, and insisted its reforms plan was "merely in the interest of good government" and to maintain "its historical position as Liberia's next friend." Under these circumstances, it is understandable why the Liberians were eager to send a delegation to the Paris conference.

It came as a surprise to official America when it became known that Clemenceau had given his permission for the congress to convene. In fact, officials at the Quai d'Orsay even declared that the French prime minister had not actually given his approval. Ambassador Polk "notified his superiors in Paris that the Pan-African Congress was to convene without the approbation of the United States Government."[113]

The Pan-African Congress, which held its inaugural session at the Grand Hotel on the boulevard des Capucines in Paris on 19 February 1919 and lasted until 21 February 1919, was very much another of the symbolic acts used by African Americans to influence United States and, in this case, world policy toward Africa. Its executive committee consisted of M. Blaise Diagne, president; Dr. W. E. B. Du Bois, secretary; Mrs. Ida Gibbs Hunt, assistant secretary; and M. E. F. Fredericks. Of the fifteen countries with fifty-seven delegates at the congress, the United States had the largest number of delegates, sixteen, with the French West Indies coming in second at thirteen. Both France and Haiti had seven delegates each, Liberia had three, the Spanish colonies had two, and Abyssinia, Algeria, the Belgian Congo, British Africa, Egypt, England, French Africa, the Portuguese colonies, and San Domingo all followed with one delegate each.[114]

Judging from Du Bois's report, while sympathetic to the goals of the congress, the delegates took care not to be too critical of the white masters of the world and in a few cases praised what the imperialists were attempting to do. Blaise Diagne, conscious that among the French delegates at the congress was the chairman of the Committee of Foreign Affairs in the French National Assembly, "opened the Congress with words of praise for French colonial rule. He expressed the hope that the ideal of racial unity would inspire all of African origin throughout the . . . world." The French officials in the Office of Foreign Affairs echoed some of Diagne's sentiments and emphasized that his country's commitment to equality and liberty existed long before the French Revolution and was demonstrated by the presence of six colored delegates, including Diagne. The delegates from Guadeloupe and Martinique, who were also deputies in the French National Assembly, insisted that "color should not be considered in the maintenance of human rights." Two other deputies from the French West Indies "expressed their inability to understand how Americans could fail to treat as equals those who in common with themselves were giving their lives for democracy and justice."[115] The only French person who did not quite join in this chorus of self-congratulation was Mme Jules Siefried, president of the French National Association for the Rights of Women. Bringing sororal greetings from her organization, then meeting in Paris, she declared that "no one could appreciate better than women the struggle for broader rights and liberties."[116]

M. Overgergh, the Belgian delegate, who was an official of the International Geographical Society and conscious of Belgium's dismal record in the Congo, could not suggest that the Africans there enjoyed equality and liberty. His emphasis was on the reforms underway in the colony. Dr. George Jackson, speaking about his experiences in the Congo, held that the native people there had come to hate aspects of European culture. As an American, he was often distressed by the behavior of whites in his homeland. Echoing the theme of "lusotropicalism," or the notion that the Portuguese in the tropics knew how to colonize without resorting to racism, M. d'Andrade, the Portuguese colonial delegate, told the congress about "the opportunities and liberties given the natives in the Portuguese colonies." Mr. Archer, ex-mayor of Battersea, London, and the delegate from England, had to concede that "while England accords many rights to her citizens of color, she does not give them as much representation as France." He advised the congress that it was important to continue demanding equal rights for all people of color throughout the world, starting with the United States and England: "We must fight for our just rights at all times."[117]

The delegates from the United States of America echoed the sentiments of Archer in their criticism of race relations in their homeland. Du

Bois's own assessment was reportedly quite harsh. William Walling ventured that although he was embarrassed to hear his country arraigned, there were changes taking place in the United States, and "in time Americans, whether willingly or not, would have to submit to the opinion of the world and accord to her colored contingent full justice and equality." Suggesting that while France had six colored representatives in its parliament, the United States, with a larger black population, should have "at least ten colored representatives in her legislative body." Walling predicted that America "must yield or go down before the darker races of the world." Charles Russell called upon the congress to help kill the vicious notion that "one race is inferior to another." He viewed the congress as a splendid step that should be continued. He concluded, "It is a duty for Africa and for world democracy, for black and white alike. Insist upon your rights." Mrs. Addie W. Hunton, speaking for white women in America, declared that those interested in reconstructing and regenerating the world, must of necessity seek the counsel and cooperation of women.[118]

C. D. B. King, secretary of state for Liberia, who headed his country's delegation both to the Paris Peace Conference and to the Pan-African Congress, felt that he was in a better position than Blaise Diagne to speak in the name of colonized Africans, and attempted to share with the congress the dangers these Africans faced from colonists or encroaching imperialists. King expressed the hope that African peoples the world over would not only take pride in "that little independent black Republic" but would in every possible way "aid her future development." Suggesting that Liberia be henceforth considered "a home for the darker races in Africa," he told the congress that it was its duty to help: "We are asking for rights, but let us not, therefore, forget our duties, for remember wherever there are rights, there are also duties and responsibilities."[119]

Although conscious of their limited power, the participants in the Pan-African Congress took their aims seriously. In the preface to a list of nine resolutions, which they adopted unanimously and submitted to Paris Peace Conference, they wrote:

> The Negroes of the world in Pan-African Congress assembled demand in the interests of justice and humanity, for the purpose of strengthening the forces of Civilization, that immediate steps be taken to develop the 200,000,000 of Negroes and Negroids.[120]

The resolutions adopted were essentially those contained in the memorandum prepared by Du Bois and presented to the NAACP and officials in the State Department before he left the United States. These resolutions covered African concern over land, capital, labor, education, medicine and hygiene, governance or the "State," and culture and religion. Article 8 emphasized that wherever persons of African descent were "civilized and able to meet the tests of surrounding culture, they shall be accorded the same rights as their fellow-citizens." In other words, they should have full equality. Article 9 recognized and approved the prospective role of the League of Nations, especially its "sacred mission of civilization," in securing the advancement of all peoples. Blaise Diagne, president, and W. E. B. Du Bois, secretary, signed the list of resolutions.[121]

Du Bois was delighted with his accomplishments in Paris, especially with the resolutions which he, self-congratulatory, declared were heard by the entire world. He was later to declare that he had distributed one thousand copies of the resolutions to the representatives of thirty-two nations and to newspapermen.[122] His greater desire, however, was to be able to present the resolutions from the congress to the Peace Conference. The issue, once again, in Paris, was the possible reaction of the United States delegation to Du Bois's enterprise. That the White House was aware of his activities is evident from the note he received from Walter Lippmann, a reporter on the White House staff, on 20 February 1919, the second day of the congress: "I am very much interested in your organization of the Pan-African Conference, and glad that Clemenceau has made it possible. . . . Will you send me whatever reports you may have on the work."[123] By 26 February 1919 Joel E. Spingarn was writing Du Bois that George Louis Beer, the chief adviser on colonial affairs in the United States delegation, who noted that American Negroes were "restive" and whose views had to be taken into consideration, was interested in the proceedings of the congress and wanted to meet him.[124] On 1 March 1919 Du Bois did talk to Beer about the congress and about his views about the future of Africa, but Beer did not care for Du Bois's emphasis on the important role that educated blacks should play in the governance of Africa, preferring the "tutelage" concept of the imperial Europeans.[125] Following Spingarn's advice, Du Bois also spoke to Colonel Edward M. House, who was apparently sympathetic to his plan to appear before the Peace Conference, provided the president of the conference approve.[126]

Du Bois did his best to present his resolutions to the Peace Conference because he believed this essential to their propaganda value. He did manage to communicate indirectly with David Lloyd George, the British prime minister, who promised to give the resolutions "his careful consideration."[127] Du Bois's efforts to enlist the aid of Clemenceau failed, perhaps because Du Bois had to return home to resume the editorship of the *Crisis*. Nevertheless, Du Bois remained convinced that the Allied officials had effectively sabotaged his attempts to appear before the Peace Conference.

From many indications, the powerful European nations at Paris were not overly concerned about the possible effects of the Pan-African Congress either on their subjects or on citizens of African origin. Harry F. Worley, an official of the United States Department of State, then serving as financial adviser of the Liberian republic and also as Liberia's chief negotiator in Paris, who monitored the Pan-African Congress, reported to William A. Phillips, assistant secretary of state, that Du Bois had made a strong speech against conditions of blacks in the United States, but he added: "I cannot learn of any specific action taken looking toward the world improvement of the position, politically, or socially of the Negro Race."[128] This white Virginian conveyed the same views to President Wilson, with whom he was on good terms, and to Beer whom he also knew.[129] Due, in part, to his efforts, Section 4, Articles 138–140, of the Treaty of Versailles was devoted to Liberia. Germany was obliged to renounce "all rights and privileges arising from the arrangements of 1911 and 1912 regarding Liberia, and particularly the right to nominate a German Receiver of Customs."[130] But the Liberians got little else. From the observations of the French colonial official and Africanist Maurice Delafosse, who attended the Pan-African Congress, the French saw little to fear from its resolutions. After all, their man, Blaise Diagne, was president of the organization, and its seat was in Paris, from where its activities could be monitored.[131]

From the perspective of the descendants of Africa who had gathered in Paris to defend their interests, they had accomplished a great deal—after all, they did manage to use their limited power to hold a congress. Nevertheless, it is doubtful whether they had any impact on the final decisions in Paris, especially on the mandate system that was to loom so large in the future history of the continent. Writing some forty-four years after the event, one historian remarked, "Of all the sideshows at the circus of the Paris Peace Conference of 1919, the African peace settlement perhaps attracted the least attention." For President Wilson, "the disposition of the German colonies [in Africa] was not vital to the life of the world in any respect. It was the determination of the pressing European questions which was all-important."[132] True, the United States had no formal colonies in Africa, and wanted none, despite the occasional imperialistic impulses of some of its white diplomats.[133] The problem was that the Europeans were never sure of this and, for the security of their own colonies, "frankly urged the Americans to accept a mandate or to establish some form of a protectorate [over Liberia]."[134]

It is highly ironic to note that while Du Bois and his associates dreamed of having a substantial say in what happened in a post–World War I Africa, the American delegation in Paris found that "Liberia was the skeleton in the United States colonial closet":

> There we already had obligations, and if we were to insist that France, England, Belgium and Italy should be responsible to the League of Nations for their trusteeship in the case of the lands they held in Africa, there was much force in the contention that the power which stood behind the oligarchic negro government of Liberia should be in some degree answerable as well to the same international supervision. This argument was enforced by the common charge that the existing government of Liberia was notoriously corrupt; a charge which, true or not, placed the United States in an individuos light so long as it seemed to shield the native government from the very kind of oversight which it was imposing on others.[135]

In an effort to keep the "Liberian situation as a whole out of the peace conference," American Secretary of State Robert Lansing instructed George Louis Beer to meet with C. D. B. King (the principal Liberian delegate) and negotiate the loan treaty between the United States and Liberia, as well as one between the United States, Britain, and France. The problem for Beer was how to make it possible for Liberia to sign the peace accord as a sovereign nation, while accepting a strict supervision of its affairs by the great powers, especially the United States. He wrote in his diary, "We are proposing what is virtually a protectorate while at the same time asserting the sovereignty of Liberia." What Beer did not expect was that he would have to deal with King, a man who had honed his skills in palace intrigues in Monrovia. Beer noted that King was " 'a diplomatic old beggar' who bitterly resented the interference of Britain and France in Liberia's affairs," but "evidently . . . wants our money and advice, while preserving intact Liberian independence."[136]

Beer was correct about the willingness of Secretary King and about his determination to preserve Liberia's sovereignty. Pressured by Beer, King wrote President Howard:

> We shall have to give America a free hand in our affairs and be prepared to make some sacrifice of what we have called our sovereign rights. We shall have to put up with some of the bitter drugs which may be found necessary to put us on our feet in a sound and healthful condition.[137]

Beer's frustration turned to chagrin when the State Department, more aware of the feelings of African Americans about Africa given the presence of Du Bois and others in Paris, flatly rejected his draft of an American-Liberian treaty:

> In view of the fact that your proposed treaty would establish American control by American officers in practically every important department of the Liberian government—a control which is more extensive and intimate than the control of the U.S. in Caribbean countries—it is believed by us doubtful if the Senate would approve such a treaty for a country in Africa.[138]

Beer's mistake was to misjudge the political realities surrounding United States relations with Liberia. He was convinced that the State Department had "botched" his work by not suggesting that the United States assume proper responsibilities for Liberia and for failing to understand the diplomacy of the Europeans, especially the French. Beer felt that "a mandate would be the best solution."[139] Obviously, the State Department was more aware than Beer of the possible hostility of African Americans to the subject of such a mandate. Beer had rejected Du Bois's views about the whole question of mandates and probably did not believe that African Americans had any political clout to influence the behavior of United States senators. Ironically, it was these same senators who ultimately refused to ratify Wilson's League of Nations.

There is no evidence that Du Bois knew about the negotiations between King and Beer, but had he known about them, he would have been satisfied that the "diplomatic old beggar" did not permit himself to be taken in and that the United States-Liberian negotiations were not concluded in Paris. For himself, Du Bois was satisfied that he had done as much as was possible at what he called the First Pan-African Congress. He and Diagne convened a meeting at Diagne's office at 19 rue de Bourgogne on 12 March 1919, even though the permanent office was at the Hotel Malta, 63 rue Richelieu. Undoubtedly, meeting at the office of an important personage in the French republic gave Du Bois the setting for establishing the Pan-African Association of which the recent meeting was only the first. The officers of the association, along with its executive committee and such interested parties as Rayford W. Logan, discussed plans for making the organization truly international and planned to hold the next meeting in Paris in 1921. Meanwhile, the task was to diffuse news of what took place in Paris and to mobilize to protect the rights of African peoples the world over. In an excursion into hyperbole, Du Bois said that had the black people in Paris "a central headquarters with experts, clerks and helpers, they could have settled the future of

Africa at a cost of less than $10,000." Meanwhile, in an effort to reach elite blacks, they proposed to publish an international quarterly, *Black Review,* in English, French, "and possibly Spanish and Portuguese."[140]

News of Du Bois's activities in Paris preceded his return to the United States. He was to be lionized by his friends and supporters, and lambasted by his detractors, when he finally reached home. As Mary White Ovington said to him when he reported to his board:

> As I wrote you after you had sailed, what you needed to do was to get something over in Paris. That you have done magnificently. Your work at the Congress and with the soldiers has given you a bigger reputation than you had before.[141]

On 29 April 1919 he addressed an enthusiastic overflow crowd at the Bethel Literary Society in Washington, D.C., about his experiences in Paris. According to a reporter of the Washington *Bee* who was present: "It was truly a demonstration for one who had been, and seen, and conquered. . . . The thousands of people who heard him will long remember the evening of 29 April 1919."[142] The May 1919 issue of the *Crisis* gave his reading public a full report on the Pan-African Congress.

Reports also reached Du Bois from Africa about the reaction of the leaders there to his enterprise. From Kimberley, South Africa, came a letter dated 19 May 1919 from Sol Plaatje, an emerging leader of the South African Native National Congress, regretting his inability to "get to Paris in February. It is all owing to the backwardness of our race," he complained, "a backwardness that is intensified by our tribal and clannish differences. However, I take this opportunity to thank you in the name of our people for the wide ground covered and the success up to date." Plaatje felt "certain that much more would have been effected had you any information about the semi-slavery extant in South Africa."[143]

Casely Hayford, the moving figure in the West African National Congress, was already on record as regretting that no representatives from British West Africa had been present in Paris. He expressed the desire to "have a strong representation of West Africans at the next Pan-African Congress" and hoped that Du Bois would be able to address the West African National Congress in the Gold Coast. Du Bois was pleased with Hayford's statement, "I have always looked forward to the time when representative and responsible members of our race could meet together upon a common platform for the discussion of common problems affecting us all, and I am sure I am not singular in this wish."[144]

There were, however, a number of blacks in the United States, including members of the board of the NAACP, who either felt that blacks had too many problems at home to attempt to deal with the problems of others or who did not like Du Bois's intellectual approach to Pan-Africanism. Archibald Grimké, a partisan of Booker T. Washington and former U.S. consul in Santo Domingo, refused to support Du Bois's activities and continued to do so for years after.[145] Miss Nannie H. Burroughs, the black president of the National Training School for Women, who had attended Du Bois's lecture on the Pan-African Congress, felt that he was too egotistical to lead the masses.[146] She was so disappointed that Du Bois had failed to mention in his speech that the Reverend William H. Jernagin, who had introduced him to the Bethel crowd, was also present in Paris that she and others left the building with a feeling of disgust. She swore: "I made up my mind then not to have anything more to do with the Pan-African Congress until it had as its chief promoter a man who has more respect for his fellows and more common sense in handling a public situation than was shown by Du Bois on that occasion."[147] Nevertheless, these criticisms paled in comparison with the attacks made on Du Bois by Marcus Garvey and stalwarts of the UNIA.

Whereas Du Bois had the luck or pluck to get to the Paris Peace Conference, and others of his supporters were able to join him later on, only one of the delegates chosen by Marcus Garvey and the UNIA to go to Paris actually got there—and really too late to do much of anything. Not yet aware that his delegates would not receive their passports, Garvey spent much of December 1918 and January and February of 1919 raising funds for their work. On 18 December 1918 he and Ida B. Wells-Barnett appeared before the Baltimore Branch of the UNIA at the Bethel Church in Baltimore to drum up support for the delegation. As reported by the agents of the United States military intelligence, Garvey erroneously suggested that "DuBois and Moton were in France to prevent Negroes from getting the fruits of th[ei]r sacrifices on the battlefie[l]ds" and that he would guard his language to prevent "the Department of Justice or others taking measures to deprive her [Mrs. Wells-Barnett] of her passport."[148]

During the month of January 1919, while Eliezer Cadet was in communication with Haiti and being properly accredited to go to Paris as interpreter and secretary (really high commissioner) to the UNIA and African Communities League at the Peace Conference, Garvey and a whole team of speakers, including A. Philip Randolph, Chandler Owen, and William Monroe Trotter, ranged from Boston to New York City, to Newark, to Washington, D.C., to Chicago, and to Louisville addressing the various branches of the UNIA and raising money for the delegates. Noting on 21 February 1919 that President Wilson was planning to submit a draft of the constitution of the League of Nations, which he had presented to the Peace Conference on 14 February, to the Congress of the United States when he returned on a temporary visit, Garvey sent that body a petition urging it to reject the draft because it failed to do justice to African peoples.[149] The lack of any response from Congress did not prevent Garvey from pursuing his objectives.

Finally, on 28 February 1919, Garvey was able to report to his "Fellowmen of the Negro Race" that he was instructed by the UNIA that its high commissioner, Eliezer Cadet, had made addresses to the "people of France" and to the "people of England" urging them to support the petitions that the UNIA was laying before the Peace Conference. On 13 March 1919 Cadet wrote to the UNIA reporting on discrimination against blacks in Britain, on problems facing black soldiers waiting for ships back home, and even of prejudice among the French. These reports greatly disturbed Garvey, who bitterly criticized the "Pieces Conference" for having deprived peoples of their liberty, thereby preparing the way for Bolshevism which, he prophesied, "is going to spread until it finds a haven in the breasts of all oppressed peoples, and then there shall be a universal rule of the masses." He warned his followers to be prepared for the next war, so that when it came, whether "between Asia and Europe, or Europe and Africa," they would be prepared to take care of themselves, be able to fight the good fight and "be always in readiness for the bugle call of Mother Africa."[150]

What really disturbed Garvey and his followers was the report from Eliezer Cadet that when he had presented the "aims of the race, which were well received" by the Peace Conference, W. E. B. Du Bois sabotaged his work by repudiating his statement and "by defeating his articles in the French newspapers." Reacting to this news, Garvey called a meeting attended by Miss Amy Ashwood, W. A. Domingo, Allan Whaley and A. Philip Randolph, during which the following resolution was carried unanimously and cabled to the French press:

Resolved, That 3,000 American, African, West Indian, Canadian, and South and Central American Negroes, in mass convention assembled, express the complete support of Mr. Eliezer Cadet, their elected representative at the Peace Conference, and register their complete repudiation of Dr. W. E. B. Du Bois for placing obstacles in the way of the elected representative efficiently discharging his already difficult duties on behalf of the Negro race.[151]

The *Negro World* of 5 April 1919 not only carried the story of the resolution in support of Cadet and the criticism of Du Bois but blasted Belgium for retaining the Congo and of preparing for the next world war, and predicted that "when the 900,000,000 of yellow and brown peoples of Asia line up against the white ones of Europe and America not a Negro will be found fighting on either side."[152]

Cadet's charge that Du Bois had sabotaged his statements to the French press is difficult to confirm since "a search of the French papers of that period fail to reveal the publication of any articles by Eliezer Cadet."[153] Moreover, with the possible exception of Du Bois's warning to the NAACP that he welcomed only qualified black delegates to Paris, Cadet's activities while in Paris appear to have escaped Du Bois's attention. There is no reference in his correspondence to Cadet even though the two of them were in Paris at the same time, Du Bois leaving for the United States on 22 March 1919, just about the same time that Cadet cabled Garvey about him.

Du Bois's attitude toward this charge can be gauged when, in December 1920, he took the occasion of an assessment of Garvey's character to comment about it:

> Of Garvey's curious credulity and suspicions one example will suffice: In March 1919, he held a large mass meeting at Palace Casino which was presided over by Chandler Owen and addressed by himself and [A.] Philip Randolph. Here he collected $204 in contributions on the plea that while in France, W. E. B. Du Bois had interfered with the work of his "High Commissioner" by "defeating" his articles in the French press and "repudiating" his statements as to lynching and injustice in America! The truth was that Mr. Du Bois never saw or heard of his "High Commissioner", never denied his nor anyone's statements of the wretched American conditions, did everything possible to arouse rather than quiet the French press and would have been delighted to welcome and co-operate with any colored fellow-worker.[154]

What is intriguing is whether Du Bois had heard that Cadet did request and did receive an audience with the Liberian delegation to the Paris conference. Harry F. Worley mentioned in his report on the Pan-African Congress to William A. Phillips that Cadet, who styled himself "Grand Commissaire en France" representing the UNIA,

> left several copies of the publication [the *Negro World*] with the Liberian Delegates and each containing large headlines and inflammatory wording, emphasizing the wrongs of the negro Race, calling on them for retaliation, and prophesying a day of judgement and retribution for the American people. Cadet called on Secretary King and endeavored to arouse him in some sort of movement but I think did not receive much encouragement. Secretary King asked him, if the American Negroes were so thoroughly dissatisfied with the

social and political conditions, why they did not go to Liberia, which is a Negro Republic founded by the United States, and become citizens there where they would have social and political equality.[155]

Thus, ironically, through the person of Cadet, Secretary King of Liberia, who had met Du Bois for the first time in Paris, would learn about Garvey, the second of this pair destined to come into conflict not only over black leadership in the United States and in the world but also over methods by which African Americans could influence American foreign policy and the foreign policies of European imperial states toward Africa. Garvey would long regard the League of Nations spawned by the "Pieces Conference" as a "vile thing."[156] He found no reason to retreat from his position that the Senate of the United States should not ratify it. Du Bois, for his part, felt that in Paris he and his collaborators were "but weak and ineffective amateurs chipping at a hard conglomeration of problems about to explode in chaos. At least we were groping for light."[157] He did think that the proposed league was "not the best conceivable—indeed, in some respects it is the worst. But the worst International is better than the present anarchy in international relations." Du Bois felt that the proposed league was "oligarchic, reactionary, restricted and conservative," and that it gave imperialism, especially that of Britain, too much power. But criticizing as "Jingoes" those opposed to the league, he declared: "Let us have the League with all its autocracy and then in the League let us work for Democracy of all races and men."[158]

Notes

1. W. E. B. Du Bois, "The Pan-African Congress," *Crisis* 17 (April 1919): 274.
2. "Petition by Marcus Garvey," New York, 21 February 1919, in Robert A. Hill, ed., *The Marcus Garvey and Universal Negro Improvement Association Papers* (Berkeley and Los Angeles: University of California Press, 1983–89) 1:369 (hereafter cited as *Marcus Garvey Papers*).
3. W. E. B. Du Bois, "Booker T. Washington," *Crisis* 11 (December 1915): 82.
4. Ibid.
5. Ibid.
6. Marcus Garvey, "UNIA Memorial Meeting for Booker T. Washington," reprinted from the *Daily Chronicle*, 24 November 1915, in *Marcus Garvey Papers* 1:166.
7. Ibid.
8. Marcus Garvey, "The Negro's Greatest Enemy," *Current History* 18 (September 1923): 951–57.
9. Like many Jamaicans of his day, Marcus Garvey believed that "unlike the American negro, the Jamaican lives in an atmosphere of equality and comradeship, hence the outrages that are characteristic of America are quite unheard of in the island." White American tourists allegedly discovered that "all negroes are not pugnacious and vicious," with the result that they befriended and

associated with "the black natives just the same as they do with people of their own race" ("The Evolution of Latter-day Slaves Jamaica, A Country of Black and White," *Tourist,* London, June 1914, cited in *Marcus Garvey Papers* 1:43). For this statement, he was taken to task by many black Jamaicans. One W. G. Hinchcliffe wrote to the *Gleaner* on 13 July 1914 suggesting that Garvey could not have been "in his sane moments" when he wrote that article in an English paper. Charles S. Shirley also criticized Garvey in the *Gleaner* on 15 July, declaring: "There is actually no comparison between the condition of the black man in Jamaica, and his brother in America. In America he is better off in every respect than he is in Jamaica. And one who says he isn't either doesn't know or doesn't care to state the facts." In responding to his critics, Garvey insisted that he was not one who was ashamed of the "blood Afric" and claimed that during a short visit to the United States (a visit unverified by his biographers) he was aware of the economic standing of the African American. Nevertheless, he felt that while he knew that America offered good opportunities to its citizens, "I do not know if the average American negro Citizen take full advantage of same" (*Marcus Garvey Papers* 1:43–49).

10. Garvey to Booker T. Washington (BTW), 8 September 1914, ibid., 66–67.
11. BTW to Garvey, 17 September 1914, ibid., 71.
12. Garvey to BTW, 12 April 1915, ibid., 1:116.
13. Garvey to BTW, 27 September 1914, ibid., 153.
14. BTW to Garvey, 2 October 1915, ibid., 156–57.
15. Garvey to Emmett J. Scott, 4 February 1916, ibid., 173.
16. Ibid.
17. "Visit to Jamaica of R. R. Moton, Principal, Tuskegee Institute," *Gleaner,* 26 February 1916, in ibid., 175–76. Again, it is not clear whether Garvey met Moton during the latter's visit to Jamaica. But when Garvey visited the United States, he asked Moton to be a patron at a benefit concert he gave on 26 June 1917 (Garvey to R. R. Moton, 1 June 1917, ibid., 203).
18. Garvey to Moton, 29 February 1916, ibid., 177–83.
19. Ibid.
20. Pamphlet by Marcus Garvey, "A Talk With Afro-West Indians," [ca. July-August 1914], in ibid., 57. Errol Hill suspects that by early 1914 Garvey might have read Du Bois's "The Suppression of the African Slave Trade," written in 1897, and have known about his relations with the Pan-African Conference in London in 1900 (*Marcus Garvey Papers* 1:63).
21. Garvey to W. E. B. Du Bois, 30 April 1915, ibid., 120.
22. Ibid., 183, but cf. Manning Marable, *W. E. B. Du Bois: Black Radical Democrat* (Boston: Twayne Publishers, 1986), 113–14.
23. Garvey to Du Bois, 25 April 1916, *Marcus Garvey Papers* 1:187–90.
24. W. E. B. Du Bois's Private Secretary to Garvey, 29 April 1916, ibid., 190.
25. Marcus Garvey, "The British West Indies in the Mirror of Civilization," *African Times and Orient Review,* October 1913, in ibid., 27–33.
26. Bureau of Investigation Reports, *Marcus Garvey Papers* 1:285ff.
27. W. E. B. Du Bois, "Of the Children of Peace, *Crisis* 8 (October 1914): 289–90; "World War and the Color Line," *Crisis* 9 (November 1914): 28–30.
28. Du Bois, "World War," 28–30.
29. Richard B. Morris, ed., *Encyclopedia of American History* (New York: Harper and Bros., 1953), 302.
30. W. E. B. Du Bois, "The African Roots of the War," *Atlantic Monthly* 115 (May 1915): 707–14.

31. Du Bois, "World War," 28–30.
32. Bundy to Secretary of State, 882.032/15, no. 151; Bundy to Secretary of State, 882.00/496; Bundy to Secretary of State, and Secretary of State to Ambassador Page, 882.00/498, *Foreign Relations of the United States, 1915,* 626–30.
33. Bundy to Secretary of State, 882.00/513; 882.00/515; 882.00/519; 882.032/15, no. 154, United States Department of State, Decimal File, 1910–29, Record Group 59, National Archives (hereafter abbreviated RG 59, NA). See also Raymond Leslie Buell, *Liberia: A Century of Survival, 1847–1947* (Philadelphia: University of Pennsylvania Press, 1947), 25.
34. Ibid.
35. Although President Wilson had profited from the support of such black leaders as W. E. B. Du Bois, William Trotter, and Alexander Walters, who felt that the Republicans had abandoned blacks, he quickly turned against blacks and, among other things, wanted to appoint whites to the United States consulates in Haiti and Liberia. In June 1915 Bishop Walters wrote Wilson urging him to reconsider this plan and appoint blacks to these positions. Walters said, "In every instance since the adoption of the 14th and 15th amendments . . . except one, a colored man has represented our country at Port-au-Prince. The residents are bone of one bone and flesh of one flesh." Walters recommended James L. Curtis to Wilson for the Liberia post and enclosed to William Phillips, assistant secretary of state, the candidate's rather impressive vita. In response Wilson told Phillips that "my own inclination would be to appoint Bishop Walters himself to the post in Liberia if he were willing to accept it. . . . I, of course, know nothing about Mr. James L. Curtis but would be perfectly willing to consider his appointment if you and the secretary think that my idea about Walters is not wise or practicable." Notified of the President's offer, Walters responded, "In justice to Mr. James L. Curtis, an excellent young man for whom I have made an active campaign, I must decline the honor, to act otherwise would seem to be base treachery." Walters, acting on behalf of the National Colored Democratic League, thanked the administration for appointing Curtis to the post. On 13 September 1915 Curtis recommended to Wilson that Walters be named as a member of a commission studying conditions in Haiti (Applications and Recommendations File, Department of State, 1915, National Archives).
36. Secretary of State to Minister Curtis, 4 April 1917, 882.00/562a, no. 23, *Foreign Relations of the United States, 1917,* 877–83.
37. Ibid.
38. Secretary of State to Curtis, 9 July 1917, 882.00/565, no. 112, ibid., 883–84; Curtis to Secretary of State, 13 August 1917, 882.00/567, no. 127, ibid., 884–86; Secretary of State to Curtis, 22 August 1917, 882.00/565, no. 29, ibid., 886.
39. Curtis to Secretary of State, 3 October 1917, 882.00/575, no. 140, ibid., 886.
40. Benjamin Nnamdi Azikiwe, *Liberia in World Politics* (London: A. H. Stockwell, 1935), 86.
41. Ibid.
42. Ibid., 87–88.
43. John Hope Franklin and Alfred A. Moss, Jr., *From Slavery to Freedom* (New York: Alfred A. Knopf, 1988), 292.
44. W. E. B. Du Bois, *Dusk of Dawn* (New York: Harcourt, Brace, 1940), 239. See also his letter to President Wilson on 3 August 1915 in which he declared: "I am so deeply disturbed over the situation in Hayti and the action of the

United States that I venture to address you. It seems to me that the United States in this case, even more than in the case of Mexico, owes it to herself and humanity to make her position absolutely clear" (Herbert Aptheker, ed., *The Correspondence of W. E. B. Du Bois, Selections, 1877–1934* [Amherst: University of Massachusetts Press, 1973], 1:211–12).

45. W. E. B. Du Bois, "The Perpetual Dilemma," *Crisis* 13 (April 1917): 270–1.
46. W. E. B. Du Bois, "A Philosophy in Time of War," *Crisis* 16 (August 1918): 164–65; "Close Ranks," *Crisis* 16 (July 1918): 111.
47. W. E. B. Du Bois, "The Black Soldier," *Crisis* 16 (June 1918): 60. See also W. E. B. Du Bois, "An Essay Toward a History of the Black Man in the Great War," in Julius Lester, ed., *The Seventh Son: The Thought and Writings of W. E. B. Du Bois* (New York: Random House, 1971), 2:115–71; cf. Manning Marable, *W. E. B. Du Bois: Black Radical Democrat*, 90ff, for a discussion of the criticism Du Bois received.
48. Ibid.
49. J. E. Spingarn to Du Bois, France, 9 October 1918, Aptheker, *Correspondence of W. E. B. Du Bois* 1:230–31.
50. Ibid., 231–32. On 15 November 1918 Du Bois wrote to Stanford seeking the help of a black student to help him with this project. Professor Ephraim Douglass Adams responded either naively, or ingenuously, that he had the "regret to state that no colored man or woman has ever received training in the History Department of Stanford University, . . . a remarkable fact and I do not know the reason for it; yet it is true so far as I know, in my fourteen years in the History Department of this University, that we have had no colored students in this department" (W. E. B. Du Bois from Ephraim D. Adams, 21 November 1918, Aptheker, *Correspondence of W. E. B. Du Bois* 1:231).
51. Clarence G. Contee, "Du Bois, the NAACP, and the Pan-African Congress of 1919," *Journal of Negro History* 57 (January 1972): 13–28.
52. W. E. B. Du Bois, "The Future of Africa," from the *Advocate of Peace* (Washington, D.C.) 81 (January 1919): 12–13, in *Writings by W. E. B. Du Bois in Periodicals Edited by Others*, ed. Herbert Aptheker (Millwood, N.Y.: Kraus-Thomson, 1982), 2:122–24.
53. Ibid.
54. Ibid., 123.
55. Ibid.
56. Ibid.
57. Ibid.
58. Ibid.
59. Ibid.
60. Ibid.
61. Minutes of the Board of Directors of the NAACP, 11 November and 9 December 1918, Records of the NAACP, Library of Congress.
62. W. E. B. Du Bois, *The Autobiography of W. E. B. Du Bois: A Soliloquy on Viewing My Life From the Last Decade of Its First Century* (New York: International Publishers, 1968), 271.
63. J. P. Tumulty to Du Bois, 29 November 1918, in Aptheker, *Correspondence of W. E. B. Du Bois* 1:232.
64. W. E. B. Du Bois, "The Negro's Fatherland," *Survey* (New York) 39 (November 1917): 141.
65. Cited in Contee, "Pan-African Congress," 16.
66. Ibid.

67. *Marcus Garvey Papers* 1:300ff. Between his arrival in New York in March 1916 and December 1916, Garvey had established himself as an important figure in black politics. He had also tried without success to interest such figures as Nicholas Murray Butler, president of Columbia University in New York (to whom he had sent at least four invitations and had received replies), and former president Theodore R. Roosevelt (to whom he had sent an equal number) to take an interest in his activities. By this time, also, Garvey was under surveillance by the Federal Bureau of Investigation and other state and local intelligence agencies. The authorities were aware that Garvey had claimed that the UNIA was "THE GREATEST MOVEMENT IN THE HISTORY OF THE NEGROES OF THE WORLD." They were also aware that the UNIA held that "the negro question is no longer a local one, but of the Negroes of the World, joining hands and fighting for one common cause. . . . [T]he negroes know that they cannot attain Democracy unless they win it for themselves, and that some of their members are willing to give up their lives so that the others may be free." Nevertheless, by the end of the war, Emmett Jay Scott, then special assistant to the secretary of war, reported to his superiors that based on intelligence reports, "The activities of THE UNIVERSAL NEGRO IMPROVEMENT ASSOCIATION AND AFRICAN COMMUNITY LEAGUE, in my opinion, should not be seriously regarded."

68. Garvey to Nicholas Murray Butler, New York, 5 November 1918, and reply 6 November 1918, in *Marcus Garvey Papers* 1:283–84 and *passim.*

69. Bureau of Investigation Reports, 12 November and 5 December 1918, made by D. Davidson, ibid., 286–91, 305.

70. Ibid., 345, cited from the *New York Age,* 15 March 1919.

71. Ibid., 308ff.

72. Contee, "Pan-African Congress," 19.

73. Stephen R. Fox, *The Guardian of Boston: William Monroe Trotter* (New York: Atheneum, 1970), 226ff.

74. Du Bois, *Dusk of Dawn,* 260–61.

75. Ibid., 261.

76. Aptheker, *Correspondence of W. E. B. Du Bois* 1:232.

77. Contee, "Pan-African Congress," 20–21.

78. Ibid., 17.

79. Baltimore *Sun,* 22 January 1919, 2; New York *World,* 12 December 1918, 4; and New York *Herald,* 12 December 1918, 6, cited in ibid., 17.

80. Ibid., 18.

81. Imanuel Geiss, *The Pan-African Movement: A History of Pan-Africanism in America, Europe and Africa,* trans. Ann Keep (New York: Africana, 1974), 234ff.

82. W. E. B. Du Bois, "Memorandum to M. Diagne," *Crisis* 17 (March 1919): 224ff.

83. Ibid.

84. Ibid.

85. Cited in G. Wesley Johnson, "The Ascendancy of Blaise Diagne and the Beginning of African Politics in Senegal," *Africa* 36 (October 1966): 235–53.

86. Du Bois, *Dusk of Dawn,* 262.

87. Morris, *Encyclopedia,* 310–17. According to Stephen Fox, *The Guardian of Boston,* 226, William Monroe Trotter was disappointed that President Wilson did not add a fifteenth point advocating the ending of discrimination of African Americans and other oppressed people.

88. Morris, *Encyclopedia*, 311.
89. Minutes of the Board of Directors of the NAACP, 9 December 1918, Records of the NAACP, Library of Congress.
90. Ibid.
91. Contee, "Pan-African Congress," 20–21.
92. W. E. B. Du Bois, *The World and Africa* (New York: International Publishers, 1965), 8–9; "Opinion by Editor," *Crisis* 18 (May 1919): 7–8.
93. Du Bois, *The World and Africa*, 8.
94. General Records of the Department of State, 1919, C540.16/1–10, Record Group 256, National Archives.
95. Ibid.
96. Chicago *Tribune*, 19 January 1919, cited in Du Bois, *The World and Africa*, 8.
97. Ibid.
98. Contee, "Pan-African Congress," 21.
99. W. E. B. Du Bois, Editorial, *Crisis* 17 (March 1919): 215.
100. Contee, "Pan-African Congress," 21.
101. Clarence G. Contee, "Documents—The Worley Report on the Pan-African Conference of 1919," *Journal of Negro History* 55 (April 1970): 141.
102. Du Bois, "Pan African Congress," 225.
103. Du Bois, *The World and Africa*, 9–10.
104. Bundy to Acting Secretary of State, Peace Conference I, 6 December 1918, 763.72119/3641, RG 59, NA; Acting Secretary of State to Bundy, 14 December 1918, 763.72119/2912; and Bundy to Acting Secretary of State, 23 December 1918, 763.72119/3187.
105. *Foreign Relations of the United States, 1918,* 510ff, cited in Raymond Leslie Buell, *Liberia: A Century of Survival, 1847–1947* (Philadelphia: University of Pennsylvania Press, 1947), 26.
106. Liberian Consul General to Secretary of State, 20 November 1917, 882.51/762, *Foreign Relations of the United States, 1917,* 895.
107. State Department to President, 9 August 1918, 882.51/875a, *Foreign Relations of the United States, 1918* 2:545.
108. Bixler, *Foreign Policy,* 39.
109. Wilson to Polk, 14 August 1918, 882.51/819, cited in ibid.
110. Buell, *Liberia,* 27.
111. James A. Padgett, "Ministers to Liberia and Their Diplomacy," *Journal of Negro History* 12 (January 1937): 87; Jusserand to State Department, 27 November 1918, 882.77/25, *Foreign Relations of the United States, 1919,* 2:505ff.
112. Charles S. Johnson, *Bitter Canaan: The Story of the Negro Republic* (New Brunswick, N.J.: Transaction Books, 1987), 107–8.
113. Contee, "Pan-African Congress," 23.
114. Du Bois, "The Pan-African Congress," 271–74. Among the sixteen Americans were six members of the NAACP, including Dr. John Hope, president of Morehouse College; Mrs. Addie W. Hunton, a black member of the YWCA in France; Joel E. Spingarn of the United States Army, the former (white) chairman of the board of the NAACP; and two other white members of the NAACP, William E. Walling and Charles E. Russel. The other Americans included Mrs. Ida Gibbs Hunt, an important feminist leader; George Jackson, a sometime missionary in the Congo; and Rayford Logan, a black soldier in the United States Army stationed in France.
115. Ibid.
116. Ibid.

117. Ibid.
118. Whether he felt that the readers of the *Crisis* would have expected the African Americans present to "defend" the race, or whether they would have been more interested in hearing how white Americans dealt with the issue of race relations in the United States at an international congress, Du Bois did not report on the views of such African Americans as John Hope and Rayford Logan.
119. Ibid.
120. Ibid.
121. Ibid.
122. Du Bois, "My Mission," *Crisis* 18 (May 1919): 9.
123. Walter Lippmann to Du Bois, in Aptheker, *Correspondence of W. E. B. Du Bois* 1:233.
124. Contee, "Pan-African Congress," 25.
125. William Roger Lewis, "The United States and the African Peace Settlement: The Pilgrimage of George Louis Beer," *Journal of African History* 4 (1963): 413–33, cited in ibid., 25–26.
126. Contee, "Pan-African Congress," 26.
127. Ibid.
128. Harry F. Worley to Woodrow Wilson, 5 April 1919; Wilson to Worley, 14 April 1919, Woodrow Wilson Papers, Series VB, box 26, Manuscript Division, Library of Congress; 736.722119/5119, RG 59, NA, cited in ibid., 25.
129. Contee, "Pan-African Congress," 25.
130. Azikiwe, *Liberia in World Politics*, 89. See also M. B. Akpan, "Black Imperialism: Americo-Liberian Rule Over the African Peoples of Liberia, 1841–1964," *Canadian Journal of African Studies* 7 (1973): 217–36.
131. John D. Hargreaves, "Maurice Delafosse on the Pan-African Congress of 1919," *African Historical Studies* 1 (1968): 233–41.
132. Lewis, "The United States and the African Peace Settlement," 413.
133. A careful reading of the archives of the Department of State shows that while several white officials suggested that given the difficulties facing Liberia, it would have been better had the United States taken over that country, very few African American diplomats made that suggestion.
134. Lewis, "The United States and the African Peace Settlement," 422.
135. James T. Shotwell, *George Louis Beer. A Tribute to His Life and Work in the Making of History and the Moulding of Public Opinion* (New York: Macmillan, 1924; this book is a memorial volume published after Beer's death), 103.
136. Lewis, "The United States and the African Peace Settlement," 423.
137. Charles S. Johnson, *Bitter Canaan*, 108.
138. Acting Secretary to Commission to Negotiate Peace, 24 April 1919, no. 1722, *Foreign Relations of the United States, 1919* 2:474.
139. Louis, "The United States and the African Peace Settlement," 423.
140. W. E. B. Du Bois, "My Mission," 7–9.
141. Report of W. E. B. Du Bois, Minutes of the Board of Directors, 11 April 1919, Records of the NAACP, Library of Congress, cited in Contee, "Pan-African Congress," 27.
142. *Washington Bee*, 3 May 1919, 4.
143. Brian Willan, *Sol Plaatje, South African Nationalist, 1876–1932* (Berkeley and Los Angeles: University of California Press, 1984), 231.
144. Quoted in Geiss, *Pan African Movement*, 240–41.
145. *Dictionary of American Negro Biography*, ed. Rayford W. Logan and Michael R. Winston (New York: W. W. Norton, 1982), 273.

146. Contee, "Pan-African Congress," 28.
147. Ibid., 188.
148. *Marcus Garvey Papers* 1:332–34. It is understandable why, in light of his experiences with Du Bois and Moton in Jamaica, Garvey would erroneously lump them together in their Paris activities. By this time Garvey knew or suspected that he was the subject of surveillance since he warned his auditors, "You know in time of war we usually shoot spies, and it would be a good thing if by some reason the Negroes could get rid of the spies—of his writing and telling everything to the white man."
149. Ibid., 358ff.
150. Ibid, 377–81, 391–92.
151. Ibid., 392–93.
152. Ibid., 398.
153. Ibid., 400.
154. W. E. B. Du Bois, "Marcus Garvey," *Crisis* 20 (December 1920): 58–60.
155. *Foreign Relations, 1919* 1:248–53; 763.72119/5119, RG 59, NA, cited in Contee, "Worley Report," 141.
156. *Marcus Garvey Papers* 1:455.
157. Du Bois, *The World and Africa*, 12.
158. W. E. B. Du Bois, "The League of Nations," *Crisis* 19 (November 1919): 336–37.

11

Congresses and Conventions:
The Symbolic Battleground

For the security of our racial strength, economically[,] commercially, educationally, and in every way, we have decided to concentrate on the building of the great Republic of Liberia, and to make
Liberia one of the great powers of the world. We believe that the
Negro is entitled to national protection. Whether we be citizens or
denizens of America, we suffer from the abuse of an alien race . . .
We therefore believe that the time has come when the 400,000,000
of us—the millions of America, the millions of the West Indies, of
South and Central America, and of Africa—should unite our physical, moral and financial strength for the building up of a great government, a great nation that will protect us, whether we be in the
United States of America, in Great Britain, or under any other
alien government. (Declaration of Marcus A. Garvey)[1]

I am writing to apprise you of these facts because of some public
misapprehension of our aims and purposes. The Pan-African Congress is for conference, acquaintanceship and general organization.
It has nothing to do with the so called Garvey movement and con-
templates neither force nor revolution in its program. We have had
the cordial cooperation of the French, Belgian and Portuguese governments and we hope to get the attention and sympathy of all colonial powers.
    If there is any further information as to our objects and plans
which you would wish to have I will be very glad to write further or
to come to Washington and confer with any official whom you might
designate. (Letter of Du Bois to Secretary of State Charles Evans
Hughes)[2]

Liberia was to emerge for both Du Bois and Garvey as a symbol of a free
Africa and a test of United States intentions toward Africa and its far-
flung peoples. Du Bois felt that the Americo-Liberians were "kith and
kin" and that African Americans should use all their energy to construct
and protect the struggling West African black republic from imperial

Europe.[3] For Garvey and the UNIA, the acquisition of land in Liberia was a necessary first step in the realization of his dream of Africa for the Africans. With this foothold, the UNIA hoped to spread its influence and finally "kick out" the Europeans from the continent of Africa.[4] Moreover, Garvey judged Harlem, U.S.A. to be the place where the most important blacks in the world could provide help for his cause.

Given W. E. B. Du Bois's status as a native-born American, educated person, and leader in the NAACP, it was understandable that the Liberian delegation at the Paris conference welcomed his attention and saw him as a defender of their cause vis à vis the United States government. It was also understandable that the Liberians initially rejected the overtures of Eliezer Cadet and the UNIA; though speaking in the name of Garvey, neither Cadet nor his sponsor was an American native, and neither had any contact with the establishment in the State Department of the United States. The Liberians understood only too well that regardless of symbolic actions and the conflict between Du Bois and Garvey, the independence and solvency of their country depended upon the will and power of the government of the United States.

Liberia emerged from World War I as impecunious and anxious about its future as ever, though proud that it was able to attend the concert of nations at Versailles. In his annual message to the Liberian Senate on 16 December 1919, outgoing President Daniel Edward Howard declared:

> The recognition accorded Liberia at the World's Great Peace Conference which convened at Paris in February, 1919, must be a source of satisfaction and congratulation to every Liberian. It establishes for all time the status and relation of the Republic towards the Nations of the earth. Our Delegates . . . reflected credit upon themselves and the people and race whom they represented.[5]

However, President Howard felt that he had to share a number of grave concerns with his people. He lamented that despite the public utterance of the world's statesmen about self-determination, justice, and equity, and France's insistence on regaining Alsace-Lorraine, both France and Great Britain refused to adhere to the boundaries defined by the Manno and Cavalla rivers in conformity to what he called "International Law." Graver still was Howard's fear of Vice President Charles Dunbar Burgess King's jaundiced views toward "the Great American Republic which has begun to take an ever-increasing interest in the success of Liberia and the rehabilitation of our affairs." He felt constrained to "utter a word of warning that we should not let our traditional attitude of excessive suspicion cause us to swerve from the consequence of a policy which the Government was compelled to enter upon by the insistence of public opinion."[6]

Howard was aware that Vice President King had returned from Paris and Washington disturbed by American policies. As noted above, King was disappointed and alarmed by what he had heard while in Paris of the imperalist attitude of George Louis Beer. It is also possible that he was seduced by Blaise Diagne's claims about the economic benefits to be derived from the French, in contrast to those offered by the United States. Moreover, King had "furiously repudiated" the protocols of the loan agreement with the United States, claiming that "he had been deceived about its terms."[7] No doubt King knew about the alleged formation of the Liberian Development Corporation, whose goal was to develop the resources of Liberia. This entity was allegedly capitalized at $10 million, of which sum 60 percent was American and 40 percent British and French. It was also said to be affiliated with a subsidiary American corporation believed to be capitalized at $2 million, which contemplated constructing railways and other public works and desired to start a survey at once.[8] It is also possible that while in Paris King was convinced by his meeting with Du Bois and Cadet that African Americans could be relied upon to help in any confrontation with the United States.

When King finally became president he was prepared to test the limits of any accord that Liberia could forge with its "best friend." The inevitable conflict between the United States and Liberia turned upon the need of the president to reward his political allies. In order to do so, he needed unbridled control of his country's economy and sovereignty. The desire of the United States, on the other hand, was to secure financial stability and accountability in Liberia to avoid having to provide it with aid.

As early as 1917 the State Department had suggested to the Liberians that they combine their departments of War and the Interior under one head. But for reasons of local politics, the Liberian legislature, by law, had combined the departments of the Interior and Education. As soon as the legislature had adjourned, then-President Howard, by executive order, had assigned the duties of secretary of war to the head of Interior and Education, thereby placing all three departments under one head. On 26 December 1919 President Howard verbally notified Joseph L. Johnson, the American Minister that President-elect King had "advised him that next administration would again establish [an] Education Department and separate War from Interior and each of these three Departments would have head of Cabinet rank." In view of the rumor that King had approached the American State Department on this matter and, receiving no negative response, was planning to adopt these measures, Johnson sought the guidance of Washington.[9] The response of the American State Department was curt and to the point. It informed Johnson that it was "very important that administrative expenses of Liberian Government be maintained at a minimum." It advised that the status quo ante be maintained, at least for the time being, but that "any deviation from [the] Reform Program" should be made only with the concurrence of Worley, the financial advisor, and "after submission to Department."[10]

When Johnson informed the Liberians of the United States' position, he was told that President King had officially confirmed his intention to separate the three departments and to have each administered by a cabinet officer as "required by [the] Liberian Constitution." Moreover, the Liberians asserted that since King had the "distinct impression" that the Department of State had agreed to his proposal, the "suggestion to keep War, Interior and Education Departments combined places President King in [a] most embarrassing position." Johnson reported that while the Liberian government endorsed the view "that any deviation from [the] reform program should be made only [with the] concurrence [of the] Financial Adviser and after submission to the [American State] Department," this procedure was subject to any "suggestions in [the] reform program as were accepted and adopted by Liberian Government."[11] In other words, the Liberians insisted upon the supremacy of their constitution and sovereignty over any suggestions that came from the United States.

In stark contrast to some of his early predecessors who had political clout, Minister Johnson did not appear to support the insistence of the Liberians that their sovereignty be scrupulously defended. He agreed with the view of his legation's staff that the Liberians' declaration that their constitution gave them the right to have separate departments for War, Interior, and Education was "a subterfuge," since the constitution mentioned only "departments" and it was not unconstitutional to combine them. Worley insisted that the obvious motive "behind [the] attempt to separate Departments is [the] desire of [the] President to create offices mainly for political purposes." Johnson reported to the State Department that attempts to forestall King's actions had been rejected by the president. Worley then recommended that the Department of State pressure the Liberians by insisting that "sanction cannot be given to [a] budget which includes salary for more than one Cabinet minister to administer War, Interior and Education Departments." Johnson concluded that

> if [the] President of Liberia succeeds in separating Departments and elects
> what suggestions in reform program Government may adopt then presence of
> American administrative assistants is useless and rehabilitation [of] Republic
> impossible. This matter may be considered test cased and if Department
> withdraws from position already taken or compromises, American prestige
> here gravely implicated and position [of] American agents shortly would be
> untenable.[12]

Once this issue was joined, relations between President King and the United States deteriorated. Apparently convinced that he had the clout to withstand pressure from Washington, King and the Liberian Congress took a number of actions that annoyed the legation. These included raising presidential and cabinet ministers' salaries without the approval of the financial adviser and granting a concession to the Mountain Mining Company to construct a railway and engage in banking, again without approval of the legation. This latter action allegedly benefited British capital and the chief justice of the Supreme Court of Liberia. Moreover, King reportedly gave "strong encouragement" to the legislature to approve a concession to a French cable company at Monrovia to construct and operate for thirty years a telegraph line serving fifty-eight towns along the Liberian coast and ultimately extending to the Ivory Coast. Finally, the president appointed persons to the customs office without Worley's approval and ignored "the friendly advices of the United States and the principles laid down in the Reform Program of 1917."[13] Responding to these reports from Monrovia, the acting secretary of state in Washington instructed Johnson to take Worley with him to call on King in order to ascertain whether the Liberians wished to abide by the recommendations of the United States officials. They were to warn the Liberians that "a clear and unambiguous statement from the President is considered imperative at this time before further steps under the loan arrangements are taken."[14]

Embattled as he was with the United States over the loan, King could not resist the blandishments of the UNIA. With remarkable speed, the activities of Marcus Garvey and the UNIA had become known in Africa in general and in Liberia in particular. A chapter of the UNIA was established, and in April 1920 the Reverend Dr. Lewis G. Jordan, secretary of the National Baptist Convention, who had just returned from Liberia, told a gathering at Liberty Hall in New York City that during a dinner in Monrovia he had informed President King that "Mr. Garvey and his people say they are going to put their headquarters here after August," to which King responded, "Well let them come." To the applause of his auditors, Jordan revealed that he was testing King to discover whether the president had been swayed by the anti-Garvey propaganda. Turning to Garvey on the podium, Jordan remarked, "I find that Liberia stands ready to welcome you." He added that not only was Liberia the "hope of Africa" but its effect on that continent was comparable to the effervescing of soda in a glass of water. "Whatever goes out from there would spread all over Africa, and all Africa would be blessed if you strike Liberia."[15]

Garvey welcomed Jordan's report because he was planning an "International Congress of Negroes" to be attended by delegates from all over the world, after which plans would be made to transfer the UNIA headquarters to Liberia. With that in mind, Garvey had despatched Elie Garcia as his "Commissioner to Liberia" on 17 April 1920 to examine the conditions that would permit "the future establishment of the Headquarters of the Association in the Republic of Liberia."[16] Receiving warm welcomes from the UNIA chapters in Liverpool and in Sierra Leone, Garcia was pleased but a bit disturbed to be welcomed by two rival local delegations of the UNIA when he arrived at Monrovia on 27 May 1920. He promptly proceeded to reconcile the two groups before holding his first meeting. In the chair at this meeting was Gabriel Moore Johnson, father-in-law of the president of the republic, mayor of the city of Monrovia, and president of the local UNIA chapter. Attending were such members of the Liberian establishment as ex-President Arthur Barclay and Mrs. Anna Howard, "the Associate Chief Justice of Liberia."[17]

Garcia's immediate tasks were to rebut hostile charges against the UNIA published in the *Liberia Commercial News* and to arrange to meet President King. His defense of Garvey was so eloquent that the Liberian secretary of state spontaneously declared that "any Negro who fails to see the benefits to be derived from the Association [is] a consummate fool." Then on 9 June 1920, through the good offices of Gabriel Moore Johnson, Garcia was able to meet President King and to present to him the memorandum from the UNIA. In brief, the memorandum described the UNIA and the African Communities League as consisting of three million members scattered throughout the United States of America, South and Central America, the West Indies, Great Britain, and Africa. It hoped to assist in "civilizing the backward tribes of Africa"; to help develop the independent Negro nations and communities; to establish universities and train people; and to use the resources of the Black Star

Line, capitalized at $10 million, and the Negro Factories Corporation, capitalized at $1 million, to help countries such as Liberia.

What the UNIA was requesting from Liberia, said the memorandum, was permission to "transfer its headquarters to the City of Monrovia or to any other convenient township of Liberia." And because of rumors in the United States that Liberia would not welcome the UNIA, the memorandum requested of the Liberian government "a written assurance that it will afford us every facility for procuring lands for business, agricultural or industrial purposes and that the Government will do everything in its power to facilitate the work of the Association along these lines." In return for such facilities, the UNIA promised to ask its three million members to lend financial aid to build educational facilities and development corporations. Finally, the UNIA "would be prepared to do anything possible to help the Government of Liberia out of its economic plights and to raise subscriptions all over the world to help the country to liquidate its debts to foreign governments."[18] This request was backed by ex-President Barclay.

After praising the UNIA, President King roundly condemned the articles hostile to the UNIA, arguing that these were not the sentiments of the Liberian people. The president expressed his best wishes for the work of the UNIA and, true to his word, sent an answer to the UNIA's memorandum four days later. He instructed his secretary of state, Edwin Barclay, to say to the UNIA that "the Government of Liberia, appreciating as they do the aims of your organization as outlined by you, have no hesitancy in assuring you that they will afford the Association every facility legally possible in effectuating in Liberia, industry, agriculture and business projects."[19] King allegedly reminded Garcia that while in the United States in August 1919 on a visit to President Wilson, he had met Garvey and had "advised him to come to Liberia."[20] Garcia left Monrovia for Sierra Leone on 27 June 1920 en route to the United States.

An astute observer, Garcia prepared a rather critical report on Liberia intended for the eyes only of Garvey. Intriguingly, this report on the Americo-Liberians was similar to those sent to the State Department by J. Milton Turner, the first minister resident and consul general to Liberia, and by most of his successors. Noting that the commonality of Liberians had a strong revulsion "for any kind of work," even extending so far as to import their national food, rice, from elsewhere, Garcia reported that the educated "Americo-Liberians, also called 'Sons of the Soil,' " as contrasted with the "natives," constituted "*the most despica-*

ble element in Liberia." He alleged that most of these people, educated in England and other places, were dishonest and only wanted government jobs where they could receive "*graft.*" Moreover, he reported, they were hostile to any attempt on the part of American and West Indian immigrants to get involved in local politics. He warned: "This fact is of great importance *and I dare suggest that words must be given to any one going to Liberia in the interest of the U.N.I.A. to deny firmly any intention on our part to enter into politics in Liberia.*" Such an approach was necessary, he counseled, to prevent any opposition to the UNIA getting a "foothold in the country to act as we see best for their own betterment and that of the race at large." Again, the UNIA was counseled not to say anything about the native peoples who were being treated as slaves and human chattels, because the Liberians were opposed to any element which could end "*their political tyranny, their habits of graft and their polygamic freedom.*"[21]

But as critical as Garcia was about the Americo-Liberians, he was more bitter still about the attitudes and actions of the white imperial powers. He remarked, "If Liberia ever needed help, it is at this present time when the small Republic is the object of a close contest between America, England and France." He reported on the general hope of the Liberians that the United States, "their best friend," would give them a loan, thereby permitting them to avoid dealing with Britain and France. The Europeans, however, were waging a propaganda battle against this possibility and were promising Liberia generous aid in the hope of finally taking over the country. Garcia told Garvey that faced with the possibility that the UNIA might help, the French, while outwardly friendly, had issued an order that he not visit any of their colonies in West Africa.

The UNIA commissioner for Liberia reserved his greatest scorn for the United States. Someone from the Liberian foreign office had permitted him to read the "famous memorandum" that the American chargé d'affaires, Richard Carlton Bundy, had recently presented to the Liberians. Garcia called it "from beginning to end . . . the most insulting and humiliating document ever presented to a free people for ratification." He then recounted what the memorandum demanded from the Liberians: all debts to be investigated before being paid by the United States; a receiver general to be appointed by the United States with the right to fix salaries of all Liberian officials and to collect all revenues; the local senate to have no rights to make concessions and so on. Garcia expressed the fear that if the Liberians accepted the demands of the

United States, it "will mean the election of a white king over Liberia, and will be a great inconvenience to the U.N.I.A." Meanwhile, he feared that the British and the French were attempting to extend their already great influence in Liberia as they felt that the Liberians would reject the Americans' memorandum.[22]

Garcia ended his report by stating that he had received a tip that Gabriel Johnson, who had been chosen to be the Liberian delegate to the UNIA convention, "was secretly empowered by the Government to see what help could be gotten from the U.N.I.A." The commissioner felt pity for Liberia, "hard up against three strong white nations determined to choke her. Should she have the best chance at it? This is the problem. May God help her! for, as it is, any one of the three will be harmful to her later." He concluded:

> However, the American memorandum, though insulting as it is, proves that the United States are well informed of the unreliability of the Liberians in handling money. I make this statement to impress you, Mr. President, with the fact, that whatever finance is to be given by the U.N.I.A. to the Government, we must keep an eye open on the use made with the help so given and even manage to have a voice in the disbursements: otherwise, it will be only fattening the purses of a few individuals.[23]

Garcia believed that the "people of Liberia welcome sincerely the U.N.I.A. and expect much from it." He insisted that they needed help urgently, but he sympathized with their fear of "political domination" from their helpers, whether "blacks or whites." In view of this, Garcia felt constrained to report to Garvey that a news article in the *Negro World* dealing with the draft of a constitution for the UNIA referred to the *"powers of the Potentate"* and the *"election of a ruler for all black people [which] have been a troublesome nightmare to them."* Nevertheless, Garcia felt that "with diplomacy and also modesty and discretion on the part of those who will represent the U.N.I.A. in Liberia, *our work is bound to be successful along ALL lines* [emphasis his]."[24]

Meanwhile, in New York, Garvey continued to plan furiously for the month-long convention of the black people of the world to come to New York to represent the race. He was aware that agents of the federal government of the United States had penetrated his organization and had access to his plans.[25] Nevertheless, he was determined that "the American Negro . . . will elect a leader for himself . . . And on the same day we elect a Negro for the American Negroes, we shall elect a leader for all the Negro peoples of the world."[26] This was necessary, he felt, so that when such great powers as England, France, or Germany desired to deal with Negroes, "they will have to address their diplomatic note to the leader of the Negro peoples of the world, and we will debate the question and give suitable reply."[27] Garvey said neither who the African American could be nor who could be the leader of the entire black world. Nevertheless, Cyril V. Briggs of the African Blood Brotherhood and a harsh critic of Garvey wrote in his paper, the *Crusader,* that Garvey wanted to become a "Paramount Chief" of the Negro race. Briggs felt that the convention was being called for the purpose of electing "His Supreme Highness, the Potentate, His Highness, the Supreme Deputy, and other high officials, who will preside over the destiny of the Negro peoples of the world until an African empire is founded."[28]

While Garvey rejected Briggs's allegation, he lost no opportunity to drum up support for the convention. Asserting that he needed no less than $2 million for this enterprise, Garvey beseeched his followers to give whatever they could in support of the cause. He promised that at the convention the "Magna Charta of Negro rights will be written. A consti-tution will be given to the world by which the present and future genera-tions of Negroes shall be governed."[29] Ignoring the possible presence of government agents, Garvey seldom bit his tongue while inveighing against those he considered enemies of blacks. He was, however, both-ered by the problems facing his fledgling Black Star Line but felt that he was doing his best to make sure that the books were in order. Neverthe-less, he was branded by government agents as an agitator of the worst sort, even though they did not question his honesty. What concerned and amused these agents was Garvey's hold on his followers. As one wrote:

> Most of these people haven't any idea of the geographical location of Africa or under what conditions Africa i[s] governed by the several European countries. Some of these people really believe that after this convention they will have elected a president for Africa and all they will have to do is to go over there and set up their government.[30]

It is possible that many of Garvey's followers, like those of Chief Alfred Charles Sam or earlier emigrants, did believe that he advocated mass migration of New World blacks to Africa. But Garvey always insisted that he was too wise to recommend such a move. On one occa-sion he declared:

> It does not mean that all Negroes must leave America and the West Indies and go to Africa to build up a government. . . . [We] say to all Negroes in America, the West Indies and elsewhere, seize all opportunities that come to you, but remember our success educationally, industrially and politically is based upon the protection of a nation founded by ourselves. And that nation can be nowhere else but in Africa.[31]

As the 1 August deadline for the opening of the convention approached, Garvey looked about to find an African American whose name could be placed in nomination as leader. Perhaps out of a sense of humor, or perhaps with genuine hope, Garvey wrote a letter to Du Bois on 16 July 1920 telling him about the "International Convention of Negroes" to be held in August and informing him that delegates from the Negro people of the forty-eight states of the Union would elect a leader to be the "accredited spokesman of the American Negro people. You are hereby asked to be good enough to allow us to place your name in nomination for the post."[32] Du Bois responded a week later saying, "I thank you for the suggestion but under no circumstances can I allow my name to be presented." But his anger was clearly visible when, in response to Garvey, he wrote that his magazine, the *Crisis,* had received several inquiries concerning Garvey and his organization, and "I desire to publish in the *Crisis* some account of you and your movement." Du Bois appended a list of questions that he wished Garvey to answer and in a postscript asked the president general of the UNIA for a recent photograph and an account of his life.[33] Almost immediately afterward, Du Bois began to make enquiries from several sources about the financial status of the UNIA and especially about the Black Star Line.[34]

On 1 August 1920, a date commemorating the abolition of slavery in the West Indies, the International Convention of Negroes opened in what the *Negro World Convention Bulletin* called a "Blaze of Glory." The newspaper added that in attendance were "more than 10,000 Negroes, representing every class of the race from all over the United States, Africa, Central and South America and the West Indies." Welcoming the delegates to Liberty Hall, Garvey summarized the goal of the representatives of the Negroes of the world:

> They are here for the purpose of discussing the great problems that confront the Negro; they are here for the purpose of framing a bill of rights for the [N]egro peoples of the world; they are here for the purpose of laying plans for the redemption of the great continent of Africa. We assemble ourselves together because we believe this is the age in which the Negro, like all the other oppressed peoples of the world, should strike out for, his own redemption. From the four corners of the world come delegates who are imbued with the spirit of liberty.[35]

The program of that day and the following days included a "silent parade" of all members and delegates; divine services; a mass parade of all the delegates and members; and a "big public mass meeting in Madison Square Garden." Declaring that some of the parades were the largest ever sponsored anywhere in the world by blacks, the *Negro World* reported on contingents of military units, military bands, Black Cross nurses, and thousands of onlookers waving handkerchiefs.

The real business of the convention took place during the following days and involved reports by delegates from most of the forty-eight states, and from the West Indies, Central and South America, Canada, and Africa, especially Nigeria and Liberia. Most of the New World delegates had apparently emigrated to the United States years before. Nevertheless, they had vivid memories about conditions such as discrimination and segregation in their homelands and beseeched the UNIA to help. One of the more eagerly awaited reports was the one from Gabriel Moore Johnson, mayor of Monrovia. In introducing Johnson, Garvey remarked that "the Divine Architect and Creator has seen fit in His great wisdom to preserve at least one spot on the West Coast for the Negro."[36] After congratulating the delegates and Garvey, Johnson explained that although he occupied an official position in Monrovia, he was at the convention "solely as a delegate from the local division of the Universal Negro Improvement Association in Monrovia." Declaring that although he was not able to give the delegates "any guarantee of the Republic of Liberia in any official capacity, or from the government officials there," he could outline the problems and possibilities of his country. He expressed the hope that the UNIA would "take on the right spirit and with concerted action on [its] part" Liberia would some day "grow and prosper and be what we all desire it to be—a great Republic."[37]

Occupying the minds of most of the delegates to the convention were such issues as a constitution for blacks, the "back to Africa" question, and the selection of officers for the association. One of the most troubling clauses in the "bill of rights" was one stating "that no Negro shall engage himself in battle for an alien [*sic*] race without first obtaining the consent of the leader of the Negro people of the world, except in a matter of national self-defense." Fearing that this clause would jeopardize their citizenship or resident status in the United States, many delegates questioned the wisdom of it. Nevertheless, it was adopted as Clause 47 of the declaration. The first clause declared that "all men, women and children of our blood throughout the world free denizens" were to be considered "free citizens of Africa, the Motherland of all Negroes." To ensure this right, it was declared that all the "duly accredited representatives" of the UNIA "be given proper recognition in all leagues, conferences, conventions or courts of international arbitration wherever human rights are discussed." All fifty-four clauses spelled out in clear detail what the UNIA considered to be "fair and just rights," as well as the treatment it proposed to demand for blacks "of all men in the future." When the document was finally presented to the convention on 20 August 1920, Garvey vowed that it might take fifty years to put the clauses into effect but that he was prepared for the effort.[38]

The "Declaration of Rights of the Negro Peoples of the World" spelled out clearly that the members of the UNIA believed in the freedom of Africa for the black people of the world and, by extension, the principle of Europe for the Europeans and Asia for the Asians. It therefore demanded "Africa for the Africans at home and abroad." Nevertheless, Garvey explained to the delegates at the convention,

> the doctrines of going "Back to Africa" must be clearly understood. We are not preaching any doctrines to ask all the negroes of Harlem and of the United States to pack up their trunks and to leave for Africa. We are not crazy, because we have to wait until we get a Lenox Avenue and a Seventh Avenue before we could get the Negroes of Harlem to leave for Africa. . . . But we are asking you to get this Organization to do the pioneering work. The majority of us may remain here, but we must send our scientists, our mechanics, and our artisans and let them build railroads, let them build the great Educational and other institutions necessary and when they are constructed, the time will come for the command to be given, "Come Home" to Lenox Avenue, to Seventh Avenue.[39]

Intriguingly, Garvey's attitude toward the possibility of blacks "returning to Africa" was similar to that of the early "exodusters"—Lott Carey, Henry Highland Garnet, Henry McNeal Turner, Chief Alfred Charles Sam. He believed, as they did, that a "free and redeemed Africa" was necessary because "no security, no success can come to the Black man, so long as he is outnumbered in the particular community where his race may become industrially and commercially strong." Thus the need to formulate a "Bill of Rights in order to build up a Free and Independent Africa."[40]

The refusal of W. E. B. Du Bois to permit his name to be placed in nomination as leader of African Americans did not stop Garvey from asking other important blacks to consider the honor. John E. Bruce declined the nomination, insisting that "a younger and more active man than I know myself to be should be selected to fill this post." Nevertheless, he pledged to Garvey that he was "at one with the organization in all that it is attempting, has attempted and will attempt" under his leadership, to unite the race "for the ultimate redemption of Africa from the plunderers and buccaneers of an alien race who would barter their

God for his image in gold."[41] There were allegations that Robert Russa Moton, president of Tuskegee, was offered and refused $10,000 to attend the convention and to permit his name to be placed in nomination as "leader of the American negroes in this Universal world movement."[42] The man ultimately nominated and elected to this office was the Reverend James W. H. Eason of Philadelphia, an early supporter of Garvey and chaplain general of the UNIA. He was authorized a yearly salary of $10,000, and it was rumored that he planned to live in Washington in a "symbolic Black House."[43]

The Honorable Gabriel Moore Johnson, the most important delegate directly from Africa, was chosen by acclamation the "Potentate Leader of the Negro Peoples of the World and head of the U.N.I.A." George Osborne Marke, from Sierra Leone, was chosen "Supreme Deputy of the U.N.I.A. and second World Leader of the Negro Peoples of the World," again by acclamation. It was the position of president of Africa that created a great deal of excitement and dissension. Somewhat self-servingly, Garvey insisted that "a native born African should not be elected as President of Africa, as in his opinion, such a man would be under very grave suspicion by England, France and other European countries who own territory there." Garvey said that he feared that such a person would be quickly eliminated by the Europeans since his task would be to found a republic in Africa, which would involve spreading propaganda for that purpose. While this proposition appeared reasonable to many New World delegates, some African delegates felt that "Africans can better understand the nature of African chiefs, kings etc. who would resent an outsider." This did not sit very well with Garvey, and his position won the day though not without opposition from Africans and the black press.

Garvey was elected "Provisional President of Africa and President General of the U.N.I.A." much to the hostility of the black press and a number of Africans. One African who called himself "Prince" was "greatly enraged at the fact that Garvey had elected himself President of Africa without giving the honors to them."[44] These complaints were simply ignored in the general jubilation of people caught up in the drama and excitement of what they considered to be a history-making convention. In the words of an editor of the *Negro World,* Garvey had "proved himself, more than ever before, a born orator and leader of his race. There is no other man in the race today who is his equal in this respect[,] Prof. [W]. E. [B.] Du Bois and the Hon. Robert Mot[o]n, president of Tuskegee Institute, notwithstanding."[45]

Official Washington, while somewhat amused by the events at the convention, was kept fully informed by its agents of what was taking place in New York. One federal bureaucrat sent a list of questions concerning the composition of the UNIA, its goals, foreign allies, and future prospects for which he wanted answers. One of the government's most trusted informers, Special Agent P-138 reported:

> So far as I can see the movement has ceased to be simply a nationalist movement but among the followers it is like a religion. . . . I am fully convinced that Garvey's teaching is without doubt a purely anti-white campaign and the Negro World is the instrument employed to spread the propaganda . . . That he is flirting with the leaders of the Irish, Egyptian, Indian and Japanese only so far as to further his aims. . . . That his followers are under the impression owing to Garvey's statement from the platform, that he has defied state and Government, outwitted the State District Attorney[,] hence he is looked upon as a black Moses. That the convention and movement is only stirring up race hatred and widening the gap between the Races which the other intelligent leaders took years to build up.[46]

At the end of the convention, the various agents appeared to have reached a consensus: that both the announced and covert aims of the movement were to redeem Africa from European rule and eventually to establish on the African continent a strong Negro government; that it planned to establish an International Negro Business Corporation to run a steamship company, banks, stores, etc.; that Garvey's election as chief of the organization was unquestioned; that its members, while initially primarily lower class West Indians, had started "to attract many people who formerly regarded him as a joke and they are speaking more seriously of his work;" and most important for the people in Washington, that there "appears to be nothing in this movement that should give the American government concern" and that the entire aim of the movement "is directed toward the goal of liberating Africa from European rule and all the propaganda is shaped along that line."[47]

A number of newspapers and private persons in New York City, as well as elsewhere in the country and overseas, began to take Garvey's activities more seriously than did the United States government. One of the complaints of the government's agents was that "the white daily newspapers, viz: New York World, Globe, Post, etc. are doing more to spread this anti-white propaganda by advertising and boosting Garvey, reporting his meetings, etc., than even Garvey himself." Sympathizers of the UNIA eagerly bought these papers whenever articles on Garvey appeared and claimed that "he must be a powerful man, a man who is right when white newspapers speak and write of him."[48] Of course, these papers often wished only to increase their circulation, but they contributed to the symbolic value and propaganda notions of Garvey.

As important to African Americans were the attempts of the media and ideologues and publicists of various kinds, both black and white, to exploit the real and imagined divisions among them created by the rise of the Garvey movement. Charles Mowbray White, a rightist lecturer on socialism and radicalism, succeeded in interviewing and publicizing the views of Du Bois, Garvey, Chandler Owen, and A. Philip Randolph about the UNIA. Garvey briefed White about his plans for blacks and Africa. He criticized Du Bois as representing "the ante-bellum negro," while since World War I, blacks had developed a "new spirit" for world independence and a nation of their own. Owen told White that Garvey was "either a fool or a rogue" and that the "New Negro" would not be gulled into action by emotionalism and utopian dreams. Owen attempted to impress his interlocuter by claiming that he was for socialism and "for equality in all things with the whites, even intermarriage." Speaking on behalf of himself and Randolph, Owen insisted, "We don't believe in the cry of the Garvey gang—'Africa for the Africans,' no more than we accept the cry of America for the Americans. We are not nationalists but internationalists." Criticizing Du Bois for being the lackey of capitalist liberals, even though he was involved with the "anti-white" NAACP, Owen stated that Garvey meant to kill all the mulattoes in the world and that, given its extreme positions, the UNIA was bound to fail within three months.[49]

If the transcript of Du Bois's interview with White about Garvey is to be believed, the editor of the *Crisis* was still ambivalent about the UNIA and its leader. On the one hand, he reportedly said, "I do not believe that Marcus F [*sic*] Garvey is sincere. I think he is a demagogue, and that his movement will collapse in a short time." On the other hand, he reportedly told White, "It may be that Garvey's movement will succeed. I shan't raise a hand to stop it." Du Bois added that hundreds of colored persons had asked his opinion about the UNIA but that he was obliged to reply that he did not have sufficient information by which to advise anyone.[50]

What was instructive, however, was that in talking to White, Du Bois attempted to put Garvey's movement in perspective for the average white reader. He insisted that the UNIA movement was not "an American movement in any sense of the word" and that most of Garvey's followers were West Indians. Moreover, Du Bois reportedly said that he felt that the UNIA's alliances with Bolsheviks and Sinn Feiners could not possibly improve the condition of blacks. Du Bois felt that the strength of the movement lay in the disgust of blacks at constant lynchings and black soldiers "return[ing] from France filled to the boiling point with hatred for the white Americans never before dreamed of." Du Bois told White, "The time has come when the negro must be placed on an equal footing with the white man, socially and otherwise . . . There should be no distinction between peoples because of color differences." With these words, Du Bois allegedly gave White an advance copy of the 15 September 1920 issue of the *Crisis,* which for the first time dealt with the Garvey question.[51]

While it is clear that White's reports indicated a racist preoccupation with intermarriage, he did manage to get an initial reading about some of the thinking of African American leaders toward Garvey and the UNIA. Some of these leaders could not deal effectively with what E. Franklin Frazier called the first true mass movement led by a charismatic leader and attributed the phenomenon of the UNIA to its West Indian membership.[52] Yet Du Bois's attempt to attribute part of the movement's success to the postwar climate of racist repression suggests that Du Bois was aware either that the movement appealed to many African Americans or that the West Indians were able to articulate the inchoate feelings of their American-born neighbors. In any case, White was not impressed by any of the four black leaders he interviewed. He considered them "utterly unfitted for their work because of their close sympathy and affiliation with the ultra-radical forces."[53] With respect to Garvey, he wrote:

> In my opinion the first thing that should be done in this matter is that the English government should be warned to prevent Marcus Garvey, the leader of the World Negro plan to possess Africa, from landing in Africa. He is leaving for there in several months, he told me today, to set up a Republic. [(]Without him as leader the plan will not be so formidable.)[54]

Given his personal pride and the sacrifices he had made on behalf of blacks in the United States, in Africa, and in the rest of the African diaspora, Du Bois could not help being affected by the rise of Marcus Garvey. As he would later admit, he was deeply troubled by Garvey's pageants in Harlem and at Madison Square Garden. Moreover, Garvey's invitation to him to consider the nomination as leader of African Americans, presumably under Garvey's leadership, frankly rankled. Apropos of this, when Garvey was told that Du Bois had allegedly been spotted at the Madison Square Garden extravaganza, he remarked that "Du Bois was no more to him than anyone else; that 'we only think of those Negroes who feel that the hour has come for Negroes to stick by Negroes.' "[55] Du Bois also could not have relished being made the butt of hilarity at the convention, and as he promised Garvey in his letter rejecting the nomination, he was planning to respond to this challenge of his status. In the first place, he was not less than ingenuous in his statement to White that he had not given advice to people concerning the UNIA. Initially, at least, considering Garvey to be a fraud, Du Bois appeared to be more interested in the financial activities of the Black Star Line than in the other activities of the Jamaican immigrant.

It is therefore interesting to note that Du Bois, very much the intellectual, overcame his pique at Garvey when, instead of criticizing him in the September issue of the *Crisis,* Du Bois entitled his article, "The Rise of the West Indian." Noting that there were then more than one hundred thousand foreign-born blacks in the United States at that moment, most of whom were West Indians, Du Bois felt that it was necessary for American blacks to understand the nature of "this new ally in the fight for black democracy." Asserting that in contrast to South America, where the black minority sought assimilation, the black majority in the West Indies eschewed this process and, especially after World War I, ignored their old mulatto leadership and started to migrate to the United States. Du Bois admitted that the West Indians' "new cry of Africa for the Africans" startled "America's darker millions." But he mused that this movement, "yet inchoate and indefinite," had tremendous possibilities and that it was "not beyond possibilities that this new Ethiopia of the Isles may yet stretch out hands of helpfulness to the 12 million black men of America."[56]

It was not until December 1920 that Du Bois felt that he had enough evidence to tackle Garvey and the UNIA. He dutifully recounted what he knew about Garvey's background, including the convention of August 1920. Then Du Bois revealed what had been uppermost in his mind, namely, Garvey's inception of the Black Star Line. According to Du Bois, "The public for a long time regarded this as simply a scheme of exploitation, when they were startled by hearing that Garvey had bought a ship." Then when Garvey also hired a black captain and crew and announced that there would now be trade between the colored peoples of America, the West Indies, and Africa, his popularity and that of his association "increased quickly." Du Bois admitted that he asked himself, Is the UNIA "an honest and sincere movement?" "Are its industrial and commercial projects business like and effective?" But most important to Du Bois was, "Are its general objects plausible and capable of being carried out?"[57]

Du Bois volunteered that it was "a little difficult to characterize the man Garvey."[58] He found no reason to believe that Garvey was dishonest and engaged in graft—to the contrary, he found him "essentially an honest and sincere man with a tremendous vision, great dynamic force, stubborn determination and unselfish desire to serve."[59] What Du Bois could not understand was Garvey's inability to recognize what to Du Bois were contradictions in his modus operandi: a recognition that he knew nothing about the shipping business but a refusal to seek competent help; a desire to "unite all Negroes" but contempt for the work of blacks in the United States, where he "finds asylum and sympathy"; a belief that African American leaders were jealous of him, when, according to Du Bois, these leaders were "simply afraid of his failure, for his failure would be theirs . . . and if in addition he wants to prance down Broadway in a green shirt, let him—but do not let him foolishly overwhelm with bankruptcy and disaster *one of the most interesting spiritual movements of the modern Negro world* [emphasis added]."

Du Bois's basic attitude toward Garvey, and one he did not substantially change, was that the head of the UNIA here was a "sincere, hardworking idealist" but a man who was also "a stubborn, domineering leader of the mass." Du Bois felt that Garvey's "dreams of Negro industry, commerce and the ultimate freedom of Africa are feasible; but his methods are bombastic, wasteful, illogical and ineffective and almost illegal." Du Bois also believed that Garvey was an inexperienced businessman who needed to make capable and effective friends rather than enemies. He expressed the hope that Garvey would learn by experience and suggested that if he did, then some of his schemes could be accomplished. "But," Du Bois warned, "unless he does these things and does them quickly he cannot escape failure."[60]

Du Bois had the greatest difficulty understanding Garvey's views about international relations. He could not understand why and how, as a British subject eager to trade with British territories, Garvey constantly (and, to Du Bois, needlessly) antagonized and insulted Britain. Unaware of the mission that Garvey had sent to Liberia, Du Bois questioned whether it was wise of him to propose setting up a headquarters in Liberia. Du Bois wondered whether Garvey had "asked permission of the Liberian government?"

> Does he presume to usurp authority in a land which has successfully
> withstood England, France and the United States,—but is expected tamely
> to submit to Marcus Garvey? How long does Mr. Garvey think that
> President King would permit his anti-English propaganda on Liberian

soil, when the government is straining every nerve to escape the Lion's Paw?

And finally, without arms, money, effective organization or base of operations, Mr. Garvey openly and wildly talks of "Conquest" and of telling white Europeans in Africa to "get out!" and of becoming himself a black Napoleon![61]

Du Bois knew a great deal about Liberia because he had kept himself informed about conditions in that country. Charles Young, military attaché in the United States legation, had written to Du Bois on 20 July 1920 complaining of harassment by the Liberians on account of an article on Haiti in the *Crisis* to which they had taken exception. The result, said Young, was that "the cry of the man in the streets," egged on by Liberian politicians, and the English and French, was whether Young was "a spy here drawing maps and plans for the U.S. to take us over as happened in Haiti?" The attaché blamed his discomfort on the "propaganda of the English and the French being staged here to put a screwdriver and a monkey-wrench in the Liberian Legislative machinery in order to defeat the prospective loan of 5 million of dollars asked for by the Liberians in 1918 for rehabilitation of the country." Young felt that the game of the Europeans was "to make America cast off Liberia for good and all and then England and France are to proceed to gobble it up, because Liberia will have no powerful friend to turn to and no sponsor to stand for her and give aid, advice and counsel to her." In this climate Young feared that he could do little good in Monrovia.[62]

In fact, relations between the legation and the Liberian government had deteriorated so badly that the American secretary of state, Bainbridge Colby, had written to the secretary of the navy requesting a warship to visit Monrovia for a week, so that its commander could accompany the American minister resident and consul general when he went to deliver the financial plan to the Liberian government. The secretary of state's rationale was

that by the action requested the critical political situation which has existed for several months in the Republic of Liberia might be extensively improved and the propaganda and other means employed by foreign representatives to disturb the friendly relations which have for over one hundred years existed between the Republic of Liberia and the United States Government might be effectively countered.[63]

Relations between the legation and the Liberians deteriorated even further after Minister Johnson returned to the United States, leaving Richard Carlton Bundy, an African American, in charge. Bundy was convinced that President King was misleading "the Liberian people and

Legislature to further his own questionable ends." Bundy advised the Department of State to take a much tougher stance toward the president. He went as far as to warn the Liberians that since the United States had "a deep interest in seeing Liberia a self-supporting country ultimately independent of all foreign financial control," the Liberians should realize that failure to comply with American wishes "may cause the revival of the question of establishing a mandate or protectorate over the Republic which the United States through its friendly activities at the Peace Conference prevented." Bundy reported to Washington that the legation had the support of ex-President Howard and Vice President Samuel Alfred Ross, and only waited for orders to put pressure on President King.[64]

King was much tougher than Bundy realized, and the State Department did not appear too eager to put pressure on the Liberian ruler. No doubt both King and the Department of State were aware that Liberia had received good publicity during the Garvey convention in New York. The department was concerned that "the Liberian Government was sending information to its consul general in the United States [Ernest Lyon, who had served as minister in Monrovia] for the purpose of propaganda among American Negroes to bring pressure for a change in the plan."[65] Meanwhile, in Monrovia, Bundy was livid when he heard that the president had not only rejected the financial plan but was considering sending a commission to Washington, D.C., to consult with the United States government. Bundy then took the unusual step of advising the Department of State to refuse American visas to the commissioners either in Monrovia or en route to the United States. Moreover, he requested "that cruiser be sent immediately to Monrovia with instructions to impress President that Department's representations through Legation must be heeded." He warned, "If cruiser is not sent President likely to send commission despite anything Legation may do."[66]

Bundy had lived so long in Liberia and was so frustrated that he appeared to have lost perspective. Like an earlier African American diplomat, Minister Charles H. J. Taylor, Bundy complained to the department that all the American officials except two were so disgusted by the "gross carelessness, deliberate obstruction, and quibbling of the Liberian Government that they have expressed to Legation desire to leave Liberia." He intimated that had these diplomats not wished to carry out the department's plans for rehabilitating the country, they would have long since resigned. Bundy reported that he was "credibly advised" that President King had said that "only by the use of force" would Americans control the finances of Liberia. Moreover, King had intimated that he had ensured that such authority would never be granted by the Liberian Congress. "This reported statement," wrote Bundy, "is the crux of the situation and it moves Legation to say it has *reluctantly come to conclusion that nothing substantial can be done to institute reforms or rehabilitate Republic unless [and] until mandate is established over Liberia or effective intervention undertaken* [emphasis added]."[67]

Bundy suggested to the department that if its plans could legally be put into operation without the consent of the Liberians, then he and the other Americans at post would recommend it, despite the recent action of the legislature. He felt that this should be done primarily to protect "the native population now rapaciously despoiled and without defenders." Then, in a statement that some former African American diplomats who had served in Liberia would have hesitated to make, given their desire to protect the black nationality, Bundy concluded: "It seems apparent that effort to aid Ethiopians [meaning the Americo-Liberians but could well mean all black people] through suggestion and advice is signal failure. Without exception all foreigners in Liberia openly ridicule and criticize our policy."[68]

Reacting to a number of pressures—the attitudes of African Americans toward Liberia; rumors that the Liberian government was attempting to relieve its financial condition by negotiating for a loan from the Bank of British West Africa and that the "Liberian International Corporation of London" was attempting to have the Liberians accept a British financial plan; surprise that they could not understand President King's opposition to the American plan—officials at the Department of State decided to receive the Liberian commission to discuss "proposed modifications of the loan plan."[69] In turn, the Liberian commission, under the active chairmanship of President King, asked for and was given plenary powers by the Liberian legislature to reach a definite agreement with the United States. It sailed for the New World on 28 January 1921.

Whether to establish or cement diplomatic relations with European powers, or to demonstrate to the United States that Liberia had other options, President King and his entourage took their time getting to the United States. They visited Spain and France where they met royalty and officials, finally arriving in New York on 6 March 1921. The following day at Union Station, Washington, D.C., the delegation was "met by the representatives from the State Department and a number of prominent American Negro Citizens." Among these blacks were no doubt supporters of President-elect Harding, who, in the words of Du Bois, wanted to be "Recorders of Deeds, Registers of the Treasury, Assistant Attorneys-General and Fiscal Auditors."[70] The editor of the *Crisis* wrote, "Slowly but steadily and with unflinching determination the American Negro is returning to political power" and predicted more gains in the future. But, added Du Bois, African Americans wanted from the Republican party not "*offices but deeds.*" These would include abolition of Jim Crow, more representation in Congress and in the field of foreign affairs, and help for black countries.[71]

Charles Evan Hughes, the new secretary of state, received the Liberian commissioners on 16 March 1921. This meeting went as well as the Liberians could have expected, with the secretary apologizing for his inability to present them to the equally new president, whose duties kept him occupied. When the commissioners met with Harding on 15 April, the Liberian president repeated the homily that "the Government and people of Liberia have always been keenly solicitous of having the goodwill and friendship of the United States Government and of the continuation of that peculiar interest which it has uniformly manifested in the welfare of Liberia." King expressed the hope that this would continue under the new administration. Harding responded that he was well aware of the role that the United States had played in the establishment of Liberia and assured his guests that his administration "stands always ready to support, as far as it can, any country which, like yours, is endeavoring to uphold the true standards of democracy."[72]

The problem that confronted the Liberians, however was that both the American president and people wanted to forget World War I with all of its ghosts and memories. This meant, among other things, that the Senate Committee on Foreign Relations was considering an estoppel on all foreign loans and credits to countries such as Liberia, Greece, and Czechoslovakia that had not yet been made. It also wished to halt the disbursement of funds to foreign countries in the shape of loans by the American government and called upon the Treasury to report on all negotiations then in progress. This action effectively prevented the State Department from continuing its negotiation with the Liberians about their loan. The best the State Department could hope for was to persuade Congress that Liberia's loan should "not be included among the general foreign credits which were to be cancelled."[73]

The Liberians were aware of the animosity that existed between the legation in Monrovia and the Department of State under Colby, and although the arrival of Bundy to work on their loan disturbed them, they decided to put the best face on the situation. They let it be known that they found Charles Evans Hughes's collaborators "most sympathetic, and that fact of itself was a great help to the Commission and the situation." The commissioners professed to accept the will of the American people as expressed through the Congress against further loans. Nevertheless, they wanted to persuade all Americans that the offer of the loan had been made in good faith and that that faith should be respected. Ignoring King's role in delaying the loan's approval, the Liberians concluded that "the moral influence of the United States, which was involved in the proposed loan credit, by far outweighed the purely financial benefits that would seem to accrue to [them]. . . . [They] were disposed, without any show of impatience, to await results."[74]

While the Liberians were waiting, Congress on 2 July 1921 ended the state of war that had existed between the United States and Germany. Concerned that this would kill the loan, on 25 July President Harding sent the Liberians a copy of his special message to Congress explaining why Secretary of State Hughes felt that the United States was morally obligated to assist their country with a loan of $5 million. On the basis of this letter, the Liberians and the State Department negotiated an agreement and signed it on 28 October 1921. The joint communiqué by President King and Secretary of State Hughes indicated that the United States had satisfied "all the Constitutional objections made by the Government of Liberia to the Plan formerly submitted, but also those which appeared to unnecessarily offend the susceptibility of the Liberian people." The new plan eliminated the notion of a "receivership" that was so distasteful to the Liberians and substituted the concept of a "Financial Commission." The amount of the advances to be made by the United States Treasury to the Liberians was increased, but the number of American officials to oversee the plan was also increased from thirteen to twenty-two. Unfortunately, this meant that their salaries, which totaled $109,700, and the $250,000 interest on the loan would be greater than the customs revenue of the country. The loan agreement was to be submitted to both the United States Congress and the Liberian legislature, and this was expected to take many months.[75]

The person Harding appointed on 26 October 1921 as his representative in Monrovia at this critical juncture was the Reverend Solomon Porter Hood of New Jersey. Born in Lancaster, Pennsylvania on 30 July 1856, he graduated from Lincoln University in 1876, remaining there to complete his theological degree in 1880. Hood spent four years as a missionary in Haiti and came to national attention as the chief organizer of the fiftieth anniversary celebration of Negro emancipation.[76]

Even while President King and his commission were in Washington, D.C., both Garvey and Du Bois planned conferences for the summer of 1921. Garvey's Second International Convention was due to start on 1 August in New York City, and Du Bois's Second Pan-African Congress was scheduled for Europe at the end of August. These conferences would pit the two men together for leadership of black peoples, and would reveal how they planned to influence United States policy toward Liberia and the attempts of the imperial European powers to take over that country.

Although plagued by the financial problems of the Black Star Line and aware that the United States and European colonial powers were concerned about the UNIA's programs, Garvey planned to leave the United States in January 1921 for an extended visit to the West Indies and Central America and then proceed to Africa.[77] He allegedly told a meeting in Philadelphia that he was "about to put into operation the plans laid at the August Convention in New York, namely, the construction and probably the conquest of Africa." He declared: *"We are sending men there from New York, January 20th, 1921.* The time has come to cease talking and do something. This nation must be built between 1921 and 192[2]."[78] With this in mind, Garvey wrote to inform Gabriel Moore Johnson that a UNIA delegation led by "His Highness the Supreme Deputy," George Osborne Marke, and including, among others, Mr. Cyril A. Crichlow, appointed "Commissaire and Secretary," was departing for Liberia via Cadiz, Spain, to set up headquarters in Monrovia. Garvey declared that it was time for Marke to "take up his residence along with you [Johnson] in the Capital City of Monrovia."[79] He informed Johnson of the need for a concession of land near Monrovia, and indicated that funds were being provided for that purpose and for the salaries of the delegation. Garvey added that one thousand acres of land were needed by the UNIA to start a township of its own and beseeched Johnson to use his "good offices with President King, in getting this concession."[80]

Garvey's plans to leave the United States on the SS *Kanawha* to visit his followers in Central America and the Caribbean did not pass unnoticed by British intelligence. On 26 January 1921 the governor-general of Bermuda sent a telegram to Winston Churchill, then secretary of state for the colonies, proposing that Garvey be prevented from landing in Bermuda. Churchill dutifully asked the Foreign Office to keep his bureau informed about the activities of the UNIA. The British ambassador in Washington, D.C., was also informed about Garvey's plans. Meanwhile, Garvey's advisers were apprehensive about his trip, as well as a possible subsequent visit to Africa, and warned that he might not be permitted to reenter the United States.[81]

As Garvey's advisers had feared, some United States officials wanted to get rid of Garvey for good. Reacting to lawsuits over the finances of the Black Star Line, lawsuits against Du Bois and the *Crisis,* cables from British officials along Garvey's route voicing concern about the UNIA head's activities, and reports of conflicts between Garvey and some of the crew who were American citizens, the American State Department grew increasingly perturbed. It agonized whether its consuls should grant Garvey a visa to reenter the United States. On 25 March 1921 the Department of State advised the American consul in Kingston, Jamaica, that in view of "the activities of Garvey in political and race agitation, you are instructed to refuse him a visa and to inform at the same time the Consul at Port Antonio of your action."[82]

On 22 June 1921, frustrated at being forced to remain in Kingston when he felt that he should be in New York planning his conference, Garvey sent the following cable to Secretary of State Charles Evans Hughes: "Could you instruct Consul here to visa my passport[?]"[83] After an exchange of cables between Washington and Kingston, an official in the State Department instructed its consul that "with reference to Marcus Garvey . . . I really think by insisting upon exclusion, we would martyrize him."[84] The official suggested that Garvey "be allowed to return and his case will receive the undivided attention of the Department of Justice with a view to taking up this matter and if possible secure a conviction thereby, utterly discrediting him once and for all."[85]

Meanwhile, the African American establishment, especially Du Bois, whose article on Garvey had provoked a lawsuit by the UNIA, actively sought to curb the association. Du Bois succeeded in getting Liberian President King, who was still negotiating the loan in Washington, to "correct" for the American people some "wrong impressions [that] seem to exist about the present conditions in Liberia."[86] President King complied. He declared that while his country considered itself "the natural refuge and center for persons of Negro descent the world over," it never considered surrendering its sovereignty to any other nation or organization; that while Liberia needed trained immigrants, it was not in a position to "receive large, miscellaneous numbers of immigrants."[87] King insisted that under no circumstances would Liberia "allow her territory to be made a center of aggression or conspiracy against other sovereign states," presumably Britain and France. He concluded that Liberia wanted to develop "for Liberians and to live at peace with the rest of the world."[88]

The American State Department and J. Edgar Hoover of the Department of Justice continued to investigate the UNIA and Garvey's activities and programs in Liberia. On 25 May 1921 Robert Woods Bliss sent the following telegram to Joseph L. Johnson, minister resident and consul general at Monrovia:

> You are instructed to watch closely and report fully all activities of the United Negro Improvement Association in Liberia.
>
> The Department desires to know the names of persons in Liberia connected with this apparently subversive movement and wishes to be informed especially with regard to Gabriel Johnson, Mayor of Monrovia, who is reported to have taken an active part in furthering the aims of this movement.[89]

The State Department did not yet know that the affairs of the UNIA in Monrovia were then in disarray because of a disagreement between Crichlow and Gabriel Moore Johnson. On 21 March 1921, three UNIA commissioners, Crichlow, Johnson, and George Osborne Marke, met with the Liberian cabinet to discuss plans for the activities of the UNIA, especially the request for five thousand acres of land. The UNIA had transferred funds to Monrovia to get the projects started, but the Liberians opposed granting the land. The Western European Affairs Division of the American State Department, which was closely following UNIA affairs, wrote the American assistant to the secretary of state that many local Liberians, except for two members of the Liberian cabinet, opposed granting the land. The division concluded, "We must be careful about this U.N.I.A."[90]

Meanwhile, in Monrovia, Crichlow and Johnson appeared to have fallen out over the disbursement of funds. On 10 May 1921 Crichlow sent a cryptic confidential cable to New York indicating that he had some private information for the executive council of the UNIA that could not be forwarded either by cable or by mail. He indicated that he wanted funds to return home by 1 June and that "Potentate's [Johnson] presence New York unnecessary."[91] Crichlow said that he had complained to Johnson that being kept ignorant of official messages from New York raised the question of whether in fact he was not just a figurehead. Crichlow submitted his resignation to the executive council of the UNIA on 12 June 1921 claiming that Johnson had approved it.[92]

The UNIA in New York refused to accept Crichlow's resignation and invited Johnson to come to New York, sending him the necessary funds.[93]

Apparently at the end of his tether, Crichlow sought the advice of the American minister, Joseph L. Johnson. Crichlow said that he had hoped to conduct the affairs of the UNIA without approaching the United States government. But finding himself in an "intolerable and unbearable" situation, he said that he found it necessary to "fall back on my Government to see that I get a square deal." His concern was that he was being supplanted as commercial head of the UNIA in Monrovia; that the affairs of the UNIA were being conducted outside the commissariat not only in violation of Garvey's orders but in a way that prevented him from keeping good records; that he was prevented from drawing funds from the bank; and that he was being "ditched" in Monrovia with scarcely enough funds to pay his passage home or even to pay for telegrams to New York. Crichlow felt that in view of these developments, and as an American citizen, he should ask the minister to use his "good offices, to see to it that I am fairly dealt with in the premises."[94]

Crichlow's letter to Garvey, a copy of which is in the State Department's files, recounted a tale of woe that in many ways resembled those of former African American diplomats in Monrovia. Over and above his report that Gabriel Moore Johnson and George Osborne Marke were guilty of backbiting, nepotism, and corruption, Crichlow reported that while the Liberians welcomed money from African Americans and West Indians, they were hostile to their benefactors. According to him, the Liberians felt that New World blacks "believed they knew too much and were more aggressive and progressive . . . than the Liberians: and the Liberians were in league to tame them down." This is why, wrote Crichlow, the wings of Colonel Charles Young, the American military attaché, "had to be cut: . . . why Mr. Bundy, the secretary of the American legation was *persona non grata*"; and why other African Americans had been forced out. Because of these experiences, Crichlow felt he should advise Garvey to keep Johnson as head of propaganda but to use either African Americans or West Indians for practical purposes. He was convinced that Liberia had to be developed and that "the world of Negroes must accomplish it." Nevertheless, he was determined to resign, even though he was normally prepared to "overlook any personal differences for the larger welfare of the race and the Universal Negro Improvement Association."[95]

Aware of the situation in Monrovia and leery of the role that Johnson was slated to play as "High Potentate" during the convention in August

1921, the United States government sought to prevent his leaving Monrovia and, if possible, to scuttle Garvey's plans for holding the convention. On 29 June 1921 officials in Washington instructed the legation in Monrovia "that immediate steps be taken to stop Gabriel Johnson's voyage" to the United States. They were disturbed that Gabriel's brother, F. E. R. Johnson, associate justice of the Liberian Supreme Court, then in Washington, D.C., negotiating the $5 million loan, was "very anti-American and opposed to the loan." They suspected that Gabriel, being involved with the UNIA, would also be "opposed to the loan, and is probably being brought over by the Garvey people in an endeavor to negative [negate?] the Department's plans." The State Department instructed its officials to refuse Johnson a visa or to cancel it if it had already been granted, and to notify authorities along Johnson's route to do both.[96]

While the State Department wanted to frustrate the activities of both Johnson and Garvey, at least one African American resident of Monrovia had other views about the mayor. Writing to a friend in the United States, he wrote that while Johnson, the "potentate," had allied himself with the UNIA and had been honored by that organization, it was important to remember that the mayor was an ultraconservative, a "Liberian official first, and in very close touch with his associates in office[,] many of whom are his near relatives."[97] The correspondant said that he hated "to be so critical" but was convinced that Johnson "would foster the work of the U.N.I.A., only so far as it will lend itself to the will of this coterie of Liberians."[98]

Contrary to the wishes of the State Department, Johnson arrived in the United States on 13 July 1921, having successfully avoided United States consuls along his route. He was promptly detained by immigration officials when the ship docked and questioned about his relationship with the UNIA. Johnson did acknowledge his association with the UNIA but equivocated by stressing that he did not know how long this connection would last since he did not agree with the way in which the organization was run. He informed his interrogators that he was really in the United States on family business since President King of Liberia, then in the United States, was married to his daughter and that Justice Johnson (also with the King commission) was his brother. The only negative action the immigration authorities could take was to send Johnson to Ellis Island, thereby preventing him from using a military escort of the UNIA detailed to meet him. They had no blanket orders to bar UNIA members, including Garvey, from the United

States. The next day immigration officials were forced to release the potentate.[99]

Meanwhile, en route to the United States by sea, Garvey turned his attention to preparing for the second convention of the UNIA. Cabling his followers that the "task of organizing the four hundred million Negroes of the world is gigantic and requires the combined wisdom of all our forces," he requested that they notify "all Negro communities, societies, lodges, churches, fraternities and newspapers to send delegates to this convention."[100] Then, as soon as he arrived in New York, Garvey met with the executive council of the UNIA and its members. To their cheers he announced that between 1 August and 31 August 1921, thirty to fifty thousand delegates would attend his second international convention and that it would be opened by "His Highness, the Potentate, Hon. Gabriel Johnson, Mayor of Monrovia, Liberia."[101] Garvey also once again invited members of the African American old guard such as Du Bois, Moton, and Kelly Miller. He asserted that this was not the time for differences but a time "to pitch in now to save the Negro race from the doom that threatens."[102]

The Second International Convention of the Negroes of the World opened as planned with a mammoth parade on the streets of Harlem reminiscent of the previous one. Numerous placards carried in the procession proclaimed, among other things, "Long live the republic of Liberia!" "Honor to the Stars and Stripes!" and "Duty requires every Negro to fall in line." There was also one demanding, "Why a Pan-African Congress in Paris?" Gabriel Moore Johnson assured the delegates in his speech opening the convention that "the headquarters of the movement just established in Monrovia under my direction is doing all that is possible to impress the government and peoples of the country of its sincerity of purpose and deep interest in the welfare of the republic." Elaborating upon the theme that blacks were living in trying times and needed to prepare themselves for a bitter struggle, the potentate asked on behalf of the "President General and Administrator" for their "hearty support in all matters that have for their aim the emancipation of our race and the redemption of our Motherland, Africa."[103]

Garvey made Du Bois the subject of his opening speech to the convention. He had been convinced that members of the black establishment, as well as some members of the UNIA,[104] were behind his difficulty in reentering the United States. Also stung by the article in the *Crisis,* Garvey boldly asserted that the UNIA had no intention of using any one country in Africa as the site for the battleground of African freedom, because anywhere he landed in Africa would be such a place. He applauded world leaders who defended their people and vowed to lead the "new Negro" who was demanding "Africa for the Africans." Declaring that the old leadership of Du Bois and Moton had been buried in 1914, Garvey criticized Du Bois and associates for calling a congress of the Negro race in European cities. This, he intimated, had as its main purpose the goal of social equality for its organizers rather than for the Negro race. Garvey dismissed the congress as representative of the black peoples of the world since for him, "W. E. B. Du Bois, Secretary of the so-called Pan-African Congress, and those associated with him, are not representatives of the struggling peoples of the world."[105] Moreover, Garvey felt that they had received no mandate to call the congress and asked the convention to adopt the following resolution:

> Be it Resolved: That we, the duly elected representatives of the Negro peoples of the world, from North America, South America, Central America, West Indies, Asia, Europe, Australia and Africa, assembled in open conclave on this 1st day of August, 1921, . . . do hereby place on record our repudiation of a Pan-African Congress to be held in London, England, Sunday and Monday, August 28 and 29; Brussels, Belgium, Wednesday, Thursday and Friday, August [3]1, September 1 and 2; Paris, France, Sunday and Monday, September 4 and 5. As also the Special Committee of said Congress to visit the Assembly of the League of Nations, Geneva, Switzerland, after September 6.[106]

Very much concerned that he and his organization were the subject simultaneously of fear and attacks, Garvey launched a veritable public-relations blitz to improve his image. Writing in the name of the representatives "OF THE 400,000,000 NEGROES OF THE WORLD ASSEMBLED IN THIS OUR 2nd ANNUAL INTERNATIONAL CONVENTION," he sent greetings to such world figures as President Warren G. Harding of the United States; Eamon de Valera, the Irish nationalist; George V, king of England; Mahatma Gandhi, the Indian nationalist; and many others, wishing them good health or good luck in their several endeavors.[107] Closer to home, Garvey advocated sending a delegation to the connectional council of the AME Zion Church and welcomed the program of Cyril V. Briggs of the African Blood Brotherhood, an allegedly secret organization advocating a worldwide federation of all Negro organizations.

Much to the amusement of his followers but not to the secret agents of the United States government who were present, Garvey gave the floor to Mrs. Rose Pastor Stokes, who spoke on behalf of the Soviet Union and world communism. Taking the floor afterward, Garvey said that having heard in the person of Mrs. Stokes, "a Soviet professor," and professors from the "four corners of the world," he announced that the convention would hear later from professors from the Republicans, Democrats, and from "monarchial systems." Mrs. Stokes had, he said, argued well the cause of the Soviets; he hoped the capitalists would make out theirs—"but when they come to Negroes they will find keen judges."[108]

More serious for Garvey, however, was the need to persuade his followers that he was making progress in Monrovia with the Liberians. Gratified that Gabriel Moore Johnson had come to the convention, Garvey was able to report that "everything is working splendidly in Liberia." Moreover, he noted that of a $200,000 Liberian Construction Loan authorized by the executive council of the UNIA, $137,458.22 had already been subscribed to by the membership. However, Garvey was concerned that a message from President Harding to the U.S. Congress on 3 August 1921, urging that it approve the $5 million to Liberia because of the commercial and military importance of the port of Monrovia to the United States, would interfere with his fund-raising efforts.[109]

Garvey was distressed that President King, then still in Washington, D.C., attempting to negotiate the loan from the United States, was being pressured to repudiate the UNIA. He wrote him insisting that despite misrepresentations, the UNIA stood by the views of the "Potentate and President General, that the purpose of the Universal Negro Improvement Association with respect to the Republic of Liberia, is solely and purely industrial and commercial, with a view of assisting the peoples of Liberia in strengthening and improving their country, generally."[110] King had his secretary assure the convention that the president was satisfied with the declaration made "over the signatures of the official heads of the association" and the clause which read that the UNIA was generally only interested in assisting the people of Liberia. King's secretary had underscored the president's view that the declaration was "most opportune, in view of the representations that have become current as to its [UNIA's] political aims in Liberia and Africa generally." The letter concluded with the ominous statement:

The Republic of Liberia, as a sovereign state with corresponding international responsibilities, could not permit its territories to be used as a center of hostile attacks upon other sovereign states, by any organization now operating or which may desire to operate within its political and territorial jurisdictions, . . . a fact which the President of Liberia hopes that your association will fully appreciate.[111]

Garvey apparently took all such warnings in stride and in articles in the *Negro World* gave the impression that he believed that most of the declarations opposing the UNIA by some black leaders were simply cynical attempts to placate the more powerful whites. Meanwhile, he went on with his convention and proudly reported to the delegates that their activities in New York were attracting the attention of the outside world.[112] Garvey read to them letters from Chinese nationalists and other important persons and organizations congratulating the UNIA. Garvey was especially pleased to announce that the League of Nations had acknowledged the receipt of the UNIA's protest against the Pan-African Congress and against the notion that Du Bois represented the "present-day Negro."

In the closing session of the Second International Convention of the Negroes of the World that took place on Wednesday, 31 August 1921, a number of resolutions were unanimously adopted. The UNIA protested the decision of the Supreme Council of the League of Nations to distribute countries in Africa among the white nations of the world. The convention insisted that "Africa, by right of heritage, is the property of the African races, and those at home and those abroad are now sufficiently civilized to conduct the affairs of their own homeland."[113] The delegates reiterated their belief in the right of Europeans to have Europe; to have Asia; and of Africa for Africans at home and abroad. The convention declared that at a time when "humanity everywhere is determined to reach a common standard of nationhood . . . 400,000,000 Negroes demand a place in the political sun of the world."[114]

W. E. B. Du Bois had already left for his own Pan-African Congress in England by the time Garvey's convention ended on 31 August 1921. Over the preceding months the thought uppermost in his mind had been the challenge of Garvey and the reaction of the outside world to the UNIA. Du Bois was therefore determined not to emulate Garvey and alienate the powerful persons and groups that could either help or hurt his movement. He was also determined to encourage a greater number of Africans from the continent to attend his congress. On 16 June 1921 Du Bois had written to Sir Auckland Geddes, Britain's ambassador to the United States, informing him of plans for the congress and seeking British support through representation from the Colonial Office.[115] More important, perhaps, was his letter to Charles Evans Hughes informing the American secretary of state about the congress. Enclosed for the information of the secretary were the resolutions passed by the First Pan-African Congress in Paris and a note indicating that Colonel House of the American Peace Commission had thought well of them. Du Bois also enclosed the program of the forthcoming congress to be held from 29 August to 6 September 1921. Secretary of State Hughes acknowledged Du Bois's letter on 8 July 1921 and suggested that the State Department "shall be glad to have any further information which from time to time you may have at your command." [116]

Looking back on these preparations some years later, Du Bois wrote: "We went to work in 1921 to assemble a more authentic Pan-African Congress and movement. We corresponded with Negroes in all parts of Africa and in other parts of the world and finally arranged for a congress to meet in London, Brussels, and Paris in August and September." [117] Unfortunately for Du Bois, this date was inconvenient for Blaise Diagne and Gratien Candace, possibly because of the French penchant for considering August holidays sacrosanct. Some of the British, especially Reverend Harris, secretary of the Anti-Slavery and Aborigines Protection Society, also disliked the idea of holding the congress in the summer. He indicated a preference for a smaller conference in order to avoid the presence of "persons with impractical ideas," presumably the Garveyites. For his part, Du Bois insisted on retaining the date for the congress. He too was leery of having undesirable and unreasonable individuals at the meeting but he wanted as many delegates as possible. [118]

Whether because he "always had pronounced socialist views" as was suggested [119] or because, as Du Bois claimed, he wished to deal with the "question of the relation of white and colored labor," there was a pre-conference meeting with members of the international department of the English Labor party and the Anti-Slavery and Aborigines Protection Society. Included in these meetings were Beatrice Webb, Leonard Woolf, one Gillies, and Norman Leys, an expert on Kenya. And while Du Bois remained relatively silent on the result of these meetings, it has been suggested that he did not get either the reception or support he had expected. [120] Du Bois did note, however, that the climate in Europe was not favorable for his venture. He felt that the Europeans had decided to recoup their losses from World War I "by intensified colonial exploitation." Consequently, they were suspicious of "native movements of any sort," especially in light of the threat posed by the relative success of the Garvey movement. [121]

From Brussels came word that the Belgians were especially alarmed about the congress. Du Bois believed this was due to their fear that it was associated with, or was part of, the Garvey movement. Nevertheless, an article in the Brussels *Neptune* on 14 June 1921 tells a slightly more complicated story:

> Announcement has been made . . . of a Pan-African Congress organized at the instigation of the National Association for the Advancement of Colored People of New York. It is interesting to note that this association is directed by personages who it is said in the United States have received remuneration from Moscow (Bolsheviks). The association has already organized its propaganda in the lower Congo, and we must not be astonished if some day it causes grave difficulties in the Negro village of Kinshasa composed of all the ne'er-do-wells of the various tribes of the Colony aside from some hundreds of laborers.[122]

This report from Brussels was only one of a series of indications that Du Bois might have been a bit too optimistic that the European colonial powers would approve his program. Nevertheless, he persisted, and the London meetings of the second congress opened in the precincts of Central Hall, Westminster, on 28 and 29 August 1921. Among the gathering of 113 delegates in London were 41 from Africa, 35 from the United States, 24 blacks living in Britain and Europe, and 7 from the West Indies. In addition there were a number of European Socialists and sympathetic former British colonial officials. Dr. John Alcindor from Trinidad, president of the African Progress Union, who presided at the first session, was present at the 1900 Pan-African Conference. Lamenting the absence of Diagne and other francophone Africans, Alcindor said that the European governments were often as inimical to the progress of black people as blacks themselves. The object, as he saw it, was for African peoples to meet, articulate their problems, and fight to solve them.[123]

Du Bois chaired the sessions on the second day and was assisted by J. R. Archer of Battersea, England, a former president of the African Progress Union. Du Bois echoed some of the Alcindor's sentiments and described his own efforts and those of the NAACP to articulate the problems of African peoples both at the Paris Peace Conference and before the Senate of the United States. Then, probably with Marcus Garvey in mind, Du Bois sought to impress upon the delegates the need for educated blacks to inform themselves about the problems African peoples faced around the world. This theme was picked up by such West Africans as Peter Thomas from Lagos, W. B. Mark from Sierra Leone, and Albert T. Marryshaw from Grenada, among others. Then followed several resolutions and the now-customary "Declaration to the

World."[124] Known as the "Manifesto of the Second Pan-African Congress," it proclaimed, in part:

> The absolute equality of races,—physical, political and social—is the founding stone of world peace and human advancement. No one denies great differences of gift, capacity and attainment among individuals of all races, but the voice of science, religion and practical politics is one in denying the God-appointed existence of super-races, or of races naturally and inevitably and eternally inferior.
>
> That in the vast range of time, one group should in its industrial technique, or social organization, or spiritual vision, lag a few hundred years behind another, or forge fitfully ahead, or come to differ decidedly in thought, deed and ideal, is proof of the essential richness and variety of human nature, rather than proof of the co-existence of demi-gods and apes in human forms. The doctrine of racial equality does not interfere with individual liberty, rather, it fulfills it. And of all the various criteria by which masses of men have in the past been prejudged and classified, that of the color of the skin and texture of the hair, is surely the most adventitious and idiotic.[125]

While parts of this declaration were pure Du Bois—for example, the insistence that a group of people can only advance if their intelligentsia are recognized as their "natural leaders"—other parts echoed Garvey's indictment of the West. Du Bois criticized England for its vaunted Pax Britannica, which sadly failed to grant the right of self-government to colonial peoples. Belgium, which according to Du Bois congratulated itself in taking responsibility for the Congo from a tyrant, had to bear the opprobrium of subjecting its wards to exploitation by banks and great corporations. And while Spain and Portugal did not have official color-caste lines, Portugal did permit foreigners to exploit her African colonies. France was given credit for treating some blacks as equals but was criticized for alienating African land and for using Africans as forced laborers and conscripts. The United States was castigated for enslaving black people, for freeing them without the means to take advantage of their freedom, and for discriminating against them while permitting their participation as soldiers in war.

The manifesto lamented the promulgation of the Treaty of London, which "practically invited Italy to aggression in Abyssinia" while failing to indict America for "unjustly and cruelly" seizing Haiti, murdering, and for a time "enslaving its workmen." It insisted that the independence of Abyssinia, Liberia, Haiti and San Domingo, was a categorical prerequisite to "any sustained belief" on the part of blacks in the "sincerity and honesty of the white[s]." The manifesto ended with eight resolutions. They ranged from one asking for "the recognition of civilized men as civilized despite their race or color," to a call for local self-government for the colonies, "deliberately rising as experience and knowledge grow to complete self-government," to the establishment under the League of Nations of an "international institution for the study of Negro problems," and a labor bureau to protect native labor.[126]

As one would have expected, many whites in the audience and many white journalists could see little difference between the Pan-African ideas of Du Bois and Garvey's UNIA. These were viewed as two sides of the same coin. Du Bois admitted later that while the "whole press of Europe took notice of these meetings and more especially of the ideas behind the meeting[s]," it was only "gradually [that] they began to distinguish between the Pan-African Movement and the Garvey agitation. They praised and criticized."[127] Sir Harry Johnston, who was sympathetic to Du Bois but generally suspicious of New World blacks, sought to put his own spin on the controversy: "This is the *weakness* of all the otherwise grand efforts of the Coloured People in the United States to pass on their own elevation and education and political significance to the Coloured Peoples of Africa: they know so *little about the real* Africa."[128] What the American diplomats at the Court of St. James's knew and thought about this matter or the congress is not to be found in the State Department's archives.

Some Britishers in the audience were especially angry with Du Bois for believing that France's colonial policies were much better than their own. No doubt Du Bois's views were a mixture of pride in his own French Haitian ancestry and gratitude for the help he had received from Clemenceau and Diagne in 1919 to hold his Paris congress despite American opposition. It was alleged that "although fervent endeavours had been made to enlighten him about the true state of affairs in the French colonies, Du Bois had turned a completely deaf ear."[129]

It was, however, this francophilic attitude that helped Du Bois when the congress moved to the continent. He met a storm of protests from the Belgian press for his reference to the Congo during the sessions that were held in the Palais Mondial in Brussels from 31 August to 3 September 1921. With Blaise Diagne now in the chair and two sympathetic Belgians in attendance, attempts to rescind the criticism of Belgium's colonial policy were sidetracked. Fearing that the Belgian press would convince the world that the congress was a Bolshevik front for Africa, Diagne accepted a mild amendment to a manifesto which called for "common efforts by blacks and whites to develop Africa."[130]

What Du Bois could not avoid in Brussels, however, was the widespread belief that his ideas were similar to those of Garvey. Apparently there was at least one Jamaican participant in the debate who, "without identifying himself completely with his compatriot Garvey, delivered a speech full of bitterness about the situation in his country" and confessed to occasionally thinking of "resorting to murder as a weapon in the struggle."[131] Another person referred to as " 'un noir français à la parole souple et mordante' demanded that Garvey be invited to the next Pan-African Congress" to expound his views. The speaker expressed the desire to hear "this Black man with red ideas." Du Bois argued against this on the grounds that the congress did not entertain the views of returning to Africa. And while he was supported by both Blaise Diagne and Gratien Candace, it appeared that many delegates wished that Garvey be invited to the next congress so he could "defend his views."[132]

Diagne was in the chair when the Paris session of the Second Pan-African Congress convened in the Salle des Ingénieurs civils, rue Blanche, on 4 September. He took the opportunity to remark upon the "absolute freedom which the Congress enjoyed on French soil," presumably in contrast to Brussels. Referring to his role in World War I, Diagne told the delegates that "the 300 million coloured people in the world could no longer be ignored" because they came to the aid of the Allies when asked to do so. Diagne asked rhetorically whether African peoples did not have the right to ask for help during peacetime. To emphasize the role that blacks played in World War I, the delegates made a visit to the tomb of the French Unknown Soldier. They held that it was possible that he was of African origin since death did not ask the skin color of persons who defended France.[133]

Picking up on this theme, Du Bois presented the Pan-African agenda of African Americans. He explained that this called for, among other things, "absolute" equality in the United States, the development of the masses, political power for all colored peoples, self-government for Africans in Africa, and the return of lands that had been expropriated. Du Bois concluded that he was "against racial separation" but that if the colonial powers refused full citizenship for Africans, then "there would be no alternative" to separating blacks from whites. This theme inadvertently awakened the specter of Garveyism and the UNIA that had not been exorcised in Brussels. Senegalese and Haitian delegates passionately attacked Garvey and all that the UNIA stood for.[134]

When both the New York *Sun* and the New York *Tribune* published these stories based on reports from the Associated Press, Garvey rose to the attack. Claiming that Du Bois had engineered opposition against him at the Pan-African Congress in Paris, he read the following excerpts from the papers to his followers:

> Thirty American colored men and women, delegates to the Pan-African Congress in session here, today, headed by Dr. W. E. B. Du Bois of New York, repudiated the plan of Marcus Garvey, Provisional President of Africa, of "Africa for the Africans!". . .
>
> France's two Negro deputies do not agree with Marcus Garvey's contention of "Africa for Africans!" Diagne, the colored deputy from Senegal, and Candace, from Guadaloupe[,] today declared:
>
> "We do not hate the white race. What we seek is conciliation and collaboration. Our evolution and development depend upon relations with the white race. We would lose everything if we were isolated in Africa."
>
> Instead of sacrificing present nationalities, the Congress insists Negroes must endeavor to take greater advantage of their opportunities under prevailing conditions. The body is firm against efforts of the Negro extremists to ally themselves with the Russian Bolsheviki.[135]

Garvey apparently enjoyed the scandal, especially Candace's revelation that if asked about his identity he would reply, "I am black, but I am French first." Not in his wildest dreams could Garvey imagine that a real black man could make such a statement. Garvey resented attacks on his programs and upon his title as "Provisional President of Africa," and was infuriated by the statement that Liberia was "less developed than the French colonies that have black populations." What particularly incensed him was the report that Du Bois had allegedly declared that "the colored population cannot withstand the African climate. We cannot oust the Europeans, and do not desire to do so."[136]

Nevertheless, Garvey perceived the irony of the Europeans confusing his movement and ideas with those of Du Bois. Much to the amusement of his followers who had gathered in Liberty Hall, Garvey remarked: "We had two conventions this year. We had one in New York and we had one in Europe, and we sent Dr. Du Bois over to Europe to take care of the one we held there while we were busy with the one we had here."[137]

Du Bois naturally took comfort in the support he received from the congress in attempting to convince the world of the differences between his approach to helping African peoples and Garvey's. He was also pleased to go to Geneva with Dr. Dantes Bellegarde, a delegate to the congress who also served as Haitian ambassador to France and permanent representative to the League of Nations, to present a petition to the Mandates Commission of the League. The petition declared that, in view of the widespread feeling that "it is permissible to treat civilized men as uncivilized if they are colored and more especially of Negro descent," self-government be granted to African majorities in the mandated areas and that persons of "Negro descent, properly fitted in character and training, be appointed . . . member[s] of the Mandates Commission as soon as a vacancy occurs." The petition added that while its framers recognized the limited power of the League of Nations to adjust such matters, they felt that the "vast moral power of world opinion" could prevail upon the League to ask the colonial powers "to form an International Institute for the study of the Negro problem, and for the evolution and protection of the Negro race."[138]

Before returning to the United States, Du Bois and a committee of the delegates of the Second Pan-African Congress established a Pan-African Association, with provisions for creating branches throughout the world. It was stipulated that any branch with over 250 members could send one delegate to future meetings. Isaac Béton, a Martinican who taught in Paris, was appointed secretary and given the task of arranging the third congress in 1923. What was not resolved was the problem of funding. It was not clear that the NAACP, which had provided funds for earlier congresses, would continue to provide money. Noted also was the escalation of both the psychological and ideological differences among the delegates that had surfaced during the meetings in London, Brussels, Paris, and Geneva. These would increase and create difficulties among the principals.[139]

Available data seem to indicate that while United States officials in New York and Washington kept close tabs on the Garvey movement and its conventions, those in London and Paris exhibited less concern about the Pan-African Congresses. The State Department apparently did not follow up the secretary of state's suggestion that it contact Du Bois if that proved necessary. Apparently the American officials in Paris did not believe that the Pan-African Congress posed any threat either to the United States or to its European allies. What is significant, however, is that even while Du Bois was in Europe, the State Department had sent a confidential note to its embassy in Paris citing a reliable source "that Garvey is contemplating leaving for Europe this month, for the purpose of visiting France, Belgium and England." Describing Garvey as "a negro agitator for 'Africa for Africans' " and for proposing to "kick out all 'whites'," the note expressed the hope that before the information reached Paris, "Garvey may be wrapped in the warm but confining embraces of the authorities here on a charge of white (negro) slavery"—the reference here was to an indictment charging Garvey with violating the Mann Act for taking an unmarried woman across state lines. The United States government did not prosecute Garvey for his marital and romantic proclivities, but on 15 February 1922 Garvey and several of his officials were indicted in the district court of the United States in New York for conspiracy and using the mails to defraud.[140]

Notes

1. "International Convention of Negroes Opens in Blaze of Glory," in *The Marcus Garvey and Universal Negro Improvement Association Papers,* ed. Robert A. Hill (Berkeley and Los Angeles: University of California Press, 1983), 2:478–79 (hereafter cited as *Marcus Garvey Papers*).
2. Herbert Aptheker, ed., *The Correspondence of W. E. B. Du Bois, Selections, 1877–1934* (Amherst: University of Massachusetts Press, 1973), 1:250–251.
3. W. E. B. Du Bois, "Sensitive Liberia," *Crisis* 28 (May 1924): 9–11.
4. Clarence Garner Contee, "W. E. B. Du Bois and African Nationalism" (Ph.D. diss., American University, 1969), 248ff.
5. Nathaniel R. Richardson, *Liberia's Past and Present* (London: Diplomatic Press, 1959), 131.
6. Ibid., 130.
7. Charles S. Johnson, *Bitter Canaan: The Story of the Negro Republic* (New Brunswick, N.J.: Transaction Books, 1987), 108.
8. Monrovia to State Department, 26 December 1918, 882.00/12, United States Department of State Decimal File, 1910–29, Record Group 59, National Archives (hereafter abbreviated RG 59, NA).
9. Ibid.
10. U. S. Secretary of State to Minister Johnson, 7 January 1920, 882.00/626.
11. Johnson to U.S. Secretary of State, 20 January 1920, 882.00/632.
12. Ibid.
13. Johnson to U.S. Secretary of State, 28 February 1920, 882.602/34; Acting Secretary of State to the Minister in Liberia (Johnson), 2 March 1920, 882.51/1074.
14. Acting Secretary of State to Minister Johnson in Liberia, 28 February 1920, 882.00/626.
15. *Marcus Garvey Papers* 2:293–94.
16. Ibid., 660.
17. Ibid., 661–62.
18. Ibid., 662–63; Elie Garcia to President C. D. B. King, 8 June 1920, ibid., 345–47.
19. Edwin Barclay to Garcia, 14 June 1920, ibid., 347.
20. Garcia to Garvey and the UNIA, August 1920, ibid., 663–64.
21. Ibid., 667–68.
22. Ibid., 668–70.
23. Ibid., 670.
24. Ibid., 672.
25. Tony Martin reported that as early as October, J. Edgar Hoover wrote:

    Garvey is a West-Indian negro and in addition to his activities in endeavoring to establish the Black Star Line Steamship Corporation he has also been particularly active among the radical elements in New York City in agitating the negro movement. Unfortunately, however, he has not as yet violated any federal law whereby he could be proceeded against on the grounds of being an undesirable alien, from the point of view of deportation. (*Race First* [Westport, Conn.: Greenwood Press, 1976], 174)

26. Report of UNIA Meeting, 29 April 1920, *Marcus Garvey Papers* 2:302.
27. Ibid.
28. Exchange Between Marcus Garvey and Cyril V. Briggs, *Crusader,* April 1920, ibid., 301–2.
29. Editorial Letter by Marcus Garvey in the *Negro World,* 22 June 1920, ibid., 390.
30. Report by Special Agent 800, New York City, 21 July 1920, ibid., 429–30.
31. See Marcus A. Garvey, *Negro World,* 6 February 1926, 4; Rupert Lewis, *Marcus Garvey: Anti-Colonial Champion* (Trenton, N.J.: Africa World Press, 1988), 71–72.
32. Garvey to W. E. B. Du Bois, 16 July 1920, *Marcus Garvey Papers* 2:426.
33. Du Bois to Garvey, 22 July 1920, ibid., 431–32.
34. Ibid., 433–35. In retrospect, Du Bois did not believe that Garvey was dishonest, but in his hour of pique he did write to one H. L. Stone, stating:
    First, you remember that some time ago you spoke to me concerning Marcus Garvey and the Black Star Line. I have got to write something on the subject for *The Crisis* and I am afraid that Garvey is financially more or less a fraud. I want, therefore, to follow up his operations very carefully.
35. Opening of the UNIA Convention, ibid., 477.
36. Address by Gabriel Johnson, 3 August 1920, ibid., 526–29.
37. Ibid.
38. UNIA Declaration of Rights, 13 August 1920, ibid., 571–80; Reports of the Convention, 15 August 1920, ibid., 583ff.
39. Reports of the Convention, 8 August, ibid., 559.
40. Ibid., 559–60.
41. John E. Bruce to Garvey, 17 August 1920, ibid., 601.
42. Interview with Frederick Moore by Charles Mowbray White, 23 August 1920, ibid., 622–23.
43. Edmund David Cronon, *Black Moses: The Story of Marcus Garvey and the Universal Negro Improvement Association* (Madison: University of Wisconsin Press, 1968), 67.
44. Reports by Special Agent P-138, 19, 21, 25 August 1920, *Marcus Garvey Papers* 2:608, 612, 628.
45. Report of the [UNIA] Convention, ibid, 648.
46. Report by Special Agent P-138, 6 August 1920, ibid., 546–47.
47. Capt. H. A. Strauss to the Director, Military Intelligence Division, 27 August 1920, ibid., 630–33.
48. Report by Special Agent P-138, 23 August 1920, ibid., 625– 26.
49. Interview with Chandler Owen and A. Philip Randolph by Charles Mowbray White, 20 August 1920, ibid., 609ff; Interview with Marcus Garvey by Charles Mowbray White, 18 August 1920, ibid., 602.
50. Interview with W. E. B. Du Bois by Charles Mowbray White, 22 August 1920, ibid., 620–21.
51. Ibid.
52. E. Franklin Frazier, "Garvey: A Mass Leader," *Nation* 123 (18 August 1926): 147–48, cited in John Henrik Clarke, ed., with the assistance of Amy Jacques Garvey, *Marcus Garvey and the Vision of Africa* (New York: Vintage Books, 1974), 236–41.
53. *Marcus Garvey Papers* 2:604; cf. *New York Times,* 15 July 1920.

54. Interview with Marcus Garvey by Charles Mowbray White, 18 August 1920, ibid., 602.
55. Reports of the [UNIA] Convention, 3 August 1920, ibid., 525.
56. W. E. B. Du Bois, "The Rise of the West Indian," *Crisis* 21 (September 1920): 214–15.
57. W. E. B. Du Bois, "Marcus Garvey," *Crisis* 21 (December 1920): 58–60 and 21 (January 1921): 112–15.
58. Ibid., 21 (December 1920): 58–60.
59. Ibid.
60. Ibid., 21 (January 1921): 112–15.
61. Ibid.
62. American Legation, Office of the Military Attaché, Monrovia, Liberia, 20 July 1920, reel 9, frame 296.
63. Secretary of State to Secretary of the Navy (Daniels), 17 April 1920, 882.51/1906A, RG 59, NA.
64. The Chargé in Liberia (Bundy) to the Secretary of State, 23 July 1920, 882.51/1150, and 24 July 1920, 882.51/1151, *Foreign Relations of the United States, 1920* 3:83.
65. Raymond W. Bixler, *The Foreign Policy of the United States in Liberia* (New York: Pageant Press, 1957), 49.
66. Bundy to the Secretary of State, Monrovia, 21 August 1920, 882.51/1169, *Foreign Relations, 1920* 3:86–88.
67. Ibid.
68. Ibid.
69. Bixler, *Foreign Policy of the United States*, 49.
70. W. E. B. Du Bois, "Political Rebirth and the Office Seeker," *Crisis* 21 (January 1921), 104.
71. Ibid.
72. Richardson, *Liberia's Past and Present*, 135.
73. Ibid.
74. Ibid., 135–37.
75. Ibid., 136, and Raymond Leslie Buell, *Liberia: A Century of Survival, 1847–1947* (Philadelphia: University of Pennsylvania Press, 1947), 28–29.
76. James Padgett, "Ministers to Liberia and Their Diplomacy," *Journal of Negro History* 1 (July 1916): 87–88. The young Reverend Hood became a pastor in churches in Pennsylvania, New York, and New Jersey. He also taught school, serving as a district superintendent in New Jersey and as principal of the Beaufort Normal Industrial School.
77. Report by Special Agent J. T. Flournoy, 7 June 1921, *Marcus Garvey Papers* 3:458–59. The United States government was intrigued to discover that the Belgian embassy in the United States was subscribing to the *Negro World* and investigated the matter. The investigator was told that the Belgian ambassador monitored "the contents of the paper . . . from time to time, as he found that this paper was being circulated in the Belgium [*sic*] possessions and was stirring up the negro inhabitants by the circulation of propaganda against this country and Belgium."
78. Report by Bureau Agent H. J. Lenon, 18 January 1921, ibid., 134.
79. Garvey to Gabriel M. Johnson, 18 January 1921, ibid., 135.
80. Ibid.
81. Sir James Willcocks to the British Secretary of State for the Colonies, 26 January 1921, ibid., 140; Reports by Special Agent P-138, 31 January 1921, ibid., 146–47.

82. Wilbur J. Carr to Charles L. Latham, 25 March 1921, ibid., 277. While there was a great deal of sentiment in the State Department against permitting Garvey to reenter the United States, on 11 June 1921, one William C. Matthews, assistant counsellor general in Boston, requested Harry A. McBride, Visa Control Office, Department of State, to honor the request of the board of directors of the Black Star Line to permit Garvey to return to the United States to deal with problems concerning the ship to be named *Phillis Wheatley* (ibid., 463).
83. Garvey to Charles Evans Hughes, 22 June 1921, ibid., 482.
84. Fred K. Nielsen to Richard W. Flournoy, Jr., 23 June 1921; William W. Heard to Hughes, 23 June 1921; William L. Hurley to Harry A. McBride, 24 June 1921, ibid., 483–84. On 25 June 1921, the State Department authorized its consul at Kingston to grant a visa to Garvey. Apropos of this, Robert P. Skinner, who had helped the United States to establish consular relations with Ethiopia, and was consul general in London in April 1921, interviewed Mr. Duse Mohamed Ali about Garvey's earlier stay in Britain. He reported, "Marcus Garvey is an alien [who] may perhaps be of some utility to the Department of Labor, since if he is an objectionable person, he might very properly be deported" (ibid., 491, 340).
85. Ibid., 484.
86. "An Open Letter From the President of Liberia," *Crisis* 22 (June 1921): 53. King told a representative of the Department of State that he was especially concerned that "Foreign countries, particularly France and England, might become anxious with regard to the position of Liberia in connection with this [Garvey] movement" (Memorandum by the Division of Western European Affairs, Department of State, 8 April 1921, *Marcus Garvey Papers* 3:348).
87. "An Open Letter From the President of Liberia," 53.
88. Ibid.
89. Robert Woods Bliss to Joseph L. Johnson, 25 May 1921, *Marcus Garvey Papers* 3:425.
90. Memorandum by John Cooper Wiley, 12 May 1921, ibid., 416.
91. Cyril A. Crichlow to Garvey, 10 May 1921, ibid., 396.
92. Crichlow to Gabriel M. Johnson, 11 June 1921, and to UNIA Executive Council, 12 June 1921, ibid., 465.
93. UNIA Executive Council to Gabriel M. Johnson, 15 June 1921, ibid., 470.
94. Crichlow to Joseph L. Johnson, 20 June 1921, ibid., 479–80.
95. Crichlow to Garvey, 24 June 1921, ibid., 485–91.
96. John C. Wiley to Hurley, 29 June 1921, ibid., 493.
97. Cyril Henry to O. M. Thompson, 1 July 1921, ibid., 500–504.
98. Ibid.
99. Report of Agent Starr, 14 July 1921, enclosed in J. Edgar Hoover to Hurley, 20 July 1921, ibid., 545–48.
100. Cable by Marcus Garvey, 10 July 1921, ibid., 521.
101. Speech by Marcus Garvey, 24 July 1921, ibid., 553.
102. New York *Call*, 1 August 1921, cited in ibid., 584.
103. Report on the Convention Parade of the UNIA, 1 August 1921, ibid., 566–68; Keynote Speech by Gabriel M. Johnson, 1 August 1921, ibid., 570–76.
104. Official Convention Report by Marcus Garvey, 4 August 1921, ibid., 615. Garvey was aware that opposition to his reentry to the United States was fairly broad-based. In his official report to the convention on 4 August 1921 he declared:

I have learned that not only enemies from without did make representations to the government against my returning to the United States, but that members and officers of the Universal Negro Improvement Association did encourage and engage themselves in such representations to the government. Through the misrepresentation made to the State Department, all the American Consular Agents in Central and South America and the West Indies were instructed by the State Department not to vise my passport for a return to this country.

105. Speech by Marcus Garvey, 1 August 1921, ibid., 582–83.

106. Ibid., 583.

107. Ibid., 585ff.

108. Convention Speech by Rose Pastor Stokes, 19 August 1921, ibid., 681.

109. Official Convention Report by Marcus Garvey, 4 August 1921, ibid., 617ff. See also Nancy Kaye Forderhase, "The Plans That Failed: The United States and Liberia, 1920–1935" (Ph.D. diss., University of Missouri, 1971).

110. Garvey to King, 4 August 1921, *Marcus Garvey Papers* 3:619–20.

111. Gabriel L. Dennis to Matthews, 12 August 1921, ibid., 655.

112. Convention Report, 2 August 1921, ibid., 590–91. While the United States government had completely penetrated the Garvey movement and was leery of it, many white Americans failed either to take it seriously or to be afraid of it. A reporter for the New York *Globe* who interviewed Garvey on 2 August 1921 wrote sympathetically that the UNIA, while interested in taking over Africa for the Africans, envisaged a republic run along American lines and not on the Soviet model (ibid., 588–90).

113. Speech by Marcus Garvey, 31 August 1921, ibid., 734–40.

114. Ibid.

115. Herbert Aptheker, *Correspondence of W. E. B. Du Bois, Selections, 1877–1934* (Amherst: University of Massachusetts Press, 1973), 1:251–52.

116. Ibid., 252.

117. W. E. B. Du Bois, *The World and Africa: Inquiry Into the Part Which Africa Has Played in World History* (New York: International Publishers, 1965), 236.

118. Imanuel Geiss, *The Pan-African Movement: A History of Pan-Africanism in America, Europe and Africa*, trans. Ann Keep (London: Methuen, 1974), 242.

119. George Padmore, *Pan-Africanism or Communism?* (London: Dennis Dobson, 1956), 129.

120. Geiss, *The Pan-African Movement*, 242.

121. W. E. B. Du Bois, *The World and Africa*, 236. George Padmore, *Pan-Africanism or Communism?* 128, suggested that in addition to the Garvey movement, Europe had other reasons to worry: a number of revolts had broken out in the French West African colonies and the Belgian Congo; and led by J. E. Casely Hayford, a delegation from the West African National Congress, including persons from The Gambia, Gold Coast, Nigeria, and Sierra Leone, had visited Lord Milner, the secretary of state for colonies, demanding constitutional and other reforms.

122. W. E. B. Du Bois, *The World and Africa,* 237. While it is clear that the *Neptune* did confuse aspects of the Garvey movement with those of the NAACP, it may have been correct in noting the presence of UNIA cells in the Congo. Cf. Tony Martin, *Race First,* 116.

123. Geiss, *The Pan-African Movement*, 240ff.

124. Ibid.

125. W. E. B. Du Bois, "To the World: Manifesto of the Second Pan-African Congress," *Crisis* 23 (November 1921): 5–10.

126. Ibid.
127. Du Bois, *The World and Africa*, 239. There were, however, journalists in London who got the impression that "although Du Bois rejected Garvey's crude methods, he was in his way just as determined to help the Africans attain their rights by peaceful and constitutional means." See also Geiss, *The Pan-African Movement*, 246.
128. Du Bois, *The World and Africa*, 239.
129. Geiss, *The Pan-African Movement*, 242.
130. Ibid., 246.
131. Ibid.
132. Ibid.
133. Ibid., 247.
134. Ibid.
135. Speech by Marcus Garvey, 7 September 1921, *Marcus Garvey Papers* 4:31–33.
136. Ibid., 32.
137. *Negro World*, 8 October 1921, 2.
138. Du Bois, *The World and Africa*, 240–41; Padmore, *Pan-Africanism or Communism?* 134–35. Apparently, Du Bois's personal position at Geneva was tougher than indicated in the text of the petition. According to Geiss, *The Pan-African Movement*, 242, "When Du Bois came to Geneva to hand in a petition to the League of Nations, he seems to have behaved in such a way that even some of the best friends of the 'negro race' dissociated themselves from him."
139. Geiss, *The Pan-African Movement*, 248–51.
140. *Marcus Garvey Papers* 4:29.

12

In the Whirlwind: Du Bois and Garvey

The United States made a gesture of courtesy; a little thing, and
merely a gesture, but one so unusual that it was epochal. President
Coolidge, at the suggestion of William H. Lewis, a leading colored
lawyer of Boston, named me, an American Negro traveler. Envoy
Extraordinary and Minister Plenipotentiary to Liberia—the highest
rank ever given by any country to a diplomatic agent in black Africa. And it named this Envoy the special representative of the
President of the United States to the President of Liberia, on the
occasion of his inauguration; charging the Envoy with a personal
word of encouragement and moral support. It was a significant action. It had in it nothing personal. Another appointee would have
been equally significant. (Du Bois on being appointed envoy).[1]

Remember that I have sworn by you and my God to serve to the end
of all time, the wreck of matter and the crash of worlds. . . . If I die
in Atlanta my work shall then only begin, but I shall live in the
physical or spiritual to see the day of Africa's glory. . . . I repeat, I
am glad to suffer and even die. Again, I say, cheer up, for better
days are ahead. I shall write the history that will inspire the millions that are coming and leave the posterity of our enemies to
reckon with the hosts for the deeds of their fathers. With God's
dearest blessings, I leave you for awhile. (Garvey on his way to
prison.)[2]

Garvey sensed he would be imprisoned for his activities and wanted to
go to Africa to establish a UNIA base in Monrovia. However, he was
unwelcome by the Europeans either in their homelands or in their African colonies. But American State Department officials responsible for
African affairs had less cause for worry, since Cyril A. Crichlow, now
alienated from the UNIA, had told them that "Garvey had not had a
chance to bring about his so-called Monrovian settlement, as the British
Government would make every possible effort to keep him and his
followers out of there."[3]

469

Garvey was also increasingly persuaded that African American leaders of all political persuasions wished to destroy his movement and to have him declared an undesirable alien. He had a bruising battle with Cyril V. Briggs, head of the African Blood Brotherhood, over the issue of Communist influence in, or control of, black organizations. This quarrel ended up in court on charges of libel. Garvey and James Weldon Johnson traded jibes in the New York *Age* over whether or not the UNIA leader supported white racism. For his part, Du Bois denied ever having said that African Americans were not adaptable to the climate of Africa. Nevertheless, he went on to say that Garvey and his movement were more detrimental to the future of blacks in America than ever before.[4] Soon after his release on bond, an embattled Garvey felt obliged to make a speaking tour of the United States in order to raise money for his legal defense, for his Liberian settlement, and for his Third International Convention to be held in August 1922.

Garvey's association with the Ku Klux Klan during this tour created an uproar among African American leaders; it also created division within the ranks of the UNIA.[5] Very much a race man, Garvey refused to understand how and why other black persons, whether in the United States, the Caribbean, Europe, or Africa, could willingly tolerate prejudice, discrimination, and lynching rather than go to Africa and build a black nationality. Not only was he scandalized by what had taken place at the Pan-African Congress in London, Brussels, and Paris, but he felt betrayed by Blaise Diagne who, Garvey insisted, had gained power and prestige in France for having taken a battleship "to his native land to recruit black people to die for Frenchmen."[6] The head of the UNIA was therefore prone to see the logic of a Klansman who believed "America to be a white man's country" and who also advocated that "the Negro should have a country of his own in Africa."[7] Because Garvey also believed that whites had no business being in an "Africa for Africans, at home and abroad," he was willing to support white American senators who advocated sending blacks to Africa.[8]

Du Bois certainly understood Garvey's rage, but he could not help being embarrassed by, and detesting, the UNIA leader's bombast and tactics. The editor of the *Crisis* saw the plight of the race in a larger perspective: he agonized about "fifty-nine Negroes lynched in Tulsa"; was hurt when President Harding, speaking in Birmingham, refused to concede racial equality to blacks; was bitter about "helpless Haiti" then under United States occupation; and was frustrated by the "delay of [the] Liberia Loan."[9] Occasionally, and in a manner not unlike Garvey, Du Bois would abandon his intellectual calm and vent his spleen against America and the whole white world.[10]

Du Bois's frustration with the delay of the Liberian loan was undoubtedly shared by Secretary of State Charles Evans Hughes, who was attempting to draft a bill presentable to the Congress of the United States. On 18 June 1921 Hughes finally forwarded all the documents relating to the loan to the president for approval and for transmission to Congress for action.[11] The secretary warned that "it seems likely that foreign interests not in favor of the plan will endeavor to obstruct it unless by timely action on the part of this Government, the loan provided for in the plan is made available at an early date."[12] What the secretary did not reveal to President Harding was the continued scheming of both Britain and France to subvert Liberian sovereignty.[13]

Garvey, for his part, attempted to help Liberia in his own symbolic way. His tour across the United States in March 1922 to raise funds for his domestic activities and foreign ventures in Liberia, and to drum up support for his forthcoming international convention, was not to be as successful as he had hoped. Aside from being closely monitored by the FBI, he occasionally ran into trouble from blacks who opposed his views of the Klan and racist whites who detested blacks—whatever their ideology. Meanwhile, from New York, Duse Mohamed Ali, who was in charge of organizing the convention, sent out a steady stream of invitations to prospective delegates and to hoped-for supporters such as Du Bois, Robert Russa Moton (Tuskegee), Nicholas Murray Butler (Columbia University), Albert Beacon Fall (secretary of the interior under Harding), Charles Evans Hughes, Giovanni Amendola (Italian secretary of state for the colonies) and the French minister of the colonies, among others. Like Garvey, who would not take "no" for an answer, Duse Mohamed pestered those who did not send him a polite excuse of their inability to attend.[14] Garvey himself notified Harding of the convention and asked him to receive "a delegation elected from this 3rd Annual International Convention, to visit you in Washington, and to lay before you certain facts appertaining to the race." He sent a similar request to Sir Eric Drummond, secretary general of the League of Nations.[15]

The Third International Convention of the UNIA opened in New York on 1 August 1922 with the usual fanfare. But there was an air of crisis due to Garvey's indictment and "a few nosebleeds" because of fisticuffs between those who supported and opposed his warm relations with the Ku Klux Klan.[16] In his opening speech, the Honorable Gabriel Moore Johnson, mayor of Monrovia and UNIA high potentate for Africa, lamented that the Liberians did not understand that there was no relationship between the proposed United States loan and funds being collected by the UNIA for Liberia. The high potentate also regretted that "a large portion of money" sent by the UNIA to Liberia had to be used in "other channels" than those for which it had been designated. This, he explained, led to a delay in the work in Liberia and caused the association to be "looked upon by many of the people there as a huge joke." Then borrowing a line from Garvey, Johnson appealed for "race solidarity" rather than the attitude of some "high-class" blacks who sought "social equality" with whites. He praised the Black Star Line and urged UNIA leaders to use discretion when discussing association matters with outsiders. In conclusion, he wished and hoped that the convention would be harmonious and would accomplish those things which "will tend toward the redeeming of our benighted land, Africa."[17]

Contrary to the wishes of Johnson, the convention was marked by both internal strife and outside criticism. Garvey sought to impeach members for "disloyalty" and was himself subject to impeachment proceedings.[18] This excitement caught the eye of J. Edgar Hoover of the FBI, who told his New York agent that his "attention has just been called to the renewed activities of *Marcus Garvey*, whose case is in your office in connection with an effort to defraud the mails." Hoover accused Garvey of being "a notorious negro agitator, affectionately referred to by his own race as the 'negro Moses.' " The head of the FBI noted reports of Garvey's propaganda among the "negroes" and an income of $1,000 per day, and revealed that he wanted to hasten "the prosecution which is now pending, in order that he [Garvey] may be once and for all put where he can peruse his past activities behind the four walls in the Atlanta clime."[19]

Meanwhile, a number of black leaders, such as William Pickens of the NAACP and A. Philip Randolph of the *Messenger* magazine, under the aegis of the Friends of Negro Freedom, organized four meetings with the theme, "Marcus Garvey Must Go!"[20] Some of these leaders railed at statements Garvey had made about them at the convention and contemplated bringing charges of libel against him. Garvey, in turn, filed suit against the New York *Times*, the Amsterdam *News*, the New York *Call*, Pickens, Randolph, and Chandler Owen. In the middle of all of this confusion, Garvey had to appear in court to answer a summons by the Pan Union Company about the activities of his ship, SS *Yarmouth*.[21] These sideshows did not, however, prevent the convention from going through its agenda. The various committees submitted their reports, and the UNIA sent off its delegation to Geneva to "attend the September sitting of the

Assembly of the League of Nations representing the interest of the Negro Peoples of the world."[22]

At the end of an extra session required to complete the work of the convention, a rather pensive Garvey admitted to his audience the existence of many unpleasant differences within the organization and the danger of division. Nevertheless, he urged his followers to depart the convention "with a new mission, with a new determination, swearing new allegiance to this great cause of ours and so as to be able to prove our faith and confidence, all those who will stand firm in this new year for the Universal Negro Improvement Association in its activities and in its program for the advancement of the cause of Negro humanity."[23]

The projected American loan to Liberia, which Garvey hoped was one of the programs that would advance the cause of Negro humanity, was having such rough sledging that its prospects were really in doubt. Garvey was therefore pleased when, on 10 May 1922, he heard that "America has come to the rescue in loaning Liberia five million dollars so as to put her house in order, thereby making a new start toward the goal of national security." His paeons of praise to "a philanthropic and liberal minded America, whose honesty of purpose in international politics should be better trusted than any other nations" was viewed as naive by other African American leaders. They could not believe that Garvey was serious in what they considered to be his obvious attempts to manipulate powerful whites into helping Africa either by accepting white prejudices, flattering them, or viciously attacking Europeans.[24]

President Harding appeared willing to go to great lengths to secure the loan for Liberia. At one time he even suggested to Secretary of State Hughes that there were enough votes in Congress for the approval of the loan and that the State Department could ensure this action by preparing a dossier for Congress. This document was intended to express "the views not only of the present administration but also [of] President[s] Roosevelt, Taft and Wilson" that the United States had a moral responsibility to assist Liberia. Administration officials who testified before the House Ways and Means Committee stressed the "moral obligation of this country" toward Liberia. Harding even wrote a letter to Congress urging the necessity of the loan in order "to deal with the Republic of Liberia in the good faith which is becoming of a great Republic like ours."[25]

To the chagrin of President Harding and the State Department, Liberian President King and his delegation, who had spent many months in Washington, D.C., lobbying for the passage of the bill, were running out of funds. A loan of some $3,000 that they had received from the State

Department was exhausted, and because of political shifts against King in Monrovia, the commission planned to return home. Faced with this urgent situation, the State Department and the Liberians compromised on a revised bill and sent it to the Treasury for review. This was acceptable, and on 28 October 1921 the Liberian mission and American officials signed the loan plan and a supplementary depository agreement at the State Department.

Unfortunately for the Liberians, the Treasury Department reported to the State Department that even though Liberia had withdrawn some $26,000 from the projected credit of $5 million, the delay in signing the agreement had resulted in the withdrawal of that credit. The Liberians were understandably disappointed with this decision and enquired whether it would be possible to obtain a private loan under the same rate of interest if Congress refused to extend the loan. The Department could not commit itself to this matter but arranged to make $8,140 available to the Liberians to settle their accounts in the United States. It also arranged for the USS *Denver* to take the commission to Monrovia on 15 November 1921.[26]

Once in Monrovia, President King and his commission were able to convince the Liberian legislature that it should approve the agreement without amendment. Secretary Hughes was notified of the development, and he informed the Liberians that on 15 February 1922 the President had sent the bill to Congress. The problem for the American administration, however, was that meanwhile a strong bipartisan opposition had developed against the bill. This was led by Furnifold M. Simmons, a Democrat from North Carolina, and southern Democrats who opposed the loan in retaliation for the Dyer antilynching bill then under consideration. They were joined by George Norris, a Republican from Nebraska, and midwestern Republicans who felt that their farming states needed more assistance than did far-off Liberia.[27] These opponents were joined by still others, such as Mississippi's Senator Pat Harrison, who felt that no money should be loaned to "pay a Bad Debt of an Insolvent Debtor of J. P. Morgan and Kuhn, Loeb, and Company." Moreover, they expressed the concern that the loan to Liberia would establish a dangerous precedent in which special interest groups hoping for patronage could influence the policy of Congress and the administration.[28] Despite this opposition, it appeared for a while that the bill would pass. On 12 May 1922 the State Department learned that the bill had passed the House of Representatives. The Senate was to prove more difficult, however.

Both the State Department and the White House showed a keen interest in the reaction of African Americans to the battle over the Liberian loan.

In fact, in submitting the bill to the White House to send to Congress, Secretary Hughes wrote, "The close relation which the prosperity of Liberia has to all that pertains to the advancement of the Negro race makes the situation of that Government a subject of vivid and constant concern.[29] A report in the State Department files indicates that an attempt was made to assess how "certain political factors affecting our negro citizens will probably press for consideration" of the loan. The first, and "by far the most important faction," was the one headed by Robert Russa Moton of Tuskegee. The relationship of this group to the Republican National Committee was reported to be "close," but Moton himself was viewed as personally apolitical and someone who disinterestedly gave advice in matters relating to "negro interests, including appointments to public office." Close to Moton was said to be Dr. Jesse Jones of the Phelps-Stokes Fund in New York, listed as "our best authority on negro education." He was reported to have made a thorough study of Liberia's problems and was interested in having philanthropic groups help the Liberian republic. The third member of this trinity was a Mr. Robert R. Church, who was "very influential with the negro voters and it is understood that the Republican National Committee" often suggested that he be consulted on appointments and "in affairs of vital interest to the negro voters."[30]

The second faction identified by the analyst for the State Department was the one headed "by Dr. DuBois of New York, editor of 'The Crisis,' a radical negro journal." Allied to Du Bois was said to be James Weldon Johnson, "who has so severely arraigned this Government's policy in Haiti." This radical group, allegedly operating mainly through the NAACP, was judged to be seeking, "without any very great success, to build up a strong following among negro voters." And while the analyst felt that the "influence of this faction with the National Republican Committee is understood to be limited," he advised the State Department that Moton and his friends might be encouraged to show a greater interest in Liberia because of their mutual friendship with such partisans of Du Bois as Emmett Jay Scott, Ernest Lyon, William H. Lewis, and James A. Cobb. This latter group was said to be quite interested in supporting the claim of Lewis, who expected the fee of $150,000 for his alleged role in lobbying the Wilson administration to approve the loan for Liberia. The analyst concluded that this claim was "preposterous" and predicted that the Moton faction had "no sympathy with the plans of these men and [would] withhold support from them."[31]

While Moton may have appeared less controversial than Du Bois with respect to the loan, he did have an interest in Liberia. On 22 September

1922 he had written acting secretary of state William Phillips to support
the candidacy of one William H. Baldwin as financial agent in Liberia in
the event the loan were approved. His reasons are revealing:

> It is very important—and certainly you know this as well as I—to name the
> right sort of white man. It is important to insure the best results in dealing
> with Liberia with any matter regarding the race question that the right kind of
> white man be selected for the task. I, therefore, would suggest that Mr.
> Baldwin from every point of view, I think, would be a satisfactory
> representative of our government, who will cooperate in the most helpful
> way with colored men and with white men in furthering the ends our
> government has in view in carrying out such plans and policies as [are]
> absolutely essential to that little Negro republic. . . .
>   I have been much gratified at the deep interest that the State Department
> has manifested in Liberia and Haiti. As I have said before when I see you on
> the Haitian matter I hope you will permit me to speak to you in person
> regarding Liberia and Mr. Baldwin.[32]

Despite such evidence of black support, President Harding had serious difficulties persuading the Senate of the morality of honoring the
pledges of the previous administrations to Liberia. He wrote Charles
Evans Hughes about his efforts to secure the support of Senators John
McCormick and Henry Cabot Lodge, both by letters and personal appeals. Among the reasons he gave were to prevent an unpleasant political condition in Liberia, to avoid threatening international complications, and to avoid putting the whole country of Liberia into a feverish
state of irritating anxiety. With such White House pressure, the Republican leadership in Congress held a special night caucus and defeated the
largely Democratic opposition to the bill. Nevertheless, attempts by the
president through both letters and personal interviews to encourage a
joint resolution in favor of a Liberian aid bill failed. The best the president could promise a beleaguered State Department was that the matter
would be taken up when Congress reconvened in November 1922.[33]

The Liberians exerted a great deal of pressure on Minister Solomon
Porter Hood to come to their aid. On 31 May 1922 he cabled the State
Department that Liberia was on the point of collapse and that in view of
the "traditional and moral responsibility" the United States had always
had in Liberia, he was obliged to report that its government was on the
"verge of bankruptcy, which if the crash came would involve serious
international complications."[34] Then to the consternation of Washington, Hood approved of Liberia's decision to use German funds seized in
wartime as collateral to secure a loan from the bank of British West
Africa. His action so alarmed the State Department that on 13 July 1922

it instructed him "to take no action without permission of Washington." The telegram stated that the department was "doing everything in its power to expedite the consummation of the loan and expects that favorable action by the Senate upon joint resolution establishing the credit will shortly be taken."[35]

Hood, like many previous African American heads of mission in Liberia, was aware of, and objected to, the degree of cynicism in the State Department about Liberia. He must have known that the director of the consular service had advised Washington that owing to "reports of extravagant and irregular use of public funds," the Department of State should approach "methods to relieve financial crises [in Liberia] with caution."[36] Hood explained to the department that he had taken the action in question because, as his legation understood, the policy of the United States toward Liberia, as far as it could legitimately be pursued, was to "save and preserve" Liberia as "an independent autonomous state." He indicated that he profoundly regretted the disapproval expressed by the department, but noting the time it took to communicate with Washington about events in Monrovia, he did what "at the time seemed to be the best and only course that could be taken."[37]

The Liberians were furious to learn that the State Department had censured the legation in Monrovia for coming to their rescue in time of dire need. They were especially incensed by the implication that it was their profligacy that had made the legation's action necessary. The Liberians insisted that their activities were approved by the American agents in Monrovia, who were "in a better position to know the actual facts than those in the Department at Washington." The Government of Liberia asked Hood to send a telegram to Washington that said in part:

> The policy which the Liberian Administration understood was to be adopted, was one of helpfulness, of collaboration for the furtherance of its essential interests. Furthermore, the Government of Liberia does not understand why the very unusual step of communicating the censure of your Government upon its official representative here be made to it. The Liberian Government finds itself most embarrassed by such procedure, and it could not, without violating official proprieties attempt to vindicate the actions of the American Official Representative.[38]

Hood must have felt vindicated when the department was proved wrong in its assessment of the mood of the Senate about the Liberian loan. When it reconvened, a bipartisan coalition criticized certain parts of the loan's provisions, with some members alleging that the entire transaction under which the money had originally been advanced was illegal. Then on 24

November 1922 it was moved that the entire bill be recommitted to the Senate Finance Committee, with the proviso that it be carried forward to 27 November for a final vote without further debate. Noting that the bill was recommitted without instructions, the State Department notified the Liberians that it held out little hope for them to secure the proposed loan of $5 million and suggested that they look elsewhere.[39]

Secretary of State Hughes was disappointed that the loan agreement failed since he had believed the Senate would approve it. He finally had to inform Hood that "the proposed loan [now] has no prospect of success." Consequently, he felt that the State Department could not "encourage the Liberian Government to delay further its efforts to arrange financial aid from other sources which may be available," including interested "private sources" in the United States. Nevertheless, anxious not to repeat the disaster he had just experienced, Hughes refused to give any assurance "as to whether such a loan could be arranged."[40]

Hood was caught in a dilemma. He had to take bad news to the Liberians, but as was the case for many of the early black diplomats in Liberia, he discovered that the instructions he was ordered to transmit to his hosts had already been leaked to them. Mr. Sidney de la Rue, financial adviser to Liberia in the legation, wrote to a colleague:

> Please remember that the Department never advised this Government nor the Legation of the failure of the loan until after the local merchants had received full details from their home offices in England, Holland and Germany. When it failed therefore, the trouble the American officials had was the entire loss of prestige and confidence. . . . [The] people thought we were not in the confidence of Washington. From that time to this the Minister never hears a thing until long after it happens. That several days loss was a thing we've never caught up with yet. You may recall that Dr. Hood cabled Washington saying that the Dutch Consul had given out that the loan had failed and that he wished to be authorized to deny it. The answer to that cable of his was the first official information we had.[41]

Once Hood had relayed Hughes's cable to the Liberians, their first concern was whether the United States would or should take such measures as were deemed adequate "to mitigate any pronounced evil effect on the international relations of Liberia arising out of the apparent rebuff."[42] Once again, the minister was caught in the middle. The Liberians asked for a clarification of the cryptic statement about the State Department being unable to encourage them "to arrange the desired financial aid from the other sources which may be available." They wanted to know whether the Department had any specific bankers in mind, and if so, whether the Liberians should take the initiative to approach them. Finally, but of great importance to the Liberian Government, was the need to be reassured that the failure of the loan did not indicate any change in the "traditional friendly sympathetic attitude of the American Government toward Liberia or the withdrawal of its diplomatic support and counsel."[43]

Conscious of the imperialistic designs of both Britain and (especially) France[44] on Liberia, and of the United States' failure to help that country, the State Department quickly responded to Hood's telegram. It instructed him to assure the Liberians that the failure of the loan was not indicative of any change in the traditionally friendly attitude of the United States government toward Liberia and it pledged always to "look with sympathetic interest at any attempts of the Liberian Government and people to promote the real interests of the Republic." As far as the possibility of raising private funds "for constructive purposes" was concerned, Hood was instructed to inform the Liberians that if they would "appoint an agent with proper qualifications to conduct negotiations, the [State] Department will be glad to refer any interested parties to him."[45]

Sensing that Hood might take some unilateral action to help the Liberians deal with the failure of the loan proposal, the State Department took care to caution him about following instructions. The department's telegram to Hood underscored United States traditional policy toward Liberia. But it warned:

> As the representative of the United States at Monrovia it is, of course, expected that you should properly reflect this attitude but in so doing it is desired that you should not undertake obligations, assume responsibilities, or make commitments with respect to Liberian questions without instructions.
>
> Although the Department appreciates that motives of helpfulness prompted you, association with the efforts made to meet the difficulties of the situation which followed the failure of the loan, it is believed that your most effective service would be rendered by representing the views of this Government on such Liberian matters as may be of concern to it, and not as it appears from our reports, by actively participating on your initiative in the formulation of policies or measures for adoption by the Liberian Government.[46]

Meanwhile, back in the United States, many African American leaders were disappointed with the Senate's vote against Liberia. Emmett Jay Scott went so far as to accuse some southern senators of misrepresenting the Liberian case to "certain negro politicians" rather than admit that they were against any aid to Liberia.[47] Du Bois, who was still engaged in a running battle with President Harding, considered the failure of the Liberian loan, along with the large number of lynchings and other atrocities, as one of the "debits" for blacks in 1922. He also took the opportunity to review United States policy toward Africa, to call attention to European imperialist motives in Africa, and to criticize Garvey, while at the same time attempting to make a modest proposal about salvaging something of the Black Star Line fiasco.

In a letter to Secretary of State Hughes, Du Bois declared that as "an American citizen of Negro descent, and a member of the Executive Board of the Pan-African Congress," he was very alarmed by the failure of the American Congress to confirm the Liberian loan. He explained that the main reason for his concern was the "open secret that the British and French Governments" had only been held back in their aggression against Liberia by the prospect of active aid from the United States. Now that this possibility was closed, Du Bois said that he feared that British banking interests, such as they were in Liberia, would make that country "practically . . . a British protectorate with complete absorption looming in the future." Convinced that the prospects of Congress approving a future Liberian loan were slim, Du Bois wondered "what the colored people of the United States could do to avoid this contingency?"[48]

Du Bois's modest proposal was that if the private resources of African Americans could be safeguarded from the exploitation that could arise in a commercial venture, then he was convinced that the tremendous resources of Liberia would repay any loan that African Americans could make to that country. Du Bois proposed the creation of a "small company in which colored people had representation" to establish a direct commercial intercourse between America and Liberia. That company could do a number of things: participate in direct commerce; transport passengers back and forth, not so much as immigrants but as various types of consultants; and provide America with a "museum" of Liberian resources to let both black and white Americans know about the future industrial potential of tropical Africa. There was no telling what such a successful venture would hold for the future.[49]

Presuming that the Secretary of State had heard that the Black Star Line was now bankrupt, Du Bois explained that the difficulty was that its leader, "Marcus Garvey, was not a business man and turned out to be a thoroughly impractical visionary, if not a criminal, with grandiose schemes of conquest." The result, according to Du Bois, was that nearly a million dollars garnered from the "hard-earned pennies of Negro laborers" was locked up in absolutely worthless Black Star Line stocks now scattered around the country. This to Du Bois was a shame, since the United States owned thousands of ships, any one or two of which might be used for the scheme he was proposing. What he had in mind, and what he wanted to know from Hughes, was whether there was any feasible and legal way for the United States government to guide or plan the procurement of at least two ships for a tentative beginning of commercial commerce between Liberia and America. Du Bois felt that if this could be arranged, then it would restore the confidence of the "mass of American Negroes in commercial enterprise with Africa, possibly having a private company headed by men of highest integrity, both white and colored, to take up and hold in trust, the Black Star Line certificates." He admitted to the secretary that it was quite possible that this matter was outside the "purview and power of the State Department, but I have ventured to address you, Sir, because of the pressing importance of the matter."[50]

Du Bois's suggestion to Hughes to mobilize funds from black people to help Liberia was apparently a view that was widely held by African Americans. Robert P. Skinner, the United States consul in London, reported to the department that Mr. D. G. Garland, an African American who visited his office on 5 December 1923, felt that

> there are upwards of ten million of colored people residing in the United States many of whom are prosperous and wealthy, and who as a body are desirous that the Government of Liberia should be stabilized and its prosperity assured. . . . Inasmuch as the irresponsible adventurer, Marcus Garvey, secured an enormous amount for his association without difficulty, it should not be out of the question for a responsible association of colored citizens to raise 5 million dollars by making proper appeal and furnishing the proper safeguard.[51]

Here then was another instance of collaboration of blacks, both as diplomats and symbolic actors, to attempt to influence United States policy toward Liberia. As we have seen, Hood had been publicly sanctioned for his efforts to induce the United States to help Liberia. Nothing apparently came from Du Bois's efforts to convince Secretary of State Hughes to help in this effort.

It would later be left to Garvey to attempt to implement his plans to establish both trade and colonies in Liberia, but in January 1923 he was under pressure from the legal officials of the United States. They suspected him of involvement in the assassination in New Orleans of the Reverend James W. H. Eason, who had been impeached at the convention in 1922 and who was scheduled to testify against Garvey on the charge of fraud. As it was, United States prosecutors were never able to prove that Garvey had anything to do with Eason's death. And while two UNIA adherents, William Shakespeare and Constantine F. Dyer were initially charged with manslaughter in the assassination of Eason, they were later acquitted. United States officials suspected that the real assassin was one Esau Ramus, a "minor UNIA official" who had been sent to New Orleans by Garvey. In any case, Garvey denounced the assassination, attributing it to a "woman affair."[52]

Garvey's travail worsened when on 13 May 1923 he together with Elie Garcia, George Tobias, and Orlando M. Thompson were indicted in the United States District Court in the Southern District of New York "for a scheme to defraud . . . poor persons to part with their money and invest in the stock [of the Black Star Line.]" Garvey told his followers that he was "not concerned a bit about the trial" but was prepared to face "the arrows of 'hell' for the principles of the Universal Negro Improvement Association." He blamed "the National Association for the Advancement of Colored People, the cheap Negro politicians in Harlem and the brainy white men who have sense enough to know what they want and how to get it."[53] Much to the dismay of many supporters, Garvey ignored their feeling that any man who defends himself has a fool for a client and acted as his own lawyer. On 19 June 1923, after a twenty-seven-day trial, he was convicted and sent to Tombs prison. Garvey was allowed bail of some $5,000, even though the prosecutor thought that as a non-citizen of the United States he might flee the country. On 21 June he was sentenced to five years in a federal prison and fined $1,000.[54] Garvey decided to appeal his conviction and was freed on bail.

Garvey's trial and conviction caused somewhat of a sensation in New York and attracted the attention of his followers and detractors both locally and internationally. He was convinced that he was "a victim of an international 'frame-up,' a conspiracy, not only engaged in by members of the opposite race, but including selfish and jealous members of my own." While sympathetic to the Zionist convictions of American Jews, Garvey had long believed them unsympathetic to him, preferring Du Bois. While still in the Tombs, he wrote to his supporters that he was being punished for the crime of "the Jew Silverston, who during my absence in the West Indies took $36,000 of the Black Star money. . . . I was prosecuted in this by Maxwell Mattuck, another Jew, and I am to be sentenced by Judge Julian Mack the eminent Jewish Jurist." Garvey could not resist a play on the biblical verse when he wrote, "Truly I may say 'I was going down to Jeric[h]o and fell among friends."[55]

West Indian leaders in New York took exception to some newspaper reports that while "American Negroes in Harlem were elated . . . over Garvey's conviction," those "nine-tenths of Garvey's army [who] are

West Indian Negroes" were not happy about it. One minister wrote to the New York *World* that while it was not credible to say that American Negroes were elated . . . over Garvey's difficulties, it was also not true to imply that the majority of West Indians were in sympathy with either the aims or methods of Garvey. Then sounding a note similar to that of Du Bois, the minister explained that many West Indians, even Jamaicans, were opposed to Garvey's aims and found them to be "crude" and "mischievous." Nevertheless, even these persons could "have no feeling of elation and cannot rejoice over the fall and degradation of a man who had so unique an opportunity to serve his race but whose colossal conceit and remarkable pigheadedness neutralized to his ruin the many good qualities he possessed."[56]

The French ambassador in Washington, Jean-Jules Jusserand, breathed a sigh of relief when he heard of Garvey's indictment and conviction. Writing to the president of the council in the French Ministry of Foreign Affairs, he saw an end to a condition in which his embassy had had, "on more than one occasion, to occupy itself with the 'Pan-Negro' movement, organized by a black West Indian, Marcus Garvey, who has awarded himself" such titles as "Provisional President of Africa" and who "organized propaganda fervently hostile to countries having African possessions." Jusserand reported that not only had Garvey managed to raise $1 million for the Black Star Line, capitalized for $10 million, but that he gave away grandiose titles just for the asking and founded a periodical, the *Negro World*, to "celebrate his merits and the beauty of his undertakings." He claimed Garvey had bought for his Black Star Line "ships incapable of sailing, and led the sort of life suited to a Provisional President of such vast populations." Garvey's downfall, according to the French envoy, came because he continued to sell shares "when he knew that the company was indebted and the shares worthless." The result was his sentence to "5 years in prison on the 21st of this [June] month."[57] Judging from the spate of letters from the British foreign offices to the governors in the Caribbean and Africa about Garvey and his *Negro World*, the British were undoubtedly equally relieved to believe that they had heard the last of him.[58]

What many people did not count on was the tenacity of Garvey in pursuing his dreams, even while in prison appealing his sentence. The UNIA's head continued to plan for the future and attempted to pacify the powerful white world, while at the same time castigating the black leaders deemed reponsible for his plight. On 11 June 1923 Garvey had informed his followers that there would not be an annual meeting of the

UNIA in New York that year but that all local divisions should hold their own meetings. He assured them that he was making plans to assemble all "Africa's sons and daughters in our next annual international convention not in America, not in the West Indies, but in Africa. That shall be in August, 1924."[59] Garvey also despatched the Honorable Jean Joseph Adam to serve as the UNIA's permanent delegate to the League of Nations as well as to be the association's permanent representative in France. And much to the chagrin of Great Britain, Garvey named the Reverend Richard Hilton Tobitt ambassador to England with the title Sir Knight Commander of the Sublime Order of the Nile, and sent a letter to the British colonial secretary announcing this fact. The UNIA's ambassador presented his credentials to the Colonial Office, but officials there refused to grant him an interview.[60]

Garvey and his supporters sought every opportunity to appeal to the good offices of the American White House for help during this difficult period. A hospitalized John E. Bruce wrote President Harding's secretary requesting that the refusal of U.S. district attorney to grant bail to the UNIA leader be brought before the nation's chief executive as a "very grave injustice." When Harding died suddenly of a stroke on 2 August 1923, Garvey wrote to Mrs. Harding associating the millions of Negroes throughout the world with her sorrow and regret in losing a husband viewed by them as a great American statesman on the race question. Garvey also wrote to, and received a reply from, President Coolidge regretting the death of his predecessor and expressing best wishes for his new duties.[61]

No sooner was he released on bail on 8 September 1923 than Garvey undertook a nationwide tour that took him from St. Louis, to Oakland, California; to Portland, Oregon; and on to Tuskegee. His straightforward request to Robert Russa Moton for lodgings at the institute was honored by Moton, who also gave him permission to speak at the chapel. During his speech Garvey praised Booker T. Washington but insisted that blacks had and needed "men in different walks." He defended his views about the future of African peoples, comparing them with the views of other world leaders about their own people, and concluded with the hope that the faculty and student body of Tuskegee would give Dr. Moton the "courage to go through the country and speak not only to us but to speak to the white race; speak to the nation and the world." Garvey sent a gracious note of thanks to Moton with a donation for the institute. Moton was equally appreciative in his response.[62]

Other black leaders, however, were not prepared to be civil to Garvey or to be sympathetic to his conversations with racist white senators about black emigration to Liberia. On 9 November 1923 James Weldon Johnson wrote to Robert L. Vann, editor of the Pittsburgh *Courier*, praising his criticism of Garvey for engaging in the "sort of insidious propaganda that appeals to the . . . egotism of the white man" and vowing "to oppose and to counteract" Garvey's program.[63] Vann stated editorially that his paper had always attempted to be neutral in the Garvey controversy, believing that if some blacks wanted to go to Africa at their own expense, it had nothing to say: "Since some Negroes just delight to be fleeced, we are as [con]tent to see Garvey fleece them as any one else." It was another thing, Vann said, when Garvey attempted to engage the federal government in his enterprise and possibly attempted to interest senators by "selling his whole race for a pardon." Vann vowed that the Pittsburgh *Courier* would not stand still for that.[64]

Not only did Garvey pursue his emigration strategy with several senators, but he despatched a delegation to Monrovia to parley with President King. This group, led by Robert Lincoln Poston and including J. Milton Van Lowe and Lady Henrietta Vinton Davis, left New York on 11 December 1923. In a letter to President King, Garvey indicated that the delegation's mission was to "assist in the development of Liberia, industrially, and commercially, by the settlement in some parts of the country of a large number of American and West Indian Colonists who desire repatriation to their native land, Africa, for the establishment of their permanent homes." Garvey lamented that the UNIA's work in Liberia was handicapped by misunderstanding and misrepresentation by such men as Cyril A. Crichlow and Elie Garcia but believed that the twenty or thirty thousand families each provided with $1,500 would greatly help Liberia. He hoped that with a favorable understanding on the part of the Liberian president, the emigration could begin between September and December 1924.[65]

Like many of the other African American leaders, Du Bois resented Garvey's willingness to consort with the Ku Klux Klan and racist senators who were willing to exploit any back-to-Africa sentiment to advocate the expulsion of blacks from the United States.[66] Du Bois was also infuriated by the Europeans' penchant for making no distinction between his Pan-Africanism and Garvey's. Again, he was alarmed that blacks in New York City who knew that he suspected fraud in the activities of the Black Star Line had started to blame him for Garvey's indictment and trial. Despite these concerns, Du Bois obviously felt that his status as the foremost black intellectual in the country demanded that he explain Garvey and the UNIA convention to the ordinary (white) observer who might have mistaken these antics "for the dress rehearsal of a new comic opera, and looked instinctively for Bert Williams and Miller and Lyles [well-known black comedians]."[67]

Du Bois used the format of an article, "Back to Africa," to review and contrast the history of race relations in the Caribbean with that in the United States, and to explain why Garvey "oppose[d] white supremacy and the white ideal by a crude and equally brutal black supremacy and black ideal." But he also sought to demonstrate what racism does to people caught in its vortex. Du Bois declared that in the world of black masses of West Indians in New York City, and with a small number of African Americans, there arose a movement around a sentiment that had at its core "something spiritual, however poor and futile to-day." Greater than a need for "homes and stores and churches," insisted Du Bois, was the need for "manhood—liberty, brotherhood, equality." It was this "call of the spirit" that linked the black man with all men who were "despised and forgotten, seeking, seeking. Misled they often are, and again and again they play in microcosm the same tragic drama that other worlds and other groups have played."[68]

It was possibly Du Bois's sense of rhetoric and drama that led him to describe the Liberty Hall setting and Garvey in words that would later be much criticized by Garvey and others. Du Bois related that the members of the UNIA were drawn to a

> long, low, unfinished church basement, roofed over. A little, fat black man, ugly, but with intelligent eyes and big head, was seated on a plank platform besides a "throne," dressed in a military uniform of the gayest mid-Victorian type, heavy with gold lace, epaulets, plume, and sword. Beside him were "potentates," and before him knelt a succession of several colored gentlemen. These in the presence of a thousand or more applauding dark spectators were duly "knighted" and raised to the "peerage" as knight-commanders and dukes of Uganda and the Niger. Among the lucky recipients of titles was the former private secretary of Booker T. Washington.[69]

Du Bois was caustic in his depiction of the eloquence that brought Garvey's masses to their feet cheering and believing a siren's song: "We are going to Africa to tell England, France, and Belgium to get out of there." He lamented that Garvey and his followers were cheated into buying old and leaky ships for the Black Star Line. Although Du Bois was generally contemptuous of Garvey's "monkey-shines," he considered him to be a "sincere, hardworking idealist," but a man who was also "a stubborn, domineering leader of the mass."[70]

Du Bois insisted in his article, "Back to Africa," that the American Negro had survived two grave temptations, "the greater one, fathered by Booker T. Washington, which said, 'Let politics alone, keep in your place, work hard, and do not complain.' " This meant to Du Bois "perpetual color caste for colored folk by their own coöperation and consent . . . and the inevitable debauchery of the white world." The lesser temptation, fathered by Garvey, was, "Give up! Surrender! The struggle is useless; back to Africa and fight the white world." Du Bois, the intellectual visionary, believed that this advice was a chimera. As he saw it, the world had long experienced a process of "economic unity and cultural solidarity. The process has involved slavery, peonage, rape, theft, and extermination, but it is slowing uniting humanity." To rail against it, he believed, would not only doom the world to racial struggle but would deny the contemporary "yellow, black, and brown worlds" the advantages of having the white world, with its "economic technic and organization," economically dependent upon them. He firmly believed that the "super-diplomacy of race politics to-morrow is to transmute this interdependence into cultural sympathy, spiritual tolerance, and human freedom, Not in segregation, but in closer, larger unity lies interracial peace."[71]

Du Bois would discover that not many people in the world of the 1920s shared his vision of interracial brotherhood. A surprising number of African Americans, including the Garveyites, were furious with him for portraying their leader as an ugly, fat black man and had tired of the bickering between the two leaders. One irate woman wrote to Du Bois declaring that it would have been better if he had spent his time arousing interest in the NAACP than in "sending Mr. Garvey to jail and trying to wreck the universal negro improvement association especially as to the cowardly way in which it was done while writing letters to District Attorney, Judge Mack and to others who were in authority." She denied having any interest in Garvey, his organization, or his methods but expressed concern that Du Bois's actions would discredit him and the NAACP and "cause everlasting enmity between the West Indian and the American negroes which feeling will take a long time to eradicate."[72]

Du Bois was disingenuous in his denial that he had written to the officials mentioned "or to anyone else in authority with regard to Marcus Garvey, nor have I had anything whatsoever to do with the prosecution of the case against him."[73] The Richmond *Planet* would not have bought this denial, however. The paper said that it had finally had enough of the continuous squabbling between the two camps. It declared editorially: "To the DuBoisites we say, 'Let Garvey and his followers alone; they are joined to their Africa!' To the Garveyites we say, 'Let the DuBoisites alone; they are joined to the Constitution of the United States and the guarantee to all men, black as well as white, thereunder.'"[74]

Garvey's trial and conviction, and the obvious failure of the Black Star Line effort, apparently convinced Du Bois that his own efforts on behalf of Pan-Africanism were more realistic. In fact, his trial balloon in asking Secretary of State Hughes to see whether it was possible for the United States to rescue the bondholders of the Black Star Line could be viewed as an attempt to rescue Garvey's flawed efforts. But when he turned to the task of convening his third biennial Pan-African Congress, Du Bois found that the lack of continuity from the second congress posed problems. For one thing, the membership dues for the association were minimal; for another, the officials in Paris were squabbling among themselves when they were not asking Du Bois to raise funds for administrative purposes. This was difficult for Du Bois, because it was clear that the NAACP would not provide any more money unless it was matched by contributions from other organizations. Moreover, many African Americans who had attended the previous Paris conference refused support on the grounds that they had been mistreated by the francophone Africans. Isaac Béton conceded this but felt that the Pan-African Association was such an important instrument for the future for the race that African Americans should overlook any hard feelings.[75]

Du Bois had apparently been misled by Béton, who as late as 8 May 1923 had written that the meetings would take place, as planned, during the last two weeks of September. Then at the beginning of August Béton wrote cancelling the congress, resigned his position, and blamed Candace, Diagne, and Du Bois for lack of support. What had apparently also upset Béton was Du Bois's desire to convene the third congress somewhere in the Caribbean, without troubling to sell the idea to the association in the pages of the *Crisis*. Faced with this disaster in Paris, Du Bois was thrown back on his own slender resources and his personal network, and redoubled his efforts to save the congress.

Hoping that Béton would reconsider, Du Bois asked Rayford W. Logan, then living in Paris, to seek the aid of Robert Broadhurst to arrange the London session and for Diagne to organize the Paris meeting. This time, however, Diagne refused to cooperate. A French newspaper had written that "Du Bois was a disciple of Marcus Garvey," and

Diagne refused to have anything to do with anyone associated with the head of the UNIA. Perhaps Diagne had other reasons for his action, but according to Logan, it gave the "coup de grâce" to any chance of a Paris session.[76] (It should be noted that by this time Diagne had already warned Garvey that "French natives" wished to remain French since France had given them the kind of liberty it reserved for its European children. Moreover, Diagne had told Garvey that American blacks, "at the head of whom you have placed yourself," had no authority to demand that French Africa be placed solely under the control of Africans.[77])

Faced with the prospect that the work of six years spent in attempting to "establish some common meeting ground and unity of thought among the Negro . . . was about to be lost,"[78] Du Bois elected to ignore Paris and to hold sessions in both London and Lisbon. He was on good terms with many Britishers, and the Liga Africana, composed of blacks and mulattoes from Portugal's five overseas provinces, had invited him to hold a session in Lisbon. Besides, Du Bois was sympathetic to an organization committed to fighting injustice in the Portuguese colonies and was especially impressed by its leader, Professor José de Magalhaes, who taught tropical medicine at the University of Lisbon.[79]

On 30 August 1923 Du Bois announced that the Third Pan-African Congress would take place in November. He gave as the reason for the delay Béton's failure to realize that the congress was not "an established institution" but only "a great dream." Du Bois expressed the hope, however, that a large number of people would attend the sessions. His own way was paid to Europe by the Circle for Negro War Relief, and by a committee of the National Association of Colored Women.[80] This group of women had kept up an interest in the Pan-African movement, and Du Bois did not ignore their support when inviting delegates to the congress. Among the women invitees were the very influential Mrs. Adelaide Casely Hayford, then living in Sierra Leone, and Mrs. Ida Gibbs Hunt, wife of the United States consul at St. Étienne, France.

Du Bois was not as successful as he had hoped in getting a large number of delegates from the African continent. Among the attendees were Chief Amoah III of the Gold Coast; Kamba Simango of Portuguese East Africa or Mozambique; John Alcindor, president of the African Union of the Pan-African Congress; B. F. Seldon; Rayford W. Logan; Lord Sidney Olivier, former governor of Jamaica; Harold Laski, the left-wing political thinker; J. H. Tawney, the historian; H. G. Wells of the Fabian Society; Gilbert Murray, vice president of the Anti-Slavery Society; and Isaac Béton. Du Bois claimed that eleven countries were represented, but one commentator noted that the Africans came primarily from the Gold Coast, Nigeria, and Sierra Leone.[81]

The London session of the Third Pan-African Congress that convened on 7 and 8 November in Denison House, the headquarters of the Anti-Slavery Society, was narrower in scope than previous sessions. And despite the names of Candace and Béton on the printed invitations as officers of the Pan-African Association, it was clear that African Americans, especially Du Bois, Ida Cribbs Hunt, and Logan, were in charge. Du Bois spoke about the history of the Pan-African movement and about the present situation of blacks around the world. He explained that the main reason for black America's interest in Pan-Africanism and in the plight of other colored peoples in the world was their experience as a colored minority in the United States. Logan addressed the need of the Pan-African Association for a better organization and increased activities. Ida Gibbs Hunt urged support for the League of Nations, which she felt was still a force for world peace despite its many failures. Harold Laski presented a critical analysis of the mandate system and the activities of Lord Lugard in Nigeria. Finally, Kamba Simango talked about the situation in Portuguese Angola.[82]

It was clear to Du Bois and other commentators that the London session of the congress lacked much of the spark of earlier meetings. This was due in part to the poor turnout but also to the lack of firsthand knowledge of Africa among African Americans. But perhaps the most important reason for the malaise in London was the general concern over the Garvey movement. This became clear when John Alcindor broached the subject of the constitution for the Pan-African Association. Du Bois declared that it was not the organization's structure that gave it strength but rather its flexibility. He felt that there were no definite objectives beyond the congress's aim to be "an attempt to unite in periodical conference representatives of the main groups of peoples of African descent for purposes of information."[83]

The congress reiterated most of the demands of prior sessions. These included a call for Africans to have "a voice in their own governments" and for the development of Africa "for the benefit of Africans, and not merely for the profit of Europeans," and concluded with a criticism of South African Jan Christian Smuts, who was then "striving blindly to build peace and goodwill in Europe by standing on the necks and hearts of millions of black Africans." The delegates saw no other road to peace and progress until "black folk be treated as men."[84] It was noted, however, that only the Americans—Du Bois, Ida Gibbs Hunt, and Logan—signed the resolutions.[85]

Concerned that the Pan-African movement could be irretrievably damaged if such important French Africans as Blaise Diagne and Gratien Candace withdrew from it, Du Bois decided to stop in Paris en route to Lisbon. There he held a mini-conference with Isaac Béton and Deputy Jacque Boisneuf. He did not meet either Candace and Diagne, who were diplomatically "out of town," no doubt because they were unwilling to meeting anyone viewed by the French as supporters of Garvey and the UNIA. Du Bois later observed:

> In justice to the rank and file of French Negroes it must be said that they themselves showed at the Paris sessions of the Pan-African Congress of 1921 the keenest desire to co-operate. It is their political leaders who hang back, whether for reasons of self-interest, or those of politics, or for lack of funds as they asserted, when the preparations were being made for this Congress—it would be hard to say.[86]

Ironically, Garvey had often expressed the same thoughts about the difference between the African American masses and their leaders.

The curious shadow that lay over the Lisbon session of the Third Pan-African Congress led some observers to call it the "smallest and the quietest."[87] Some Portuguese commentators even claimed that "no 'Congress' took place at all in Lisbon,"[88] despite the presence of delegates from some of the Portuguese colonies, such as Goa, as well as delegates from Nigeria, the United States, and of course, Portugal itself.[89] Undoubtedly one of the reasons for this confusion was that since the Congress had been postponed from September to the end of November, its organizers in Lisbon had not had enough time to notify their fellows in many colonies. Another reason was the Portuguese government was unhappy with British Quaker delegates who had criticized forced labor and slavery in the Portuguese colonies. Official Portugal regarded this charge as a subterfuge by the Quakers to partition their colonies among the Germans and the British, "with Sao Thoma allegedly earmarked for the . . . chocolate firm Cadbury." Du Bois himself was suspect because of his close association with the British. Despite these problems and his inability to provide the *assimilados* with the support they expected, Du Bois called the Lisbon session a success. He noted the presence of two former ministers of the Portuguese colonies.[90]

When the American minister in Lisbon asked Du Bois to call at the embassy and, during a pleasant meeting, informed him that President

Coolidge had chosen him to be his envoy extraordinary and minister plenipotentiary at the inauguration of President King of Liberia, the editor of the *Crisis* was delighted. It has even been suggested that one of the reasons Du Bois insisted on a Lisbon venue for one of the sessions of the Third Pan-African Congress was that it lay on the route from London to Monrovia.[91] In any case, he had been in touch with President King over Garvey's plans for Liberia and was very much hoping to attend King's inauguration for a second term in Liberia at the end of the Lisbon session. Of course, one problem with this scheme was how to pay to get to Monrovia and back to the United States, given Du Bois's small salary.

The actual process by which Du Bois became a presidential envoy was not usual but was interesting nevertheless given his reputation. Apparently Du Bois had written the State Department about his projected visit to Liberia, offering his service in case it would be accepted. Then, according to what he told an American official he later met in Monrovia, the department sent him "a formal answer stating that there was a Minister" in Monrovia and that "said Minister could attend to any necessary duties &c."[92] In other words, the Department of State brushed him off. It is not known whether this was the same reply that the Department of State had sent to Solomon Porter Hood, then minister resident and consul general for the United States, who may have made the usual suggestion to the Department of State that it would be in America's interest for President Coolidge to send a personal representative to the inauguration of President-elect King.

What is known, however, is that James Weldon Johnson, secretary of the NAACP, wrote to James W. Wadsworth, United States senator, recommending that President Coolidge appoint Du Bois his envoy. This the senator suggested to the State Department on 25 September 1923. On 2 October 1923 the Department advised Johnson, as it had advised Du Bois, that "this Government has a Minister Resident and Consul General at Monrovia, who will represent the United States at the inauguration."[93] Apparently neither Du Bois nor his allies were willing to take the word of the State Department that a special envoy would not be sent to Liberia.

The next actor in this episode was William H. Lewis, an Ivy League-trained Republican who had served under both Roosevelt and Taft and who now interceded with Coolidge on Du Bois's behalf. This was interesting, because although the NAACP was publicly known to be sympathetic to the Democratic party, many politicians believed that it still backed Republicans for office.[94] Du Bois himself was as usual not very happy with Republican administrations, including that of Coolidge. Du Bois had bitterly attacked the appointment of former Congressman Campbell B. Slemp as Coolidge's secretary and principal adviser in the White House.[95] Nevertheless, on 4 October 1923 Lewis wrote Du Bois stating that he had raised the issue of his appointment with Slemp, who apparently had reacted favorably toward it. Lewis admitted to Du Bois, however, that he had touched base with Emmett Jay Scott, Booker T. Washington's protégé, and with Perry W. Howard, a Fisk graduate and prominent Republican, because "I wanted to make sure that there would be no knocks in the machine when it got started. I was able to say to Secretary Slemp, that all the different elements of our people were united in your appointment to this mission."[96]

Lewis's letter to Coolidge on Du Bois's behalf is interesting since it demonstrates the administration's methods in appointing envoys:

My dear Mr. President:—

It has come to my attention that Dr. William E. Burghardt Du Bois, the distinguished publisher and scholar of the colored race, and indeed of America, intends to make a visit to the Republic of Liberia in the near future, and will probably attend the inauguration of the new President of the Republic, the Honorable C. B. D. [sic] King, who recently visited this country as a member of the Liberian Commission.

I am sure you must know that Dr. Du Bois has been for many years connected with the National Association for the Advancement of Colored People, and is editor of the Crisis, a very influential publication among our people.

It occurs to me that it would be a very graceful thing if our government could make Dr. Du Bois its special representative at the inauguration of President King, which takes place, I think, about the first of January next. It would be a splendid opportunity to show the Liberian Republic, that notwithstanding the failure of the five million dollar loan in the Congress, yet the Government of the United States still continues to maintain a kindly and friendly interest in that Republic.

At the same time, I feel certain that our Government would make no mistake in honoring such a man as Du Bois as its special representative upon such an occasion.

I have gone over with Secretary Slemp more in detail additional reasons for this appointment.

I very earnestly recommend to your early and favorable consideration the appointment of Dr. Du Bois to be the special representative of the United States at the inauguration of President King.[97]

Du Bois had to leave for the Third Pan-African Congress in early November 1923 before receiving confirmation of his appointment as envoy to Liberia and, while happy about it, could not conceal his pique at his earlier rebuff. In a conversation with the customs receiver in Monrovia, later reported to the State Department, Du Bois declared that President Coolidge's secretary had invited him to Washington for a conference before he left for Europe, but he had made an excuse to get out of it. Du Bois related that he did the same thing when invited to meet the secretary of state. The reason he allegedly gave for his behavior was that he was refused the appointment "until his political value was brought to the notice of the Presidents [sic] Secretary whereupon he believed he was to be brought to Washington to be placed in the position of being committed to the side of the Republican party in his writings and [sic] negro newspapers throughout the U.S."98

Because he had left for Europe, Du Bois also missed a letter from President-elect King approving his intended trip to Monrovia. This letter stated in part that "visits to Liberia by leaders of our racial group in the United States, will undoubtedly lead to a better and clearer understanding of Liberia and the Liberians, and also serve to draw both your and ourselves in a ban [sic "bond"] of closer union for the political, financial, social and economic advancement of our common race."99

It is clear that Du Bois hoped to accomplish a number of things by seeking appointment as Coolidge's envoy: to get to Africa under the most advantageous personal conditions; to push the cause of Pan-Africanism; and to vindicate his position as leader of the African American establishment, as opposed to Garvey's leadership of the mass of African Americans. Du Bois would later say that what Coolidge did was "just a gesture of courtesy," but it was clear that Du Bois was flattered by this "gesture" (which he had worked for but which modesty compelled him to see as "a little thing"). Nevertheless, his stressing the fact that he was "an American Negro" and the "personal" envoy of the president of the United States showed that he recognized why the gesture was "one so unusual that it was epochal." As was noted above, Du Bois knew firsthand about the reluctance of American presidents to name blacks as their envoys. He had reportedly supported Woodrow Wilson for the presidency of the United States in the hope of receiving a diplomatic post in Haiti. Nevertheless, Du Bois's role as personal representative of Coolidge to Liberia had all of the hallmarks of the structural ambivalence noted above.

President Coolidge's decision to appoint him special envoy to Liberia, came at a most propitious time in the long and often agonizing relationship between the United States and Liberia. And despite Secretary of State Hughes's attempt to persuade the Liberians that the refusal of the loan did not imply that the United States had abandoned its "traditionally friendly attitude" toward them and would continue to look with sympathy at their attempts to promote the "real interests" of their people, they remained unconvinced.[100] Both the Liberians and Du Bois knew that the United States was also not sympathetic to the blandishments of Garvey. Despite repeated efforts, Garvey never gained any influence with the United States government with respect to Liberia. Thus his petition to President Coolidge to appeal to the Liberian legislature to support his colonization scheme fell on deaf ears. Here then was Du Bois going to Africa with the blessings of the United States government, when Garvey could not get its support. Du Bois would later write that after the end of the Third Pan-African Congress, "as a sort of ambassador of Pan-Africa" he turned his face "toward Africa."[101] He apparently took time off to get calling cards printed with his title as an envoy of the United States of America.[102]

After a pleasant trip South, Du Bois saw Africa for the first time in his life at 3:22 P.M. on 22 December 1923. Overcome with emotion Du Bois remarked, "When shall I forget the night I first set foot on African soil—I, the sixth generation in descent from my stolen forefathers."[103] On the same day in Washington, the under secretary of state ordered the draft of "a telegram to the American Legation at Monrovia, Liberia, appointing Mr. du Bois, who has just arrived in Monrovia, special representative of the President at the inauguration of President King." The under secretary wanted it "made clear that there is to be no salary attached, and that du Bois does not take precedence over the Minister, but is merely a special representative at the ceremonies." Minister Hood was also instructed to send to the Liberian minister of foreign affairs the following message in lieu of autographed credentials, which were to be forwarded by the first mail for delivery to him:

Great and Good Friend,

I have made choice of Dr. W. E. B. Du Bois as my Special Representative, with the rank of Envoy Extraordinary and Minister Plenipotentiary on the occasion of your inauguration, for another term, as President of the Republic of Liberia. I have entire confidence that he will render himself acceptable to Your Excellency, in the distinguished duty with which I have invested him.

I, therefore, request Your Excellency to receive him favorably and to accept from him, the assurance of the high regard and friendship entertained by the Government and People of the United States, and the sincere felicitations which they, and I, in their name, tender to Your Excellency, of this historic occasion.

May God have Your Excellency in His safe and Holy Keeping.

Your Good Friend
Calvin Coolidge

The under secretary of state instructed Hood to advise Du Bois of his nomination and took care to repeat that there was no salary attached to the office and that Du Bois did not take precedence over him.[104] Hood did as he was instructed and was able to report to Hughes that Du Bois was "enthusiastically accepted and most courteously treated by the Liberian Government and all representatives of foreign powers here."[105]

In many respects Du Bois's reaction to being named envoy extraordinary did not differ from that of most of the ministers resident and consuls general who had been sent to represent the United States in Liberia. He reveled in having the commander of the Liberian frontier force his special aide and felt especially honored when a company of that force presented arms before the American legation and then escorted him and Hood to the presidential mansion. Du Bois, as the personal representative of the president of the United States, was senior enough to have the secretary of state of Liberia present the consuls of England, France, Germany, Spain, Belgium, Holland, and Panama, and members of the Liberian cabinet, to him in order of precedence. When President King appeared decked out in frock coat with the star and ribbon of a Spanish order on his breast, and Du Bois was introduced to him, the special envoy of the American president declared:

> The President of the United States has done me the great honor of designating me as his personal representative on the occasion of your inauguration. In so doing, he has had, I am sure, two things in mind. First, he wished publicly and unmistakably to express before the world the interest and solicitude which the hundred million inhabitants of the United States of America have for Liberia. Liberia is a child of the United States, and a sister Republic. Its progress and success is the progress and success of democracy everywhere and for all men; and the United States would view with sorrow and alarm any misfortune which might happen to this Republic and any obstacle that was placed in her path.
>
> But special and peculiar bonds draw these two lands together. In America live eleven million persons of African descent; they are citizens, legally invested with every right that inheres in American citizenship. And I am sure that in this special mark of the President's favor, he has had in mind the wishes and hopes of Negro Americans. He knows how proud they are of the hundred years of independence which you have maintained by force of arms and by brawn and brain upon the edge of this mighty continent; he knows that in the great battle against color caste in America, the ability of Negroes to rule in Africa has been and ever will be a great and encouraging reen-

forcement. He knows that the unswerving loyalty of Negro Americans to their country is fitly accompanied by a pride in their race and lineage, a belief in the potency and promise of Negro blood which makes them eager listeners to every whisper of success from Liberia, and eager helpers in every movement for your aid and comfort. In a special sense, the moral burden of Liberia and the advancement and integrity of Liberia is the sincere prayer of America.[106]

Du Bois added his own best wishes to King for his coming mandate and wished happiness for the Liberian people. He listened with a sense of pride to the response of King recounting the problems of the Liberians, who attempted "amidst most perplexing and difficult circumstances and conditions and practically unaided, to establish upon this great continent a Republic founded by Black Men, maintained by Black Men and which holds out the highest hopes and aspirations for Black Men."[107]

Resident Americans and the foreign diplomatic community in Liberia speculated whether Du Bois's speech "was the instructed message of the U.S.A. and if there was to be an active policy along the lines which were apparently indicated in the address mentioned and in the subsequent addresses both formal and informal which followed." The customs receiver, who reported Du Bois's words to the state department, felt at a loss to understand what had happened during Du Bois's visit and admitted being "mystified at the sudden friendly change." The President of Liberia appeared greatly flattered by Du Bois's visit and words and "lost no chance to read the telegram of congratulations from President Coolidge, making special mention in his inaugural address of both the Special Envoy and the telegram."[108] From all indications, then, Du Bois was an effective personal representative of the president of the United States of America.

Even before he left Monrovia, Du Bois wrote King suggesting certain projects dealing with the economic development of Liberia. He recommended that a railroad line be built between Monrovia and neighboring towns; that Liberia contact colored bankers to develop a financial institution to become a fiscal agent of the government and to be a depository for its funds; and that Liberia form a joint corporation to furnish the country with consultants in various fields and to study its resources and markets for about twenty-five years. Finally, he offered his services if the President wished to open official communications with the specialists he suggested.[109] Interestingly, some of these recommendations were not too different from those he had sent to Secretary of State Hughes in a letter lamenting the inability of the United States to loan money to Liberia and the disaster of the Black Star Line.

As one would expect, Garvey's supporters immediately apprised him of Du Bois's visit to Monrovia. On 2 January 1924 John E. Bruce urged Garvey to cable J. E. Casely Hayford about the visit in order "to break the force of Du Bois' influence in Gold Coast." Bruce told his "Chief" that Du Bois was "bent on mischief, due to failure of his 'Pan African Congress.' " Declaring that Du Bois was financed "by Joel Spingarn, a Jew, and other interests (white) inimical to African Independence," Bruce warned Garvey to "watch him" but not to make any comment.[110] While there is no documentary evidence that Du Bois attempted to scuttle the UNIA's plans while in Liberia, it is difficult to believe that he did not do so in light of an earlier request to King to discourage the Garveyites.

What mainly concerned Garvey when he heard of Du Bois's visit to Monrovia was the possible effect it would have on the mission that he had sent to Monrovia under the chairmanship of Robert Lincoln Poston and the implications for his emigration scheme. Because of shipping schedules, the UNIA delegation sailed to Monrovia by way of Lisbon and while there met members of the Liga Africana. Garvey was later to claim that the delegation had obtained some African land concessions from the Portuguese government.

The UNIA emissaries arrived in Liberia on 1 February 1924, while Du Bois was still there, but he apparently ignored their presence.[111] They reported to Garvey that they were received joyously by thousands of UNIA supporters and later had a fruitful discussion with Chief Justice James J. Dossen, ex-Presidents Barclay and Howard, and several senators and other important personages. Other reports from Monrovia indicated, however, that President King was leery of receiving them, and when he finally bowed to pressure from prominent Liberians to do so, he issued a statement declaring that the meeting would be "informal and between private individuals." King added that he rejected in advance "any proposal for the settling of 3,000 immigrants to Liberia." He wanted to make clear that he was mindful of "the Obligation of Liberia to the Great Powers, and as such to the maintenance of the Independence of the Republic."[112]

There is internal evidence in the delegation's report to the UNIA that they were concerned about King's reservations about meeting them but decided to put the best face on the meeting. They insisted that the president had cautioned them not to believe reports that the UNIA was not welcome in Liberia. They also reported that the president had established a local committee composed of Vice President Henry T. Wesley,

Chief Justice Dossen, ex-Presidents Barclay and Howard, and several other persons to deal with the offer. Members of the delegation intimated that King had attempted to impress upon them the sensitivity of his task as president and the diplomacy involved in having to appease the Great Powers while determined to accept the UNIA. They reported that while they were in Monrovia, "the English and French consuls danced around trying to find out what was going on." The delegation left Monrovia satisfied with their visit and treasuring the agreements they had made with the Liberians.[113]

The report they brought back from Monrovia, signed on 16 February 1924 by Barclay, Howard, and Dossen, among others, specified that "every emigrant before leaving America shall subscribe to an oath that they will respect the established authority of the Liberia government." In a letter dated 28 February, Dossen wrote to Garvey indicating that the "friends of emigration" in Liberia welcomed the opportunity to give blacks abroad "the pure atmosphere of manly freedom." Dossen recommended that "the first settlement be established on the Cavalla River. This locality offers many advantages to Traders, Miners, Farmers and other men of industry. Besides the climate is healthy." The local Liberian Committee "sent a letter in May setting out their plans to receive a batch of colonists in September."[114] The committee allegedly advised the UNIA to "first send material, artisans to lay out the land and build homes for those people, so that when they came they would have somewhere to go and would not be left to the mercy of others."[115]

Much to the regret of Garvey and the delegation that went to Monrovia, its chairman, Robert Lincoln Poston, died at sea on 16 March 1924, while en route to the United States. Garvey eulogized him at one of the meetings organized at Madison Square Garden to hear the delegation's report and posthumously awarded him the title, "prince of Africa." Garvey also took the opportunity to circulate copies of a petition he had sent to President Calvin Coolidge seeking support for black emigration to Liberia. This action led the Belgian ambassador to the United States to report to his foreign minister that Garvey's stay in prison in no way "dampened his enthusiasm" for "Africa for the Africans."[116]

After reading the delegation's report, Garvey replied to President King. He expressed satisfaction at the reception given the envoys and stated that the local committee had laid before the UNIA "certain suggestions . . . which fit in splendidly with the plans of our association, and which we are pleased to adopt, and to inform you of the same." He also revealed to the Liberian president the UNIA's alarm at news reaching New York indicating that the president was unwilling to "see the delegates and that American and West Indian Negroes are not wanted in Liberia." Declaring that these reports were circulated by Du Bois in the *Crisis* and by the NAACP, Garvey indicated that he was not responding to the allegations and would say nothing that would embarrass either the president or his government.[117]

Garvey wrote the president that he was pleased with the overall tenor of the local committee report, but asked whether it was possible to approve a number of amendments: that the UNIA be granted five or six additional sites in Liberia for "the purpose of building townships for the settlement of colonists as citizens and natives, for the development of Liberia," and that these townships be developed with plans approved by the local committee; and that additional lands be given in the neighborhood of these settlements "for the exclusive development of the Association agriculturally and industrially, as a source of revenue" by which the UNIA could meet some of its "current expenses" for its plan to work for "the good of the country and its citizens." Garvey suggested that if the President approved these amendments, they then be signed by the UNIA's representative, Arthur J. Barclay, and that copies of the agreement be sent to New York.[118] Finally, Garvey informed King that he would be sending "the first group of colonists" in September.[119]

On 2 May 1924 Dossen acknowledged receipt of Garvey's response to the committee's report and suggested amendments. He said that he generally approved of them, and he promised to lay them before the local executive committee.[120] The problem here was that Garvey's letter and request for amendments to the committee's recommendations could have been read to suggest that the UNIA had views about "the good of the country and its citizens" that did not fully respect Liberian sovereignty. Given the touchiness of the Liberians on such matters, which Du Bois was keenly aware of, it is not surprising that there is no evidence that President King ever agreed to Garvey's suggestions.[121] In fact, it appeared as though the Liberians might have even hardened their opposition to the UNIA and Garvey's plans.

Meanwhile, in the United States, Garvey moved his emigration plans into high gear. On 10 May 1924 an advertisement appeared in the *Negro World* inviting all members of the UNIA who were desirous of going to Liberia later that year to fill out a form attached. This campaign was too much for Du Bois. He blasted the leader of the UNIA in an article that appeared in the *Crisis* of May 1924, entitled "A Lunatic or a Traitor." Appearing to be at the end of his rope, Du Bois asserted that he had to jettison the journal's policy of leaning over backward to avoid attacking the UNIA leader, who had kept up a "persistent and unremitting repetition of falsehood after falsehood as to the editor's beliefs and acts and as to the program of the N.A.A.C.P." [122]

Du Bois suggested that one reason for these attacks was that Garvey wanted "to keep himself out of jail," but he felt that Garvey had gone too far. The editor of the *Crisis* asserted that Garvey and the UNIA had made threats against anyone who opposed them, that they were accused of assassinating a member of the UNIA, that they had flirted with the Ku Klux Klan, and that they had made threats against Du Bois's own life when he returned home from Africa. Du Bois wrote that he had decided, against the advice of friends who feared for his life, to take action by writing the article. He declared that if the day had come when he could not "tell the truth about black traitors it is high time that I died." [123] His conclusion: Garvey was "without doubt, the most dangerous enemy of the Negro race in America and in the world" and "should be locked up or sent home." [124]

Garvey did not immediately respond to Du Bois's tirade and took several months to comment upon Du Bois's visit to Liberia. He was busy fending off the attacks on the UNIA and the banning of his emissaries and newspaper from the British colonies, and occupied with his own plans for Liberia. On 4 June 1924, during a speech at Liberty Hall, New York City, Garvey announced that he was sending a team of technicians to Liberia. These were to include carpenters, builders, and civil and mining engineers. This was followed by an article in the *Negro World* in which the UNIA announced that it was raising $2 million to build the first colony in Liberia as "a permanent home for scattered Negroes of the world who desire to live in a country of their own where they may enjoy the benefits of real freedom, liberty and democracy." The object was to emulate Jews who were settling people in Palestine, and the intention was to build four colonies, each costing $2 million, under the direction of the Liberian Government, with all persons observing the laws of that country. [125]

Garvey linked his drive for funds for his Liberian colony with plans for the Fourth International Convention of the Negro Peoples of the World, which was to convene on 1 August 1924 in New York City. It was during this convention, however, that it became clear that Garvey's emigration plans could not and would not succeed. The convention opened with the now customary fanfare, but there was a note of doom in Garvey's opening speech. He observed that the Negro was "extremely miserable" because the world was "closing fast around him." For this he did not blame the white man but selfish black politicians who were building "upon sand." Garvey said that he understood the aspirations of blacks in America to someday occupy the White House, to be members of the cabinet and to be elected to the Senate and the House, and how the inability to gain equality had led leaders like Du Bois and James Weldon Johnson to establish organizations such as the NAACP. Garvey believed that this was a chimera given the terrible odds against blacks in the United States. Insisting that blacks had to seek an outlet of their own, he claimed that the recent gains made by blacks in the United States were attributable to the agitation of the UNIA. He was asking of others that they be fair to black people and their aspirations as the blacks were fair to the other races of people.[126]

Intriguingly, at least one white paper in New York City suggested that perhaps it was shortsighted to make fun of Garvey and his "high-sounding titles and . . . extravagant claims," even though some of those had "come to grief." The paper suggested that no other man of his race "in the past century succeeded in assembling a more representative gathering of his people." It concluded that "even the worst enemy of Garvey must admit that there was logic and truth in the statements he made to the convention."[127]

Garvey received two severe shocks during the convention. On 5 August 1924 he was arrested on a charge of filing a fraudulent income tax return for 1921 and, after pleading not guilty," was released on $2,500 bail. Garvey and his followers could not help feeling that attempts were being made to scuttle the convention. More serious for Garvey was the announcement by Edward G. Merrill, the Liberian consul in New York, that he and other Liberian consuls had received instruction from Ernest Lyon, Liberian consuls general in Baltimore and former United States minister resident in Monrovia, not to issue visas to Liberia to Garvey or any other members of the UNIA because their "proposed African Republic would endeavor to supplant the constitutional regime of President King of Liberia."[128] This was obviously a sequel to a news release on this matter that Lyon had issued on 10 July 1924. What created concern was the news that three of the original five UNIA members who arrived in Monrovia on 25 July were immediately put under police guard by the Liberians and ordered expelled on the next ship bound for Hamburg. The portable sawmill and some agricultural implements the UNIA had shipped to Liberia were deemed not deliverable and would be held in bond and probably sold at auction if not claimed.

The Liberian government had obviously decided to rupture all relations with Garvey and the UNIA and was taking advantage of the convention to do so. Whether the arrival of the machinery had confirmed fears among the Liberians that the UNIA was serious about emigration, and with that the specter of Garveyite imperialism in Liberia, is still open to speculation. In any event, on 25 August 1924 Ernest Lyon issued another press release indicating that he was instructed to deliver a message from the Liberian secretary of state to United States Department of State officials, which read:

> The Government of Liberia, irrevocably opposed both in principle and in fact to the incendiary policy of the Universal Negro Improvement Association headed by Marcus Garvey, and repudiating the improper implications of its widely advertised scheme for the immigration of American Negroes into the Republic under the auspices of this Association, which scheme apart from not having the sanction of the Liberian Government, does not appear to be bona fide and has in addition a tendency adversely to affect the amicable relations of the Republic with friendly States possessing territories adjacent to Liberia, desire to place on record their protest against this propaganda so far as it relates to Liberia, and to express their confidence that the Government of the United States will neither facilitate nor permit the emigration under the auspices of the Universal Negro Improvement Association of Negroes from the United States with intent to proceed to Liberia.[129]

In his memo to Secretary of State Charles Evans Hughes, which accompanied Lyon's message, the chief of the Division of Western European Affairs, William R. Castle, Jr., reported that the Liberians were so disturbed over the prospective arrival of several hundred migrants that they requested help in circulating the message. The question facing the department was whether to nip this scheme in the bud in order to forestall difficulty when prospective migrants asked for passports. Castle added that it was his understanding that the Liberian government was determined to prevent any arriving migrants to land. His recommendation, endorsed by the secretary, was to give the message to both the Associated Press and the United Press for distribution to newspapers.[130]

Reports reaching Washington indicated that Garvey was devastated by the Liberian consul's decision not to grant visas to himself and to the members of the UNIA. He believed that both Minister Solomon Porter Hood and W. E. B. Du Bois, as members of the NAACP, had prevailed upon President King to oppose the UNIA. Garvey admitted that the position of Liberia, a "little black republic" surrounded by powerful bullies such as Britain and France posed "a question of diplomacy that calls for the exhibition of statesmanship." Nevertheless, he felt that the UNIA had to defend its itself, especially since many persons were looking for a scapegoat to explain why the UNIA's Liberian project failed and why the Firestone Rubber and Tire Company of Ohio was able to get "one million acres of land to exploit for rubber and minerals." This, said Garvey, would explain "the hypocrisy and double-dealing of certain people." No doubt Garvey had both Hood and Du Bois in mind. [131]

The failure of the UNIA to establish settlements in Liberia and the presumed success of the Firestone rubber and mineral projects were the major concerns of the last few days of the Fourth International Convention of Negroes of the World. And Du Bois was the villain in the play. He of course never minced words about how he felt about Garvey, the UNIA, and emigration to Liberia. But he denied that he had played any role in the decision of the president to bar Garvey and UNIA. Years later, Benjamin N. Azikiwe, who was writing a dissertation on Liberia, asked Du Bois whether it was true, as frequently alleged, that during his mission as envoy extraordinary and minister plenipotentiary to Liberia he used his influence with Minister Hood to scuttle Garvey's colonization scheme. Du Bois responded that he had "nothing to do at all with the relations of Garvey and the Republic of Liberia." Du Bois insisted that Garvey's colonization scheme "had already been rejected by Liberia before 1 went there and before there was the slightest intimation of my appointment." He told Azikiwe that his relations with Liberia "were purely formal and I did not mention Garvey to Mr. King or to any Liberian official during my stay there." [132]

It is difficult to believe that Du Bois did not discuss Garvey while in Monrovia in light of an earlier request to King to discourage the Garveyites. Moreover, he had continued to correspond with King. When on 30 June 1924 the Liberian President responded to a letter from Du Bois dated 4 April 1924 about collaboration between African Americans and Liberians, King made it quite clear that one of the problems of having skilled help or consultants from the United States was, as Du Bois had pointed out, that "this system of advice should not be a more or less concealed attempt to take the functions of Government out of the hands of the Liberians," but that it should be "real advice of the highest order given by men of *training* and *understanding* and offered to Liberia with the idea that America wishes her progress and is pointing out the way." [133]

Apropos of Du Bois's concern that in view of the failure of the loan project Liberia needed capital, the president informed Du Bois that

recently the Liberian Government had come to "a most liberal understanding with the personal representative of Mr. Firestone of 'Firestone
Rubber Tire Company' of Akron, Ohio, U.S.A. for rubber cultivation in
Liberia on extensive plans." King indicated that he had read Du Bois's
article, "Sensitive Liberia," in which the editor of the *Crisis* had promised to publish articles from time to time in order to counteract "the
propaganda of which Liberia has been the unhappy victim." Finally, the
president expressed the hope that occasional visits to Liberia of "our
racial group in the United States, will undoubtedly lead to a better
understanding of Liberia and Liberians, and also serve to draw both you
and ourselves in a ban[d] of closer union for the political, financial,
social and economic advancement of our common race."[134]

In view of his earlier letter to Secretary of State Hughes and to President King himself, Du Bois obviously had mixed feelings about King's
decision to enter into negotiations with Firestone about economic activities in Liberia. Nevertheless, he attempted to hide his disappointment.
In feeling that blacks should play a major role in the development of
Africa, Du Bois was, paradoxically, not too different from Garvey. Du
Bois did acknowledge that Liberia needed capital for development but
felt the country was caught in a bind. It would be at the mercy of the
"great white nations" if it borrowed money from them and would face
the same kind of pressure if money came from private corporations in
white countries.[135] According to Du Bois, the English investors themselves would not have to be fair since the colored people of the British
Empire had no influence on imperial policy. The same thing would be
true of the French, because while some colored persons occupied positions of influence in France, they were "so thoroughly French in their
thought and action," and they knew so little about their own race, that
only white Frenchmen could "make France act fairly toward colored
countries."[136] On the other hand, speculated Du Bois, if white Americans did invest in Liberia and attempted to get the United States government to support unfair practices there, "the Negroes of America have
enough political power to make the government go slowly. American
Negroes are also beginning to understand and sympathize with Liberia."[137] Given these options, Du Bois recommended to King that "Liberia should apprehend least danger from American capital and should
proceed to encourage its investment under proper restrictions."[138]

There was, however, no way that the delegates to the Fourth International Convention could learn about Du Bois's attitude toward Firestone.
Thus when the two members of the Poston delegation to Liberia reported

to the convention about their mission, they criticized the "terrible amount of double-dealing and intrigue" and the search for a scapegoat to rationalize Liberia's plight.[139] Both of them expressed the belief that President King was sincere in welcoming the UNIA, and the protocols they brought were said to confirm these views. Moreover, they both insisted that if Chief Justice Dossen had not died, the UNIA would have been sustained because Dossen was "a man who loved his race" and a man who was "ready to lay down his life for the Republic of Liberia and the preservation of the Negro peoples of the world."[140] But the people now in control had no guts or backbone. Beholden to England and France to the tune of some $2 million, they permitted Firestone to come in and exploit both the land and labor of Liberia. These were the people, said the delegates, who wanted to keep out "American Negroes, who know about the price of labor and of union labor and high wages."[141]

The delegates who had been to Liberia sounded a theme that became the swan song of the convention. Theirs was a story of betrayal picked up and echoed by Garvey, who viewed himself as "a man of sorrow" but one who looked upon God Almighty to make it possible for Ethiopia to stretch forth its hand. Du Bois was viewed with disdain, and the delegates, borrowing his comments about Garvey from the *Crisis*, declared that the "man Du Bois is the greatest enemy of his race 'that God Almighty has ever made.' " They accused him of writing in the *Crisis* that it was the intention of "Garvey men to go to Africa and drive out all the whites from there. That is the man who gave the argument to the English and French to tell President King." Suggesting that neither President Coolidge nor King could live forever, the delegates vowed that the UNIA "will fight, and, even if the devil in hell tries to prevent us, we will kick him out of hell. In "keeping with the popular refrain of the 'Blues'—We are going home, going home' "—the gathering gave three cheers for Liberia and shouted, "Down with traitors to the Negro race!"[142]

In the closing sessions of the Fourth Annual International Convention of the Negro Peoples of the World, the delegates heard reports of the history of the relations between the UNIA and Liberia purporting to show that it was not true that there was no agreement with the Liberian government to colonize Liberia. The delegates passed resolutions asking President Coolidge for help, requesting both houses of the Congress of Liberia to repudiate President King's decision to bar the UNIA, condemning Du Bois and the NAACP, and appealing to the conscience of white America not to let Firestone do to Liberia what had been done in the Congo and in Haiti. With the singing of the anthem, "Ethiopia, Thou Land of Our Fathers," the convention ended.[143]

As a sequel to the convention, the members of the UNIA sent a petition to President Coolidge recounting the painful history of blacks in the United States; predicting that only in emigration to Liberia could the situation be improved; complaining that the president-general of the organization, Mr. Garvey, "has been wickedly persecuted by Agencies under the control of your Government"; and indicating why he and the Congress of the United States should ask the government of Liberia to create an open door for American emigrants to help solve the race problem.[144] Finally, they drew the president's attention to "the unfriendly attitude of . . . Your Excellency's recent representatives in Liberia, Solomon Porter Hood and W. E. B. Du Bois, in working against the interest of the Universal Negro Improvement Association . . . and who used their official positions to create prejudice against our cause because of jealousy and rivalry."[145]

The State Department, which, like the Justice Department, was carefully following the activities of Garvey and the UNIA, did not agree with the contents of the petition. William R. Castle, Jr., Chief of the Division of Western European Affairs, wrote Secretary of State Charles Evans Hughes that President Coolidge should be advised that "Mr. Garvey's statement that his movement is opposed only by a few politicians is nonsense."[146] In the event that the secretary was willing to send the UNIA's petition to the president, Castle felt that Hughes should be informed that "Mr. Du Bois is a much more important man than he [Garvey] is in this country and certainly we cannot consider the Government of Liberia, with which we are on friendly terms, as 'a few politicians.' "[147]

There is no evidence that President Coolidge did respond to this petition from the UNIA. Neither did the president intervene with the Liberians on behalf of Garvey and the UNIA. Not surprisingly, neither the State Department nor Coolidge paid any attention to the pleas of the Garveyites to sanction Hood or Du Bois. Initially, President Coolidge ignored the agitation surrounding the conviction of Garvey by a federal court, and his imprisonment on 8 February 1925 to serve a sentence of five years. Finally, on 18 November 1927, Coolidge heeded the pleas of hundreds of people to grant Garvey a presidential pardon. He commuted the remainder of the UNIA leader's sentence "to expire at once."[148]

Not being an American citizen, Garvey had to be deported from the United States. He was not permitted to return to his headquarters in New

York City but was taken directly to New Orleans where he was placed on the SS *Saramacca* bound for the West Indies and Panama. Garvey thanked the tearful crowd of admirers who had come to see him off for their loyalty and friendship. His words of farewell were: "To the millions of members of the Universal Negro Improvement Association throughout the world, . . . I can only say: Cheer up for the good work is just getting underway. Be firm and steadfast in holding to the principles of the organization. The greatest work is yet to be done. I shall with God's help do it."[149] Writing in an editorial in the *Negro World* on 2 December 1927, Garvey compared his travail to that of Jesus Christ and used metaphors of the resurrection to portray the future: "I promise you as God liveth that I shall, with the leadership of Christ . . . blast a way to African freedom. . . . Negroes, keep your heads high. . . . Believe that our work is just started. . . . Carry on, carry on, and let the standard of the Red, Black and Green Fly!"[150]

Notes

1. W. E. B. Du Bois, *Dusk of Dawn* (New York: Schocken Books, 1968), 122–23.
2. Editorial Letter by Marcus Garvey in the *Negro World,* 10 February 1925, in *The Marcus Garvey and Universal Negro Improvement Association Papers,* ed. Robert A. Hill (Berkeley and Los Angeles: University of California Press, 1986), 6:96–98 (hereafter cited as *Marcus Garvey Papers*).
3. George F. Ruch to W. W. Grimes, Bureau of Investigation, 23 September 1921, ibid. 4:72.
4. Ibid., 79.; Article by James Weldon Johnson in the New York *Age,* 24 September 1921, ibid., 107.
5. Ibid., 679. On June 1922, Garvey sent a cable to his headquarters reporting on a meeting with the acting Imperial Wizard of the Knights of the Ku Klux Klan. He asserted that the klansman "denied any hostility toward the Negro as a race" or that his organization ever officially attacked the Negro. Garvey added that the Imperial Wizard not only expressed "sympathy for the aims and objects of the Universal Negro Improvement Association" but believed that since America was a "white man's country," the Negro "should have a country of his own in Africa." Garvey indicated that he had invited the Wizard to speak at the forthcoming convention.
6. Speech by Marcus Garvey, 2 October 1921, ibid., 99.
7. Cable from Marcus Garvey to [UNIA] Chairman, 25 June 1922, ibid., 679.
8. Article in the *Negro World,* 18 March 1922, ibid., 574; Editorial Letter by Marcus Garvey, 18 April 1922, ibid., 610.
9. W. E. B. Du Bois, "The Year 1921 in Account With the American Negro," *Crisis* 23 (February 1922): 154–55.
10. Harold Isaacs, "Pan-Africanism as 'Romantic Racism,' " in *W. E. B. Du Bois: A Profile,* ed. Rayford W. Logan (New York: Hill and Wang, 1971), 237. Isaacs writes that "Du Bois liked to see himself as a cool human spirit with an icy mind contemplating squirming men from a high lonely seat behind the veil.

But he has on occasion allowed himself the luxury of an outburst of good, hot hate."

11. Department of State Decimal File, 1910–29, 882.51/1422a, Record Group 59, National Archives (hereafter abbreviated RG 59, NA); *Foreign Relations of the United States, 1921* 2:366.

12. Secretary of State to President Harding, 4 January 1922, 882.51/1370b, RG 59, NA; *Foreign Relations of the United States, 1922* 2:606.

13. Charles Young to Dr. W. E. B. Du Bois, 20 July 1920, United States Department of State, Despatches from United States Ministers in Liberia, reel 9, frame 296, National Archives.

14. Duse Mohamed Ali to Du Bois, 27 March 1922, *Marcus Garvey Papers* 4:581, and reply, 11 April 1922, ibid., 597. Garvey seemed to have taken refusal to attend his events with a wry sense of humor or cynicism. Thus when Duse Mohamed Ali invited Du Bois to take part in the convention, he referred to the latter's "enthusiasm for matters Racial" as an excuse for infringing upon his valuable time. He ended the invitation by declaring, "It is written, 'Blessed are the Peacemakers.' Thanking you in anticipation, with all good wishes, believe me Yours faithfully." In contrast to his earlier letters, which pleaded being out of town for his inability to attend functions of the UNIA, Du Bois replied through his secretary: "Dr. Du Bois directs me to acknowledge your letter of March 27th and to express his regret that he will be unable to accept the invitation contained therein."

15. Garvey to Harding, 31 May 1922, ibid., 645, and to Sir Eric Drummond, 23 May 1922, ibid., 639.

16. Ibid., 781. Cited in an article in the *New York World* of 2 August 1922, headlined: "GARVEY REVIEWS HIS NOBILITY AMID A FEW NOSE-BLEEDS." Garvey was under no illusions about the racism of the Klan and shared with his followers many of the vitriolic letters he received from klansmen. He was convinced, however, that

the Ku Klux Klan is the invisible government of the United States of America. The Ku Klux Klan expresses to a great extent the feeling of every real white American. The attitude of the Ku Klux Klan is that America shall be a white man's country at all hazards, at all costs. The attitude of the Universal Negro Improvement Association is in a way similar to the Ku Klux Klan. Whilst the Ku Klux Klan desires to make America absolutely a white man's country, the Universal Negro Improvement Association wants to make Africa absolutely a black man's country. (Speech by Marcus Garvey, 9 July 1922, ibid., 707–15)

17. Opening Speech by Gabriel M. Johnson, 1 August 1922, *Marcus Garvey Papers* 4:760–66.

18. Convention Reports, 2 August 1922, ibid., 783ff.

19. J. Edgar Hoover to John B. Cunningham, 10 August 1922, ibid., 841.

20. New York *Times*, 7 August 1922, in ibid., 816–17. The article reported that police had to quiet the audience when Garvey was accused of being an ally of the Ku Klux Klan.

21. Baltimore *Afro-American*, 25 August 1922, in ibid., 999.

22. Garvey to Drummond, 29 August 1922, ibid., 1024.

23. Convention Reports, 1 September 1922, ibid., 1055–60.

24. Enclosure by Garvey in Confidential Informant 800 to George F. Ruch, 16 May 1922, ibid., 631–34.

25. Hughes to Harding, Washington, 4 January 1922, *Foreign Relations, 1922* 2:606–11; Harrison to McBride, Washington, 9 February 1922, 822.51/1396, RG 59, NA; Hughes to Stephen G. Porter (R-Penna.), Chairman, Foreign Affairs Committee, House, and Henry Cabot Lodge (R-Mass.), Chairman, Senate Foreign Relations Committee, Washington, 6 February 1922, 882.51/1383a.
26. 882.51/1825, 882.51/1829, 180, 882.51/1411, 882.51/1338, RG 59, NA; *Foreign Relations of the United States, 1921* 2:389, 391.
27. Nancy Kaye Forderhase, "The Plans That Failed: The United States and Liberia, 1920–1935" (Ph.D. diss., University of Missouri, 1971). See also *Marcus Garvey Papers* 4:634. At the same time, Garvey was scathing in his criticism of the British and Boer in South Africa for crushing a revolt by the Blondelswarts "Hottentots" in 1922 and for other atrocities committed by other Europeans in Africa (Editorial Letter by Marcus Garvey, 13 June 1922, ibid., 672–77).
28. There is some evidence that Senator Pat Harrison was concerned that African Americans such as "Emmett Jay Scott, William H. Lewis, James A. Cobb, Ernest Lyon, and William H. Houston would all receive $6,500 for their activities in 'buttonholing' certain United States congressmen and getting them to support the measure for economic aid to Liberia." See James E. Walker, "Emmett Jay Scott: The Public Life of a Private Secretary" (M.A. thesis, University of Maryland, 1971), 312–13. See also 882.51/1395A, 882.51/1477, RG 59, NA.
29. The Secretary of State to Harding, 4 January 1922, *Foreign Relations, 1922* 2:608.
30. Memorandum: Political Factors Interested in Liberia, 25 October 1922, 885.51/-, RG 59, NA.
31. Ibid.
32. Robert R. Moton to Honorable William Phillips, 22 September 1922, 882.51/1677.
33. Harding to Secretary of State Hughes, 26 July 1922, 882.51/1512.
34. Hood to Secretary of State, 31 May 1922, 882.51/1506.
35. State Department to Hood, 13 July 1922, 882.51/1506.
36. The Director of the Consular Service to the Secretary of State, 3 July 1922, 882.51/1534.
37. Minister Hood to Secretary of State Hughes, 7 September 1922, 882.51/1555.
38. Ibid.
39. *Congressional Record,* 67th Cong., 3d sess., 23 November 1922, pt. 1, 63:48, 62; ibid., 24 November 1922, 127; ibid., 27 November 1922, 277, 287.
40. Secretary of State Hughes to Hood, 8 December 1922, 882.51/1575a, RG 59, NA.
41. Sidney de la Rue to Mr. Castle, 882.51/1657.
42. Minister Hood to Secretary of State Hughes, 13 November 1922, 882.51/1568.
43. Hood to Secretary of State, 14 December 1922, 882.51/1576.
44. Ibid. The French continued to pursue an aggressive policy toward Liberia, using the issue of resolving the Franco-Liberian dispute as the reason. See correspondence between the State Department and the French Ambassador in Washington, D.C., 15 November 1921, 751.8215/1771/2; 3 December 1921, 751.8215/173.

45. Secretary of State Hughes to Hood, 26 December 1922, 882.51/1576, *Foreign Relations, 1922* 2:633.

46. Phillips for the Secretary of State, to Hood, 22 May 1923, 882.51/1605, RG 59, NA.

47. See James E. Walker, "Emmett Jay Scott," 314; an anonymous "former resident of Liberia," writing in the *Crisis* for March 1923, remarked that "the failure of the U.S. loan to Liberia is a financial misfortune of no small degrees to the Republic" (25 [March 1923]: 210).

48. From Du Bois to Hughes, 5 January 1923, in Herbert Aptheker, ed., *The Correspondence of W. E. B. Du Bois, Selections, 1877–1934* 1:260–61.

49. Ibid.

50. Ibid.

51. Consul Robert P. Skinner (London) to Secretary of State, 21 December 1923, Department of State Numerical File, 882.51/1645.

52. *Marcus Garvey Papers* 5:xxxiii–xxxiv, 10, 166ff.

53. Ibid., 301ff. According to Aptheker, "Eight prominent Black individuals—including John E. Nail, in real estate; Robert S. Abbott, the Chicago publisher; and William Pickens and Robert W. Bagnall, of the NAACP—had petitioned the United States Attorney General to 'push the government's case against Marcus Garvey'" (*Correspondence of W. E. B. Du Bois* 1:271).

54. *Marcus Garvey Papers* 5:365–84. Sympathy for Garvey's plight came from an unexpected source, the white-owned *Financial World,* which drew attention to the great disparity in the sentences meted out to Garvey and to Fuller and McGee. The latter were described as "plundering brokers" who bilked their customers out of more than $6 million and received a sentence of less than one year after pleading guilty. In contrast, "Marcus Garvey, an intellectual negro," was sentenced to five years after being found guilty of using the mails to "defraud his colored brethren." The moral of this story, according to the newspaper, was that the smaller the sum of money and the more difficult the crime, the tougher the sentence. The brokers stole a lot of money by easily encouraging people to buy stocks. In contrast, Garvey had a more difficult time investing in a scheme to establish a new republic for blacks in Africa. "In this respect," the paper concluded, "the black culprit's mentality was superior to that of the white rogues in Ludlow Street jail" (reprinted from the *Financial World,* 39, no. 26 [30 June 1923]: 817, in ibid., 386–87).

55. Ibid., 365. Garvey was not immune to the anti-Semitism abroad in the United States. Moreover, it appears that he had read the rabidly anti-Semitic *Protocols of the Elders of Zion.* After he had been expelled from the United States and was living in London, Garvey allegedly told Joel A. Rogers of having to refrain from attacking Jews "because of the harm it might have done in places such like Harlem." Garvey believed emphatically that "the Negro must beware of the Jew. The Jew is no friend of the Negro, though the Negro has been taught to believe that. . . . When they wanted to get me, they had a Jewish judge to try me, and a Jewish prosecutor [Mattuck]. I would have been freed but two Jews on the jury held out against me ten hours and succeeded in convicting me, whereupon the Jewish judge gave me the maximum penalty" (quoted from a pamphlet by J. A. Rogers, "Additional Facts on Marcus Garvey and His Trial for Using the Mails to Defraud," Negroes of New York Writers Program, New York, 1939, in ibid., 367).

56. Ibid., 367–68. Reprinted from the New York *World,* 22 June 1923.

57. Ibid., 378–79.

58. Ibid., 561. These countries ranged from Nigeria, to Gold Coast, The Gambia, and others.

59. Ibid., 320–21.

60. Ibid., 547–48, 561. Tolbert presented his letters on 19 February 1914 and was given a warm welcome by the London branch of the UNIA, but the British government did not recognize the right of Garvey to deal with matters affecting black people in the various colonies in the British Empire.

61. Ibid., 396, 416–18, 433.

62. Ibid., 479, 490ff. The British consul in St. Louis extracted sentiments from the St. Louis *Star,* which indicated that Garvey was conducting an active campaign, and sent these to the British embassy in Washington. He also sent a copy to the British passport office in New York, which had asked that the activities of the Garveyites be monitored.

63. Ibid., 497.

64. Ibid., 498.

65. Ibid., 507–10.

66. There was enough rancor between the two men to lead Dr. E. U. Essien-Udom to characterize Du Bois as one of Garvey's "arch-enemies" in his introduction to the second edition of *Philosophy and Opinions of Marcus Garvey or Africa for the Africans,* ed. Amy Jacques Garvey (London: Frank Cass, 1967), xxvi.

67. W. E. B. Du Bois, "Back to Africa," *Century Magazine* (New York) 105 (February 1923): 539–48.

68. Ibid.

69. Ibid.

70. W. E. B. Du Bois, "Marcus Garvey," *Crisis* 21 (December 1920): 58–60 and 21 (January 1921): 112–115.

71. Du Bois, "Back to Africa," 539–48.

72. Ida May Reynolds to Du Bois, 5 July 1923, in Aptheker, *Correspondence of W. E. B. Du Bois* 1:271–72.

73. Ibid., 272.

74. *Marcus Garvey Papers* 5:579.

75. Imanuel Geiss, *The Pan-African Movement: A History of Pan-Africanism in America, Europe and Africa,* trans. Ann Keep (New York: Africana, 1974), 248–51.

76. Rayford W. Logan, "Historical Aspects of Pan-Africanism: A Personal Chronicle," *African Forum* 1 (Summer 1965): 97.

77. Edmund David Cronon, *Black Moses: The Story of Marcus Garvey and the Universal Negro Improvement Association* (Madison: University of Wisconsin Press, 1968), 127–28. Surprisingly, Diagne's letter to Garvey dated 3 July 1922, quoted in Raymond Leslie Buell's *The Native Problem in Africa* (New York: Macmillan, 1928), 2:81, does not seem to appear in Hill's otherwise excellent edition of the *Marcus Garvey Papers.*

78. *Crisis* 26 (October 1923): 248; ibid., 27 (December 1923): 57–8.

79. Clarence Garner Contee, "W. E. B. Du Bois and African Nationalism" (Ph.D. diss., American University, 1969), 307–8; George Padmore, *Pan-Africanism or Communism?* (London: Dennis Dobson, 1956), 97.

80. *Crisis* 26 (October 1923): 248 and 33 (December 1926): 63; Jessie Fauset to Mary White Ovington, 1923, *The Crisis File, Records of the NAACP,* Library of Congress, as cited in Contee, "W. E. B. Du Bois," 310.

81. Geiss, *The Pan-African Movement,* 251.

82. Ibid., 252–54.

83. *West Africa,* 10 November 1923, 1352.

84. Padmore, *Pan-Africanism,* 140.
85. See the views of Contee, "W. E. B. Du Bois," 311–12.
86. "Africa," *Crisis* 27 (January 1924): 122.
87. Contee, "W. E. B. Du Bois," 313.
88. Ibid.
89. Geiss, *The Pan-African Movement,* 254–56.
90. Ibid., 255; Padmore, *Pan-Africanism,* 141–42.
91. Geiss, *The Pan-African Movement,* 255.
92. Memorandum for Wm. R. Castle, Jr., from Receiver of Customs, Monrovia, 26 January 1924, NA.
93. Ibid., 2 October 1923, in reply to WE 882.001/18, RG 59, NA.
94. James Weldon Johnson, "The Gentlemen's Agreement and the Negro Vote," *Crisis* 28 (October 1924): 260–64.
95. Du Bois, *Crisis* 26 (October 1923): 248–49.
96. William H. Lewis to Du Bois, 4 October 1923, in Aptheker, *Correspondence of W. E. B. Du Bois* 1:277–78.
97. Ibid., 278–79.
98. Report on W. E. B. Du Bois, from Customs Receiver, 26 January 1924, 882.00/743, RG 59, NA.
99. C. D. B. King to Du Bois, 30 June 1924, Aptheker, *Correspondence of W. E. B. Du Bois* 1:281–82.
100. Raymond Leslie Buell, *Liberia: A Century of Survival, 1847–1947* (Philadelphia: University of Pennsylvania Press, 1947), 29.
101. W. E. B. Du Bois, "Pan-Africa in Portugal," *Crisis* 27 (February 1924): 170.
102. Clarence Contee reportedly found one of these cards among the Du Bois papers at Fisk University, in Contee, "W. E. B. Du Bois," 257.
103. W. E. B. Du Bois, "Africa," *Crisis* 27 (April 24): 247–54.
104. Under Secretary of State to Hood, 27 December 1923, 882.001–18, RG 59, NA.
105. Hood to Secretary of State, 4 January 1924, 882.001/20.
106. Du Bois to the Honorable Secretary of State, 12 April 1924, 882.00/739. See also W. E. B. Du Bois, *Dusk of Dawn,* 124–25.
107. Ibid.
108. Report on W. E. B. Du Bois, from Customs Receiver, 26 January 1924, 882.00/743, RG 59, NA.
109. Du Bois to King, 21 January 1924, Aptheker, *Correspondence of W. E. B. Du Bois* 1:279–80.
110. *Marcus Garvey Papers* 5:513.
111. Ibid., 568–71. A special agent did report that Garvey had indicated that the delegation "secured an important concession of African territory from the Portuguese Government," but there is no indication that the Garveyites had even met Portuguese officials while there.
112. Ibid., 590–91.
113. *Marcus Garvey Papers* 5:786ff.
114. Amy Jacques Garvey, *Garvey and Garveyism* (Kingston, Jamaica: United Printers, 1963), 142.
115. *Marcus Garvey Papers* 5:789ff.
116. Ibid., 573.
117. 882.5511/15, RG 59, NA, quoted in *Marcus Garvey Papers* 5:799.
118. Garvey, *Philosophy and Opinions of Marcus Garvey,* 373–77.
119. Ibid.
120. Ibid., 378–79.

121. *Marcus Garvey Papers* 5:590-91.
122. W. E. B. Du Bois, "A Lunatic or a Traitor," *Crisis* 27 (May 1924): 8-9.
123. Ibid.
124. Ibid.
125. *Marcus Garvey Papers* 5:581-98.
126. Ibid., 631-38.
127. Ibid., 639, citing Editorial in the New York *Evening Bulletin* for 2 August 1924.
128. *Marcus Garvey Papers* 5:689.
129. 811.108G 191/34, RG 59, NA, transcript, in ibid., 774.
130. Ibid., 773.
131. Ibid., 787-88.
132. See W. E. B. Du Bois, *The Autobiography of W. E. B. Du Bois: A Soliloquy on Viewing My Life From the Last Decade of Its First Century* (New York: International, 1968), 272; Ben N. Azikiwe to Du Bois, 6 November 1932; Du Bois to Azikiwe, 11 November 1932, in Aptheker, *Correspondence of W. E. B. Du Bois* 1:464-65.
133. King to Du Bois, 30 June 1924, Aptheker, *Correspondence of W. E. B. Du Bois* 1:280-82.
134. Ibid.
135. Du Bois to King, 29 July 1924, ibid., 282-83.
136. Ibid.
137. Ibid.
138. Ibid.
139. *Marcus Garvey Papers* 5:787.
140. Ibid., 791.
141. Ibid.
142. Ibid., 796-99.
143. Ibid., 827ff.
144. Ibid. 6:6-7.
145. Ibid.
146. 882.5511/10, RG 59, NA, cited in ibid., 12.
147. Ibid.
148. Ibid., 608-10.
149. Edmund David Cronon, *Black Moses*, 142.
150. *Marcus Garvey Papers* 6:618-21.

Conclusion

The attempts of the early generation of African American leaders to influence the foreign policy of the United States toward Africa were more difficult and persistent than is often realized. Persons barely out of slavery and battling for their right to be considered Americans were badly placed to attempt to deal with foreign policy, an aspect of any nation's life historically reserved for its leaders and elite. With very few exceptions, these persons had been barred from the academies and universities that provided the educational background needed to deal with foreign policy. As it developed, African Americans interested in the foreign policy of the United States had to educate themselves in the delicate and complicated craft of diplomacy.

African American leaders and the immigrant blacks who joined them in the United States also faced the difficult task of attempting to protect Africa at the height of European imperialism. They had to struggle against a consensus in the Western world that Africa and its peoples had no place in national politics or within the global political system. Africa and African peoples were judged fit only to be colonized and civilized and to be "hewers of wood and drawers of water" for the masters of the world. Nevertheless, a number of early African American leaders dared to believe that they had the ability to protect a black nationality only barely imagined by most persons of African descent. Again, while concerned that their association with, and interest in, Africa would encourage bigoted white Americans to advocate repatriation schemes, these

515

early African Americans hoped that by helping to create a strong and developed Africa, they would contribute to the salvation of its people the world over. They often argued among themselves about the wisdom of so acting, but in activities largely unknown to contemporaries and to later generations, they also collaborated in an attempt to use both their limited political power and their considerable symbolic means to influence United States foreign policy toward Africa.

With almost no exception, the early African American leaders who participated in attempts to influence United States policy toward Africa were acutely aware of the link between their activities and their struggle to change their own status among fellow white Americans. Africa's political weakness haunted a people whose every attempt to advance within America was frustrated, for the most part, because of their African origin. As a result, almost all the early African American leaders who worked at advancing the race in the United States kept a leery eye on Africa. Some felt strongly that emigrationism was one of the most effective ways to secure equality for African Americans, as well as to help Africa. Others were equally convinced that it was better for African Americans to remain in the United States, developing a position of strength from which they would be able to aid Africa. These people were determined to prevent the repatriation of the mass of their fellows to the African continent.

Some of the African American educators and missionaries whose activities are recounted in this book were willing to cooperate with powerful whites in order to help Africa and, accordingly, were charged with helping to shoulder the white man's burden. Clearly, however, their object was not to bolster white power but rather to help Ethiopia stretch forth its hand and rid itself of the burden and shame of white domination. While their approaches often differed, these African Americans were united in striving to protect what they perceived as the black nationality.

Black leaders who sought to serve in that most elite of American national institutions, the foreign service, had the most challenging task. Historically, the conduct of foreign policy was reserved to sovereign figures judged to embody the salient values of their societies. When for any reason sovereigns could not personally fulfill their obligations, they normally chose as collaborators equally important persons. It was an honor to be chosen by a sovereign figure as an envoy to a foreign land.

The structural challenge for African Americans chosen as envoys was that they also had to serve a nation that denigrated them and Africa itself. They realized that overcoming this dilemma called for extreme prudence. Nevertheless, African American leaders sought and welcomed the opportunity to serve as diplomats of the United States. Martin Delany, an important Republican politician, believed that his service to the party merited a diplomatic post, so he pioneered the call for affirmative action in the foreign service. Henry Highland Garnet, a preacher, inveighed against racism among both Republicans and Democrats in the United States but also sought the opportunity and the honor of representing the United States abroad.

Many African American leaders sought diplomatic posts not only because of the honor it brought them personally but because of what it did for their community, for the United States, and for Africa. Partly because of the ambiguous and complex issues and power relationships involved, few of their white fellow citizens or contemporary nation-states were prepared to give them the opportunity to do so. Ironically, even to serve as minister in Liberia (Haiti was the only other nation-state that welcomed African Americans as chiefs of mission) often required white support. This support was frequently tainted by condescension and paternalism. It was only later, when Booker T. Washington had enough symbolic power to recommend African Americans for diplomatic positions in Africa, that many of them felt that they and their sponsors had the same goal: greater freedom for people of African descent.

While many of the early leaders who sought to mediate United States policy toward Africa could have been called "race persons," they were not torn by the dilemma of dual allegiances or the "hyphenate" complex. Diplomats such as J. Milton Turner, Henry H. Smyth, and Ernest Lyon were openly confrontational with the State Department to achieve their objectives. They endeavored to prove that they could serve faithfully as American foreign service officers even while protecting the black nationality. Turner's despatches were as much designed to educate the officials in the State Department about the realities of Liberia as to enlist the help of his government for the Liberians. As we have seen, this group of ex-American settlers in Liberia often tried his soul. Smyth not only insisted that seeking America's interest and protecting the black nationality held no conflict for him—that is, no more conflict for him than could or should be expected from Americans descended from peoples of Europe—but he also insisted that he had to prevent the bigotry of whites from harming America's national interests. In a few instances he did betray an arrogance that seemed to suggest that he believed he had a better grasp of national interests than did the officials in the State Department. Smyth was prepared to use local Africans to serve as United States consuls in still-independent African countries where American officials feared for their health.

Almost all the early diplomats in Africa, especially the consul in Madagascar, badgered the United States to take a stronger stand in protecting the areas they served. These men understood fully the complexity of United States policies, but they often felt that it was racism and United States complicity in European imperialist designs, rather than the country's national interest, that dictated policy. As was alleged, Consul John L. Waller may well have been afflicted with the nineteenth-century "robber baron" disease, but there is no doubt that it was his attempt to use United States power to prevent France's seizure of Madagascar that led to his imprisonment in France. The activities of two non-diplomats, William H. Ellis in Ethiopia and George Washington Williams in the Congo, were certainly motivated as much by personal ambition as by their racial interests. Nevertheless, Ellis did succeed in carrying the first Americo-Ethiopian commercial treaty to Addis Ababa, and Williams's criticism of Leopold II's rule helped to end the Belgian monarch's tyranny there.

While most African heads of state appreciated the assignment of African American diplomats to their countries, many Africans were only too well aware of the problems of status involved. The first diplomat to Liberia, J. Milton Turner, was told, "Six times seven, thou art made welcome to our shore," but he often had difficulty convincing his hosts that he was doing his best on their behalf. Turner, and no doubt others, had to bear the obloquy of some Africans who did not appreciate having a second-class American as a foreign diplomat. Fortunately for Turner, a wise American secretary of state understood the paradoxes involved. The Liberians had to recognize that if the United States held African Americans in contempt, it also held Liberians in contempt. The reverse side of this paradox was the case of Minister Taylor who, despite being a self-proclaimed race man, could not conceal from the State Department his shock at conditions in Liberia and the behavior of its citizens. Taylor was fortunate in not having been declared persona non grata (an action that was not taken against any black diplomat even though some of them were difficult characters). Nevertheless, it took all the skill of his successor to overcome the pique of the Liberians.

The archives of the State Department amply demonstrate that many African American diplomats seriously questioned certain policies of their hosts. Almost to a man, the ministers resident in Liberia objected to the settlers' treatment of the aboriginal inhabitants. Turner agonized about, but helped to frustrate, the attempts of the indigenous populations to reject settler rule and to seek the protection of the Europeans. Smyth's diplomatic faux pas in a similar case earned him the wrath of the American

Secretary of State. He was rescued by the Liberians, who recognized his concern for the black nationality. Ernest Lyon felt betrayed by the Liberians who dealt with the British behind his back, and Clark was furious when he learned that they had sold land to the French without his knowledge. Some of these diplomats secretly harbored the suspicion that the European interlopers might have done a better job than the settlers in ruling the aborigines, but they invariably concluded that in the long run it was better to protect the black nationality from outsiders.

The issue of the emigration of African Americans to Liberia posed a problem for almost all of the early diplomats. Most of them opposed the pro-emigration policies of the American Colonization Society, of members of the United States Congress, of African leaders, and of some African Americans. While the diplomats sympathized with the desire of the Americo-Liberians to increase the number of settlers and hopefully thereby attract increased support from the United States, they remained suspicious of the motives of the American Colonization Society and of members of Congress. The frequent anti-emigrationist stance of these diplomats often infuriated the Liberians, but the envoys were not prepared to help bigoted white Americans get rid of African Americans. On the other hand, a few of the ministers and others were not above using the emigrationist card when they felt they could get support for their activities. They were not above suggesting to the Department of State and to white Americans that a prosperous Africa would be attractive to potential African American migrants.

African American envoys and important members of their community often collaborated closely in the effort to influence United States foreign policy. Ernest Lyon, a protégé of Booker T. Washington, became adept at "back-channel" manipulation, that is, establishing important contacts outside the State Department in order to effect policy. Lyon knew how to exploit Booker T. Washington's strong support among both northern and southern African Americans, and his accommodationist attitude toward the white power structure, to accomplish his goals.

The Wizard of Tuskegee, for his part, was as adept in dealing with aspects of United States foreign policy as he was in influencing its domestic concerns. True, his focus was primarily upon the condition of African Americans within the United States, but he was not blind to the need to protect the black nationality, especially when he could be convinced that collaboration among people of African origin would prove universally beneficial. From the outset, Washington demonstrated something that scholars are only now coming to terms with—that there were, and are, various levels in the global system—a local level, a national level, and a global level; that each level has its own reality; and that these must be recognized and dealt with as such. Washington did not have an easy task because many of his white patrons did not believe that he should be involved in foreign policy except under their auspices, and not even then. Nevertheless, he showed that while remaining opposed to the emigration of African Americans to Africa, he was willing to work with white imperialists on behalf of Africa and even to send his students to do so. Moreover, while being his cautious self in counseling moderation to young black South Africans, he clearly expressed the view that whites were wrong if they believed that Africans could long be treated as inferiors on their own continent. As is well known, Washington was less sanguine about the ability of African Americans in the United States to push rapidly for full equality given demographic and other factors.

What many did not realize was that Washington did support and sponsor congresses as symbolic structures on behalf of African "redemption." He sought by these means to heighten the consciousness of the world to the plight of Africans on the continent and in the diaspora. Almost in spite of himself, Washington became involved with the London-based Pan-African movement launched by persons of African descent from the New World. Thanks to his efforts, W. E. B. Du Bois was able to go to Paris from where he proceeded to participate in the 1900 congress. This congress not only enabled Du Bois to project his vision of the global problems for African peoples and others in the dawning twentieth century, but also prepared him to organize and to participate in future congresses that would plan the independence of Africa.

During this early period, a surprisingly large number of African Americans who visited Africa consciously or unconsciously used symbolic structures as a means of seeking to influence United States policy toward that continent and its peoples. The sailors, miners, railroad workers, soldiers in the Boer War, missionaries, and various groups of jubilee singers presented to both blacks and whites in Africa novel notions of what blacks could accomplish. These activities often got them into difficulties with colonial and white government officials. In the event, they were not reluctant to enlist the power of the United States to help solve their problems. Curiously, State Department officials both in Africa and at home showed greater consideration for the rights of African Americans in Africa than they would have shown in the United States.

Bishop Henry McNeal Turner of the AME Church and hundreds of unsung African American missionaries did much to sensitize the Department of State to the problems of Africa. Believing as he and his fellow missionaries did in Ethiopia's outstretched hand, it is understandable why, in addition to preaching Christ crucified, these clerics would also preach "Africa for the Africans" and would use the pulpit and the schoolroom to educate and heighten the political awareness of Africans. Turner and some AME missionaries often used Aesopian language in their pronouncements, and when challenged, "Peter-like" they denied preaching sedition against the imperialists. Yet in the first decade of the twentieth century, these preachers were accused of fomenting riots in Natal, and out of their schools and churches would come many of the future leaders of the South African Native National Congress. Meantime, in the Congo, William H. Sheppard had so identified with the plight of the Congolese that only the intervention of American missionaries and the State Department kept him out of Belgian jails.

The battle waged between W. E. B. Du Bois, a Harvard- and Berlin-trained natural aristocrat, and Marcus Garvey, a charismatic Jamaican-born immigrant, for accession to the leadership mantle of Booker T. Washington was one of heroic proportions. Each was convinced that he possessed all of the attributes for dealing with American domestic race relations and its foreign policy. Du Bois used his dominant role in the elite National Association for the Advancement of Colored People to fight for full equality for African Americans within the United States, and to use this platform to launch a series of Pan-African Congresses to address the world on behalf of African peoples around the globe. Marcus Garvey, taking his inspiration from Booker T. Washington, was no less determined to move the race from slavery and colonization to preeminence in the world. His instruments were to be the Harlem-based Universal Negro Improvement Association, the Black Star Line, and a series of international conventions.

Due to the absence of African Americans in the halls of the government in the United States, Du Bois and Garvey could do little more than use symbolic structures, such as conferences and brilliant hortatory rhetoric, to pursue their goals. Du Bois was able to profit from his academic and intellectual achievements to aggregate and mobilize elite members of the African and African American communities to establish a dialogue with members of the white American and European imperial elite. He acknowledged that African peoples lacked the power to challenge the might of America and Europe and therefore sought to convince the leaders of the world that change, even if gradual, was in the best interest of all concerned. Du Bois recognized the importance of diplomacy and very often acted as though he believed that the State Department and European colonial officials would take him and his proposals seriously. It is surprising to discover how persistently Du Bois sought to keep these persons informed about his Pan-African activities.

For his part, Garvey apparently felt that he could appeal to the masses and convince a mighty race that it could accomplish what it willed. His messianic and millenarian vision of an Africa for Africans, at home and overseas, with its own flags, anthems, businessmen, diplomats, and men and women of affairs was one Du Bois did not share. Garvey, however, was prepared to fulfill his dreams, and using the pen and the pulpit, he exhorted his followers to take pride in themselves. He organized giant parades to give them a sense of accomplishment and dignity, started a newspaper to spread his message, and sought support to launch ships to create a trading network within the black world. Garvey did succeed in creating the largest mass movement among African Americans the world had ever seen.

One of the paradoxes that face scholars who look at this material is the difficulty of evaluating how much faith Garvey placed in the readiness of American whites or European imperial powers to help him realize his dreams for African peoples. Garvey fumed when the European powers and the League of Nations scorned or ignored his demand of Africa for Africans. Despite his lack of power, Garvey insisted that he and other blacks should be consulted about the future of the African continent. Sometimes it appeared that Garvey preferred angry verbal combat and failure to a courteous diplomatic approach yielding few results. It often appeared as though Garvey's goal was to demonstrate to the world that African peoples did aspire to full equality among the nations of the earth, and that even if the world had the power to ignore him and his movement, the world would have to learn to take African peoples seriously at some time in the future.

It was not surprising that Du Bois, the intellectual, was initially intrigued by Garvey's ability to mobilize the masses of Harlem, especially the immigrant West Indians. This, he believed, might furnish a charge to galvanize African Americans and to propel them to higher levels of consciousness. What increasingly troubled Du Bois, however, was his fear that the movement might become an end in itself and dash itself to pieces on the shoals of international power realities. He became harshly critical of Garvey's stewardship of the Black Star Line's finances and lost his temper over Garvey's extravaganzas in Harlem and elsewhere. Finally, an intemperate Du Bois reeling under the ridicule of

Garvey openly declared that the man and his movement should be destroyed.

Given their differences, both in style and outlook, and their lack of communication except by invective in the pages of the *Crisis* and the *Negro World,* it is surprising how similar the views of Du Bois and Garvey often were regarding the steps necessary to ameliorate the condition of African peoples. Du Bois never forgot that had it not been for his color he would have been a recognized member of the American elite, and his announcements and pronouncements acknowledged this fact. Garvey's rhetoric often concealed a close reading of the newspapers and a keen analysis of world events. His mastery of the King James version of the Bible and his acquaintance with the liturgy and practices of the Anglican church often gave a prophetic tone to his utterances. But their ideas about the problems and prospects black people faced now that World War I was upon them were basically in agreement, and their recommendations for action were almost the same. The difference was that while both sought to have their views considered by the United States and European imperialists, Du Bois felt it his due, and Garvey appeared more interested in demonstrating to the white powers his political and diplomatic acumen. In contrast to Du Bois, who was prepared to go to Versailles, London, Paris, Brussels, and Lisbon, Garvey never actually confronted either the American or European imperial elite. Again, Du Bois and Garvey both agonized over the failure of the United States to provide aid to debt-ridden Liberia. True to form, Du Bois attempted to use his limited clout to get the loan but failed. Likewise, Garvey exhorted his followers to give what money they could to aid Liberia, but he ran aground on the shoals of diplomacy and power politics, and his plans were scuttled.

Despite the different approaches of Du Bois and Garvey, many members of the white establishment, especially the Europeans, could not distinguish between their programs. Du Bois was deeply disturbed by this confusion and railed against it. He went to great lengths to point out to the Europeans, and also to the State Department, the wide differences between his opinions, philosophy, and modus operandi, and Garvey's. What plagued Du Bois, however, was that white power—both in the United States and in Europe—refused to concede anything. His attempts at dialogue were ignored, and his entreaties went unheard or rebuffed. Paradoxically, it often seemed that both the European and American governments evinced a greater anxiety or fear of Garvey and the UNIA than they did of Du Bois and the NAACP. Obviously what they feared most from Garvey and his movement was civil strife. For Du Bois, Garvey represented an intolerable approach; confrontation was not Du Bois's style.

The mischievous UNIA leader, for his part, could not conceal his wry amusement at the confusion of the Europeans and the embarrassment of Du Bois. He had brought with him from Jamaica grave reservations about the ability and willingness of the "brown" middle-class to seriously challenge white supremacy. Therefore, he saw Du Bois's reticence to accept him and his movement as representing the same condition. More prone to combat bigotry, prejudice, and white domination directly than to use diplomacy, Garvey held Du Bois, the NAACP, and the black establishment in disdain. No doubt he was confirmed in his opinion by the worsening race relations in the United States after the war and the seeming inability of the NAACP and the black establishment to do anything about it. Garvey took pleasure in poking fun at Du Bois, and understandably, this exacerbated relations between them.

In their separate and often contradictory ways both Du Bois and Garvey sought freedom and justice for African peoples the world over; in the end they both had to deal with the stark reality that symbolism, especially in the short run, lacked the power to move governments. The American government, fearful that Garvey might stir its citizens to rage or worse, incarcerated him on a charge of using the United States mails to defraud. The Liberian government, fearful of antagonizing the European imperial powers, prevented the UNIA from establishing a base from which to strive for the liberation of Africa. A dejected Garvey lamented that he had become a man of sorrow, acquainted with grief. Later, stirred by humble petitions for a presidential pardon, Calvin Coolidge released Garvey from an Atlanta prison and deported him. Garvey departed, beseeching his followers to hold high the red, black, and green and predicting that his black star would rise again. Garvey never did get to Africa, but his ideas did reach there, and in time his symbolic actions did achieve some of the results he sought.

Du Bois was more fortunate than Garvey. He would live long enough to see his Pan-African dreams come alive and would witness independent Africans shouting Garvey's praise in Black Star Square in Ghana. What was significant about Du Bois's attempts to influence the foreign policy of the United States toward Africa during this period was that his membership in the American establishment was finally and reluctantly admitted and recognized. Yet even he admitted that it was a "little thing" when the same Calvin Coolidge who had pardoned Garvey appointed him to proceed to Liberia as an envoy extraordinary and minister plenipotentiary of the United States of America. Du Bois fully understood that this was a symbolic act by the president of the United States. Nevertheless, he recognized that this act was viewed by the United States as important to its African policy and that it was appreciated by many African Americans and the Liberians. Du Bois also recognized that this act did not result in great benefits for the Liberians. The best he could do at the time was to warn the Liberians against the overtures of Firestone Rubber and suggest that they should take into consideration the political potential of African Americans to influence United States foreign policy. This was an admission by Du Bois that it was power and not symbolism that was ultimately important in foreign affairs.

Viewed in historical perspective, it is important to recognize that while still bearing the scars of slavery and concerned that their very presence in the United States was being questioned, black Americans both within the diplomatic service and without did their best to influence United States policy toward Africa. That the story is not widely known is as much a function of ignorance as it is of disinformation on the part of those who prefer not to see peoples of African descent as collaborating with each other to end the worldwide disdain in which they are still held. This study and those like it, are not only attempts to fill a lacuna in diplomatic scholarship, but they seek to challenge three assumptions: (1) that African Americans simply turned their backs on Africa; (2) that in contrast to some other ethnic groups in America, they did not involve themselves in the struggles of African peoples to gain freedom and dignity; and (3) that they did not consciously attempt to influence the United States' role in the larger world. What this book shows is how a people, initially excluded from American society, not only became members of it but never lost sight of their relationship to Africa and sought to save that black nationality as they sought to save themselves. This was not possible without aggressive attempts on the part of African Americans to understand and to influence, where possible, America's expanding involvement in world affairs.

Future studies should demonstrate equally how, despite being an embattled minority in the United States, African Americans did attempt to ensure that their country understood and sympathized with the plight of their ancestral land. They did so because their very fate was viewed as intimately linked to the position of Africa in the minds of their fellow citizens and the global community. That this story is not known or acknowledged only demonstrates the complexity of the issues involved. Nevertheless, it is quite possible that knowledge of the attempts of African

Americans to use both diplomatic and symbolic means to protect and advance the cause of a black nationality, both on the continent of Africa and in the diaspora, is part of the continuing effort by African Americans to achieve full equality in the United States.

Bibliography

Notes on Sources

Although the purpose of this book was to deal primarily with the attempts of African Americans to influence United States policy toward Africa that came to the attention of the State Department or other government officials, it was surprising to discover the amount of data available. This was true despite the general absence of papers (which may or may not exist) by some of the early diplomats. It is also true that many of the attempts of ordinary African Americans to influence United States foreign policy remain unknown because these were never taken seriously by government officials, who were often convinced that African Americans had no business dealing in foreign affairs. Attempts must be made to search out these papers and, if they exist, to place them at the disposal of scholars.

The holdings in the stacks, rooms, nooks, and crannies of the National Archives and Library of Congress on the foreign policy activities of African Americans are rich, but they are still not organized in a manner readily accessible to the researcher. Apparently such subjects are so rarely researched that the librarians have not yet developed mechanisms to deal with them. This may change as many more such projects are undertaken.

The actual records of the State Department in the archives are fairly comprehensive, but reading the (often faded) handwriting of the early diplomats was difficult. Again, the number system is not always coherent, a problem when copy editors demand a consistency that is not there. To make matters worse, footnoting systems are in full evolution. What was intriguing was to attempt to discover why certain telegrams between the Department of State and the diplomatic posts were published in the *Papers Relating to the Foreign Affairs of the United States* and why some were left unpublished. Was it the sensitivity of the subjects? The result was that the researcher had to rotate between published and unpublished sources to follow events taking place. The result, here again, was unevenness in providing adequate documentation.

A valuable source of data was the published correspondence and papers of important actors and the organizations with which they were associated. Most helpful were the *Papers of Marcus Garvey and the UNIA*. Its editor not only collected and published most of the materials but, just as important, indicated where unpublished materials could be found. This was also the case with the *Booker T. Washington Papers*. In contrast, the W. E. B. Du Bois correspondence and papers need to be properly edited. This is especially regrettable since there have been so many collections of the writings of Du Bois.

This research profited greatly from the holdings of the Moorland-Spingarn Research Center, Howard University, Washington, D.C., and the Schomburg Center for Research in Black Culture, New York. The articles in the *Journal of Negro History* turned out to be more valuable than anticipated. Some of the unpublished doctoral dissertations used were so valuable that it was difficult to understand why they were not published. Finally, the secondary sources were invaluable.

Government Documents

U.S. Department of State. *Foreign Relations of the United States,* 1865–1925. Washington D.C.: Government Printing Office, 1934 (published annually).
———. Record Group 59. Despatches from U.S. Consuls in Monrovia, Liberia, 1852–1906. Roll 3. National Archives, Washington, D.C.
———. Record Group 59. Despatches from U.S. Ministers to Liberia, 1863–1906. Rolls 2–14. National Archives, Washington, D.C.
———. Record Group 59. Notes from Madagascar Legation in United States to Department of State. Microcopy T806, 1883–94.
———. Record Group 59. Notes from Foreign Legation in Tamatave. Microcopy T60, 1853–1906.
———. Record Group 59. Numerical File (1906–1910). National Archives, Washington, D.C.
Cases 1352–1379. Roll 161 (Liberia)
Cases 2911–2927. Roll 281 (Congo)
Cases 3513–3536. Roll 326 (Liberia)
Cases 4676–4695. Roll 405 (Liberia)
Cases 7872–7910. Roll 584 (Congo)
Cases 12024–12053/60. Book 792 (Congo)
Cases 12053/61–12074. Book 793 (Congo)
Cases 12075–12083/150. Book 794 (Liberia)
Cases 12083/151–12083/360. Book 795 (Liberia)
———. Minor File (1906–1910) Vols. 32–34. National Archives, Washington, D.C.
———. Record Group 59. Decimal File (1910–1929). Box 1755. National Archives, Washington, D.C.

————. Record Group 84. Despatches from U.S. Consulate at Cape Town, South Africa. National Archives, Washington, D.C.

————. Miscellaneous Letters and Domestic Letters, Madagascar, Microcopy 400.

————. Miscellaneous Letters of the Department of State. Roll 1182. National Archives, Washington, D.C.

U.S. Presidents. Messages and Papers. *A Compilation of the Messages and Papers of the Presidents.* New York: Bureau of National Literature, 1897–1926.

A Report of the Commission of Inquiry Appointed by the Congo Free State Government. New York: G. P. Putnam's Sons, 1906.

Books and Edited Volumes

Ade Ajayi, J. F., and Ian Espie, eds. *A Thousand Years of West African History.* London: Ibadan University Press, 1965.

Anderson, Robert Earle. *Liberia: America's African Friend.* Chapel Hill: University of North Carolina Press, 1952.

Aptheker, Herbert, ed. *A Documentary History of the Negro People in the United States: From Colonial Times Through the Civil War.* 2 vols. New York: Citadel Press, 1951.

————, ed. *The Correspondence of W. E. B. Du Bois, Selections, 1877–1934.* Vol. 1. Amherst: University of Massachusetts Press, 1973.

————, ed. *Writings by W. E. B. Du Bois in Non-Periodical Literature.* New York: Kraus-Thomson, 1982.

Azikiwe, Benjamin Nnamdi. *Liberia in World Politics.* London: A. H. Stockwell, 1935.

Bailey, Thomas A. *Man in the Street: The Impact of American Public Opinion on Foreign Policy.* New York: Macmillan, 1948.

Ballard, J. A. "The Colonial Phase in French West Africa." In *A Thousand Years of West African History.* Edited by J. F. Ade Ajayi and Ian Espie. Ibadan: Ibadan University Press, 1965.

Barlett, Irving H. *From Slave to Citizen: The Story of the Negro in Rhode Island.* Providence, R.I.: Urban League of Greater Providence, 1954.

Beale, Howard K. *Theodore Roosevelt and the Rise of America to World Power.* New York: Collier Books, 1956.

Bell, Howard H. *A Survey of the Negro Convention Movement.* New York: Arno Press and New York Times, 1969.

Berwanger, Eugene H. *The Frontier Against Slavery: Western and Anti-Negro Prejudice and the Slavery Extension Controversy.* Urbana: University of Illinois Press, 1967.

Bittle, William E., and Gilbert Geis. *The Longest Way Home: Chief Alfred C. Sam's Back-to-Africa Movement.* Detroit: Wayne State University Press, 1964.

Bixler, Raymond W. *The Foreign Policy of the United States in Liberia.* New York: Pageant Press, 1957.

Blyden, Edward Wilmot. *Selected Letters of Edward Wilmot Blyden.* Edited by Hollis R. Lynch. Millwood, N.Y.: KTO Press, 1978.

Boone, Clinton Caldwell. *Liberia As I Know It.* Westport, Conn.: Negro Universities Press, 1929.

Bowen, J. W. E. *Africa and the American Negro. Addresses and Proceedings of the Congress on Africa Held Under the Auspices of the Stewart Missionary Foundation for Africa of Gammon Theological Seminary in Connection With the Cotton States and International Exposition, December 13–15, 1895.* Miami, Fla.: Mnemosyne, 1969.

Bracey, John H., Jr., August Meier, and Elliot Rudwick, eds. *Black Nationalism in America.* Indianapolis: Bobbs-Merrill, 1970.

Brawley, Benjamin, ed. *Early Negro American Writers.* Chapel Hill, N.C.: University of North Carolina Press, 1935.

Brown, Isaac V. *Biography of the Reverend Finley of Basking Ridge, New Jersey.* Philadelphia, 1857.

Buell, Raymond Leslie. *Liberia: A Century of Survival, 1847–1947.* Philadelphia: University of Pennsylvania Press, 1947.

———. *The Native Problem in Africa.* 2 vols. New York: Macmillan, 1928.

Chirenje, J. Mutero. *Ethiopianism and Afro-Americans in Southern Africa, 1883–1916* (Baton Rouge: Louisiana State University Press, 1987).

Challenor, Herschelle Sullivan. "The Influence of Black Americans on U.S. Foreign Policy." In *Ethnicity and U.S. Foreign Policy.* Edited by Abdul Aziz Said. New York: Praeger, 1981.

Cookey, S. J. S. *Britain and the Congo Question, 1885–1913.* London: Longman, 1968.

Coppin, Levi Jenkins. *Observations of Persons and Things in South Africa, 1900–1904.* Philadelphia: A.M.E. Book Concern, n.d.

Cox, Oliver C. *Caste, Class and Race. A Study in Social Dynamics.* 1948. Reprint. New York: Modern Reader Paperbacks, 1970.

Cronon, Edmund David. *Black Moses: The Story of Marcus Garvey and the Universal Negro Improvement Association.* Madison, Wis.: University of Wisconsin Press, 1957.

Crowder, Michael, and Obaro Ikime, eds. *West African Chiefs: Their Changing Status Under Colonial Rule and Independence.* Ile-Ife: University of Ife Press, 1970.

Crummell, Alexander. *Africa and America: Addresses and Discourses.* New York: Negro Universities Press, 1969.

A Letter to Charles B. Dunbar. Charles Lookwood, 1861.

Curtin, Philip. *Africa Remembered: Narratives by West Africans From the Era of the Slave Trade.* Madison, Wis.: University of Wisconsin Press, 1968.

Davis, Allen F., ed. *For Better or Worse: The American Influence in the World* (Westport, Conn.: Greenwood Press, 1981).

Dean, Harry. *The Pedro Gorino: The Adventure of a Negro Sea-Captain in Africa and on the Seven Seas in His Attempt to Found An Ethiopian Empire* (New York: Houghton and Mifflin, 1929).

Degler, Carl. *Out of Our Past: The Forces That Shaped Modern America.* New York: Harper and Row, 1970.

Delany, Martin R., and Robert Campbell. *Search for a Place: Black Separation and Africa* [1860]. Edited by Howard Bell. Ann Arbor: University of Michigan Press, 1969.

Dennis, Alfred L. P. *Adventures in American Diplomacy, 1896–1906.* New York: E. P. Dutton, 1939.

Du Bois, W. E. B. *An ABC of Color: Selections Chosen by the Author From Over a Half Century of His Writings.* Berlin: Seven Seas, 1963.

———. *The Autobiography of W. E. B. Du Bois: A Soliloquy on Viewing My Life From the Last Decade of Its First Century.* New York: International, 1968.

———. *The Conservation of Races.* Occasional Papers no. 2. Washington, D.C.: American Negro Academy, 1897.

———. *Dusk of Dawn.* New York: Schocken Books, 1968.

———. "An Essay Toward a History of the Black Man in the Great War." In *The Seventh Son: The Thought and Writings of W. E. B. Du Bois.* Edited by Julius Lester. Vol. 2. (New York: Random House, 1971).

———. *The Souls of Black Folk.* Greenwood, Conn.: Fawcett, 1961.

———. *The Suppression of the African Slave Trade to the United States of America, 1638–1870.* New York: Schocken Books, 1969.

———. *The World and Africa: An Inquiry Into the Part Which Africa Has Played in World History.* New York: International Publishers, 1965.

Dyer, Thomas G. Theodore Roosevelt and the Idea of Race. Baton Rouge and London: Louisiana State University Press, 1980.

Essien-Udom, E. U. *Black Nationalism: A Search for an Identity in America.* Chicago: University of Chicago Press, 1962.

Ferguson, John H. *American Diplomacy and the Boer War.* Philadelphia: University of Pennsylvania Press, 1939.

Fields, Karen E. *Revival and Rebellion in Colonial Central Africa.* Princeton: Princeton University Press, 1985.

Fishel, Leslie H., and Benjamin Quarles, eds. *The Black American: A Documentary History.* New York: Morrow, 1967.

Fletcher, Marvin. *The Black Soldier and Officer in the United States Army, 1891–1917.* Columbia: University of Missouri Press, 1974.

Foner, Philip S. *History of Black Americans.* 3 vols. Westport, Conn.: Greenwood Press, 1975.

———, ed. *The Life and Writings of Frederick Douglass.* 5 vols. New York: International Publishers, 1950.

Ford, Paul L. *The Works of Thomas Jefferson.* 12 vols. New York: G. P. Putnam's Sons, 1904–1905.

Fox, Stephen R. *The Guardian of Boston: William Monroe Trotter.* New York: Atheneum, 1970.

Franklin, John Hope. *George Washington Williams: A Biography.* Chicago: University of Chicago Press, 1985.

———, and Alfred A. Moss, Jr. *From Slavery to Freedom.* New York: Alfred A. Knopf, 1988.

Fry, Joseph A. *Henry S. Sanford: Diplomacy and Business in Nineteenth-Century America.* Reno: University of Nevada Press, 1982.

Garnet, Henry Highland. *A Memorial Discourse by Reverend Henry Highland Garnet, Delivered in the Hall of the House of Representatives.* Philadelphia: Joseph M. Wilson, 1865.

————. *The Past and Present Condition and the Destiny of the Colored Race: A Discourse at the 50th Anniversary of the Female Benevolent Society of Troy, New York, 14 February 1848.* Troy, N.Y.: J. C. Kneeland, 1848.

Garrison, Wendell Phillips. *William Lloyd Garrison, 1805–1879: The Story of His Life Told by His Children.* 2 vols. New York: Century, 1885.

Garvey, Amy Jacques. *Garvey and Garveyism.* Kingston, Jamaica: United Printers, 1963.

————, ed. *Philosophy and Opinions of Marcus Garvey or Africa for the Africans.* London: Frank Cass, 1967.

Gatewood, Willard, B., Jr. *Black Americans and the White Man's Burden, 1898–1903.* Urbana: University of Illinois Press, 1975.

Geiss, Imanuel. *The Pan-African Movement: A History of Pan-Africanism in America, Europe and Africa.* Translated by Ann Keep. New York: Africana, 1974.

Gerson, Louis L. "The Influence of Hyphenated Americans on U.S. Diplomacy." In *Ethnicity and U.S. Foreign Policy.* Edited by Abdul Aziz Said. New York: Praeger, 1981.

Glazer, Nathan, and Daniel P. Moynihan, eds. *Ethnicity: Theory and Experience.* Cambridge, Mass.: Harvard University Press, 1975.

Harlan, Louis R. *Booker T. Washington: The Wizard of Tuskegee, 1901–1915.* New York: Oxford University Press, 1983.

————, and Raymond W. Smock, eds. *Booker T. Washington Papers.* 13 vols. Urbana: University of Illinois Press, 1972–1989.

Harris, Sheldon H. *Paul Cuffe: Black America and the African Return.* New York: Simon and Schuster, 1972.

Heard, William H. *The Bright Side of African Life.* New York: Negro Universities Press, 1969; originally published by the A.M.E. Publishing House, 1898.

Herskovits, Melville J. "Study of United States Foreign Policy in Africa." *Committee on Foreign Relations of the United States Senate.* 86th Cong., 1st sess., 23 October 1959.

Hill, Adelaide Cromwell, and Martin Kilson, eds. and comps. *Apropos of Africa: Sentiments of Negro American Leaders on Africa from the 1800s to the 1950s.* London: Frank Cass, 1969.

Hill, Robert A., ed. *The Marcus Garvey and Universal Negro Improvement Association Papers.* 6 vols. Berkeley and Los Angeles: University of California Press, 1983–1989.

Hilton, Ralph. *Worldwide Mission: The Story of the United States Foreign Service.* New York: World Publishing, 1971.

Jacobs, Sylvia M. *The African Nexus: Black American Perspectives on the European Partitioning of Africa, 1880–1920.* Westport Conn.: 1981.

————, ed. "The Historical Role of Afro-Americans in American Missionary Efforts in Africa." In *Black Americans and the Missionary Movement in Africa.* Westport, Conn.: Greenwood Press, 1982.

Jessup, Philip C. *Elihu Root, 1905–1937.* 2 vols. New York: Dodd, Mead, 1939.

Johnson, Charles S. *Bitter Canaan: The Story of the Negro Republic*. New Brunswick, N.J.: Transaction Books, 1987.

Johnston, Harry H. *The Negro in the New World*. London: Methuen, 1910.

Jordan, Winthrop D. *The White Man's Burden: Historical Origins of Racism in the United States*. New York: Oxford University Press, 1974.

————. *White Over Black*. Chapel Hill: University of North Carolina Press, 1968.

Karis, Thomas, and Gwendolen M. Carter, eds. *From Protest to Challenge: A Documentary History of African Politics in South Africa, 1882–1964*. 4 vols. Stanford, Calif.: Hoover Institution Press, 1972.

Keiser, Robert L. *Liberia: A Report on the Relations Between the United States and Liberia*. Washington, D.C.: United States Government Printing Office, 1928.

Kennan, George F. *Memoirs, 1958–1963*. Boston: Little Brown, 1972.

Kipling, Rudyard. *The White Man's Burden*. Stanza 1. In *Poems and Complete Verse*. New York: Anchor Press, [1899] 1940.

Kissinger, Henry A. *American Foreign Policy*. New York: W. W. Norton, 1969.

Lewis, David Levering. *The Race to Fashoda*. New York: Weidenfeld and Nicolson, 1987.

Limoli, Donald A. "Francesco Crispi's Quest for Empire—and Victories—in Ethiopia." In *Partition of Africa: Illusion or Necessity*. Edited by Robert O. Collins. New York: John Wiley and Sons, 1969.

Logan, Rayford W. *The Negro in American Life and Thought: The Nadir, 1877–1901*. New York: Dial Press, 1954. Reprinted as *The Betrayal of the Negro*. New York: Collier Books, 1965.

————. *W. E. B. Du Bois: A Profile*. New York: Hill and Wang, 1971.

————, and Michael R. Winston, eds. *Dictionary of American Negro Biography*. New York: W. W. Norton, 1982.

Lynch, Hollis, ed. *Black Spokesman, Selected Writings of E. W. Blyden*. London: Frank Cass, 1971.

————. *Edward Blyden: Pan-Negro Patriot, 1832–1912*. London: Oxford University Press, 1967.

————, ed. *Selected Letters of Edward Wilmot Blyden* (Millwood, N.Y.: KTO Press, 1978).

Marcus, Harold G. "Imperialism and Expansion in Ethiopia From 1865 to 1900." In *Colonialism in Africa*. Vol. 1, *1890–1960*. Edited by L. H. Gann and Peter Duignan. Cambridge: University Press, 1969.

————. *The Life and Times of Menelik II, Ethiopia 1844–1913*. Oxford: Clarendon Press, 1975.

Marks, George P., ed. *The Black Press Views American Imperialism, 1898–1900*. New York: Arno Press, 1971.

Martin, Tony. *Race First*. Westport, Conn.: Greenwood Press, 1976.

————. *The Pan-African Connection: From Slavery to Garvey and Beyond*. Dover, Mass.: Majority Press, 1983.

Madison, James. *The Federalist Papers*. Edited by Henry B. Dawson. New York: Charles Scribner, 1863.

Marable, Manning. *W. E. B. Du Bois: Black Radical Democrat.* Boston: Twayne, 1986.

Mathurin, Owen Charles. *Henry Sylvester Williams and the Origins of the Pan-African Movement, 1869–1911.* Westport, Conn.: Greenwood Press, 1976.

Meier, August, ed. *Negro Thought in America, 1880–1915.* Ann Arbor: University of Michigan Press, 1963.

Miller, Floyd J. *The Search for a Black Nationality: Black Emigration and Colonization, 1787–1863.* Urbana, Ill.: University of Illinois Press, 1975.

Miller, Jake C. *The Black Presence in American Foreign Affairs.* Washington, D.C.: University Press of America, 1978.

Morison, Elting E., ed. *The Letters of Theodore Roosevelt.* 6 vols. Cambridge: Harvard University Press, 1951–54.

Morris, Richard B., ed. *Encyclopedia of American History.* New York: Harper and Bros., 1953.

Morris, Roger. *Uncertain Greatness: Henry Kissinger and American Foreign Policy.* New York: Harper and Row, 1977.

Mutibwa, Phares M. *The Malagasy and the Europeans: Madagascar's Foreign Relations, 1861–1895.* London: Longman, 1974.

Noer, Thomas J. *Briton, Boer, and Yankee: The United States and South Africa, 1870–1914* (Ohio: Kent State University Press, 1978).

Ottley, Roi. *New World A-Coming.* Boston: Houghton Mifflin, 1943.

Padmore, George. *Pan-Africanism or Communism?* London: Dennis Dobson, 1956.

Peden, William, ed. *Notes on the State of Virginia by Thomas Jefferson.* Chapel Hill, N.C.: University of North Carolina Press, 1955.

Plischke, Elmer. *Conduct of American Diplomacy.* New York: Van Nostrand, 1950.

———. *United States Diplomats and Their Missions.* Washington, D.C.: American Enterprise Institute for Public Policy, 1975.

Porter, Dorothy, comp. *Early Negro Writing, 1760–1837.* Boston: Beacon Press, 1971.

Redkey, Edwin S. *Black Exodus: Black Nationalist and Back-to-Africa Movements, 1890–1910.* New Haven: Yale University Press, 1969.

———, ed. *Respect Black: The Writings and Speeches of Henry McNeal Turner.* New York: Arno Press and the New York Times, 1971.

Richardson, Nathaniel R. *Liberia's Past and Present.* London: Diplomatic Press, 1959.

Roosevelt, Theodore. *The Winning of the West.* 4 vols. New York: G. P. Putnam's Sons, 1896.

———. *The Works of Theodore Roosevelt: National Edition.* 13 vols. New York: Charles Scribner's Sons, 1926.

Roux, Edward. *Time Longer Than Rope: A History of the Black Man's Struggle for Freedom in South Africa.* Madison, Wis.: University of Wisconsin Press, 1964.

Shaloff, Stanley. *Reform in Leopold's Congo.* Richmond, Va.: John Knox Press, 1970.

Sheppard, William H. *Lovedale, South Africa, 1841–1941.* Cape Province, South Africa: Lovedale Press, 1941.

———. *Pioneer Missionary to the Congo.* Louisville, Ky.: Pentecostal, 1917.

Shepperson, George, and Thomas Price. *Independent African: John Chilembwe and the Origins, Setting, and Significance of the Nyassaland Native Rising of 1915* (Edinburgh: University Press, 1958.

Shick, Thomas. *Behold the Promised Land.* Madison: University of Wisconsin Press, 1977.

Shotwell, James T. *At the Paris Peace Conference.* New York: Macmillan, 1937.

———. *George Louis Beer: A Tribute to His Life and Work in the Making of History and Moulding of Public Opinion.* New York: Macmillan, 1924 (this book is a memorial volume published after Beer's death).

Skinner, Elliott P. *Afro-Americans and Africa: The Continuing Dialectic.* New York: The Urban Center, Columbia University, 1973.

———. "Black Foreign Policymakers." In *Reflections on Black Leadership.* Edited by Ronald Walters and Robert Smith. *The Urban League Review.* New York: National Urban League Research Department, 1985.

———. "Ethnicity and Race as Factors in the Formation of United States Foreign Policy." In *American Character and Foreign Policy.* Edited by Michael P. Hamilton. Grand Rapids, Mich.: William B. Eerdmans, 1986.

———. "Personal Networks and Institutional Linkages in the Global System." In *Dynamics of the African, Afro-American Connection: From Dependency to Self-Reliance.* Edited by Adelaide M. Cromwell. Washington, D.C.: Howard University Press.

Skinner, Robert P. *Abyssinia of Today.* London: Edward Arnold, 1906.

Slade, Ruth M. *English-Speaking Missions in the Congo Independent State, 1878–1909.* Brussels: A.R.S.C., 1959.

Smythe, Hugh H., and Elliot P. Skinner. "Black Participation in U.S. Foreign Relations." In *The Encyclopedia of the Black American.* Edited by Mable M. Smythe. Englewood Cliffs, N.J.: Prentice-Hall, 1978.

South African Native Affairs Commission (SANAC). *Report of the Commission, 1903–5.* 5 vols. Cape Town: Cape Times Limited, 1905.

South African Native Races Committee, ed. *The South African Natives: Their Economic and Social Condition.* London: John Murray, 1909.

Staudenraus, Philip J. *The African Colonization Movement, 1816–1865.* New York: Columbia University Press, 1961.

Stuckey, Sterling. *The Ideological Origins of Black Nationalism.* Boston: Beacon Press, 1972.

Sundkler, Bengt G. M. *Bantu Prophets in South Africa.* London: Lutterworth Press, 1948.

Taylor, Charles H. *Whites and Blacks and the Question Settled.* Atlanta, Ga.: n.p. 1889.

Ullman, Victor. *Martin R. Delany: The Beginnings of Black Nationalism.* Boston: Beacon Press, 1971.

Varg, P. A. *Foreign Policies of the Founding Fathers.* East Lansing, Mich.: Michigan State University Press, 1963.

Walker, James E. "Appeal, in Four Articles, Together With a Preamble to the Colored Citizens of the World, but in Particular, and Very Expressly to Those of the United States of America." In *Great Documents in Black American History*. Edited by George Ducas with Charles Van Doren. New York: Praeger, 1970.

Walters, Alexander. *My Life and Work*. New York: Fleming H. Revel, 1917.

Ward, W. E. F. "The Colonial Phase in West Africa: 'Political Developments.' " In *A Thousand Years of West African History*. Edited by J. F. Ade Ajayi and Ian Espie. Ibadan: Ibadan University Press, 1965.

Washington, Booker T., N. B. Wood, and Fannie Barrier Williams. *A New Negro for a New Century*. New York: Arno Press and the New York Times, 1969.

――――. *The Future of the American Negro*. New York: Negro Universities Press, 1969.

――――. *The Story of the Negro: The Rise of the Race From Slavery*. 2 vols. New York: Negro Universities Press, 1909, 1969.

――――. *Up From Slavery: An Autobiography*. New York: Doubleday, 1949.

Washington, George. *Washington's Farewell Address: The View From the Twentieth Century*. Edited by Burton I. Kaufman. Chicago: Quadrangle Books, 1969.

Weisbord, Robert G. *Ebony Kinship: Africa, Africans and the Afro-Americans* (Westport, Conn.: Greenwood Press, 1973).

Willan, Brian. *Sol Plaatje, South African Nationalist, 1876–1932*. Berkeley: University of California Press, 1984.

Williams, Walter L. *Black Americans and the Evangelization of Africa, 1877–1900*. Madison: University of Wisconsin Press, 1982.

Woodson, Carter G. *The Mind of the Negro As Reflected in Letters Written During the Crisis, 1800–1860*. Washington, D.C.: Association for the Study of Negro Life and History, 1926, 161–63.

――――. *Negro Orators and Their Orations*. Washington, D.C.: Associated Publishers, 1925.

――――, and Charles L. Wesley. *The Negro in Our History*. 2d ed. Washington, D.C.: Associated Publishers, 1966.

Younger, Edward. *John A. Kasson: Politics and Diplomacy From Lincoln to McKinley*. Iowa City: State Society of Iowa, 1955.

Zeidler, Frank P. "Hysteria in Wartime: Domestic Pressures on Ethnics and Aliens." In *Ethnicity and War*. Edited by Winston A. Van Horne and Thomas V. Tennesen. Milwaukee: University of Wisconsin, 1984.

Articles

Akpan, M. B. "Black Imperialism: Americo-Liberian Rule Over the African Peoples of Liberia, 1841–1964." *Canadian Journal of African Studies* 7 (1973): 217–36.

Blakely, Allison. "The John L. Waller Affair, 1895–1896." *Negro History Bulletin* 33 (February–March 1974): 216–18.

Booth, Joseph. "Industrial Missions in Africa." *Missionary Review of the World* 9 (April 1896): 290–94.

Carter, Jimmy. "Farewell Address." *Vital Speeches* 47 (February 1981): 226–28.

Chalk, Frank. "Du Bois and Garvey Confront Liberia: Two Incidents of the Coolidge Years." *Canadian Journal of African Studies* 1 (1967): 135ff.

Contee, Clarence B. "Documents—The Worley Report on the Pan-African Conference of 1919." *Journal of Negro History* 55 (April 1970): 141.

———. "Du Bois, the NAACP, and the Pan-African Congress of 1919." *Journal of Negro History* 57 (January 1972): 13–28.

———. "The Emergence of Du Bois as an African Nationalist." *Journal of Negro History* 59 (1969): 51.

Coppin, Levi Jenkins. "American Negro's Religion for the African Negro's Soul." *Independent* 54 (27 March 1902): 748–58.

Davis, R. Hunt. "The Black American Component in African Responses to Colonialism in South Africa." *Journal of Southern African Affairs* 3 (January 1978): 21–32.

Du Bois, W. E. B. "The African Roots of the War." *Atlantic Monthly* 115 (May 1915): 707–14.

———. "Back to Africa." *Century Magazine* (New York) 105 (February 1923): 537–48.

———. "The Inter-Racial Implications of the Ethiopian Crisis." *Foreign Affairs* 14 (1935): 88, 92.

———. "Marcus Garvey." *Crisis* 21 (December 1920): 58–60 and 21 (January 1921): 112–15.

———. "The Pan-African Congress." *Crisis* 17 (April 1919): 274.

———. "The Present Outlook for the Darker Races of Mankind." *Church Review* (Philadelphia) 17 (October 1900): 95–111.

———. "To the World: Manifesto of the Second Pan-African Congress." *Crisis* 23 (November 1921): 5–10.

Ellis, George W. "Dynamic Factors in the Liberian Situation." *Journal of Race Development* 1 (January 1911): 268–69.

Emerson, Rupert. "American Interests in Africa." *Centennial Review.* 4 (1960): 416.

Frazier, E. Franklin. "Garvey: A Mass Leader." *Nation* 123 (18 August 1926): 147–48.

Garrett, Stephen A. "East European Ethnic Groups and American Foreign Policy." *Political Science Quarterly* 93 (1978): 307.

Gatewood, Willard B., Jr. "Black Americans and the Boer War, 1899–1902." *South Atlantic Quarterly* 75 (1976): 226–31.

Hamedoe, S. E. F. C. C. "The First Pan-African Conference of the World." *Colored American* 1 (September 1900): 223.

Hargreaves, John D. "Maurice Delafosse on the Pan-African Congress of 1919." *African Historical Studies* 1 (1968): 233–41.

Harlan, Louis R. "Booker T. Washington and the White Man's Burden." *American Historical Review* 71 (January 1966): 441–67.

Johnson, G. Wesley. "The Ascendancy of Blaise Diagne and the Beginning of African Politics in Senegal." *Africa* 36 (October 1966): 235–53.

Kirk-Greene, A. H. M. "America in the Niger Valley: A Colonization Centenary." *Phylon* 23 (Fall 1962): 225–39.

Lewis, William Roger. "The United States and the African Peace Settlement: The Pilgrimage of George Louis Beer." *Journal of African History* 4 (1963): 413–33.

Logan, Rayford W. "The Historical Aspects of Pan-Africanism: A Personal Chronicle." *African Forum* 1 (1965): 90.

Manheim, Frank J. "The United States and Ethiopia: A Study in American Imperialism." *Journal of Negro History* 17 (April 1932): 141–155.

Marable, W. Manning. "Booker T. Washington and African Nationalism." *Phylon* 35 (1974): 398–406.

McC. Mathias, Charles, Jr. "Ethnic Groups and Foreign Policy." *Foreign Affairs* 59 (1981): 97.

Mehlinger, Louis R. "The Attitude of the Free Negro Toward African Colonization." *Journal of Negro History* 1 (July 1916): 276–301.

Noble, Frederick P. "The Chicago Congress." *Our Day* 12 (October 1893): 279–300; *Voice of Missions* (October 1893); *A.M.E. Quarterly Review* 4 (October 1893): 120.

Padgett, James A. "Ministers to Liberia and Their Diplomacy." *Journal of Negro History* 12 (January 1937): 74–92.

Pankhurst, Richard. "William H. Ellis—Guillaume Enriques Ellesio: First Black American Ethiopianist?" *Ethiopian Observer* 15 (1972): 89–121.

Psalm 68:31.

Redkey, Edwin S. "Bishop Turner's African Dream." *Journal of American History* 54 (September 1967): 271–90.

———. "Critique of the Atlanta Compromise." In *Respect Black: The Writings and Speeches of Henry McNeal Turner.* New York: Arno Press and the New York Times, 1971, 165–78.

Sanford, Henry S. "Report of the Hon. Henry Shelton Sanford, U.S. Delegate from the American Branch to the Annual Meeting of the African International Association in Brussels, in June 1877, to the Hon. John H. B. Latrobe, Brussels, July 30, 1877." *American Geographical Society Journal* 9 (1877): 103–8.

Scheiner, Seth M. "President Theodore Roosevelt and the Negro, 1901–1908." *Journal of Negro History* 47 (1962): 169–82.

Scott, Emmett J. "Is Liberia Worth Saving?" *Journal of Race Development* 1 (January 1911) 288ff.

Sheppard, William H. "Into the Heart of Africa." *Southern Workman* 12 (December 1893): 182–87.

———. "Light in Darkest Africa." *Southern Workman* 24 (April 1905): 218–27.

Shepperson, George. "The American Negro and Africa." *British Association for American Studies* 8 (June 1964): 3–20.

———. "The Centennial of the West Africa Conference of Berlin, 1884–1885." *Phylon* 46 (1985): 38–48.

———. "Notes on Negro American Influence on the Emergence of African Nationalism." *Journal of African History* 1 (1960): 299–312.

Sherwood, Henry Noble. "Paul Cuffe." *Journal of Negro History* 8 (April 1923): 153–299.

———. "The Formation of the American Colonization Society." *Journal of Negro History* 2 (1917): 211.

Skinner, Elliott P. "Strangers in African Societies." *Africa* 33 (October 1963): 307–20;

Taylor, Senator. "The Race Question in the United States." *Arena* 10 (September 1890): 385–98.

Verner, S. P. "The Affairs of the Congo State." *Forum* 36 (July–September 1904): 150–59.

———. "The White Man's Zone in Africa." *The World's Work* 7 (November 1906): 8227–36.

Wade, Richard C. "The Negro in Cincinnati, 1800–1830." *Journal of Negro History* 39 (January 1954): 53.

Walshe, A. P. "The Origin of African Political Consciousness in South Africa." *Journal of Modern African Studies* 7 (1969): 592–94.

Washington, Booker T. "Cruelty in the Congo Country." *Outlook* 78 (October 1904): 375–77.

Wesley, Charles H. "The Struggle for the Recognition of Haiti and Liberia as Independent Republics." *Journal of Negro History* 2 (October 1917): 375.

Woods, Randall B. "Black America's Challenge to European Colonialism: The Waller Affair, 1891–1895." *Journal of Black Studies* 7 (September 1976): 57–77.

Woodward, Walter C. "The Rise and Early History of Political Parties in Oregon." *Oregon Historical Quarterly* 12 (1911): 146.

Dissertations

Beecher, Lloyd N., Jr. "The State Department and Liberia, 1908–1914: A Heterogeneous Record." Ph.D. diss., University of Georgia, 1970.

Coan, Joseph R. "The Expansion of Missions of the African Methodist Episcopal Church in South Africa, 1896–1908." Ph.D., Hartford Seminary Foundation, 1961.

Chalk, Frank. "The United States and the International Struggle for Rubber, 1914–1941." Ph.D. diss., University of Wisconsin, 1970.

Contee, Clarence Garner. "W. E. B. Du Bois and African Nationalism." Ph.D. diss., American University, 1969.

Forderhase, Nancy Kaye. "The Plans that Failed: The United States and Liberia, 1920–1935." Ph.D. diss., University of Missouri, 1971.

Keto, Clement Tsehloane. "American Involvement in South Africa, 1870–1915. The Role of Americans in the Creation of Modern South Africa." Ph.D. diss., Georgetown University, 1972.

Karanja, J. Njuguna. "United States' Attitude and Policy Toward the International African Association, 1876–1886." Ph.D. diss., Princeton University, 1962.

McStallworth, Paul. "The United States and the Congo Question: 1884–1914." Ph.D. diss., Ohio State University, 1954.

Journals, Papers, and Magazines

African Repository
American Colonization Society Bulletin
A.M.E. Church Review
A.M.E. Zion Quarterly Review
British Parliamentary Papers
Christian Recorder
Colored American
Congressional Globe
Crisis
National Cyclopaedia of American Biography
Our Day
Phylon
Urban League Review
Voice of Missions (October 1893)
West Africa
Who's Who in America

Index

541